PAPERS AND CORRESPONDENCE
OF
WILLIAM STANLEY JEVONS

Volume VII

PAPERS AND CORRESPONDENCE
OF
WILLIAM STANLEY JEVONS

Volume VII
PAPERS ON POLITICAL ECONOMY

ECONOMIC PAPERS HITHERTO UNCOLLECTED
EXTRACTS FROM THE PERSONAL DIARIES, 1856–60
LIST OF ADDITIONAL WRITINGS
JEVONS AS EXAMINEE AND EXAMINER
REVIEWS OF *THE THEORY OF POLITICAL ECONOMY*

EDITED BY
R. D. COLLISON BLACK

in association with the Royal Economic Society

First edition 1981
Reprinted 1984

Published by
THE MACMILLAN PRESS LTD
London and Basingstoke
Companies and representatives
throughout the world

ISBN 0 333 19979 0

Printed in Great Britain by
Antony Rowe Ltd
Chippenham

CONTENTS

Preface   vii

List of Abbreviations   xi

Errata to Volumes I–VI   xii

ECONOMIC PAPERS HITHERTO UNCOLLECTED   1

    I   Contributions to the Sydney *Empire* (1857)   3
   II   Mr Gladstone's New Financial Policy (1866)   11
  III On Coal (1867)   18
  IV On the Probable Exhaustion of our Coal Mines (1868)   28
    V On the Progress of the Coal Question (1875)   36
  VI The Importance of Diffusing a Knowledge of Political
          Economy (1866)   37
 VII Two Lectures on Political Economy (at Hyde, Cheshire
          1869)   54
VIII On the International Monetary Convention and the
          Introduction of an International Currency into this
          Kingdom (1868)   65
  IX The Progress of the Mathematical Theory of Political
          Economy (1874)   75
    X Remarks on the Statistical Use of the Arithmometer   85
  XI The Solar Influence on Commerce (1879)   90
 XII Preface to the English translation of Cossa's *Guide* (1880) 98
XIII List of Selected Books in Political Economy (1882)   101
XIV The Solar-Commercial Cycle (1882)   108

EXTRACTS FROM THE PERSONAL DIARIES, 1856–60   113

LIST OF WRITINGS ADDITIONAL TO THOSE INCLUDED IN
APPENDIX B TO THE *LETTERS AND JOURNAL*   121

JEVONS AS EXAMINEE AND EXAMINER   129

    I Paper sat by Jevons at University College London,
       1860   131

II Papers set by Jevons for the Moral Sciences Tripos, Cambridge, 1874 and 1875   132

REVIEWS OF *THE THEORY OF POLITICAL ECONOMY*   139

  I By Alfred Marshall, 1872   141
  II By John Elliot Cairnes, 1872   146
  III Anonymous, 1871   152
  IV By T. E. Cliffe Leslie (of the second edition), 1879   157

General Index (Volumes I–VII)   163

PREFACE

Apart from the 1875–6 lecture notes contained in Volume VI, the Jevons Papers include only one other previously unpublished piece of economic work – this is the draft article entitled 'The Solar Influence on Commerce' printed as Chapter XI of the first part of this volume. In 1881 Jevons had formed the idea of collecting into two volumes some of the fifty and more papers on economic subjects which he had written since 1857.[1] The preparation of fourteen articles on monetary questions for incorporation into *Investigations in Currency and Finance* was almost complete before his death and was finished by H. S. Foxwell in 1884.

Jevons had presumably himself made the decision not to include his uncompleted paper on 'The Solar Influence on Commerce', evidently written in 1879, and Foxwell did not alter this, although he did include another unfinished item entitled 'Sir Isaac Newton and Bimetallism' as well as various fragments on the latter topic. However, it seems right that the whole of Jevons's writings on his sunspot theory should be accessible, rather than just the four items which were included in *Investigations*. So this unfinished and hitherto unpublished item is included here, as well as a brief paper from *Nature*, 1882 (Chapter XIV below), which, as suggested there, may only have been published after Jevons had decided on the form which *Investigations* was to take.

The second volume of papers which Jevons proposed to collect comprised those which he had written on social questions; these were edited by his wife after his death and published in 1883 under the title of *Methods of Social Reform*. The remaining papers on economic subjects, which have never previously been republished, are now collected in the present volume. Inevitably they form a miscellaneous collection, lacking the unity of theme which characterised *Investigations* and *Methods*; on the other hand they have the merit of allowing the reader to see Jevons at every stage of his intellectual development and displaying almost every facet of his wide-ranging interests in economic questions.

The very first pieces which Jevons wrote on economic questions, when he was a young settler, are included here. Following these are a group of papers connected with *The Coal Question*, the book which first gave Jevons

[1] See H. S. Foxwell's Introduction to the First Edition of *Investigations*, p. xx.

a national reputation as an economist and which he himself thought to have influenced his election as Cobden Professor in 1866. [2]

On his appointment to that Chair Jevons found himself obliged to present political economy in a fairly popular form to primary school teachers and others. Examples of his teaching at this level, which did not win him much popularity with the representatives of the working class to whom it was primarily directed, are incorporated as Chapters VI and VII.

In sharp contrast to these is the paper on 'The Progress of the Mathematical Theory of Political Economy' (Chapter IX), which shows Jevons as an internationally recognised authority on economic theory using the Manchester and London Statistical Societies to propagate the mathematical approach to his subject which he found so much more readily accepted abroad than at home.

For the rest, the collection includes another paper, that on international currency, which might well have found a place in *Investigations* but somehow did not, and some short pieces which exemplify that 'many-sidedness' which Keynes praised in Jevons. One shows Jevons the practical statistician explaining prophetically to the Statistical Society of London the value of a simple calculating machine in connection with the method of least squares, while others display his wide knowledge of the literature of economics, both English and European.

In the Preface to Volume I, I pointed out that 'the works of Jevons, published during and after his lifetime, display the finished products of his mind. The papers published here enable the reader, for the first time, to see the workshop in which they were produced.' [3] This is particularly true of the papers which make up the latter part of this volume. The diary entries with which it opens are quite distinct from the Journal which formed the main text of Volume I but of similar interest in the understanding of Jevons's intellectual development.

Jevons used his journal as an occasional record of his thoughts and of events of special significance. He was never a regular diarist, but between 1856 and 1860 he used a series of Letts' diaries to jot down records of his work and reading, which serve now to throw valuable light on the early growth of his interest in social and economic studies and the sources from which he derived some of his knowledge and ideas. All the entries which seem significant in this regard are reproduced here; such a selection seemed preferable to publishing the whole text of the diaries, which include many trivia such as jottings of daily or weekly expenditures.

While the diaries contain much information on Jevons's early reading, information about his writings, beyond what has previously been known,

[2] Cf. Letter 253, Vol. III, p. 101.
[3] See Vol. I, p. xii.

proved to be contained in a plain black-covered exercise book in which he kept a record of all his activities as an author. This not merely supplements the incomplete lists of Jevons's writings given by Mrs Jevons in *Letters and Journal* and by H. S. Jevons as an appendix to the fourth edition of *The Theory of Political Economy*, but also enables a number of pieces published anonymously by Jevons to be identified.

Finally, the opportunity has been taken to bring together some related items published elsewhere. Reference has already been made to the well-known story of the 'sad reverse' which Jevons felt he had suffered in the political economy examination at University College London in the summer of 1860. In view of this, special interest attaches to the examination paper set on that occasion by Jacob Waley,[4] and it is therefore reproduced here.

Fourteen years later, his reputation as an economist firmly established, Jevons was invited to act as one of the examiners for the Moral Sciences Tripos at Cambridge in 1874 and 1875. Three papers on political economy were then part of the Moral Sciences Tripos and special interest also attaches to these, not only because of Jevons's part in setting them, but also because among the candidates were, in 1874, Mary Paley (afterwards Mrs Alfred Marshall), and in 1875 John Neville Keynes.

The circumstances of the 1874 Tripos examination have again been classically related by John Maynard Keynes in *Essays in Biography*. Of the four examiners two placed Mary Paley in the first class and two in the second, leading Dr Kennedy (of Latin Grammar fame) to compose the verses which ended—

Were they at sixes and at sevens?—
O Foxwell, Gardiner, Pearson, Jevons![5]

Keynes's *Essays in Biography* also contains some well-known references to the reception of *The Theory of Political Economy* and particularly to Marshall's 'tepid and grudging' review of the book. This review is re-produced here along with that of Cairnes, as the last representative of the classical school, that of Cliffe Leslie, representing the historical school, and the anonymous critique of the *Saturday Review*, which Edgeworth regarded as sufficiently able to merit special comment in his *Mathematical Psychics*.[6]

The index to Volumes I–VII, which appears at the end of this volume, has been prepared by Mrs Barbara Lowe of Cambridge. I should like to record my thanks to her for the great skill and meticulous accuracy with which she has carried out the very large amount of work involved.

[4] See Letter 256, n. 5, Vol. III, p. 106.
[5] *Collected Writings of J. M. Keynes*, vol. x, *Essays in Biography*, p. 237.
[6] pp. 83–6.

In conclusion, I should like to return to two points which I made at the end of the Preface to Volume I – first, to stress again that for any errors and imperfections in editing which remain in these volumes, the responsibility is mine alone; and last, but most certainly not least, to put on record my continuing gratitude to my wife and family for the support and encouragement they have given me during the years that this project has been under way.

Queen's University, Belfast   R. D. COLLISON BLACK
12 November 1975

LIST OF ABBREVIATIONS
used throughout the volumes

Relating to Jevons material

LJ   *Letters and Journal of W. Stanley Jevons*, edited by his wife (1886).

LJN   Previously published in LJ; manuscript not now in Jevons Papers, or other known location.

LJP   Previously published in LJ, but only in part; fuller text now given from the original manuscript in the Jevons Papers or other indicated location.

WM   From a manuscript made available by Dr Wolfe Mays, University of Manchester.

Investigations   *Investigations in Currency and Finance*, by W. Stanley Jevons. Edited, with an Introduction, by H. S. Foxwell (1884). All page references to first edition.

Methods   *Methods of Social Reform and other papers*, by W. Stanley Jevons (1883).

T.P.E.   *The Theory of Political Economy* by W. Stanley Jevons (1st ed. 1871, 4th ed. 1911). All page references to fourth edition, unless otherwise stated.

Relating to other material

BM   British Museum, London (now British Library).

FW   Fonds Walras, Bibliothèque Cantonale de Lausanne.

HLRS   Herschel Letters, Royal Society, London.

JRSS   *Journal of the London* (later *Royal*) *Statistical Society*.

KCP   Palgrave Papers in the Library of King's College, Cambridge.

LSE   London School of Economics, British Library of Political and Economic Science.

MA   Archives of Macmillan & Co. Ltd.

NYPL   New York Public Library.

RDF   From a manuscript made available by Mr R. D. Free.nan.

TLJM   Isabel Mills, *From Tinder Box to the 'Larger Light'. Threads from the Life of John Mills, Banker* (Manchester, 1899).

Walras Correspondence   *Correspondence of Léon Walras and Related Papers* edited by William Jaffé (3 vols, Amsterdam, 1965).

Figures following any of these abbreviations denote page numbers.

ERRATA TO VOLUMES I–VI

I, 7n.4	for *Experience* read *Experiences*
I, 14 line 3	for treacher read teacher
I, 32n.2	*Annual* not italicised in line 3; line 4 to be deleted –
lines 3, 4	repeat of line 3
I, 79n.2	for p. 187 read p. 87
I, 240–1	Jevons Family Tree: parentheses wholly or partly omitted in the following entries:
	Anne (1796–1826)
	Charles Thomas, Mary Emily (Apr 1832–May 1833)
	Mary Catherine (b. 1870)
	James Edward (b. & d. 1875)
II, 61n.3	for forces read forced
II, 66n.10	for *Chime* read *Chemie*
II, 110n.3	for Jhon read John
II, 123n.10	settled in: insert space
II, 131n.16	for ovdr read over
II, 176n.13	for Jevon's read Jevons's
II, 191n.6	for Tainity read Trinity
II, 198n.6	for *Magazing* read *Magazine*
II, 224n.3	for Boscha read Bochsa
II, 230n.14	for 1961 read 1916
II, 306n.10	for H. Pouillet read C. S. M. Pouillet
II, 369n.1	for Hendal's read Handel's
II, 401n.3	various times: insert space
II, 403n.1	for *Ecomonica* read *Economica*
II, 450n.1	for 1826–77 read 1862–77
III, 6n.2	for 1873 read 1863; for I p. 172 read I p. 190
III, 197n.3	free trade: insert space
III, 197n.5	for Chancellors read Chancellor's
III, 201	for Rosung read Roswag
IV, vi Letter 363	for Herbert Spencer read Herbert Jevons; for 27 June read 25 June
IV, 3n.1	for p. 00 read p. 22
IV, 5n.3	for or Reprints read of Reprints
IV, 33 line 3	for Machester read Manchester
line 8	for Hebert's read Herbert's

IV, 38n.2	for *The Life and Letters of Herbert Spencer*, n, 162–4 read . . . II, 162–4
IV, 52n.3	for sidely read widely
IV, 130n.1	for p. 000 read p. 141
IV, 183n.1	for 183 read 182
IV, 225	heading: for Letter 50 read Letter 508
IV, 244	line *Correspondence of Harold Wedergaard* (sic) *1878* should be deleted
IV, 273	for n.4 read n.6
IV, 303n.2	for tor read to
IV, 304n.5	for Friedrich von Weber read Carl Maria von Weber
V, 92n.3	for as basis read as a basis
V, 96n.6	for Walras, *Eléments d'économie politique appliquée* read *Etudes d'économie politique appliquée*; for *Eléments d'économie sociale* read *Etudes d'économie sociale*
V, 96n.7	for billtet read billet
V, 108n.1 line 3	for 1872 read 1827
V, 111n.2	for 1880, Rylett . . . read 1880. Rylett. . . .
V, 118n.1	for see read See
V, 124n.3	for Franais read Français
V, 163n.3	for 1822 88 read 1822–88
V, 165n.4	for denisty read density
VI, 36n.2	for n.i, p. 000 read n.3, p. 163

ECONOMIC PAPERS HITHERTO UNCOLLECTED

I CONTRIBUTIONS TO THE SYDNEY *EMPIRE*

On 17 June 1857 Jevons wrote to his sister Henrietta: 'the subject I have been most of all concerned in for the last six months is political economy'.[1] Three short pieces in the Sydney *Empire* are the first published results of that interest. As might be expected, they are examples of vigorous criticism rather than profound original thinking. Jevons had not at this time developed his own system of economic ideas, nor had he perhaps a very extensive acquaintance with those of other economists. Thus he showed no acquaintance with the theory of systematic colonisation of Edward Gibbon Wakefield,[2] on which the policy of an 'upset price' for public lands in Australia was founded, and his whole approach was empirical rather than analytical.

The background to, and bibliography of, these pieces has been set out by Professor J. A. La Nauze in his *Political Economy in Australia* (Melbourne, 1949). As Professor La Nauze states, the Sydney *Empire* was a daily newspaper, edited at this time by Henry Parkes: from September 1856 until it ceased publication in August 1858 the *Empire* included a weekly Meteorological Report written by Jevons. Not long before his death, Jevons wrote to Parkes 'I have always felt indebted to you for the kindness with which you used to publish my first efforts in science and political economy' (Jevons to Parkes, 18 June 1882, Parkes Collection, Mitchell Library, Sydney: quoted in La Nauze, op. cit., p. 39).

The first of these contributions, a comparison of the land and rail policy of New South Wales, which appeared on 8 April 1857, is reproduced in Volume II as Letter 103, pp. 282 – 7. The other two, dealing respectively with the public lands of New South Wales and with railway economy, in June and December of the same year, are reproduced below.

W. S. JEVONS TO THE EDITOR OF THE *EMPIRE*[3]

[From a Correspondent.]

THE LAND LAWS AS THEY ARE.

1. At present the waste lands of this colony are treated as a vast estate or fund, portions of which are to be economically sold or expended from

---

[1] See Vol. II, Letter 105, p. 292.
[2] See R. C. Mills, *The Colonization of Australia* (1915); D. N. Winch, *Classical Political Economy and the Colonies* (1965).
[3] Published on 24 June 1857: cf. Vol. II, Letter 107, n. 9, p. 297.

year to year, to afford a revenue for the general purposes of the community.

2. To ensure economy a minimum price of one pound per acre is imposed upon all land, which, together with any additional sum obtained by open competition, is to be paid down before occupation.

3. The extent or supply of waste lands being altogether boundless in comparison with the demand under this regulation, the upset price of land is not the *natural exchange value* of the land but a monopoly price.

4. As this monopoly price of nearly £1 per acre is paid to Government, it is properly denominated a *tax on the act of occupying and cultivating lands* otherwise useless (or very nearly so) to all. In short *price* is not the proper name, and tends to mislead persons.

5. The tax on the act of occupation though not large in comparison with the value of the produce which may be easily raised from the land, has the great fault of withdrawing capital at the very moment when it is most required for effectively commencing cultivation.

6. It is thus not an uncommon case in the country to find men who have purchased small but rich farms and expended almost their whole capital in paying the Government price or tax, obliged in consequence to defer cultivation, and in the meantime to raise a little money and support themselves by working at their former trades, even under great disadvantages. When it also happens, as I have myself known it, that these would-be farmers are living upon imported American or Chilian flour, the effects of the land-laws reach a climax of absurdity.

7. The result is shown from a statistical point of view in the following table.

Country	Year of Estimate	Population	Estimate of Acres in Crop	Proportion of Acres to each Person
New South Wales	1856	266,189	180,000	68
England and Wales	1846	16,920,879	13,300,000	·78
Canada	1848	723,332	1,281,504	1·77
Prussia	1849	16,285,013	29,782,444	1·83
France	1834	33,152,234	63,099,110	1·90

N.B. – The "acres in crop" for New South Wales are roughly estimated by adding about 10,000 to the returns for 1855, as given in the Census Report.

The other estimates are from M'Culloch, except where it was necessary to calculate the population from the nearest census.

From the above few examples it will appear probable that New South Wales is less advanced in agriculture than almost any other country in the world.

8. By the operation of the land laws is probably explained, also, the extraordinary fact, disclosed by the late census, that the rural and pastoral population only form 55 per cent. of the whole.

Population of Sydney 69,173
Ditto ditto country towns 51,391
Ditto rural and pastoral 145,625

Total of New South Wales 266,189

The number returned as engaged in agricultural occupations was only 16,728, or 6·3 per cent of the whole.

Even in England, the greatest of manufacturing countries, the rural population was just equal in 1851 to the town population, each being therefore 50 per cent. of the whole.

9. The only real benefit of the upset price is, that the sale of Crown lands yields at present about £184,000 per annum, or about one-sixth part of the revenue. The amount is, however, uncertain and fluctuating, and yields a false support, since to expend this for the ordinary purposes of government, is like a man living on his capital instead of the interest of it.

10. The chief additional argument urged in favour of the upset price is, that it prevents *land-jobbing*, and is really no impediment to those who have sufficient capital to commence farming properly. In short, that it rather ensures than obstructs the distribution of land to those who will make the best use of it.

In answer it may be said that, even supposing persons of moderate or considerable fortune are not much inconvenienced by the payment of the tax, there must always be numbers of persons of just such an amount of means that the payment or not of the tax will decide whether they can or cannot become farmers. And in the case of those who are not altogether prevented from occupying land, the effect of the tax or increased price of land is not the less injurious in proportion, as we have before instanced.

As to land speculation—

First – An upset price or tax cannot prevent speculation, but only impedes it in proportion as it impedes all sales or transactions with land from the greater sums of money involved in them.

Secondly, if it be allowed, as surely it must be, that the interests of the State lie in the distribution and cultivation of the lands, the business of the speculator is really identical with that of the Government, merely with the difference that the work will be performed a hundred times as efficiently by the former, who himself receives a portion of the profits, as by a Government Department. That much money might be made by land-jobbing is perhaps undeniable, but this implies increased gain and value in some direction, and necessarily increased cultivation; and better so than that the land should remain untouched and in every way useless. It is certain that land would now be more accessible to all classes if no upset price had ever been imposed, and that the prosperity and the revenue too of the country would be much larger than it is.

THE LAND LAWS AS THEY SHOULD BE

11.   The waste lands are useless to the community, excepting the comparatively small profits which they yield as squatting runs, whereas every acre cultivated yields produce, and supports increased population, which may be taxed in a more or less direct manner for the increase of the revenue.

12.   It being one of the chief duties of Government to raise the revenue in the least injurious and inconvenient way possible, the upset price or tax on the occupation of land should be entirely abolished.

13.   Large quantities of land, however, having been purchased for many years past on the understanding that this price would always be maintained, it would be a breach of faith to throw a practically inexhaustible supply of new lands into the market at their natural or almost nominal value, unless either compensation be offered to all previous purchasers, which is clearly impossible, or the value of all such purchased land be by some means artificially raised by the same amount.

14.   This may be most easily accomplished by imposing a perpetual yearly tax of one shilling per annum per acre, in place of the present upset price, which is equivalent to demanding the interest at 5 per cent., instead of the capital.

15.   Every facility to be offered to persons to acquire any piece of waste land they may desire in the colony, but to prevent unfair dealing as well as to ascertain the real value of the land, all sales or rather leasings had better be still made by open auction. The charges on land would therefore be as follows:—

I. Cost of survey, &c., to be paid down.
II. Fixed rent of 1s. per annum per acre.
III. Premium bid at auction.

If the third sum were required to be paid down, it would either act injuriously in withdrawing capital, or lead poor persons to select bad land purposely. It should be, therefore, turned into a yearly rent on the same terms, or the land should be leased to the person bidding the highest rent.

16.   The continual leasing of lands in this manner would yield a steady and perpetually increasing revenue of a perfectly unexceptionable character. It would be of the nature of the *tax on the increase of rent,* proposed and recommended by Mill, the great modern authority in political economy, and as the average value of all lands gradually increased from the growing numbers of the population, the land-tax might be now and then increased, say one penny per acre at a time, the increase being laid of course on all appropriated land whatever. Those portions, however, purchased previously to the change of laws would still enjoy the exemption of one shilling, which is equivalent to a repayment of the upset price.

17.   A land office should be established in which all sales and conveyances of lands would be registered, and their respective rents recorded; any purchaser of land will therefore be liable for the rent or tax, until a transfer is made in this office and accepted by the new owner.

18.   The tenure of the land to be perfectly secure and complete, and no reservations whatever to be made, but for roads and similar public purposes. The rent or more properly the tax to be only recoverable as any ordinary tax or other debt.

19.   Every facility will be offered by the Land Office for the transfer and division of land in any manner that may be desired by the owner, provided that no transfer be allowed for a less quantity than 10 acres in one piece. This is to prevent too minute a subdivision of agricultural lands, which is known to be injurious to productiveness.

20.   Land rent to be remitted on any piece of land not exceeding one acre, upon which a house or other erection of the least value of £100 shall be built, the area of land exempted to increase in some proportion if the house be of greater value than £100.

21.   Land may thus be freed from the Land Office regulations and divided in any manner for building purposes, but will be registered and assessed in a separate department of the Government, charged with collecting a moderate house tax.

22.   The sudden failure of one-sixth part of the revenue ensuing from such a change of laws, would, of course, be inconvenient for the first one or two years. Such large quantities of land would, however, be almost immediately taken on lease, as soon to remedy this. In the meantime the occasion would be a legitimate one for resorting to further loans, as the perpetual interest on the money borrowed by 5 per cent. debentures, would only be equal to the perpetual rents of the average quantity of land at present purchased every year. But much larger quantities would certainly be taken up, and instead of running in debt, the revenue would

be really gaining just as much as if the whole were paid for at the upset price.

23. Great precautions should be taken in making the change of regulations gradually, for instance, by limiting for a few years the total quantities of land allowed to be leased, lest over excitement or a crisis should be occasioned.

24. If laws were carried out on the above roughly sketched principles, it might be confidently said that New South Wales had laid the foundations of the most unexceptionable system of direct taxation in the world. The spontaneous increase of the rent or value of land, and the expenditure of each family as measured by the condition of their dwelling-house, being proved by Mill to be most desirable sources of revenue. With the assistance of duties on spirits and tobacco they might in time provide the whole.

25. And if the lands were thus thrown open to the use of all who have just enough capital to use them, the total produce would be immensely increased, and numbers would find employment in agricultural pursuits who now crowd the towns and depress wages and business in many trades (thus putting a stop to all further clamour about protection).

It is needless to enter into the benefits to the colony and all concerned in it, from the stream of emigration which would spontaneously turn hither from England, as well as from the neighbouring colonies. New South Wales would assume a new importance and a fresh position in the world.

Sydney, June 23, 1857.

W. S. JEVONS TO THE EDITOR OF THE *EMPIRE*

[29 December 1857]

[From a Correspondent.]

A short time since I wasted some trouble in trying to prove that considerations of economy may be desirable even in accepting such a magical gift of science and skill as a locomotive railway. Indirect benefits, and specious appearances of progress and improvement, seemed to me a very shadowy recompense for a most direct and tangible pecuniary loss. And not only do they seem so, but logical arguments from the most indisputable truths of Political Economy lead to the same irresistible conclusion. This was clearly and completely shewn in Professor Pell's paper, read to the Philosophical Society, and lately published in the *Sydney Magazine* for November.

But opinions which will not be accepted for mere words and arguments are now beginning to be impressed upon the public mind by a variety of slight untoward signs. Debentures, secured upon the whole consolidated revenue of New South Wales, are falling in price, or even unsaleable. The stream of capital is, in fact, dried up, indicating a want of confidence in commercial men, which is indeed well accounted for by the actual results of the speculation, viz., 38½ miles of railway in working condition for £1,049,194, with working expenses amounting to 66 per cent. of the total receipts, and leaving £38,439 as an "annual charge on revenue to defray interest." It is almost useless now to re-open the whole question of Government extension of railways, to which we are already more or less committed. The experiment is in progress, and I shall, therefore, only avail myself of opportunities as they occur, to show what the results are, and to prove by a *reductio ad absurdum* that the first principles of common sense, as well as of economical science, have been violated from the commencement. On the present occasion I shall only notice a statement on the subject which, as proceeding direct from head-quarters, perhaps requires all the more a little close criticism.

The statement I refer to is from Captain Martindale's report, as follows:—

	£	s.	d.
Annual charge on revenue to defray interest	59,670	13	7
Estimated gain to community by improved communications, per annum	362,907	11	8
Gain to community by the construction of railways after payment of all expenses, per annum . . .	303,236	18	1

The improved communications referred to in the above being "the entire of the railways existing, in progress, or at present proposed (to be constructed)."

Now, if Captain Martindale were to favour us with the full details of the calculations by which he has arrived at the above satisfactory conclusion, we should probably be smothered with such a complexity of statements as to sections and estimates, gradients, fish-jointed rails, cross sleepers, rolling stock, traffic, &c., &c., as none but the mind of a Royal engineer can fairly grapple with. I will not, therefore, prefer such a hazardous request, but proceed to treat the point after my own method. I regard the above statement as reducible at once to the following three-horned dilemma:— 1st. A fallacy in all Captain Martindale's estimates and calculations. 2nd. Absurd mismanagement in the regulation of the railway tolls. Or, 3rd. An absurd infatuation on the part of the public employing or that might employ the railway.

Having just stated this, I need scarcely explain it further. We are required to believe that a certain portion of the public, possessing, we may fairly suppose, an average share of common sense, may be expected to travel upon and employ the railways which are proposed to be immediately constructed, and we are informed that they will derive therefrom an annual benefit, pecuniarily estimated at £362,907; yet such railways will be insolvent to the extent of nearly £60,000 per annum. The public using the railway, or receiving benefit from it, coolly pocket £362,907, and are shameless enough to refuse even £60,000, or 20 per cent. of it, to pay the fair expenses, leaving this as a charge upon the remainder of the public whom the railways may positively injure by unequal competition. The alternative is evident. Raise the tolls to the extent of about 25 per cent., and maintain them by the force of legislative authority, and as sure as human nature is governed by the law of self-interest, the most of those who formerly used the railway, will disgorge a small proportion of their former profits rather than obstinately relinquish the whole. Captain Martindale may rely upon the public performing their part of the negotiation with discrimination and common sense, and the third alternative is, in short, utterly inconceivable. I will not attempt to decide between the other two alternatives.

But I shall probably be answered, "Oh, you are under a mistake. This prosperous (but inconceivable) state of affairs is what *is to be* when the extensions already proposed are completed." Well, this I must acknowledge alters the case entirely; there is such a very striking and essential difference between what *is to be* and what eventually *comes to pass,* as cannot better be illustrated than by the difference between the present financial condition of our railways and what Captain Martindale might anticipate according to his own statement if he ventured to raise the tolls. And the same difference might be still better illustrated if we could trace back the first origin and rise of the railway mania in New South Wales, which resulted in that financial phenomenon – the Parramatta railway. I have often wondered, for it does not come within my colonial experience, who they could be that first proposed that undertaking, or by what enticing statements and calculations, on a par with Captain Martindale's "gain to the community," they allured the shareholders who were only saved from loss by the unfortunate adoption of the present Government railway policy.

In the condition of things anticipated by Captain Martindale, a proper regulation of the tolls might undoubtedly render the railways solvent and even pecuniarily profitable, like the Post Office in England. I ask, could the same result be in any degree expected from raising or regulating the tolls on the present railways? If so, it is the height of folly not to do so immediately. Supposing the receipts of the railways were once rendered sufficient to pay working expenses and interest, can we doubt that capital would immediately be offered at a fair rate from every quarter, where the speculation is profitable, and an additional national security is included. Or again, taking Captain Martindale's "annual charge" at £60,000 and annual "gain to community" at £300,000, is it conceivable that capitalists should now show any signs of distrust, or that, on the contrary, capitalists, contractors, or whole organised railway companies would not rush in to secure such a useful and profitable field for speculation. The only conclusion I can draw is that Captain Martindale's statement is fallacious and even inconceivable, which cannot but throw a shadow of uncertainty over his other conclusions and recommendations so far as connected with finance and economy.

At the same time, I gladly allow that wherever Captain Martindale's technical engineering knowledge and skill are alone concerned, the report seems to be the most sensible and impartial paper on the subject, of which we have the benefit. If there is one glimpse of hope for the substantial yet judicious and economical improvement of our internal communications, it is in the proposal first made, I think, in this report, to introduce here the plank-road of the United States. A party of common fencers, one would imagine, could lay down such a line upon the existing roads, almost as rapidly and easily as they would fence them in. Surely the suggestion of plank-roads should not be lost sight of.

AN EXACT THINKER.

II   MR GLADSTONE'S NEW FINANCIAL POLICY

Macmillan's Magazine, Vol. 14 (June 1866) 130–4

This article was written at the time when the public interest aroused by *The Coal Question* was at its height. The background to it is given by the entries in Jevons's Journal for 5 and 11 March and 20 April 1866 (Vol. I, pp. 202–3 and 205) and by his correspondence with Alexander Macmillan and Gladstone (Letters 233, 238, 241–3, 245 and 257, Vol. III, pp. 84–120). In his Budget statement on 3 May 1866 Gladstone referred to Jevons's arguments on future coal supplies as a reason for redeeming debt rather than reducing taxation; this is the 'new financial policy' to which this article refers.

Of the three subsequent papers, the first two largely restate the essential arguments of *The Coal Question* in a more condensed and more popular form. The third, of which only a brief abstract was published, was written almost ten years after that book had appeared. In it Jevons sought to show that his predictions had been vindicated by the movements of coal production during the intervening years.

The *Standard* newspaper remarks that Mr. Gladstone, having worked out one vein of financial expedients – the remission of taxes – is about to pursue another line of *sensational finance*, by attacking the National Debt. It would be hard to express in fewer words so high an eulogy of both the party and their leader to whom the *Standard* is opposed.

The *Saturday Review* points out how cleverly Mr. Gladstone marked this turning-point in his financial career. "After preparing the minds of his hearers by an exordium of more than Gladstonian mystery, he kept curiosity in suspense for more than an hour while he dilated on the national importance of untaxed pepper and the reduction of the omnibus duty to $\frac{1}{4}d$. per mile." The petty character of these and other minute fiscal modifications "had, however, a special rhetorical meaning, and served to point the great thesis of the speech, that the period of fiscal revision which we have passed through with such brilliant results is drawing to a close, and that we have now entered upon a new age, in which our chief duty is, and our leading policy should be, to see to the reduction of our National Debt."

Like a musician in composing a symphony, Mr. Gladstone announces the termination of one movement by prolonged cadences, which raise expectation while they defer a new and striking movement. And the new key-note was doubtless struck with consummate skill and with effect. "In the part of his speech," says the *Spectator*, "relative to the exhaustion of coal, when he explained that the misfortune to be apprehended must fall chiefly on landowners – since labour, if wages fall, may emigrate; capital, if profits fall, will emigrate; but land cannot emigrate, and rents must fall if population and capital depart – the country gentlemen looked not only 'rather blue and dejected,' but a little indignant, as if under cover of science the Chancellor of the Exchequer had wantonly invented some new and refined species of torture for them, which they did not know how either to escape or revenge."

Now as regards this proposal to commence a new and vigorous effort for the liquidation of our debt, the *Saturday Review* remarks:—"What Mr. Gladstone says upon this subject is little more than an effective reproduction of Mr. Mill's speech on the Malt Duties."

The *Times,* again, makes it appear that Mr. Gladstone has undergone a sudden conversion. "The fervour with which he enforced, on Thursday last, the duty of paying off our obligations was new, and men are apt to distrust these sudden conversions. If all that Mr. Gladstone said was true, how came it, they ask, that he now impresses it upon us for the first time? Great financiers have before now been misled."

"It is not necessary," the *Times* continues, "to stake the adoption of Mr. Gladstone's plan for the conversion of permanent into terminable obligations upon the perfect trustworthiness of his speculations on coal. It is tolerably certain that he has exaggerated the rate at which the exhaustion of our coal-fields is proceeding by assuming, with Mr. Jevons, that the consumption will continue to increase in its present rate of geometrical progression; but, on the other hand, it is quite conceivable that some readier means of getting at the heat-power of coal may be discovered, entirely destroying our local advantages as a manufacturing nation. The true point to be considered, is whether the plan of conversion of the Chancellor of the Exchequer is good in itself."

The *Saturday Review* similarly says that "the great coal argument" may be put aside altogether, and that the main point – whether posterity will be better for cancelling the debt – is evaded by Mr. Gladstone and Mr. Mill.

We will accept the suggestion, and put aside "the great coal argument." At the same time it may be remarked that, after the emphatic challenge which Mr. Mill addressed to the House of Commons and the country on the 17th of April, we must wait for a refutation before the question can be shelved. "If Mr. Jevons's conclusions could be shown to be fallacious in any way by an honourable member, it would be most desirable that it should be done; but up to the present time no answer had been given to him which led to more than a comparatively short extension of the time during which a supply of coal may be expected."

But putting the question aside, we hold that it is altogether erroneous to say that Mr. Gladstone has suffered any sudden conversion, or displayed any inconsistency. There is no charge against this great minister more common than that of impulsiveness and inconsistency. In this case, at least, it seems to be wholly unfounded. There are some persons indeed, and even some ministers, who have only one idea, and they are consistent only as long as they pursue that idea.

Mr. Hutton, in his admirable critique on the Chancellor's character, reprinted from the *Pall Mall Gazette,* has beautifully expressed how Mr. Gladstone's mind has something in common with every phase of feeling in the country. He is emphatically a man of many ideas; and when one great idea, that of unimpeded commerce, is confessedly approaching re-alization, what is more natural and consistent than that the next most important idea should rise into prominence? The consistency of a broad mind is necessarily different from that of a narrow mind. It is fixed upon foundations which others cannot see.

There is every reason to believe that for years back Mr. Gladstone has looked forward to a reduction of the National Debt as an appropriate sequel to his great Free Trade measures. In his Budget of 1864 he explicitly stated his views. After explaining that the nett sum applied in that year to the liquidation of the debt was 4,146,000*l*., he added, "The House was pleased last year to give its sanction to more than one measure intended for the purpose of furthering and renewing that policy which aims at the reduction and extinction of debt by the conversion of Perpetual into Terminable Annuities; and I have to acquaint the House that, in consequence of those measures, we have during the last year converted Perpetual into Terminable Annuities, to the extent of 433,000*l*. *The National Debt appears to me to be a very formidable burden, grave and serious even in the midst of our wealth and prosperity, and likely to become even more grave and serious in its pressure if our prosperity turned out to be less permanent and less stable than most of us are disposed to believe.*"

The policy, the measures for carrying it out, and the views which led to its adoption, are identical with those of his last financial statement, only less full and explicit. And there is every reason to suppose that, in this emphatic reference to a "less permanent prosperity" than most of us were disposed to expect, he had his own impressions concerning our coal mines.

Let us remember how strongly Mr. Gladstone's attention must have been drawn to this subject of coal in 1860, when he was carrying the French Treaty of Commerce through Parliament, and debates arose concerning the 11th clause, which prohibits us from laying a tax on the export of coal.

Notions concerning the exhaustion of our coal seams were then freely bandied about, and Mr. Hull was led to undertake his able and successful inquiry as to the total contents of our coal-fields. Most persons, too, must remember the thrill of vague dread which ran through the nation when Sir W. Armstrong, in his address to the British Association in the autumn of 1863, speaking among the scientific and practical men of England assembled at the metropolis of the coal trade, referred to the time when that busy trade must become less busy.

There can be no doubt, too, that Mr. Gladstone's mind has for a considerable time been occupied by independent reflections on the subject of coal. Hawarden Castle lies in the Flintshire coalfield, where exhaustion is proceeding so steadily and palpably that Mr. Hull assigns forty years as the probable duration of the present supply.* It would be

---

* In this estimate no account is taken, on the one hand, of the increasing demand for coal, nor, on the other hand, of the possible increase of supply by mining under the river Dee.

hardly possible for Mr. Gladstone to shut his eyes to what was going on round his own walls. It happens that his reflections were distinctly stated. On December 30th, 1864, Mr. Beckett, F.G.S. of Wolverhampton, gave a lecture at Mold upon the Flintshire coalfield; and the Chancellor, who was present as an auditor, moved a vote of thanks. After a remarkable speech, displaying the most intimate knowledge of the conditions of the Flintshire coalfield, he said,† "He hoped that 200 years were not to see the exhaustion of the mineral wealth of England, for – having immense confidence in the resources of this country, as well as in the character of the people, which, under God, was the best of all its resources – he did think that there was nothing certainly which he for one should contemplate with such apprehension as the exhaustion of its mineral wealth, and especially of its supplies of coal."

It only needs to be considered further whether the financial arrangements of the country have reached such a point that a change of policy is natural. Fortunately the country is now so well instructed in the doctrines of Free Trade, that almost every one can discern the difference of a tax imposed purely for the purpose of raising revenue, and one which protects a certain branch of industry, and thus tends to alter the application of labour and capital.

The corn tax not only diminishes the consumption of corn by raising its price, but it also causes much corn to be grown within the country under disadvantages which would have been imported from abroad. In a twofold manner it thus cuts down our imports; our exports correspondingly diminish, and it is on these that our manufacturing population are employed. But the tax on tea has no effect beyond that of simply reducing the consumption of this article. The whole that we do use is still imported, so that our foreign trade and the employment of our population are affected only in a simple and minor manner.

It is of course desirable to do away with all taxes as soon as possible, for they all press more or less upon industry and enjoyment. But the general opinion of the public appears to accept what is probably the truth – namely, that all the taxes of exceptional hardship and of distinctly protective tendency are now removed. Future remissions of taxation will affect our enjoyment of luxuries rather than the strength of the springs of industry. The question thus arises whether we are to enjoy everything which the lavish use of coal can give, or whether we are to have some thought for our great-grandchildren.

"What has posterity done for us?" is a question that suits well the bantering tone under which an Englishman loves to hide a subject of serious concern. But why does our aristocracy uphold every vestige of

† *Times*, January 2, 1865.

feudal power? Why does it almost over-esteem every element of stability in our Constitution, unless it be to defer a little later that advent of popular power which centuries hence they fear may considerably modify the form of our society? Why do our great governing families cling to the law of entail if they have no thought of their grandchildren? And yet it is folly to cling to the shell when the kernel is gone; and the kernel of this country, as some think, is being insidiously filched away.

The only question that remains, then, is whether our posterity will really be richer by our raising revenue now, to invest it in the payment of debt "Where there is a will there is a way," and endless fallacies will doubtless be brought forward by those who have the will to show that it is better to owe than to pay. The main strength of these fallacies, however, lies in one plausible phrase, "that it is better to leave the money to fructify in the pockets of the people."§ This phrase will doubtless appear sufficient to those who never look beyond the first aspect of a question, and imagine that there must necessarily be a loss if we take money from merchants and manufacturers who are making 10 per cent. upon it and invest it in funds at 3 or 4 per cent.

But a moment's thought will show that, even supposing taxes come at one end out of capital, yet, in paying off the National Debt, it is returned at once to the fund of productive capital. In proportion as the debt is paid off an equivalent amount of capital will be set free for other investments, and, through the multifarious channels of the Stock Exchange and the Money Market, will find its way into the hands of those best able to use it.

The fact is, however, that only a minor portion of the revenue comes out of the fund of capital. For if a tax be remitted, it is not to be supposed that every one will lay by the whole amount which he formerly paid to the Government. Some may, but most will simply live rather more luxuriously than before. So, in imposing a tax or retaining one already imposed, the savings of some individuals will be reduced and the capital fund affected, but the Government will receive a large sum which individuals would have spent unproductively. Now if the Government invests the proceeds of such a tax by payment of debt, it is obvious that the capital of the country will receive a considerable increase.

It is the stomach, then, rather than the pocket which will suffer by our abstaining from a continuous and excessive reduction of taxes. If we can make up our minds to abstain even in a very slight degree from the full immediate enjoyment of the wealth which Free Trade is developing from our stores of coal, we shall have reason to expect that our grandchildren will enjoy an increased capital fund, and an immunity from a galling

§ See J. S. Mill *Of a National Debt*, Principles of Political Economy, Book v. chap. vii.

burden which we have already too long borne. Even were "the great coal argument," as it is called, put aside, our duty would hardly be less plain. This argument may not possess a definite numerical certainty; we apprehend that no one attributes such to it. But when we consider that our unprecedented wealth is gained by a consumption of fuel equally unprecedented, and exceeding that of all other countries put together; when we consider the depth our mines have already reached, and the still greater depths we must penetrate to if we are to meet the ever-growing demand, while the shallow fields are being worked out; and if we finally remember that in a Transatlantic land are coal-fields many times the extent of our own, shallow, and in the easiest condition for working: we must feel that our present peculiar supremacy must be of limited duration. It is not a foreign people we fear as competitors – it is our own people: the coal-miners and the iron-workers of Staffordshire and South Wales and Northumberland and Scotland are those we have to fear. For they will go, and they do go, and perhaps they ought to go, where high wages and expanding employment are enjoyed.

Let us not then be rendered thoughtless by the power and wealth which is undoubtedly ours at present and for some time to come. Our forefathers incurred this debt in great part for the purpose of securing the liberties we enjoy. Our fathers could not undertake its repayment, and our children and grandchildren will hardly be as well able as we now are to set the stone rolling. "Well begun is half done," and public opinion with singular unanimity allows that we should now make a good beginning. There is even that sign of perfect conviction which consists in imagining that the new thought is a familiar old one. Newspaper editors are just beginning to remember how often they impressed upon their readers the duty of repaying the debt, and the average political Englishman may be heard to exclaim that he always thought we were very neglectful about it.

What has wrought this change? Is it Mr. Neate's motion, or Mr. Mill's profoundly thoughtful and memorable speech; or the "coal argument;" or the lapse of time and the natural change and reaction of public opinion? Whatever it is, there can be no doubt it is Mr. Gladstone's financial skill which has brought us so soon to the crisis when a new policy may be wisely adopted. And it would be folly and ingratitude indeed if we should fail to acknowledge that, so far as appears, the new policy has proceeded consistently from him. If he has suffered a conversion, it must have been in progress years before any one else thought about it. In him we have a leader whose varied feelings and powers fitly represent the many interests of the British nation. To the minutest care and comprehension of our pecuniary interests he unites the highest aspirations towards the future greatness and moral elevation of his country. And on this question of the National Debt, at least, the party of his warm supporters should include the whole country.

III   ON COAL

Lecture delivered in the Carpenters' Hall, Manchester, 16 January 1867

Originally published as Lecture IX in *Science Lectures for the People,* first series (Manchester, 1871) pp. 107–18.

PROFESSOR ROSCOE, who presided, introduced the lecturer, and stated that his subject would be "Coal, its economical value, and its importance in the arts and sciences." Professor Roscoe added that the lecturer had made a special study of the subject of coal, and had published a book which had attracted great and deserved attention from scientific men, manufacturers, and the Government, and had led to the appointment of a Royal Commission for inquiring into the subject of coal, the amount of its consumption, its probable duration, &c.

Professor JEVONS explained that his remarks would be a continuation of what Dr. Roscoe had told them in his lectures about coal, its numerous uses, and the great power evolved from it by its conversion into heat and motion. Perhaps, continued Professor Jevons, the best way of showing you what coal does for us is to enumerate a few of the principal uses of coal as we apply it. First of all is its domestic use. We use it for warming our dwellings and for cooking. I think that during the present severe weather nobody will mistake the value of coal in warming our houses. I see a great number of carts of coal going about the streets – everybody seems to be trying to get a good supply; but Dr. Roscoe tells me that his coal cellar is empty, much to his inconvenience. I am afraid that a great many others may be in that unfortunate position, with the thermometer near zero. I will give you an idea how much coal is used for domestic purposes. According to the common estimate, the average consumption of coal for each person annually is one ton, which would make about 30,000,000 tons per annum, in the United Kingdom. It is obvious that we should not know what to do without coal, for there is not timber enough in the country to supply the fires. If we burnt wood, we should need to plant nearly the whole of the country with trees. In France wood is still used as fuel, and much valuable land has to be given up to the growth of forest trees. Even in the United States, which used to be considered an inexhaustible country, the scarcity of wood is becoming felt in some parts, and the Washington government has recommended the planting of trees in some of the states. But the domestic use of coal constitutes a small part of its utility. The next use I may mention is in the working of the metals – for instance, in the blacksmith's forge. From the earliest times coal seems to have been used for the blacksmith's fire. It is peculiarly suitable for making that sort of "breeze" or small coal which is necessary for the blacksmith. It is very probable that the abundance of coal in Staffordshire and Yorkshire assisted in the formation of the iron trade, and the production of those numerous hardwares for which Birmingham, Wolverhampton, and Sheffield are celebrated. But in the present day we use coal in a much more extensive way than formerly, in the coal blast furnace, in making iron. Another use of coal is in the salt trade, which is confined to a limited district, where the salt rock occurs in Cheshire; but that small district supplies the greater part of the world with salt. Salt was originally derived from sea water, through evaporation, by the sun's rays; instead of the heat of the sun we now use heat from coal, which is employed for boiling the salt pans. Without this cheap fuel, salt could not be produced at its present low cost, so that we are able to send salt to India, Australia, and South America, and almost every part of the world. We use coal again in the chemical manufactures of this neighbourhood. It is almost impossible to carry on any chemical operation without an abundant supply of heat, for boiling, melting, evaporating, dissolving, &c. The chief chemical manufactures are situated between Manchester and Liverpool and on the Tyne, the banks of which river are covered with them, as is evident from the fumes and the great heaps of refuse. But far more important is the iron manufacture, or the smelting of iron with coal. This mode has arisen within the last 100 years. It was not until the middle of the last century that men succeeded in making iron by the use of coal; previously it had been done by charcoal. To such an extent has this trade grown that during the last year 28 million tons of coal were used in smelting and puddling iron, that is making it into wrought iron. In all these trades coal produces heat, which is used directly.

The next use is where we turn the heat into force, as in the steam-engine. I need not in Manchester remind you how much the steam-engine does for us. It is used to do the greater part of our work, and such is its force that the people of England are said to perform as much work by the aid of the steam-engine, as all the people in the world could effect by hand labour. I will enumerate a few of the uses of the steam-engine. First of all the engine pumps for us, that is to say, it gives us the power of raising water. You may not at first appreciate the full importance of that use, but the engine was invented for the sole purpose of pumping the water from mines, and without the pumping-engine we could never have had our mines to anything like their present depth. The iron trade, again, is impossible on a large scale without the engine; of course iron was made before the engine was invented, but not to the same extent. The utmost difficulty was felt a century ago in commanding blast power sufficient for iron works, and it was only by the engine that the power could be obtained which is necessary for producing large iron plates in the rolling mill. It would be utterly impossible to obtain this power by means of wind mills. From 20 to 50 wind mills would be required to produce the power often needed in a mill, and during one-half of the year there might be no wind at all, and the works would come to a stop. Again, the engine is necessary for all our machinery in Manchester. Steam-boats depend entirely on coal, for not only are their hulls and engines made of iron, but they are propelled by coal. I do not think that sailing vessels will be used much longer for passenger traffic and the conveyance of the more valuable class of goods. There will be as little travelling by sailing vessels as there is now by canal boats. If any of you remember the Liverpool harbour and docks 20 years ago, and know what they are now, you will realize how important a part coal plays in our steam navigation. Again, I need not remind you that our inland conveyance is carried on by coal. The locomotive is made by the use of coal, and it burns coal; the railroad is also made by the use of coal for it is an iron road; and although our railways do a great deal for us, I think they will yet do much more. I do not think we have reached the limit of railway construction even in this country, and as to the rest of the world, with the exception of a few countries, they have yet to make their railways. Probably you think that I have mentioned enough uses of coal, but you must not forget that this room is lighted with coal, and that all our best means of illumination are now derived from coal. For nearly 50 years we have had gas illumination, and it has been gradually extending until now every small town in the country is lighted with gas. But during the last twenty years we have commenced the production of petroleum or paraffin oil, that now fill our lamps. I think you can get a good lamp for sixpence, and a better light than by any tallow dip for about a farthing per night. Candles used to be made of wax, spermaceti, and other expensive materials; as fine looking candles, and much cheaper ones are made from paraffin, which is derived from coal. Nor can we see any end to the uses to which the oil derived from coal may be applied. The thicker oils are used as lubricants, taking the place of palm and other oils. We have used tar for a long time as a kind of paint to preserve wood, but it is only of late years that it has been found to yield a multitude of valuable things, such as colours and scents. The beautiful mauve and magenta colours are derived from coal-tar, as well as the pine apple and other flavours that are used in the manufacture of sweetmeats. We used to think that all the wealth came from India; it comes rather from the "black diamond," as coal has been appropriately named. The coal mines are our Indies. Dr. Roscoe told you the other night that the diamond was nothing but carbon. A diamond hardly larger than your finger end would be worth thousands of pounds, but I think that, according to a just estimate of utility, a ton of coal is far more valuable. Yet you can in some places get a ton of coal at the pit's mouth for five shillings.

Now, considering all these things that coal is capable of producing, we cannot be surprised to find that the coal fields are the chief seats of our industry. I can give a very simple reason for that, namely, that if you carry coal far its price is very much enhanced. Coal at the pit's mouth is perhaps the cheapest thing we use, but its transit to any distance doubles its price. Iron costs £8 a ton; copper, lead, and other metals nearly £100 a ton, yet coal, which is capable of producing all these things costs but 5s. a ton. Although we have developed ways of carrying things cheaply, you cannot carry coals to London without about doubling its price. The best coal, which will be 9s. or 10s. at the pit's mouth, will cost about 20s. in London. In Brighton Dr. Roscoe informs me that coal is 32s. a ton; it is obvious, therefore, that no business can be profitably carried on in Brighton which requires a great consumption of coal. A large number of iron ship-builders in London (15,000 it is said) are out of work. Various reasons have been assigned for this, but I believe the real cause is the high price of coal and iron in London, owing to the cost of carriage. Iron cannot be carried to London without increasing its price about 15s. per ton. The quotations of iron in the London market are always higher than in the Staffordshire market and in the other iron and coal fields. Coal is also dearer in London, consequently shipbuilders cannot compete with builders on the Mersey and the Clyde. I could never quite understand why the masters established iron ship-building in London, where the articles used are so much dearer; and it is not surprising that several of them have failed. The unfortunate result of this misplaced trade is, that when bad times come, and the demand for iron ships falls off, thousands of workpeople are idle and suffering. To show you how the trades arise upon our coal fields and stick to them, I will show you a plan of the English coal fields. [Professor Jevons exhibited on the illuminated screen a series of maps showing the coal fields and the grouping around them of the great trades of England.] There was no part, it appeared, where population was so concentrated as about Manchester. The South Wales coal fields were said to be inexhaustible. In Staffordshire the coal was 30ft. thick and near the surface. The fields in Yorkshire, Shropshire, Durham, Cumberland, and Scotland, were pointed out. There was a small field of coal in the Forest of Dean, a tract of country which was formerly very celebrated. An immense trade had sprung up in South Wales. The Newcastle field was the oldest. For five centuries Newcastle had supplied London with coal through the coasting trade. From the Whitehaven field Ireland was supplied. The Scotch fields were in Ayrshire, Fife, and the Lothians.

The Professor next pointed out the scarcity of manufacturing towns in the agricultural districts, such as Lincoln and Bucks. In the agricultural counties there were handicrafts carried on, such as straw platting, making boots, gloves, lace, &c. These trades were unknown in the mining and iron districts, where they had more profitable trades. He mentioned instances to show how trades shifted their locality through the discovery of coal. The woollen trade of England, he said, was for many centuries its staple trade. The Lord Chancellor sits upon a woolsack, as an emblem of England's power. The wool trade was formerly most prosperous in Norfolk, but it had almost disappeared from that county, and was transferred to Yorkshire, because the weaving, &c., was now done by steam power, for which a new and cheap supply of coal was necessary. A more surprising instance was the iron trade. Formerly the iron used in England was made by means of charcoal, and the chief seat of the trade was Sussex. The charcoal was got from the woods, taken to a small forge, and power was got from a waterwheel. About 200,000 tons were thus yearly produced in this country a century ago, not more than is now turned out of one iron works. The iron trade has now removed to Staffordshire, South Wales, Newcastle, and Scotland, and there is not a ton of iron now made in Sussex, or anywhere near it.

It is difficult to express what a contrast Lancashire now presents to its former condition. About the year 1400, four centuries and a half ago, it was looked upon as a kind of morass or waste, and the people were supposed to be so uncivilized that travellers did not like to venture into it. Some ancient documents recently discovered, show it to have been about the poorest county in England.* One of the most reliable early English writers was Camden. In his "Britannia," a celebrated book, he speaks of Lancashire as "that country lying beyond the mountains towards the western ocean." He spoke of the people of Lancashire as if they were but half civilized. He says, "first of all, the people whom I approach with a kind of dread. However, that I may not seem wanting, I will run the risk of the attempt, hoping that the divine assistance which has favoured me hitherto will not fail me now." That is the way in which he regarded our forefathers – for I have the pleasure of being a Lancashire man.

An enlarged map showing the localization of the trades was then shown. Almost every trade was found around Manchester, excepting the great iron trade. He did not know why the metal trades were not more numerous on the Lancashire coal field – but perhaps it was because we

* See Professor Roger's History of Agriculture and Prices in England.

had so many other things to do. These trades were, however, springing up, and one of the finest steel works in the country, was that lately built at Gorton. He had hoped to have another map showing the railways, but the snow had prevented it being photographed. This map would have displayed the remarkable fact that the railways were most ramified and numerous close upon the coal fields. In the agricultural districts the railways were fifteen to twenty-five miles apart. The lines that paid best were those connected with the coal fields. Some of the earliest railways, such as the Great Western and the Great Eastern, which ran through agricultural counties, were now the most unfortunate, although at one time great hopes were entertained of their success. On the other hand the railways that ran through coal fields, or were connected with them, especially the London and North-Western, appeared to have the power of developing an endless amount of traffic. This connection of railways and the coal trade, the Professor added, is more intimate than you think. The fact is we owe the railway to coal. Railways were invented two centuries and more ago for the purpose of carrying coal and for no other purpose, and for nearly two centuries they were used only for carrying coal and a few other minerals. Again, it is by the use of the locomotive, another product of coal, that we have been able to spread railways. And what I want to point out is that the railway system is still necessary for the coal trade, for we could not carry the weight of coal we require by any other means. Twelve of the great railway companies last year carried 50,000,000 tons of coal, the remainder was carried by the other companies, and by canal and sea. The enormous amount of coal we raise depends greatly on the railways for its conveyance to the several towns and villages of the country, and it is only by extending our railways still further that we can develop the coal trade in a way that the coal owners desire. There are at present several schemes afloat for extending our coal railways: one line is to run all the way from Newcastle to London, purposely to carry coal; another is to run right through the Lancashire district, in order to carry coal to Liverpool and to ship it there, as well as to supply the steamers. Another line is designed to carry coal from South Wales to London. Now it is plainly by the use of railways that we develop the coal trade, and it is the coal trade that favours the extension of the railway system; they work one into the other. I will point out another proof of the result of the use of coal depending upon the density of population.

On an average of the whole kingdom there are 344 persons to a square mile. In Lancashire we have 1,280, that is nearly four times as many as in the rest of the kingdom. Staffordshire has 652, the West Riding 564 persons to the square mile. Now contrast that with some of the agricultural counties:—Bucks 230, Hereford 147, Dorset 192, Lincoln 148.

The most striking proof perhaps of what coal is doing for us is shown in the progress of population. All the coal producing counties are increasing very rapidly. Lancashire in the ten years from 1851 to 1861 increased in population 20 per cent, Staffordshire 23 per cent., West Riding 14 per cent, Durham 30 per cent. Glamorganshire 37 per cent. Now of these counties Durham and Glamorganshire are the two counties where the trade has been developed most rapidly. Compare those numbers with the following for the agricultural counties:—Bucks 3 per cent, Hereford 7, Dorset 2, Lincoln 1, Somerset no increase at all; but that is a great deal better than a falling off, which we find in a good many counties. Suffolk diminished 2 per cent in population, Wiltshire 2, Cambridge 5 per cent.

I might go on to point out the changes in towns. It is curious that the larger towns are the more rapidly they increase proportionately to their size. I will read a sentence from the census report:— "The towns where silk and woollen goods and gloves are made increased slowly; the towns famous for cottons, for stockings, shoes, and straw plait increased more rapidly. The increase of population was most rapid in the seaport towns, and in the mining districts, where hardware is made, in that direction the tide of natural industry has recently flowed."

I might show you in another way what coal does for our manufacturers, by accounts of the quantities of goods produced, by showing in short upon what we live. It is obvious that we live to a certain extent upon the wheat, barley, oats, potatoes, cattle, and garden produce of our fields, gardens and dairies. We also spin and weave the wool of our own sheep, and the flax grown in Ireland. But it is obvious that these products are not capable of much increase. On the other hand we use every year a great quantity of foreign produce, not only wheat but things that do not grow in England. Thus we get sugar from the West Indies, tea and silk from China, rice and spices from the East, and cotton from almost all parts of the world. How do we get these things? Of course we have to pay for them. For every £100 worth of material brought into the country we must send out £100 worth in return. To India we send a great deal of gold that we get from Australia, and we send silver got from South America. But how do we get the gold and silver? We must pay for them. We get them by means of our coal produce. We work all these materials up into things which other nations desire to buy, and it is only by constantly shipping more and more goods that we get more and more additions of material and food. The consequence is we must go on using more and more coal in our manufactures.

I will now draw your attention to the quantity of coal we use, and the value of it.

Perhaps you might say that it is not our coal alone that is so valuable, but our copper, iron, and lead mines. But these are unimportant in comparison with coal. I can tell you exactly what these things are worth. Mr. Hunt, of the Mining Record Office, in London, states that in 1865, the value of the ores raised was:—iron, copper, lead, &c., £7,821,000; coal £24,537,000; so that the value of coal is three times as much as the other minerals. You may see this in another way. We not only use our own copper, lead, iron, and other ores, but we import largely from other countries. The fact is that the Cornish copper mines are beginning to fail, and we can get metals cheaper elsewhere. Many years ago there prevailed a notion that we were using a great deal of coal, but there were only wild guesses as to the quantity, until 1854, when the first return was made at 64,600,000 tons. Since then we have had accurate accounts of the consumption of coal every year. The following table shows the quantity of coal raised and exported in Great Britain from 1854 to 1865:—(See Postscript, p. 28)

COAL TRADE OF GREAT BRITAIN.

Year.	Coal raised.		Coal exported.	
1854	64,661,000	tons	4,309,000	tons
1855	64,453,000	,,	4,976,000	,,
1856	66,645,000	,,	5,879,000	,,
1857	65,394,000	,,	6,737,000	,,
1858	65,008,000	,,	6,529,000	,,
1859	71,979,000	,,	7,081,000	,,
1860	83,208,000	,,	7,412,000	,,
1861	85,635,000	,,	7,222,000	,,
1862	83,638,000	,,	7,694,000	,,
1863	88,292,000	,,	7,529,000	,,
1864	92,787,000	,,	8,063,000	,,
1865	98,150,000	,,	8,585,000	,,

Last year people were rather alarmed to find that the consumption had risen to 98 million tons. It is hard to form a notion of what a million is. At the Crystal Palace they have printed a piece of calico with a million dots, to enable people to see how many a million is, but you cannot take in the number with the eye at all, consequently you cannot conceive what a hundred millions would be. But to give you some notion of what the weight and size of this coal would be, I have drawn here a representation of the Great Pyramid of Egypt, and another picture by the side of it, of the much greater coal pyramid which we consume every year. The Great Pyramid, it is said by Herodotus, was twenty years in building, and it took 100,000 men all that time to raise it. It contains 3,394,307 cubic yards of stone. The coal raised last year would make a Pyramid of 100,000,000 cubic yards, since a cubic yard of coal weighs very nearly a ton. The quantity of coal we raised is therefore thirty times as much as the Great Pyramid, which is considered one of the greatest works ever erected. The largest stone work in England is said to be the Plymouth Breakwater, but the Great Pyramid contains six times as much stone as that; yet our coal raised in one year was thirty times as much as the stone in the pyramid!

The question has been suggested by a number of writers as to whether sooner or later, we shall not get to the bottom of our coal mines. A hundred million tons of coal is an enormous quantity to consume every year; but it is not this amount that is so alarming as the rate at which the consumption increases year by year. In 1865 we used half as much again as in 1854. Now if we go on in that sort of way – if in 1876 we use half as much again as we do now, and still went on in that way, we should get to amounts that would be alarming to contemplate. Some people say we shall not do so – that we shall economise our coal, use it more carefully, and get more power out of it in the steam engine. The fact is, we are doing that now. Iron is now made by much less coal than it used to be, yet we use more coal than ever. Engines are better now than they were in 1854, but this has not cut down our coal consumption; then what is the likelihood that it will do so in the future? The fact is that coal is a thing of such value to us that we cannot help spending it – there is more temptation than we can resist. It is such a useful substance that we find wealth in it more and more every year. The consequence is there is one trade that always seems brisk. If you read the trade reports in the newspapers, you will see that the Cardiff steam coal trade always seems to be brisk. But, I ask myself, is it really favourable for us to be spending our capital at this rate, and will it always be so?

And again, it is not so much the amount of coal that we use, as that compared with the coal produce of other countries which is astonishing. It is obvious that our enormous power of coal partly explains our extraordinary position in the world. You will appreciate what I mean when I compare the total produce of coal in Britain and in the world. We used 98 millions; now the known coal produce of the whole world is said to be 164 millions, so that we used 60 per cent of the coal used in the whole world, although we are only 30 millions of people out of about 1,220 millions. All the Anglo-Saxon nations together use 116 millions, or 70 per cent – seven parts out of ten are used by one race. This may explain, in some degree, the advance of this race in material power and possessions. But then we ought to look at the comparative quantity of coal in different parts of the world. Professor Jevons referred to a map showing the proportion of the coal in various countries. Russia was said to have a large quantity of coal, but scarcely any of it was worked. Australia has a certain supply. New Zealand has a small deposit. The maker of this map has indeed inserted a large black tract, or coalfield, in the interior of

Australia. Now, if he is correct, and there are really those extensive coalfields, Australia will probably become the first country in the world. But I am very much afraid it is a mistake. But when you come to North America we have the most solid reality as to the extent of coal. In the interior there are great expanses of coal of the most perfect quality, and in circumstances most suitable for working, such as the Pennsylvanian and Mississippi fields. The better way will be to compare the relative extent of coal produced in different countries:— Great Britain, 98 million tons; Zollverein, 20; United States, $16\frac{1}{2}$ (rapidly increasing); France, 10; Belgium, 10 (also rapidly increasing); Australia, $4\frac{1}{2}$; Russia, $1\frac{1}{2}$; Spain, 300,000; New South Wales, 250,000; Ireland, 123,000. The last quantity is as much as one respectable colliery in England would turn out. It is said that there is a large area of coal in Ireland, but it certainly is not worth much. Among all the reasons given for Irish misfortune, this absence of coal goes a considerable way.

Now let us compare these products of coal with the quantities believed to exist in different countries. I have represented the extent of the English coal measures by a black square indicating 5,400 square miles; Prussia contains 1,370, much less than England; so with France, 984. The United States contain the largest area of coal in any country – viz., 196,000 square miles. They have the means of developing the coal trade almost indefinitely.

The only thing that remains to be said is as to what we ought to do under the circumstances. The fact is that if other nations go on increasing their yield of coal – especially if America develops her resources, as she must do – then we cannot hold such a prominent position as we do now. I do not say that we cannot always be pretty well off, but we cannot take the lead in the markets of the world, and have the largest shipping and coal trades, and the largest manufactories, because not only shall we find it difficult to get coal for ourselves, but they will be getting a great deal more, and coal will be much more valuable 50 or 100 years hence, because it will be more and more a source of power. Some people think that we ought to begin cutting down our produce of coal, and that we ought to prohibit the exportation to France and other countries. But that is a very narrow-minded view of the question. I do not know that we have a right to keep things to ourselves in that manner. I think it is the duty of every country to use its wealth to the best purpose, and to communicate it in the way of free trade. We do not give them our coal for nothing – we get something for it; and it would be in every way a most short-sighted policy to violate those admirable doctrines of free trade which Manchester has done so much to establish. But if by increasing our trade we are diminishing our wealth for the future, then we ought to be thinking about that. It strikes me that the best way to prepare for future time is by taking every advantage of the present. I do not think that our descendants will blame us if we take proper precautions to use our coal economically, and to get the best possible return for it – that is to say, the most force and the most wealth, and not to burn it needlessly upon waste heaps, as is sometimes done. And, secondly, when we get this wealth from our coal, we must take care to turn it to the best account. We must use our wealth as it ought to be used. If we use it in mere luxury and mismanagement, such as in our dockyards, we shall be justly blamed; but if we use it in improving the condition of every one, so far as it can be improved – if we use it in providing education, in improving the dwellings; and if we could by any possibility use it so as to do away with pauperism, and to provide libraries and institutions or anything that will increase the power and improve the character of our people, then I think we shall never be blamed for using our coal too fast. This is the way in which we shall best provide for any future difficulties under which our country may labour.

A vote of thanks to the lecturer, moved by one of the audience, and carried with applause, concluded the proceedings.

POSTSCRIPT. – Several years having elapsed since the delivery of the above lecture, the following additional figures can be given to show the subsequent progress of the coal trade of the United Kingdom.

Year.	Coal raised.		Coal exported.	
1866	101,630,000	tons	9,367,000	tons
1867	104,500,000	,,	10,565,000	,,
1868	103,141,000	,,	10,967,000	,,
1869	107,427,900	,,	10,744,000	,,

IV ON THE PROBABLE EXHAUSTION OF OUR COAL MINES

Lecture delivered at the Royal Institution, 13 March 1868

Originally printed in *Notices of the Proceedings at the Meetings of the Members of the Royal Institution of Great Britain,* with Abstracts of the Discourses delivered at the Evening Meetings, vol. v, 1866–1869 (1869) pp. 328–34.

I. THE coal raised from the coal mines of the United Kingdom in the year 1866 amounted to more than *one hundred million tons* (more exactly 101,630,544 tons), according to the excellent returns published by Mr. Robert Hunt, of the Mining Record Office. Reflecting upon the full significance of this fact it may be asserted:—

1. That the coal trade of this kingdom is the greatest trade, in regard to the bulk and weight of the commodity, ever carried on.

2. That every pound of that vast quantity of coal may be regarded as a pound of the most intrinsically useful and valuable substance ever discovered.

3. That the power and usefulness of coal is felt in every branch of industry, and in almost every operation which we carry on.

4. That Britain possesses the aid of this most invaluable substance in an altogether peculiar degree; and –

5. That we cannot hope to stand very long in this most happy position.

II. So vast a quantity as 100,000,000 tons cannot be represented to the eye or mind. Its bulk is 30 times as great as that of the greatest single work of human hands, the Pyramid of Cheops. Greater quantities of commodities are brought into British ports at present, than are recorded in the history of any nation, and yet it would take more than seven times as many vessels as those which enter our ports in a year to carry the quantity of coal we use.

More than half of the whole carrying power of the railways of the United Kingdom, devoted to goods traffic, is occupied in the conveyance of coal. So far as we can judge from returns, which do not always distinguish the kinds of goods carried, the goods traffic of the railways of the United Kingdom in 1865 was as follows:—

General Merchandise*	36,800,000
Minerals	18,300,000
Total	55,100,000
Coal and Coke	59,500,000
Total	114,600,000

III. This vast trade in coal can only be accounted for by considering the wonderful qualities with which coal is endowed. It is the MAINSPRING OF OUR MATERIAL INDUSTRY. It may be called the real Philosopher's Stone, which supplies us cheaply and plentifully with everything that can

---

* Not including live stock, of which the weight is not ascertained.

conduce to the service of man. This extreme usefulness of coal is due –

1. To the enormous power which is latent in it, and is brought forth when we burn it;

2. To the fact, now so clearly revealed by science, that *force is the key to all the changes of matter.*

By aid of the mechanical equivalent of heat, we can ascertain that good coal contains latent force sufficient to raise its own weight 11,422,000 feet, or about 2100 miles against the force of gravity. The coal raised in 1866 may further be calculated to contain force equal to that which would be exerted by 530,000,000 horses, or 2,650,000,000 men, working eight hours a day for 300 working days in the year.

IV. This vast power is turned to use in an indefinite multitude of ways, which may thus be rudely classified.

CLASSIFICATION OF THE USES OF COAL

(I.) AS SOURCE OF HEAT.

1. *For Household Use.* – Warming and ventilating houses, churches, public buildings, &c.
2. *For the Alteration of Cohesive Condition of Substances.*
   Melting and casting of metals; softening and forging of metals – the blacksmith's fire.
   Manufacture of glass, bricks, earthenware, &c.
   Boiling salt, soap, &c.; brewing; distilling; drying substances.
   Chemical manufactures.
3. *For the Production of Power by the Steam, Gas, or Hot-air Engine.* Pumping water; draining mines; supply of water; removal of sewage.

Steam navigation.

Railways, and road locomotives.

Hammering, rolling, and working metals.

Mill and factory labour.

Hydraulic and pneumatic machines.

Small machines moved by gas engine.

Machine agriculture; steam ploughing, &c.

Manufacture of ice.

(II.) AS REDUCING AGENT; SOURCE OF HEAT, WITH CHEMICAL AFFINITY.

Smelting of the metals – iron, copper, lead, zinc, &c.

Chemical manufactures.

(III.) As Indirect Source of Electricity by Magneto-Electric Machines.

> Electro-telegraphy.
> Electro-metallurgy.

(IV.) As Source of Light.

> Gas manufacture; petroleum; paraffin candles.
> Electric light-house illumination.
> Photography by artificial light.

(V.) As Source of Material.

> Tar, pitch, naphtha, lubricating oils.
> Ammoniacal manures; carbolic acid; aniline dyes; ethereal
>> odours and flavours, &c.

It is only by thus collecting together the multitudinous uses of coal that we can gain an adequate idea of its importance to us and the certainty that its use will extend.

V. Comparing, now, the present yield of coal (100,000,000 tons annually) with the quantity which Mr. Hull believes to lie in these islands, within 4000 feet of the surface and in workable condition (83,544,000,000 tons), we find that we might continue to consume coal at our present annual rate for 835 years at least; but when we remember that our consumption has increased by 36 millions in the last twelve years (from about 65 millions in 1854 to 101,000,000 in 1866), and that the causes of increase still continue in existence, we cannot attribute any importance to the above calculation. There is no appearance that steam navigation or railways have at all approached their full development in this country; while in the steam-plough, in schemes of steam-drainage or water-supply, the employment of steam-produced hydraulic pressure, in the use of small gas-engines in workshops, and in a multitude of other ways, we have some indication of the increased future demand for coal.

VI. Economy, it may be pointed out, does not tend to reduce the industrial consumption of coal, but acts in the opposite direction: by increasing the profitableness of coal-labour, it extends its use. Almost every improvement in the engine for the last century and a half has been directed to economizing the consumption of coal; and yet the use of the engine and the quantities of coal consumed advanced *pari passu* with its economical performance.

It is altogether irrational to argue that progressive economy, which has coexisted with and been the partial cause of advancing consumption in the past, will have the opposite effect in the future.

VII. As regards the law of increase of coal consumption, both experience and theory lead us to believe that the increase takes place in a geometrical series, by multiplication rather than by mere addition. The following numbers will illustrate the difference in question:—

| *Arithmetical Series*, increasing by addition .. | 1 2 3 4 5 6 7 8 |
| *Geometrical Series*, increasing by multiplication | 1 2 4 8 16 32 64 128 |

The following table will show that when we can get accurate statistics of the consumption of coal we find the increments indefinitely increasing, in the manner rather of a geometrical than of an arithmetical series.

Year	Total quantity of coal imported into London.	Increase in fifty years.
	Tons.	Tons.
1650	216,000	—
1700	428,100	212,100
1750	688,700	260,600
1800	1,099,000	410,300
1850	3,638,883	2,539,883
1863	5,119,887	5,696,170*

The above and other statistics quoted in the 'Coal Question,'† Chapters IX. X. and XI., show that our industry grows by multiplication, and by multiplication at a rising rather than at a falling rate. The temporary depressions of trade which occur at intervals may sometimes seem to check the rapidity of this increase; but we have only to wait a year or two to see our industry advancing again with growing strides.

No statements of the total amount of coal produced in this kingdom are the least to be relied on, except those collected by Mr. Robert Hunt, the Keeper of Mining Records, and the following is a statement of the general progress of the coal trade of the United Kingdom as ascertained by him:§—

Year.	Coal raised. Tons.	Coal exported. Tons	Year.	Coal raised. Tons.	Coal exported. Tons.
1854	64,661,000	4,309,000	1861	85,635,000	7,222,000
1855	61,453,000	4,976,000	1862	83,638,000	7,694,000
1856	66,645,000	5,879,000	1863	88,292,000	7,529,000
1857	65,394,000	6,737,000	1864	92,787,000	8,063,000
1858	65,008,000	6,529,000	1865	98,150,000	8,585,000
1859	71,979,000	7,081,000	1866	101,630,000	9,367,000
1860	80,042,000	7,412,000			

It is impossible to view, without some degree of alarm, so rapid an increase of the coal trade as the preceding figures indicate. Without doubt our production will advance to 200 millions before very many years are past; and the alarming calculation may be made that if we went on

* Increase as for fifty years, if continued at same rate as during the thirteen years experienced.
† 'The Coal Question: an Inquiry concerning the Progress of the Nation, and the Probable Exhaustion of our Coal Mines.' By W. S. Jevons, M.A. 2nd ed. revised. London, 1866. (Macmillan.)
§ I am kindly informed by Mr. Hunt that when the returns of the consumption of coal in 1867 are completed, the total will probably amount to 104,000,000 tons, showing continued increase in spite of the depression of trade.

increasing our production of coal for 110 years as rapidly as we have done during the last 12 years, our coal seams would be worked out to a depth of 4000 feet. But such a supposition is put forward, not as a serious possibility, but as a *reductio ad absurdum*. The conclusion to be drawn from it is simply that the nation cannot possibly progress in material wealth for 110 years more as rapidly as it has done in the present century. The limited extent of our coal-fields would not allow us to go on increasing the draught of coal as lavishly as we have done. But it is the very necessity of changing from a highly progressive to a less progressive or stationary condition, that is most grievous. Population and production, when once set in motion, move with a certain impetus, and it is the check to such motion which is distressing and threatening.

VIII. The subject wears a more serious aspect still when we consider the coal resources and production of other countries as well as our own.

According to the latest returns which are at hand, it would seem that the total known produce of coal in the world is thus distributed over the chief nations:—

	Tons.
Great Britain	101,630,000
United States	25,800,000
Prussia and the Zollverein..	20,610,000
France	10,710,000
Belgium..	9,935,000
Austria	4,500,000
British North America	1,500,000
Russia	1,500,000
Spain	300,000
New South Wales	250,000
Ireland	123,500
Total	176,858,500

It would appear then that of the total *known* produce of coal in the world we raise considerably more than half (57 per cent.), although we form probably not more than one in forty of the population of the world. If to our own coal produce we add that of the United States and our colonies, we may conclude that the Teutonic race enjoys 73 per cent., or almost 3 parts out 4, of the coal raised. It is hardly possible to over-estimate the forces acting in our favour which are represented by this partial monopoly of the most powerful material agent of civilization.

The total quantity of coal existing can hardly be said to be known in the case of any one country; but some notion of the comparative coal resources of different countries may be gained from the following statement of the area of the coal-measures in the chief coal-producing countries, as estimated by Professor Rogers:—

	Area of Coal Lands in square miles.
United States	196,650
British North American Possessions	7,530
Great Britain	5,400
France	984
Prussia	960
Belgium..	510
Bohemia.	400
Westphalia	380
Spain	200
Russia	100
Saxony	30

Though Great Britain is far more abundantly provided with coal than any continental nation, our resources sink into insignificance beside those of North America, and no very long period will elapse before this comparative poverty in coal will make itself felt.

IX. It is continually suggested, indeed, that before coal is at all likely to be exhausted, some substitute will be found for it, and appeal is made to some old proverb, like *Necessity is the mother of invention*. But it requires very little philosophy to see that the proverb is very partially true. We live in a chronic state of necessity and difficulty, and the great discoveries which we enjoy are but so many exceptional instances in which we have been unexpectedly relieved from labour and evil. We have no real ground for supposing that when one exceptional advantage is withdrawn from us, another will immediately be extended to us.

The favourite notion that electricity will be the future source of power is entirely fallacious; for the coal-driven engine moving the magneto-electric machine is now the cheapest source of electricity, and by gradual improvements, such as that in Mr. Wilde's machine, coal will become a still cheaper source of electricity. Even the elements of the electric battery have always been practically furnished by the reducing power of coal. If coal then become, as there is every reason to suppose it will, a cheaper and cheaper source of electricity, it is obviously absurd to suppose that electricity should supersede the power of coal.

It is conceivable, indeed, that in the course of ages some wholly new source of power might be discovered; but there is no reason to suppose that this island, which forms but the one four-hundredth part of the total land-area of the globe, would be as richly endowed with the new source of power as it is with coal. If the sun's beams are in the future to be the direct source of power, it is the plains of Africa or of Australia that will be the seats of industry and not this cloud-obscured Isle.

X. The conclusions we must come to on this subject are then as follows:—

1. The power of coal is extending itself and making itself more widely and deeply felt every day. It is more and more taking the place of wind, horse, or manual power, and is becoming the universal assistant.

2. We are naturally led every day to extend our consumption of so invaluable a substance, and experience shows that the more we use the more extensive are our augmentations.

3. Our consumption is already commensurable with our total supply; that is to say, we can form some notion how long our supply will endure with a stationary consumption.

4. As this consumption increases by multiplication, our national life becomes shortened, and it is apparent that the increase cannot go on very long at the present rate.

5. The moment we are forced to draw in, other nations, possessing far more extensive fields of coal compared with their annual consumption, will be enabled to approach and ultimately to pass us.

6. The exhaustion of our mines, as it will probably manifest itself within the next hundred years, will consist not in any stoppage of supplies, but an increase of cost, and the impossibility of increasing the consumption each year as at present.

XI. At some future time then, when coal will be even a more useful agent than at present, we shall stand in a position of comparative inferiority. For such a time we can best prepare ourselves, not by short-sighted restrictions on the consumption or evaporation of coal, but by freeing the nation from its burdens of debt and ignorance and pauperism. We have many great tasks to perform, which can only be undertaken with a fair hope of success when the nation is in a state of high prosperity and progress. It will be too late to think of such great undertakings when our progress is checked, and the pressure of population and the want of employment are grievously felt. It is in a period of free expansion like the present that we can alone take any effectual measures for raising appreciably the standard of education, comfort, and morality of the people; and if we do not use the abundant wealth which our coal resources now afford us to fulfil such duties, we undoubtedly misuse it.

V   ON THE PROGRESS OF THE COAL QUESTION

A paper read before Section F of the British Association for the Advancement of Science, Bristol, 1875.

Abstract printed in Report of the 1875 Meeting, *Transactions of Sections*, p. 216.

The purpose of this paper is to compare statistical facts concerning the recent progress of the output of coal with various predictions and theories which had been published on the subject in the previous fifteen years. The quantity of coal raised in the United Kingdom in the year 1873 amounted to the enormous weight of 127,000,000 tons, according to the mineral statistics of Mr. Hunt. Professor Hull, in his valuable work on the English Coal-fields, had questioned the power of the coal-fields to admit of a much greater drain in any one year than 100,000,000 tons, at which rate he believed the supply would be sufficient for eight centuries. Facts now entirely negative the hypothesis of any such fixed limit.

Sir W. Armstrong, in his Presidential Address of 1863, put forward his celebrated calculation, that the produce of coal was advancing by a uniform arithmetic annual addition of $2\frac{3}{4}$ millions of tons, at which rate the coal in the country, as then estimated, would last only 212 years. According to this law of increase the produce in 1873 ought to be 119 millions, which is 8 millions *less* than the truth, the increase in the interval being at least 41 millions, instead of 33 millions, as it would be according to Sir W. Armstrong's method of calculation. The annual average addition to the output is now nearly $3\frac{1}{2}$ millions of tons, instead of $2\frac{3}{4}$ millions; but the true law cannot really be that of arithmetic increase, which, if followed backwards, would lead us to zero about the year 1830.

The true law of increase is that of a geometrical series, with the average annual ratio of $3\frac{1}{2}$ per cent. According to this law, as described in the 'Coal Question' in 1865 (1st ed. p. 213, 2nd ed. p. 240), it was calculated that the produce of coal in 1871 would be about 117·9 millions. According to Mr. Hunt's statistics it proved to be actually 117,352,028 tons. On the same method of calculation the produce of 1873 would be about 126·3 millions; and the actual quantity raised, as already stated, exceeds this by about 700,000 tons. In spite of the extraordinary rise of price of coal in the years 1872 and 1873, the law of geometric increase is thus remarkably verified.

In the Report of the Royal Commission on Coal some calculations of Mr. Price Williams are put forward, in which the average consumption (apart from exportation) of coal per head of the population is assumed as rising from 3·9636 tons in 1871, to 4·4266 tons in 1881, 4·5786 tons in 1891, and so on, to a maximum of 4·6526 tons in 1941. But, according to this method, the *consumption* (not including coals exported) of the year 1873 would be nearly 6 millions less than the truth. Mr. Price Williams believed that the rate of increase of consumption of coal per head had passed its maximum, and was declining, whereas the most recent statistics show that between 1869 and 1873 the advance was more than double that in the interval 1865–69. The whole theory of Mr. Williams rested upon the assumption that there was a continuous decrease in the rate of increase of the population, whereas his own tables showed that this increase was, in the last decade (1861–71), 11·736 per cent., compared with 11·197 per cent., that of the decade 1851–1861.

It is further pointed out that the remarks of the Commissioners upon the "Coal Question" proceed from an entire misapprehension of the arguments given in that book. No one asserted that the production of coal in Great Britain ever would rise to the higher quantities given by the geometric law of increase. The true conclusion drawn was, *"that we cannot long maintain our present rate of increase of consumption; that we can never advance to the higher amounts of consumption supposed. But this only means that the check to our progress must become perceptible within a century from the present time."*

In the year 1872 the price of coal rose in many places to a height two or three times its previous highest amount. This rise was in some respects exceptional, but was mainly due to the increased demand which, in spite of the enormous price, advanced 5 per cent. per annum. The great increase in the number of collieries produced by the extraordinary demand, will no doubt render the price more moderate for some time to come; but the coal famine of the years 1872–73 may be regarded as the first twinge of the scarcity which must come, and it has taught us that coal has now become the first necessary of life in this kingdom.

VI THE IMPORTANCE OF DIFFUSING A KNOWLEDGE OF POLITICAL ECONOMY

Delivered in Owens College, Manchester, at the opening of the session of Evening Classes, on 12 October (originally published as a separate pamphlet, Manchester, 1866).

This is the full text of the introductory lecture to public primary school teachers which 'brought some little criticism from the Radicals' on

Jevons. The full circumstances are detailed in Vol. I, pp. 207–8; see also Letters 269 and 270, Vol. III, pp. 132–8.

I HAVE been requested by our Principal to give the opening lecture of the present session of Evening Classes, because, by the appointment which I have recently had the honour to receive in this College, my connection with these Evening Classes becomes of a permanent and somewhat peculiar character. The Cobden Memorial Committee have given a certain endowment to the Professorship of Political Economy in Owens College, and have laid it down as a condition that all teachers in schools supported by public funds or contributions in Manchester or Salford shall be admitted to an evening course of lectures in Political Economy without payment of the class fee.

As Professor of Political Economy, I thus become likewise the Cobden Lecturer on the same subject, and have to undertake the work of carrying out, as far as possible, the excellent intentions of those who have founded this Lectureship. While I may safely say that there is no occupation which I should undertake with more pleasure and prosecute with more effort, I must also add how well I am aware of the difficult work to be done.

It seems very appropriate that I should take the present opportunity to enter at once upon the work of the Lectureship by explaining the exact purpose and nature of the course of lectures which I have to deliver. I have endeavoured to ascertain as closely as possible the object which the Cobden Memorial Committee have in view, and to this of course I shall adhere, as far as my ability may go.

The founders of the Cobden Lectureship desire to take a step towards disseminating through the community, and especially among the working classes, a comprehension of the principles of political economy which govern the relations of employers and employed, of rich and poor, of buyer and seller, of debtor and creditor – those social and industrial relations on which the prosperity of every one and of the whole nation depends.

It is thought desirable that instruction in political economy should be given, at least in the case of the poorer classes, at a very early age, – almost as soon, in fact, as a boy has acquired the power of reading with facility. It is desired that all teachers of boys from about eight years of age and upwards should devote a certain portion of time to instructions in social economy, and should qualify themselves for the purpose by attendance upon a course of lectures. Though the teacher will of course only have to communicate to his boys lessons and maxims of a very simple character, it is almost indispensable that he should himself acquire a thorough comprehension of the science from which his lessons are drawn. Incidentally I may say that there seem to be at least three strong reasons why a teacher should know far more of a science than he can ever hope to communicate to young pupils.

Firstly, he ought conscientiously to assure himself of the truth of what he is going to deliver, and not repeat the lessons by rote, as if he had no further concern with them.

Secondly, without a knowledge of the science the teacher cannot have any feeling of its value, and will probably think his time and trouble uselessly spent in trying to teach social economy to boys. Bacon, indeed, says of studies – "they teach not their own use; but that is a wisdom without them and above them, won by observation." While on the one hand it is obvious that if a person keeps entirely to one study or science he cannot well know its value or use comparatively to other studies, it must be allowed on the other hand that those who know nothing of a science cannot possibly judge whether it will be useful or not, nor whether it can be taught to any given pupils. I fear that to most persons political economy is a mere name and suggests hardly the slightest notion of what the science is.

Thirdly, the lessons will come with far more force and clearness if they come from a powerful comprehension of their nature and foundations in truth. I need say nothing to establish this.

The instructions of the Cobden Lecturer are to be opened freely to all teachers in public schools in this neighbourhood, in order that they may have some inducement to begin or proceed with the study with such slight advantages as I can give them. It is hoped that many may thus gain both the desire and the power to introduce the subject successfully into their schools. Those teachers who disregard or are prejudiced against this movement will undoubtedly be those most ignorant of the nature of political economy.

I propose now to describe as well as I can the special reasons, as I conceive them, for promoting the diffusion of a knowledge of political economy. In stating these reasons I shall indeed feel as if I were attempting to add a sequel to the very able Introductory Lecture lately given by my colleague, Professor Ward, in the Town Hall. His subject was "National Self-Knowledge." Γνῶθι σεαυτὸν, "Know thyself," was the famous precept, the importance of which he proved by illustrations drawn from the history of ancient and modern nations and persons. He showed how a mistake as to our own nature and powers leads pretty surely to failure and ruin. It is indispensable that in every thing we do we should obey the natural laws under which we are placed, and we cannot be sure we obey them unless we know them.

Si vis omnia subjicere, subjice te rationi – 'If you wish to conquer all things, subject yourself to reason,' – is a wise maxim, the meaning of which has been even better expressed in one line by Tennyson, who speaks of

"Ruling, by obeying nature's powers."

Now, it is obvious that these great precepts, *Know thyself* and *Obey thy own nature*, must be observed not only in the policy of a great nation but in every slight act of an individual. Where we do not observe them we are as likely as not to make nature herself our opponent and to incur the reward of ignorance and presumption.

Knowledge, indeed, cannot do everything, and we need something above knowledge. Still, the greater part of the misfortunes and unhappiness of life may be avoided by knowledge, and our appointed way to avoid them is by energetic efforts to gain the necessary knowledge, and to act according to it.

We have been endowed at our creation with powers of observation and reasoning which seem capable of penetrating by degrees all the secrets of nature. When we are suffering under or are threatened with any evil we should not content ourselves with hoping or praying for its removal only, but we should set in action all our faculties, and by first acquiring and then diffusing all the knowledge we can gain of its nature and causes, we should place in the hands of men the means of averting it. It is not our own power we use, it is the Divine power of knowledge.

As man by intelligence and cultivation delivers himself from positive physical want and becomes capable of a higher life and activity, he seems to incur at the same time new dangers. The first man, for instance, who mounted a horse has caused the death of many careless and unskilful riders, but he has contributed to the advantage of infinitely more. Ships have on the whole grown more useful and more safe from the time when our Celtic ancestors paddled about in coracles. But nowadays when a vessel is faultily fitted in some small particular, or carelessly managed, we have a catastrophe like the sinking of the "London" or the burning of the "Amazon." Our ancestors, again, could hardly imagine the benefits which we derive from railways, but they could hardly, on the other hand, conceive to themselves a disaster so instantaneous and terrible as a railway collision. The carelessness of a single man, the disorder of some delicate mechanism, or the breaking of a single pin or bar, may bring the most dreadful slaughter and mutilation to hundreds.

The greater our triumphs over nature the worse the punishment we incur for any remissness or faulty ignorance.

The same is exactly true of moral and social affairs. Our population multiplies, our towns spread, our industry grows and diversifies indefinitely by the aid of knowledge and skill. But there is hardly an advance which is not qualified by some risk or disadvantage incurred. We cannot fail to be proud of our vast metropolis and other great towns; but the overcrowding of people occasions sanitary evils with which we can hardly cope.

The progress of our commerce, again, brings us at intervals into dangers and distresses comparable in intensity to the advantages which it usually provides for us. Thus the cotton famine was an event that had long been dreaded, and I think reasonably dreaded. Its worst results were, however, averted when the time came, by a loyal love of order on the part of the suffering operatives, by a liberality on the part of the country generally, and by a skilfulness and energy in organization on the part of gentlemen on the spot, which cannot be too much admired.

But when, last April, the very greatest of our financial houses, a very pillar of the money market, as it was thought, broke down – when a monetary panic set in which might have stopped the industry and exchanges of the whole country, and when the Bank of England itself might have been obliged to suspend payments, – then we must have felt that we had a vast machine in operation in our midst the working of which we did not fully understand and could not safely control. Nor do the unreasoning acts of speculators and merchants, and even bankers, or the various and absurd opinions expressed by most persons as to the causes and remedies of the catastrophe inspire us with much hope that similar disasters will be avoided for the future.

The best example which I can give, however, of the evils and disasters which may accompany progress is to be found in trade unions and the strikes they originate and conduct. Of these I may say, in the words of a recent article of the *Times,* that "every year sees these organizations more powerful, more pitiless, and more unjust. Such atrocities as that reported from Sheffield are but the extreme cases of a tyranny which is at this very moment paralysing the large part of the trades of the country."*

In mentioning trade unions I must advert to their political bearings on the present occasion, because as I am considering the importance of the science of economy I must look beyond it, according to the maxim of Bacon. But I must add that in my classes I make a point of keeping within the subject and taking a perfectly neutral position with respect to political questions, just as in all the classes of the College my colleagues and myself are bound by the will of the founder to abstain from inculcating any theological doctrines.

While these unions are in many respects proofs of admirable self-control on the part of the working classes, they cause great uneasiness

* This quotation has been interpreted as meaning that the trades unions were responsible for the occurrence of trades-outrages; but I did not attribute this meaning to it, nor had I the least intention of making such an assertion. The useful purposes which unions may serve are adverted to on pp. 48 and 49.

among those entrusted at present with the government of the country. England, we are fond of believing, is the country in which exists the truest liberty and the truest toleration, and we may well be happy in the belief that this liberty becomes year by year truer and greater. By liberty I do not mean merely what is vulgarly regarded as liberty by many, the privilege to vote for a representative in Parliament. I mean what Mr. Mill upholds as true liberty, in that noble essay which is perhaps the best of his great works. According to Mr. Mill, human liberty comprises – first, liberty of conscience, absolute freedom of opinions on all subjects; secondly, "liberty of tastes and pursuits, of framing the plan of our life to suit our own character;" thirdly, from this liberty, says Mr. Mill, follows the "liberty . . . of combination among individuals, freedom to unite for any purpose not involving harm to others." He adds, "no society in which these liberties are not, on the whole, respected is free, whatever may be its form of government, and none is completely free in which they do not exist absolute and unqualified. The only freedom which deserves the name is that of pursuing our own good in our own way, so long as we do not attempt to deprive others of theirs, or impede their efforts to obtain it."[1]

This is the kind of liberty and toleration which we desire to cherish in this country. It cannot but happen indeed that where perfect individual liberty of this kind is enjoyed many must err and injure themselves by their error. It is for no want of regret for such error, or want of care for what we think the true and good that we uphold liberty which tolerates the false and, possibly, the evil. Toleration reposes on a profound trust in the value and strength of truth, a trust that truth will prevail and that error will show its worthlessness.

It may be confidently asserted that almost the whole of the upper classes of this country not only desire to uphold and advance the liberty of opinion and combination, but even to introduce a large part of the working classes within the governing power of the state by giving them the franchise. Mixed, however, with the strong desire to achieve progress such as this, is a fear that political power may be misused through ignorance. We wish every working man to be not only free, but privileged; but to this end he must have intelligence and education, else he is not free but in name. He must know what are the true principles of free thought, and free action, and free combination. He must learn to see that in the trade unions, in which he chiefly places his hope at present, there is no true individual freedom, but that he is entirely at the mercy of the prevailing opinions of his fellow-workmen, often in fact of a few leaders of the union.

---

[1] J. S. Mill, *On Liberty* (ed. R. B. McCallum, Oxford, 1946), p. 11.

I have enumerated many great disasters arising from a want of knowledge; but there is one great disaster almost the greatest that I can figure to myself. It is that our working classes, with their growing numbers and powers of combination, may be led by ignorance to arrest the true growth of our liberty, political and commercial. This fear is not so chimerical as it might seem. If we look to the English colonies in Australia we see that the extension of the franchise has been followed by the overturn of free trade and the establishment of protective tariffs. Having personal acquaintance with some of the Australian colonies, and having noticed from the first the rise of the protection doctrines there, I may venture to assert with the more confidence that there is hardly any part of the earth's surface where such doctrines will do more harm. The doctrines of protection, whatever they may be elsewhere, are wildly irrational when applied to Australia. Yet they are in the ascendant there among a body of electors who are through ignorance doing all they can to retard the progress of rising states which are in all other respects the source of the greatest pride to Englishmen.

I might point again to the United States as an example of a great nation where the true commercial interests of all classes are sadly misconceived from an ignorance of the principles of economy and freedom of trade as they have been discovered, expounded, and put in practice, with the utmost success in Europe.

To avoid such a disaster as the reversal of the free policy of the country we must diffuse knowledge, and the kind of knowledge required is mainly that comprehended in the science of political economy. The working classes are doing harm to themselves and the country by the want of such knowledge; they have done harm ever since (by advancing freedom) they had the opportunity, and as freedom advances further they will do more and more harm, to an extent we cannot measure, unless they act from a better knowledge of their position and true interests. They act from wholly mistaken notions of their relations to their fellow-workmen and their employers. Not only is this to be regretted in itself as tending to sap the foundations of the industrial prosperity of the country, but it is to be regretted because it tends to retard the extension of the franchise and the advent of many true social reforms.

I hope that I may never be found among those who would wish to stay that progress towards all that is noble and free, which marks the course of English history. But the more I desire that this nation may attain the highest possible point of development, morally, politically, and industrially, the more do I regret any tendency which seems to me to be contrary to that development. And truth compels me to admit, against my inclinations, that those numerous classes of the population, whose hopes are usually thought to be on the side of liberty, do not always estimate the character of liberty aright. I fear especially that they are prone to act in a manner directly contrary to the laws of free industry.

Having thus attempted to point out the necessity for a better comprehension of social laws among our population, I should like, if I could, to put before you the extreme difficulty which there is in overcoming the unreasoning prejudices of men on the subject. In questions which have economical and political bearings, the dictates of science and reasoning, are not calmly listened to. Every man thinks himself alike able and privileged to form his own opinions by his own unaided intelligence. Yet it is not so in any other branch of learning or science. So great and frequent have been the triumphs of physical science that the most ignorant crowd would feel some deference for the superior knowledge of a chemist, an electrician, or an astronomer on their own subjects. No sane man disputes the calculations of the Astronomer Royal and the predictions of the "Nautical Almanack," for people are aware not only how often astronomers have been proved right, but that astronomy itself is a science which cannot be understood without long study.

How unenviable would be the position of the Astronomer Royal if he had not only to ascertain and predict the moon's place to a nicety, but had every now and then to convince a crowd of persons at the hustings of the truth of his predictions by making plain to their untutored intellects the minutest details of the lunar theory. How much worse would it be if, when he failed to convince them of some point in the problem of the three bodies, they forthwith accused him of inventing the whole for interested purposes, to maintain his own emoluments or the privileges of his class. Such, however, is really the unfortunate position of any person who endeavours to discuss a question of social economy with an uneducated mass of persons. The teacher of physical science is never in such position. When an astronomer predicts an eclipse or a comet, when the analytical chemist detects poison or adulterations, when the meteorologist discovers the approach of a gale, they are listened to with almost unquestioning deference; and even one scientific man hardly ventures to question the results of another whose subject of study is at all remote from his own.

A little reflection will show how different it is in the case of the social sciences. These sciences, in the first place, deal with subjects far more difficult than the physical sciences. To convince you of this I would refer you to Mr. Mill's chapters upon the logic of the moral sciences, at the conclusion of his great treatise on Logic. Political economy is an older science than chemistry, and is far older than the science of electricity and several other most prolific branches of physical science. Yet so difficult is the subject that we have not yet advanced safely beyond the lowest and simplest generalisations. Political economy is not yet an exact science.

But the difficulty of his subject is not the worst difficulty in the way of the political economist. The worst difficulty is the obstinacy, prejudice, and incredulity of those he has to convince. Bentham has said, with regard to moral science and jurisprudence – "Gross ignorance descries no difficulties; imperfect knowledge finds them out and struggles with them; it must be perfect knowledge which overcomes them."

The best student and teacher of social science is but struggling with his difficulties and imperfect knowledge; as to the rest of the population they are involved in that state of mind which descries no difficulties at all, and is but too ready to act accordingly.

The mechanic, for instance, finds no difficulty in comprehending his social and economical position. He sees that his employer gives him just as little wages as he can. It is obvious then that the workmen of a trade should combine and refuse to work for so little and then they will get more. Common sense is quite sufficient to show that.

A workman, again, sees that a machine, requiring the attendance of one or two men, does the work of many. If such a machine comes into use his own sense tells him, he thinks, that many will be thrown out of work, and himself probably among them. The instinct of self-defence leads him to destroy the machine.

The tradesman sees that the more a rich man buys from him the more profit there is to trade, the more employment to men. Common sense shows that free expenditure sets trade going, and there arises a feeling of approbation in the community in favour of those who live well and spend freely, as compared with those of a saving disposition.

The merchant feels that the more money he can borrow to trade upon the more he can gain. An extended issue of paper money is what he thinks requisite for diffusing activity of trade and general prosperity.

As regards the poor and dependent classes of the population, it is clear that a gift gives satisfaction to the receiver. Few, then, of charitable disposition can realise the fact that charity, unless it is given with the utmost discrimination, does far more harm than good. And who is there that is not offended by the political economist when he proves that a poor law must be harsh and niggardly if it is not to undermine the sources of our welfare? Even the most eminent men – such as Mr. Dickens and Mr. Hughes – have enlisted their common sense and high talents against the conclusions of the political economist.

Common sense yet rules in social discussion, and few can be made to see that economical science is but founded on common sense, refined and more intensely applied. Every workman and person of common intelligence has felt his way roughly to certain conclusions, so obvious to him that he refuses to look further. He cannot be made to see that he has reached only the beginning of a series of results and effects, of which the last would very much surprise him by its difference from the first. He would find too often that what is evidently beneficial in the beginning is immensely and widely hurtful in the end.

It is the duty of the political economist to try to trace out the ultimate effects of actions, and conditions, and laws on the wealth of individuals and the nation. This is well expressed in the title of an admirable little work of M. Bastiat, "What is seen, and what is not seen." This work has been translated by Dr. W. B. Hodgson, and was published first in the columns of the *Manchester Examiner and Times* in 1852, and afterwards in a separate form. I shall have to direct the attention of my classes to it, because, with a simple clearness of language, and a brilliancy of wit and illustration to which no English economist can lay claim, M. Bastiat contrasts, in a number of different incidents, the apparent and the unapparent results, and leads the most unwilling reader to confess that the prepossessions of his common sense are proved by a more penetrating course of reasoning to involve error and injury.

There was a time not many centuries ago when men thought that the earth stood still, and the sun moved round it. Their common sense told them so, and they were prejudiced in favour of this opinion to the extent of imprisoning and persecuting those who thought otherwise. There is hardly a child who does not know the contrary now, and in place of a mistaken prejudice we have now a noble science. It is for us to endeavour to overcome similar prejudices which lie in the way of the social science, and thus to bring on the time when the natural laws which govern the relations of capital and labour, and define inexorably the rates of profits and wages, will be obeyed.

I should like now to spend a few minutes in putting before you the proofs how much the opinion and will of the workman in these economical questions influence and will influence the prosperity of himself and his country.

In the first place, I think it is hard to exaggerate the extent to which the progress of industry and invention is hindered by the antipathies of workmen to the introduction of machinery and improvements. It is true that we do not now have bands of Luddites collecting after dark and destroying whole factories full of machinery. In the textile and certain other trades the use of machinery is so fully established that there is little or no further difficulty in the matter. I believe, too, that trade unions often now refuse to support their members in opposing the introduction of new machines. But there is still an immense force of passive resistance in occupations to which the use of machinery is new. Workmen are usually able to destroy machinery in an underhand manner, by over-loading or over-running it, or by secretly inserting a bar among the wheels and hidden parts. Employers are thus much deterred from erecting new expensive machines. Only two or three weeks ago I saw, in the Dudley Midland Exhibition, samples of chain cable of which the links were very successfully shaped and forged by machinery. Only four miles off I saw a fine new works in course of erection for the manufacture of cables by hand forging. The proprietors of the new works were fully acquainted with the success of the new machine, but hesitated to introduce them in their Staffordshire works, fearing the hostility of the many chain-makers in the neighbourhood. If introduced at all, these machines will probably be erected in works at a distance from Staffordshire. Thus will the ignorance of the chain-makers tend to drive away an important branch of manufacture from its ancient seat.

In the Great Exhibition of 1862, many must have noticed the very interesting type-composing and distributing machines. It would be of the greatest advantage to the diffusion of knowledge to lower the cost of setting type; but the use or even the fair trial of these machines has been prevented by the absolute refusal of compositors to work in a shop where they are tried.*

At the late Social Science Meeting it was stated that attempts had been made to lower the cost of erecting workmen's dwelling and lodging-houses, and thus improve their domestic condition by employing bricks of a larger size than usual. The insuperable difficulty was at once encountered that no bricklayers could be found who would set such bricks.

Many must be the cases of inventions and improvements which, when once frustrated by opposition, have been abandoned and forgotten. I am peculiarly acquainted with the case of a machine for making horse-shoes invented by an American gentleman many years ago. My father purchased the patent for the United Kingdom, and had no difficulty in making shoes as good and cheaper than they can be made by hand. On trying to introduce these, however, he found that every farrier in the kingdom declined to have anything to do with machine-made shoes. As those who shoe horses are almost invariably the same men who make the shoes, it was soon seen to be hopeless to overcome the prejudice, and the attempt, I believe, has never been repeated.

It avails not to say that in these or any other cases the machines did not work successfully or cheaply enough. It is only after long experience and improvement by actual working that a machine can be brought near its maximum of efficiency. There is cost and difficulty enough in bringing any invention or improvement into use without the opposition of the whole series of labourers and tradesmen on whom its use depends. If a composing machine, a brick-making machine, a chain-forging machine,

---

* A compositor, writing in the *City News*, has denied that the trial of the machines was prevented, but he allowed that the rules of the Printers' Trade Society prohibited the employment of women to work or attend upon the machines in any way.

or any other machine, will not and cannot succeed, why should workmen hesitate to try it and demonstrate its failure. The fact is they needlessly hate its success, and will not allow it even to be tried.

Had I time I should like to advert again to strikes and trade unions, and point out by examples and details how contrary they are to the principles of industrial freedom. It will be, however, our work in the classes to consider this fully. I will only say that they are in their nature and present designs directly contrary to the principles of free labour, the promulgation and establishment of which by Adam Smith has led in a main degree to our present prosperity. In the 10th chapter of the 1st book of the "Wealth of Nations," Adam Smith pointed out with all his beautiful clearness of argument and illustration the evils which the policy of Europe has inflicted upon labour, "by not leaving things at perfect liberty." Those are his words. "The property," he says, "which every man has in his own labour, as it is the original foundation of all other property, so it is the most sacred and inviolable. The patrimony of a poor man lies in the strength and dexterity of his hands; and to hinder him from employing this strength and dexterity in what manner he thinks proper without injury to his neighbour, is a plain violation of this most sacred property. It is a manifest encroachment upon the just liberty both of the workman and of those who might be disposed to employ him. As it hinders the one from working at what he thinks proper, so it hinders the others from employing whom they think proper."

These remarks were aimed against the incorporated trades and guilds, or universities, as they were called, which, by strict regulations and restrictions as to the admission of apprentices and members, tried to secure their own advantage, indifferent to the public good. Such things are swept away in this country, and there are hardly any laws now existing in this kingdom which can be said to press upon the free employment of labour. But Dr. Smith could not have anticipated, when more than a hundred years ago he opposed laws and customs then in existence, that a hundred years afterwards there would arise among free bodies of workmen unions and corporations of vast extent, distinctly aiming at the restriction of employment.

Let it be distinctly understood that it is not the existence of combinations the political economist protests against. We cannot have too much co-operation and combination among men for purposes in accordance with the laws of nature and the laws of the country. All classes of people, all districts, towns, and villages, should have their unions, institutions, and societies, and meetings of various kinds. And it is highly desirable, at the same time, that every class of tradesmen and workmen should meet in their societies and unions to exchange information and assistance, and to concert every means of really and permanently benefiting their own body and the community. Any matter concerning the convenience and health of the workman – such as the length and arrangement of the hours of labour and the time for meals, the allowance of holidays, the mode and time of paying wages, the wholesomeness and safety of factories – should be discussed by workmen among themselves in their unions. But this is where a want of a knowledge of economy and the laws of the working of society is so indispensable. When they pass from these matters in which an employer should consult the welfare of his men collectively, to regulate or raise the rate of wages, to enforce equality of work and wages, they bring their own and others' welfare into peril; and what I want you especially to see is, that, with the increasing intelligence and habit of co-operation among labourers, there is the more urgent need of a knowledge of economy, that they may restrain their power within natural laws – that they may, in short, know themselves.

It is only knowledge that can enable workmen to draw the rather nice boundary between what their unions may very properly interfere with, and what they should not touch.

As it is, however, the unions are becoming every day more arrogant in their attempts to coerce their employers and rule their own trades by exclusive corporations or universities, embracing the whole labour of each trade in one inflexible and resistless body. I quoted to you a sentence from the *Times*, which, I believe, is quite within the truth. It is hardly possible to take up a newspaper without seeing several accounts of strikes, dissensions, and sometimes even of trade outrages.

In order to show you how the matter is regarded by persons engaged in trade, and competent to judge, I will read you extracts from a letter I happened lately to receive. "In our business as iron merchants," says the writer,[2] "we are continually hearing of the despotic tyranny they display in their conduct towards the ironmasters, who are now positively afraid of them, and hardly dare speak to them. There is a strike now pending in the Cleveland iron district against a reduction of wages, the issue of which is very uncertain, though it has continued for several months. The manufacture of iron has become a losing business with the masters, owing to the long-continued depression of business and the competition with foreign manufacturers; and yet the men will not submit to any reduction of wages from the highest point. We know it for a fact, from our own experience, that the French and Belgians have been supplying the Continental demand for iron for the last two or three years, and have supplanted English iron almost entirely by their lower prices. Our business with the Continent has dwindled away to nothing, owing to that cause; and we have many letters telling us, in reply to our quotations and

---

[2] Timothy Jevons. See Letter 265, Vol. III, p. 127.

solicitations for orders, that the writers can buy what they want cheaper in France and Belgium. What, then, is to be done? Until lately, England was the cheapest market in the world for iron, and now we are undersold by our nearest neighbours. The wages now demanded by our workmen are far more than what their fathers and predecessors were paid for the same kind of work; and yet they will not submit to any reduction. Is England, then, to lose its prestige in one of its most important productions, owing to the unreasonable conduct of its workmen. In our own business, the common labourers whom we employ in the warehouse in handling and weighing iron, to whom we for a long time paid 3s. 6d. a day, have lately demanded 4s., and have compelled us to pay it, for they will not permit a strange man to be employed at all, though we could get plenty at less money. And this kind of thing is not confined to the iron trade: it pervades almost every branch of trade and manufactures. You have probably seen in the papers what riots have recently taken place in the South, from the introduction of some foreign navvies, on a railway. Such is the spirit that pervades our whole labouring population. It seems probable that they will deprive the country of all the benefit of our free-trade policy. We certainly want free trade in labour quite as much as we wanted free trade in corn twenty years ago."

We must remember that the trade of this country will have difficulties to meet in future years from which it has in times past been comparatively free. The very staple commodity on which it works, coal, will before very long rise in price, if it is not already rising. Not only in France and Belgium have we competitors whom it never occurred to us to fear, but in the United States there are mineral resources, inventive skill, and mercantile energy which may easily leave us behind. Let us remember, too, that our productive population, and our productive capital, have a great tendency to emigrate and increase the powers of our competitors. If, then, there be superadded to all these tendencies which will act against us, a truculence and tyranny on the part of the workmen unknown in other countries, we need nothing else to make us fear that capitalists will gradually withdraw their capital from home employment and invest it in the colonies, United States, and foreign countries.

It will be our work in the class to consider the nature of capital and the strong reasons which economists have discovered for believing that the average rate of wages in a trade cannot be raised by strikes and unions, and that thus the strikes and contentions which have occurred between employer and employed since the combination laws were repealed in 1824, represent a vast loss to workmen as well as to capitalists and the country in general.

I have wished by this and previous instances to make plain that advancing intelligence and freedom may but lead our operatives into loss and disaster unless they are furnished with appropriate knowledge of natural laws which they cannot escape from, and must ultimately obey. Men think that by the repealing of human laws they become free to act as they like. They must learn that there are natural laws even of human nature which they cannot break, but against which they can easily, through ignorance, throw themselves to their own destruction.

I will now only consider, in conclusion, how we may best hope to impress upon the people generally a knowledge of economy. To publish cheap treatises, though they be the very best treatises, like the People's Edition of Mr. Mill's works, will not have the desired effect, for in few cases will they be bought by the working classes. We cannot expect that men working hard during the day, should spend their evenings in the study of abstruse and difficult treatises. Mr. Mac Culloch published, some twelve years or more ago, a sixpenny work on wages and labour, intended to be generally read among the working classes. "There are none," he says in the preface, "who are more deeply interested in having the truth, as respects their situation, honestly and fairly stated, than the workpeople. It will be seen that at bottom they have no exclusive interests, and that their prosperity is intimately connected with, and is indeed inseparable from the prosperity of the other classes." But this work was not much read by those for whom it was intended, nor was its style well adapted to the purpose.

Miss Martineau made a very different and clever attempt, more than thirty years ago, to spread a knowledge of political economy in a series of tales entitled "Illustrations of Political Economy." The tales are very interesting and readable, and the doctrines clearly inculcated and sound. But like many other moral tales, they have not been so much read as they deserved, nor have they been read by the classes in whom we are concerned.

The works of M. Bastiat, especially his "Harmonies," and his tract before mentioned, "What is seen and what is not seen," are excellently adapted for general readers, and have, I believe, been much read in France. They have been both translated into English, but in spite of Dr. Hodgson's efforts, are not so well known as they should be.

Dr. John Watts, again, of this city, the secretary of the Cobden Memorial Committee, has published cheap tracts on trade societies, machinery, co-operative societies, and strikes, excellently adapted for reading among the working classes, by whom several of them I believe were favourably received.

Still it must be apparent that efforts like these, even when attaining the measure of success hoped for, cannot produce any deep and wide-spread influence upon the opinions of a large population. We must begin upon children, and impress upon them the simple truths concerning their social position before the business of life has created insuperable prejudices.

The first writer, so far as I know, who produced a work on social or political economy suited to the use of children was Archbishop Whately, than whom a sounder and more judicious thinker and writer never lived. We may be sure that we are doing nothing wild or impracticable when we are following him. Many years ago he printed, through the Society for Promoting Christian Knowledge, a little book entitled "Easy Lessons on Money Matters for the use of Young People." It was, by the bye, my own first text book on the subject when I was certainly not more than ten or twelve years of age, possibly only eight. In 1843 it had reached the 7th edition, and it is still in common use, having reached the 16th edition.

An extract from the preface to this little work will show very distinctly Whately's opinion on the subject of this lecture:— "The following short lessons," he says, "were designed, and have on trial been found adapted, for the instruction of young persons from about eight years of age and upwards. Care has been taken to convey elementary knowledge on the subjects treated of, in such simple language that it is hoped these lessons will be found, with the help of explanation and *questioning* on the part of the teachers, easily intelligible, even to such as have but the ordinary advantages in point of education; and there are few subjects on which it is for all classes of people more important to inculcate correct principles, and to guard against specious fallacies. All persons in every station must, when they grow up, practically take some part, more or less, in the transactions in question. The rudiments of sound knowledge concerning these may, it has been found by experience, be communicated at a very early age: and that they should be inculcated early is the more important, because at a later period there are more difficulties in the way of such elementary instruction. Many, even of what are called the educated classes, grow up with indistinct, or erroneous and practically mischievous, views on these subjects; and the prejudices any one may have casually imbibed are often hard to be removed at a time of life when he imagines his education to be completed. When such simple elementary principles as those here taught are presented to him he is likely contemptuously to disregard them as childish 'truisms;' while the conclusions deduced from those principles are rejected by him as revolting paradoxes. Those, therefore, who are engaged in conducting, or in patronising or promoting education, should consider it a matter of no small moment to instil betimes just notions on subjects with which all must in after-life be practically conversant, and in which no class of men, from the highest to the lowest, can, in such a country as this at least, be *safely* left in ignorance or in error."

I conceive that the success which has attended the use of this little book is sufficient to show that social economy can be taught to children even from the age of eight years.*

Of late years an effort has been made by Mr. William Ellis, the patron of the Birkbeck Schools, by Dr. W. B. Hodgson, Mr. Shiel, lately a teacher in University College School, London, and others to introduce the teaching of Social Economy into schools for young boys generally. Though only some half dozen schools have been tried in this movement the success has been so encouraging as to lead the founders of the Cobden Lectureship to desire its general introduction in this neighbourhood. We do not in fact need to go far for an example of success. For in the Manchester Free School, in Deansgate, about five minutes' walk from here, the teaching of social economy was introduced by Mr. Templar, of Manchester, with complete success. On Mr. Templar's promotion the teaching has been continued with like success by the present head master, Mr. Mellor. At the Liverpool meeting of the Social Science Association, in 1858, Mr. Templar pointed out most distinctly the importance of the views now more widely adopted. He showed not only the utility of the information which may be given, but also its suitability for the purpose of exciting and exercising the thoughts of the pupils.

Those who are at all incredulous about the possibility of teaching such a subject to young boys should be present at one of Mr. Mellor's lessons and hear with what accuracy and interest a number of little ragged boys out of Deansgate and other parts will answer questions concerning the variety of wages in trades, the division of labour, the use of money, and so forth. The subject is taught in this school to all boys who have learned to read with facility a small work called "Reading Lessons in Social Economy for the use of Schools," prepared for the purpose by Mr. Templar. A portion of the lesson is read over by the boys in turn, and its meaning and contents fixed in the mind by numerous questions.

It may be confidently said that if schoolmasters generally would make themselves acquainted with the doctrines and value of economical and social science, they would at once perceive the inestimable service which they might perform to their pupils and the community generally by introducing it as a subject of their lessons. And I will add a word to remind those engaged in elementary education, that in their hands lies the destiny of the country. Any one who has followed the late admirable debates on education in the meeting of the Social Science Association, or any one who only reflects on what is seen every day, must feel that our only chance of a permanent amelioration is by a comprehensive and thorough system of education for all.

---

* I may also especially recommend a little work entitled *Outlines of Social Economy*, published by Messrs. Smith, Elder, and Co., as written in a peculiarly clear and excellent manner.

In these days of high wages I believe there is nothing to prevent any mechanic or operative, as a general rule, from saving money by degrees. He may invest it in Savings' Banks or the Government Annuities, and insurance office, or better still in co-operative stores and undertakings. He may thus secure himself and his family from the accidents of life, and may even become a capitalist sharing in the profits of capital as well as labour; able again by the funds at his disposal to move and establish himself where he likes, or if he prefers, to emigrate with comfort and advantage. There is nothing in short but prejudice to prevent him gaining a position enviable for its independence. But it is distressing to think how much might be done by appropriate education when we see how little is done. No country ever enjoyed wealth and opportunities at all approaching to what the various classes of English society now enjoy. The working classes alone have been calculated to earn £400,000,000 sterling, and it is a reasonable estimate that £80,000,000 annually are spent upon drinks and tobacco. It is assuredly then not the want of means and money that makes our population so different from what it ought to be. It is the want of knowledge.

VII   TWO LECTURES ON POLITICAL ECONOMY

Delivered at the Mechanics' Institute, Hyde, Cheshire (*North Cheshire Herald*, 6 February and 13 March 1869)

Of these lectures Mrs Jevons wrote – 'In February and March 1869, he (Jevons) gave a course of lectures on political economy to working men at Hyde, near Manchester. Some influential gentlemen of that neighbourhood desired that a course of such lectures should be given, and when they asked Mr. Jevons' help he would not refuse it, for no one felt more strongly than he did the need of extending political economy to the working classes' (LJ, p. 246). Of this course, only the report of two lectures, published in a local newspaper, has survived.

I

The PROFESSOR commenced by expressing his sorrow at disappointing them a few weeks previously by not attending according to announcement, but added that as he was ill at the time, he had no alternative. He then proceeded to say:— In the present lecture we will attempt to give some notion of the subject we have to treat, and the arrangement of the course. Political Economy means, of course, the economy of the State. The very common word "political," is derived from a Greek word signifying city or State. Again, economy means management. In reality it means management of the household, from the Greek words for house and law, or regulation. Good economy means a thrifty management, in which we get the best for our money. But we also apply the word generally, as in the economy of a factory, of a farm, rural economy, and when we wish to speak of the house especially, we call it household economy. It may perhaps partially explain the meaning of the name if we say with Mr James Mill (Elements of P. E. p.1), "Political Economy is to the State what domestic economy is to the family. The family consumes, and in order to consume it must be supplied by production. Domestic economy has, therefore, two grand objects in view, the consumption and supply of the family." But I think there is a difference. In the economical management of a house we look only to the wise spending or consumption of income. But the economy of the State, even a more important branch of the subject, regards the gaining of the income, or production. We ought to take care that we do not form an exaggerated notion of what we can do in Political Economy. To suppose that it could treat of the whole management of State affairs, of all that concerns the welfare and prosperity of a nation, would be absurd. There are a number of sciences which are more or less conducive to such welfare. Moral philosophy considers the grounds of men's duties and obligations towards each other, and the effects of their characters and actions on the general good. Jurisprudence shows how some of the more definite and important rights and duties of men may be embodied in laws and enforced by the united power of the community or State. International law contains a system of moral rules which ought to guide the actions of nations towards each other. Political philosophy treats of the power by which laws are made and enforced, the mode by which the judgments of the country may be most wisely evoked. In our country, the Government has proceeded through so long a course of almost unbroken progress – 800 or 1000 years – that its growth becomes almost the subject of a science, as you will find in Mr. Hearn's work on the Government of England. Social and statistical science, such as it is treated at the meetings of the Social Science Association, is hardly a science, but a great collection of facts – concerning the condition of the people, evils, and their remedies. Sanitary science is a branch of social science. After all the administration of State affairs, though it should always be guided by the results of these various sciences, is really an art, and a very difficult art, in which no abstract principle must be allowed to govern alone, but regard must be had to all the circumstances of the time, the state of public opinion, the foreign relations of the country, the state of trade, &c., &c. The navigator would indeed be foolish who should calculate the bearings of his port, and then declare that he must go straight to that port, or not at all. He must have regard to all the rocks and intervening headlands, to the tides and currents, and the winds. So the statesman has to be conversant indeed, and has ever to be actuated by the principles of the several social sciences, but he must be aware also of the rocks and currents of public prejudice, and all the facts and circumstances of the time. I have gone into these remarks that you may not misapprehend the scope of Political Economy, and imagine that any sensible teacher of it would set it up as an invariable rule for the management of State affairs. Political Economy treats only of wealth, or as we may say of the weal or welfare of the nation, so far as it depends upon the plentiful supply of commodities and services. We consider men as governed by the want of food, and clothing, and shelter, or as actuated by a greater or less desire for possessions, for a comfortable house, furniture, adornments, amusements, literature, in short, a supply of most various commodities. To obtain these commodities he is endowed with the muscular power of his body, the intellectual powers of his mind, and the possession of the land with its materials and forces. We have to consider how he may best apply his labour to satisfy his wants. How, in short, he may acquire most wealth at the expense of the least labour. Thus Political Economy treats only of wealth. This can easily be shown from some of the definitions. Adam Smith's great work was called the "The wealth of nations," and he says in its opening, that according as the produce of the labour of the country "bears a greater or smaller proportion to the number of those who are to consume it, the nation will be better or worse supplied with all the necessaries and conveniencies for which it has occasion." To come down to one of the most recent, Mr. J. S. Mill says, prelim. p. 1., "Writers on Political Economy profess to teach, or to investigate the nature of wealth, and the laws of its production and distribution, including, directly or remotely, the operation of all the causes by which the condition of mankind, or of any society of human beings, in respect of this universal object of human desire, is made prosperous or the reverse."[1] But you will observe that it is only welfare so far as is dependent on wealth that is considered. Many persons have objected to Political Economy as a low and narrow minded science, because it treated only of wealth. But this is a most superficial objection. As Archbishop Whately says in his lectures, p. 11, "This sounds very much like a complaint against mathematicians for treating merely of quantities, or against grammarians for investigating no subject but

---

[1] J. S. Mill, *Principles of Political Economy* (People's Edition, 1865), 'Preliminary Remarks', p. 1.

language." Each science must treat one subject, or there would be such a confusion of facts and principles that no science could exist. But then we must not suppose that one science will give absolute indications of what should be done. It does not follow that because war interrupts trade and the accumulation of wealth that we are never to go to war, for the maintenance of freedom, and justice, and of moral principles, which are above wealth, may be involved. It does not follow that because the poor rate subtracts from the wealth of the country that we are to have no poor rate. Poor relief and voluntary charity is [*sic*] given for the most part on moral considerations with which Political Economy has nothing to do. But Political Economy will show, to some extent, how it may best be raised and expended. Political Economy thus gives us qualified or partial advice, and the statesman or the individual should take it into account *quantum valeat*, or for as much as it is worth. "It is thus," says Whately, "we judge in all other cases. When a physician tells his patient 'You ought to go to the sea,' or 'You ought to abstain from sedentary employment,' he is always understood to be speaking in reference to health alone. He is not supposed to imply, by the use of the word 'ought,' that his patient is morally bound to follow the prescription at all events, which would imply the incurring of ruinous expense, or the neglect of important duties." I will not promise, however, to confine myself in this class entirely to the strict subject. We shall show that the wealth of the community is promoted by industrial freedom, that is, by allowing every man to engage in whatever trade, or manufacture, or occupation he wishes. In a purely economical point of view a man's own instincts and self-interest is the best guide to his occupation, both as regards himself and the community. But from other considerations many restrictions are imposed even by Government; thus, by a new Act just come into operation, no one can begin to act as a pharmaceutical chemist without passing an examination. The price of drugs may thus be raised a little perhaps, but then we shall run less chance of being poisoned by an ignorant druggist's assistant. We shall have to discuss the very nice question how far the various restrictions imposed by trades' unions are warranted by economic or other considerations. As a general rule it will be shown that individuals or companies working for their own profit do best and most cheaply, but we shall find striking exceptions to this in the post-office and other monopolies, and we must consider how to draw the line here if possible. In many cases we shall find that classes of men are possessed by prejudices opposed to the true interest of the nation. Then every tradesman naturally rejoices in the high prices of his goods, as he gets more profit thereby, and there is an impression that low prices are ruinous to everyone. But a little reflection will show that the truth is directly the opposite of this, and that all improvement of industry aims at reducing prices, and everyone is benefitted – not by the money wages or profit he gets, but by what he can buy with that money. There is a strong prejudice afloat against capital. The capitalist seems to be drawing a large part of the produce of labour without doing anything for it. I have seen it said that past labour has no right to rob present labour; that the dependence of labour on capital is altogether wrong and tyrannical – if it means anything, this means that capital should be done away with. But we shall readily see that capital means the very subsistence on which we live, while they are engaged on a long work or series of operations; it means those tools, machines, buildings, and works of various kinds, which no one can deny to be necessary. What mechanic, or what body of mechanics, will undertake to make a locomotive without tools, lathes, planing machines, steam hammers, and all the buildings necessary to hold them. Again, what mechanic did you ever meet who was willing or desirous to forego [sic] receiving wages until the locomotive was done and sold. Capital was required to advance his wages during the progress of the work. Since the necessity of possessing the tools and other capital cannot be denied, either the men must possess them, or they must consent to hire them from those who do. We shall find, therefore, that the possession of capital in the product of past labour gives advantages, power, productiveness, and independence which cannot be replaced by anything else. Then, in the present state of things, men must either possess capital, or they must depend upon those who do. I will say a word or two about the value of the study of political economy. Some persons may be inclined to run it down as a very poor sort of science. My colleagues at Owen's College, for instance, in chemistry and natural philosophy, who are accustomed to prove a thing to one thousandth part of a grain or one thousandth part of a foot, may think that is not a science which cannot exhibit exact numbers. I shall often have to admit the imperfections of a science. There are many questions on which the most diverse opinions are held, and wherever such difference of opinion exists we have hardly got to a scientific basis. But on the other hand we cannot doubt that even a slight insight into Political Economy is better than none at all. There is an excellent proverb that "half a loaf is better than no bread," and we may apply it to Political Economy. Even the few economical doctrines, which are placed on a sure footing, are far better than nothing at all. Let us remember that we are every day, and every waking hour, doing things, or having dealings with other men in which the principles of the science are concerned. We are acting with or against those principles, and are either benefitting or hurting ourselves and others. It is impossible, therefore, that we should ignore the existence of a science which alone can show us whether we are acting rightly or wrongly. And it is a fact too that those who have no knowledge of a scientific Political Economy almost invariably have a Political Economy of their own. There is not a member of Parliament, a tradesman, a mechanic, nor even a labourer, but has a Political Economy of his own, generally a very narrow one. The banker thinks that things are going on very well when the rate of discount is high, and there are plenty of bills to discount. The merchant's one idea of Political Economy is running up the price when he has got a good stock of goods. The shopkeeper thinks that the country is prosperous when his customers are spending freely, and his stock moves off quickly. The mechanic sometimes supposes that a good close trade, active demand, and a difficulty in supplying the wants of the public is the great thing to be desired. Now these are all small, narrow systems of Political Economy, but they are all short-sighted. Every tradesman acquires a most acute sagacity in regard to the immediate causes of his own success, but he cares not to look further. It has often and truly been said that science is after all but a better kind of common sense. Every man's peculiar notions of Political Economy are only common sense applied to his own affairs. But in order to have a true Political Economy we require to look further, and trace out the less apparent results of things. We may then see that the high rate of discount, so pleasing to the banker, is ruinous to the merchant; that the high price of goods is so much loss to the consumer; that the lavish expenditure in which the tradesmen delight diminishes the productive capital of the country; and that the close union and high wages earned in some trades is not only burdensome to the community as a whole, but unfair to the rest of the working-classes, who are excluded. Every trade for itself is the rough Political Economy of common life. The good of the whole country is the aim of the Political Economist. I cannot too much recommend to your notice a little work entitled "What is seen and what is not seen in Political Economy, in one lesson," by the excellent French writer, Bastiat. It has been translated by Dr. W. B. Hodgson, and is published by the *Examiner* Office, where it is to be had at a low price. Here Bastiat beautifully shows that the ultimate effect often differs strangely from the immediate. A boy throws stones and breaks a window, or a hailstorm comes and breaks many. That improves the glazier's business; if there were no windows broken the glazier's business would be nearly done away with. Hence the impression arises that to set trade a-going, even at the expense of breaking windows, is good rather than bad. Bastiat beautifully shows the absurdity of this when we look a little further. So he considers the immediate and real result of dismissing soldiers; of discontinuing unproductive public works; of opposing the introduction of machines, of establishing protection doctrines, and so on. In dealing with this subject it will be well to adopt as a text book Mr. J. S. Mill's work on Political Economy. That is the generally recognised treatise on the subject, and is published at 6s., but perhaps it might be purchased for 5s.

There was another little work issued by Professor Rogers that costs 4s. 6d., and many chapters in it were excellent. If you could meet with Professor Fawcett's "Manual of Political Economy," that contains the substance of Mr. Mill's work, written in simpler language. I am in the habit of recommending students in my own classes to take notes of the subject advanced. It is almost indispensable in attending lectures to take notes more or less, and it is invariably done in college classes. I think those who attend the classes are almost sure to lose the memory of what they hear before very long if such means were not taken to retain it. But taking notes is also necessary in getting clear notions of what you are learning. Then again, I think it is desirable to have discussion at the end of each lecture. In the evening classes at college I ask questions during the lecture if it does not interfere with the subject, but it will perhaps be better to have a quarter of an hour's discussion upon what has been brought before you. I shall be very glad to answer any question to-night.

There were no questions asked.

II

The PROFESSOR commenced by referring to the lecture of the previous week, which was on partnerships between masters and men, and stated that during the week he had received the report of a company established on the principle, which showed that nothing above five per cent on the capital employed in the business had been realised during the two years it had been in operation. Still it had the advantage of being a means to prevent strikes, and the promoters seemed to have great confidence in the scheme. He proposed to notice in the present lecture the division of labour, and its effect on wages and profits in different employments. They had seen that wages were turned into commodities used by the people, therefore anything that increased the production of articles used increased also the comforts of the people. Among the things that increased the production the division of labour was the most important. The term simply meant dividing any kind of work into different parts, so that one man should do one part of the work, and another man another part. The agriculturist or farmer did every kind of work on his farm, but the man occupied with the labour in a factory did one kind of work only. They had a good instance of the division of labour in pin making, as conducted in the Birmingham factories, for in the making of a pin ten or twelve persons were employed, some to make the head, others to fasten it on, &c. That division of labour ran throughout the whole of society, and not only had every factory different kinds of work, but different kinds of work were divided among different factories, and there was now an inclination for one firm to take up one branch of a business only. It was important to notice how it was that it was so advantageous. The advantages had been described by Adam Smith, and afterwards by other writers. The first advantage was in the dexterity that was acquired by repetition. Everybody knew that when a man or a woman first tried at anything they felt very clumsy, but if he or she continued at work of the same kind they would accomplish it better. There was a good example in the case of making nails, which was considered by Adam Smith. A person not accustomed to use a hammer could hardly make a nail, and even a good blacksmith who was familiar with the use of the hammer could not make more than 200 or 300 nails a day, yet a nailer made 2,300 a day of some sorts of nails, or a man accustomed to the work would make ten times as many nails as the blacksmith. The second advantage was that which arose from the saving of time in changing tools, and passing from one kind of work to another. Everyone must be aware that when one kind of work was once begun, time would be saved by keeping at that work, instead of passing from it to something else, and if they had to change tools many times during a day, considerable time would be lost in that way also. The third advantage arose from the invention of machines that tended to facilitate labour, and enabled one man to do the work of many. It would be apparent that if they only had to do a particular kind of work they would be able to do much more by the aid of elaborate tools and machines than they would with ordinary manual labour. Where a factory had a particular kind of work to do it had an enormous demand for that kind, and a considerable amount of money could be spent in machines to do it in the best way. Then, again, it was said that a man occupied with one kind of work was more likely to invent machines that would facilitate that kind of labour. Those were the three advantages that Adam Smith had named, but he (the lecturer) would mention a fourth, which was of great importance – it was the power that arose from doing a great many things at a time, and thus multiplying results, as when the same thing was done for a great many people. There was a remarkable instance of that in the post-office. It seemed impossible to send a parcel to any part of the country for a penny, or indeed for a halfpenny – for one halfpenny was paid to Government for every letter – and it could only be done from the fact that a man could carry a hundred letters instead of one. If they appointed a messenger to carry a letter for them it would cost as much as if the messenger carried letters for the whole town, and in that way there was an enormous saving. There was also an instance of that advantage in the employment of police or a guard of soldiers, for it was obvious that a few police could protect a man much better than he could protect himself, or even better than a large number of people could protect themselves. The fifth advantage arose from repeating the operation in a machine-like manner, as it were – it was what they might call the multiplication of efficiency from repetition. He meant to say that when once they got a machine in work they might produce many things from the same mould with a comparatively small amount of labour. The printing press was a remarkable instance of this. In former times it was necessary, in order to have a copy of a book, either to copy it, or else get someone else to do so. At that time £50 of our present money would have been a cheap rate for a book. Books were now very much cheaper, simply because when the type was once set the number of copies could be readily multiplied *ad infinitum*. The same applied to a variety of other things, such as the coining of money, engraving and striking medals from moulds, as in the manufacture of the small Birmingham goods, where there seemed to be no end to the number of articles that could be produced. The sixth advantage that arose from a division of labour was what he called personal adaptation – it gave everyone an opportunity of choosing the kind of work for which he was best adapted: that was to say, when there was a variety of trades and professions which could not be the case in a primitive state of society, when every man had to do much the same as every other man. But in the present state of the country everyone had a chance of choosing what he would do, according to the abilities he might possess. It was obviously to the advantage of society in general that every person should have an opportunity of exercising his ability or strength in the most profitable way, for it was evident the greatest amount of wealth would be created, and the greatest amount of good would be done, if everyone could get into the right place. There were two ways of getting men in the right place, one of which was by Government promotion – though that did not work very well – and the other was by competition, which he apprehended was the most practicable. There was a further advantage from the division of labour that might be noticed, namely that of local adaptation. Every place was more or less suited to some particular kind of industry of its own. No one thought of producing wine, or to grow silk in England. If they were wise they would leave each country to provide what was best grown there. This gave rise to what was called territorial division of labour, and resulted in making one a corn-growing country, another a wine-growing country, and another a coal and iron-producing country, such as this country is. These were the advantages which resulted from a division of labour, but one of the results was that considerable difficulty existed in different trades as to the profits, that was what portion should be set apart for wages, and what for interest of capital employed in a trade. Several weeks ago he had said a little about what regulated wages, and he then stated that it depended upon the amount of capital in the country compared with the number of those who were supported on that capital. It was, as it were, a sort of dividend of money appropriated to pay wages divided among those who were to receive it. But that only determined the average rate that should be paid to each, and did not determine who should get the biggest share of the money paid. In different trades there was always an extreme in the rate of wages paid, which depended more or less on the demand and supply. Of some kinds of men there were much larger supplies than of other kinds, and if there happened to be more of one trade than there was work for, some would have to take any other kind of work they could get. They would see how it was that supply and demand of persons in different trades were governed, and to understand that they would consider the circumstances that had been laid down by Adam Smith as governing them. The first circumstance that governed supply or demand was the agreeableness or disagreeableness of employments. By that was meant that if an employment was very agreeable there would be sure to be a large number flocking to it, if they could only get into it. In this way they could account for various employments being readily taken up. There were several occupations that would present examples, for instance the occupation of a barrister was poorly paid in reality, yet they were attracted to it by a certain position which it gave them. Secondly, there was the easiness or cheapness by which a trade could be learned. If a trade were difficult to learn there would be fewer able to do it, but if it were easy to learn there would be many people to do it. The poor wages paid to seamstresses was an example, for there were sure to be an extraordinary supply of those who could sew so long as their labour was necessary; they therefore could not expect to get as high wages as in some other kinds of labour that was more difficult to learn. He supposed the science of a soldier or a policeman was not very difficult to learn, which would account for the low wages paid to them. The third law they must notice was the constancy or inconstancy of an employment in trade. If a man had a trade in which he would be more liable to be thrown out of work than another, he would require more wages whilst he was in work, and on the other hand if an employment was constant he would be satisfied with less wages. That accounted for the low rate of wages paid in many employments, as for instance that of the schoolmaster, and some others. Fourthly, they had to notice the small or great trust that might be reposed in a man. If a man was required for a trustworthy situation he must possess a character for being trustworthy, which was worth money. Fifthly, there was the probability or improbability of success in trade. If a man entered a trade in which there was a probability of failure, then he must be attracted to it by a prospect of more profits than he would be likely to meet with in ordinary trade. These circumstances rendered it impossible for there to be a uniformity of wages in all trades; for instance it was impossible that a man should go to a great expense in learning a business if he were only to receive the same as other people who had not been at such expense. If there were not great degrees of success or great rewards to be occasionally had, no one would be led to exert his faculties more than another, or if all were insured [*sic*] a certain amount of wages, there would be no particular motive for hard work. This touched upon a subject that often turned up, namely what were called socialistic ideas. Schemes had been proposed with the view of arranging people in the places they should hold; and that promotion should be conducted on some arbitrary system, but competition, after all, seemed to offer something better. He thought all would admit that the motive for pushing their way and exerting their talents was what really conduced to the wealth of the country. In connection with this he might notice what governed the profits in different trades. That was a similar question to the one of wages, because it really would depend upon supply and demand in the same way. If there was any business or manufacture that seemed to offer more than ordinary advantages or profits, or was more agreeable than others, then there was sure to be people looking out for an opportunity for the use of their capital, who would turn their attention to it. First of all they might consider which business yielded the greatest profits, and judge as best they could from the knowledge they possessed. It might be that agreeableness in business influenced the capitalist as well as the labourer. It might be that an employment in London might be more agreeable than one in the provinces, but he thought that as a general rule the profits would be pretty sure to govern everything else. They required to look into the matter a little before they could make out the profits of any business. If they were to investigate the books of a firm they must first of all make allowance for the capital advanced, a part of the remainder went to pay rent, and another part to pay wages. When all these were paid there should remain interest of capital employed, and beyond that there should be a certain amount of profit. It might be asked, "Why do men want more than the ordinary interest for their capital?" A little reflection would show that a man using his money in business must look for interest and for something else. Interest means what a man could get by lending his money, or by investing in ordinary security, such as railway shares. If a man had money he could get five per cent for it without any trouble, then if he employed that money in business, and spends his whole time in using it to the best advantage, of course he looked for something that would remunerate him. In this way a man's profit in business consisted of two parts – interest for his money and remuneration for his trouble. This was well illustrated by the partnership scheme already referred to, in which the employers took five per cent as a fair remuneration before there was a division of the profits. Then there came in an element beyond that, namely, the risk a capitalist underwent in being employed in any trade. When they looked at the number of bankrupts that were published, they would see that there was a great risk, and there was hardly any employment where there was not occasional losses. The risk of a business becoming a losing one was a disagreeable circumstance, which had a tendency to keep people out of it, and if there was one business more risky than others, people would avoid it and put their money into a surer business. – There was a short but interesting discussion afterwards.

VIII ON THE INTERNATIONAL MONETARY CONVENTION, AND THE INTRODUCTION OF AN INTERNATIONAL CURRENCY INTO THIS KINGDOM

Read before the Manchester Statistical Society, 13 May 1868. Published in *Transactions of the Manchester Statistical Society, 1867–8*, pp. 79–92.

The increase in the gold supply and the number of trading countries whose currency was effectively based on gold had made the possibility of an international coinage a real one in the eighteen-sixties, and Jevons was a prominent supporter of this proposal. The background to, and details of, it are fully set out in this paper. It was in connection with it also that Jevons undertook, during the year 1868, an extensive statistical study of the amount and condition of the gold coinage in circulation in the United Kingdom. The results of this were published in a paper read before the Statistical Society of London (afterwards the Royal Statistical Society) on 17 November 1868, and entitled 'On the Condition of the Gold Coinage of the United Kingdom, with reference to the question of International Currency' (*JRSS*, 31 (1868) 426–64).

This latter paper was included in *Investigations* and a note attached to it there states that 'part of the substance of this paper . . . had been previously communicated to the Manchester Statistical Society. . . . To prevent repetition, the Manchester paper is not reprinted in this volume.'[1] In fact the extent of repetition is very small, and the two papers were more complementary than overlapping.

It does not seem to be sufficiently known to the English public that changes of the utmost importance are taking place in the systems of metallic currency of continental nations. They amount to a complete revolution in the ancient and customary standards of value of most

---

[1] *Investigations*, first edition (1884) p. 244.

countries, and they open a fair prospect of ultimately attaining that which has hardly hitherto been conceived possible, namely, a world-wide *uniform currency*. These changes have been partly brought about by the deliberations of the International Statistical Congresses; they have been much forwarded by a natural cause, namely, the excessive supply of gold from California and Australia, but they seem to me to be very much due to the enlightened views of M. de Parieu and the French Government. With the aid of an able pamphlet on the subject, privately printed by Mr. Frederick Hendriks together with some official documents, I will first describe how the scheme arose, and then consider the motives which might lead us to join and promote it. The disturbances in continental currencies commenced in the year 1850, when the Belgian Government demonetized their gold coinage, and made silver the sole legal standard. This was done from a fear that the value of gold would be extensively depreciated and all contracts falsified. But as the Belgian coinage is nearly identical with the French coinage and the countries are conterminous, it was found impossible to prevent the French gold coin from passing into Belgium. Thus it came to pass, that in 1861, Belgium found it desirable to accept the French system of currency, including the double standard of gold and silver. Somewhat similar difficulties had at the same time been experienced by Switzerland and Italy, which also possessed a coinage resembling that of France, or were partially conterminous with France. As to France itself, it is well known that the action of the alternative double standard since 1850, has been such as to convert a coinage substantially consisting of silver into one consisting chiefly of gold.

Under these circumstances, the French Government readily accepted a suggestion that France, Belgium, Italy and Switzerland should undertake a joint investigation and arrangement of their currencies. The result was the convention signed on the 23rd December, 1865, which established what has been called the Latin Monetary Convention, or, as M. de Parieu names it, the Latin Münzverein. By this first step towards an uniform currency, the four nations in question bound themselves to issue from their several mints an uniform series of coins on the basis of the franc, these coins to be accepted indifferently by the Public Treasuries of the four governments. A year or two previous to the accomplishment of this convention, namely, in September, 1863, the International Statistical Congress had arrived at clear views as to the mode in which it was best to attempt the great problem of an international coinage. It was felt to be hopeless to choose any one system of currency and expect all nations at once to adopt it. But it was observed that the principal unit coins already in use were nearly multiples of the franc or half-franc, and were consequently connected by simple ratios with each other. Thus, approximately—

$$2\tfrac{1}{2} \text{ francs} = 1 \text{ florin.}$$
$$5 \quad ,, \quad = 1 \text{ dollar.}$$
$$25 \quad ,, \quad = 1 \text{ pound sterling.}$$

Slight alterations in the coins would thus enable the franc, florin, dollar, and pound sterling, to pass as multiples, or sub-multiples of each other, and the identically same coins might be current in almost all countries, the name alone altering as they passed from one to the other. Thus, one pound would pass in France for 25 francs, in the United States as a half eagle, in Austria as a 10 florin piece. This scheme seemed so feasible, that the French Government suggested the assembling of a conference to consider it during the period of the International Exhibition. No less than twenty states, including all the principal European nations together with the United States, sent representatives, and the whole subject of international monetary arrangements was minutely discussed, and decided with a degree of unanimity which could hardly have been anticipated. I will now give a brief outline of the results as made known to us in the official report of the Master of the Mint and Mr. C. Rivers Wilson, who attended the conference as representatives of the British Government. The possibility of creating a single uniform system of universal currency was first discussed, but however great the advantages of such a scheme might be if accomplished, the difficulties were soon felt to be insuperable. The conference therefore came to the conclusion that—

"Monetary unification may be most readily attained by the adjustment of existing systems, taking into consideration the scientific advantages of certain types, and the number of the populations by which they have already been adopted."

It was however felt, at the same time, that the system of French currency claimed a preponderance of attention, both on account of its theoretical perfection, and because it was already accepted by four nations included in the convention of 1865, with a population of 72 millions of persons, in addition to the Papal States and the Kingdom of Greece, which have since acceded to that convention.

The conference next proceeded to consider what metal should be recommended as the general standard of value. So equal are the claims of gold and silver to serve this office, that the best economists have never been able to arrive at any distinct and well-founded opinion in favour of either. In most European countries, indeed, silver was from early times the standard, and in England, the adoption of a gold currency arose at the first unintentionally. To habit and prejudice, rather than to deliberate judgment, we must attribute the preference for gold which many English writers, including Lord Liverpool, have expressed. The statesmen of the

French Revolution indeed endeavoured to combine the use of both metals as standards, by making both legal currency, at the fixed rates of $15\frac{1}{2}$ parts by weight of silver to 1 part of gold, and so late as last May, the Imperial Commission, which has lately been inquiring into the whole subject of the French currency laws, pronounced in favour of this system. Of all the countries represented at the conference, only two, viz., Great Britain and Portugal, actually possessed an exclusively gold standard, and it is very surprising to find under these circumstances, that the conference unanimously decided in favour of a gold standard. If this decision were the sole result of the meeting, it might yet be said to have effected a revolution in the currencies of the globe; but the full significance of the fact will only be apparent to those who know the eagerness with which the battle of the standards has been waged in monetary discussions, and the invincible differences of opinion to which it gave rise. Of the soundness of the decision there can hardly, I apprehend, be any doubt. Natural circumstances rather than theoretic arguments have brought about unanimity. The extraordinary supplies of gold thrown on the market since 1849, have not only furnished abundance of this metal, but have also to some extent depreciated both gold and silver. At the same time, the general increase in the wealth and activity of trade in many parts of the world has naturally led to the increased use of the more intrinsically valuable and portable metal.

Gold, thus tended by the force of uncontrollable natural events to become the general medium of exchange, and it will probably prove that the members of the conference showed the highest wisdom in promptly accepting the necessary changes. We may congratulate ourselves that we already employ gold and silver in our currency in the very method recommended by the conference; gold as the absolute standard, silver as the material for the fractional token coinage, passing as legal tender to a limited sum ($£2$). Eighteen nations have unreservedly adopted a standard of value hitherto upheld almost solely by ourselves; this surely should be sufficient to appease the pride of Britons, and prevent them from rejecting with their customary scorn the slightest suggestion from abroad that our laws and customs could be amended.

The first point in which we should need to make a slight concession in accepting the provisions of an international currency regards the proportion of alloy in our coins, which at present is $\frac{1}{12}$ part in the case of gold. But all other civilized nations now coin gold with $\frac{1}{10}$ part of alloy, and the practice has been adopted by our own mint at Hong Kong in the coinage of silver dollars. The higher fineness of our gold coins has hitherto been upheld on the ground that they are rather harder than coins of $\frac{9}{10}$ fineness, but Mr. Graham, than whom there can be no higher authority, considers that this opinion has arisen from a misapprehension of experiments made more than half a century ago, and he holds that the advantage lies rather the other way. There cannot be a doubt that we shall be wise in accepting the foreign system and adding $\frac{1}{60}$ more alloy to our coins, a change of wholly inconsiderable importance in itself, but indispensable to the introduction of international currency.

The most difficult point upon which the conference touched was the common unit of value which might be recommended for ultimate adoption. The majority were in favour of the five franc piece, or gold dollar, and a resolution was passed that the common coin of five francs should be made a legal tender throughout the countries which might unite in a monetary convention. In this vote the English representatives did not join, and their opinion is in favour of a higher unit of value. The point which is of most immediate importance to us next came under consideration, namely, the introduction into the international system of a 25 franc piece. It is that coin which forms the possible link between the British and international currency, and the conference adopted the general currency of the 25 franc piece, avowedly on the ground that the adhesion of Britain might thus be received. It is also most important to note that Mr. Ruggles, the American representative, warmly supported its adoption, and informed the conference that the United States were prepared to lower their coinage 3 per cent. and re-coin the whole of the gold, provided the convention gave currency to the new 25 franc piece, which would pass in their country as a half eagle.

Passing over points of minor importance to us, we have now to consider the difficulty which arises in assimilating our sovereign to the future 25 franc piece. It is well known that according to the par of exchange—

$$£1 = 25\cdot2079 \text{ francs.}$$

so that our sovereign is ·825 per cent. too heavy, when newly and accurately coined, to circulate as international money. The difference is only ·988 of a grain of pure gold, worth about 2d. Even this small difference between the sovereign and 25 franc piece would prevent their common and indifferent currency, so that it would be indispensable either to raise the franc a little, or to lower the sovereign. For us to demand the former would be quite out of the question, because the French currency is nicely adjusted in connexion with the metrical system of weights, and is adopted by six nations representing a much larger population than that which now uses the sovereign. It would be, moreover, a far more difficult task to raise a currency one per cent. than to lower it by so much. If we are to join the convention, then we must lower our sovereign 2d. in the pound, and it is for the government to decide by the aid of the Royal Commission now sitting whether the advantages of an international currency are worth the inconvenience of making this change.

I will now briefly enumerate the inconveniences and advantages so far as they are known to me, beginning with the former. When the lowering of the currency is officially proclaimed, it will be necessary, supposing the present system of free coinage be maintained, to authorize every creditor to add 2d. in the pound to the nominal amount of his debt. Suppose the change were effected on the 1st January, 1870, then every debt of £1000 contracted before that day would become £1008 6s. 8d., the sovereign having been lowered, so that this sum only represents as much pure gold as £1000 did before. But the necessity for any disturbance of contracts will be altogether avoided by the proposed imposition of a seigniorage, or charge for coinage of one per cent. At present the cost of turning bullion into coin in London is only $1\frac{1}{2}$d. per standard oz., or $\frac{1}{6}$ per cent., the commission allowed to the bank in acting as the agent of the mint, and the government bear the whole costs of the coinage of gold. This is quite contrary to the practice of other countries; in France, according to the information obligingly furnished to me by Mr. Hendriks, the cost of converting bullion into coin is at least one per cent; in the Philadelphia mint the charges altogether amount to one per cent.; and in our own branch mint at Sydney, N.S.W., the charge is one per cent on sums below £10,000, and $\frac{3}{4}$ per cent. on larger sums. The present free coinage system of the British mint has really failed in practice. It has no effect in keeping our currency up to its full weight, because the new and heavy coins, instead of driving out the old and light ones, are picked out for melting and exportation, and are used in preference by gold beaters, electro-gilders and others. The Master of the Mint says:—

"There is reason to believe that large masses of new British sovereigns are occasionally treated, so as to separate out the heavy pieces, and these are disposed of as bullion; while the lighter pieces, which may still be all of legal weight, are preserved and put into circulation. This fact will not surprise those persons who are aware of the small margin of profit upon which bullion transactions are often conducted."

It is absurd that the nation should be at the expense of coining money which to the extent of many millions is only to be melted down again for the profit of bullion speculators. In entering the monetary convention, it is most reasonable that we should impose a mint charge equal to what other nations now impose, and that the mint regulations of all countries should be reduced as nearly as possible to complete uniformity by treaty obligations. At present it appears to be difficult if not impossible to say what the real par of exchange between nations is, because in addition to all other complications the mint charges are variable and very uncertainly known. All such uncertainty would be removed by the adoption of uniform mint regulations, and the coins of one country would be enabled to pass into the currency of another without any depreciation. Thus the objections to a mint charge raised by Lord Liverpool in his celebrated Letter on the Coins of the Realm, fall to the ground almost entirely. He opposes a mint charge for four reasons—

1st. – Because the principal measure of value would not in such case be perfect.

2nd. – Because merchants in exporting the coins would lose the mint charge, and would raise the price of foreign goods in order to transfer the loss to consumers.

3rd. – Because a reduction in the weight of the sovereign would be necessary, and consequently –

4th. – A re-coinage would be requisite.

Of these reasons it will be observed that the third and fourth are now altogether annulled, or rather reversed. We wish to reduce the sovereign and we shall require to re-coin a portion of our gold currency. The imposition of a seigniorage facilitates in a most remarkable manner the desired alteration, and renders the re-coinage a profit instead of a loss.

The second reason is also entirely annulled, because under uniform mint regulations contemplated by the monetary convention, coins will not lose in value by exportation. It is no doubt true, that in theory free coinage gives the most perfect measure of value, but inasmuch as our mint cannot manufacture coins of perfectly equal and accurate weight, inconveniences arise in practice, described below. The views of Lord Liverpool were adopted in the law of 1816, which at present regulates our metallic currency, but it is probable that had he regarded the question from the point of view which we now enjoy, he would no longer have opposed a mint charge.

The second inconvenience would consist in the requisite recoinage of a portion of our gold currency, the silver coinage being unaffected. In the report of the English representatives, the amount of our gold circulation is vaguely stated as lying between £80,000,000 and £120,000,000; but facts have, I believe, recently come to light showing that large quantities of newly coined sovereigns have been melted for exportation. An investigation which I have recently made leads me to believe that the gold currency is really under eighty millions. I have, moreover, evidence kindly furnished to me by a number of bankers and other gentlemen in many parts of the kingdom, showing that something like one gold piece in every three is on an average too light to be legal tender, but would serve as a 25 franc piece. Separate evidence is derived from careful weighings of 280 sovereigns, which I made upon an excellent chemical balance in Dr. Roscoe's laboratory, at Owen's College. Out of 280 sovereigns drawn on three occasions from Manchester banks, I find that there are—

Weight or above weight....................	6 per cent.
Within remedy.................................	68 ,,
Below weight....................................	26 ,,
	100

Comparing the weight of these sovereigns with the weight of the future 25 franc piece, and allowing a remedy of $\frac{1}{2}$ per cent. in excess or defect, I find the following results:—

Sovereigns too heavy to pass as 25 franc piece.........	54 per cent.
Of proper weight..	38 · ,,
Too light	8 ,,
	100

It thus appears that we have actually in circulation in Manchester sovereigns which are lighter than 25 franc pieces, and there is every reason to believe that in other parts of the country where there is no branch Bank of England in the immediate neighbourhood, the proportion of old to new or light to heavy coins would be greater. The half sovereigns there is no doubt are rather worse than the sovereigns.

To be brief, I will only say that I believe our present currency law has broken down; that the practice of weighing and rejecting light sovereigns is almost entirely discontinued, except at the Bank of England and in a few localities in Ireland; and that we now have a currency which is wearing more and more light every year. I need hardly say too, that it is very difficult to drive light coins out of use, because no individual and no bank will incur the loss of 4d. or 6d. in the pound if they can contrive to pass off the coin again at its full value. Every device is therefore employed to keep light coins back from the Bank of England which invariably weighs them, and at the same time the melter and exporter of sovereigns has an equal interest in picking out the new ones. I am inclined to think that there is no fair and reasonable mode by which the currency of the kingdom may be raised again to its legal weight but by the Government undertaking the work and bearing the loss, which would probably amount to £200,000 or £300,000. From this loss we should, in a certain sense, be saved by reducing the sovereign. In fact as the mint expenses for coinage amount only to $\frac{1}{3}$ of a penny per sovereign, there would be a profit by calling in our present coinage and issuing 25 franc pieces, whereas, before long a formidable loss must be incurred in the re-coinage of sovereigns if we resolve to adhere to our present system.

There remains the inconvenience which might arise in effecting the change of currencies. Two modes present themselves: —

1st. – On the day fixed for proclaiming the change, to make the light sovereigns between 121·58 and 122·80 grains a legal tender, and to authorize the currency of heavier sovereigns at a nominal increase of value of 2d.

2nd. – To lower the limit of the legal currency of sovereigns to 121·58 grains, and to leave the heavy ones temporarily current as at present, until they be reduced by wear, or melted, or exported. The fact is, that if the mint began to issue a plentiful supply of new 25 franc pieces, the heavier coins would rapidly disappear from circulation, and as the Government now practically permits the circulation of sovereigns varying between 119½ grains and 123½ grains, and every person who has a light sovereign now is liable to a loss of 4d. to 6d. upon it, I conceive that it would be needless and over-scrupulous for the Government to secure to every holder of a heavy sovereign its slight difference of value compared with the 25 franc piece.

The profit on melting and exporting heavy sovereigns would not really fall exclusively to the bullion dealers. By rendering the export of gold profitable, it would tend to reduce the quantity of coin in circulation and raise its value. So long as there were heavy sovereigns to export, the lighter ones would really bear in trade the value of the heavy ones; only when the supply of heavy coins was exhausted, would the value of the currency fall 2d. in the pound.

I have now only to advert to the advantages which would arise from the introduction of an international currency. There seems to be a great difficulty in appreciating these advantages; for merchants, and especially bullion brokers and those engaged in business connected with the foreign exchanges, affirm that it would be no advantage, and that they get on very well as they are at present. I believe, however, that just as we find it convenient to have an uniform currency within the kingdom, we shall in time find the highest benefit in having something like a world-wide currency. The advantages I can enumerate are four or five in number.

First, and least, I place the convenience to travellers in being able to pass the same money in whatever country they may visit. We find it a great convenience already that the sovereign will generally be received for 25 francs, at a loss of 2d.; but if we accede to the convention, the new sovereign will probably be received all the world over for its full value.

Secondly. – The reduction of sums of money from their expression in one currency to another will be simplified. To turn pounds sterling into francs, florins, or dollars, it will only be necessary to divide by 25, 10, and 5, respectively, and as these are all multiples of 5, both multiplication and division may be effected by one significant figure with alteration of the decimal point. This convenience, however, will not be fully experienced until we have a decimal subdivision of our unit of value.

Thirdly. – The international currency of coins would render the adjustment of the exchanges more rapid and accurate. So long as there is gold in each of two countries, the exchanges can never vary between them more than by the cost of transmitting gold from one to the other. At present a large part of the gold and silver trade consists in the transmission of bars, and the trade falls into the hands of a special class of dealers, who, no doubt, make a fair profit out of it, in addition to paying the costs of melting and assaying when necessary. Another portion is transmitted as foreign coin, of which the Bank always holds a considerable value, counted among the bullion. Still large quantities of British gold coins are annually exported and re-imported. Thus in the year 1866, the exports and imports of gold were in value as follows:—

	EXPORTS.		IMPORTS.
Bullion.	£5,282,164	. .	£9,099,064
Foreign Coin	3,452,806	. .	10,356,854
British Coin	4,007,089	. .	4,053,723
	£12,742,059	. .	£23,509,641

The bullion brokers assert that they can transmit bars just as easily as coin; why then do we find the larger part of the trade already conducted in coin? It must be because the transmission of coin is more easy and less costly, and coin would evidently be still more suitable for foreign trade if it were indifferently current in all countries.

But I conceive, that after all the greatest advantages are the indirect and ultimate ones, which will arise from the world-wide extension of the monetary convention. The adhesion of Austria is already secured by a preliminary treaty, signed at the termination of the conference; the United States are perfectly willing to join, and if we, with our wide-spread colonies and all-pervading trade, lend our aid, a general reform and unification in the currencies of the world is almost a necessary result. It must be remembered that by far the largest part of the gold supplies of the world is in the hands of the British Empire and the United States, and the sovereigns coined on an uniform system will pervade the world somewhat in the same manner that the Spanish dollar has for two centuries or more been the international currency, and has been of the greatest services to trade.

As from natural causes, gold is replacing silver as the main medium of currency, some gold coin will take the lead, and if we are only wise enough, we shall make the sovereign suitable for this purpose. We must remember, that the advantages are not to be experienced within this kingdom so much as by the promotion of our foreign trade. We have admitted foreign vessels and foreign goods, and have thrown ourselves unreservedly upon foreign trade, as our main stay: we are now as much interested in the welfare and prosperous course of trade in other countries as in our own. Exchange is always mutual, and if there is anything wrong at one end, harm will be felt at the other end. If trade is injured by a bad and depreciated currency, we are liable to suffer through the losses of our merchants. In the great scheme of international money, I consider we are far behind our proper place. It is England that should have suggested free trade in money to the world; it is Manchester that should have suggested it to England, as it has suggested other great ideas before. The unification of currencies is the appropriate sequel to the introduction of free trade. It is a new step in the *rapprochement* of nations and the spread of civilization.

We have lost the opportunity of initiating this great reform, but if we refuse to accept it when offered by an enlightened foreign government, whether it be from the shortness of our vision, or the pride of our hearts, I hold that we shall stultify ourselves, and act unworthily of that proud position which we occupy in the commerce and civilization of the world.

IX. THE PROGRESS OF THE MATHEMATICAL THEORY OF POLITICAL ECONOMY

Read before the Manchester Statistical Society, 11 November 1874. Published in *Transactions of the Manchester Statistical Society, 1874–75*, pp. 1–19, and reprinted in *JRSS*, 37 (1874) 478–88.

The full title of the paper adds 'with an Explanation of the Principles of the Theory'. As Jevons states in the opening paragraph, it was largely the outcome of his becoming acquainted with the work of Walras and other continental mathematical economists to whom Walras directed his attention. On 13 September 1874, Jevons wrote to Walras: 'I have been thinking how I could make [your book] known in this country, but am sorry to say that there are only one or two publications which I could ask to admit an article on so unpopular a subject.'[1] On 9 October Jevons wrote to Johan d'Aulnis de Bourouill: 'I am about to prepare a memoir, to be read to the Statistical Society of Manchester, upon the subject of the mathematical theory of political economy, and if the book which you are proposing to publish is sufficiently advanced I should much like to draw the attention of the Society to it.'[2] The paper does contain one or

[1] See Letter 391, Vol. IV, p. 65.
[2] See Letter 393, Vol. IV, p. 70.

two mentions of d'Aulnis, but without any enlargement or explanation of his work.

Jevons later made extensive use of this paper as a means of propagating the ideas of Walras and himself, sending copies to G. H. Darwin, Alfred Marshall and others likely to be interested.[3]

The very recent publication of an important work on "Political Economy," by M. Leon Walras, the ingenious professor of the science in the Academy of Lausanne, induces me to draw the attention of the society to the mathematical theory of economy. The work of M. Walras is entitled "Eléments d'Économie Politique Pure," and although constituting only the first part of a complete treatise, it is divided into three books, which discuss respectively the "Objets et Divisions de l'Economie Politique et Sociale," the "Théorie Mathematique de l'Echange," and lastly the subject "Du Numéraire et de la Monnaie." The first of these divisions is a general discourse upon the subject and method of the science; the second contains a highly remarkable mathematical analysis of the laws of supply and demand and the conditions of value; the third applies the result of this analysis to the special case of the currency.

It is to the second of these essays, that I wish particularly to direct your attention. Commencing with a sketch of the operations which take place and the motives which govern those operations upon any extensive market, like that of the French Rentes at the Paris Bourse, M. Walras proceeds to attach definite ideas to the familiar terms value, price, effective offer, effective demand, satisfaction of wants, &c. Regarding all these notions as strictly mathematical, as they certainly must be, because they deal with definite quantities, he proceeds to invent a notation, accurate and ingenious, but perhaps a little complicated, for expressing their relations in the briefest and most general manner. He shows also that the variation of the quantities can be very clearly expressed graphically by curves representing the supply and demand of any commodity at different prices. The causes of these variations are next investigated, and discovered to depend upon the extension and intension of utility of the commodities, which notations, again, are represented by curves of the variation of utility. The intensive utility of an article is stated to be identical with its rarity, arising from the limited character of the supply. Finally, M. Walras arrives at this fundamental theorem, that the current prices of commodities, or the prices *in equilibrio*, are equal to the ratios of the rarities, or, as otherwise expressed, the values in exchange are

---

[3] See Letters 399, 415 and 416, Vol. IV, pp. 81, 99 and 100.

proportional to the rarities. It is a remarkable circumstance concerning this theorem that, although expressed in different language and reached by a different course of reasoning, it is yet precisely identical with the chief result of the mathematical theory of political economy of which the first brief outline was made known at the Cambridge meeting of the British Association for the Advancement of Science in 1862, and of which a fuller exposition, under the name "The Theory of Political Economy," was published in 1871. I cannot help reiterating here my feeling that in England the progress of true economical science is being immensely retarded by the excessive popular reputation attaching to the writings of the late Mr. Mill. So peculiar was the power excited over his friends and readers by Mr. Mill's zeal, his fearless independence of opinion, his high moral character, and his lucid, persuasive, and apparently logical style of composition, that his works have acted upon English readers like a spell, which it may take many years to break. Already, however, his exposition of the wage-fund theory has been overthrown by Professor Cliffe Leslie, and his fundamental propositions concerning capital have been shown to involve various fallacies and self-contradictions by Mr. George Darwin, and quite recently by Governor Musgrave, of South Australia. After studying the writings of Mr. Mill for twenty years, and teaching from them for more than ten years, as I am unfortunately obliged to do by the public recognition which they receive at the Universities, I feel bound to express my confident belief that they will in the course of time be allowed to consist to a large extent of a series of ingenious sophisms.

In our own subject of political economy, it has been much too commonly assumed that Adam Smith founded the science, that Ricardo systematised it, and that Mill finally expounded it in a nearly perfect form. An orthodox economical creed has thus been established, and all who can call its truth in question are too likely to be treated as noxious heretics, or, at the least, as harmless crotcheteers. But in spite of all danger of being thus regarded, I maintain that it is only by going back and reconsidering the primary notions of the science that we can arrive at a true theory of economy, and be enabled to distinguish between the true and the false in ancient doctrines. It is probably a mistake to put forward the new views of the science as forming specially a mathematical theory. In truth, there is nothing more theoretical, and but little more mathematical, in the views of M. Walras, M. d'Aulnis, and myself than in the ordinary doctrines. The laws of political economy must be mathematical for the most part, because they deal with quantities and the relations of quantities. If we turn to the explanations given of the principal elements of the subject in any of the chief authors, we shall find that they deal continually with quantities. Adam Smith says, "The value of any commodity to the person who possesses it, and who means not to use or consume it himself, but to exchange it for other commodities, is equal to the quantity of labour which it enables him to purchase or command. Labour, therefore, is the real measure of the exchangeable value of all commodities." Again, he says, "Equal quantities of labour, at all times and places, may be said to be of equal value to the labourer." Ricardo does not entirely agree with Smith's opinion on the origin of value, but his own ideas are not the less mathematical. "Possessing utility," he says, "commodities derive their exchangeable value from two sources – from their scarcity and from the quantity of labour required to detain them." And he proceeds to consider how the question of value is affected by the varying price given for different quantities ·of labour. There is hardly a page of his well-known treatise in which Ricardo does not reason about the equality or inequality, the proportionality, or the manner of variation of quantities of commodity, labour, value, utility, money and so forth. If we examine the treatises of Senior, of M'Culloch, of Say, of Mill, or of any other economist, in fact, we shall find that quantity is almost the sole theme, but that the manner of treating quantitative relations is of the crudest character, and that little or no aid is derived from the recognised modes of mathematical expression, which are found essential in all the other sciences dealing with quantity. Thus the chief difference between the old and the new doctrines is, that the old ones involve a crude and partially false mathematical theory, and the new ones, as I venture to maintain, a true mathematical theory. This difference arises, as I believe, from overlooking the importance of a thorough analysis of the notion of utility.

Economists, with few exceptions, have described utility as if it were a fixed and invariable quality of a substance, like its colours, density, hardness, or conductivity. They have probably confused utility with those fixed physical properties on which its utility is founded. Mr. Mill, for instance, on reaching the critical point of his theory of value, introduces a long quotation from that strange writer De Quincy [sic], who, in his "Logic of Political Economy," illustrates the relations of price, utility, and difficulty of attainment. Here, again, we have crude mathematical reasoning. We are told "the inertness of D (that is, difficulty of attainment) allowed U (that is, utility) to put forth its total effect. The practical compression of D being withdrawn, U springs up like water in a pump, when released from the compression of air;" and so forth. In parts of this curious passage De Quincy speaks of symbol U as denoting intrinsic utility, implying that the utility treated by economists is intrinsic or deeply seated within the objects and commodities which are the subject of the science. In this use of the term he is in perfect accordance with the generality of economists. Adam Smith says, "Nothing is more useful than water," meaning, in the absence of qualification, that all water has qualities which render it exceedingly useful. In the works of Smith and most English writers it is indeed difficult to find any precise definitions of utility.

Turning to French economists we find clear, though it may be mistaken, definitions. According to Say, utility is "Cette faculté qu'ont certaines choses de pouvoir satisfaire aux divers besoins des hommes." Garnier still more clearly sums up the opinions of most economists when he says: "L'ensemble des qualités qui rendent les choses propres à satisfaire nos besoins et à procurer des jouissances, se nomme utilité." According to all such writers, then, utility is the *ensemble* of physical qualities which are capable of making the substance possessing them suitable to the wants of men. Among English writers there is one who, without perhaps being aware of the whole importance of the change, has given a different definition of utility. Nassau Senior, in the admirable introduction to his treatise on political economy, describes utility somewhat vaguely as "the power, direct or indirect, of producing pleasure;" but then he goes on to make the following most important remark: "Utility, however, denotes no intrinsic quality in the things which we call useful; it merely expresses their relations to the pains and pleasures of mankind. And, as the susceptibility of pain and pleasure from particular objects is created and modified by causes innumerable and constantly varying, we find an endless diversity in the relative utility of different objects to different persons, a diversity which is the motive of all exchanges." It is from the notions expressed in these two sentences, when fully interpreted and followed out, that a true theory of economy is unfolded. To illustrate the importance of the change, let us go back to De Quincy and his "intrinsic utility." He imagines a little romance in his agreeable style, and represents the reader as travelling upon Lake Superior in a steamboat, making his way to an unsettled region 800 miles ahead of civilisation. "One fellow-passenger, whom you will part with before sunset, has a powerful musical snuff-box. Knowing by experience the power of such a toy over your own feelings, the magic with which at times it lulls your agitations of mind, you are vehemently desirous to purchase it. In the hour of leaving London you had forgotten to do so: here is a final chance. But the owner, aware of your situation not less than yourself, is determined to operate by a strain pushed to the very uttermost upon U, upon the intrinsic worth of the article in your individual estimate for your individual purposes." Here we find, clearly, that the musical box possesses intrinsic utility and intrinsic worth; but if these words mean anything, each musical box of exactly the same physical construction must have exactly the same intrinsic utility, however many boxes of the same sort you may previously possess. Even then, if you had brought a box with you from London, you would be equally anxious to buy a second exactly similar one from your fellow-passenger — nay, twenty such if they had come in your way. Now, what possible use can attach to twenty exactly similar musical boxes in the wilds of the Rocky Mountains? You cannot set them all going at once, for the discord would be terrible. If you try to use them all, by starting first one and then the other, the monotonous and constant repetition of the same tunes would be equally intolerable. If you only have them going occasionally, then a single one will serve for many years; and if you keep a second and a third to meet the case of the first being worn out or broken, the remaining seventeen will be simply useless. It is true that if you have neighbours, these surplus boxes may be sold or given to them; but it is as regards your neighbours that they now acquire utility, and the very ground of the change of ownership is that what is useless to you will be useful to them. In short, then, utility, as Senior said, is not an intrinsic quality at all; it is accident of a thing arising out of its relation to the wants of an individual. Utility only exists when there is on the one side the person wanting, and on the other the thing wanted; and the utility consists in the *ensemble* of all the qualities and circumstances which actually do enable it to quench the thirst or relieve the hunger or satisfy any of the wants of some person. Just as the gravitating force of a material body depends not alone upon the mass of that body, but upon the masses and relative positions and distances of the surrounding material bodies, so utility is an attraction between a wanting being and what is wanted.

Now this view, properly followed out, leads to startling conclusions. We cannot stop at musical boxes, but we must allow that even food and water are continually varying in utility according as there are people who want them or do not want them. Imagine a man in total solitude upon an island in the Pacific Ocean, where there are twenty bread-fruit trees. If the fruit of one tree is amply sufficient to sustain him, then we must allow that the fruit of the other nineteen trees has no utility. In the ordinary circumstances of an industrial community the same principles hold true; but the question is complicated by the practice of exchange, which renders useful to one man what is useless to another. We must now take a further step, and allow that each different portion of the one same commodity may possess a different degree of utility. If a man, imprisoned or otherwise cut off from all other supplies of food, receive only one pound of bread per day, he could barely maintain life upon it; a second pound per day would therefore possess extreme utility for him in satisfying his hunger and maintaining his strength. Supposing, however, that a third pound of bread be offered to him daily, will it possess equal utility with the second? Clearly not; for though he may eat some of it still further to supply his need of nourishment, yet he can hardly eat three pounds of bread per day. As to a fourth pound per day it would be absolutely useless, and would not be touched. We find, then, that the very same uniform commodity varies in utility according to the quantity which is already in possession. Exactly the same considerations apply to all other commodities in a more or less marked manner. One pair of boots is requisite; a second is very useful to replace the first when worn out, or temporarily unavailable; a third, and a fourth, and a fifth might be conceivably useful, though this would depend much upon the variety of construction adapted to serve a variety of purposes. No one can find equal use for 20 or 100 pairs of boots, as would be the case if the utility were intrinsic. We come, then, to the conclusion that the utility of a commodity is no intrinsic or unchangeable quality, but rather a relation which is essentially variable in degree and dependent upon the intensity of the want felt, which again depends upon the quantity of commodity which has been already consumed. Theoretically at least this variation must be regarded as taking place in the very smallest portions of the commodity. Not only is each pound of bread less useful than the pound already consumed, but each ounce than the previous ounce. The decline in the degree of utility may be regarded as approximately continuous, and is properly represented by a curve which more or less rapidly declined towards zero. While the height of this curve at any point above the base line represents the intensity or degree of utility of the commodity, when a certain quantity has already been consumed the area of the curve up to that point measures the total quantity of utility in the form of useful effect derived from its consumption.

We must observe that useful effect is a quantity of two dimensions – namely, the quantity of commodity consumed, and the degree of utility of each part of the commodity; in this sense their utility is correctly represented by an area. Degree of utility, on the contrary, is a quantity of one dimension, and is to be represented by a line. It is by thus giving precision to our ideas of utility that we can alone arrive at a correct comprehension of the relation between utility and value, upon which depends the solution of all the problems of political economy.

If these views concerning utility be accepted, the main branches of the science of political economy resolve themselves into the theory of the equilibrium of utility. The theory will apply, for instance, to the determination of the proper distribution of the same commodity when it is applicable to several different purposes. The commodity ought to be so divided and consumed that the final degree of its utility in each employment is the same. Each want should be satisfied up to the same point of satisfaction, because if one want is ever so little more pressing than another, there will be an increase of useful effect in applying a little more commodity to that, and a little less to some want which is not so acutely felt. The same principle holds true of the consumption of a store of commodity at different times. We ought so to consume the commodity that in each day or other interval of time the wants of the individual are satisfied up to the same point. It is, then, a general principle that in the case of each individual the degrees of utility are to be equalised, and this is also the key to the theory of value. If a person has a great deal of one commodity and little or none of another – say a great deal of bread and very little tea – the degree of utility of part of the bread will be low, and he will readily part with some, whereas more tea will have to him a high degree of utility, and he will be very desirous of obtaining more. If, then, he happen to meet with a second person who has plenty of tea and little bread, there will be evident increase of useful effect in the exchange. So far there is no mystery. But how are we to determine how much bread shall be given for so much tea, or *vice versâ*. The principle of equilibrium again applies, and each will give of his superfluous commodity until, if he gave either more or less at the existing ratio of exchange, the useful effect would be diminished. The matter is complicated, however, by the fact that the price of one commodity in terms of the other may be higher or lower. Thus if 2 oz. of tea be given for 39 oz. of bread, then in order that utility shall be maximised the utility of 2 more ounces of tea must be exactly equal to the utility of 39 oz. of bread; and this must hold true of each person separately. Now, the total utility or useful effect of 2 oz. of tea is found by multiplying the degree of utility of each ounce (assumed, for the moment, to be of equal degree of utility) by two, the number of ounces; the useful effect of the bread, in like manner, is found by multiplying the degree of utility of the bread by 39, the number of ounces. When equilibrium is attained, the products will be equal; from which it follows as an evident inference that the quantities exchanged will be inversely proportional to the final degrees of utility of the commodities.

It is also to be observed that in an open market there cannot be at the same time two ratios of exchange for the same uniform commodity. Hence the whole quantities of commodity exchanged, will bear the same ratio as the last small quantities. Now, the value of a thing, as we use the term, is greater as we give less of that thing for a given object, and less as we give more. Thus the values of things are inversely as the quantities of them given, and therefore directly proportional to the final degrees of utility.

Now, as the final degree of utility is only another expression for what M. Walras calls the rarity of a commodity, we have arrived at the theorem that the values in exchange are proportional to the rarities. It is evidently impossible that I should in a brief paper give all the requisite explanations concerning a general theory of this kind; it is still more out of the question that I should develop the consequences to be drawn from the theory. The deductions are only in a very partial way exhibited in the work of M. Walras, or in my "Theory of Political Economy." I should mention, however, that the laws of supply and demand, as generally accepted by economists, are easily deduced from the theory of exchange, so that the theory is verified by experience and statistical science. One all important point, however, is the relation between value and labour spent in production. Adam Smith vacillated between utility and labour as the causes and measures of value, and what perplexed Smith has perplexed subsequent writers. Thus we find Ricardo laying down that commodities derive their exchangeable value from the quantity of labour required to produce them, except in the case of commodities of which the supply cannot be increased by labour, and in these cases scarcity is the cause of value. The result of our theory, however, is to show that value always depends upon degree of utility, and labour has no connection with the matter, except through utility. If we can readily manufacture a great quantity of some article our want of that article will be almost completely satisfied; so that the degree of utility, and consequently its value, will fall. Production operates upon value only by varying the intensity of our desires for more of the same commodities; and it is plain that, in deciding how much of each kind of goods is to be produced, the principle of equilibrium of utilities must again guide us, so that each want shall be satisfied up to the corresponding point. Regard must now be paid, however, both to the ratios at which commodities exchange, and to the comparative quantities of different commodities which can be produced by the same labour.

The same kind of investigation which has been applied to the analysis of utility can also be applied to labour regarded as varying both in duration and intensity of painfulness. The general result, as explained in the "Theory of Political Economy," is to confirm the prevailing doctrine that the values of commodities tend to become approximately equal to their cost of production. The most important critic who has raised objections to this theory is certainly Professor J. E. Cairnes, who as I have said, altogether repudiates it in the very first chapter of his new work. He commences by remarking that I follow M. Say in maintaining that value depends entirely upon utility, and that he had regarded Say's views as long ago disposed of by Ricardo. So far, Professor Cairnes may be in a manner quite correct. M. Walras, M. d'Aulnis, and I do follow Say and several other eminent writers in regarding value as totally dependent on utility; but it is the exact nature of this dependence which is the all-important point, this which Mr. Cairnes has wholly misapprehended, or rather not apprehended at all. Altogether missing the distinction between total utility or aggregate useful effect, and the remaining degree of utility, which attaches to fresh supplies of the commodity, he remarks:—"A use of language according to which water is only useful where it is paid for, and in proportion as it is paid for; according to which atmospheric air is only useful in diving-bells, mines, and other places, whither it is costly to convey it; according to which meat and corn are less useful commodities in the United States than in England, and clothing and cutlery less useful in England than in the United States; according to which diamonds are more useful than coal, and iron is the least useful of the metals – such a use of language, it will be admitted, requires strong reasons for its justification." No doubt; but anything more wide of my use of the term useful cannot be conceived. Water, in a certain quantity, is infinitely useful to every person; but when enough has been received, further supplies are not useful, and may be hurtful, as in the case of a flood, a damp house, or a wet mine. A person living by a stream of pure water pays nothing for water, because he experiences the total useful effect of water without paying. For like reasons we seldom pay for air, because, though infinitely useful at every moment of our lives, the portions of air requisite to produce the useful effect of respiration can be drawn straight from the atmosphere without cost, and further supplies would not be useful. In diving-bells, mines, and elsewhere, we pay to get air, because otherwise we should not have enough, and additional quantities are worth paying for. The same explanation applies to all Mr. Cairnes' other objections. Coal is vastly more useful than diamonds in its total usefulness; but as we have for the present plenty of coal and not plenty of diamonds, we may still want one small diamond more than we want an additional ton of coals. With his own interpretation of my use of the term utility, it is no wonder that Mr. Cairnes holds my theory of value to be groundless. It amounts to this, he thinks, "That value depends on utility, and that utility is whatever affects value." In other words, the name utility is given to the aggregate of unknown conditions which determine the phenomenon, and then the phenomenon is stated to depend upon what this name stands for. I am wholly unable to see how Mr. Cairnes reaches this view of the matter. Value does depend upon the degrees of utility of the commodities valued, and these degrees of utility depend upon the quantities of commodities available as compared with the wants of consumers. But, in reality, so long as Mr. Cairnes fails to distinguish between the total useful effect of a commodity and its remaining degree of utility, and so long as he interprets my employment of the term utility in a way which is totally opposed to my own use of it, there is no possible common ground of discussion between us.

I will only further add a few words as to the value of the theory itself. It might seem that it leads us to no new conclusions, because we found that the principal inferences from the theory were the laws of supply and demand, and the doctrine of the relation of value to cost of production already so well known in political economy. But though many parts of economical doctrine as now accepted will be confirmed by the theory, other parts will probably be shown to be groundless. The results of any such theory must be of a triple character, destructive, conservative, and constructive; but it is yet too soon to attempt to trace out the actual character and extent of its effects in each direction. It might be thought, perhaps, that, being a mathematical theory, it cannot be of use until reduced to exact numbers and mathematical formula. Though numerical precision would be very vauable if it could be secured, yet it is no more requisite to this theory than to the old doctrines of economy, which are mathematical so far as they are anything at all. A true mathematical theory without numerical results can correct, or if necessary overturn, a false mathematical theory without numerical results. The laws of supply and demand are the best established part of the prevailing doctrines, although they have never been defined or analysed with any numerical precision; but, so far as they are known to be true, they form the verification in experience which ought to be applied to every theory. There is nothing, then, more theoretical, more speculative, more mathematical, more removed from experience or common sense in the new than in the old views. The new views simply arise from a more close and thorough analysis of the conditions of utility and its relations to value and labour. Ricardo said, "From no source do so many errors and so much difference of opinion in that science proceed as from the vague ideas which are attached to the word 'value.'" It will be a result of quite sufficient importance for the present if the new theory enables us to test the truth of prevailing doctrines concerning value, and to reject those which are false. It is quite doubtful whether the new theory will always lead us to such precise and dogmatic conclusions as we find in some of the principal treatises on political economy; but it will be allowed that precise and dogmatic conclusions do more harm than good if they be false, and that there is nothing of more worth in scientific matters than the touchstone which can decide between truth and error.

X REMARKS ON THE STATISTICAL USE OF THE ARITHMOMETER

Read before the Statistical Society of London, 19 November 1878. Published in *JRSS*, 41 (1878) 597–601.

If the previous paper displayed Jevons as a pure economic theorist, this one shows him as the applied statistician, very much alive to the value of aids to computation. The 'arithmometer', invented by Thomas de

Colmar about 1850, represented a very real advance on previous calculating machines. It employed the mechanical principle of toothed-wheel gearing, the wheels being engaged by setting stops to the figures.

It seems desirable to draw the attention of statists to the great saving of time and mental labour, which may be effected by the use of the Arithmometer, or French calculating machine. There is no great novelty in this machine. In principle it is the same as the original arithmetical machine invented by Blaise Pascal,* at the age of 19 or 20, about the years 1642–45, and imitated by several later mechanicians. The Arithmometer too, as actually manufactured by the late M. Thomas, of Colmar, has been a good deal used by actuaries, engineers, and others. It was made known to many people at the Paris Exposition of 1867, and to many more at the recent Exposition. English astronomers are now just beginning to use it for the tedious computations continually going on in observatories. Yet mercantile men, statists, and the English public at large remain unaware of the immense saving of labour which may be derived from the expenditure of 16*l.* or 20*l.* upon this beautiful machine.

It is true that the machine is of little use except for simple multiplication and division. The work proceeds entirely by addition and subtraction, which, when repeated time after time, constitute multiplication and division. But there is seldom any saving of time by employing the machine to perform simple addition or subtraction, because a computer of very moderate skill accomplishes this work rapidly on paper, and the transfer of the numbers from paper to the machine would occupy a good deal of time. The machine may be used also to extract square and cube roots; but it only does so by going through all the steps of the ordinary arithmetical processes, which are lengthy, and when not done on paper liable to blunders. For these and various other operations, logarithms would be more advantageous.

Nevertheless, the most common and troublesome operations of the computer consist in multiplication and division, and it is in this work that the machine can render inestimable service. A long sum can be put on the machine in ten seconds, and then a few turns of the handle give the product or quotient almost infallibly correct, and to as many places of figures as can possibly be required. The work for which the statist will find the machine most useful, is that of drawing percentages or ratios. There is little or no significance in any statistical number, except as compared with some other similar number, and in almost all cases that comparison

* "Œuvres Complètes de Blaise Pascal," vol. iii, pp. 185–208, &c. Paris, 1864.

should be made by calculating the ratio of one to the other. If then a statistical table is to be really intelligible and useful, every column of absolute numbers should be accompanied by a column of ratios. This accordingly is done to a certain extent in the Census Reports, the publications of the Registrar General's office, and some other important statistical tables; but it is never done as much as would be desirable. The reason is obvious. Each ratio can only be obtained by a tedious long division sum, or by the use of logarithms. Many hours of tedious mental labour must be endured before a large statistical table can be reduced to its proper intelligible form. The result is that, in the absence of an office full of clerks, the labour is almost always shirked, and the reader of our statistical publications is left to extract their meaning as well as he can – which means very badly.

With the Arithmometer at hand, however, the work becomes rather amusement than labour, especially to those at all fond of ingenious and beautiful mechanism. The amount of time saved will vary with the character of the operation and the nature of the calculations; but about the saving of mental exertion there can be no possible doubt. The machine will also be of great use in effecting the reduction of numbers from one denomination to another, as from pounds to francs, dollars, rupees, &c.; tons to kilogrammes, yards to metres, &c., &c. It is requisite, however, that all numbers should be expressed in the purely decimal form, so that our absurd systems of money, weights, and measures, present obstacles to the easy use of the machine. When frequent alterations of any numbers in a definite ratio have to be made, it will often be best to calculate at the outset a table of the multiples of that ratio; this can be done with the utmost facility by the machine, because each turn of the handle gives a fresh number for the table. A reduction table can thus be prepared as fast as the numbers can be written down, and all further labour of calculation is saved by reference to this table.

I should like to add, that if our science of statistics is to progress in the spirit of the times, frequent use must be made of the Method of Least Squares. This method is merely the method of means or averages employed 'in a more complete and elaborate way, to disentangle the probable values of several unknown quantities which happen to be involved together in our statistical data. The working of the process, as described in Merriman's "Elements of the Method of Least Squares" (Macmillan, 1877), in De Morgan's "Essay on Probabilities," and many other works on the same subject, can be carried on by mere rule of thumb; but it requires a great amount of multiplication. With Thomas' Arithmometer, however, the requisite calculations can be readily accomplished, and I conceive, therefore, that in this as well as in other cases, the frequent use of the machine is indispensable as a condition of any distinct advance in statistical inquiry. Familiarity with the arithmetical machine would gradually lead to the undertaking of intricate numerical inquiries, which are practically impossible without its aid.

The use of the machine as employed by actuaries has already been described by General Hannyngton in the "Journal of the Institute of Actuaries," vol. xvi, p. 244, and a very able paper "On the Arithmometer of M. Thomas (de Colmar) and its Application to the Construction of Life Contingency Tables," was printed by Mr. Peter Gray, in the journal of the same Society for 1874, and issued separately as a pamphlet. The operations therein described are, however, far more complicated than what the statist will usually need to perform.

The working of the machine is so easy, that it can be learnt by any person of ordinary intelligence in the course of an hour, and with a few little precautions, which are stated in the explanatory book of instructions delivered with the machine, there need be no fear of its getting out of order. It is said that machines are often worked daily for many years in succession, without any mishap or error occurring; but other operators find that certain springs are apt to break, and require replacement. The machine, though constructed only in Paris, can be inspected and purchased at a depôt in London. The smallest machine now made gives a product not exceeding twelve places of figures, which would be sufficient for most purposes; but the medium-sized machine, giving a product of sixteen places, is said to be more convenient in use, as there is greater scope and freedom of action. My own limited experience of the machine leads me to think that this may be so.

I have been induced to bring the Arithmometer under the notice of the Society, by the feeling that there must be many who are (as I was myself a few months ago) imperfectly acquainted with the value of the machine. Had I purchased a machine when I first saw it at the Paris Exposition of 1867, I should have been saved a great deal of mental fatigue during the eleven subsequent years, and I might have undertaken statistical inquiries which are beyond the power of a private unaided arithmetician. The conviction that this machine must prove no inconsiderable factor in the progress of statistical and social science, renders it desirable for those acquainted with its value, to endeavour to overcome the inertia, which, especially in this country, impedes the introduction of any new labour-saving invention. A machine which was in its essential features invented by the youthful genius of Pascal, in the year 1642, is only now coming into use. For *two hundred and thirty-six years* (236 years!) practical men have ignored what may prove one of the most practically useful, as it is certainly one of the most beautiful products of human reason.

PROFESSOR JEVONS'S DESCRIPTION *of the* CALCULATING
MACHINE; DISCUSSION.

Dr. Farr said the Society was indebted to Professor Jevons for bringing
forward the machine and explaining its uses. It was of great use in the
Registrar-General's office in determining the ratios and the percentage of
deaths, births, marriages, and so on, and this was done on a very large
scale. The clerks were allowed to work by logarithms or by arithmetic,
but they invariably preferred the machine. Undoubtedly in order to
make it of universal application, there should be a decimal system of
calculation in weights, measures, and money; but at present he
recommended its use for calculations on a large scale.

Dr. Balfour said that for the last five or six years, when he was at the
head of the Army Medical Department, they could make all their
calculations as quickly as they could by the machine, but he thought it
minimised the chance of error. In working out logarithms there was a
source of error, which was avoided by using the machine. All the time it
was used in the office under his charge he never had any cause to
complain of it except that the springs that were worked on the pegs were
apt to go wrong. He was indebted to General Hannyngton, who pointed
out how this could be remedied, and after he had done so he had never
found the machine to go wrong once. On one occasion the clerk of the
Department said that the machine had gone wrong, but it was afterwards
found that the error was on the part of the clerk, and not on the part of the
machine. In working out ratios it minimised the chance of error, which
was a consideration of great importance.

Mr. Walford said he had been familiar with the machine some years
ago. He had seen some sixty calculating machines, but he thought on the
whole that the one exhibited was the most available for general purposes.
He did not think it was a safe thing to use, except by persons familiar with
it, because if it was not set with great care errors would arise, and if one
number was wrong, the whole would be wrong. He would minimise that
difficulty by having two machines to commence at decennial points, and
work the one with the other – not, however, by the same operator – and if
the results were both the same, they might be pretty well sure that they
were correct. It would save a great amount of labour, money, and
thought, and simply required care.

Mr. A. H. Bailey, President of the Institute of Actuaries, said that the
machine grew upon people the more they used it. There was a variety of
purposes to which it could be applied. It was very useful in the
distributing of a bankrupt's estate, for instance, and one of its great uses
would be to introduce a decimal system of arithmetic; but even with our
present system of weights and measures, and of pounds, shillings, and

pence, the machine could be used. It should, however, be understood that it was entirely a decimal machine.

The President, in moving a vote of thanks to Professor Jevons, said that he had shown that it was an extremely valuable instrument, and he thought it might be looked forward to as one of the principal instruments in Government offices. Although it might not save time, it would save a good deal of mental labour, and that was one of the greatest considerations in a Government department.

XI   THE SOLAR INFLUENCE ON COMMERCE

This paper is hitherto unpublished. In December 1878 Jevons was contemplating the preparation of a paper to be entitled 'The Sun's Influence on Commerce' for the *Princeton Review*.[1] From internal evidence there seems little doubt that the following, of which the manuscript is in the Jevons Papers, is the one in question; but for reasons which are not now apparent Jevons left the article unfinished and it was never published. It is clear that it was written after the first two papers on his sun-spot theory which Jevons published in 1878[2] and thus at a fairly early stage in the development of that theory. Jevons was evidently attempting to set the theory out in a fairly popular form and it may be that he was not satisfied with the result.

The recent and present condition of industry in Great Britain imperatively demands the careful attention of economists and men of science. A vast calamity[3] has to be investigated, and its recurrence as far as possible provided against. Artizans have been thrown out of employment by tens of thousands, if not by hundreds of thousands. Through no apparent fault of their own, they find themselves suddenly reduced to pauperism, with families which can only be saved from starvation by public or private charity. To them the present state of trade would simply mean famine, did not the semi-socialistic organization of modern society provide a refuge against actual starvation. To other classes of people the state of things is almost equally disastrous. The breaking of several large

[1] See Letters 566 and 567, Vol. IV, pp. 303–304.

[2] 'The Periodicity of Commercial Crises and its Physical Explanation'; read before Section F of the British Association, Dublin, 19 August 1878; 'Commercial Crises and Sun Spots', *Nature*, XIX, 33–7. Both are reprinted in *Investigations*.

[3] replaces 'evil', deleted in original manuscript.

banks has reduced many shareholders to complete ruin, has swept away the savings of a lifetime or the widows' provision which can not be restored. Even when establishments are not broken up they have in many cases been reduced, and highly paid clerks, receiving two, three, four or more thousands of dollars annual salary are cast adrift in the decline of life. Pauperism in fact is not confined to the operative classes.

The state of things is not equally bad in all parts of the country; it chiefly affects Lancashire & Yorkshire where industry depends much upon foreign trade. No doubt, too, the destitution will be very temporary. In the United States the depression of trade seems already to have passed its worst point, and the collapse although long drawn out has not culminated in a crisis so severe as the English markets have been just enduring.

But when the lives and fortunes of so many are concerned, & when in fact the prosperity of the whole trading world is at stake we must not be contented with superficial discussion. We must not lay to the charge of trades-unions, or free trade, or intemperance, or any other pretext, a fluctuation of commerce which affects countries alike which have trades-unions & no trades-unions, free trade and protection; as to intemperance and various other moral causes, no doubt they may have powerful influence on our prosperity but they afford no special explanation of a temporary wave of calamity. We can hardly doubt that it will be temporary because on looking back thirty or forty years we find that crises of very similar character, followed by a temporary interruption of industry have repeatedly recurred. The distress of the Lancashire operatives in the years 1841 & 1842 has never been forgotten and it recurred in a less severe form in the years 1848–9, and again in 1858. Now it has come back again with a severity which almost promises to equal that of 1842.

The most casual inquirer can hardly fail to be struck by the fact that these epochs of distress are periodic. The crisis or collapse of credit which ushers in a period of destitution is more definite in date than the interval of destitution itself, and if we remember that there was, especially in the United States a collapse in 1837, another in 1847, another in England 1857, & again in 1866, and now a most distinct one in 1878, we may be tempted to carry our thoughts still further back to 1825–6 when there was likewise a most fully developed crisis followed by depression of industry. These events have thus recurred at intervals successively of say 12, 10, 9, and 12 years, and the approximation to an average period of about 10½ years is so remarkable, that no one who really contemplates the facts can fail to be struck by the fact. But many who have been forced to admit the periodic character of these events have shown a strange unwillingness to enter upon any scientific examination of its causes. They say that they do not want mere theory; it is to facts, and to daily experience they look; to mention the sun or planets to them is only to call forth a denunciation of astrological speculations. Practical men must have practical arguments, which expression being interpreted, means arguments not going beyond the memory of the last few months, or at most the last few years. But I now make it my business to show that it is these so-called practical men who are the baseless theorisers, and that it is the astrological speculators who really base their explanations upon a large range of experience, upon facts widely gathered and carefully collated. I need not inform my readers that a series of eminent astronomers, meteorologists, and physicists of different ranks & branches of science, have gradually established the fact that the sun is a variable star, having a period of variation somewhere between ten and twelve years, as Professor Loomis states the fact in his newest work on astronomy. An eminent meteorologist, Mr J. A. Broun, lately the Director of the Magnetic Observatory at Trivandrum in the Madras Presidency estimates the period, as we shall see precisely at 10.45 years, and this period so closely agrees with the commercial period already pointed out, that a strong presumption of causal connection at once arises. It will obviously be impossible in an article to adduce the best array of facts by reference to which we can alone validly judge the worth of this presumption, and I must therefore confine myself to attempting to sketch out the course of inductive argument and enquiry which leads almost conclusively to a belief in the solar origin of commercial fluctuations.

In the first place, we must look to the general principles of inductive logic by which our inquiries must necessarily be guided. The relation which we are attempting to establish is one of cause and effect, and both cause and effect are supposed to be periodic in character, and the one is supposed to produce the other. To this case there applies a general principle of mechanics [which is][4] called *the principle of forced vibrations*, which has been clearly stated by the late Sir John Herschel in several of his works.[5] One statement of the principle is given in my "Principles of Science", but a more simple statement is found in Herschel's *Meteorology* (§ 144) where he says – "It is a dynamical law absolutely universal, and one which extends even beyond the domain of mere dynamics, that all periodicity in the action of a cause propagates into every, even the remotest, effect of that cause, through whatever chain of intermediate arrangements the action is carried out." I have elsewhere explained that Herschel was mistaken in stating this law as an *absolutely universal* one,

---

[4] deleted in original manuscript.

[5] Herschel, 'Sound', *Encyclopaedia Metropolitana*, (1845) IV, 811; *Outlines of Astronomy*, fourth edition (1851) pp. 410, 487–8; 'Meteorology', reprinted from the *Encyclopaedia Britannica* (Edinburgh, 1861) p. 197.

since his own discovery of fluorescence, or epipolarization of light as he originally called it, shows that a vibration of less period may under certain unknown conditions produce one of longer period; calorescence again as investigated by Professor Draper proves that heat vibrations may produce more rapid & small light vibrations, & many casual phenomena of water and other waves likewise furnish exceptions to the general principle of periodicity. Nevertheless the principle of forced vibrations holds perfectly true as a general law of mechanics and nature. The direct simple effect of any periodic cause is likewise periodic, and in the absence of disturbing causes, the period of the effect will be exactly equal to that of the cause. It will not usually be simultaneous, because an interval often elapses between the moment of action of a cause, and the manifestation of the effect which strikes our attention. If, for instance, a loaded repeating rifle be discharged at exact minute intervals against a distant target, the bullets will strike the target at intervals of one minute each and the sounds of those strokes will also be heard at similar intervals; but a second or two will intervene between the discharge and the stroke, and again between the stroke and the sound as heard at a distant spot. Now the solar influence, assuming it to be periodic in amount, will undoubtedly produce variations in industry, which variations will be periodic, but the several effects will follow in a chain at successively greater intervals after the occurrence of the cause. The greater intensity of the sun's rays will alter the condition of the atmosphere; this will affect the growth of crops, the price of vegetable food, subsequently the price of animal food; the currents of trade will then be varied in amount & direction, and the influence, if sufficiently great, will more or less manifest itself in the most complicated transactions of currency, credit & speculation. But it is, of course, quite likely that many of the remote effects of solar variation will be beyond the power of our insight, owing to great disturbing causes, such as wars, social disturbances, changes in currency and other social institutions, mutations of fashion, & habit, etc, etc.

But we have not yet done with pure theory; we have only learnt from an eminent physicist that a periodic cause will have periodic effects. When we perceive the existence of a periodic effect, such as commercial crises appear to be, how shall we proceed to discover its cause? We must proceed upon the great principle of inductive method, as laid down by Laplace and the several great mathematicians who created the theory of probability. This principle is to the effect that the most probable cause of an event which has happened is that cause which if it existed would most probably lead to that effect. This principle is at once the perfection of commonsense, and the most general result of the theory of inductive logic. If, for instance, a mariner at sea hears reports of guns at exact intervals of a minute, he infers at once that there is somewhere near a vessel in distress. The reasoning, if carefully analysed, amounts to this, that if there were such a vessel in distress, she would in all probability fire minute guns, and the reports of those guns, if not too distant, would be heard at minute intervals; on the other hand, it is not easy (indeed almost impossible) to conceive any other cause which would be likely to produce reports regularly recurring at that precise interval in the middle of the ocean. If afterwards the mariner descries a vessel from which proceed puffs of smoke at minute intervals, it becomes practically certain upon a like method of inference, that she is the vessel in distress producing the periodic gun-reports. The outcome of inductive method as it affects our present subject is simply this, that if we perceive a distinctly periodic effect, and can discover any cause which recurs at exactly equal intervals, and is the only discoverable cause recurring in that period, this is probably the cause of which we are in search. Such is the *prima facie* result, drawn simply on the ground that such a cause if existing would have effects with the required period, and there is no other cause which could be supposed with any probability to give that result. But this *prima facie* probability is immensely strengthened if we can give other reasons for believing that a cause of the nature supposed, apart from the question of its period, is likely to have effects of the kind we are attributing to it. In short, mere equality of period is a perfectly valid ground of inductive reasoning; but our results gain much in probability if we can analyse and explain the precise relation of cause and effect.

In a paper read at the last meeting of the British Association (Dublin, 1879) and in a distinct article published in *Nature*,* I have given reasons for believing that the average period of recurrence of commercial crises in England between the beginning of the 18th century and the present time is about 10.46 years, whereas Mr J. A. Broun's latest investigations of the sun-spot period convince him, as I shall afterwards explain, that its period is about 10.45 years. These numbers are so closely equal that there arises at once a strong presumption of causal connexion, so strong that, supposing the observations to be well made & discussed without bias, they would almost establish the connexion however discrete and apparently remote the phenomena thus brought into theoretical relation. But, as just explained, it lends much strength to such an inference if we can show that a variation of the nature in question, namely sunspot variation, would be likely to produce variations in commerce which might constitute a commercial crisis. It will be most convenient to take the latter part of the investigation first, and to inquire whether sunspot variations are likely in their physical nature to affect commerce.

* *Nature*, 14 November 1878, vol. XIX, pp. 33–37. [This note was inserted by Jevons himself in the margin of the manuscript.]

It strikes me forcibly that those would-be 'practical men' who smile and sneer as soon as ever they hear the sunspots or planets mentioned in connection with trade, must either know, or else think, very little about the constitution of the solar and terrestrial system of which they form a part.[6] The very men who laugh at the notion of sunspots ruling their destinies are probably profound believers in that little formula, given in many almanacks, and falsely called Herschel's Weather Table. Upon no foundation either of fact or theory they will attribute the changes of weather to the moon, while they set down almost as lunatics those who attribute tides in human affairs to the sun's influence. The very name 'lunatic' embodies the popular impression that the periods of the moon do affect us, at least in certain states of health. No doubt the regular periodic appearance of the moon in its several phases has always impressed the imagination of man in a profound manner. To the moon we undoubtedly owe the chronological period of the month of 28 days, and there can be little doubt that the week is simply the fourth part of the month. If so, we owe to the moon the whole periodic variation of industry which completes itself within the week, the fortnight or the month. It need hardly be pointed out, too, that there are in the human constitution certain changes, which according to our inductive formula must be attributed with high probability to the lunar influence.

But, if the potency of the moon in human affairs is thus considerable, how vastly greater must be that of the sun. Let us consider the relative powers of these bodies. So far as we know at present, there are only three modes in which one cosmical body can possibly affect another cosmical body, namely (1), by gravitation; (2) by radiation; (3) by the actual communication of matter. Now, as regards gravity, it is true that the moon is about 400 times nearer to us than the sun, so that, in respect of this fact, its gravitating power is about 160,000 times as great as that of the sun. But then the mass of the sun is so enormous, namely 31,134,986 (thirty one million times) as great as the mass of the moon, that the actual force of gravity exerted by the sun on a particle of the earth comes out at about 194.6 times as great as the similar force of the moon.[7] So far, indeed, as such force is uniformly exerted upon all the particles composing the earth, it is incapable of creating any variation of phenomena in them, so that it is in fact only the differential force of gravity, that is the difference between an exterior body's gravity as exerted in one part and the other of the earth, which can be perceived by us. Now owing to the comparative nearness of the moon it is true that its differential force of gravity upon the earth is about three times that of the

---

[6] replaces 'one of the most insignificant parts', deleted in original manuscript.

[7] In the original manuscript Jevons here wrote 'sun'; 'moon' has been written above this in pencil possibly by another hand.

sun. Yet the absolute amount of this force is very small being only about one four millionth part of the sun's total attractive force upon the earth. So small indeed are these differential attractions that there is no phenomenon excepting the tides of the sea and atmosphere, which they have been observed to produce. Only through the tides then can the moon's gravitation affect human industry, so far as we know.

It seems excedingly unlikely then that either the moon or sun should by its mere force of gravity have any influence on human affairs except through the tides which of course affect navigation and commerce in a certain degree. Proceeding then to radiational power, comprehending under this expression both the heat and light rays of the spectrum, there cannot of course be the slightest doubt that the sun is almost incomparably superior in influence. The moon's rays are but a faint reflection of the sun's rays falling upon its surface. Wollaston long ago estimated the suns light as 810,072 times that of the full moon, and Bouguer made it 300,000 times. The more recent determination of this ratio by Professor G. P. Bond at the Harvard College Observatory† comes between these numbers, being 470,980. The considerable discrepancies between these results is of no importance to us, because in any case it is certain that the radiative influence of the moon is a wholly inconsiderable fraction of the suns power. The unaided eye is no safe measure in such a question, since in bright sunshine the pupil is contracted to its smallest dimensions, while in the brightest moonlight it would be found to be comparatively dilated.

In the second place the positive evidence of variation comes from many independent sources. There is the direct evidence of the eyes to the effect that during some total eclipses of the sun, enormous protuberances of a splendid pink colour are suspended in the suns atmosphere; during other eclipses these protuberances are seen to be comparatively insignificant. We have thus direct proof that in the sun there are periodic meteorological changes involving such immense masses of matter in such an intense state of heat and agitation that it is hopeless to attempt to form to the mind any adequate idea of this "Soul" of our system. The much ridiculed solar spots again can be no matter of ridicule to those who know what they are. Their magnitudes vary from the least which can be observed up to enormous cavities 40,000, or 50,000 miles or more in diameter. Spots have been observed so gigantic in dimensions that a score of bodies equal to the earth might be conceived as dropped in without filling them up. Now long continued telescopic observation completely establishes the fact that these inconceivably vast agitations of the solar surface only take place during certain intervals of years. In one year the

---

† *Monthly notices of the Royal Astronomical Society*, 10th May 1861, vol. XXI, pp. 199–200. [This note was inserted by Jevons himself at the bottom of the page of manuscript.]

spots occasionally grow so large that they may be seen by the naked eye; from five to seven years afterwards a telescope will not disclose anything to be called a spot. But it is well known now to every tyro in science that the numbers of spots when ascertained from records as completely as possible show a periodic variation almost as well marked and regular, at least in certain parts of the 18th and 19th centuries, as the rise and fall of the tides.

Most unfortunately astronomers and physicists have omitted to make any long series of direct experiments upon the heating power of the sun's rays as would prove the fact of variation and show clearly that the rays are more powerful whether in heat, light or actinic effect, in one state of maculation as compared with other states. Pouillet showed how the heating effect might be accurately measured in 1838, by performing the operation, with his Pyrheliometer, as described in his [8]

However these more speculative questions may be resolved it requires a very moderate acquaintance with physical science to know that almost all the motions and changes going on upon the earth's surface are ultimately referable to the energy of the sun's rays. We must except the tides, volcanic, and a few other inconsiderable phenomena; the winds & ocean currents are in some degree referable to the earth's own energy of rotation. But it is quite clear that vegetable life, & through that animal life is wholly dependent on solar radiation. True vegetable growth goes on only under the direct excitation of the suns rays, the so called actinic or chemical energy of which accomplishes the decomposition of carbonic acid. Hence the origin of all heat furnished by combustion whether in the wood fire, the coal fire, or the animal body. Long ago George Stevenson acutely anticipated the results of subsequent scientific inquiry when he said that coal was but sunshine bottled up; now it is among the mere common places of science that all the motions & energies of life, whether it be that of the windmill, the waterwheel, the steam engine, the beast of burden, or the human operative, are directly or indirectly derived from the sun. Happily did Milton describe that orb as "of world, both eye and soul." In a physical point of view it is simply the soul, the fount, the mainspring of life & energy of the planetary system. To our part of the material universe it is what the spring is to the watch, the weight to the clock, the water to the mill, the fuel to the engine. What then is there absurd or fanciful in the supposition that if the sun varies in power of radiation, those variations will in virtue of the principle of forced vibrations, manifest themselves in the course of industry and trade. The sun is altogether the body to which all scientific influence would point as

---

[8] In the original manuscript Jevons left a space of three lines at this point. For the reference to Pouillet's work which he may have intended to insert in it, see *Investigations*, p. 234.

the most probable cause of any periodic variations perceptible in animal & vegetable life but of course we must not assume without a full investigation of evidence that the sun does vary in power. In the last thirty or forty years however a constantly accumulating body of evidence has been forthcoming tending to constitute constructive proof that the sun is a variable star, or at all events that its energy as showered down upon the earth is periodically variable. The limitation of space will not allow me to do more than briefly indicate the several sources and kinds of this evidence.

In the first place the analogy of other variable stars renders the hypothesis of solar variation an *a priori* reasonable one. A great number of fixed stars are now known to go through well marked variations of brightness, in periods of a few days, a few years, or it may be many years. The remarkable star Algol has a regular period of just 2.86 days. As long ago as 1596, the star O Ceti or Mira was observed to vary, and it reaches a maximum of brightness about twelve times in eleven years, its period being therefore about 331.3 days. Rudolf Wolf has gone so far as to point to the star of *Argus Navis* as one whose complex periodic variations are not improbably similar to those of our own sun. But however this may be there is certainly no antecedent improbability attaching to the hypothesis of periodic variation in a series of complex periods.

XII PREFACE TO THE ENGLISH TRANSLATION OF COSSA'S *GUIDE*

On 5 May 1879 Luigi Cossa, Professor of Political Economy at the University of Pavia, wrote to Jevons seeking to enlist his help in securing the publication by Macmillan of an English translation of his *Guida allo Studio dell' Economia Politica*.[1] Jevons considered the proposal worthy of support, for, as he later wrote to Alexander Macmillan, 'the *Guide* contains a great deal of information quite inaccessible hitherto to English ordinary students.'[2]

The 'former lady student . . . of the Cambridge Society for the Extension of University Teaching' who prepared the translation was Margaret A. Macmillan.[3] It was published as *Guide to the Study of Political Economy* by Macmillan & Co., London, in 1880. The short preface which Jevons contributed to it is interesting as showing both his desire to make the work of Continental economists better known to English economists

[1] See Letter 610, Vol. V. p. 59.
[2] W. S. Jevons to A. Macmillan, 24 March 1880, Letter 643, Vol. V. p. 94.
[3] Cf. Letters 603 and 651, Vol. V. pp. 53 and 101.

and his great respect for, and interest in, the historical method. This latter point has often been overlooked, mainly because of the rigorously deductive character of his *Theory of Political Economy*.

To a reader fairly acquainted with the English Literature of Political Economy it will be evident why this translation of an Italian text-book has been undertaken. The sufficient reason is that no introduction to the study of Economics at all approaching in character to Professor Cossa's *Guida allo Studio dell' Economia Politica* is to be found in the English tongue. This work presents, in a compendious form, not only a general view of the bounds, divisions, and relations of the science, marked by great impartiality and breadth of treatment, but it also furnishes us with an historical sketch of the science, such as must be wholly new to English readers.

Every economist would grant that we have in English the works of the father of the science, Adam Smith, and of not a few successors or predecessors who have made the science almost an English science. But this fact, joined perhaps with the common want of linguistic power in English students, has led our economic writers to ignore too much the great works of the French and Italian economists, as well as the invaluable recent treatises of German writers. The survey of the foreign literature of the subject given in this *Guide* will enable the English students to fix the bearings of the point of knowledge which he has reached, and to estimate the fraction of the ocean of economic literature which he has been able to traverse.

Of course it is not to be expected, nor even to be desired, that English students of Economics should at once endeavour to master treatises in the French, German, Italian, and other languages. A few may be able thus to extend their studies; and it is believed that they will find in Dr. Cossa a safe pilot to the course of reading they may best pursue for their special purposes. The ordinary student must necessarily be contented with a second-hand and superficial acquaintance with the masses of literature here indicated. But it would be a mistake to treat such knowledge as worthless. The late Professor De Morgan said, or at least very happily repeated the saying, that "true education consists in knowing everything of something and something of everything." Applying this maxim to our science, the judicious student of Economics must necessarily select the works of Adam Smith, of Ricardo, of J. S. Mill, of Cairnes, or of some one or a very few leading English economists, and must study them, so to say, completely. They will be the something of which he must learn everything. But, when this has been sufficiently accomplished, he cannot do better than learn the something of everything in economic literature, which is admirably given in this *Guide*.

One valuable result which will probably be derived from the reading of Professor Cossa's work is the conviction that the *historical method* must play a large part in economic science. Without for a moment admitting, with some extreme advocates of that method,* that there is no such thing as an abstract science of Economics, the student will readily become convinced that in such matters as land tenure, agriculture, the organisation of industry, taxation, &c., theory must be applied with very large allowances for physical and historical circumstances. National character, ancient custom, political condition, and many other conditions, are economic factors of great importance. Although some of our best English economists were fully alive to this fact, there is nevertheless an almost inevitable tendency to regard the complicated industrial organisation of England as if it were the natural and best organisation, to which other nations have failed, in a more or less serious degree, to attain. Wider study will show that economic as well as political and social development must bear relation to the historical and physical circumstances of the race. It is surely time to abandon the idea, for instance, that the landlord system of land-tenure of England, even supposing that it is the best for English agriculture, is necessarily the best for France, Belgium, Norway, India, Australia, Ireland, and the rest of the habitable world in general. In the fourth chapter of the First Part Dr. Cossa has very clearly refuted some of the prevailing errors on the subject of the historical method.

Now and again we meet opinions and expressions in the *Guide* in which it is impossible to coincide. On page 124 of this translation, for instance, the author speaks of "the notable advantages to industrial organisation and progress," which he thinks have been conferred in its time by the Protective System. Few, or probably no English economist, would now accept this opinion, unless with qualifications and explanations which would really reverse the writer's meaning. Nor is this, as we think, the only scientific or doctrinal blemish of the work. Yet after all exception is taken it must be allowed that the author has performed his difficult task in a most judicious and impartial manner.

As Dr. Cossa has passed over without mention most of his own economic labours, it should be stated that he has been, since the year 1858, Professor of Political Economy in the University of Pavia. During nearly a quarter of a century he has devoted himself entirely to the promotion and dissemination of economic science, and not a few of the rising economists of Italy owe their success to his instructions. Among his principal works may be mentioned the *Primi Elementi di Economia Politica*,

---

* See, for instance, Professor Cliffe Leslie's Essay on the "Philosophical Method of Political Economy," in *Hermathena*, No. iv., 1876.

first published at Milan in 1875, of which a fourth edition, considerably augmented, appeared in 1878. Spanish and German translations were printed in 1878 and 1879. His second work was the *Primi Elementi di Scienza delle Finanze* (1875), of which a third edition is about to appear. Various essays on economic subjects have been reprinted in a volume under the title *Saggi di Economia Politica* (Milan, 1878).

The *Guida allo Studio dell' Economia Politica*, of which the following pages contain an English version, was originally published at Milan in 1876; a second revised and enlarged edition being issued in 1878. A Spanish translation was printed at Valladolid in 1878, and it is said that a German translation by Dr. Edward Moormeister is to appear during the course of the present year at Freiburg. The considerable use which is thus evidently being made of Professor Cossa's text-books will not surprise a reader who can appreciate the extraordinary extent and accuracy of Dr. Cossa's knowledge of the economic literature of almost all nations. This characteristic of his works may be partly explained by the fact that he was in early life a pupil of that most learned and eminent economist, Professor Wilhelm Roscher. In England we cannot hope to compete with the polyglot learning of a Roscher or a Cossa, but it is to be hoped that not a few English students of economics, who are seldom polyglots, will use this translated *Guide* in order to make themselves a little less insular than they would otherwise be.

The work of translation has been carried out by a former lady student in one of the excellent classes of Political Economy, conducted under the superintendence of the Cambridge Society for the Extension of University Teaching. Acknowledgments are due to Professor Cossa for corrections and additions, which bring up the work to the present year.

XIII LIST OF SELECTED BOOKS IN POLITICAL ECONOMY

Monthly Notes of the Library Association of the United Kingdom, III (1882) 105–11

An enthusiastic book collector who had amassed a considerable private library, Jevons was always interested in libraries and bibliography. He was a member of the Library Association, and occasionally attended its conferences; for these reasons, no doubt, Ernest C. Thomas, the editor of the Association's *Monthly Notes*, turned naturally to Jevons for a list of economic works to guide public librarians.

Adam Smith's *Wealth of Nations*.

The basis of every economic library. The best "library" edition is that of Thorold Rogers, in two vols. (Clarendon Press). 1st ed., pp. xlvi., 423; viii., 594. McCulloch's one vol. edition is valuable for reference chiefly on account of the good index. Gibbon Wakefield's edition, in four vols. (12mo. London, Knight, 1843), should be secured when it is met with; the notes are good. There is a very cheap (3s. 6d.) reprint edition, pp. 781 (Ward and Lock), which gives the text complete; but there are plenty also of good old three-volume editions.

J. S. Mill's *Principles of Political Economy*. (Longmans.)

The cheap "People's Edition" is, except as regards type, equally good with the more expensive library editions.

The following works are recommended as treating of the science generally:—

Some Leading Principles of Political Economy newly Expounded. By J. E. CAIRNES. (Macmillan.) 1874. Pp. xix., 506.

Harmonies of Political Economy. By FRÉDÉRIC BASTIAT. Translated from the 3rd edition of the French, by P. J. STIRLING. 2nd ed. Edinburgh (Oliver Boyd). Pp. 528.

Economic Sophisms. By FRÉDÉRIC BASTIAT. Translated from the 5th edition of the French by P. J. STIRLING. Edinburgh (Oliver and Boyd). 1873. Pp. viii., 235.

The Wages Question: A Treatise on Wages and the Wages Class. By FRANCIS A. WALKER, Yale College. (Macmillan.) 1878. Pp. 428.

The Economics of Industry. By ALFRED MARSHALL and MARY PALEY MARSHALL. (Macmillan.) 1879. Pp. xiv., 231

Political Economy. By NASSAU WILLIAM SENIOR. 5th Edition. London (Griffin). 1863. Pp. viii., 231.

Indispensable as a student's text book. The original edition of the book is found in the "Encyclopædia Metropolitana" (Division – Useful Arts).

James Mill's *Elements of Political Economy*. 3rd Ed. 1826. Pp. viii., 304.

Easily procured and excellent.

For the history of Political Economy it is desirable to have the following works:—

Principles of Political Economy. By WILLIAM ROSCHER. Translated by JOHN J. LALOR. Chicago (Callaghan and Company). 1878. 2 vols., pp. xxi., 464, 465.

The chief value of the work lies in the foot notes, which are replete with information and references.

Histoire de l'Economie Politique en Europe. Suivie d'une Bibliographie raisonnée des principaux Ouvrages. Par BLANQUI. 4th Ed. Paris (Guillaumin). 1860. 2 vols., 12mo, pp. 384, 412.

This work has been recently (1880) translated into English by E. J.

Leonard, with a Preface by David Wells (George Bell and Sons). But this edition is said to lack the bibliography which adds value to the original.

Guide to the Study of Political Economy. By Dr. LUIGI COSSA. Translated from the Second Italian Edition. With a Preface by W. STANLEY JEVONS. (Macmillan.) 1880. 12mo, pp. xvi., 237.

Principles of Political Economy. With sketch of the Rise and Progress of the Science. By J. R. McCULLOCH.

There is a cheap (3*s*. 6*d*.) edition (Ward and Lock), pp. 360.

The Literature of Political Economy: A Classified Catalogue of Select Publications in the different departments of that Science, with Historical, Critical and Biographical Notices. By J. R. McCULLOCH. London (Longmans). 1845. Pp. xiii., 407.

Indispensable to an economic library, but difficult to obtain. Though far from being complete and perfectly accurate, it is practically the only bibliography of Economics in English.

Dictionnaire de l'Economie Politique. Publié sous la direction de MM. Ch. COQUELIN ET GUILLAUMIN. Paris (Librairie de Guillaumin). 1852. 2 vols., pp. 971, 896.

A very valuable work, especially as regards the biography and bibliography of economic writers. The later edition appears not to be superior to that named.

The Romance of Trade. By H. R. FOX BOURNE. London. (Cassell, no date.) Pp. vi., 379.

A readable and instructive book.

The Growth of English Industry and Commerce. By W. CUNNINGHAM, M.A., Cambridge, at the University Press. 1882. Pp., xiv., 492. 3 Charts and 2 Maps.

In spite of its extensive and therefore somewhat expensive character, it is impossible to omit mentioning the following great economico-historical work:—

A History of Agriculture and Prices in England from the Year after the Oxford Parliament (1259) *to the commencement of the Continental War,* 1793. Compiled entirely from Original and Contemporaneous Records. By JAMES E. THOROLD ROGERS, M.A., Oxford, at the Clarendon Press. Vols. I. and II., 1876. Pp. xvi. 711; xviii., 714. Vols. III. and IV., 1882. Pp.xvii., 775; xx., 779.

Passing now to books treating of special departments of the Science we must note:—

The Economy of Machinery and Manufactures. By CHARLES BABBAGE. 3rd Ed. London, 1832. Pp. xxiv., 392.

A work of great excellence. Easily purchased second-hand, but said to be still in print.

History of the Middle and Working Classes; with a Popular Exposition of the Economical and Political Principles which have influenced the Past and Present Condition of the Industrious Orders. By JOHN WADE. London, 1833. Pp. xx., 604.

A book which, though old, has not been superseded by anything better. It is partly founded on Eden's celebrated work. There is a cheap reprint, 4th ed., 1842. Edinburgh (Chambers). Pp. 174, double col.

Political and Social Economy; its Practical Applications. By JOHN HILL BURTON. Edinburgh (Chambers). 1829. Pp. xii., 345.

Political Economy for Plain People. Applied to the Past and Present State of Britain. By G. POULETT SCROPE, F.R.S. 2nd ed. London (Longmans). 1873. Pp. xxv., 353.

English Factory Legislation. By ERNST EDLER VON PLENER. With an Introduction by ANTHONY JOHN MUNDELLA, M.P. London (Chapman). 1873. 12mo, pp. xxiv., 175.

Essays in Political and Moral Philosophy. By T. E. CLIFFE LESLIE. Dublin (Hodges, Forster and Co., University Press Series). 1879. Pp. xii., 483.

Contains some valuable articles on gold, prices, wages, philosophical method of political economy, &c.

Essays in Political Economy, Theoretical and Applied. By J. E. CAIRNES. London (Macmillan). 1873. Pp. xi., 371.

Treats of depreciation of gold, land, free trade, &c.

The Character and Logical Method of Political Economy. By J. E. CAIRNES. 2nd and enlarged Edition. London (Macmillan). 1875. Pp. xvii., 229.

Essays on some Unsettled Questions of Political Economy. By JOHN STUART MILL. (Longmans.) 1844.

The Conditions of Social Well-being; or, Inquiries into the Material and Moral Position of the Populations of Europe and America, with Particular Reference to those of Great Britain and Ireland. By DAVID CUNNINGHAM. (Longmans.) 1878. Pp. xv., 357.

As regards economic statistics, it is especially recommended that every library should have a copy of the following very cheap annual Parliamentary paper:—

Statistical Abstract for the United Kingdom. 8vo. (Price in 1881, 10d.)

There are several other almost equally valuable and cheap official publications, such as the *Statistical Abstract of the Colonial Possessions of British India*, &c.

For the older economic statistics the best work is *The Progress of the Nation.* By G. R. PORTER. New ed. (Murray.) 1847. Pp. xxiii., 846 (Later edition, 1851.)

MacCulloch's Commercial Dictionary, contains a mass of information. The earlier editions are to be easily found, and any edition is better than none. There is a quite new edition, edited by A. J. WILSON. (Longmans.)

There are numerous books, taking various views of socialistic discussions, but the following can be confidently recommended:—

Robert Owen, and his Social Philosophy. By W. L. SARGANT. London (Smith, Elder & Co.). 1860. Pp. xxiv., 446.

Social Innovators, and their Schemes. Same author and publisher.

On the Land Question the following works are to be named:—

The Land Question, with Particular Reference to England and Scotland. By JOHN MACDONNELL. (Macmillan.) 1873. Pp. 250.

Primitive Property. Translated from the French of EMILE DE LAVELEYE by G. R. L. MARRIOT. With an introduction by T. E. CLIFFE LESLIE. (Macmillan.) London, 1878. Pp. xlvii., 356.

One of the best works of the so-called historical school of political economy; to which also belongs the following earlier but very excellent book:—

An Essay on the Distribution of Wealth, and on the Sources of Taxation. By the Rev. RICHARD JONES. London, 1831. Pp. xlix., 329 (49).

The following was published under the sanction of the Cobden Club:—

On the Agricultural Communities of the Middle Ages, and Inclosures of the Sixteenth Century. Translated from the German of E. NASSE by Colonel H. A. OUVRY. London (Macmillan). 1871. Pp. 100.

Systems of Land Tenure in Various Countries. A series of essays published under the sanction of the Cobden Club. Edited by J. W. PROBYN. London. (Cheaper edition, 1876, title page undated, Cassell.) Pp. viii., 418.

All the other publications of the Cobden Club are desirable acquisitions. The larger volumes, such as the "Cobden Club Essays," 1872, and the Essays on "Local Government and Taxation" are not easy to find, but there are numerous minor publications. The secretary of the Club is Mr. Richard Gowing, 53, St. John's Park, London, N.

Among the more useful and readable works on finance, money, &c., may be named:

Goschen's *Theory of the Foreign Exchanges*. Any edition.

James Wilson on *Capital, Currency, and Banking*. London, 1844.

Laing's *Theory of Business for Busy Men*. 2nd Edition. (Longmans.) 1868. Pp. viii., 285.

Bagehot's *Lombard Street*. 6th Edition. (Kegan Paul & Co.)

Chevalier's *Cours d'Economie Politique*. 3me Tome, "La Monnaie." Paris.

Essays in Finance. By ROBERT GIFFEN. London (George Bell & Sons). 1880. Pp. xii., 347.

Money. By FRANCIS A. WALKER. New York (Henry Holt & Co.); London (Macmillan). 1878. Pp. xv., 550.

Money in its Relation to Trade and Industry. By F. A. WALKER. New York

(Henry Holt & Co.). 1879. 12mo. Pp. iv., 339.

A Treatise on the Coins of the Realm; In a Letter to the King. By Charles, First Earl of LIVERPOOL.

A masterly work, which contains by far the best history and general account of the English Currency. The original edition (4to, 1805: Oxford, pp. 268) is scarce; but the 8vo reprint, issued by the Bank of England (Effingham Wilson, 1880, pp. xii., 295) is fortunately to be had.

Turning to the subject of Banking:—

The Principles and Practice of Banking. By J. W. GILBART.

Any of the later editions; but the best is a new edition by Michie (George Bell and Sons).

The Scottish Banker; or, A Popular Exposition of the Practice of Banking in Scotland. By W. H. LOGAN. New Ed., 1850.

A small but good book.

The Practice of Banking. Embracing the Cases at Law and Equity, bearing upon all Branches of the Subject. By JOHN HUTCHISON. London (Effingham Wilson). *Title undated,* 1880? Pp. xxviii., 526.

Banking Reform: An Essay on Prominent Banking Dangers, and the Remedies they Demand. By A. J. WILSON. London (Longmans). 1879. Pp. vi., 192.

The history of banking may be found either in *Lawson's History of Banking,* which is scarce, or in

The Theory and Practice of Banking. By HENRY DUNNING MACLEOD. 2 vols. Longmans. 1855. Pp. xxiv., 436; lxxxii., 542.

In regard to Finance and Taxation, the works to be sought for are as follows:—

The Financial Statements of 1853, 1860–63; *to which are added a Speech on Tax Bills,* 1861, *and on Charities,* 1863. By W. E. GLADSTONE. London (Murray). 1863. Pp. 462.

Twenty Years of Financial Policy: A Summary of the Chief Financial Measures passed between 1842 and 1861; with a Table of Budgets. By Sir STAFFORD H. NORTHCOTE, Bart. London (Saunders, Otley and Co.). 1862. Pp. xvi., 399.

National Finance: A Review of the Policy of the last Two Parliaments. By JOHN NOBLE. London (Longmans). 1875. Pp. 368.

A book which has not been superseded is

The History of the Public Revenue of the British Empire. By Sir JOHN SINCLAIR. Third Edition. Three vols. 1803. Pp. xvi., 532; viii., 411, 63; viii., 320, 196.

The third volume contains a valuable bibliography of works on Finance.

On Free Trade the best treatise is—

Free Trade and Protection. New and Cheaper Edition. By the Right Hon.

HENRY FAWCETT. London (Macmillan). 1882.

The following works by AUGUSTUS MONGREDIEN are published by Cassells, or by the Cobden Club:—

Free Trade and English Commerce. History of the Free Trade Movement in England. 5th Ed.

Pleas for Protection Examined.

Among a multitude of works relating to labour and capital, the following only can be mentioned here:—

The Labour Laws. By JAMES EDWARD DAVIS. London (Butterworths). 1875. Pp. xv., 335.

The Conflicts of Capital and Labour. Being a History and Review of the Trades Unions of Great Britain. By GEORGE HOWELL. London (Chatto and Windus). 1878. Pp. xviii., 520.

An excellent cheap little work or primer, giving the elements of the labour question, is—

Political Economy for the People. By JOHN LANCELOT SHADWELL. Reprinted from the *Labour News.* London (Trübner). 1880. 12mo. Pp. v., 154.

The most compendious French text book of the science is—

Traité d'Economie Politique, exposé didactique . . . Par JOSEPH GARNIER. 5me Ed. Paris (Guillaumin). 1863. Pp. xii., 748.

The theory of the science, partly according to the recent French views, may be well studied in

Plutology; or, The Theory of Efforts to satisfy Human Wants. By W. E. HEARN, Professor of Political Economy in the University of Melbourne. London (Macmillan). 1864. Pp. xii, 475.

Having specified some of the more indispensable works, the following are added as books which may safely be purchased when they are met with at reasonable prices.

Henry Thornton's *Inquiry into the Nature and Effects of Paper Credit,* 1802.

Thoughts and Details of the High and Low Prices. By THOMAS TOOKE, and the other minor writings of the same author. Tooke and Newmarch's *History of Prices,* in 6 vols. is sold at absurdly high prices.

Torrens' *On the Production of Wealth.*

Whately's *Introductory Lectures on Political Economy.*

Nicholls' *History of the Poor Law.*

Eden's *State of the Poor.* 3 vols. 4to. 1797.

The last is an invaluable work, and contains a bibliography of books on the subject. Unfortunately it is scarce and expensive.

XIV   THE SOLAR-COMMERCIAL CYCLE

Nature, vol. XXVI, pp. 226–8, 6 July 1882.

This article, typical of Jevons's work on his 'sun-spot' theory of the trade cycle, is in fact an addendum to two articles on 'Commercial Crises and Sun-Spots' which had appeared in *Nature* in November 1878 and April 1879, and were reprinted as item VIII in *Investigations in Currency and Finance*. The reasons for excluding the present paper from the set in *Investigations* are not clear: it is possible that Jevons, who selected the papers for that volume himself, had completed the collection before this paper was published. It was in fact his last completed publication on an economic subject.

In an article printed in NATURE (vol. xix., pp. 588–90) I gave a table of the prices of wheat at Delhi, from 1763 to 1835, quoted, or rather calculated from data given in a brief paper of the Rev. Robert Everest, contained in the *Journal* of the (London) Statistical Society for 1843, vol. vi. pp. 246–8. Between the years 1763 and 1803 there was evidence of wonderful periodicity in the recurrent famine and abundance at that part of India. When recently engaged in examining more minutely the relation between these prices and the variations of solar activity, as indicated by Prof. Wolf's numbers, it has occurred to me that an inference may be drawn which I overlooked on the previous occasion.

In the accompanying diagram[1] I have exhibited the prices in question together with Wolf's numbers as stated in the *Monthly Notices* of the Royal Ast. Soc. vol. xxi. pp. 77, 78. I have also indicated the dates of the Commercial Crises of the time according to the article on the subject in Mr. H. D. Macleod's "Dictionary of Political Economy," vol. i. pp. 627–8. It need hardly be said that the coincidence between the three classes of recurrent phenomena is of a very remarkable character, and goes far in supporting the relation of cause and effect which I had inferred to exist, both on empirical grounds and from the well-known fact that it is the cheapness of food in India, which to a great extent governs the export trade from England to India. But although the coincidence of commercial Crises in Western Europe with high corn prices at Delhi is almost perfect, it will be noticed that after 1790, the correspondence of the solar curve with that of prices is broken. Wolf does not recognise the existence of any sun-spot maximum between 1788 and 1804, and he believes that

[1] See below, p. 112.

there was a minimum at 1798. According to Wolf's later researches (*Memoirs* Roy. Ast. Soc., vol. xliii. p. 302), these dates are respectively, maximum 1788·1, minimum 1798·3, and maximum, 1804·2.

But now arises the question to which I wish to draw attention. If the eleven-year solar periodicity was really interrupted in this long interval of 16·1 years, how comes it that the meteorological periodicity, as manifested in the corn prices at Delhi, was not interrupted. It is true that the price maximum of 1803 was a comparatively small one; but this was quite to be expected, considering that if there were an intervening solar maximum, it must have been a small one. May we not reverse the argument and infer that the evident relation between the previous sun-spot maxima and the succeeding scarcities at Delhi, would lead us to expect a minor solar maximum about the year 1797?

Standing alone, the presumption thus created would, doubtless, be of a somewhat slight character. But it is in the first place well known, that the data upon which Wolf based his numbers about this time, are less conclusive than in other parts of his series. His results, too, from 1801 to 1807 are expressly marked as doubtful, so that extrinsic information which might have little weight where there was abundance of reliable solar or magnetic observations may come in very usefully where doubts already exist. Now it happens that the late Mr. J. A. Broun inquired very carefully into the facts known about the solar variation at this time, his results being given in the *Transactions* of the Royal Society of Edinburgh, vol. xxvii. pp. 563–594, and in his article printed in NATURE (vol. xvi. pp. 62–64). Broun inferred from the observations of Gilpin, and from other data, that there was a small maximum about 1797, and that there were grounds for believing that the subsequent maximum "may really have occurred after 1806, when Gilpin's series terminated." Now, what Broun deduced from totally different data, is exactly what we should infer from the Delhi prices. If we are to believe that Indian meteorology depends upon solar variations, then it almost follows that there was a solar maximum about 1797. The consequence of this inference, however, is very important, because it goes to support the views of Lamont, Broun and others, that the solar period is about $10\frac{1}{2}$ (10·45) years and not 11·1 as calculated by Wolf. It should also be pointed out that the temperature observations of Prof. Piazzi Smyth lead to a like result. The epochs of the heat waves are, according to him (NATURE, vol. xxi., p. 248), 1826·5, 1834·5, 1846·4, 1857·9, and 1868·8, giving an average interval of 10·57 years.

I may take this opportunity of asserting that the progress of events confirms belief in the eastern origin of the great commercial Crises.* In

* As it is impossible to reproduce the explanations and qualifications contained in the article

his important work, the "Précis du Cours d'Economie Politique" (vol. i. pp. 604–5), M. Cauwès while partially accepting the doctrine of periodicity criticises the particular views here advocated. He says:—

"Depuis longtemps les économistes ont signalé la périodicité de ces évolutions: MM. Juglar et Jevons prétendent même pouvoir la calculer d'une manière précise. Selon M. Jevons, l'ensemble des phénomènes serait renfermé dans un cycle de dix années et demie. De fait, les grandes crises économiques du siècle (1806, 1817, 1825–7, 1836–37, 1847, 1857,) s'échelonnent à dix années d'intervalle ou à peu près, mais les dernières, 1866 et 1873, seraient venues un peu avant l'heure, et celle de 1873 s'est prolongée au delà de toute attente." M. Cauwès in short accepts the six earliest crises of this century as sufficiently agreeing with the theory. The crisis of 1866 no doubt came about a year before it would be expected, which is a divergence of reasonable amount. The year 1873, however, is one which it would be impossible to introduce into the series. Now there doubtless were both in America and England in that year, a state of commercial stringency, a relapse of prices and other disturbances which might be mistaken for the signs of a true crisis. But such as it was, this crisis turned out to be just one of those exceptions which prove the rule. The following statistics of bankruptcy in the United Kingdom, as collected by Messrs. Kemp, and published in the *Mercantile Gazette*, show conclusively that the real collapse came in exact accordance with the decennial theory in the autumn of 1878 or early in 1879:—

Year.	Number of bankruptcies.	Year.	Number of bankruptcies.
1870	8,151	1876	10,848
1871	8,164	1877	11,247
1872	8,112	1878	13,630
1873	9,064	1879	15,732
1874	9,250	1880	12,471
1875	9,194	1881	11,632

It will be remembered that the crisis of 1878 was precipitated by the failure of the City of Glasgow Bank owing to great losses of their customers in the Indian trade, the depression of that trade being caused by the recent famine in India.

As a good deal of misapprehension has arisen concerning the American

---

quoted above, or that at pp. 33 - 37 of the same volume of NATURE (vol. xix.), it is assumed that this article is read subject to those qualifications and explanations. In p. 588 col. *b* of the same volume, a *seer* of wheat was by a typographical oversight stated to be equal to 21 lbs. instead of the true weight 2 lbs.

Crisis of 1873, it is well to quote the following valuable statistics from the Annual Circulars of Messrs. R. G. Dun's mercantile agency:—

Year.	Number of failures	Amount of liabilities in dollars.
1873	5,163	228,589,000
1874	5,830	155,239,000
1875	7,740	201,060,353
1876	9,092	191,117,786
1877	8,872	190,669,936
1878	10,478	234,383,132
1879	6,658	98,149,053
1880	4,735	65,752,000
1881	5,582	81,155,932

Although the amount of liabilities involved in the failures of 1873 was larger than in any subsequent year except 1878, the number of failures was less than in any year named except 1880. The average liability of each failure in 1873 was $44,274 compared with 22,369 in 1878. It is thus apparent that the crises differed entirely in character, and I believe that the collapse of 1873 was mainly due to the breakdown of values of properties necessarily following sooner or later upon the contraction of the paper currency. In any case there was a very distinct maximum of failures in 1878, succeeded by a sudden reduction, and it occurred at a time differing by less than a year from the corresponding collapse in England. In the Dominion of Canada there was a very strongly marked maximum of failures at the same time as in England, namely, in 1879.

The theory of the solar-commercial cycle and of the partially oriental origin of decennial crises has received such confirmation as time yet admits of. I am, however, fully alive to the weight of some of the difficulties and objections which have been brought forward against the theory. These objections are far from being conclusive, and I may hope to give them in due time a satisfactory answer. But such answer must involve more detail than can be put into a brief article.

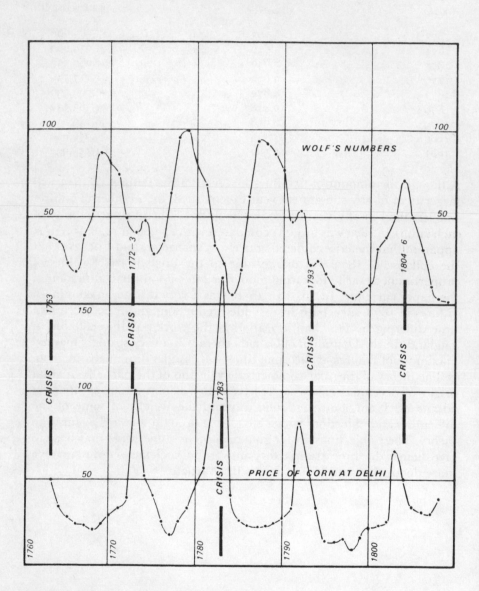

EXTRACTS FROM THE PERSONAL DIARIES
1856–60

EXTRACTS FROM THE PERSONAL DIARIES

1856

6th January

In town during middle of day, where fairly began "Smith's Wealth of Nations".

21 January

Had a day's work at Mint, but read a little of Smith's Wealth of Nations, on "value".

18 February

Sat up till 3 a.m. writing letter to Lucy consisting of two sheets letter paper, which I finished.[1] Recommenced reading Smith's Wealth of Nations at the Mint.

22 February

Reading Wealth of Nations at Mint regularly. In evening did some work at Meteorological Reports.[2]

25 March

Recommenced work at Mint. Read Smith's Wealth of Nations.

25 April

In evening worked at German writing etc. etc. Commenced British Empire by MacCulloch.[3]

27 May

Had a long discussion with F. B. M[iller][4] on Taxes. I am for the total abolition of all indirect taxation by Customs, excise &c &c.

1 June

Did little in morning but commenced letter concerning the Governors lecture on Railways.[5]

18 July

I have lately become much interested in a discussion on the introduction of railways into this colony; this evening it increased to the point of writing a short letter to the Herald on it.

26 July

[Jevons's account of his weekly expenses for this date includes an entry 'Chambers Pol. Econ. 2/6'.[6]]

---

[1] See Vol. II, Letter 81, pp. 208-11.

[2] See Vol. II, Letter 79, n. 6, p. 198; Letter 92, n. 2, p. 239.

[3] J. R. McCulloch, *A Descriptive and Statistical Account of the British Empire* . . . 2 vols (1837) and other editions to 1854.

[4] Assayer to the Branch Royal Mint, Sydney, 1854-65. See Vol. II, Letter 27, n. 6, p. 49.

[5] See Vol. II, Letter 90, pp. 235-7 and notes thereto; cf. Diary entry below.

[6] William and Robert Chambers, *Chambers's Information for the People*, published in 100 parts, 2 vols (Edinburgh and London, 1848-9).

31 July

Commenced reading Mayhews "Great World of London"[7] in which my idea of a science of Poliography or a *Topographical* Description of the districts of a city seems to have been anticipated.

6 September

Commenced reading Whewells Philosophy of the Inductive Sciences.[8]

11 September 1856

Subscribed for "Empire" £1. Subscribed for Waugh and Coxes New Sydney Directory[9] from which I intend to make up my "social maps of Sydney".[10]

19 November

Occupied during evening with a letter to Herald concerning Debentures & terminable annuities, which however I did not complete or send.

24 November

London Directory 15/- which I bought with the intention of commencing the study of towns and preparing myself for the study of Sydney in particular.

28 November

In evening copied music & commenced catalogue & statistic of trades of London in which I am in hopes of doing something.[11]

[At the end of the diary for 1856 is a page headed 'Work to be done 1856'. Among the entries on this page are the following:

Letter on railways.

Social map of Sydney &c

Social statistics of London.

Write work on "Formal Economics"

Only the first of the entries has been checked off by Jevons as completed, and at the beginning of his diary for 1857 a page headed 'Work to be done during 1857' repeats the last three entries given above; again these have not been checked off as completed.]

1857

4 February

Drew from Library Mill's Political Economy Vol. II.

7 February

Not doing much, except commencing a letter to "Empire" on the

[7] Henry Mayhew, *The Great World of London*, parts 1-9 (1856).

[8] William Whewell, *The Philosophy of the Inductive Sciences founded upon their history*, 2 vols (1840).

[9] *Waugh and Cox's Directory of Sydney and its Suburbs, 1855* (Sydney, 1855), continued as *Cox and Co.'s Sydney Post Office Directory, 1857* (Sydney, 1857).

[10] See Vol. II, Letter 107, n. 10, pp. 297-8.

[11] See Vol. I, p. 17.

"Western Railwayline, & the general policy of government railway extension".[12]

9 February

Engaged at Mint during afternoon in finishing and writing out letter on Railways which I sent to Empire office, finding it published in 2½ columns of large type next day.

13 February

Bought MacCulloch's Account of the British Empire; in getting this as well as other expensive books, I wish to turn my attention to statistics and other similar subjects and the ultimate value to me of every scrap of knowledge of this kind obtained now will amply repay the few pounds I spend somewhat freely. Besides, on returning to England these books will be available there and are therefore a perfectly good investment.

15 February

In the evening music and Political Economy.

3 March

[An account of purchases made on this date includes the entry 'Heeren's Political System 15/-'.[13]]

6 March

Finished reading Mills Economy; many parts but carelessly and rapidly read but not without some advantage I think.

12 March

Returned Mill's Economy to School of Arts.

22 March

In evening continued letter upon Land and Railway Policy, with some success.

27 March

Whewells lec^{rs} on Political Economy 10/-.[14]

28 March

Wrote and sent letter to Empire with view of shutting up writers about Protective Humbug.[15]

31 March

In evening wrote an article on the regulation of public houses, inns, etc. & the sale of spirituous liquors with the view to the prevention of habitual drunkenness.

[12] See Vol. II, Letter 98, pp. 262-8.

[13] Arnold Hermann Ludwig Heeren (1760-1842), *A Manual of the history of the political system of Europe and its colonies, from its formation at the close of the fifteenth century to its re-establishment upon the fall of Napoleon.* Translated from the fifth edition by D. A. Talboys (1846).

[14] Jevons definitely wrote '*Whewell's* lec^{rs} on Political Economy' but no work with such a title had been published by Whewell at this date. It seems probable that Jevons, who had been reading Whewell's *Philosophy of the Inductive Sciences*, wrote 'Whewell' in mistake for 'Whately' since the diary entry for 5 April and a special entry in his Journal (Vol. I, pp. 157-9) show that he had been reading the latter's *Introductory Lectures*. Cf. below, n. 16.

[15] See Vol. II, Letter 102, p. 281.

5 April

Read a good deal of Shakespeare and Whateley.[16]

Writing etc. Proceeded with letter upon Land & Railway Policies.[17] Much engaged.

22 April

A list of purchases made on this date includes the following entries: "Lardner's Railway Economy 14/-[18]

Census tables of N S W 3/6"

29 April

Commenced reading Malthus essay on population.

Busy considering the subject of Roads & Internal communication in a financial point of view.

1 May

Commenced writing article on resolutions of meeting in favour of protection.

2 May

Finished writing out an Article on the absurd resolutions passed at a Protection Meeting. Delivered at office.

7 May

Read Malthus. Afterwards through town.

18 May

In evening commenced reading Mills Pol. Economy Vol. I. Introductory remarks not very remarkable or useful as far as I see.

21 May

In evening proceeded with the Introduction of my book on Anthropology or the general consideration of Man in the concrete, comprising Political & Social Economy, Moral Philosophy, & parts of ethics & metaphysics.

22 May

In evening reading Mills & writing on Economy.

26 May

Reading Mill, Thackeray. Also account of Dr. Livingstone's Explorations in Central Africa.[19]

6 June

[A list of purchases at this date includes the entry: 'Dr. Chalmers Work 7/6'.[20]]

---

[16] Richard Whately, *Introductory Lectures on Political Economy* (1831). See Vol. VI, Lecture 1, p. 4.

[17] See Vol. II, Letter 103, pp. 282–7.

[18] Dionysius Lardner, *Railway Economy: A Treatise in the New Art of Transport* (1850).

[19] Possibly *Sketches of Dr. Livingstone's missionary journeys and discoveries in Central South Africa* (1857).

[20] Thomas Chalmers, *Political Economy in connexion with the Moral State and Prospects of Society*, 2 vols (Glasgow, 1832). Presumably this is the 'Work' referred to, although it could also have been Chalmers's *Bridgewater Treatises* of 1833.

9 June

Finished 1 Vol of Malthus which is certainly a great & useful work if it was really the first exposition of so important a principle of human nature as that of over population.

In evening alone & much reading of Thackeray's Newcomes[21] etc. Wrote part of a letter on Land regulations.[22]

14 June

Chiefly during morning. "Newcomes" Mill etc.

Evening. Well on with my most comprehensive work on Man in Society which on the most moderate estimate would take two lifetimes to finish.

20 June

Finished Mill Political Economy Vol. I.

21 June

Reading Mill's Logic.

23 June

[A list of purchases made on this date includes the entry: 'Census of Great Britain 10/6']

6 July

Commenced working again at Industrial Statistics.

14 July

Very busy every evening with classification of occupations as returned in Census of 1851 in Great Britain.

2 August

[A list of purchases made on this date includes the following: 'Quetelet's Treatise on Man[23] Philosophy of the working classes.']

16 August

Worked at *Division of Labour*.

30 August

Wrote a good deal of article on Division of labour in morning.

13 October

Working hard at the "Division of labour" and engaged adding up totals of returns of employment from the British Census. These total results when finished will be quite complete giving the number of persons of, male and female separate, for every order of every section and class. The trouble however is very great.

[21] William Makepeace Thackeray, *The Newcomes. Memoirs of a most respectable family* . . . 2 vols (1854–5).
[22] See 'Contributions to the Sydney *Empire*' above, p. 3.
[23] Lambert Adolphe Jacques Quetelet, *A Treatise on Man and the Development of his faculties* . . ., first English translation (Edinburgh, 1842).

1858

Jevons's diary from 1 January to 4 February 1858 contains no entries relating specifically to political economy. At this point there is an entry reading 'after this diary discontinued but again used in London for the year 1860'.

1860

February 3rd – 5th including Sat. & Sun. – was almost entirely engaged in commencing a work on Pol. Econ to be established on a demonstrative basis, in the form of connected & distinct propositions. Value to be established on the basis of labour and the problems of rent wages interest etc. to be solved as mathematical functions. Am very sanguine of its success.

11 February

A short walk in Kensington Gardens. Some work at Latin, Greek and Pol Econ.

16 February

Math. & Pol. Econ.

18 February

Geometry, Econ. etc

19 February

At home all day & working chiefly at Economy, arriving as I suppose at a true comprehension of *Value* regarding which I have lately very much blundered.

25 February

Drill in the morning for 13th time.

Platoon exercise as in square.

De Morgan.

Latin, & Pol. Econ. rest of day.

LIST OF WRITINGS ADDITIONAL TO THOSE INCLUDED IN
APPENDIX B TO THE *LETTERS AND JOURNAL*

ADDITIONAL WRITINGS

Appendix B to *Letters and Journal* is entitled 'Mr. Jevons' Writings', but in fact the list given there is not complete; neither is that given in Appendix IV to the *Theory of Political Economy* (fourth edition), which extends only to 'Works and Papers upon Economical Subjects'.

Jevons did, however, keep a notebook in which he entered details of all his publications. In his early years he appears to have been scrupulous in making all the entries fully, but in later life he does not seem to have kept the notebook regularly. However since the bibliographies mentioned above are mainly deficient with respect to Jevons's earlier writings, the notebook provides a valuable supplement to previously published lists. All the entries in it which are not to be found in those lists are therefore reproduced here, in the order in which Jevons made them.

1856

July 19	'The Railway Discussion', letter in *Sydney M. Herald*.
Oct. 2	'Lead poison in the Sydney Water, vindicating Dr. Smith' *Empire*
Nov. 20	'Red tapeism & the Newcastle Lifeboat.' *Empire*

1857

March 28	'Observations on the Total Eclipse' *Empire*
May 1	On the 'Resolutions passed at the Protection Meeting', Sydney *Empire*
Aug. 1	'Remarks on the Barometer & on Meteorology generally' *Empire*
„ 8	'On a Sungauge' *Empire*
	Reprinted in the Summary for England.

1857

September	Meteorology of Australia	*Empire*
„	Letter on a local subject	„
„	'Gunpowder and lightning'	„
„	'Railway Economy'	„
„	'Cure for the Revenue'	„
„	'The Royal Prerogative of Mercy'	„
	'New Facts concerning the interior of Australia, viz Copper coloured Races and Gregory's Expedition.	
	'On the Philosophical Society of N.S.W.'	„

1858

June 23   Letter concerning Mr. Scott's criticisms *Sydney Magazine*

October   Review of the *Sydney Magazine of Science and Art* – In the *Sydney Morning Herald.*

                   'The Social Cesspools of Sydney'   *S. M. Herald*

Oct.   'Canoona Diggings in a Scientific Aspect'   *S. M. Herald*

1859

February   'Meteorological   Observations   in   Australia'   supplementary to those in Waugh's Almanack

March   do.   continued   *Sydney Magazine*

1861   Notice of a work on Indian Whirlwinds – *Economist*

                   [Note to December entry for 'On the Deficiency of Rain in an elevated Rain-gauge' – 'See *Athenaeum* No 1770 Sept. p. 412']

December 9   Note on Sunspots 'Standard'.

                   [Note to entry on Watt's Dictionary articles – 'Arts. in Watts Chemical Dictionary noticed in the Philosophical Mag. vol. xxvi p. 309 Oct. 1863']

1862

May 3   *Chemical News*   Letter pointing out Thomas Melvill as first discoverer in the subject of spectrum analysis.

1862

September.   The following papers were forwarded to the meeting of the British Association at Cambridge. I was informed by the Secretary that they were read before the F Section, and that the second was approved of.

    „   1.   Notice of a *General Mathematical Theory of Political Economy*   (p. 158.

    „   2.   On the study of Periodic Commercial Fluctuations with five diagrams   (p. 157

    „   Brief abstracts are contained in the Report of the Proceedings, 1862, pp. 157–8.

    „   A fuller explanation and publication of the above - mentioned theory is deferred until a more suitable period for establishing a matter of such difficulty.

1862

Sept. 13.   'Clerk of the Weather Office' in *Spectator*

                   Statistical diagrams are noticed in Spectator of August 1862.

1863   Review of Dove's Law of Storms
                                Economist
[Note to April 16 entry "A Serious Fall . . . . ."
  Edw. Stanford, 6, Charing Cross S. W. London.
Noticed in *National Review*   October 1863
Noticed in *Westminster Review* Jan 1864.
"Serious Fall" noticed by Dr. Farr in Reports of the
English Delegates to the International Statistical Con-
gress, Berlin.
            Journal Stat. Soc., Dec. 1863 p. 415
"Prices have been investigated by Mr. Jevons . ."
quote continues down to "from the best authorities".
            Discussed by Dr. E. Laspeyres, Prof. in Basel in
Essay – "Hamburger Waarenpreise 1851–63".]

1863 Dec.   18 – [following entry on *Pure Logic*:]
                 Noticed by Prof. de Morgan – *Athenaeum*.
                    Spectator – March 12, 1864
1864   Reader?

        March 5   Notice of Hearn's Plutology
                                Spectator – March 5
        March   Statistics of Shakespearean Literature
                       No 1898 *Athenaeum*   12 March 1864 p 373–374.
        March 11th *Spectator*
                       Notice of Robertson's 'Laws of Thought' 1864.

1865   The Coal Question
                   First attention given to subject in 1861 or 1862. Inquiry
                commenced in January 1864. Chiefly carried out at
                Museum Library June and July 1864. Writing completed
                before Christmas. Transmitted to Mr. Macmillan about
                Dec. 28.   Accepted Jan. 6th 1865. Printing commenced
                Jan.   First proof Jan. 27.
                        Announced in *Macmillan's Mag.* Febr. 1.
                   Athenaeum Febr. 4th.
                     copied into *Examiner* (Manchester)
                                Inquirer
                April   Coal Question published during the week
                        April 24th – 30th
                May 1 Publisher's Circular   ⎫ Cuttings pasted
                Cty News (London) June 3rd 1865   ⎬   in.
                Quarterly Review   April 1866 p. 435
                        Art "Coal and Smoke"
                        (quote from p. 464).

Review   *London Quarterly Review*   April 1874
No. LXXXIII, p. 121
News cutting dated "Liverpool, 19 March 1866" and headed "Literary and Philosophical Society" recording that "Professor Jevons then gave a "Preliminary Account of certain Logical Inventions", the *Logical Abacus* and *Logical Machine"*

1867

December 11th 1867.   Diagrams in paper of Mr. John Mills on Credit Cycles
Manchester Statistical Society

1868

November 3rd 1868   Remarks on Mr. Baxendell's Laws of atmospheric ozone
Manchester Lit & Phil Society
Proceedings, p. 33.

1867   27 April. Article in *Spectator* newspaper on "Early Presentiments of the Electric Telegraph"
pp. 475–6 as Review of George Dodds Railways, Steamers & Telegraphs.

1869   Nov 18th *Nature* – Letter on the Personal Error in astronomical observations Vol. 1. p. 85   See answer 27 Jan 1870 p. 337.

1869   Dec 30th Nature – Article – p. 231
A Deduction from Darwin's Theory

1870   [After entry on Mechanical Perf. of Logical Inference] see Proceedings Nature 27 January 1870 p. 343
Printed in the Philosophical Transactions for 1870   pp. 497–518 Plates 32–34.

1870   Feb 10th 'Oversight by Faraday'   Nature vol. 1 p. 384.

1870   Glasgow Herald – Notice of Mrs. Fawcett's "Political economy for beginners"

1870   Nature – Notice of Whitworth's Choice & Chance.

1870   [After note of Pres. Address to Section F.] –
Statistical Journal Vol. XXXIII p. 309
Nature Vol. II p. 428   Sept 22, 1870.
see Pall Mall Gazette   16 Sept 70 p. 10
27 Sept 70.

1871

14 October 1871 – The Theory of Political Economy
New Editions
> Review in West^r Rev[iew] Jan 1880
>> New series Vol. VII   pp 226–7.

1875

[After cutting from Publisher's Circular announcing *Money and the Mechanism of Exchange:*]
"Geld und Geldverkehr" von W. Stanley Jevons
Leipzig – F. A. Brockhaus 1876 (May.).

1874

[Above cutting from Publisher's Circular of 2 February announcing the *Principles of Science*] "Title chosen in April 1868"
British Quarterly Review April 1874 No. CXVIII p. 546.
The above by James Collier.
Hull Criterion 4th July 1874, No. 27 p. 3.
Letter concerning Mill's Logic and the Principles of Science.

1876

Bonamy Price on Currency and Banking
Notice in Manchester Guardian 24 March 1876.
Letter in Spectator June 1876 on the alleged Poisoning of the Natives of Queensland.
"The Prospects of the Telegraph Department"
Letter dated March 20, 1876, published in Manchester Guardian.
After the entry for the *Primer of Logic* (1876) the entries are few and scattered. The next entry relates to *Studies in Deductive Logic* under date 26 October 1880 and the next again to Cossa's *Guide* (both publisher's announcements). The final entry (in W. S. J.'s handwriting) is –
> The Silver Question
>> Banker's Magazine Dec 1877
>> vol XXXVII   pp 989–996.

JEVONS AS EXAMINEE AND EXAMINER

I   PAPER SAT BY JEVONS AT UNIVERSITY COLLEGE LONDON, 1860[1]

POLITICAL ECONOMY.

1.   How is wealth defined by political economists?

2.   Discuss the proposition that "all men desire wealth", and the mode in which, and extent to which, its habitual assumption by political economists affects the soundness and generality of their conclusions.

3.   Mention the general causes in operation which tend to elevate wages, and those which tend to depress wages.

4.   Mention some of the circumstances which give rise to difference of wages in different occupations.

5.   Show that profits have a minimum limit; and discuss the circumstances which, in wealthy and industrious communities, influence their approximation to and recession from that limit.

6.   State and reply to the arguments for the proposition, that improvements in machinery are often injurious to the interests of the working classes.

7.   Show that the natural tendency of manufacturing industry is to concentration at a few points, and of agricultural industry to diffusion.

8.   Describe the system of gold, silver, and copper coinage in this country, with particular reference to the mode in which it ensures the joint circulation of gold and silver coin.

9.   Mention some of the leading forms of credit in use in commercial countries.

10.   Show that in general the exchanges must be unfavourable to the mining countries and those carrying on a transit trade in the precious metals.

11.   What were the objects aimed at in the Bank Charter Act of 1844?

12.   State your views as to the working of that Act.

13.   "These different movements in the distribution of the precious metals to the points to which the exchanges of the world direct them, are all determined by broad general principles, which are self-acting, and which any artificial attempt to disturb or control can only tend to derange."

Give a sketch of the principles referred to as determining the distribution of the precious metals, and indicate the circumstances which regulate local prices.

14.   State Adam Smith's four maxims of taxation.

15.   Sketch the arguments for and against levying an income tax by an

---

[1] *Calendar of University College, London, 1860–61*, p. 167.

equal per-centage on permanent and temporary incomes; and on incomes earned in a business or profession, and those derived from realized property.

16.   Describe the warehousing system, and point out its advantages.

N.B.   *Where the answer is matter of opinion, it should be accompanied by a statement of reasons.*

JACOB WALEY, *Professor.*

II   PAPERS SET BY JEVONS AS EXTERNAL EXAMINER AT CAMBRIDGE UNIVERSITY[2]

MORAL SCIENCES TRIPOS.

TUESDAY, *Dec.* 1, 1874.   1 to 4.

POLITICAL ECONOMY.

1.   EXPLAIN briefly but precisely the relations between the sciences of Ethics, Economics and Politics. Illustrate your answer by discussing the action of the Government of India in saving a part of the population from famine, which has been described as "a setting aside of the laws of political economy." In giving your opinion upon this subject, take into account the assertion of some eminent authorities that the population of the famine districts is becoming excessive, and that a recurrence of such famines appears to be inevitable.

2.   Give a very brief account of the origin of Trades-Unions. Point out the conditions of their successful action on the rate of wages: and examine how far this action can be legitimate and permanent.

3.   It has been said that the difficulty of preventing a commercial crisis lies more in moral than in physical or commercial forces.

Describe the different stages of a commercial crisis, and the effects produced by the 1844 Bank Act, so as to illustrate this remark.

4.   What are the chief circumstances affecting the value in England of a bill of exchange on France?

5.   "As a physical fact, capital will consist chiefly of gold." A. Musgrave. Examine this statement.

6.   What are the conditions of an effective monopoly? The character of the demand being given, show upon what principles the price should be fixed, in order that the greatest gross profit may be made by the sale of the commodity.

---

[2] *Cambridge University Calendar for the year 1875.* pp. 156 62. and *for the year 1876.* pp. 154 60.

What modifications are required in the cases (*a*) of a limitation in the monopoly – e.g. railways. (*b*) Of a limitation in the commodity – e.g. coal?

7. Investigate the principles which should govern a banker in the investment of his funds. In what respects, and why, is the case of the Bank of England a peculiar one?

8. It is stated that the clauses of the Irish Land Act facilitating the purchase by tenants of the freehold of their farms have proved nearly inoperative. Analyse the probable causes of this failure and the difficulties which stand in the way of the spread of peasant proprietorship.

9. Because wages are lower and the hours of labour longer in Mulhouse or other continental towns, it is asserted that continental manufacturers can undersell English manufacturers. Examine the truth of this inference.

10. It has been adopted almost as an axiom by many recent writers on political economy that no taxes should be laid upon the necessaries of life. Examine this question; and give all the reasons which occur to you for or against such a fiscal rule; taking as instances of necessaries of life, corn, salt, and coal.

MORAL SCIENCES TRIPOS.

THURSDAY, *Dec.* 3, 1874. 9 to 12.

POLITICAL ECONOMY.

1. WHAT are the chief practical axioms or principles of action upon which our present economical intercourse is based? Show how far these differ from the principles hypothetically assumed by the scientific economist: and contrast them, on the one hand, with those of any previous historical state with which you may be acquainted, and, on the other, with those of any ideal economic state.

2. "Capitalists can never exact from labourers the whole advantage which their capital confers."

Explain this position; and show the form in which it is proved by Adam Smith and Bastiat.

3. "The quantity of money must in every country naturally increase as the value of the annual produce increases. The value of the consumable goods annually circulated within the society being greater, will require a greater quantity of money to circulate them."

Comment upon this passage from the Wealth of Nations.

4. Give a concise statement of the wage-fund theory; and examine

any objections to the theory which have been brought against it in recent years.

5. How far, and why, are the principles which apply to international trade different from those which hold true of the internal trade of a country?

Is the trade between London and Melbourne, or between London and Dublin international?

6. What are the principal new theories or additions to economical doctrine due to Ricardo? How far have such novel doctrines been countenanced by subsequent leading writers?

7. Give your opinion in detail as to how far the present revenue of the United Kingdom is raised in conformity with the views enunciated by Adam Smith one century ago.

8. Investigate minutely the action of the system of metallic currency known as *the double standard system*, and give your opinion as to its effects upon the values of gold and silver relatively to each other and also relatively to commodities in general. State the time at which such a system was in operation in England; and describe how it came to exist and to terminate, and what effects followed from it.

9. Give Adam Smith's account of the manner in which the public debt of Great Britain was contracted. What are the economical reasons for and against a rapid reduction of the debt by increased taxation? and how is the reduction effected at present?

10. It has been said that the *vocabulary* of commerce is framed almost wholly from the capitalists' stand point. Show, by illustrations, how far this is true of economic science as usually expounded: and how far this was the *real point of view* of the following economic writers:— Adam Smith, Ricardo, Bastiat.

MORAL SCIENCES TRIPOS.

FRIDAY, *Dec.* 4, 1874.   1 to 4.

POLITICAL ECONOMY.

1. DESCRIBE and contrast the methods of Adam Smith, Ricardo and Bastiat. What are the chief advantages to be derived by the use of the Historical and Comparative methods in Political Economy?

Give examples showing what parts of the science admit of treatment by Mathematical methods; and point out the nature and limits of the advantage gained by this treatment.

2. MacCulloch and some other English writers have asserted or

implied that Political Economy is entirely a modern science, and was quite unknown to the Greeks and Romans. Give your opinion upon this point, supporting it by adequate statements of the doctrines of classical authors.

3.   Form a classification of the principal theories which have been held concerning the mutual relations of *utility, labour* and *value*. Give the names of some of the principal writers who have upheld each distinct theory: and criticise them from your own point of view.

4.   What are the chief economical and social consequences which might be expected to result from the considerable increase of industrial partnerships, or co-operative *producing* societies?

5.   Wages and profits in different employments and neighbourhoods are not uniformly proportional to the efforts of labour and abstinence of which they are the respective rewards.

Classify the circumstances which prevent this uniform proportionality; and show (a) how far their effect is likely to be reduced by economical progress, (b) how far they occasion the differences of value of the same commodity in different markets.

6.   If it were required to suddenly double the revenue of this country, upon what principles should the new Budget be framed, and from what sources chiefly would it be best to derive the additional revenue?

7.   State as precisely as possible the general principles upon which poor-law relief is at present administered in England: describe as far as may happen to be known to you the difference between the classes of paupers who are allowed to have indoor and outdoor relief, and discuss the expediency and probable effect of altogether prohibiting outdoor relief.

8.   Adam Smith generally maintains that it is best to leave individuals perfectly free in their economical relations. What are the precise assumptions on which this conclusion depends? how far do they require qualification? and how far is their truth affected by the increasing solidarity of society?

What exceptions to his general principle are recommended by Adam Smith? Would you extend the list?

MORAL SCIENCES TRIPOS.

TUESDAY, *Nov.* 30, 1875.   1 to 4.

POLITICAL ECONOMY.

1.   ADAM SMITH enumerates among the kinds of fixed capital, "the

acquired and useful abilities of all the inhabitants or members of the society." Discuss this statement in connection with the common saying that "Labour is capital".

2.   "In proportion to the increase of capital, the absolute share of the total product falling to the capitalist is augmented, and his relative share is diminished; while, on the contrary, the labourer's share is increased both absolutely and relatively".

Give Bastiat's "demonstration" of both parts of this theorem, and examine its validity.

3.   It has been held that the demand for labour can be increased and the rate of wages consequently raised by the trades-union expedient called "making work". Examine the soundness of this doctrine, and indicate some of the consequences to which its adoption would logically lead. Point out some of the various forms which the process of "making work" may assume.

4.   What is the doctrine summed up in the expression *laissez-faire?* State your opinion as to the limits, if any, within which its application should be restricted.

5.   Examine the grounds upon which the government or the municipal authorities in many places regulate the charges of cabmen, boatmen, porters, guides, &c., instead of leaving them to the action of free competition.

6.   Give an abstract of Smith's account of the Bank of Amsterdam, and explain how far, or in what way, similar functions are performed by the English banking system at the present day.

7.   What are the four principles of taxation laid down by Adam Smith? How far do they lead us to a preference of direct for indirect taxation?

8.   Explain the assertion that "an *ad valorem* tax on commodities generally would be amongst the most unequal and mischievous duties that could be imposed," causing "a change in the values of most descriptions of commodities".

MORAL SCIENCES TRIPOS.

THURSDAY, *Dec.* 2, 1875.   9 to 12.

POLITICAL ECONOMY.

1.   ADAM SMITH commonly describes wealth as "the annual produce of land and labour". In what respects must this definition be regarded as faulty?

2. Give Mill's analysis of Cost of Production and the purport of Cairnes' criticism upon it. Explain how the transfer of labour and capital from one trade to another, so frequently assumed by economists, is affected by actual experience.

3. Analyse the circumstances upon which depends the amount of difference between the wholesale and retail prices of a commodity.

4. It has been held by some that exchange can produce no benefit, because the values of the goods exchanged are equal. Others have argued that what one gains the other must necessarily lose. What is really the nature of the gain which a country derives from its foreign trade? Is it possible to determine the amount of such gain?

5. Point out the connection which exists between the business of banking and the doctrine of probability, and investigate precisely the nature of the principal risks and difficulties to which bankers are subject.

6. What are the chief provisions of the Bank Act of 1844? Discuss the dictum that "the business of the banking department of the Bank of England should be conducted on precisely the same principles as that of any other bank".

7. Examine the advantages and drawbacks of the Funding System as compared with the plan of raising the supplies within the year. On what grounds has the National Debt been sometimes represented as a source of benefit to the community?

8. What was the Sinking Fund of Price and Pitt? Describe some of the other principal schemes by which it has been proposed or is actually attempted to reduce or eventually complete the payment of the National Debt.

9. Give an outline of Professor Cairnes' views as to the logical method of political economy.

MORAL SCIENCES TRIPOS

Friday, *Dec.* 3, 1875. 1 to 4.

POLITICAL ECONOMY.

1. WRITE a brief article in which the editor of an American newspaper is supposed to advocate the policy of protection to native industry.

2. Supposing the price of a commodity within a country be high, inquire under what circumstances, if any, the prohibition of its exportation would tend to lower the price. Among other instances of commodities consider corn and horses.

3.   In what manner can you explain the high level of wages and prices in the United States or England as compared with that in Switzerland, Norway, Russia or Bengal?

4.   Specify the objections which have been urged against the so-called Ricardian theory of rent by Dr. Whewell and Professor Rogers. "Shew me in any part of the world land which has not been subjected directly or indirectly to human action, and I will shew you land destitute of value." How does Bastiat endeavour to reconcile the existence of different degrees of fertility of land, and of a consequent residual value of the superior qualities not resolvable into remuneration of anterior labour, with the doctrine implied in the above quotation?

5.   What is a coin? It has been urged that the supply of coinage, like that of other commodities, should be left to the free action of competition, instead of being a government monopoly. Point out any grave objections which in your opinion attach to such a proposal.

6.   Mention some of the popular explanations of the rise in general prices which has occurred during the last twenty-five years, and discuss their force.

7.   The fact that the silver price of gold has remained comparatively unaltered has been regarded by some writers as a proof that no fall in the value of the metal has taken place. Consider the validity of this reasoning, and state what are, in your opinion, the means by which the question, whether depreciation has or has not occurred, may be decided.

8.   Is a government justified under any circumstances in maintaining roads, telegraphs, railways, or other means of communication, which cannot be made to pay the ordinary return to labour and capital? If so, under what circumstances?

REVIEWS OF *THE THEORY OF POLITICAL ECONOMY*

I   MR JEVONS' THEORY OF POLITICAL ECONOMY

by Alfred Marshall, *The Academy*, 1 April 1872

THIS book claims to "call in question not a few of the favourite doctrines of economists." Its main purpose is to substitute for Mill's Theory of Value the doctrine that "value depends entirely upon utility." The rate of exchange of two commodities will, when the equilibrium has been attained, be such that the utility to each individual of the last portion of the commodity which he obtains is only just equal to that of the last portion of the other commodity which at this rate he gives in exchange for it. The utility of a commodity is in part "prospective," that is, dependent on the benefit which will at a future time accrue from its possession: and this depends partly upon the difficulty that there might be in obtaining something before that time to supply its place. Though "labour is often found to determine value," it yet does so "only in an indirect manner by varying the degree of the utility of the commodity through an increase in the supply." Bearing in mind what has been said about prospective utility, it is almost startling to find that the author regards the Ricardian theory as maintaining labour to be the origin of value in a sense inconsistent with this last position. But the language of Ricardo on this point was loose with system: and that of many of his more prominent followers differs from his only in that its looseness is not systematic. By a natural reaction, attempts have been made by a series of able men to found the theory of value exclusively upon the neglected truth.

Although the difference between the two sets of theories is of great importance, it is mainly a difference in form. We may, for instance, read far into the present book without finding any important proposition which is new in substance. But at length he definitely commits himself: at the end of his Theory of Exchange we read—

> Labour affects supply, and supply affects the degree of utility which governs value, or the ratio of exchange. But it is easy to go too far in considering labour as the regulator of value; it is equally to be remembered that labour is itself of unequal value . . . I hold labour to be essentially variable, so that its value must be determined by the value of the produce, not the value of the produce by that of the labour.

The confusion here implied is not merely one of words. He returns again in his concluding remarks to his attack upon the ordinary theory of the variation of wages in different employments, and says "the wages of a working man are ultimately coincident with what he produces after the deduction of rent, taxes, and the interest on capital." He does not see that, since rent, taxes, etc. are not paid in kind, we must have before us a complete theory of value in order that we may perform this subtraction. He does not speak of the amount of the wages, and the exchange value of the products as varying elements, the variations of each of which affect those of the other. He considers that value is determined absolutely and independently, and that wages are determined afterwards. He goes on:

> I think that in the equation,
>
> $$\text{Produce} = \text{profit} + \text{wages},$$
>
> the quantity of produce is essentially variable, and that profit is the part to be first determined. If we resolve profit into wages of superintendence, insurance against risk, and interest, the first part is really wages itself; the second equalises the result in different employments; and the interest is, I believe, determined as stated in the last chapter.

The attempt, here referred to, to give an account of interest independent of any theory of wages or value, is bold and subtle. The reasoning is mathematical; but the argument may be expressed by the following example. Suppose that A and B employ the same capital in producing hats by different processes. If A's process occupies a week longer than B's, the number of hats he obtains in excess of the number obtained by B must be the interest for a week on the latter number. Thus the rate of interest is expressed as the ratio of two numbers without the aid of any theory of value – expressed, but not determined – yet in the passage quoted it is spoken of as determined. The relative productiveness of slow and rapid processes of manufacture is but one of the determining causes of the rate of interest: if any other cause made this fall, B's process would be abandoned. The rate of interest affects the duration of the remunerative processes of manufacture no less than it is affected by it. Just as the motion of every body in the solar system affects and is affected by the motion of every other, so it is with the elements of the problem of political economy. It is right and necessary to break up the problem; to neglect for the time the influence of some elements; to investigate the variations of any one element which must, *caeteris paribus*, accompany certain assumed variations in one or more others. Such investigations give results which, even as they stand, are roughly applicable to certain special cases. But this does not justify us in speaking, in general, of one element as determined by another; as, for instance, of value as determined by cost of production, or of wages as determined by value. It is difficult to remember a prominent Ricardian writer who has not attained brevity at the expense of accuracy by employing the former of these expressions. Professor Jevons' use of the latter of them will have done good service if it calls attention to the danger of such parsimony.

The main value of the book, however, does not lie in its more prominent theories, but in its original treatment of a number of minor points, its suggestive remarks and careful analyses. We continually meet with old friends in new dresses; the treatment is occasionally cumbrous, but the style is always vigorous, and there are few books on the subject which are less open to the charge of being tedious. Thus it is a familiar truth that the total utility of any commodity is not proportional to "its final degree of utility," *i.e.* the utility of that portion of it which we are only just induced to part with, or to put ourselves to the trouble of procuring, as the case may be. But Professor Jevons has made this the leading idea of the costume in which he has displayed a large number of economic facts. In estimating, for instance, the benefit of foreign trade, we must pay attention to the total utility of what we obtain by it, as much as to its final utility, which alone is indicated by the rate of exchange. His attack on Mill on this point is worth reading, though it is in parts open to criticism; and though, while Mill pleads the difficulty of the subject in excuse of his neglect of the total utility of international trade, Jevons does not overcome the difficulty. Again, the whole advantage of capital to industry – its total utility – cannot be measured by the rate of interest, which corresponds only to its final degree of utility. Again, the final degree of utility to a labourer of his wages diminishes as their amount increases, while the final degree of pain resulting from the labour, at all events after a certain time, increases as the amount becomes greater: consequently, the artisan as soon as his real wages have ceased to be barely sufficient for his support, strikes for shorter times, rather than for the further increase in wages.

Among his more interesting incidental discussions are those on the difficulties Thornton has found in the theory of value, and on the economy of muscular effort. He contributes to the definition of the terms "market," "labour," "capital," "circulating capital," but he does not keep sufficiently distinct the various connections in which each of them is employed. His lucidity serves to render darkness visible; to make us conscious of the absence of a specialised economic vocabulary, perhaps, on the whole, the severest penalty that the science has paid for its popularity. He supplies, indeed, one expression which, with a little more care, might be rendered a useful one. Capital which "consists of a suitable assortment of all kinds of food, clothing, utensils, furniture, and other articles which a community requires for its ordinary sustenance," he calls "free capital," because it "can be indifferently employed in any branch or kind of industry." The term "value," indeed, he considers as hopeless, and he expresses an intention, to which he does not adhere, of avoiding its use.

Value in exchange expresses nothing but a ratio, and the term should not be used in any other sense. To speak simply of the value of an ounce of gold is as absurd as to speak of the ratio of the number seventeen.

There does not seem to be any greater absurdity in speaking of the value of an ounce of gold, or of a cubic inch of gold, than there is in speaking of the weight of a cubic inch of gold. In each case reference is made to some unit conventionally adopted at some particular place and time. He complains that "persons are led to speak of such a nonentity as intrinsic value": but the examiner, who has asked for a definition of specific gravity, is fortunate if he has not heard of "intrinsic weight." The abuse of a term is not a sufficient cause for its rejection. We cannot afford to dispense with the phrase "the rate of wages," though Ricardo has employed it in a forced sense, which Professor Jevons himself has failed to catch.

He has done good service, moreover, in protesting against Mill's saying:—"Happily there is nothing in the laws of value which remains for the present or any future writer to clear up; the theory of the subject is complete." It is probable that Mill intended this to be interpreted in a very narrow sense; but anyhow, it is unfortunate. As Jevons says, it would be rash to make such a statement about any science. It would be very rash to make it about the law of gravitation. Mill would probably have been more correct if he had stated that, taking into account only questions which have already occurred, there is no one side of the theory of value which does not require for its completion a greater amount of scientific investigation than has, up to the present time, been applied to the whole of political economy—that there is scarcely any question which can be asked with regard to value to which a complete answer is forthcoming. Take, for instance, a question which Professor Jevons has made prominent—What is the influence which a rise in price of hats, owing to an increased demand, has on the wages of hat-makers? Of course one element to be considered is the facilities which exist for introducing new workmen into the trade. How far, then, is this dependent on the number of parents occupied in this and other employments who have been able to give their sons an education sufficiently good to fit them to become hat-makers, but not a much better one. What is the relation between the cost of production of an average skilled labourer and his remuneration? This is but one question out of many. We know, perhaps, in what direction to look for the answers: but the point is that they are not yet formulated. And who can tell what difficulties will have to be overcome before they are formulated?

Professor Jevons has expressed almost all of his reasonings in the English language, but he has also expressed almost all of them in the mathematical. He argues at great length and with much force the applicability of mathematical method to political economy:

> If there be any science which determines merely whether a thing be, or be not – whether an event will happen, or will not happen – it must be a purely logical science; but if the thing may be greater or less, or the event may happen sooner or later, nearer or farther, then quantitative notions enter, and the science must be mathematical in nature, by whatever name we call it.

He insists that mathematics have been successfully employed in physical sciences of which the data are very inexact; and what innumerable possibilities of economical statistics exist already half tabulated in the books of mercantile houses great and small. His remarks on these and some similar points are singularly good. In general, indeed, he makes but little use of mathematical methods of reasoning. And he has not even fully availed himself of the accuracy which he might have derived from the use of the language. He does not always point out what are the variables as a function of which his quantities are expressed. It is often necessary to understand independently the whole of his reasoning, in order to know whether he means his differential co-efficients to be total or partial; and in several cases he seems almost to have himself forgotten that they are total. He has expressed the fact that "the last increments in an act of exchange must be exchanged in the same ratio as the whole quantities exchanged" by the equation

$$\frac{dy}{dx} = \frac{y}{x}.$$

He does not indicate the existence of any relation the $\triangle y$ and $\triangle x$, of which he considers dy and dx to be the limits, which can constitute $\frac{dy}{dx}$ a differential co-efficient: the mathematical phrase merely confuses. Some amusement has been derived from the absurd result which is obtained by integrating the equation. But this implies a misapprehension. A point on a locus may be determined by an equation with a differential co-efficient in it. If we integrate the equation, we get, not this locus, but some other intersecting it at the point to be determined. An instance of a different kind of inaccuracy, for which his making use of mathematical language leaves him without excuse, occurs in his investigation of the influence on the rate of international exchange exerted by a tax on imports. He tacitly assumes that the government levies the tax in kind, and destroys it, or, at all events, consumes it in such a way as not to interfere with the demand there would otherwise have been in the country for it.

We owe several valuable suggestions to the many investigations in which skilled mathematicians, English and continental, have applied their favourite method to the treatment of economical problems. But all that has been important in their reasonings and results has, with scarcely an exception, been capable of being described in ordinary language: while the language of diagrams, or, as Professor Fleeming Jenkin calls it, of graphic representation, could have expressed them as tersely and as clearly as that of the mathematics. The latter method, moreover, is not well adapted for registering statistics until the laws of which they are instances have been at least approximately determined: and it is not intelligible to all readers. The book before us would be improved if the mathematics were omitted, but the diagrams retained.

ALFRED MARSHALL.

II NEW THEORIES IN POLITICAL ECONOMY

by John Elliott Cairnes, *Fortnightly Review*, n.s., XI (January 1872) pp. 71–6.

IN the concluding remarks of Professor Jevons's able and original work he enters a protest against "the too great influence of authoritative writers in political economy," urging, as a plea for the boldness of his own speculations, the existence of a "tendency of a most hurtful kind to allow opinions to crystallise into creeds." I should be inclined to deprecate quite as strongly as he does the tendency in question, could I perceive its existence; but I own I am quite unable to do so. So far from this, what strikes me as the most notable feature in recent economic publications – almost the only circumstance, indeed, which they have in common – is the entire freedom manifested by the writers from any such subserviency to authority as Mr. Jevons deprecates. With the single exception of Professor Fawcett's manual and Mrs. Fawcett's smaller treatise, I am unable to recall a single work published within the last twenty years in which principles, more or less fundamental in what Mr. Jevons would call the accepted system of political economy, have not been freely brought in question. In the writings, for example, of Mr. McLeod, of Professor Rickards, of Professor Rogers, of Mr. Thornton, of Mr. Longe, of Mr. Jennings, of Professor Hearne, and of Professor Jevons himself, not to mention French and American publications, I think it would be difficult to discover indications of that subservient and timid spirit against which we are warned. Indeed, I must frankly own that my apprehensions take an entirely different direction; and that what I should be disposed to deprecate in the treatment of economic questions is something the exact reverse of excessive deference for authority – an eagerness to rush into difficult speculations, and to propound crude solutions of complicated problems, in entire disregard, or at all events without due study, of what has been done towards elucidating those subjects by previous thinkers. Not indeed, that I consider political economy to have spoken its last word – very far from this – or even to have received in any of its branches final and definite form; and still less that I desire to see a "despotic calm" in economic speculation, but that I think impatience of authority may in science be carried too far. What appears to be due to the great names in any province of thought is that their opinions should be candidly studied before being set aside, and that, so far as is consistent with scientific convenience, the new developments of doctrine, suggested by enlarged investigation, should be built upon the results of past thought, where these are found to be sound. It appears to me that no presumption can be greater than that of a writer who, dealing with problems of extreme difficulty, which have been the subject of the prolonged and intense meditation of some generations of able men, coolly thinks he may disregard all that has been done, and strike out at a heat, by his unassisted genius, solutions which they have failed to discover; and it is towards this extreme, as it seems to me, far rather than towards servile acquiescence in established doctrines, that the intellectual habit prevailing among those who engage in economic discussion tends at the present time. It is, indeed, true that we find abundant appeals on all hands to "the established principles of political economy;" but what is the value of such appeals? The dogmas appealed to are, in the great majority of cases, no more principles of political economy than they are principles of the black art, but, as Mr. Jevons would no doubt be the first to admit, the merest plausibilities – platitudes, for example, about supply and demand – either evolved at the moment from the moral consciousness of the reasoner, or which have somehow got current, possibly as having what is considered the proper scientific ring. I am, therefore, wholly unable to join in the present protest against the alleged servile spirit of modern economic speculation. It is anarchy, as it seems to me, rather than despotism, with which we are menaced. Mr. Jevons, indeed, thinks that in the "republic of the sciences sedition and even anarchy are commendable." But in this view I cannot concur. As I regard the matter, sedition is only commendable when preceded by knowledge of the principles against which the revolt is made, and perception of their inadequacy; nor can I think that anarchy is commendable at all; at best it is only preferable to absolute stagnation.

It would seem, therefore, that our author has no need to be apprehensive of his views failing to receive the attention they undoubtedly deserve from any indisposition on the part of economists to entertain novel doctrines. Every one will acknowledge the perfect competency of so able and accomplished a writer to challenge any principle of political economy, it matters not by what names it may be endorsed; and he will, on his side, no doubt be prepared to find opinions, deviating so widely as some of his do from those which have been held by some very able men, severely and even jealously canvassed. Mr. Jevons has diverged from the beaten track in two directions – on the question of the method by which political economy ought to be cultivated, and also on some of its substantive doctrines. As regards method, he thinks that economic principles may be best developed by means of mathematics; while he has propounded, on the subject of value in exchange, as well as on some other doctrines of the science, some views of more or less novelty. A few remarks on his doctrine of value are all I shall venture on, on the present occasion.

The phenomena of exchange-value involve two perfectly distinct problems, which, one is surprised to find, Mr. Jevons does not discriminate – the problem as to normal or average, or (to use Adam Smith's phrase) "natural" values, and that as to fluctuations of value, or, as it is commonly expressed, "market values". Of course all exchanges whatever, at least all with which political economy is concerned, take place in a market, and therefore all values are in a sense "market values;" but the exchanges of the market may be considered either with a view to the law of their fluctuations, or with reference to that which governs them as average or normal phenomena, when taken over periods long enough to allow disturbing causes to neutralize each other. It is one thing to inquire why the price of wheat is higher to-day than yesterday, this year than last; it is an entirely different inquiry why its price is *on an average* higher than that of oats, or why gold is *on an average* of higher value than silver, silver than copper, copper than iron. These two problems I say are distinct. It is of course conceivable that a solution may be found which shall embrace both; and, as Mr. Jevons has ignored the distinction, this, I presume, is what we are to understand his theory as undertaking to do.

That theory is not absolutely new; at least it seems to me that I perceive in it a conception of the law of value at bottom the same with that propounded by Bastiat in his "Harmonies Economiques."* But in form, and in the exposition, the doctrine now advanced appears, so far as I know, for the first time. It is briefly as follows:— Exchange-value, or, as Mr. Jevons prefers to call it, "the ratio of exchange," depends upon utility – that is to say, corresponds with, and expresses the relative utility of, the commodities exchanged; but "utility" is here to be taken, not as ordinarily understood, as expressing the capacity in general of a commodity to satisfy a human desire, but in a sense which will be gathered from the following passage:—

* Examined in the *Fortnightly Review*, October 1870.

"We can never say absolutely," says Mr. Jevons, "that some objects have utility and others have not. The ore lying in the mine, the diamond escaping the eye of the searcher, the wheat lying unreaped, the fruit ungathered for want of consumers, have not utility at all. The most wholesome and necessary kinds of food are useless unless there are hands to collect and mouths to eat them. Nor, when we consider the matter closely, can we say that all portions of the same commodity possess equal utility. Water, for instance, may be roughly described as the most useful of all substances. A quart of water per day has the high utility of saving a person from dying in a most distressing manner. Several gallons a day may possess much utility for such purposes as cooking and washing; but after an adequate supply is secured for these uses, any additional quantity is a matter of indifference. All that we can say, then, is, that water, up to a certain quantity, is indispensable; that further quantities will have various degrees of utility; but that beyond a certain point the utility appears to cease.

"Exactly the same considerations apply more or less clearly to every other article. A pound of bread per day supplied to a person saves him from starvation, and has the highest conceivable utility. A second pound per day has also no slight utility: it keeps him in a state of comparative plenty, though it be not altogether indispensable. A third pound would begin to be superfluous. It is clear, then, that *utility is not proportional to commodity*: the very same articles vary in utility according as we already possess more or less of the same article. The like may be said of other things. One suit of clothes per annum is necessary, a second convenient, a third desirable, a fourth not unacceptable; but we, sooner or later, reach a point at which further supplies are not desired with any perceptible force, unless it be for subsequent use."

In conformity with this view as to the varying degrees of utility incident to each commodity, the doctrine of exchange-value is thus laid down:—"The ratio of exchange of any two commodities will be inversely as the final degrees of utility of the quantities of commodity available for consumption after the exchange is effected;" in other words, the greater "the final degree of utility" in the case described, the smaller will be the quantity of the commodity which will be given in exchange for others, or the higher will be its exchange-value. Such is the theory, which may be considered from either of two points of view; either, 1, with reference to its truth as an expression of fact; or, 2, with reference to its importance as a means of elucidating the phenomena of wealth.

As regards the question of fact, our decision must evidently depend on the criterion which we adopt for estimating utility. "Utility," Mr. Jevons tells us, "corresponds to and is measured by pleasure." This seems sufficiently clear; but in truth it leaves the whole question open; for how are we to measure pleasure? Most people would, I think, say that the pleasure which a man derives from, let us say, the last drop of water that satisfies his thirst – in Mr. Jevons's language, the "terminal utility" of water – is substantially the same in all times and places. A man's capacity for enjoying a drink of water does not change with his change of locality. Or, again, I think it would be generally agreed that the pleasure derived from wearing a shirt or coat – given the constitution of the man and the climate – is not sensibly different now from what it was a century ago. The satisfaction would be regarded as depending upon the constitution of the human being in conjunction with the nature of the commodity. But, estimating utility by this method, Mr. Jevons's theory is manifestly untenable, since it is matter of fact that the exchange-value of water is not the same for all times and places, and it is equally certain that the price of all articles made of cloth or calico has greatly fallen within a century. Another measure of utility, therefore, must be found if the doctrine is to be accepted. For example, this view may be taken. It may be contended that the pleasure or utility which a man derives from the use of a commodity is not properly represented by the satisfaction arising from the action of the commodity upon his sensitive frame, but depends upon his estimate of the commodity as indicated by the things which he is disposed to give in exchange for it. In other words, we may take exchange-value as the criterion of utility; and this in fact is the test which Mr. Jevons ultimately adopts. "The price of a commodity," he says (p. 140), "is the only test we have of the utility of the commodity to the purchaser." So that what we come to is this – exchange-value depends upon utility, and utility is measured and can only be known by exchange-value. With these explanations the theory may perhaps be saved, but what is the value of the doctrine thus emasculated? I own it seems to me to come so close to an identical proposition, that I am unable to distinguish it from that species of announcement. I fail to perceive in what way it throws light on any problem of economic science. What is the purpose of a theory of value? As I understand the matter, to inform us of the conditions on which this phenomenon depends. But, if the conditions the theory announces are something undistinguishable from the phenomenon itself, if their statement is merely another mode of expressing the fact, what is the importance of the information it conveys? We desire to know, for example, the course which exchange-value will take with the progress of society, or in consequence of changes in the modes and sources of production, in the case of such articles, suppose, as corn, meat, iron, coal, gold, and silver; and we are told it will correspond in each case with the "terminal utility" of the commodity. But of what avail is it to know this, unless we have some means of determining the "terminal utility," independent of the phenomenon in question? If the "terminal utility" can only be known by the exchange-value, how are we helped to a knowledge of the latter by being referred to the former? The importance of knowing the laws of Nature is that we may overcome Nature by obeying her — as Professor Huxley has put it, to avoid the boxes on the ear which Nature administers to those who neglect her warnings. But if the only intimation we can have of the law is the experience of the box, how are we bettered by our scientific knowledge?

The purely formal character of Mr. Jevons's doctrine is still more clearly brought into view in the following development of it:—

> "What is the utility of one penny to a poor family earning fifty pounds a year? As a penny is an inconsiderable portion of their income, it may represent one of the indefinitely small increments, and its utility is equal to the utility of the quantity of bread, tea, sugar, or other articles which they could purchase with it, this utility depending upon the extent to which they were already provided with those articles. To a family possessing one thousand pounds a year, the utility of a penny may be measured in an exactly similar manner; but it will be found to be much less, because their want of any given commodity will be satiated or satisfied to a much greater extent, so that the urgency of need for a pennyworth more of any article is much reduced." (P. 133.)

Thus the "terminal utility" of a commodity will vary with the circumstances of each purchaser. The "terminal utility" of a pound of tea will be greater to a washerwoman than to a fine lady; from which some readers might be disposed to infer that, according to Mr. Jevons's theory, the washerwoman ought to pay more for her tea. But this would be a wrong inference; because the "terminal utility" of the money paid for the tea would, according to the standard adopted, be also different in the two cases, since it was to be measured by that of the tea itself. If the pound of tea be more useful to the washerwoman than to her rich neighbour, so also is the money paid for it; and thus, according to the theory, the price for each purchaser ought to be, as it is, the same. The theory thus may be saved by the simple process of depriving it of meaning. It cannot be said to be at variance with fact, since it merely asserts that the fact agrees with itself; but something more than this, I apprehend, is required of a scientific doctrine.

Besides the doctrine of value, there is much in Mr. Jevons's volume that will attract the attention of economists. In particular his view as to the amenability of economic problems to mathematical treatment is well deserving of consideration. Into this question, however, I do not now enter. I shall merely say that, while not denying that some of the doctrines of political economy may be exhibited mathematically, and may possibly thus be made clearer to some minds, my own belief is that this mode of presenting economic truths admits of but very limited application. When mathematics are carried further than this in the moral or social sciences, and used for conducting processes of reasoning, without constant reference to the concrete meaning of the terms for which the mathematical symbols are employed, I own I regard the practice with profound distrust. I must, however, defer to another occasion any attempt to vindicate my objections on this score.

J. E. Cairnes.

III   UNTITLED AND ANONYMOUS REVIEW[1]

Saturday Review, 11 November 1871, pp. 624–5

Professor Stanley Jevons remarks both in the preface and in the conclusion of this book that an exaggerated respect for authority has been very injurious to the progress of Political Economy. The names of Mill, Ricardo, and Adam Smith have been hurled at the head of any unfortunate heretic, and he has frequently been hooted out of Court without obtaining a hearing. Nothing, as Mr. Jevons truly urges, can be more opposed to the true spirit of scientific inquiry. We are therefore prepared to be rather grateful than otherwise to Mr. Jevons for attacking some of the accepted views. He will have, in the opinion of many, a better claim to be heard because his divergence from the old results is scarcely so great as he seems to imply. He accepts, for example, the orthodox theory of rent. He holds a doctrine as to the relation of profit and wages which to us seems to be substantially orthodox; and even in the theory of exchange, where he professes to introduce the greatest amount of novelty, he comes to many of the old conclusions. He believes in Mr. Mill's theory of international exchanges, with a slight exception; he admits, with Ricardo, that certain commodities are exchanged in the ratio of the cost of production; and he even accepts the general reasoning as to the laws of supply and demand. In fact, we have been struck by his general agreement with the writers to whose authority he declines, and rightly declines, to yield unreasoning obedience.

In what, then, does Mr. Jevons's originality consist? First, in the fact that he approaches the subject from a new point of view; and, secondly, that this method enables him to express his conclusions in mathematical symbols. To explain the first statement we may remark that, for scientific

---

[1] Possibly written by George Wirgman Hemming (1821–1905), mathematician, law reporter and fellow of St John's College, Cambridge. Cf. Merle M. Bevington, *The Saturday Review 1855–1868* (1941).

purposes, human society may be considered as a vast piece of machinery, in which the action of the various parts is determined by the various forces which affect the will. Each man is regarded as an instrument moved by pain and pleasure; and the arrangements of society at large are determined by the aggregate impulses of all its individual members. If, then, we could calculate the effects of given causes in producing pleasure and pain, we might determine such phenomena, for example, as those of the exchange of commodities. Just so, if we knew all the molecular forces by which the various parts of the human frame are combined, we could determine the mode of circulation of the blood. The apparently hopeless complexity of the problems thus suggested has induced economists, like anatomists, to renounce the attempt of thus analysing human society into its ultimate constituent forces, and to be content with tracing the consequences of certain highly general empirical laws. They assume, for example, that an increased supply will diminish the demand for a commodity; but they do not attempt to show from any consideration of human nature by what law the intensity of desire for the commodity will be regulated. If the time should ever come at which the actions of a man could be calculated like the orbit of a comet, political economy would reach its ideal perfection, and we might, no doubt, as Mr. Jevons urges, make it part of a Calculus of Pain and Pleasure. Meanwhile he thinks that he can detect some laws which will at least start us in the right direction; though, of course, we cannot as yet expect a mathematical accuracy of solution. We will try to see what he has made of it.

Let u, he says, represent the whole utility proceeding from the consumption of a quantity x of any given commodity. Then we may assume that u is a function of x, and he defines the "degree of utility" to be the differential coefficient of u with respect to x or $\frac{du}{dx}$. This is all very well, but so far we see no clearer. When a mathematician wishes to calculate the variations of a force, he begins by telling us distinctly what is the measure of force; when, for example, we know that g means the number of feet which a body will cover in a second with the velocity derived from gravitation acting for a second, our ideas are perfectly clear. But what is the measure of utility? To this we can discover no answer in Mr. Jevons's book. The obvious reply would be that utility is measured by the price paid for the object under given circumstances. But this would be, in fact, to give up Mr. Jevons's method, and to relapse into the old mode of empirical inquiry. We must suppose that a unit of pleasure is somehow discoverable. Mr. Jevons admits that we can "hardly form the conception" of such a unit; but thinks that we may somehow compare quantities of pleasure. Undoubtedly we can tell that one pleasure is greater or less than another; but that does not help us. To apply the mathematical methods, pleasure must be in some way capable of numerical expression; we must be able to say, for example, that the pleasure of eating a beefsteak is to the pleasure of drinking a glass of beer as 5 to 4. The words convey no particular meaning to us; and Mr. Jevons, instead of helping us, seems to shirk the question. We must remind him that, to fit a subject for mathematical inquiry, it is not sufficient to represent some of the quantities concerned by letters. If we say that G represents the confidence of Liberals in Mr. Gladstone, and D the confidence of Conservatives in Mr. Disraeli, and x and y the numbers of those parties; and infer that Mr. Gladstone's tenure of office depends upon some equation involving $\dfrac{dG}{dx}$ and $\dfrac{dD}{dy}$, we have merely wrapped up a plain statement in a mysterious collection of letters. Let us, however, attempt to test the value of Mr. Jevons's conclusions by following out at some length an example which illustrates his chief principle. Perhaps we shall find that an array of symbols very terrible in appearance may be expressible in plain language when we examine them closely.

Mr. Jevons begins his inquiry by the assertion that if A. exchanges x of one commodity for y of another, the equation $\dfrac{y}{x} = \dfrac{dy}{dx}$ will necessarily be satisfied; and his reason is as follows:—"Suppose that two commodities are bartered in the ratio of x for y, then every mth part of x is given for every mth part of y, and it does not matter for which of the mth parts." Extending this to the case of indefinitely small parts, the above equation of course follows.

He then undertakes to solve the following problem. If A. has a [say] of corn and B. b of beef, and A. exchanges x of corn with B. for y of beef, what must be the values of x and y? He assumes the truth of the following principle – namely, that as the quantity of corn in A's possession diminishes, the utility of each unit will increase, although the utility of the whole may diminish. This is the equivalent of the ordinary proposition that the specific value of any commodity will increase as the supply diminishes, though the value of the whole amount will diminish. Hence the utility of the corn in A's possession will be some function of the total amount; or, if we use symbolical language, and remember that, after the exchange, he has $a - x$ of corn and y of beef, we may call the utilities of his corn and beef $\phi_1(a - x)$, and $\psi_1(y)$, where ϕ_1 and ψ_1 are some functions dependent upon the idiosyncrasies of A. Using similar symbols for B., the utility of his corn and beef will be expressed by $\phi_2(x)$ and $\psi_2(b - y)$; and Mr. Jevons proceeds to argue that, when each is satisfied, the following equation will hold good:—

$$\frac{\phi_1(a-x)}{\psi_1(y)} = \frac{dy}{ax} \text{ and } \frac{\phi_2(x)}{\psi_2(b-y)} = \frac{dy}{dx}$$

Or, since

$$\frac{dy}{dx} = \frac{y}{x},$$

$$\frac{\phi_1(a-x)}{\psi_1(y)} = \frac{y}{x} = \frac{\phi_2(x)}{\psi_2(b-y)}$$

Here are two equations to determine the two unknown quantities, x and y.

Let us now try to discover the meaning of these mysterious symbols. And, first, of that equation $\frac{y}{x} = \frac{dy}{dx}$, of which Mr. Jevons makes so much use. It follows immediately from the statement, as Mr. Jevons may learn from any book on differential equations, that $y = Cx$ where C is a constant; or, in words, that the quantities bought and exchanged have a fixed ratio. In short, he has simply put into a symbolical shape the very simple truth that, if three herrings are sold for a penny and a half, any number of herrings will be sold for the same number of halfpence. Or, to speak more generally, we may say that, if two commodities are exchanged at a given rate, any quantities exchanged will always be in the proportion so fixed. Rather an obvious truth to be expressed in so cumbrous a fashion!

When Mr. Jevons proceeds to apply this equation to the solution of his problem, he appears to us to fall into a palpable blunder. Translated into plain English, the equation $\frac{y}{x} = \frac{dy}{dx}$ means, as we see, simply that, however much corn A. gives to B., he will receive a proportionate quantity of beef in exchange. If he doubles the amount of corn, that is, he will receive twice as much beef. But the other equations are obtained on the contrary supposition, namely, that the rate of exchange will vary according to some complex law, determinable, if we could tell precisely what effect will be produced on the mind of the parties to the bargain, by the possession of varying quantities of beef and corn. In fact, x is now a function of y, as might easily be foreseen from Mr. Jevons's statement of the case, in quite a different sense from what it was before. The substitution, therefore, of, $\frac{y}{x}$ for $\frac{dy}{dx}$ is a mistake, whilst even the equations

$$\frac{\phi_1(a-x)}{\psi_1(y)} = \frac{dy}{dx} = \frac{\phi_2(x)}{\psi_2(b-y)},$$

assuming them to be legitimate, seem to us to be simply useless so long as the functions are obviously indeterminable. They are merely a round-about way of expressing what may be better said in words. In short, we are compelled to regard Mr. Jevons's equations as altogether illusory.

We will, however, attempt to discuss the problem which he examines from a different point of view, and, as we would hope, in a plainer manner. Mr. Mill, in his *Political Economy* (Book III. Chap. XVIII.), puts the following case, which, as he thinks, illustrates the "elementary principle of international values." "Suppose," he says, "that 10 yards of cloth cost in England as much labour as 15 yards of linen, and in Germany as much as 20; at what rate will cloth and linen exchange, if the trade is thrown open?" We need not follow out his argument, remarking only that according to him the exchange will ultimately be made at some intermediate rate, depending upon the mode in which a rise or fall in price affects the demand in each market. Now Mr. Jevons's hypothetical case differs from Mr. Mill's in the following way; that A. and B., who may stand for England and Germany, are each supposed to have a strict monopoly of their respective commodities, and that moreover the production can be neither increased nor diminished. His problem is therefore equivalent to this; suppose that the British Museum had all the existing remains of Greek sculpture, and the Louvre all the existing remains of Roman sculpture; at what rate would they exchange collections, no other purchasers being in existence? The problem is so far removed from reality that it may be scarcely worth considering; and certainly it cannot be taken for a normal type of exchanges that actually take place. However, as extreme cases may very well illustrate principles, let us endeavour to follow out Mr. Jevons's example by his method, though without the use of his symbols. A. has 100 of corn and wishes to exchange it for some of B.'s beef. Suppose, for the moment, that a given rate of exchange is adopted. Let it be 5 of corn for 1 of beef. When A. has made one deal on these terms, he will have 95 of corn and 1 of beef. He may be willing to continue the process till, perhaps, he has 80 of corn and 4 of beef. We may suppose that he will now be unwilling to deal further on the same terms. If he parted with more corn for beef, the "utility" of his corn would rise and that of beef decline, and therefore the bargain of 5 for 1 would no longer be satisfactory to him. Meanwhile B. has 20 of corn and 6 of beef. If this happens to satisfy him, there will be equilibrium. We need hardly say, however, that the chances are much against it, and therefore some other rate of exchange must be found which will satisfy both parties to the bargain at the same level. It may be that no such rate is discoverable. Suppose, for example, that at the point just reached, B. having a surfeit of beef is willing to offer 2 of beef for 5 of corn, but that even this attraction will not induce A. to alter the composition of his sandwiches. Then A. will be content, but B. would still be willing to exchange at a moderate rate. Neither do we see why the rate which would content both of them should ever be hit upon. In short, all we can say is that they will exchange beef and corn till one or both of them choose to leave off; but when that will be depends partly on the desire of A. and B. for beef and corn, and partly on their acuteness in higgling. This is the same result as that at which Mr. Jevons himself arrives in the case of a man wishing to sell a house to a single purchaser. If one would rather take 900*l.* than not sell the house, and the other would rather give 1,100*l.* than not buy it, there is, as he justly remarks, no way of determining from general considerations what the price will be. He thinks, however, that the difficulty is owing to the fact that the house cannot be sold by separate bricks, whereas it is really owing in our opinion to the assumed absence of competition. If any number of other houses can be built, the rate of exchange would at once be determinable, as Mr. Jevons admits, by a different set of considerations. But till that cause comes into play no rule can be given. In fact, to sum up our view of Mr. Jevons's conclusions, we should say that he wishes to determine the rate of exchange by the utility to the dealers, without introducing the ordinary play of supply and demand; he therefore imagines a case where supply and demand do not operate; he finds, as might be expected, that the only answer is, that the result depends in some way on personal peculiarities which evade examination; and he wraps up this mysterious conclusion in symbols which are mere verbiage, as they contain functions which neither are nor can be determined.

Without going further, we may conclude that, whether anything can or cannot be done in the direction indicated – and we by no means say that it cannot – Mr. Jevons has taken us a very short way.

IV   UNTITLED REVIEW OF THE SECOND EDITION

by Thomas Edward Cliffe Leslie, *The Academy*, no. 377, n.s. (26 July 1879) pp. 59–60

The high reputation of the author, and the unsettled state of opinion with respect to both the limits and the method of political economy, make it the duty of every economist to master the doctrines of this work; and that can be done only by careful study of the book itself. A reviewer limited to a few dozen sentences can at best only assist a reader to form a judgment on some of its main topics. The principal questions it raises are whether political economy should be confined within the limits that Mr. Jevons assigns to it, and whether the method which he applies to the solution of the problems within those limits is legitimate and adequate. On both questions our own opinion differs from that of Mr. Jevons; but with respect to the first, the difference, though important, is one mainly of classification and naming. For Mr. Jevons fully concurs in the necessity of historical induction to ascertain the economic phenomena of society and their laws, but would set it apart as a branch of the general science of society under the name of economic sociology, confining the term political economy - or, as he prefers to call it, economics - to a theory deduced from known facts, axioms, or assumptions respecting the conduct dictated by personal interest, such as "that every person will choose the greater apparent good, that human wants are more or less quickly satisfied, and that prolonged labour becomes more and more painful." The theory of population, accordingly, though pronounced by Mr. Jevons "as scientific in form as consonant with facts," forms, in his view, "no part of the direct problem of economics," and is not discussed in his present work. The majority of the most eminent economists of all schools – including Mr. Senior, who attempted to make political economy purely deductive, and whom Mr. Jevons estimates highly – are, it need hardly be said, against so narrow a limitation of the province of the science, and Mr. Jevons gives only the following reason for it:—

"The problem of economics may be stated thus: Given a certain population, with various needs and powers of production, in possession of certain lands and other sources of material; required the mode of employing their labour which will maximise the utility of the produce."

He adds that "it is an inversion of the problem to treat labour as a varying quantity when we originally start with labour as the first element of production, and aim at its most economical employment." The answer seems to be that land, like Labour, is a primary element of production, and the area in cultivation and the productiveness of that area are both varying quantities. Were labour, moreover, not a varying quantity - as it is, because population is so - inferior soils and costlier methods of cultivation would not have been resorted to, and rent, to which Mr. Jevons gives a high place in economics, would not have arisen. But if, for these reasons, the laws of population come properly within the pale, political economy is clearly not limited to an assemblage of deductions or calculations from self-interest. Nor can any other natural laws, directly and deeply affecting the amount and distribution of wealth, be in consistency excluded. Admit the theory of population, and all that Mr. Jevons classes apart under the name of economic sociology has a logical title to a place within the domain of political economy.

Since Mr. Jevons, however, is an advocate, not an opponent, of the most extensive historical and inductive investigation, it is, as we have said, mainly a question of naming and classification whether the term "political economy" or "economics" should be confined to a narrower field. But the question follows – Within that narrower field can we proceed, as Mr. Jevons contends, not only by simple deduction, but by mathematical process? "There can be," he says, "but two classes of sciences – those which are simply logical, and those which, besides being logical, are also mathematical. If there be any science which determines merely whether a thing be or not, whether an event will or will not happen, it must be a purely logical science; but if the thing may be greater or less, or the event may happen sooner or later, nearer or farther, quantitative notions enter, and the science must be mathematical in nature, by whatever name we call it."

Nevertheless, it can hardly be contended that Adam Smith's reasoning respecting the nature and causes of the wealth of nations is in its essence, and ought to be in actual form, mathematical; or that the process by which his main propositions are established is anything more than logical. We might add that they rest in good part on inductive, and not simply on deductive, logic; but the question before us is whether mathematical methods could properly be applied to their demonstration. That wealth consists, not of money only, but of all the necessaries and conveniences of life supplied by labour, land, and capital; that man's natural wants are the strongest incentives to industry; that the best assistance a Government can give to the augmentation of national opulence is the maintenance of perfect liberty and security; that the division of labour is the great natural organisation for the multiplication of the products of industry; that it is limited by the extent of the market; and that the number of persons employed in production depends in a great measure upon the amount of capital, and the modes of its employment – these are the chief propositions worked out in *The Wealth of Nations*, and it can hardly be said that mathematical symbols or methods could fitly be used in their proof. We need not controvert Mr. Jevons' proposition that

> "pleasure, pain, labour, utility, value, wealth, money, capital, are all notions admitting of quantity; nay, the whole of our actions in industry and trade depend upon comparing quantities of advantage or disadvantage."

But the very reference which Mr. Jevons proceeds to make to morals militates against the assumption that "political economy must be mathematical simply because it deals with quantities," and that "wherever the things treated are capable of being greater or less, there the laws and relations must be mathematical." The author instances Bentham's utilitarian theory, according to which we are to sum up the pleasures on one side and the pains on the other, in order to determine whether an action is good or bad. Comparing the good and evil, the pleasures and pains, consequent on two courses of conduct, we may form a rational judgment that the advantages of one of them preponderate, that its benefits are greater, its injurious results, if any, less; but it by no means follows that we can measure mathematically the greater or less, or that the application of the differential calculus would be appropriate or possible in the matter. We do not go the length of saying that there are no economic questions to which mathematical calculation may be fairly applied. The precious metals, for instance, move so easily between adjacent countries that the variations of the foreign exchanges might perhaps be mathematically treated. But the immense inequalities in wages and profits, and the extraordinary fluctuations of prices under the uncertain influences of credit and speculation, are enough to baffle any attempt to apply the calculus to questions of value in general.

Were the application of mathematical processes and symbols to all economic reasoning, however, possible, it does not follow that it would be expedient. Bastiat's conception of the main problem of political economy was not very different from that of Mr. Jevons, who says that "to satisfy our wants to the utmost with the least effort — to procure the greatest amount of what is desirable at the expense of the least that is undesirable — is the problem of economics." Suppose that Bastiat could have put his *Sophismes Economiques* into a mathematical form, with symbols for words and equations for syllogisms and epigrams, would not political economy and the world have suffered a heavy loss by his doing so? The *Times* might be printed in shorthand, and much ink and paper thereby saved, but would it conduce to the enlightenment of the public to make that economy? We regret that so much of Mr. Jevons' own reasoning is put into a mathematical form, because it is one unintelligible or unattractive to many students of considerable intellectual power and attainments. On the other hand, we not only concede that a mathematical shape might have been given to a great part of Ricardo's system, but we regret that it ever received any other, because his theory of value, wages, profits, and taxation is misleading and mischievous. Assume that the products of equal quantities of labour and abstinence are necessarily of equal value and price, and that exertions and sacrifices of different kinds are commensurable, and a number of mathematical equations and calculations can be based on those assumptions. But since the basis is false, the more the superstructure is hidden the better, and we should be glad to see it obscured in every treatise in which it is put forward by a liberal use of the calculus. Taking utility in the sense in which Mr. Jevons uses the word, we should acquiesce in his "general law that the degree of utility varies with the quantity of commodity, and ultimately decreases as that quantity increases." Yet in one case only are the variations of utility and value, consequent on variations in the quantity of commodity, susceptible of mathematical measurement and calculation. The purchasing power or value of currency is inversely as its quantity, because there is an unlimited demand for it; but the variations in the value of other commodities bear no regular ratio to their quantity. Davenant's estimate, to which Mr. Jevons refers, that a defect of one-tenth in the harvest raises the price of corn three-tenths, and that a defect of one-half more than quadruples its price, is useful as an illustration, and made a rough, though only a rough, approximation to truth, so long as little corn came from abroad. Now the supply comes from the harvests of the world, and a defect of one-tenth in our own harvest might be followed by a fall instead of a rise in the price of grain. Could we even get accurate statistics of the harvests of the world, it would be found that its price is affected by so many other conditions that it bears no constant mathematical ratio to the amount of supply.

On the other hand, the stress which Mr. Jevons lays on the relation between value and quantity of supply seems to us to afford an answer to an objection which Mr. Cairnes has made to the proposition for which Mr. Jevons contends, that "value depends on utility." When Mr. Cairnes asks whether commodities are exchanged for each other simply in proportion as they are useful, we should reply in the affirmative, if by usefulness is meant, what Mr. Jevons and most other economists mean by it, the power of satisfying any human desire. If, in a siege or a famine, a loaf is refused in exchange for a large diamond, it is because the loaf is more desired or more useful; if, in ordinary times, a large diamond would not be given for a thousand loaves, the reason is that the diamond is preferred, or has greater utility in the economist's sense. It may, indeed, be urged that the comparative usefulness of diamonds and loaves in the two cases gives only the proximate cause of their relative value in exchange, and that the ulterior cause is comparative limitation of supply. A loaf contains as much nourishment in a time of plenty as in a famine; but in the former case no particular loaf is much wanted, or has any particular utility, while in a famine every loaf has a utility proportionate to the amount of food it contains. Mr. Jevons' proposition is in substantial accordance with the generally accepted doctrine that value depends mainly on limitation of supply. It depends, however, also on other conditions which defy all mathematical powers of calculation. Given the supply of a commodity, the urgency of the desire for it, and the amount of the funds in the hands of the persons desirous to purchase it, its price is still indeterminate. It will vary according as buyers and sellers combine or compete, according to the activity of credit and speculation, and according to other conditions which are subject to no ascertainable laws.

A proposition laid down by Mr. Jevons, in which we fully concur, is that "economics must be found on a full and accurate investigation of the conditions of utility, and to understand this element we must examine the wants and desires of man." An urgent desideratum in political economy is certainly the substitution of a true theory of what Mr. Jevons terms "the laws of human wants" for vague abstractions, such as the love of wealth and the aversion to labour. But wide historical investigation must precede the construction of the true theory. The authors to whom Mr. Jevons refers have made some instructive suggestions respecting the sub-ordination and successions of human wants, but they seem not to have perceived that these wants vary under different surrounding conditions and in different states of society. The order which the evolution of human wants follows is one of the enquiries that await a rising historical and inductive school of economists, which happily has no opposition to encounter from Mr. Jevons. But with respect to the deductive method, Mr. Jevons does not quite fairly represent the view of that school when he says, "I disagree altogether with my friend Mr. Leslie; he is in favour of simple deletion. I am for thorough reform and reconstruction." We are, it is true, for deletion of the deductive method of Ricardo; that is to say, of deduction from unverified assumptions respecting "natural values, natural wages, and natural profits." But we are not against deduction in the sense of inference from true generalisations and principles, though we regard the urgent work of the present as induction, and view long trains of deduction with suspicion.

We have been able to touch only a few of the problems discussed in Mr. Jevons' treatise. It is one which requires a considerable intellectual effort on the part of the reader, but the effort will bring its reward, even where it may not end in entire assent to the views of the eminent author.

T. E. C. Leslie.

GENERAL INDEX

Compiled by Barbara Lowe

Alphabetisation is normally by word rather than by letter, e.g. all entries beginning with 'bank' precede entries beginning 'banker' or 'banking'. Normally, alphabetical order is used for sub-entries (e.g. vegetation), but other sequences may be preferred: chronological (e.g. Gladstone), or by subject matter (e.g. Robert Adamson). Where there is a strong or fundamental connection with Jevons himself, the sub-entry 'WSJ and' comes first, as in 'botany', but where the connection is purely incidental (as in 'Birmingham'), it takes its place alphabetically under 'w'.

Persons with a long entry usually end with a 'personal' paragraph, followed by published works (if any), and correspondence. The emphasis throughout is, naturally, on the relationship between person or subject to Jevons.

There are many cases where similar subject matter is discussed under different terms. The index is designed to guide the reader to these distinctions (even where there may not be much difference). This is particularly true of entries relating to cycles., e.g. cycles, fluctuations, periodicity, as well as particular aspects of cyclical occurrences, such as sunspots.

Married women are normally indexed under their married names, after their husband, but in special cases, where the woman is the more important character, the positions may be reversed (e.g. Anna and Henry Bishop, Mrs Gaskell and William Gaskell). On the whole, duplication of information has been avoided wherever possible, but the nature of the subject matter demands a considerable overlapping, (e.g. between 'utility' and 'value').

The abbreviation 'WSJ' is used throughout for William Stanley Jevons.

abacus, *see* logical abacus

Abdul Aziz, Sultan of Turkey, 1861–76, IV 194

Aberdeen, II 434

Aberdeen, Earl of: becomes Prime Minister, January 1853, I 87; resigns, February 1855, II 79, 122n3

abolition of slavery, II 134n7, 151, 409. *See also* slavery

Aborigines Protection Society (North Australia), IV 174, 176–7

Académie des sciences morales et politiques, IV 47, V 13

Academy
  review of *Theory of Political Economy* (Alfred Marshall, 1 April 1872), IV 5, VII 141–6; of ed. 2 (Cliffe Leslie, 26 July 1879), V 67, VII 157–62

article on Section F of British Association (Cliffe Leslie, 1878), IV 273

editor, *see* Appleton, Charles Edward

acoustics, I 91

actinometer: Bunsen's, II 124n16; WSJ's (his sun-gauge), 125n17, 161, 297n8, 344–5

actuaries, VII 88; Institute of, 89

Adam Smith Society, proposal for, *see* reprinting society

Adamson, Robert (1852–1902)
  succeeds WSJ as Professor at Owens College, IV 183, 226n1, V 55; his 'Life' of WSJ in *Owens College Magazine*, 136
  questions WSJ's formula for rate of interest, IV 226–7, his chapter on capital, 227, and his equations,

Adamson, Robert (*contd*)
228, 230–1; alterations in ed. 2 of *Theory of Political Economy* due to, 230n1, 231n2, V 61n1, 62nn2, 3
applies for examinership in Logic, University of London, IV 240
'discovery' of Gossen's utility theory of political economy, IV 267–9, 272, 278, 282; on Mill, V 61, 62; critical notice of Schröder (*Mind*, 1878), IV 231
joint editor with H. A. Jevons of *Pure Logic and Other Minor Works* (1890), I 52n5
letters from, IV 226–8, 230–1, 267–9, 299–301, V 52, 55, 60–1, 61–2
Adelaide, II 47n1, 48
Adelong goldfield, II 366, 368
Adie, John, of Edinburgh, inventor of the sympiesometer, III 147
ad valorem system of taxation, VI 136–7; abolished by Gladstone, 139
Afghanistan, IV 303
Afghan War, 303n2, V 73
Africa
annual gold product, IV 7
du Chaillu's explorations, II 436n6
locusts, II 174
WSJ tacks down the coast en route to Australia, I 102
agriculture
agrarian policy in Ireland, V 197; vendettas, 150n3
agricultural and industrial districts, VII 22; circulation of paper and coin in, IV 19; population, III 255, VII 5, 23–4; railways, 23
agricultural and manufacturing industry, VII 131
in colonial economy, II 282, VII 8; specie for transactions, III 192, 195–6
implements for, VI 24, 34; steam ploughs, 44, VII 30, 31
subdivision of agricultural land, VII 7
also mentioned, VI 21, 100
Aikin, Dr, II 440
Airy, Sir George Biddell (1801–92), Astronomer Royal, III 186n1
lecture on Eclipse of the Sun at the British Association (1861), II 435
on the French currency, III 186

Reports to the Visitor, V 100
letter from, III 186
also mentioned, IV 147
Alaska
fur trade, IV 155n1
purchase of, from Russia, IV 153–4
Albert, Prince Consort, I 71, 72, II 146n3
Alby, L., defends protectionism, IV 126
alcohol
annual expenditure on, VII 54
coal for brewing and distilling, VII 30
'Note on a new class of Alcohols' (Cahours and Hoffman), I 228n6
regulation of sales, VII 117
tax on, VI 134, 136; on wine and spirits, 137, 139, VII 8
see also beer; licensing reform; rum; wine
alcoholism, V 122n1
Aldrich, Henry (1647–1710): *Artis Logicae Compendium*, read by WSJ, II 433
Alexander II, Emperor of Russia, 1855–81: his assassination, V 143
Alexandra, Princess, of Denmark: marriage to Edward, Prince of Wales, I 190, III 6–8
Alexandria, II 132, 133n1; bombarded by the British (1882), V 200n5
Alfassa, M., joint translator into French of *Theory of Political Economy* (1909), IV 261n6
algebraic formulae as criterion of mathematical economist, IV 278, 283
Alglave, Emile (1842–1928), Professor of Public Finance at the Paris Faculty of Law, IV 86
'A Liberal M.P.', writer of a letter to *Pall Mall Gazette*, IV 150n4
alkali industry, II 134n6; Alkali Act (1863), 305n3
Allen, George Peter (1835–1905), WSJ's solicitor, IV 150
Allen, G. Peter, of the *Manchester Guardian*, I 46n1
Allen, Mrs G. Peter (Alice Boyce, 1837–1922), I 46n1. *See also* Boyce, Alice
Allen, Peter, of the *Manchester Guardian*, I 47n2
Allen, Mrs Peter (Sophia Taylor), I 47n2
Allen, Thomas, Euston Road bookseller, V 84, 159, 175, 196
Allen, William B., secretary of the Protective League, II 280n12; his letter

in the *Empire* answered by WSJ, 281

Allerton Hall, country home of WSJ's maternal grandfather, I 5, 59n5, 193

allotropy, I 69, 81n2, II 124, 159

alloys, *see under* gold

Allport, Henry Curzon (d. 1854), drawing master, settled in Sydney, II 48

Alps, I 121, II 175, 199; Mont Blanc, I 84, II 365

Alps, Australian, II 367

Altrincham, WSJ's marriage at (19 December 1867), I 211n5

aluminium, II 62n6; specimen for WSJ, I 121, II 175, 184–5, 199, 204, 357n1

Amalgamated Society of Carpenters, benefit payments, VI 73

America, *see* United States of America

America, discovery of, IV 170

American Almanac . . . , III 54

American Gas Light Journal, V 71n1

American Indians, II 384, 455

American Iron and Steel Association, IV 30, V 86n5

American Manufacturer, V 86

American Social Science Association: WSJ's paper, 'The Silver Question', read before (1877), IV 217, 266, V 187

Americans: WSJ's dislike of, II 78, 197, 206, 248, 259, 392, 430; Henry Jevons popular with, II 150; Herbert Jevons on, II 423, 'strongly Anti-American', 438

Amiens Cathedral, V 148

Amiens, Peace of (1802), V 13

Amiens, University of, I 105, II 98

'amount' in WSJ's theory of interest, IV 25

'Amphitrite', I 104

Amsterdam
  Bank of, VII 136
  commercial fluctuations, VI 117
  Exchange, IV 233
  ratio of gold to silver, VI 102

amusements
  writings on: backgammon or whist, and probabilities, II 30; popular amusements, IV 286–7; in Victoria gold towns, II 371; wages spent on, VI 61

WSJ's: blindman's buff, I 79; cards and

draughts, 103, 107, II 85; cribbage, I 106, II 424; cricket match in Sydney, 262; dancing parties, I 79; 'dissipated' at Cremorne Gardens, II 455; fishing in Minnesota, II 400, 411; a period of abstention, 410; quoits, 414; skating, I 84, 89, II 118, 303, 403, 424, V 84, Edgeworth's memories of him on the ice, 202; snowballing, I 84, 89, IV 303; a Spanish bull-fight, II 376, 396

other skaters, II 424, 439, V 86, 91–2; Thomas Jevons's usual rubber of whist, I 116

see also music; theatre

'Amusements of the People', *see* Jevons, W. S., Works

'An Australian Mountaineer', II 263, 264

Anderson, John, Professor of Natural Philosophy in University of Glasgow, founder of Anderson's Institution (1796), II 442n7; his theory of rent, IV 146

Anderson, John, WSJ's cabin mate on board the *Oliver Lang*, I 106, II 77, 80, 81, 82, 99

Anderson & Hunt, Messrs, I 193n6

Anderson's Institution (later, College), Glasgow: foundation, II 442n7; WSJ refuses offer of post at, 442

Andes, II 375, 387, 397

Andrew, a colonial young man, I 235, 238

Andrews, Thomas (1813–85), Professor of Chemistry, Queen's College, Belfast, II 191

'An Exact Thinker', pseudonym of WSJ, II 303n3, VII 11

Anglo-Saxon nations, VII 26
  degeneration of Saxon settlers in Australia, II 420

animals: centipede, II 207; dolphins, I 104, II 84–5, 97; dogs, tax on, VI 136, 138, WSJ's dogs, II 152, 181–2, 206–7; gorillas, du Chaillu's discoveries, II 436; grampus, I 108, II 100; locusts, II 174; oxen, VI 96; sheep and pigs, III 192; whale, II 375; wild cattle, 365

animal labour, VI 24, 37, VII 97

see also birds; horses; snakes

Annales des Ponts et Chausées, IV 192, 196, 249

Annali di Statistica, V 167

Annangrove Cottage, WSJ's second home in Sydney, I 21, 24, 111, 113, II 146–7, 158, 166, 176; his harmonium, I 32, II 147, 158, 162; meteorological observations taken from, 172, 269, 272; WSJ leaves, 270

Annette, at Mrs Mackenzie's lodging house in Gower Street, II 20

Annuaire du Bureau des Longitudes de 1878, V 13, 14, 16

annuities: Gladstone's plan for conversion of perpetual into terminable, VII 13–14; working-class investment in Government annuities, VII 54

Ansdell, Mr, inventor of instrument for detecting fire-damp, III 147

anthropology, WSJ's proposed book on, I 27, VII 118, 119

Antietam, Battle of (1862), II 454n7

Appleton, Charles Edward (1841–79), editor of the *Academy*, IV 273

Appleton and Company, American publishers, V 69

apprenticeship, VI 69–70, VII 48

Arabi Pasha, V 200n5

Arabs in Egypt, V 200

Araluen Valley, II 365

Arber, Edward (1829–1912), Professor of English Language and Literature, Birmingham University: reprints of rare books, V 73, 87

letter to, V 87

Arbuthnot, George (1802–65), Treasury official, II 157–8

Archdall, Mervyn, and John Lodge, *The Peerage of Ireland* (1872), V 123, 124, 125

Archer, Francis, Liverpool surgeon and botanist, I 55n1, 79

Archer, Samuel (d. 1902), friend and classmate of WSJ at University College: excursions with WSJ, I 55, 57, 59–60, 61; his plant specimens, 55n1, 62–3, 79n4; 'learning to doctor', II 78

Archibald, E. Douglas, Professor of Mathematics at Patna College: letter to WSJ on his plan for coordinating research on sun spots, V 56–7

Argentine Republic: proportion of silver to gold, V 140

Argyll, 8th Duke of (George Douglas Campbell, 1823–1900), *The Reign of Law* (1867), IV 53

aristocracy, V 98, VII 15–16; opposition to corn law repeal, III 130

Aristotle: read by WSJ for M.A. degree, II 422, 437; also mentioned, III 3, 13, 113, IV 15

arithmetic
  arithmetical increase of subsistence, VI 55, 57–8
  'linear arithmetic', IV 8, 9
  Pascal's arithmetical machine, VII 86

arithmometer, paper on the statistical use of (WSJ, 1878), VII 85–90

Armitage, Benjamin, M.P. for Salford, V 115

Armitage, Messrs E. & Sons, their playground for children, IV 287

Armstrong, Sir William George (1810–1900), engineer-entrepreneur: Presidential Address to British Association (1863) on coal production, IV 127–8, VII 14, 36; his hydraulic crane, VI 25

letter from, IV 127–8

Armstrong guns, II 408

army, as a profession, VI 66–7, VII 61, 63
  English soldiers going to Turkey, II 63

Arnold, Arthur, M.P. for Salford, V 115

Ascension Island, I 102, II 101

Ascher and Company, foreign booksellers, IV 3

Asia
  annual gold product, IV 7
  famines, VI 59
  paralysed by Russia, IV 225

assaying
  apparatus, II 49–50, III 50–1; balances, II 50, 113; bone earth, 60–1, 70; cupel machine, 60–1, 107, 108; gas fittings, 108, 113; melting furnace, 107, 108; standard assay gold, 55, 231

  assay procedure, II 70n2, 126–7; in Paris, II 62, diploma examinations, 70–1; at the Royal Mint, III 218; in Sydney, I 20, 206, 227, WSJ's paper on 'comparative determination', I 247, his improved methods, 345; assays in New Zealand, III 39, 48n2, 50–1, 150

die stamp for gold ingots, II 117, 204

'Gold Assaying', article by WSJ in *Dictionary of Chemistry*, I 20n5, II 247, 345, III 50, 51

laboratories, Graham's, I 97–8, II 49; WSJ's in Sydney, II 107, 113, 171

Manual of Assaying, III 51

pyx testing, II 231, 261

Trial Plates (Sydney Mint), II 162, 231–2; (Royal Mint, London), III 222, 223, 224

see also Paris Mint; Royal Mint; Sydney Mint. For WSJ as assayer *see under* Paris Mint *and* Sydney Mint

Association for the Freedom of Exchanges (France), V 41

Association for the Promotion of Social Science, *see* National Association for the Promotion of Social Science

Astronomer Royal, *see* Airy, Sir George Biddell

astronomy

astronomical periods, IV 275

astronomical physics, V 103n1

computation by machine, VII 86

sun established as a variable star, VII 92, 98

WSJ studies, I 96, II 53

also mentioned, VI 7, VII 44

atheism, II 326

Athelstan, King of England, VI 69

Athenaeum: WSJ elected to (1879), V 26, 35, 36, dines at, 123, finds too hot in winter, 178; members shaken by Mansion House bomb, 132

Athenaeum

Coal Question announced in (4 February 1865), VII 125

Economics of Industry reviewed (8 November 1879), V 80

Pure Logic reviewed (18 December 1863), VII 125

Serious Fall advertised, III 12

'Statistics of Shakespearean Literature' (WSJ, 12 March 1864), VII 125

WSJ advertises his literary agency in, I 182

Atholl, Duchess of, I 71

Atlantic Ocean, II 385

atomic theory

Lockyer's experiments, IV 294

WSJ's 'sublime idea' for, I 51–2

also mentioned, I 14, 78

Aurora Australis, I 108, II 100

Austin, John (1790–1859), first Professor of Jurisprudence at University College, London, V 22–3

Lectures on Jurisprudence, ed. 4(1873), V 102

Australasia

Bank of, II 147n1

studies of climate, I 23–4

trade in pepper and herring, V 49

Australasian Steam Navigation Co., I 123

Australia

books on, II 52–3; Kingsley's novel on bush life, 403

climate and weather: 'regular Australian weather' (fine), I 108, II 253, clear skies, 403; storms, I 108; rainy weather, II 182; winter the best part of the year, II 182; 'true Australian climate', 272; *Some Data Concerning the Climate of Australia and New Zealand* (WSJ), I 23–4, II 240n4, 332, 340–1, 363

damper, I 143, 146, 172, 175

emigration to, I 24, II 53–4, 83, 267–8, IV 7, VII 8

entertainment: Australian tours of international concert and theatre performers, II 170n1, 181n2, 224n3, 250n22, 257–8; travelling performers at inns, I 234

Government: 'Advance Australia', II 268; Australian Colonies' Government Act (1850), 205n5; franchise and protective tariffs, VII 43; 'Responsible Government' and ministerial crises, II 247–8

Herbert Jevons in, I 10, 182n2, 189, II 447, 448, III 3, 4, 15–16, 28, 31

newspapers, WSJ's collection, II 373

railways, I 135

towns, I 24, II 233; WSJ's study of, I 17, 28, II 297n10; his dislike of I 142, II 252; 'pleasant little towns', 373; *Social Survey of Australian Cities* (unpublished), I 159n1

Australia (contd)
  trade and industry: coal fields, VII 26–7; cotton exports, II 60; foreign exchange, VI 111, 114; imports, II 281, III 19–20, VII 19; minerals, II 50; wine production, VI 32; wool exports, VI 111, 114. See also under gold
  WSJ and, I 22–32; accepts offer of post as assayer in new Australian Mint, I 96, 117; his Australian years (1854–9) in retrospect, I 110, II 374, 382, once felt himself a naturalised Australian, 313; Christmas days in, I 134, 140, II 110–11, 205, 252–3; photography of Australian subjects, I 31, II 348n12, 352–5, of gold diggings, 340, 346, 364–5, 371; decision to leave, I 179, 184–5, 189n1, II 413; chooses overland route from Sydney to Melbourne, 334, 344, 366–72, 381; his Australian Journals, I 24, 30, II 374, 386, lost at Havana, I 25, II 374n1, 390, 398
  for details of WSJ's life in Australia see New South Wales; Sydney; Sydney Mint
Australian aborigines: 'Corbow', I 227; at the gold diggings, II 365; alleged poisoning by white squatters, IV 174–7; copper-coloured races in Australia, VII 123
Australian Almanac, see Waugh (and Cox) Australian Almanac
Australian Keepsake, I 136
Australian Photographic Review, I 31
Australian Sailing Directory (The Australian Directory, Vol I), II 235
Australian Sketches (19 February 1876), illustration of fight between diggers and blacks, IV 177
Australian view of England, II 255
Australians, I 146–7, 152–3, 162, 174–5, 219, 224, 229, 235, 238, II 420; aristocracy, 208; convicts, I 152, 223, 235, II 162, 170, 221; diggers, I 222, 227–8, II 83, 122n2, 346, 365, 370–1; ladies, I 225, 235, II 250–1, 253–4; 'snobs', I 234; tramps and tourists, II 365

Austria
  coalfields, III 71; coal production, VII 33
  commercial treaty with England (December 1865), III 71
  currency, III 199; gold coinage, V 58, 59, VII 67; adheres to International Monetary Convention, 74
  Seven Weeks' War, III 125n2; Italian wars of liberation against, V 37
  also mentioned, II 417n7, III 242
Ave Maria day, II 201–2
averaging machines, VI 25.
Axon, William Edward Armitage (1846–1913), member of the Manchester Guardian staff, V 195; editor of The Field Naturalist and Scientific Student, 195n4
  article by his young son, V 200
  letters to, V 195, 196, 200

B—, Mr, II 20
Babbage, Charles (1792–1877), Professor of Mathematics at Cambridge: On the Economy of Machinery and Manufactures (1832), VI 25, 29, VII 103
Babcock, George Herman (1832–93), American inventor of the polychromatic printing process, II 171–2
Bach, Johann Sebastian: Passion music performed in Salisbury Cathedral, V 43
Bacon, Francis, II 437; Liebig's criticism, III 78, 80–1; WSJ's criticism, IV 196
  Novum Organum, III 81; 3rd Aphorism, VI 22, 23; 4th Aphorism, 23–4; 'bordering instances', 45; 'common fund', IV 210, 215; on studies, VII 39, 41
Baden Powell, see Powell, Baden
Baden-Powell, [Sir] George Smyth (1847–98), M.P., colonial administrator, V 108
Bagehot, Walter (1826–77)
  as editor of the Economist, I 36, 182n3, II 450n1, III 19, IV 160; asks WSJ to write for it, III 86
  joint founder of University College Debating Society, I 39, 187n2
  joint editor of National Review, II 416n6
  testimonial for WSJ, III 86, 106, 114;

examines with WSJ for Ricardo Scholarship, IV 124n1

death, V 184

Lombard Street (1873), IV 78, VI 98n7, VII 105

letters from, III 86

also mentioned, I 65n4, 73n1

'Bagehot principle', IV 209n1

Bailey, A. H., President of the Institute of Actuaries: on the arithmometer, VII 89–90

Bailey, Frances, *see* Martineau, Mrs Russell

Bain, Alexander (1818–1903), Professor of Logic and English, Aberdeen, III 106; testimonial for WSJ, 107

'Theory of Euclid', IV 231

Baines, [Sir] Edward (1800–90), proprietor of the *Leeds Mercury*, III 100

Baines, James & Co., Liverpool shipping company, owners of the Black Ball Line, I 19, 107, II 111n3, 116n6, 133n1, 144, 146, 446; their day over, 231

bakers

in Manchester trade disputes, III 132–3

subsidiary trades employed by, VI 34

Balaclava, Battle of (1854), II 122n3

balance of payments, IV 252

balance of trade, VI 111–12

balance sheets, VI 77

Balfe, Michael, *The Bohemian Girl*, II 181

Balfour, David Miller (1811–1902), American broker: comments on *Serious Fall*, III 54–5; his tables of prices in *American Almanac*, 54n2, IV 6–7

letters from, III 54–5, IV 6–7

Balfour, Dr, Head of the Army Medical Department: remarks on the arithmometer, VII 89

Balfour, Eleanor Mildred (1845–1935), marriage to Henry Sidgwick, IV 157n4. *See also* Sidgwick, Mrs Henry

Ballarat: goldminers' insurrection, II 112, 122; gold discoveries, 351; visit to gold diggings, 344, 370–1

Ballarat Directory (1857), donated by WSJ to British Museum Library, II 449, 450n2

balloons, II 18, VI 24

Ballyheigue, ancestral home of the Cantillon family, V 123, 124, 125, 127

Baltimore, WSJ's first stop in U.S.A., II 381, 382, 383, 399

Banfield, Thomas Charles, IV 91n3; *Four Lectures on the Organization of Industry, . . .* (1845), VI 14, 15, 16n6

'bank', origins of word, IV 210, 214n1

Bank Act of 1844, I 181n4, III 140, 141, 164, IV 10, 13, 17, 107n1, 111–12, 165n2; subdivision of Bank of England under, 12n11, 32, VII 127; suspended (1847), VI 123, (1857), 125n5, 129, (1866), III 102n1; Hincks's pamphlet on, IV 158–9; examination questions on, VII 131, 132, 137

Bank of Amsterdam, VII 136

Bank of Belgium, VI 122

bank clerks, VI 77

bank directors, IV 209, 211, 232, 252, 264, VI 125; policy on bank rate, IV 252, 264n2

Bank of England

Bank Charter: Report of Committee of Secrecy on (1832), IV 264–5, 280; Bank Charter Act (1833), IV 11n8, 252; Bank Charter Act (1844), *see above*, Bank Act

banking and issue departments, III 140, IV 160–1, VI 127–8; separated by Peel in 1844, 127; 'lender of last resort', IV 209n1, 216n1; loans to merchants, VI 129

Bank officers, I 19, III 161n3, IV 264

crises in: (1696–9), VI 116n1; (1792), 118; (1797), 118; (1825–9), 119–20; (1836–9), IV 210, VI 122; (1857), 124–5, 129; (1866), VII 41; (1875), VI 98n7; Bank of England in a credit cycle, 130–1; and commercial panics, IV 275n5

deposits, VI 127–8

diagrams showing weekly accounts, 1844–1862, and circulation of notes, I 181n4, II 426–7, 451, 452, IV 112, VI 127n1

foundation (1694), VI 15

gold assays for, II 49, III 224; and investigations into gold coin in use, 161–4, 165, 190, 194, 195–6, 201, 202–3, VII 72; and recoinage of gold sovereigns, V 180–1

governors, III 114, 162–3, IV 265, V

Bank of England (contd)
    193; Court of Governors, IV 264
Liverpool Branch, II 55
and money market, IV 77, 111n1, VI
    127–9; London money market, IV
    220
publications, III 212, 232–3, VII 106
relations with joint stock and country
    banks, III 140, 195–6, IV 77, 140,
    159, 209, VI 130
reserves, IV 18, 31, in credit cycle, VI
    130; bankers' reserves, IV 111, 159;
    gold reserves, V 188, VI 113; note
    reserves, III 203, IV 77, 161, VI
    127, 128, 129
and the South Sea Company, VI 116,
    117n4
Usury Laws, supposed petition against,
    IV 252, 265, 279, 280; partial
    exemption from, IV 252n3
also mentioned, III 213, V 193, VI
    113n8, VII 133
see also bank notes; bank rate
bank failures, VI 125, VII 90–1; Bank of
    Belgium, VI 122; City of Glasgow,
    IV 293n1; country banks, VI 118;
    Douglas, Heron & Co., 117n6;
    Overend, Gurney & Co., III
    102n1; West of England Bank, IV
    304n6; stoppages, VI 118–19
Bank of France: crises and bank reserves, V
    13, VI 98; loan to Bank of England
    (1839), VI 122
Bank of the Netherlands, IV 57, 58, 76
Bank of New South Wales, New Zealand
    branches, see under Jevons, Herbert
bank notes
    Act of 1844 regulating issues, IV 10, 111,
    158–9; as credit, VI 105; as cur-
    rency, VI 107; always represen-
    tative money, VI 96; case for uni-
    form issue, IV 18
Bank of England: note issues, II 11n8,
    18, IV 16, 111–12, VI 127, 129, in
    1720, VI 116; should be sole issuer,
    IV 77; a £10 note for WSJ, II 55
country bank notes, III 203, IV 11n8,
    12, 16–18, 118; restrictions on issue,
    IV 77; demand for, in Yarmouth
    fisheries, 78–9; in credit cycle, VI
    130
joint-stock bank notes, VI 127n1, 129

£1 notes: prohibited, IV 78, 118, V 181,
    192, 193; could be safely issued, IV
    160–1; us : in Ireland, III 190; a
    chest full (1825), VI 120
Scotch and Irish notes, III 203, IV 13,
    18, 107n1, 161; notes in Wales, III
    191–2
small notes in Canada, IV 158–9, 161–2
Walras on 'billets de banque', V 96
bank rate
in financial crises, IV 231–2, 304n6, VI
    125; varies in inverse proportion to
    reserves, 129; as means of correct-
    ing foreign exchanges, IV 251–2,
    264–5, VI, 129
and usury laws, IV 11n8, 17, VI 121
Bank of Scotland, VI 115
bankers, IV 17, V 153, VI 68, VII 59, 71,
    133; and note issues, IV 18, 77, 78–
    9, 98–9, 107n1, 118; reserves in the
    Bank of England, IV 111, 159,
    threat to close Bank of England,
    161
Bankers' balances, IV 31, 209
London bankers, IV 187, 210
Bankers' Institute, V 130, 181n2; exam-
    inations, 80. See also Journal of In-
    stitute of Bankers
Bankers' Magazine, The: edited by Inglis
    Palgrave, IV 105n4, 217n1, V 85,
    129–30; articles by Palgrave, IV
    76–7, 98, 118, 168n1, 169, by G. H.
    Pownall, V 130n2
The Silver Question (paper by WSJ read
    before American Social Science As-
    sociation, 1877), reprinted in, IV
    217–18, V 187, VII 127
Banking Almanac and Directory, edited by
    Inglis Palgrave, IV 105, V 90,
    130
banking system, III 140, VI 115; in Liver-
    pool, V 153–4
books on, VII 105; chapter on, in Money
    and the Mechanism of Exchange, VI
    107
country banks, IV 12, VI 130. See also
    under bank notes
examination questions on, VII 136, 137
Gazette returns, IV 78–9
joint-stock banks: reckless conduct, II
    140, allow too much interest, IV
    209–10; scheme for common re-

serve, 209n1. *See also under* bank notes

new banks, III 102

Palgrave's 'Notes on Banking . . .' (1873), correspondence with WSJ on, IV 10–14, 16–19

reserves, IV 12, 17, 77, 78, 159, V 181 *see also* panics, *and under* separate countries

bankruptcies

in America, V 11–12, VI 122

bankrupts' estates, VII 89

and credit cycles, VI 131

in England, IV 273–4, VI 117, 118, 119; in the Jevons and Roscoe families, I 12

in Europe, VI 117

and rise in price of corn, II 450

also mentioned, VII 64–5

Barbados, I 80, IV, 157n1, 158

Bardswell, Mary Ann, *see* Roscoe, Mrs Richard

Barham, Mr, *see* Foster-Barham, Alfred Garrett

Barker, Thomas (1838–1907), Professor of Mathematics at Owens College, I 42, III 76; on WSJ's equations, IV 87

Barned's Banking Co., Ltd., VI 126

Barnett, Morris, *The Serious Family*, II 278

barometers

WSJ's: aneroid barometer, I 216, 217, II 217, 404, recommended for measuring air pressure in pits, III 147; mountain barometer, I 159, 163, 165, 167, 175, 176; in his home in Sydney, II 113, 172, 309

Melbourne Observatory readings, II 372

ship's barometer on board the *Chrysolite*, II 386

article on, in Sydney *Empire*, VII 123

use of, to measure air pressure in coal pits, III 144–7; readings associated with pit explosions in 1866, 145

also mentioned, II 124, 180

Barrault, H. E., joint translator into French of *Theory of Political Economy* (1909), IV 261n6

Barrett, [Sir] William Fletcher (1844–1925), Professor of Physics, Royal College of Science, Dublin: letter to

WSJ on music and the weather, V 35

Barry, Sir Charles (1795–1860), architect, II 30n5

Barry, Edward Middleton (1830–80), architect, II 30n5

barter, IV 104n11; foreign trade as, VI 108, 109

Basel: WSJ visits, III 81; Thomas Jevons visits, II 199

Basile, Antonio, editor of *Economista d'Italia*, IV 84

Bass Straits, II 386

Bastiat, Frédéric (1801–50), French economist, IV 72, 91n3, V 41, 95; examination questions on, VII 133, 134, 136, 138

Economic Sophisms, VII 102, 160

Harmonies Économiques, IV 72n1, V 196–7, VII 10, 51, 148

'What is seen and what is not seen', VII 46, 51, 59

Bateson, William Henry (1812–81), Master of St John's College, Cambridge, IV 148

Bateson, Mrs William Henry, IV 148

Bath, British Association meeting at (1864), III 59

Bath Abbey, IV 129

Bathurst, New South Wales: WSJ tours, I 225–6, lodges at, 234; road and rail connections, II 217, 263, 265; also mentioned, I 24, 128, 152n1

Bathurst mail, I 230, 234

Baudeau, Abbé Nicolas (1730–92), Physiocrat, IV 91n3

Baxendell, Laws of atmospheric ozone, VII 126

Baxter, Robert Dudley (1827–75), pioneer in statistics: paper on National Debts, read to British Association at Liverpool (1870), III 242, IV 9

The Panic of 1866 . . . , III 140

letter from, III 242–3

Baynes, Thomas Spencer (1823–87), asks WSJ for contribution to *Encyclopaedia Britannica*, ed. 9, V 55

Beal, James (d. 1891), land agent, letter to, V 79

Beal, Mrs, *see* Husson, Mrs

Beardsall, Mr, of Manchester, V 25

Beaumaris, home of John and Lucy Hut-

Beaumaris (*contd*)
ton, I 11, II 460, III 30, 32, 158; WSJ visits, II 446, 447, III 14, 33–4, 48, 56–7, 59, writes *The Coal Question* at, 97, spends Christmas at, 149

Beaumont, Somerset Archibald (1836–1921), M.P.: letter from, on *The Coal Question*, III 71

Becker, Lydia Ernestine (1827–90), founder of the Manchester Women's Suffrage Committee: attends British Association meeting (1875), IV 129

Becket, Mr, F.G.S., VII 15

Beckwith, Mr, WSJ attends his private school in Liverpool, I 13, 58, 77n2, 115

Beer, tax on, III 239; brewing, VII 30

Beethoven, Ludwig van, I 178, II 314, 320–1, III 99–100
chamber works arranged for piano, IV 56; *Engedi*, II 328, 329; *Fidelio*, 296; *Letters*, III 90; *Missa Solemnis*, II 296; *Mount of Olives*, 320, 369; *Pastoral (Sixth) Symphony*, 320; piano sonatas, III 100, IV 199; Second Symphony, III 100; waltzes, II 339
song recital at St James's Hall, London, II 458

Beeton, H. R., V 106n2

Belfast
newspapers, V 111
the Queen's College, V 169n1

Belgium
coal production, VII 27, 33, 34, 50
currency: 'double standard', VI 101, VII 66; gold coinage, V 59; international money, III 212
iron manufacture, III 128
labour market, III 151n2; competition from her cheap labour, 239, VII 49–50
WSJ visits, I 211, III 158
also mentioned, VII 100
see also Bank of Belgium

Bell, Alexander Graham (1847–1922), inventor of the telephone, V 108

Bell, George (1814–90), bookseller and publisher, V 81

Bell, [Sir] Isaac Lowthian (1816–1904), industrialist: 'Notes' on industrial

resources of northern England, III 71

Bellini, Vincenzo (1801–35): *La Sonnambula*, II 181, 224; *Norma*, 224, 278n9, 298; *Puritani di Scozia*, 277, 289, 298

'Ben Carver', of the Blue Mountains, New South Wales, I 146, II 253

Bendigo: gold nuggets from, II 127n5; visit to, 344, 370, 372, 385

benevolence, in moral theory, I 132

Bengal: periodic scarcities, V 45; grain prices, 46, 51; wages and prices, VII 138

Bennett, Alfred William (1833–1902), botanist, member of the Society of Friends, II 64–5

Bennett, Edward Trusted (1831–1908), member of the Society of Friends, II 64–5

Bennett, Samuel (1815–78), revives the *Empire*, Sydney newspaper, II 341n4

Benson, —, former owner of pamphlets bought by WSJ, V 146

Benson and Mallett, Liverpool stationers and printers, II 462

Bentham, Jeremy (1748–1832)
on capital, VI 36; on ignorance and knowledge, VII 45; on population, VI 55
his term 'Utilitarian', V 75; Utilitarian theory, VII 159–60

Bentley, Mary, family servant of the Jevons, I 9, II 36, 176, 183, 214; makes bun loaves and raspberry vinegar for WSJ, II 81; laid up with a poisoned thumb, 95; visit from WSJ, 390–1; supported in retirement by Jevons family, 441; attends Roscoe Jevons's funeral, III 205

Bentley, publisher, IV 213

benzole gas, the 'New Light', II 91

Berdan, Mr, mining machinery manufacturer, II 92

Berdan Gold Machine Company, II 92n3; their machines, 92, 94

Bergen, V 143

Berkeley, George (1685–1753), philosopher, II 437, V 127

Berlin
H. E. Roscoe's account of, II 72–3

International Statistical Congress meet at, III 49, VII 125

Royal Academy of Berlin, IV 4

Society of Economists, III 197

Berlioz, Louis Hector (1803–69), V 132n4; WSJ's enthusiasm for, 131–2

Béatrice et Bénédict, V 132n3; *Childhood of Christ*, 131, 134; *Damnation of Faust*, 123, 131, 134; *Romeo and Juliet*, 134

Bermondsey, expeditions to, I 77, 84, 91; tanneries, 90n3, 91; Jacob's Island, 84, 90

Berne Convention (1886), on international copyright, V 69n1; *see also* copyright

Bessemer, [Sir] Henry (1813–98), inventor of the Bessemer steel process, VI 29

Bessemer Saloon Steamship, VI 91

Best, William Thomas (1826–97), organist, II 142

Betsy, Aunt Jane Hornblower's maid, II 28

Bible

WSJ and: reads New Testament with Aunt Jane, I 64; attempts a history of Christ, 99; finds no evidence for inspiration of the bible, 155; his faith not based on, II 312

Faith, Hope and Charity, I 30, II 258; *Genesis*, I 159, II 330–1; geology and scripture, I 156; locusts, II 174; Our Daily Bread, III 132–3; *Psalms*, II 329; sowing and reaping, V 113; sparrows, I 157; to him that hath, II 23

The Four Gospels (Livermore), III 45

Biblioteca dell' Economista: Italian translation of *Theory of Political Economy* published in, IV 94n1, 98; translation of *Quatre mémoires* (Walras), 270; also mentioned, 181

Bibliothèque scientifique internationale, proposed volume on mathematical political economy, IV 289, 290

Bibliothèque Universelle et Revue Suisse, V 21, 22–3

bills of exchange, V 153, VI 105; accommodation bills, VI 106, 114; in anticipation, 114; bills created, 130, in 1831, 120, 121; bills due, 105, 107; exemption from usury laws, IV 252n3; for foreign trade,

VI 108–11, 114–15, VII 132; inland bills, VI 130; as money, 107

bimetallism

bimetallic money, IV 163, VI 100, or double standard, 101–2

debate on, at Political Economy Club, V 191, Grenfell's suggestions, 192–3

Economist articles on, V 188

France's double standard, III 196–7, V 139, VI 100–2, VII 66, 67–8; considered for India, IV 187, V 140n3, 142

WSJ's opposition to, V 138n1, 140, 187–8; writings on, IV 266, V 188n2, 187, 189, *Investigations* intended for controversy on, 158, 159n1, 191, 201; Wagner's music an antidote to, 194; the subject not 'worth much powder and shot', 139, collapses with inflows of gold, 178

other views on: Mills's letter on, V 138–9; opposed by Chevalier, III 208n1; not recommended by Isaac Newton, V 44; supported by Cernuschi, 139, by Langley, IV 186n2, by Mallet, V 140n3

Binney, Edward William (1812–81), geologist, III 63

Biograph, The, 'Life' of WSJ (May 1881), V 136

Bird, Dr, surgeon and lodging-house keeper, II 13, 17

birds: albatrosses and Cape pigeons, I 104, II 97–8, 375; booby birds and pelicans, 375; cockatoos and others in Janbecumberre, Australia, II 365; nightingale in Hampstead, V 99

Birdwood, Sir George Christopher Molesworth (1823–1917), of the India Office, V 49n1, 54; study of early trade with India, 48, letter to WSJ on, 49–50, 54

Birkenhead

earthquake felt in, I 71

Kenyon Terrace, home of Uncle William Jevons, II 26

Melbourne compared to, II 370

visit to iron ship-building yard, I 85, 93

also mentioned, IV 250, V 99

Birmingham
  British Association meet at (1865), III
    99n2
  Brummagen politics, V 115
  factories, VII 60; hardware, 19; metal
    trades, VI 32; small manufacturers,
    VII 62
  Iron Masters meetings, I 120, II 163–4
  Roscoe Jevons's asylum, I 8, 120, II 163,
    visited by WSJ, 391
  WSJ 'stops off' at, I 85, 94
  also mentioned, II 90n1, 155, 431n16, V
    50n4
Bishop, Anna, singer (Ann Rivière, 1810–
    84), concerts in Sydney, II 224
Bishop, [Sir] Henry (1786–1855), com-
    poser, husband of Ann Rivière, II
    224n3
Black Ball Line
  clippers for emigration trade, II 111n3,
    116n6
  Oliver Lang, 1272-ton clipper, WSJ
    sails to Australia on, I 19
  ships used by Admiralty during Crim-
    ean War, II 133n1
  Startled Fawn, iron-built clipper, II 132,
    144
  see also Baines, James & Co.; ships
Blackheath, New South Wales, I 146, 237
blacksmiths, VI 30, 31, VII 19, 31, 61
Blake, William Phipps (1825–1910), Pro-
    fessor of Mineralogy and Geology
    in California; The Production of the
    precious metals, III 203
Blanqui, Adolphe Jérome, Histoire
    de l'Economie Politique en Europe, VII
    102; English translation, 102–3
Blondin, Charles (1824–97), his rope-walk
    across Niagara seen by WSJ, II 401
Bloxam, Charles Loudon (1831–87), Pro-
    fessor of Practical Chemistry at
    King's College, London, II 229
Blue Mountains, New South Wales: ex-
    peditions to, I 2; (March 1856), II
    217; (Christmas 1856–7), I 134n3,
    137–54, II 253; Blue Mountain
    Inn, I 237
  railway project through, II 263–5
  sandstone ridges, I 221, II 264
Blundel, Captain, student at Owens Col-
    lege, I 196
Blunt, of the Queen's Own Rifles, in

Vancouver Island, II 440
Board of Trade, IV 222n6, 305n1
  meteorological log for, kept by WSJ on
    board ship, II 374, 386
  President of, see Bright, John; Cardwell,
    Edward; Chamberlain, Joseph
Boccardo, Gerolamo (1829–1904), econ-
    omist and statistician, IV 48, 262
  elected to Statistical Society, V 31–2, 42,
    60
  La legge di periodicità delle crisi . . .
    (1879), copy sent to WSJ, V 32
  publishes article by Walras, IV 181
  translates Theory of Political Economy into
    Italian, IV 94, 103, and Quatre
    mémoires (Walras), 270
  letter from, V 31–2
Bochsa, Robert Nicolas Charles (1789–
    1856), harpist, II 224n3
Bodio, Luigi (1840–1920), director of the
    Central Statistics Office of the Ital-
    ian Government, IV 48, 68, 298–9
  interest in mathematical treatment of
    political economy, IV 80
  is sent Theory of Political Economy, IV 80,
    95, 97, and other pamphlets, 154, V
    198
  visits Owens College, IV 95
  statistical publications, IV 154, V 198;
    Monografia statistica della Città di
    Roma . . . (1878), IV 299, V 197–8
  treatise on savings banks, IV 154
  letters to, IV 80, 95, 154, V 197–8;
    letters from, IV 97–8, 298–9
Boehmert, Karl Viktor (1829–1918), Pro-
    fessor of Political Economy in Dres-
    den, V 15
Boers, Gladstone makes peace with, V 135
Bohemia, coalfields, III 71, VII 34
Bohn, Henry George (1796–1884), book-
    seller and publisher: his typo-
    graphy, V 81
Boisguillebert, Pierre le Pesant (1646–
    1714), Le Détail de la France (1695),
    V 149–50
Bolckow, Vaughan & Co., Cleveland iron
    firm, III 229
Bolingbroke, Henry St John, Viscount
    (1678–1751), an early allusion to
    survival of the fittest, IV 4
Bolton, Anne, family nurse of the Jevons, I
    19, II 16, 95, 111, 183, 214; sister of

Charles Bolton, I 106n4, II 341; goes to Wales with the family, I 120, II 89, 155; her cousin, 127; a box of insects from WSJ, 174, and a note, 299; retires to the country, 390-1

Bolton, Charles, brother of Anne: goes with WSJ as his assistant to Sydney, I 19, 20, 106, 109n2, II 77, 78, 81, 82, 89, 95, 107, 129, 136, 174, 195, 198-9; his salary, 162; illness and death of his wife, 295; leaves the Mint for gold diggings, I 24, II 340, 341-2, 346, 405; WSJ visits his camp, 364; returns to the Mint, 418, 451; settles in Australia, I 106n4

Bolton, Mrs Charles (Barbara Mary MacMartin), II 342; illness and death, 295

Bolton, cousin of Anne and Charles, his nuggets of gold, II 127

Bolton, —, schoolboy, fellow-lodger of WSJ at Mrs Mackenzie's boarding house, I 100n1, II 14, 17, 20, 25

Bolton family, of Liverpool, I 100n1, II 14

Bonaparte, Louis Napoleon: his *coup d'état* against the Second Republic (2 December 1851), II 30n6. *See also* Napoleon III

Bond, G. P., of Harvard Observatory, VII 96

bonds
dock, VI 106
Exchequer, VI 116
long-term public utilities, VI 106n4
perpetual, VI 104
Turkish loan, VI 113n8
U.S., held in Europe, IV 220

bons du Trésor, V 5-7

bonus schemes, III 153, VI 77-8

bookbinding, WSJ's early interest in, I 99

bookkeeping, II 78
'book credit', VI 104
capital and current expenditure in accounting, VI 47
lectures for WSJ in, II 78

Boole, George (1815-64), Professor of Mathematics, Queen's College, Cork: WSJ 'involved' in his probabilities, I 201; his equations of quantity and quality confused, III 13; his mathematical system and WSJ's new Formal Logic, 34-5, 104, 110, 111, 113; his system worked on the logical abacus, 69; also mentioned, 76n2

The Mathematical Analysis of Logic (1847), IV 231

Booth, Alfred, & Co., Brazil Steam Ships, I 77n2; WSJ speculates in, II 210n2, III 150

Booth, Charles (d. 1860), Liverpool corn merchant, uncle of Harry Roscoe, I 77n2, II 29, 292, 230n14

Booth, Mrs Charles (Emily Fletcher), II 230n14

Booth, Rt Hon. Charles James (1840-1916), statistician, co-founder of Booth Line of steamships, cousin of Harry Roscoe, I 77n2, II 29n1, 230n14

Booth, Henry (1788-1869), promoter of Manchester and Liverpool Railway, II 29n1

Booth, Thomas, cousin of Harry Roscoe, I 77n2, II 29n1; goes to University of Cambridge, II 230

Borchardt, Dr Louis, of Manchester, IV 148n8

Borchardt, Malvina Henrietta (d. 1916), pioneer student at Girton College, Cambridge, IV 148n8; a journey with WSJ, IV 148-9

Bostock, Dr John, I 60n2

Boston, U.S.A.
customers of Jevons Iron firm, II 138
shipyards, II 111n3
WSJ sails from, II 384n1, 390, 401

botany
WSJ's early interest in, I 99, 113, II 256; studies botany at University College, I 54, examination in, 55-6; wins the prize, 58, III 110; his prize books, I 66, 77; plans to continue study, 78, prefers Natural to Linnaean classification, 63; specimen collecting, I 56, 57, 59, 60, 61, 96; his herbarium, 61, 62, 64; first botanical walk round Hampstead, 95
botanising in Australia, I 145, 146, 153, II 53, 78, 106, 130, 158, 253, 256, 332, 342, 346; his Botanical tin collecting box, I 135, 141, 147, 152, II 254

botany (*contd*)
  Botanical Gardens, I 60n2 II 106, 142
  Francis Archer's natural history collection, I 79n4
Botany Bay, I 161, 162; excursions to, II 110, 196-7, 207, 208; 'lags' of, 223
Boucher, Louisa, *see* Rylett, Mrs Harold
Bouguer, Pierre (1698-1758) physicist, astronomer, VII 96
Boulogne, V 148
Boult, S. Winton (1809-76), founder of the Liverpool Fire Office, II 60, 131; his two sons, II 60
Boult, Mrs S. Winton (née Grundy), II 118, 166
Boulton, Matthew (1728-1809), founder of the Soho engineering works, VI 28
Bowen, Francis (1811-90), Professor of Natural Religion at Harvard: uses *Elementary Logic* in his classroom, III 239; recommended to Walras, IV 66
  letter from, III 239
Bowenfels, New South Wales, I 222, 223, 235
Bowman, John Eddowes (1819-54), Professor of Practical Chemistry at King's College, London, II 229
Bowring, Sir John, III 238n1
box making, V 84; 'Boy' engaged in, 132
Boyce, Alice (1837-1922), cousin of Harriet Taylor, friend of WSJ, I 46, 197; marries G. Peter Allen, 46n1
Boyce, Miss, *see* Taylor, Mrs John Edward
Bradshaw railway timetable, II 388
Braidwood goldfields, excursion to, I 24, 33, II 358, 364-5
Brande, William Thomas (1788-1866), Professor of Chemistry at the Royal Institution, II 50, III 165
Brassey, Thomas, 1st Earl (1836-1918), M.P.: letter to WSJ on regulation of wages, IV 51; publications, 51nn1, 2
Brazil
  British sovereigns in, III 162, 163
  droughts, V 65
  woods exhibited at Paris Exhibition, II 184
Brazil steam ships, I 77n2; speculation in, II 210n2, III 150

bread
  degrees of utility of, VI 85-8, VII 149, 161
  price of (1872), III 256; cheap bread and consumption in general, III 55
  also mentioned, III 20, V 53, VI 60
Bremner, fellow lodger of Herbert Jevons in New Zealand, III 39
Brentano, Lujo (1844-1931), economist, V 42
  History and Development of gilds, VI 69n1
Brewer, William Henry Brooks (b. 1842)
  awarded medal in final B.A. examinations, IV 3; acts as substitute lecturer for WSJ at Owens College, 3n1, 21, 22-4, V 177, VI ix
  list of books relating to the mathematical treatment of economics, IV 8-9, 242, 249
  appointed examiner for Victoria University, V 177
  reviews Cairnes's treatise on Political Economy, IV 60
  letters to, IV 3, 5-6, 22-4, 242, 249; letters from, III 8-9, 14-15, 19
brewers, III 159
Breymann, Hermann, Lecturer in French and German at Owens College, IV 108, 110
bricklayers, VII 47
bricks
  made by machine, VI 74, VII 30, for workmen's dwellings, 47
  production of, as indication of commercial storms, II 427, VI 123
Bridlington, Mr, Sub-Postmaster at Hull, III 180
Briggs, Messrs, colliery owners: profit-sharing schemes, III 143, 151, VI 77
Briggs, Mrs, servant of the Jevons family, II 391
Briggs, W. E., M.P., V 194
Bright, Jacob (1821-99), V 164n2
Bright, Mrs Jacob (Ursula Mellor): letter to *Manchester Guardian* on rights of married women, V 164
Bright, John (1811-89), M.P., President of the Board of Trade, III 161
  abused by the *Spectator*, II 432, and by *The Times*, III 135
  speech on foreign policy (April 1879), V

Bright (*contd*)
　49, 50n4
　letter from, III 161
　also mentioned, II 88n3, V 164n2
Brighton
　cost of coal, VII 21
　Grand Hotel and new Pier, III 46
　home of Uncle William Jevons Jun., II
　　443, 444, III 10, 46, 69, 70, 73
　libraries, *Coal Question* not available at,
　　III 72
　National Association for the Promotion
　　of Social Science meets at (1875),
　　IV 181
　WSJ's visit to (1881), V 132
Brinley, Caroline, *see* Macmillan, Mrs
　Alexander
Brinsmead, John (1814–1908), manufac-
　turer of pianos, V 190
Bristol
　British Association meet at (1875):
　　paper on 'Progress of the Coal
　　Question' read at, IV 55n6, 128n4,
　　235; abstract of paper on Sun spots
　　presented to, 128, 129; also men-
　　tioned, 181n4
　Brunel's *Great Britain* built at, II 42n4
　St Mary's, Redcliffe, IV 129
　Unitarians, II 65n7
Bristol University: Marshall becomes Prin-
　cipal and Professor at, IV 128n1; re-
　signs owing to health (1881), V 170;
　returns as Professor (1882), 170n3
Britain, *see* England; Great Britain
*British Almanac, . . . with The Companion to
　the Almanac*, V 45, VI 32
British Association meetings
　(1854) at Liverpool, I 118, 197, II 75,
　　79, 94–5, 434; Foucault's experi-
　　ments, 102–3, 104–5
　(1855) at Glasgow, H. E. Roscoe's paper
　　on light chemistry read before, II
　　191–3
　(1861) at Manchester: WSJ reports on,
　　for *Manchester Examiner*, I 25, 35, II
　　434–6; Dr John Smith's paper, I 25,
　　36, II 435; Thorold Rogers's paper,
　　III 475; WSJ's first paper 'On the
　　deficiency of rain in an elevated
　　rain gauge', 35–6, read by R. B.
　　Clifton, 187n1; du Chaillu's paper
　　on gorillas, II 436; telegraphic

　soiree, 434–5
　(1862) at Cambridge: 'Notice of a Gen-
　　eral mathematical theory of Econ-
　　omy' read before, I 37, 188n1, II
　　452, 456, III 104, 166, IV 40, V 80,
　　VII 77, 124; 'The Study of Periodic
　　Commercial Fluctuations' read
　　and approved, I 37, 188n1, III 104,
　　VII 124
　(1863) at Newcastle: *Serious Fall* quoted
　　in Fawcett's paper 'On the Effects
　　of the recent Gold Discoveries', I
　　192n2, III 36, 37, 42, 43, 44; Sir W.
　　G. Armstrong's Presidential Ad-
　　dress on the coal question, IV 127–
　　8, VII 14
　(1864) at Bath, H. E. Roscoe's papers
　　read before the Chemistry section,
　　III 59
　(1865) at Birmingham, *The Coal Question*
　　recommended in Lord Stanley's
　　Presidential Address, III 99
　(1869) at Exeter, Royal Commission on
　　the relation of the state to science
　　appointed through efforts of the
　　Association, III 237n2
　(1870) at Liverpool: WSJ's Presidential
　　Address to Economic Section, III
　　236, 243–4, VI 59n14, VII 126; Re-
　　port advocating metric system for
　　weights and measures, III 238; Bax-
　　ter's paper on 'National Debts', 242
　(1875) at Bristol, IV 104, 128–30,
　　181n4, 183; 'On the Progress of the
　　Coal Question' (WSJ), IV 55n6,
　　128n4, 235; 'On the Influence of
　　the Sun-Spot Period upon the Price
　　of Corn' (WSJ), IV 128, 129, 188–
　　9, 199, 272n2, VI ix; *Second Report on
　　Combinations of Capital and Labour*,
　　IV 130n1
　(1878) at Dublin: 'On the Periodicity of
　　Commercial Crises and its Physical
　　Explanation', paper read in WSJ's
　　absence, IV 271–2, 274, V 47, 57,
　　VII 94; Ingram's Address to the
　　Economic Section, IV 272, 273n6,
　　276, V 124n1, 125; Cliffe Leslie on
　　Section F, IV 273
British Columbia, II 439, 441, IV 157;
　land prices, IV 420
British Dominions, I 48

British Empire: Sydney sovereigns made legal tender throughout, II 127n4; gold supplies, VII 74

British Guiana, IV 157n1, 158

British Institute, I 85

British Meteorological Society, II 323n4

British Museum
  Catalogues, IV 3, V 12; errors in Cantillon entries, 120-2
  officials of the Museum, II 392n18, 436n7, V 45, 120n1, 122n1
  WSJ and: schoolboy visits to, II 9; explores Sculptures section, I 80, Nineveh sculptures, II 18; visits Greek Antiquities and Minerals, I 83, 84; meets his father by chance, II 30; commences reading in Library (1860), I 180, II 416; his source of learning, I 182, half his time spent at, 185-6; takes a violent dislike to, 189; presents printed and MS documents to, II 449-50; works on *Coal Question* at, I 43, III 58, VII 125, on *Statistical Diagrams*, II 426; regrets leaving (1863), III 10; wishes to return to, IV 107; later visits to, 279, V 120, 131
  also mentioned, III 233, 234, IV 233, 302, V 91

British Quarterly Review
  review of Macdonnell's *Survey of Political Economy* and WSJ's *Theory of Political Economy* (1872), III 246
  review of *Principles of Science* (1874), VII 127

British Record Society, IV 297n1

'British Worker, A', writer of letter to *Manchester Examiner* protesting against WSJ's Cobden lecture, III 129; reply to, 131-2, 135

Britons in Wales, II 89

Brittain, Frederick, *British Trade and Foreign Competition*, IV 251

Broadfield, Edward John (1831-1913), journalist, former student of WSJ at Owens College, III 70, 93, 99; writes testimonial for WSJ, 99, 118-19
  bereavements, IV 249-50
  collection of books on economics, IV 249
  election activities, V 97
  on Manchester School Board, V 3

letters to, IV 134-5, 249-50, V 3, 97-8; letters from, III 70, 72, 93, 199-200, V 67
  also mentioned, I 10n2

Broadfield family, V 112

Broderick family, II 125

Brodie, [Sir] Benjamin (1817-80), Professor of Chemistry at Oxford, I 81; his equations for the chemical calculus questioned, III 155-7
  letters to, III 155, 156-7; letters from, III 155-6

Brontë, Charlotte (Currer Bell), II 311-12, 337
  Jane Eyre, WSJ finds his creed in, II 310, 311, 312
  Shirley, WSJ reads, II 311
  Life of Charlotte Brontë, by Mrs Gaskell, I 178n2, II 337n1

Brooke, Gustavus Vaughan (1818-66), Irish actor in Sydney, II 170, 257; his Shakespearean roles, 278

Brotherton, Edward, I 47n3

Brougham, Lord, II 34, 322n9

Broun, John Allan (1817-79), pioneer of scientific meteorology, V 8n4; on sun-spot cycles, IV 293n1, V 8, 11, VII 92, 94

Brown, John, & Co., WSJ's investments in, V 155, 190

Brown, Mr (V 11), *see* Broun, John Allan

Brown, Mr, assistant secretary, University College, London V 137

Brown, S., advocates international coinage scheme, III 213

Brown, Thomas, Sheriff's bailiff, Sydney, II 182

Brown, W., letter to WSJ on the translation of Primers into Indian vernaculars, V 18-19

Brown, William (1784-1864), M.P., supports decimal coinage, II 155-6; letter to Thomas Jevons, II 157-8

Browning, Mr, of the Manchester Chamber of Commerce, III 183

Brunel, Isambard Kingdom (1806-59), engineer: the *Great Britain*, iron-built ship, II 42, 60; the *Great Eastern*, III 78, 124, VI 91

Brunel, Sir Marc Isambard (1769-1849), engineer, father of Isambard Kingdom:

Thames Tunnel, I 91n2, II 61n3, 449, VI 91

material relating to both Brunels donated to the British Museum Library by WSJ, II 449

Brunton, Sir Thomas Lauder (1844–1916), physician, writer of articles on social questions, V 122

Brussels, II 362n1, V 106, 138n1

Bryant, Mr and Mrs, WSJ's landlords at Porteus Road, London, II 458

bubbles
(18th century), IV 240–1, VI 116–17; (1822–5), 119; (1836–9), 121; (1854), prevented by war, 124; (1880), plenty ahead, V 90; (1881), 134
'explosions of commercial folly', V 48
limited liability bubbles, VI 125
essay question on, VI 120
see also South Sea Company

Buchan, Alexander (1829–1907), Scottish meteorologist, V 57

Buchanan, James (1791–1868), 15th President of United States, II 420, 431n15, 453n6

Buckinghamshire, VII 23, 24

Buckle, Henry Thomas, *History of Civilization in England* (1857), II 316, 437

Budgets, VII 135; Budget Party (1852), I 79, 84
see also under Gladstone, William Ewart

buds of truth, II 337

Buff, Heinrich (1805–78), Professor of Physics at Giessen, II 72
Familiar Letters on the Physics of the Earth, I 64, 67, 114

building societies, VI 75, 105

buildings: as fixed capital, VI 40, 42, 43; investment in, 105; coal heating for, VII 30
churches and houses in Lima, II 378–9, 394–6; Crystal Palace, II 11, 12; Herbert's log hut, 384; New York multi-storey buildings, 399; New Houses of Parliament, II 30; Palais de l'Industrie' in Paris, 179

Bulletin de la société vaudoise des sciences naturelles, IV 181

Bulli, New South Wales, I 162, 177–8

bullion
accumulation of, in Bank of England,

and circulation of bank notes, II 451, IV 14, 32

bullion brokers, VII 73, 74

circulation of, III 203

coins as, III 220; cost of converting into coins, VII 70

dealers in, III 202, 213

exports and imports, VII 74; drain to the East, IV 163

flow of, effect on prices, III 20, 23

and the telegraph, IV 220

Bullion Report (1810), IV 252

Bullionist (later *The Financier*) V 191

bullionists, Wolowski among, III 199

Bull Run, battles of, II 454

Bunsen, Robert Wilhelm Eberhard (1811–99), Professor of Chemistry at Heidelberg, II 66n11
H. E. Roscoe studies under, I 83n2, II 63n7, 66, 73, 74, 75, 192, 194, 244, 315, 316; projected tour together of volcanic districts, 229; his actinometer, 124n16; laboratory, 125; specimens of Plutonic rock for, 350
law of diffusion of gases, II 315–16
views on antiquity of human history, II 331
Gasometry translated into English by Roscoe, II 74, 315
'Photo-chemical Researches', articles with H. E. Roscoe (1856), II 191n4, 192n10, (1857), 315n2, (1859), 356
also mentioned, I 83n2

Bunsen burner, II 66n11

Buquoy, Georg von, V 55

Burke, T. H., Under-Secretary for Ireland, murdered in Phoenix Park (May 1882), V 189n1

Burton, John Hill, *Political and Social Economy*, 1829, I 27, III 27, VII 104

business
as a career for WSJ, I 61–2, 78, 88–9, 117, II 36–7
cycles, IV 300n2; depressions, III 128; fluctuations, I 12
specialisation in, VII 60
'what really happens in', V 192

business men, II 445, V 173, VI 68

Busk, J. R., New York agent of Rathbone Brothers and Co., III 78, 158, 185

Busk and Jevons, New York agents of

Busk and Jevons (contd)
 Rathbone Brothers and Co., I 10
Butler, Lady Eleanor (1745?–1829), 'Lady
 of Llangollen', II 153
Butler, Joseph (1692–1752), Bishop of Bris-
 tol, IV 38
Butler, Lady, see Thompson, Elizabeth
Buxton, V 99
Byrne, J. C., Twelve Years' Wanderings in the
 British Colonies, from 1835–1847, II
 52–3

Cader Idris, II 87
Caernarvon, I 108nn2, 3, 109, II 100;
 cholera in, III 149
Cahours, Auguste André Thomas (1831–
 91), Warden of the Paris Mint, II
 64, 65, 65n6; (with A. W. von
 Hofmann), 'Note on a new Class of
 Alcohols', II 228
Cairnes, John Elliott (1823–75), Professor
 of Political Economy, Queen's College, Galway, then (1866–72) at
 University College, London
 and WSJ: supports Serious Fall, I 192n2,
  notices it in Economist, III 17, 18,
  22, 23, 25, 27, 38; correspondence
  on gold supplies and prices, 16–18,
  20–1, 22–5; letters to The Times in
  support of WSJ's views, 36, 37, 42,
  44; his own articles on the subject,
  17, 21n6, 25; testimonial for WSJ
  (1865), III 64, 106, 107–8; esteem
  for him as logician, IV 113; Cairnes
  included in lecture syllabus at
  Owens College, 124, at University
  College, 143; examination questions set on, VII 137
 economic views: 'proper price of the
  market', V 30–1; on protection, IV
  126; wages fund, V 77, 80; theory of
  value, III 22, IV 87, 99, objections
  to WSJ's theory, III 246–7, VII
  148–51, has no understanding of it,
  IV 58, 99, 132; theory of utility, IV
  60–1, 62, VII 83–4, 148–51, 161;
  repudiates mathematical treatment, IV 62, 80, 81, 114, VII
  151–2
 personal: his cousin in New Zealand, III
  38; Northern Sympathies in America, 53; his health, 207, 252; illness

 and death, IV 105, 122, 123
 letters to, III 19–22, 22–3, 53–4, 64–5,
  245–7, 251–2, IV 60; letters from,
  III 16–18, 23–5, 55–6, 107–8, 206–
  7, IV 113–14
 writings:
  The Character and Logical Method of
   Political Economy (1857), III 16n1,
   19; ed. 2 (1875), chapter on 'Definition', IV 114, VII 104, 'a wonderful production for anyone', IV
   123
  'Co-Operation in the Slate Quarries
   of North Wales' (Macmillan's Magazine, 1865), III 65, VI 39n12;
   review of Chevalier (Edinburgh Review), V 17
  Essays in Political Economy Theoretical
   and Applied (1873), III 252n4, VI
   39n12, VII 104; price and wage
   statistics for, III 251–2; reviewed
   by WSJ (Manchester Guardian), IV
   60
  'New Theories in Political Economy'
   (Fortnightly Review, 1872), review of
   Theory of Political Economy, III 245,
   IV 58, V 30, reprinted, VII 146–52
  The Slave Power (1862), III 16n1, 53,
   56; ed. 2 (1863), 53n2, 56
  Some Leading Principles of Political Economy newly expounded (1874), IV 58,
   132, V 31n3, VI 112, VII 102;
   reviewed by G. Darwin (Fortnightly
   Review, 1875), IV 81n1, 87, 99, 100,
   102; WSJ on, 99, 101, 126; reviewed by Brewer (Manchester Guardian), IV 60
calculating machines, III 104, VII 86, 88,
 89. See also Arithmometer; logical
 abacus
calculus of pleasure and pain, I 35, VII 153
Calcutta
 Botanic Garden, I 60n2
 Calcutta Overland Mail, II 115, 132,
  135, 157
 Mint, III 210n2
 also mentioned, II 146n3
Caldecott, Alfred (1850–1936), Fellow of
 St John's College, Cambridge, V
 105–6
Calder Marshall, William, R. A. (1813–
 94), sculptor: in WSJ's Volunteer

Calder Marshall (*contd*)
Company, II 460–1
Caldwell, Captain, of Caldwell, Train &
Co., II 116n6
Caldwell, Hannah Eliza, *see* Roscoe, Mrs
William Stanley
Caldwell, Train & Co., I 108n3, II 100,
115, 116n6
California
gold from, II 12n6, III 55, 68n, 208, IV
6, 7, VI 101, 123, VII 66
wine growing, VI 32
also mentioned, II 60
Callao, Peru: WSJ's voyage to, from Aus-
tralia, II 364, 372, 373–6, 381, 385–
7, 394; stay in, 376, 378–9, 380,
387–8, 397; his curious French inn,
378, 387, 394
Cambridge
British Association meeting (1862):
'Notice of a General Mathematical
Theory of Political Economy' read
at, I 37 183n2, 188n1, IV 40, V 80,
VII 77, 124; 'On the Study of
Periodic Commercial Fluctuations'
read and approved, I 37, VII 124
Macleod's paper, II 456
population, VII 24
WSJ's visits to, IV 93, 95–6, 103, 126,
147, 149
Cambridge Society for the Extension of
University Teaching: Foxwell lectures for, IV 142, 145; lady students
of Political Economy, V 101n1,
VII 98, 101
see also under Macmillan, Margaret
Cambridge University
Colleges: Girton, IV 146, 148n8, 149;
Newnham, 148n2, 157n4; St
John's, IV 52n1, 146, V 105–6;
surpassed in beauty by Oxford, IV
285
economic studies in, I 37, V 22, 94; ideas
current in, IV 101, 103, 126; mathematical treatment recognised, V
24n3; economists irritated by Preface to ed. 2 of *Theory of Political
Economy*, 77–8, 79. *See also under*
Fawcett, Henry; Foxwell, H. S.;
Marshall, Alfred
Moral Sciences Tripos, IV 145; WSJ
examines for (1874), IV 52–3, 69–

70, 88, (1875), 143, 148–9; examination papers set by WSJ, VII
133–8
periodicity in boat-race victories, V 51
Philosophical Society, IV 103–4, V 8n3
philosophical teaching system, V 22,
23
University Library, V 119, 120n1
women admitted to Tripos examinations, IV 143; WSJ meets
women candidates, 148–9
also mentioned, I 54n6, 65n5, 192n2, II
230, III 5, IV 29
Cambridge University Press (Pitt Press),
IV 133, 147
Camden, William (1551–1623), VII 22
Camden Society, V 82
Camden Town, I 13; WSJ's lodgings in
(1853), 98, II 49
Cameron, General, invades Waikato, III
41n4
Campbell, Annie Sophia, of Sydney, II
279; marries Captain Ward, II
51n2
Campbell, John Francis (1822–85), II
323n4; his sungauge, 323–4, 343
Campbell, Robert, sen., (1769–1846),
merchant, II 279n10
Campbell, Robert (1804–59), New South
Wales Treasurer, II 51n2; a family
quarrel, 279
Campbelltown, New South Wales, I 167,
172
Canada
banks and note issues, IV 158, 161–2
Colonisation of North-West, II 420
monetary (decimal) system, IV 161–2,
166; silver and copper coins, 166
Oregon–Canada boundary dispute, II
408n14
population and acres in crop, VII 4
woods exhibited at Paris Exhibition, II
184
WSJ travels through, II 401
see also Hincks, Sir Francis
Canadian Monthly and National Review, IV
157n3, 158
canals
canal boats, VII 20; canal boat children,
V 169
coal transported by, VII 23
New River Canal, VI 43

Canard, Nicolas François (c. 1750–1833), pioneer of mathematical economics, IV 8, 9; Principes d'économie politique . . . , IV 9n5, 16

Canaries, I 101, II 112

candles, VII 20, 31

Canoona diggings, article on Australian gold finds, II 350–2, VII 124

Canterbury, England, visit to (1881), V 132

Canterbury, New South Wales, II 207, III 74

Cantillon, Bernard, V 130

Cantillon, Leopold Albert, student at Trinity College, Dublin (1881), V 128, 129

Cantillon, Philip: works on political economy ascribed to, V 119–22; family origins, 123, 125, 126; his will, 130, 132

Cantillon, Richard, economist: WSJ's research on, V 118, 119–22, 123–9, 130–1, 132; family origins, 123, 125, 126; his will, 130, 132

Essai sur la Nature du Commerce en Général, V 118n2, 119, 120, 122, 123

'Richard Cantillon and the Nationality of Political Economy' (WSJ, Contemporary Review, 1881), V 118n2, 120, 121n1, 123, 124, 125

'Cantilloniana' (Foxwell), V 179

Cantillon, Richard Talbot, brother of Leopold Albert, V 128

Cantillon, Robert, of Kerry (b. 1700), father of Richard the economist, V 123

Cantillon, Robert, jun., brother of Richard the economist, V 123

Cantillon family, V 120; genealogy, 123–4, 125–8

Cantilupe (Cantelupe), see Cantillon

Cape Clear, I 108, II 100

Cape of Good Hope, II 90

Cape Horn, II 42n4, 60

Cape Otway lighthouse, I 107, II 100, 113

Cape pigeons, I 104, II 97, 98, 375–6

Cape Verde Islands, I 101, II 84, 112

capital
    accumulation of: loanable, in London, IV 220; taxation on, VI 136

capital advanced, VII 58, 64

corn as, II 450

credit and, VI 104, 106

and current expenditure, VI 47

emigration of, VII 12, 50

examination questions on, VII 132, 133, 136, 137

floating capital, VI 121

'free' capital, VII 143

goods held by consumers as, VI 52–4

in industry, I 26n6, II 360; industry limited by, VI 38, 48, 62

intermediate, VI 43–7

investment in, IV 226, 230, VI 46–7; in iron products, III 141–2, in railways, I 27, in woollen manufacture, II 281; abundant openings for, III 131

law of the Interest of Capital, II 411, 422, IV 226, 230, V 156

lecture notes on, VI 35, 36–41

Mill's propositions on, VI 38–40, 48, 62; his ignorance on, IV 101; Cazenove on, 119–22; Edgeworth deep in Mill's fallacies, V 156

origin of term, VI 36–7; definitions, II 411, VI 37, 52, VII 143

as requisite of production, VII 60, 159

short dated capital, VI 126

standing, VI 51

taxation and, VII 16

theory of, and the time element, I 26, V 156, VI 22

total and final utility of, VII 143

see also circulating capital; fixed capital

capital and labour: relations between, governed by natural laws, VII 46; remedies for strife between, III 132, VI 78–9

see also co-operatives; profit-sharing; strikes

capitalisation, V 156

capitalists, VI 53, 74, 84; capitalist view of wages, VI 61; in Mill's wage funds theory, 49–51; and speculation, VII 11

workmen as, III 138, VII 54

Captain of the Chrysolite, see MacIntyre, Captain

Captain of the Collaroy, I 124

Captain of the Medway, II 397

Captain of the *Oliver Lang*, *see* Manning, Captain

Captain of the *Williams*, and his wife, I 129–30

Carbonnel, member of WSJ's Volunteer Corps, II 436

Cardiff, steam coal trade, VII 26

Cardwell, Edward (later Viscount, 1813–86), I 86; becomes President of Board of Trade, 87

Carew, Sir George, Earl of Totnes, V 125

Carey, Henry Charles (1793–1879), Philadelphia publisher and pamphleteer, III 201; condemns theory that value depends on utility, IV 58; his fallacy on protection, VI 134

Carlyle, Thomas (1795–1881), on the 'dismal science', VI 7

Carnarvon, Lord, IV 224n4

Carpenter, Mary (1807–77), daughter of Russell Lant Carpenter: reads paper on 'Industrial Schools' at British Association meeting, Bristol (1875), IV 129

Carpenter, Dr Russell Lant (1780–1840), Unitarian divine, II 167n8, IV 129n3

Carpenter, William Benjamin (1813–85), Professor of Medical Jurisprudence at University College, London, II 167

carpenters, *see* Amalgamated Society of Carpenters

Carriboo, gold from, II 439

Carrington, Richard Christopher (1826–75), astronomer: *Observations on the Spots on the Sun* . . . (1863), V 86

Cartagena, II 380, 397

Carvalho, Léon, Paris theatre manager, II 69n3

Carvalho, Mme, *see* Miolan, Marie Caroline Félix

Case, Mr, London lodging house keeper for schoolboys, II 11, 17, 19

Castlemaine, Australia, II 371–2

Cathcart, Fanny, *see* Heir, Mrs Robert

cattle, VII 24; and origin of term 'capital', VI 36–7; specie for trade in, III 192

Cavendish, Lord Frederick (1836–82), Liberal M.P.: becomes Chief Secretary for Ireland (1882), V 179n6; murdered in Phoenix Park (May 1882), 189

Cavour, Count, V 37

Cazenove, John (1788–1879), London merchant and writer on economics: letter to WSJ on Macdonell's *Survey of Political Economy*, IV 119–22

census: (1851), I 17, 28, VII 24, 119; Reports, VII 87; Census Tables of New South Wales, VII 118

ceramics
earthenware, VII 30
manufacture of earthenware and china, II 41; drain-tile Potteries, I 91
Playfair's lecture on Pottery, I 85
pottery as 'positive evidence' against biblical account of creation, II 330

Cernuschi, Henri (1821–96), advocate of bimetallism, IV 163, V 139, VI 102

Ceva, Giovanni (1647–1734), engineer: *De re nummaria* . . . (1711), included in list of mathematico-economic books, V 21–2; article on, by Nicolini, 22n2, 42

Ceylon, I 112, II 89n7, 380n1, 386

Chadwick, Sir Edwin (1800–90), architect of the Poor Law, I 16, III 238n2; member of Political Economy Club, IV 117, 202

chain makers, VII 47

Chalmers, George, VI 89n3

Chalmers, Thomas, *Political Economy* . . . (1832), VII 118

Chamberlain, Joseph (1836–1914), President of the Board of Trade, WSJ's old school friend, V 189–90

Chambers, Robert (1802–71), publisher: *Vestiges of Creation*, II 233

Chambers, William and Robert, *Chambers's, Information for the People*: 'Political Economy', VII 115

Chambers's *Edinburgh Journal*, II 51n15

Champion, Lake, II 389–90, 401

Chance, theory of, I 155, 156; Maupertuis on, IV 4; and the diamond fields, IV 258

Channing, William Ellery, II 134n7; *A Discourse on the Evidences of Revealed Religion*, . . . (1821), I 99; *Lectures on . . . the labouring portion of the Community*, II 292

Channing, William Henry (1810–84), Uni-

Channing, William Henry (*contd*)
tarian minister of Renshaw Street
Chapel, Liverpool, II 134, 151

Chapman, Edward John (1824–1904),
Professor of Mineralogy at University College, London, II 50

Chapman, Mr, lecture to working men of
Yorkshire, III 229

charcoal, VII 19, 122

charity: in the biblical sense, I 30, II 258;
in the eyes of political economy, VI
8, VII 45, 57
medical charities, III 256–7; WSJ's
view of, 256n1

Charles, Arthur, Q. C., stands for University of London (1880), V 97n2

Charley, Sir William Thomas (1833–
1904): defeated for Salford, V 115;
co-founder of Infant Life Protection Society, V 167n8

Chartists, II 81, VI 122

Chatsworth, Paxton's Conservatory, II 11,
12n5

Chaucer's tomb, I 184

Cheddar, IV 130

*Chemical Journal, see Quarterly Journal of the
Chemical Society*

Chemical News, VII 124

Chemical Society, II 75, 122, 191n3; Presidents, 49nn3, 6, 50nn8, 11, 74n16

chemistry
Brodie's chemical calculus, III 155–7;
chemical power of the future, 124;
Faraday's experiments in magnetism, I 81–2; industrial use of
chemistry, I 90,II 38, VII 19, 30;
isolation of aluminium, II 62; laboratory practice in France, II 65n6,
in Germany, 71n2, 125; Lockyer's
experiments, IV 294; the three
greatest chemists in Europe, II 193;
University College pioneer work
in, I 13–14; Williamson's lectures
at the Royal Institution, 82, 87
Liverpool College of Chemistry, II
134n6
professors of chemistry, IV 24, VII 58.
See also Bunsen; Faraday; Graham,
Thomas; Liebig; Roscoe, H. E.;
Williamson, A. W.
(H. E.) Roscoe's reports on, in Germany
and England, II 63, 65–6, 71–3,

125, 228–9, 315–16; his researches
with Bunsen in physical chemistry,
73, 74–5, 122, 124–5, 159, 190–3,
229, 243–4

WSJ's early interest in, I 113–14; experiments at home, 57, 92, 194, II 30,
35, his apparatus, 78; studies at
Mechanics Institute High School, I
114n1, at University College, London, I 54, 62, 64, 67, 69, 78, 82–3,
87, 90, 91, 94, attempts at original
research, 101; works in Birkbeck
Laboratory, 89, 94, 95, 97; examinations, 55–6, 85, 94; wins silver
medal (1852), gold medal (1853),
61n5, 114, II 31, 32–3, III 110;
suggested career as manufacturing
chemist, I 61, 110; visit to chemical
manufactory, II 435; gives up
chemistry, 244, 347, 406; surviving
notes on, I 101

Herbert Jevons studies, II 13, 15

Cheops, his Great Pyramid, VII 29

Cheque Bank (1873), IV 169, 178–9, 184–
6; liquidated, 156, 184; reconstruc-
ted as Cheque Bank Ltd (1876),
184n2

cheques: in America, IV 54, 155–6; charge
on small cheques, 169, on single
cheques, 184–5; as credit, VI 104–
5; as currency, IV 11, 17, in place of
currency, VI 107; in Germany,
178–9; for overseas payments, 185;
in Wales, III 191, 192; for Yarmouth fisheries, IV 78

Cheshire, I 71; salt trade, VII 19

Chesson, F. W., secretary of Aborigines
Protection Society, IV 174, 175,
176–7

Chester, I 85, 93

Chester & Holyhead Railway, I 93

Chevalier, Michel (1816–79), Professor of
Political Economy at the Collège
de France
Cobden–Chevalier commercial treaty
with France, II 408n12, III 208n1,
VII 14
writings on depreciation of gold, III 17,
48n1, 208n3; estimate of currency
in Great Britain, 201; on gold and
silver movements, 208–9; 'intrinsic
value' of money, VI 96

Cours d'Economie Politique . . . , VI 43, 96n4, VII 105; *Exposition universelle de 1867 à Paris*, III 209; *Traité de la Monnaie*, ed. 2, 209
letter from, III 208–9

Chicago, II 400, 419

Chicago Tribune, IV 117

Chigwell, expedition to see Barnaby Rudge's Maypole, I 55

Child, Sir Josiah (1630–99), *A New discourse of trade*. . . . (1693), V 160, 175

Children
deaths through bad nursing, VI 58–9
in factories, V 172
political economy for, VII 38–9, 51–3
protective legislation for, V 166–7, 168–9
use of opiates on, V 174
see also infant mortality

Chile, flour exports to Australia, III 20, VII 4

China
Anglo-French expedition to Peking (1860), II 417
Chinese in Australia: camps in Victoria goldfields, II 367–8, 371; a Chinaman in the gold escort, I 152; in Melbourne, II 142; merchants in Queensland, IV 177
Chinese currency (Vissering), IV 224
ginseng imports from North America, II 419n2
labour, IV 233
landscape painting, II 367
meterological variations and commercial crises, IV 293n1, V 10–11, 45, 48
pea from, II 142
prices, III 252
silk from, III 208, VII 24, and tea, III 24–5, VII 24

Chinese library at University College, London, IV 233

cholera: in England, I 16, 17, 68n1, in Caernarvon, III 149; in Italy, II 190, Thomas Jevons's death from, at Pisa, I 121, 122

Christ, I 155, II 226, 258; in Peruvian churches, 379, 395

Christian Socialists, I 16

Christian World, The, V 111

Christiania, IV 43–4

Christianity: WSJ's altered attitude to, I 52, 99, II 325–6, the 'whole system' of, opposed to Christ's teaching, 258; 'poetical' Christianity, 327; in Spanish America, 379

Christie, Charles Howard Peregrine (d. 1906): correspondence on *Theory of Political Economy*, V 30–1, 32–4; alterations due to, 34nn2, 3

Christie, Richard Copley (1830–1901), Professor of Jurisprudence and Political Economy at Owens College, II 305n8, III 121; resigns chair of Political Economy, WSJ takes his classes, I 42, 45, 205n2, 207n2, III 76, 104
letter from, III 121

Christmas: in Australia (1854), II 109, 110–11, (1856), I 134, 140–1, II 252–3, 280; in London (1862), II 460; in Beaumaris (1866), III 148–9

Chubb, Hammond (1830–1904), Secretary of the Bank of England, IV 264, 265

Church of England, V 75; clergy stipends, VI 65

Church Hill, WSJ's first home in Sydney, I 20, 21, 22, II 107, 109–10, 113, 161; moves to Annangrove Cottage, 146–7

Churchill, William Smith (1826–1914), Manchester numismatist: letter accompanying gift of coin and paper money for WSJ's collection, IV 193–5

Cincinnati, II 382, 400; threatened by Confederate Army (1862), II 453

circular notes, III 182

circulating capital, VI 40–1, 42–7; bills of exchange as, 105; Ricardo's definition, VI 42, WSJ's, VII 143; wages as, VI 47, 61, 62

City of Glasgow Bank, collapse of (October 1878), IV 293n1, 304n6

City Lands Committee, V 180–1

City News, VII 47n, 125

civil servants, VI 65

Civil Service examination, V 180

Civil Service Supply Association, VI 75

Claflin, Horace Brigham (1811–85), New York merchant, V 83n3

Claflin, H. B., and Co., of New York, V 83–4

Clanmaurice, ancestral home of Cantillon family, V 123, 124

Clarke, Hyde (1815–95), civil engineer, Vice-President of Royal Statistical Society, III 243–4; on periodicity, IV 274–6, 295–6
  letters to, III 243–4; letters from, IV 274–6, 295–6

Clarke, Rev. William Branwhite (1798–1878), geologist in Australia: meetings with WSJ, I 163n1, II 298; readings of elevations, I 167n1; gold discoveries, II 298n11
  'Notes on the Geology of New South Wales' (1855), II 134n4

Clarke, Mrs W. B. (Maria Moreton Stather), II 298

Clarke, the Misses, daughters of Mr and Mrs W. B. Clarke, II 298

class
  middle classes, II 435
  social classes in Sydney, I 29
  upper classes and political economy, III 130; views on working class suffrage, VII 42
  see also working classes

classical studies, I 98, 179; scientific education 'worth any amount' of Latin and Greek, II 244
  Greek: WSJ studies at University College, London, I 61, 62, 78, II 33, 389, 403, 406, 415, 437, VII 120, and Greek history, I 69–70, II 415; examinations, I 54, 83; a holiday from, II 30; takes elementary evening classes in, at Owens College, III 14, 29
  Latin: (WSJ's) College examinations in, I 54, II 33; preferred to chemistry, I 61; plan to continue while starting in business, 62; not compatible with scientific study, 78; takes for B.A. (1859), II 389, 403, 406, 415; classes in Latin at Owens College, III 14, 29

classification: WSJ's 'strong disposition to classify things', I 308; his remarkable powers, III 18
  in botany, I 63; of commodities, III 54, 56; of the 'general science of society', VII 158; of material for projected Treatise on Economics, I 50–1; in Social Survey of Sydney, 29; system of, for the logical abacus, III 69; of trades, I 17, 28, VI 33–5, VII 119

Claudet, Antoine François Jean (1797–1867), glass manufacturer and pioneer in photography, II 62

clearing houses, IV 302–3, V 7, 153–4, VI 107, 108; origin in Italy, IV 302, V 153n2; in London, IV 55, V 25, 153n2, 154n4; in Manchester, IV 55; in New York 43, 54, 155; a case of multiplication of efficiency, VI 30

clearing house clerks, VI 28

Clerk Maxwell, James (1831–79), physicist: letter to, on the Theory of Heat, IV 207–8

Clerkenwell, explored by WSJ, I 71–2

Cleveland Iron district: strike against reduction of wages, III 128, VII 49

'cleverness', I 58, 191, II 293–4, 307–8; 'clever fellows', 222

Clifford, William Kingdon (1845–79), Professor of Applied Mathematics at University College, London: alterations in Principles of Science, ed. 2, due to, IV 207–8; death, 207n4, 251
  'Of Boundaries in General' (1879), V 53; 'The First and Last Catastrophe' (1875) IV 207n4

Clifford Smith, J. L., secretary of the National Association for the Promotion of Social Science: letter to WSJ, V 173–4

Clifton, Robert Bellamy (1836–1921), Professor of Natural Philosophy at Owens College, I 41, III 9, later at Oxford, I 41, III 100, fellow student of WSJ at University College, III 5; reads WSJ's paper on rain gauges at British Association meeting, Manchester, I 36, 187, gets up telegraphic exhibition, II 435; supports WSJ's application for professorship at Owens College, III 100; at British Association meeting, Bristol, IV 128
  letter from, III 100

Clifton, Mrs Robert Bellamy, I 197

Clifton College, British Association *soirée* at, IV 130

climate, *see* meteorology

clocks, VI 26; logical machine constructed by clockmaker, III 157; WSJ's compensating gold watch, II 344; watchmaking, VI 28, 30, 32

clothes: ratio of exchange for, VI 81
  boot-and-glove making, VII 22, 24; cabbage-tree hats, I 135, 141; stockings, 24

clouds: WSJ's study of, on board the *Oliver Lang*, I 19, 114, in Sydney, 22, II 161, 203, on his Australian expeditions, I 147, 148, 213, 214, 216, 217, 218–9, 226, 237, off the coast of Peru, II 375, 387; his new theory of cloud formation, 244–5, 261
  papers on, *see under* Jevons, William Stanley, Works

Clough, Anne Jemima (1820–92), first Principal of Newnham College: meets WSJ at Cambridge, IV 148, 148n5

Clough, Arthur Hugh (1819–61), Professor of English Language and Literature at University College, London, 1850–2: WSJ attends his introductory lecture, I 65; also mentioned, I 9, II 443n1, IV 148n2

Clyde shipbuilding, III 228, VII 21

Clydesdale Bank, IV 108n1

Clynnog, Caernarvonshire, home of Lucy Jevons (Mrs John Hutton), I 11; WSJ stays at, I 201, III 127; too dreary in winter, III 149

coaches: mail coach travel in New South Wales, II 366, 374, 381; the gold escort, I 152; Parramatta Coach, 154; Sofala Royal Mail, 234, Harteley Mail, 235, Sydney Mail, 'the Mountain Plumb', 236–8; journey from Sydney to Ovens by mail cart, II 366–8, from Ovens to Melbourne, 368–9, to New Rush Creek, 371; in Jamaica, V 70–1. *See also* omnibuses

coal
  areas of coal measures, VII 27, 34
  in Australia, I 123n3, 125, 127, 129, 159n1, II 267, VII 26–7; in Great

Britain, III 189, V 143, VII 21, 22, 24–8, 29, 31–3, 34; in other countries, II 164, III 71, 102, VII 26, 27, 33, 34, competition to Britain from, VII 50

'bottled sunshine', VII 97; 'the Philosopher's Stone', VII 29

brown coal, III 71; gas-coal, I 50n15; steam coal, III 71

by-products, II 119, VII 20–1

as circulating capital, VI 43

consumption, III 102, 119, 251, IV 127–8, VII 18, 25, 27, 35; the 'coal pyramid', 25–6; geometric increase of consumption, VII 13, 31–2, 36, 37; by steam engines, III 188–90, VII 31; economy urged, 27–8

examination questions on, VII 133

exports, VII 24–5, 27, 28, 37; tax on, forbidden, 14

geology of coalfields, II 119, 298n11, 352, III 63; fossil fish in coal strata, II 134

prices, III 251, 256, VII 21, 37; and iron prices, III 228; and wages, VI 126n8; cost of carriage, VII 21

primary and secondary utility, IV 138; degrees of utility, 136–7

tax on, proposal for, IV 55, 222

uses for, VII 18–21, 30–1; Britain's preeminence in use, III 92, 93; as source of power, VII 30, 35; the 'first necessary of life', 37

coal miners: agitation amongst (1869), III 228; strike against wage cuts (1875), VI 126; emigration, VII 17

coal mines
  average output per colliery, VII 27; total output (1866), 29
  colliery explosions (1866), and barometric pressure, III 144–7
  increase of, to meet demand for coal, VII 37, depth working, III 139–40, 147, VII 17, 19–20, 33
  investment in sinking a mine, VI 46–7
  'our Indies', VII 21
  pits working half time, V 139
  profit-sharing schemes, III 151
  WSJ goes down a mine, II 435, III 126–7

'Coalowner', writer of a letter to *The Times*, III 249

coalowners, III 147, VII 23; profits, III
    251
Coal Question: *Coal Question* (1865) raises
    possibility of coal exhaustion, I 45,
    VII 34–5, 36–7; Gladstone on, I 45,
    III 87–8, 102, VII 11–13, 14–15;
    Marshall on, IV 234–7; substitutes
    for, out of the question, III 77, 88,
    90–1, 92–3, VII 34, a different
    view, III 125n1; the Coal Panic,
    III 102; coal famine, V 90, VII 37;
    Coal Argument, VII 17
    see also The Coal Question under Jevons,
        William Stanley, Works
Coal, Royal Commission on (1866), III
    101, 102, VII 36–7; questions, III
    154
coal trade, VII 29
    depressions in, VII 32; collapse (before
        1877), IV 210; in 1880–1, V 107;
        recovery, 155; relapse, 179, 190
    figures for 1854–1865, VII 25; for 1865–
        1869, 28, 32; for coal imported into
        London, 32
    free trade for, VII 27
    trade reports, VII 26
    WSJ's shares in, V 108, 139, 155, 190
coal, WSJ's articles on: 'Mr Gladstone's
    New Financial Policy' (1866), VII
    11–18; 'On Coal' (1867), 18–28;
    'On the Probable Exhaustion of our
    Coal Mines' (1868), 28–35; 'On the
    Progress of the Coal Question'
    (1875), 36–7
Cobden, Richard: Owens College housed
    in his former home, I 41; negotiates
    Anglo-French commercial treaty,
    II 408, III 208n1, VII 14; a Cob-
    denite on, III 130; a trade unionist
    on, 134, 135; his supposed views on
    trade unions, 161; the reforming
    Muslin Manufacturer, V 41; also
    mentioned, II 429
Cobden Club, publications on political
    economy, VII 105, 107; Cobden
    Club prize, V 129n1
Cobden Memorial Committee, III 86n1,
    131, VII 38, 51; memorial fund, III
    130
Cobden Professorship of Political Econ-
    omy at Owens College: endowment
    and terms of, III 86n1; WSJ applies

for, 103–5, testimonials, 114–20;
    his appointment to, I 207, III 121;
    Introductory Lecture as Professor,
    VII 37–54, exchange of letters aris-
    ing from, III 128, 129–38, 139
'Cobdenite, A', writer of letter of protest
    against WSJ's Cobden lecture, III
    129–31; reply to, 131–2
Cockburn, Lord, IV 173n1
coffee, III 54; from Jamaica, V 70; price,
    IV 6; tax on, III 239, VI 139
Coffin, W. E., of Boston, II 91
coinage
    Coinage Act (1816), VI 98, 100
    coins issued from the Mint in a credit
        cycle (diagram), VI 130
    copper coins, II 201, IV 194, 195
    examination questions on, VII 131, 135
    gold coins: Australian sovereigns in Lon-
        don, III 179; British guinea, V 44,
        sovereign, legal tender in other
        countries, III 163, compared with
        other coinages, 207, 217n4, 219,
        coin equivalent of £ sterling, III
        216–17, VI 98–9, 100; French, II
        184, III 219, V 59, VII 66; Ger-
        man, V 58; Irish, III 191; Italian,
        II 200; New Zealand, III 210;
        U.S.A., III 203, 219, V 58, 59, VII
        69. *See also under* Sydney Mint
    dies for stamping dates on coins, III
        165
    exports and imports, III 164, 181–2,
        213, 219–20, V 88, VII 70–3, for
        foreign payments, VI 113
    as fixed capital, VI, 45
    hoards, III 79
    as international currency, VII 69–75,
        problem of assimilating sovereign
        and franc, III 183–4, 207, VII 67,
        68–73
    investigation by WSJ into state of
        gold coinage (1868), III 159, 160,
        161–5, 179–82, 183–4, 186–7, 190–
        6, 200–3, 206–7, 210; the Gold
        Controversy of 1869, 211–21; the
        Assay Master on standard gold
        coin, 221–4
    light coins: coined before 1851, III
        218, 223; proportion to total circu-
        lation, III 193, 210n1, 211, V 88,
        181, VII 71–2, method of calcu-

lation, III 213–14; 'remedy' allowed, III 217, 223; retained by Banks, III 196, 217, V 181, kept from Bank of England, VII 72; put into circulation in preference to heavy coins, VI 99, VII 70, 72–3, Proclamation to prevent (1842), V 183; Fremantle's First Report on (1871), V 182, later Reports, 183, Memorandum on (1880), V 92; WSJ's letter to *The Times* on (1879), V 87–9; withdrawal, V 181–2, 183

melting of coins, III 162, 182, 186–7, 202, 213, 219–20, V 88, VII 70–3

recoinages, VI 98; (1774), V 182; (1844), V 88; required in 1868 for international currency, V 182, VII 66; (1882), V 180–3; cost of, V 88, 182, VII 72

Thomas Jevons's collection of coins, II 209

silver coins: English, III 193–4, 203; French franc, VI 100; German, VI 101; Hong Kong silver dollar, VII 68; Italian, II 200–1; Spanish dollar, III 183

recoinages, V 44

Colburn, Zerah, editor of *Engineering*, III 125

Colenso, Bishop, Rule of Three, III 214, 221

Collie, Alexander, & Co., East India merchants, failure of, IV 210, VI 106

Collier, James, review of *Principles of Science* (*British Quarterly Review*, April 1874), VII 127

colonies

colonial economy, II 282–3; cheques for, IV 85; copper currency, IV 166; exports to America, IV 220; Mints, III 164, Sydney gold coins made legal tender throughout colonies, II 127; postal service, II 133; progress compared with America, II 429–30; roads, VI 133

life in the colonies: 'Colonial Experience', I 110, II 216, VII 10, sharpness, I 177, 'newness', 179; 'free and easy society', IV 33; inconveniences and hardships, I 33, II 297n8, 343, 404

also mentioned, V 108n1, VII 3

see also Australia; Canada; emigration; India; New South Wales; New Zealand

Columbus, Christopher, II, 399

Colvile, Charles Robert (1815–86), M.P., IV 287

Colvill, W. H., class mate of WSJ at University College, I 54, 63, II 35, 114, 252

Combe, George, III 134

Combination Laws, VI 70; repealed, VI 71, VII 50

liberty of combination: Mill on, VII 42; workers' growing power of, 43; attitude of political economists to, 48–9

commerce

barometric indications for, IV 215, 216n1; dangers inseparable from progress in, VII 41; Madsen's 'commercial centres of gravity', V 28–9; problem of getting statistics, IV 254–5

credit for, VI 105

increase in foreign commerce, III 55

a preventive of war, II 408

proposed course in the history of, III 105

vocabulary of, VII 134

see also trade

commercial fluctuations, *see* cycles

commercial travellers, III 191; WSJ with his Botanical tin box taken for a travelling hawker, I 141, a dealer in false 'jewellry', 152, II 254

Committee of the Privy Council on Education, V 103n1

commodities: definition, VI 10; Mill's three classes, 83; degrees of utility, 92–3

'common fund', Bacon's term, IV 210, 215

Compagnie d'Occident (1717), VI 116n2

competition

with cheap foreign labour, III 239, in the iron industry, 128, 141–3, VII 49–50; due to union activity, VI 74

and cooperative associations, VI 75

and the examination system, IV 213; examination questions on, V 152, VII 133, 136, 138

in labour relations, VI 79; territorial division of labour due to, VI 36

competition (*contd*)
    for promotion, VII 62, 64
    versus monopoly for public utilities, VI
        133
    see also free trade
compound interest, VI 56
computers, *see* arithmometer; calculating
        machines
Comstock Lode, IV 187
Comte, Alexander: 'Comtists' of the
        Fortnightly, IV 250
Condillac, Etienne Bonnot de, IV 75, V 95
Condorcet, Marie Jean Antoine Nicolas
        Caritat, Marquis de, *Vie de Turgot*,
        V 129
'Confederate Rams', III 53
Conolly, Dr John (1794–1866), pioneer in
        humane treatment of the insane, I
        85
Conrad, Johannes E. (1839–1915), Pro-
        fessor of Political Economy at
        Halle: includes bibliography of
        WSJ's writings in *Jahrbucher für
        Nationalökonomie und Statistik* (1870–
        1915), IV 253, 277; doubts on
        publishing bibliography of 'Works
        on the Mathematical Theory of
        Political Economy', 263, 277–8
    letters from, IV 253, 277–8
Conservatives, I 18, VII 154; Peelites, I
        79n2; rejected as a party by WSJ,
        208; retain Hampstead (1880), V
        98n4
    Conservative Clubs, III 134
consols, IV 133, VI 118
Conspiracy and Protection of Property Act
        (1875), VI 73n5
Constantinople, threatened by Russia, IV
        224n4, 225
consumers
    consumer credit, VI 106
    consumers' and producers' surplus, IV
        5n3
    goods held by, VI 52–4
    wage increases paid by, VI 72
consumption
    and capital, VI 39–40; of workmen and
        capitalists, 72
    and production, IV 75, VI 12–13, 14,
        17, 53; all consumption unpro-
        ductive, IV 122, VI 53
    taxation of, VI 134

wasteful consumption of the Earth's
        product, III 83–4
Contemporary Review
    articles by WSJ: 'Amusements of the
        People' (1878), IV 286–7, 291;
        'Bimetallism' (1881), V 136, 187;
        'Experimental Legislation and the
        Drink Traffic' (1880), V 74, 90,
        166; 'John Stuart Mill's Philosophy
        Tested' I, 48; '–I' (1877), IV 192n2,
        221, 250, V 74; '–II' (1878), IV
        221n2, V 74; '–IV. Utilitarianism'
        (1879), V 75n1; 'Married Women
        in Factories' (1882), V 154, 161,
        172, 173, 174; 'Postal Notes,
        Money Orders and Bank Cheques'
        (1880), IV 216n2, V 99, 101; 'Rati-
        onale of Free Public Libraries
        (1881), V 123; 'Richard Cantillon
        and the Nationality of Political
        Economy' (1881), V 118n2, 119,
        120, 122, 123; 'A State Parcel Post'
        (1879), IV 303, V 3, 155n2; 'The
        Use and Abuse of Museums', in-
        tended for, but not published in, V
        132
    other articles mentioned: 'Capital: Mr
        Mill's Fundamental Propositions'
        (Musgrave, 1874), IV 126; 'Com-
        modities *versus* Labour' (G. Dar-
        win, 1873), IV 35; 'Positivism on
        an Island' (W. H. Mallock, 1878),
        IV 250; Professor Whitney on the
        Origin of Language (G. Darwin,
        1874) IV 87; 'The Study of Soci-
        ology' (Spencer, 1872–3), IV 38n2
    founder of, Alexander Strahan, V 74;
        WSJ's fellow contributors, IV 250
contract, freedom of, and Irish landlord-
        ism, V 112–15
Contzen, Karl Wilhelm Heinrich (1835–
        88), German economist, V 15
convertibility: of bankers' reserves, IV 111;
        in France and England, VI 98n7
conveyance of goods, VI 21, 24, 38; cost of
        carriage in London, VII 21
convicts in New South Wales: in the gold
        trade, I 21, II 162; shipment of,
        prohibited (1840), I 24; as road
        labour, 152, 217, II 221; convict
        settlements, I 220, 223, 237; an Inn
        kept by a pardoned convict, 235;

convict highwaymen, II 170; 'lags' of Botany Bay, 223; neighbourhood suspicions of, 405

Cook, Captain James, II 207

Cook, J. D., editor of *Saturday Review*, II 259n5

Cook's River, II 207, 239

Cookstown, North Queensland, IV 177

Coope, Q. E., M.P. for Hampstead, V 98n4

Cooper, [Sir] Daniel (1821–1901), Sydney merchant and philanthropist, II 270

Cooper, Thomas, father of Daniel Cooper, Lancashire merchant, emigrant in Sydney, II 270

co-operation, VII 74–7; or division of labour, VI 34–5; innate in Saxon nature, VI 68; panacea for workmen's grievances, III 132, 137, VII 48–9

co-operatives
banks, VI 76
Brassey's article on, IV 51
examination questions on, V 152, VII 135
friendly societies, I 16, VII 51
in Germany, IV 85
industrial partnerships, VI 76–8; mills and works, III 138, 166
newspaper, the *Reasoner*, III 165n3, 166
protective companies, VI 75–6
retail societies, VI 74–5
working-class investment in, VII 54

Copenhagen
Nationaløkonomisk Forening, IV 243
WSJ visits (1877), IV 206–7, 244

Copernicus, IV 268

copper
Cornish, VII 25; from Cumberland, VI 43; New South Wales, II 139, 142, plan for sending ore to England, 139–40; New Zealand, III 74; Wales, II 93, with gold traces, 88n3, 135n11, John Hutton's Welsh mine, III 210, Poltimore mine, I 118, II 94, 128, 142–3
copper assays, II 139; copper coins, Italian, 201, Swedish, IV 194, 195
smelting, IV 276, VII 30
trade in copper, VI 33; price, IV 232, VI 120, VII 21, 24–5

uses for: in gold refining, III 50; plating for ships' hulls, II 60n5

copper coloured races, VII 123

copyright, international, V 59, 69, 94; Berne Convention, 69n1

Coquelin, Charles (1805–52), article on commercial crises, IV 14

Coquelin et Guillaumin, *Dictionnaire de l'Économie Politique* (1854), V 13–14, VII 103

Corbet, Thomas, *An Inquiry into the Causes and Modes of the Wealth of Individuals* (1841), V 107, 176

'Corbow', Australian aborigine, I 227

Cordeaux River, I 175, 178n1

Cordier, Joseph Louis Etienne (1775–1849), French civil engineer, IV 72

Corkran, Charles Loftus (1813–1901), Unitarian minister: letter to WSJ on his plan to found a Recreation Society in East London, IV 292

corn
as capital, II 450, VI 53, 54; as standard of value, IV 170, VI 98
corn growing countries, VII 62; Australia, II 282
examination questions on, VII 133, 137
imports, IV 306, VI 58; tax on, VII 15
price of, IV 6–7, 72, VI 121; and demand for other goods, 15; as determinant of wages, VI 61, 62, 63; price in India, 89, 121, 123, 124; influence on rate of interest, II 450; rise in, expected (1865), III 65, fall in (1878), IV 293; and sun spots, IV 188–9, 204, 300, V 57
quantity of, and ratio of exchange, VI 81, 89, VII 161
statistics for, II 426, 427

Corn Laws, I 4; anti-Corn-Law agitation, III 130, 134, 161n1, 183n1, VII 50; repeal (1849), III 55, IV 6, VI 139, effect on population, VI 15; shilling duty on, abolished (1869), III 231n2

corn trade, VI 34; holding of stocks, 53–4; speculation, 123

Cornwall
copper mines, VII 25; tin and copper smelters, IV 276
Cornish engines, VI 26

Cossa, Luigi (1831–96), Professor of Politi-

Cossa, Luigi (*contd*)
cal Economy at Pavia: asks for membership of Royal Statistical Society, V 60; his error on protection, VII 100; suggestions for List of Mathematico-Economic Works, V 42–3

Guida alla Studia dell' economia politica (1876): copy sent to WSJ, V 41, 53; English translation by Margaret Macmillan, 53, 59, 60, 64, 69, 94, 101–2, 106, VII 98, 103, 127, WSJ's Introduction to, V 101n1, VII 98–101, 103; reviewed in *Journal of Royal Statistical Society* (1880), V 136; German translation, VII 101

translation of *Primer of Political Economy* (WSJ) into Italian, V 37n3, 60, 62
other publications, VII 100–1
letters from, V 41–3, 59–60
cost of living, rise in, III 256–7, IV 6–7
cost of production
defined, VI 84
of average skilled labour, VII 144; of coal, III 251
examination questions on, VII 137
and prices, III 56
as source of value, VI 90; value determined by (Ricardian theory), V 62, VI 83, VII 142, 152, limited in the long run by (WSJ), III 246, VII 83, by the most costly portion, VI 92
cottage wife, shelters WSJ from storm, I 147–9
cotton
from Australia, II 60; from India, III 208; from U.S.A., III 11, export duty on, II 429
cotton famine, VI 125, VII 41
manufacture, in Manchester, VI 33; quantity of wheaten flour used in manufacture, III 206
price, III 64–5, IV 6, 293, VI 125
trade, VI 33–4, in Liverpool, III 64–5; diagram, II 461; effect on, of rice prices in India, V 45, VI 15, of Civil War in America, III 208; classes of trade in, VI 33–4; statistics for, II 427
WSJ visits cotton mill and cotton ma-

chinery works, II 435
Coughtrey, Dr Millen (1848–1908), Professor of Anatomy and Physiology at University of Otago, New Zealand, IV 42
country gentlemen, VII 12
Courcelle-Seneuil, Jean Gustave (1813–98), IV 91, 95; *Traité Théorique et Pratique de l'Economie Politique* (1858–9), IV 59, VI 12
Cournot, Antoine Augustin (1801–77), pioneer of mathematical economics, IV 104, V 67, 80, 95; translations of his works included in mathematico-economic bibliography, V 22; examination question on, V 152; on Macleod's 'negative value', V 77; copy of *Theory of Political Economy* sent to, IV 68

Principes de la théorie des richesses (1863), V 19, 55; *Recherches sur les Principes Mathématiques de la Théorie des Richesses*, IV 3, 5, 15, 19, V 24, Dupuit's debt to, IV 197, Walras's, 46–7, WSJ's, V 80
Courtney, Leonard Henry (1832–1918), Professor of Political Economy at University College, London, IV 66, 118, 145; upholds periodic character of trade stagnation at Political Economy Club, 202–3, proposes WSJ for ordinary membership of Club, V 142; supports proposal of Inglis Palgrave for Royal Society Fellowship, 163
letter from V 142
Courts of Conciliation and Arbitration Act (1867), VI 78
Cowper, Lord, Viceroy of Ireland, V 151n4; resigns (1882), 179n6
Cowper, William, poem on his Mother, I 7
Cox, J., *see Waugh (and Cox) Australian Almanac* and *Waugh and Cox's Directory of Sydney*
Coxe, Henry Octavius (1811–81), Librarian, Bodleian Library, Oxford, IV 285
Craik, [Sir] Henry (1846–1927), General Editor of The English Citizen Series, V 157, 178; letter to WSJ on publications, V 137–8

Crane, P. M., secretary of the Irish Peat Company, II 118–19

Crawfurd, John, letters to *The Times* on the gold question (1863), III 36–7, 43–4

Creasy, [Sir] Edward Shepherd (1812–78), Professor of History at University College, London, I 69; *Rise and Progress of the English Constitution*, IV 213

credit
  consumer credit, VI 106
  and copper prices, IV 232
  as currency, VI 106–7
  examination questions on, VII 131
  for foreigners, VI 108, 109, 113
  lecture notes on, VI 103–7
  shock to, in England (1879), V 65; anticipated in 1878, IV 281

credit cycles, *see* cycles

Creed, H. Herries, *Times* correspondent in Brussels, joint author of letters on foreign competition, III 141, 151–2

Crimean War: expedition to Black Sea (1854), II 63; expeditions to Baltic (1854, 1855), 79; attempts to take Sebastopol, 103, 122n3, 162–3, 171, captured (1855), 194, 204, 206; screw steamers and guns for, 114, 133n1; 'our whole army . . . ruined', 122, 'a wretched conflict', IV 225; a Day of Humiliation and Prayer, II 132; Russians driven out of Sea of Azov, 151; alliance with France, 175n8; war prices, 194; recruits from America, 194n16; newspapers 'all for peace', 197; Peace celebrations (Treaty of Paris, March 1856), 234; also mentioned, II 53n7, 118, 175n8, 360n4, VI 113n8, 125n5

Criminal Law Amendment Act (1871), VI 72–3; repealed (1875), 73n5

crises, theory of
  capital-shortage theory, V 134n3
  comparative theory of Juglar and Wirth, IV 300, V 13
  Coquelin's article on, V 13–14
  definition of crisis, a problem, IV 300; distinguished from 'breakdown', 281

examination questions on crises, VII 132

WSJ's sunspot theory, IV 225, 293, 304. *See also* Sun-spots

see also cycles; periodicity

Critique Philosophique, La, edited by Charles Renouvier, IV 85

Crompton, Charles (1833–90), eldest son of Sir Charles Crompton, II 191

Crompton, Mr Justice (Sir Charles John, 1797–1865), II 14n2, 34, 123n12, 191; appointed Judge and knighted (1852), 31

Crompton, Mrs Charles John (Caroline Fletcher), I 14, 31, 191

Cronstadt, bombardment of, II 79

Crosby, botanical expedition to, I 59–60

Crossley, Louis John, pioneer of telephone development, V 36n5

Crowther, John, IV 279

'Crucible', WSJ's dog in Sydney, II 152, 181–2

Crump, Arthur, *The Theory of Stock Exchange Speculation* (1875), IV 133

Crystal Palace, I 4, 116, 179n1, IV 223; Paxton's glass structure, II 11, penny pictures of, 12

  Exhibition of 1851 (the Great Exhibition), I 17, II 26, 119; 'calico with a million dots' displayed in, VII 25; Koh-i-nor diamond on show, II 188; WSJ's evening walks to, 23

  French singers at, II 418; Saturday afternoon concerts, V 110, 131; Electrical Exhibition, V 148n2

  see also Great Exhibition

Crystal Palace, Paris, II 179

crystallography, I 62, 67, 78, 114

Cuba, II 381, 397, 398; slave agriculture, III 53, 56n1

Cumberland: coal mines, VII 21; copper, VI 43; lead, I 175

  Worthies of Cumberland, IV 275

Cumberland, New South Wales, II 262

Cunard shipping line, II 384n1; Steamship *America*, WSJ sails to England on, 385, 401

Cunningham, David, *The Condition of Social Well-being* (1878), VII 104

Cunningham, William, *The Growth of English Industry and Commerce*, VII 103

currency
  of bank notes, VI 107
  circulation, IV 16–19, 162; in
    Gresham's law, VI 99; of metallic
    currency, III 201, IV 10–11, 16
  cowries as, V 141, VI 97
  credit as, VI 106–7
  difference with Inglis Palgrave on, IV
    76–8
  economised by cheque system, VI 107
  England's excellent system of, V 181,
    188
  gold as; accumulation in banks, VI 128,
    coin and bullion in Bank of En-
    gland, 127–30; circulation, III 184,
    195–6, 200–1, 202–3, IV 11nn4, 7,
    16, 77–8, V 92, 213–14, VII 71–2;
    in Ireland, III 190; in Wales, III
    191–2; 'quantity in use', III 161–2
  Laws of 1816 for regulating, VII 71, 72
  periodicity in, IV 275
  and prices, IV, 170
  silver as: in Anglo-Saxon times, VI 99, in
    16th century, III 47, in 18th cen-
    tury, V 44; in modern times, III
    193–4, 201, 203, V 183, VII 68; in
    France, III 186, VI 100–1, 102–3;
    depreciation of silver governed by
    French currency, III 5, 17, 21; in
    Germany, IV 163, VI 101, 102,
    103; in India, problem of super-
    fluity, V 26–7, 59, 140, 141, 142n2,
    VI 103, 192
  Tooke's errors on, III 21
  utility, law of, applied to, VII 161
  by weight, VI 99
  in WSJ's lectures at Owens College, IV
    23
  see also coinage; international currency;
    money
Currer Bell, see Brontë, Charlotte
curves, II 427, 'pricking off curves', I 35
  demand curves: Fleeming Jenkin's, IV
    5n3, correspondence with WSJ on,
    III 166–78
  Dupuit's curves, IV 197, V 95
  Marshall's use of, IV 96, V 66
  price curves, III 53–4, 55; supply and
    price curves, VI 16
  utility curves, III 167n2, IV 5n3, 59, 62,
    64, 197, V 95, VII 81
  Walras's curves, IV 197, 270, VII 76

  weather calculation curves, II 245
Cushman, Charlotte Saunders (1816–76),
    American actress, II 134–5
Cushman, Susan Phillips, see Muspratt,
    Mrs James Sheridan
Custodi, Pietro, Scrittori classici Italiani di
    economia politica (1803–16), V 60
customs duties, VI 136, 138, 140, VII 115;
    Gladstone's reforms, VI 139
custom house, VI 112, 113, 134, 138
Cusumano, Vito (1843–1908), Professor of
    Political Economy at Palermo, IV
    84
cycles
  commercial, credit or monetary: (18th
    century), IV 224, 228–30, 233,
    240–1, VI 117–18, South Sea Bub-
    ble one of the series, IV 232, 237,
    insurance companies a clue to, 240,
    associated with Delhi wheat prices,
    V 47; (1800–86), IV 230, 232, 275,
    300, V 6, 47, VI 120–6, 127–9, VII
    91, associated with railway mania
    and brickmaking, VI 122–3, 125,
    with price of corn, 123–4; (1873–
    7), IV 232, premature, 229, or
    temporary, V 90, associated with
    excessive paper money, 147; prob-
    lem of 1877–8, IV 273–4, 274n1,
    304, associated with famines in
    India and China, IV 293n1; (1880–
    2), V 88–90, 132, 134, 147, 171,
    178–9, revival associated with de-
    mand for metallic currency, 89, no
    real crisis in 1882, 171, 178–9
  bankruptcies associated with cycles,
    IV 273–4, V 11–12, VI 118, 122,
    124
  cyclical factors affecting price chan-
    ges, I 39
  decennial series, IV 228–9, 232, 233,
    V 11–12, 45–8, 90, VI 117; Adam-
    son's doubts on, IV 300–1; Hyde
    Clarke on, 274–5; influence of ex-
    traneous circumstances, 210, VI
    118; exceptions, V 16, American
    crisis of 1873 not in the series, V 11,
    VI 126
  diagram of credit cycle, VI 130–1
  Herapath's cosmical cycles, IV 274,
    276
  Indian rainfall cycles, V 50–2;

weather cycles, II 341n3
see also fluctuations; periodicity; sun-
spots

Dahms, Dr Anna, physician: views on
married women in factories, V 166
Daily News, III 99n2; estimate of gold and
silver in circulation, 1872, IV 10,
11n4, 16; report of WSJ's paper on
sun-spots (30 August 1875), IV 129
Daily Telegraph, II 123n15; on *The Coal
Question* (20 April 1866), III 93
Dalton, John, physicist, I 65n5, II 66n13
Dangeul, Plumard de, *Remarques sur les
avantages* . . . attributed to, V 128n1
Daniell, Claremont John, of the Bengal
Civil Service: his solution to the
Silver Question, V 192–3
Daniell, John Frederic (1790–1845), Pro-
fessor of Chemistry at King's Col-
lege, London: 'Chemistry' (in 'Lib-
rary of Useful Knowledge', Vol.
IV), I 65; *Introduction to Chemical
Philosophy* (1839), I 83
Danson, John Towne (1817–98), econ-
omist, Chairman of the Council of
Queen's College, Liverpool: letter
in support of WSJ's application for
professorship at Owens College, III
86–7
Darbyshire, W., letter to *Manchester Guardian* on WSJ's article, 'Married
Women in Factories', V 163–4
Dardanelles, IV 224n4, 225n3
Darling Harbour, Sydney, I 124, 159, II
239
Darwin, Charles
doctrine of evolution, IV 42; theory of
survival of the fittest anticipated by
Maupertuis, IV 4, 15
letter from WSJ, IV 100n4; 'A Deduction from Darwin's Theory',
article by WSJ (*Nature*, 30 December 1869), VII 126
'Historical Sketch of Natural Selection',
IV 15; 'Variations of Animals and
Plants under Domestication', IV 15
also mentioned, IV 55n3, 63, 94, 102,
200n1
Darwin, George Howard (1845–1912),
mathematician, second son of
Charles Darwin

as economist, IV 35, 63, 66; difference
with WSJ on theory of interest, 24–
9, 35, 63; alterations in ed. 2 of
Theory of Political Economy due to,
230n1; reads d'Aulnis, IV 94, 96,
and Walras's 'Memoirs', 205; is
sent copy of paper on 'General
Mathematical Theory of Political
Economy', VII 76
elected Fellow of Royal Society, IV 221
writings: 'Commodities *versus* Labour',
on Mill's view of capital, IV 35,
VII 77; 'Marriages between First
Cousins' (*JRSS*, 1875), IV 35; 'Professor Whitney on the Origin of
Language' (*Contemporary Review*,
1874), IV 87; 'The Theory of Exchange Value', review of Cairnes
(*Fortnightly Review*, 1875), IV 81n1,
87, 99, 100, 102, Walras on, 180–1
letters to, IV 35, 81, 87–8, 99–100;
letters from, IV 24–9
Daulby, Daniel, cousin of WSJ, art collector and historian, I 59n5
Daulby, Mrs Daniel, sister of William
Roscoe, I 59n5
Daulby family, cousins of WSJ, I 59; send
WSJ books in Sydney, II 79; Australian shells for, 195; family grave,
III 204
Daulby–Roscoe Icelandic Collection of
books, I 59n5
d'Aulnis de Bourouill, Johan, Baron
(1850–1930)
his doctoral dissertation, 'The Income of
Society' based on WSJ's theory of
value, IV 57–9, 70, 71–4, 75–6, 81–
3; Preface, 90–1; 'note' on, for WSJ,
95; difference with WSJ on exchange of indivisibles, 58, 62–3, 70,
75, 76, 82, 90; on WSJ's solution to
problem of value, 90–1; his book
favourably mentioned by Darwin,
94, 96, 99, mentioned in Preface to
ed. 2 of *Theory of Political Economy*, V
76; agrees with WSJ and Say that
value depends on utility, VII 83
as a mathematical economist, IV 261,
282–3, VII 77; relations with
Walras, IV 45, 59, V 56, plans to
visit him in Lausanne, IV 271, 289–
90

d'Aulnis de Bourouill (contd)
  appointed Professor of Political Econ-
    omy at Utrecht University, IV 229,
    252, 271; inaugural speech on
    Kathedersocialism, 284
  projected visit to England (1880), V 104
  letters to, IV 61–3, 70–1, 81–2, 94–5,
    229–30; letters from, IV 57–60, 71–
    4, 75–6, 83, 88–9, 96–7, 282–4, V
    55–6
Davenant, Charles, political economist:
    statistics of corn prices, IV 72, VI
    89nn3, 4, VII 161
David, Psalms, II 329
Davis, Edward (1813–78), sculptor: bust of
    William Roscoe, II 128, 144
Davis, James Edward, The Labour Laws,
    VII 107
Davitt, Michael, founder of Irish Land
    League, V 150nn1, 2; Liverpool
    speech on 'land for the people', V
    196
Davy, Humphrey, II 243
Dawson, Ada, tours illuminations of Lon-
    don, III 6
Dawson, Catherine Castle, see Jevons, Mrs
    Arthur
Dawson family, of Liverpool, friends of the
    Jevons family, II 10; visit to Lon-
    don for wedding celebrations of
    Prince of Wales, III 6
Dawson, John, Liverpool merchant, II
    10n1
Dawson, Lucy, tours London illumi-
    nations, III 6–8
Dawson, Mary, tours London illumi-
    nations, III 6–8
Day, Mr, retired Shoreditch grocer: plays
    cribbage with WSJ on board the
    Oliver Lang, I 106, II 99, 112; fishes
    for dolphins, II 84
Deasy, Timothy, a Fenian, III 159n6
death, thoughts on, I 122, II 215, 241, 307,
    312
debentures, VI 105, VII 7; secured on New
    South Wales revenue, VII 9; pro-
    jected letter to Sydney Herald on
    (WSJ, November 1856), VII
    116
De Bretueils, of France, ancestors of Rich-
    ard Cantillon, V 123
de Cantelupe, ancestral name of Cantillon

family, V 123–4, 125–6, 127, 131
de Cantelupe, Mabella, V 123, 124
de Cantelupe, Raymond, ancestor of Rich-
    ard Cantillon, V 123
de Cantillon, Phillipe, see Cantillon, Philip
decennial periods, see cycles
decimal coinage
  in Canada, IV 161; in Italy, I 122, II
    200; England not yet ready for, III
    184
  Hendrick's pamphlet on, III 212, 213,
    232n2; Thomas Jevons's ideas on, I
    120, II 143, 155–6
  pound and mil system for, II 156, III
    186n1
  Royal Commission on (1856–9), II
    156n5; Professor Graham's evi-
    dence before, III 187
  William Brown's Bill for, II 155, 157–8
decimal system, necessary for use of
    arithmometer, VII 87, 89, 90
Decker, Sir Matthew, An Essay on the Causes
    of the decline of the foreign trade . . .
    (1744), V 159n2; ed. 2, 160
de Colmar, Thomas, inventor of the
    arithmometer, VII 85–6, 87, 88
Dee, River
  childhood games by, II 294
  tidal power from, III 122
definitions
  Cairnes's chapter on, IV 114
  and logical method, VI 5; discussed in
    WSJ's logic classes, III 118
  of political economy, VI 4–8; Marshall
    on WSJ's contribution to, VII 143
  Walras's plea for, IV 262
de Grey, Earl, III 237n3
Deism, II 325–6
de Jong, Dr I., mathematician, IV 57n3
de Kingsley, Sir Adam, of Cheshire, V 124
De la Beche, H. T., The Geological Observer
    (1851), I 98
De Laille (or Deleuil), supplier of materials
    for Paris Mint, II 60, 70, 71
de la Rive, Auguste, Traité d'Electricité théo-
    rique et appliquée, I 96
de la Rivière, Pierre François Joachim
    Henri le Mercier (1720?–93), VI 5
De Laski, Paris acquaintance of Thomas
    Jevons, II 58–9; WSJ too shy to call
    on his sister, 58–9
Delhi wheat prices, V 46–7, 50

de Malynes, Gerard (?1586–1641), *The Centre of the Circle of Commerce . . .* (1623), V 160

demand
for commodities; lecture notes on, VI 48–54; limit to world demand for manufactured goods, IV 237; not a demand for labour (Mill), III 119–20
demand curves: Dupuit's, IV 197, V 95; Fleeming Jenkin's, IV 5n3, 166–78; Walras's, IV 270, VII 76

demand and supply, *see* supply and demand

democracy
and attitudes to working-class franchise, I 208, III 135
democratic argument on taxation, III 239
in Minnesota, II 409; in New South Wales, II 248
and popularisation of political economy, IV 68

De Morgan, Augustus (1806–71), Professor of Mathematics at University College, London
WSJ studies under, I 15, 95, his mathematical thinking influenced by, 15, 16; attends his lectures on 'Higher Junior' mathematics, 65, 67, 69, copies out unpublished tracts, 65, 67; returns to 'Higher Senior' lectures in 1859, 403, 421, 422, VII 120, finds him 'an unfathomable fund of mathematics', II 406; WSJ's notes and extracts on the lectures, I 65n6
and WSJ as logician: classes on probabilities, II 30–1; influence on WSJ's scientific work, 31n7; testimonial for WSJ as lecturer in logic at Queen's College, Liverpool, III, 106, 108–9; his definitions discussed in WSJ's logic classes, 118; WSJ's head 'full' of his logic, V 80; on WSJ's abacus, I 206
at Faraday's evening lecture, I 82; his 'wild complexities', III 13; difference with Spencer on quantitative nature of logic, 117; on education, VII 99; resigns professorship (1867), I 206n2; H. E. Roscoe

regrets not attending to, II 66
Essay on Probabilities, VII 87; *Trigonometry and Double Algebra*, I 64
also mentioned, III 76n2, 113

Demosthenes, II 335

Dendy, John, statistics on pattern of drunkenness, V 165n4

Denison, Sir William Thomas, Governor-General of New South Wales, II 205n4, II 278n9
blows up the new Legislative Council, II 205
fears scarcity of food, III 20
President of Philosophical Society, I 23, II 249; paper on Rail Roads, I 26, II 235n1, 265
his twelve meteorological stations, II 269

Denmark
international trade, V 27
money system, V 130
rise of prices, IV 45
St Thomas, Danish island, II 381, 397
WSJ visits (1877), IV 205, 206, 291, V 65; his few words of Danish, IV 233
also mentioned, II 66n14, 431
see also Alexandra, Princess of Denmark

depreciation
allowance for, VI 47, 77
in America (1857), VI 124
of currency, VII 75; English sovereign, III 26; of Italian paper money, VI 110
examination question on, VII 138
see also under gold

depressions
distinguished from crises, IV 300; periods of, ushered in by credit crisis, VII 91; shown in chart of credit cycle, VI 130–1
in iron trade, III 228, VII 49
of 1841, VI 15–16, VII 91
see also cycles

De Quincey, Thomas (1785–1859): *The Logic of Political Economy* (1844), included in 'List of Mathematico-Economic Books', IV 278; his strange theory of utility, VII 78, 79–80

Derby: Lucy Jevons at, II 142, 145, III 149, 442; WSJ has a family holiday at Matlock, IV 271, 281

Derby, Earl of: forms Ministry (1852), I 85, 86; renders the Constitution ridiculous, II 412; resigns office over Disraeli's military policy (1878), IV 224n4

Descartes, René, I 82, II 437

Deutsche Allgemeine Polytechnische Zeitung, notice of WSJ and review of Walras (1875), IV 103, 188

Deville, Henri St Claire (1818–81), produces aluminium from bauxite ore, II 63n6

Devonshire, 6th Duke of: Paxton's work for, at Chatsworth, II 12n5; Italian sculptures at Chatsworth, IV 122

Devonshire, 7th Duke of, Chairman of the Royal Commission on science and the state (1869), III 237n3

Devonshire Committee on Scientific Instruction (1871–5), V 103n1

diagrams: for *Investigations in Currency and Finance*, V 158–9, 201; for John Mills's paper on Credit Cycles, VI 130–2, VII 126; for 'Statistical Atlas', and *Two Diagrams, see* Jevons, William Stanley, Works; in *Theory of Political Economy*, VII 146; WSJ's limited use of, V 137; diagrams and symbols, V 23–4

diamonds: chance, and the diamond-fields, IV 258; coal, the 'black diamond', VII 21; the Koh-i-Noor, II 188, 199; in a railway carriage, II 177

Dickens, Charles
concern for London poor, I 16, 17; and political economists, VII 45
Barnaby Rudge, WSJ's favourite novel, I 55; *Bleak House*, I 16; *David Copperfield*, IV 105; *Oliver Twist*, I 16, 71n6, 90n3
also mentioned, II 25n8

Dickins, Thomas, President of Manchester Statistical Society, V 25, 26n

Dieppe, *Table d'hôte* at, II 177–8

differential calculus
WSJ and: basis of his theory and statistics, I 15, 27, 34–5; works at, under De Morgan, 94, II 403; used in theory of interest, IV 25, in utility theory, VI 87; reliance on,

questioned by Cliffe Leslie, VII 160
Cournot's use of, V 24; d'Aulnis's, IV 72
see also calculus

differential co-efficients, VII 145

differential equations, II 406, VII 155

Dikins, Mr or Mrs, London lodging-house keeper, II 11

Dilke, Sir Charles Wentworth (1843–1911), 2nd Baronet, M.P., member of Political Economy Club, IV 202

Dillon, John (1851–1927), Irish M.P., released from prison, V 189n2

diminishing returns: in Ricardian theory, IV 266; in Gossen's laws of pleasure, 268; examination question on, V 152

Disraeli, Benjamin, Lord Beaconsfield
as Chancellor of the Exchequer (1852), I 85; Budget, 79, Budget Party in St James's Road, 85
legalises peaceful picketing (1875), VI 73n5
orders Mediterranean Fleet to Dardanelles (1878), IV 224; rejects war with Russia over Turkey, 225n3
purchase of Post Office telegraphs, IV 150n4
WSJ's mixed feelings on, IV 293
also mentioned, VII 154

distribution
of income, VI 60–8
tripartite division of total produce, 60, 67
of land in Australia, VII 5
of precious metals, VI 111, 112
examination question on, VII 131
of wealth, VI 12, VII 158
examination question on, V 152
wholesale and retail, labour employed in, VI 21

Dittman, Wilhelm (1833–92), laboratory assistant to H. E. Roscoe, II 315

divisibility of value, VI 94, 97

division of labour
division of employment, term preferred by Wakefield, VI 27, 34
for economical production, VI 22, VII 60–2, 159; lecture notes on, VI 26–36; disadvantages, 35
examination question on, V 152
in physical science, VI 7
taught to little ragged boys, VII 53

territorial, VI 31–2, VII 62

WSJ 'working hard' at (1857), I 28, VII 119; unpublished paper on, II 363n9

Dodds, George, *Railways, Steamers and Telegraphs*, reviewed by WSJ (*Spectator*, April, 1867), VII 126

Dolgelly: Jevons family holiday at, I 118, II 85, 86–9, 92; gold mines, II 135; also mentioned, II 132

domestic economy, VI 5

domestic servants, VI 21, 79

Donaldson, Sir Stuart Alexander (1815–67), first Minister in the new New South Wales Constitution, II 265

Donizetti, Gaetano
Don Pasquale and *Lucia di Lammermoor* performed in Sydney, II 290n4
Lucrezia Borgia included in WSJ's repertoire of music, II 224, *Don Pasquale* in his 'cheerful programmes', 339

Donkin, Bryan, & Co., engineering firm, III 187n1, 188n4; Horizontal Patent Steam Engine, 189–90

Donkin, Bryan, jun., engineer, III 187–8; Russian connections, 188n4

Dorrien, George, former Governor of Bank of England, IV 265n5

Dorset, population growth, VII 23, 24

Double Bay, Sydney, WSJ's third home in Sydney, I 22, II 248, 261–2, 270–2, 347, 355; plan of the house, 271; his parlour, 271, 278, 294–5, 309, 311, 313, sketch of, 271–2, 295; walk from, to the Mint, 272–3, 278
gold diggers from, II 346

double standard system
examination question on, VII 134
in France, VI 101
Wolowski on, III 196–8, 199, VI 102; single standard preferred by WSJ, III 198, VI 103
see also bimetallism

Douglas, Heron and Co., Scottish bank, collapse of in 1772, VI 117n6

Dove, Heinrich William (1803–79), *Law of Storms*, reviewed by WSJ (*Economist*, 1863), VII 125

Dowlais Iron Company, I 12

Dowling, Vincent, New South Wales squatter, I 127–8

Downshire, Earl of, his Irish estates, V 112–13

Doyle, Richard, *The Foreign Tour of Messrs Brown, Jones, and Robinson . . .* (1854), II 73

Dr —, ship's doctor on board the *Oliver Lang*, I 106–7, II 81, 83

Dr Williams's Library, III 12; WSJ's birth registered at, II 33

Drake, C. P., Boston electrician, makes gaslight from benzole, II 91n2

Draper, Professor, physicist, on calorescence, VII 93

Drummond, Thomas (1749–1840), inventor of the 'Drummond light', II 18

Dublin
British Association meeting (1878), WSJ's paper on sun-spots and commercial crises read at, IV 271–2, 274, VII 94
Phoenix Park murders (1882), V 189
Royal college of science, V 35n1
Soyer's soup kitchens, II 360n4
University, *Principles of Science* used as textbook, IV 286
also mentioned, II 181n2, 329n5, 392n18

Dublin Statistical Society Journal, article on Gold (J. E. Cairnes, 1859), III 17, 19, 21n6, 25

du Chaillu, Paul Belloni (1835–1903), explorer: his gorillas, II 436

Dudley, Midland Exhibition, VII 47

Dudley, Mr, neighbour of WSJ in Australia, II 405

Dumas, Jean Baptiste André (1800–84), chemist, a founder of Ecole Centrale, Paris, II 65

du Maurier, George Louis Palmella Busson (1834–96), *Punch* illustrator, IV 194

Dunedin, New Zealand: Herbert Jevons at the Bank of New South Wales in, III 38, 40, 157, 204; leaves temporarily for gold fields, 74; moves to Hokatika, 157, 158

Dunoyer, Charles (1786–1862), French economist, IV 197n4, V 39

Dupre de Saint-Maur, VI 96n4

Dupuit, A. J. Etienne-Juvenel (1804–66), engineer and pioneer mathematical economist
anticipates WSJ on utility, IV 192; his correct theory of value, 249; con-

Dupuit, A. J. (contd)
    fuses demand and utility curves,
        197, V 95
    Mémoire de la Mesure d'utilité des Travaux
        Publics . . . (1844): Walras on, IV
        85, 196–7, 205, V 95; read by WSJ,
        IV 192, 249
    'Réponse à M. Dunoyer . . .' (Journal
        des Economistes, 1861), IV 197, 205
duration: as criterion of fixed or circulating
    capital, VI 42–7; lengthening dur-
    ation of life expectancy, VI 59; see
    also time
Durham
    coal fields, VII 21
    population growth, VII 24
    WSJ visits, III 127
Dutch, see Holland
Dyer, Louis, husband of Margaret Mac-
    millan, V 101n1

Early English Text Society, V 82, VI 69
Eastbourne, visit to, IV 271, 292
East India Company, V 47, 77n5
East India merchants, V 84
East India Steam Packet Co., III 157
East India trade, VI 32
East Indies, II 184
Economic Journal
    F. Y. Edgeworth, first editor, V 98n1
    obituaries: Juglar (by De Foville, 1905),
        V 17n1; Foxwell (by J. M. Keynes,
        1936), V 106n2, 185n1
economic (economical) science, IV 235,
    VII 9
    examination questions on, VII 134
    working men's distrust of, III 130
    WSJ's plans for teaching, III 105
economic sociology, VII 158
economics
    WSJ and: term 'economics' preferred by
        WSJ to 'political economy', VII
        158; 'problem of economics' stated,
        158, 160; investigation of utility the
        foundation of economics, 161–2; his
        contribution to the professionali-
        sation of economics, VI vii, to
        economic vocabulary, VII 143,
        144; Theory of Political Economy the
        first modern book on (Keynes), I 48
    Herbert Stanley Jevons abandons
        science for, I 114n2

Macleod's 'Pure Economics', IV 115
other uses of term, VII 99, 100, 101
see also mathematical theory of political
    economy; political economy; statistics
Economist
    articles by WSJ: 'the Depreciation of
        Gold' (8 May 1869), III 82n4, 208;
        'Notice of a Work on Indian Whirl-
        winds' (March 1861), VII 124;
        obituary of Cliffe Leslie (4 Feb-
        ruary 1882), V 171; reply to Mr
        Westgarth on bi-metallism (15 Ap-
        ril 1882), V 187–8; review of Dove's
        Law of Storms (1863), VII 125;
        considers submitting statistical cal-
        culations, I 37, II 448, 452
    notices and reviews of works by WSJ:
        'Diagrams' noticed (15 November
        1862), II 448n3, 450, 459, III 4;
        paper on gold coinage noticed (12
        December 1868), III 200; A Serious
        Fall . . . reviewed by Cairnes (30
        May 1863), III 17, 18, 22, 23, 25,
        27, 38, 42
    other articles: Cairnes, on periodical
        panics (1863), III 64; 'G.', on
        Paper Currency (1875), IV 159–
        60; 'Mr Lowe on Scotch Banking'
        (1873), IV 11n5; Pownall's circular
        (1881), V 130n2; 'Questions for
        Bimetallists' (1882), V 188–9,
        192n2; Rylett, on Irish Land
        League (1881), V 157, 197; Wo-
        lowski, on income of France (1871),
        III 242
    'Commercial History and Review of
        1864', Supplement, 11 March
        1865, III 67; monthly prices
        quoted, III 82, 141–2, 252
    editors: Bagehot, II 450n1, III 19n2, 86,
        IV 160, with Richard Holt Hutton
        before 1861, I 36, 182n3, II 416n6;
        Inglis Palgrave, V 72, 73, 129, 157,
        197; assistant editor, see Giffen,
        Robert
    also mentioned, III 61, 217, 225, IV 7,
        11n4, 160–161, V 47, 194n3
Economist Annual Review (1876), Index list
    of prices, IV 170
Economist, and Joint Stock Banker's Journal
    and General Commercial Chronicle
    (1837), IV 275

Economista d'Italia, IV 84
Economiste Français, L': de Fontpertuis on British Association meeting (31 August 1878), IV 27; de Foville, 'Les Tâches du Soleil et les Crises Commerciales' (15 February 1879), V 17n1
economists
WSJ as economist: De Foville on, V 17n1; Mallet on, V 188n4; Marshall on, V 66, VII 141–6; his originality questioned, VII 152–7; *see also under* economics
Continental and English, VII 98–101; German, IV 266, 283
Hans Forssell's portraits of modern economists, IV 233–4
in the Political Economy Club, IV 134
in the Royal Society, V 184
socialistic attitudes of young economists, V 186
'third school' in Macleod's list of, IV 115
Eden, Sir Frederick Morton, *The State of the Poor* (1797), VII 104, 107
Edge, George, servant of Jevons family, at Roscoe's funeral, III 205
Edgeworth, Francis Ysidro (1845–1926)
WSJ and: WSJ's testimonials for his (unsuccessful) applications for professorships, V 98–9, 145–6; friendship with WSJ at Hampstead, V 98n1, 202; letter of condolence on WSJ's death, 201–2
'deep in the fallacies of Mill' on capital, V 156
becomes Tooke Professor of Political Economy at King's College, London, V 98n1
first editor of *Economic Journal*, V 98n1
New and Old Methods of Ethics (1877), V 145; *Mathematical Psychics* (1881), V 145, 156n1
letter to, V 156
Edinburgh
Royal Observatory, IV 296; earth-thermometer observations, 297
Royal Society of Edinburgh, IV 231, V 17; Proceedings, IV 5–6
'Torbanehill case', II 50
WSJ's visits to, in 1866, III 126, in 1876, IV 173
Edinburgh Courant, IV 173n3

Edinburgh Review: article by Cairnes (July 1860), III 17
Edinburgh University
Chair of Political Economy: Hodgson apponted to, I 13, III 235, hopes WSJ will succeed him, IV 150; not attractive to WSJ, 173
Honorary degree conferred on WSJ (1876), IV 167, 173, V 107
Library, IV 231
Edison Telephone Company, II 415n2
Edmonds, Frederick B., classmate and friend of WSJ at University College, I 54; on sun-spots, V 86, 100–1, 103
letter to, II 111–13; letters from, V 86–7, 91–2, 100–1, 103
Edmonds, Thomas Rowe (1803–89), father of F. B. Edmonds, II 111n1
Edmonds, Mrs Thomas Rowe, mother of F. B. Edmonds, V 92
education
coal for, VII 28, 35
and the examination system, IV 212–13
De Morgan on, VII 99
Elementary Education Bill (1870), III 238n2
'free trade in', III 138
as labour, VI 21
school run on Froebel and Pestalozzi principles, IV 212n1
teachers: political economy for primary school teachers, III 105, VII 37–9, 53; for WSJ as teacher *see under* Jevons, William Stanley
training through play, IV 287
Whately on, VII 52
WSJ's system 'true Republican', IV 213; advice to Henrietta on, II 360–1
see also examinations; universities
Educational Committee of the Privy Council, V 29n2
Educational Congress, Brussels (1880), V 106n1
Edward III, III 222: loans from Florentine merchants, IV 215
Edward, Prince of Wales
celebrations for his marriage to Princess Alexandra, I 190, III 6–8
patron of foundation of Royal College of Music, V 178

Edward, Mr, tutor, his debts, II 29–30
effective demand, IV 46, VI 83, VII 76;
    effective offer, VII 76
    see also demand
efficiency, multiplication of, VI 29–30,
    VII 61–2
Egypt
    alluvial floods and biblical criticism, II
        330
    British sovereigns legal tender in, III 63;
        trade with, V 50
    Great Pyramid, VII 25–6, 29
    nationalist revolt (1882), V 200
    tribute paid to Turkey, VI 113n8
Eisdell, J. S., *Treatise on the Industry of
    Nations*. . . . (1839), III 27, 31
Electrical Congress, first International,
    Paris, 1881, V 148n2
Electrical Exhibition, first International,
    Paris, 1881, V 148; Exhibition at
    Crystal Palace, 148n2
electricity
    in cloud formation, WSJ's theory of non-
        agency, II 329–30, 345
    coal for, VII 31
    electric light, for magic lantern, II 103;
        Electric Exhibition lit by, V 148
    electric telegraph, II 180, VI 25, VII 31
    Faraday's discoveries, I 81n1
    German lead in, II 125
    as a prime mover, 'an impossibility', VI
        24; cannot be a substitute for coal as
        source of power, VII 34
    Tindall's Royal Institute lectures on, II
        146
    WSJ studies at University College under
        Potter, I 83, 87; takes examination
        in, 95–6
Eliot, [Sir] John (1839–1908), Meteoro-
    logical Reporter to the Govern-
    ment of Bengal, V 51
Elizabeth I, Queen of England, VI 70
Elliott, Dr Christopher, M.D., of Bristol,
    IV 129n1
Elliott, Mrs, attends British Association
    meeting at Bristol (1875), IV 129
Ellis, Alexander, paper on spelling reform
    read before Royal Society of Arts
    (1870), III 238n2
Ellis, Mr (d. *c.* 1879), chairman of Midland
    Railway Company, V 87
Ellis, William, patron of the Birkbeck

Schools, Manchester, VII 53
Elmes, Harvey Lonsdale (1813–47), ar-
    chitect, II 95n5
Ely, Talfourd (d. 1922), master at Uni-
    versity College School, III 6–7
Emerson, Ralph Waldo, III 39; *English
    Traits*, II 259
emigration, VI 124
    to Australia, I 24, II 53–4, 267–8, IV 7,
        VII 8; boom, II 111n3; emigrant
        ships, 111n3, 116n6, 141; and land
        availability, II 282–7
    effect on price of labour, IV 7
    emigrants, II 83, 115n5, 270n2, 298n11,
        363n8; WSJ perhaps an emigrant
        to New Zealand, 417; coal miners
        and iron workers, VII 17
    internal, in America, II 419
    and productive capital and population,
        VII 50
    statistics, II 426
Empedocles, IV 15n4
Empire, Sydney newspaper, II 265, 278n9;
    WSJ unpaid Meterological Obser-
    ver for, I 23, II 198, 239–40, 244,
    303; sends copies to England, 195,
    324; subscribes to, VII 116; Mail
    numbers for England, II 297, 346,
    VII 123; paper goes bankrupt
    (1858), II 341, 346, resumes publi-
    cation (1860), 341n3
    articles and letters by WSJ: on Land
    Laws (June 1857), VII 3–6, 6–8; on
    Land Policy (7 April 1857), I 26, II
    235n1, 282–7, VII 3; 'Meteorology
    and the Herald' (25 February
    1857), II 268–9; 'Public Lands of
    New South Wales' (24 June 1857),
    II 297, VII 3–8; 'The Railway
    Discussion' (19 July 1856), II 235–
    7; 'Railway Economy' (29 Decem-
    ber 1857), II 303, VII 8–11, 117;
    reply to Mr Allen on Protection (28
    March 1857), II 281; 'On a Sun-
    gauge' (14 July 1857), II 297, VII
    123; 'The Western Line of Rail-
    way' (10 February 1857), II 262–8;
    other articles and letters from WSJ,
    I 26, VII 123
'Employer, An', letter to *The Times* on
    employer-employee relations, III
    148, 150n2, 151, 153

employers and employed, III 134, 137–8, VII 38, 43, 45

employment
  census returns, VII 119
  conditions of, and supply of persons, VII 63–4
  dependence on capital, VII 159
  Mill's 'double' employment, VI 51–2
  restrictions on, VII 48
  and the wages fund, Mill's argument on, VI 51–2

Emsley, John, Bradford businessman, V 172n1

Emu plains, New South Wales, I 143, 224–5, II 264; botanising in, I 153; a camp on, 215–17, II 220–1; races held on, I 154

Encyclopaedia Britannica, 9th edition: WSJ declines request for article on political economy, V 155; articles by Herschel, II 432n3, 434; editor (James Thomson), II 228n8

Encyclopédie Méthodique, IV 215

Encyclopaedia Metropolitana (1845), VI 3
  'Heat' (Rev. Francis Lunn), I 65,
  'Political Economy' (Nassau Senior), VII 102
  'Sound' (J. Herschel), VII 92

energy
  Joule's principle of conservation of energy, II 66n13
  and theory of labour, VI 24, 26
  Thomson's work on, II 66n12

Enfield, Edward (1811–80), moneyer at the Royal Mint, II 64n2, 140, 194
  marriage to Harriet Roscoe, I 90n4, II 64, 122; their London home, 435; in Paris, II 65; tours Northern Germany, 71n1; visits Switzerland, 230; goes with WSJ to a chemical manufactory, 435
  as member of Council of University College, London, donates blue books to Owens College, III 233–4
  letter to, III 233–4

Enfield, Mrs Edward, *see* Roscoe, Harriet

Enfield, Henry, secretary of Spicer Street Domestic Mission, I 90n4

Enfield, New South Wales, I 143

Enfield rifle, II 407, 436

Engineer, The, V 86

engineering: proposed as career for WSJ, II 38–9; plans for Engineering School at Owens College, III 150

Institute of Civil Engineering, III 187n1

Engineering: Coal Question reviewed in (15 June 1866), III 125; 'The Power of the Tides' (1866), III 122, 123

England
  and America, II 392–3; Herbert Jevons on, 423
  Australian view of, II 255–6, 279
  Day of Humiliation and Prayer for peace, II 132; newspaper campaign for peace, 197
  English chemists, their backwardness compared with German, II 125
  English people: attitudes to animals and blacks, IV 174n1; feudal power of aristocrats, VII 15; ignorance of Irish affairs, V 111–12; love of peace, IV 225; misunderstanding of liberty, VII 43 4; musical tastes, V 199; niggardly and stupid, III 147; short-visioned and proud of heart, VII 75
  and France, II 417, 418. *See also under* Great Britain
  incomes, 1841-68, III 242
  Kossuth finds refuge in, II 415n3
  landowners, V 197; landlord system of tenure, VII 100; 'old landed fogies' in Opposition Party, III 102; parks, II 365, 366
  law, civil and criminal, VI 133; criminal law revision (1879), V 23
  philosophical teaching, V 22–3
  political economy: English Economic School, I 203; WSJ's mathematical theory ignored or ridiculed, IV 61–2, except among younger mathematicians and economists, 63; interests stop at Adam Smith and Ricardo, 95; change of opinion, 103, V 144; elementary teaching in, V 15–16, 29–30, VII 38–9, 51–3; economical science overshadowed by J. S. Mill's writings, 77
  progress and wealth, II 429–30, VII 43, 55; preeminence in commerce and civilisation, 75; 'the Genius of the World', II 259; wealth of all classes, VII 54; her noonday prosperity past, II 393

England (contd)
  winter in, II 118, 125
  WSJ's feeling for, II 216, 224, 242, 334,
    386–9; an English exile in Aus-
    tralia, 313; finds Anna Bishop a
    truly English woman, 224; 'the quiet
    and solid success' back at home,
    392; dislikes servility of lower
    classes, 392
  see also Great Britain
England and Wales, population and acres
    in crop, VII 4
Englefield Green, home of Uncle Robert
    Roscoe, I 66, II 32n4, 141, 145;
    schoolboy visits to, II 9, 16, later
    visits, 389, 414, 416, 418, 425; a
    railway accident on the way,
    175
entrepreneur: definition of, lacking in
    Political Economy, IV 260, 262,
    263, V 95; note on, IV 263n4;
    translated as employer or under-
    taker, VI 67
Epping Forest, I 55
equations
  of exchange: correspondence with
    Fleeming Jenkin on, III 167n2,
    171–3, 178; correspondence with
    Walras on, IV 40, 46; similarity
    between WSJ's equation and
    Walras's équation de satisfaction
    maximum, 46, 50, 63, WSJ's pri-
    ority, 64; lecture notes on, VI 88;
    'Failure of the Equations of
    Exchange', IV 131n3
  and international traffic, V 28
  Mill's use of the term, VI 82
  in Theory of Political Economy, IV 87;
    conversation with Miss Borchardt
    on, IV 149; questioned by Adam-
    son, 227–8; Westergaard on, 255–
    8; referred to, in lectures, VI 93;
    Marshall's criticisms, VII 145; Sa-
    turday Review on, 154–6
equilibrium economics
  in Theory of Political Economy, IV 151
  Walras as creator of, IV 36n1, 65, 260n3
  R. O. Williams on theory of, IV 141
equilibrium of utilities, VII 82, 83
Errera, Alberto (1842–94), of Venice,
    economic historian and statistician,
    IV 48, 65, 67, 260, 261, 262; copy of

Theory of Political Economy sent to,
    IV 103
Essays read before the Literary and Philosophical
    Society of University College, London
    (1865), I 187n3
Euclid, I 69, IV 231, V 192
Eugenia de Montija, Empress of France:
    appears with Emperor Napoleon
    III in the Tuileries, II 69
Europe
  gold production, IV 7
  North Europe trade crisis (1857), IV
    210; prolonged crisis (1881), V 132
  prices, III 24
  war prospects (1864), III 50
Evening Post (New York), IV 293
Evening Standard, review of Theory of Political
    Economy (17 December 1871), IV 5
Everest, Rev. Robert (1798–1874), chap-
    lain to the East India Company, V
    46–7
evil, I 155, 157; dark thoughts on, 156;
    sermon to Lucy on, II 288–9
evolution: controversy between Spencer
    and Gladstone on, IV 38–9; WSJ
    accepts Spencer's philosophy, I 52,
    reads Origin of Species, 66, finds
    doctrine not inconsistent with De-
    sign, IV 42
Ewart, William (1798–1869), M.P. for
    Liverpool, I 86
examinations
  WSJ's views on: dominated by J. S. Mill
    in logic and political economy,
    I 48, III 245–6, IV 96, 115–16, V
    80–1; speech on competitive exam-
    inations at British Association
    meeting (1875), IV 130; a defence
    of the system, 212–13; pressure of,
    on examiners, V 80, 106, 116,
    118
  Bankers' Institute examinations, V 80
  Cambridge Tripos in Moral Sciences:
    WSJ's arrangements with Foxwell
    for Political Economy paper
    (1874), IV 52–3, 69–70, 88, 96,
    126, (1875), 115–16, 133, 147;
    papers set for, VII 132–8; women
    admitted to, IV 143, 146; papers
    read, lists settled, 148–9; J. Neville
    Keynes heads Tripos list (1875), V
    105, 177; comments on answers of

candidates, IV 196, V 23, 80

Civil Service examinations, WSJ refuses examinership, V 180

Indian Civil Service, logic and political economy papers, V 65

for Joseph Hume scholarship, University College, London, V 105, 109

Owens College, examination system, IV 23

Oxford University, WSJ refuses examinership, V 180

for Ricardo Scholarship in Political Economy, University College, London, II 406; won by WSJ (1860), I 34, II 416n5, 422–3, III 103; WSJ and Bagehot examiners for (1875), IV 124, WSJ and Foxwell (1881), V 147, 149, 151; question paper, V 151–3

University College, London, *see* University College

University of London: examinerships in Logic and Political Economy for M.A. degree, IV 239–40; WSJ examines in Logic, 239–40, examinership terminates (1880), V 110; examining for B.A. degree, IV 183, 291, V 65; women admitted to degrees, IV 224

Examiner, The

article attacking WSJ's address to Manchester Statistical Society, IV 91; reply (refused publication), 91–3

editors, A. W. Fonblanque, III 181n2, Henry Morley, V 73

exchange

as barter, VI 94; money as medium, 94–5, oxen as, 96; always mutual, VII 75

of indivisible commodities, correspondence with d'Aulnis on, IV 58–9, 62–3, 70–1, 75, 76, 82, 90; Williams's solution to problem, 131, 153–4

see also foreign exchanges

Exchange, The, notice of 'Two Diagrams' (1862), II 459, III 2–3

editor, II 459, III 3

exchange, theory of

in *Theory of Political Economy*, III 246–7,

IV 39–41, 104n11, VI ix, VII 141–2; law of, VI 86–7; similarity of Walras's theory, IV 39, 46–7, 49–50, 67; Cairnes's objections, III 246; d'Aulnis on, IV 72; defended by G. Darwin, 102; Williams on, 151–4; Fleeming Jenkin on WSJ's 'fluxion' theory, 167–78; discussed in *Saturday Review*, VII 152, 154–7

Dupuit's failure to reach a theory, IV 192; Gossen's theory, 269; Mangoldt's, V 104; Mill's theory of international exchanges, VII 152, 156

see also ratio of exchange

exchange value: meaning of term, III 22; interchangeable with utility, VII 150–1; Cairnes on WSJ's theory of, III 246–7, VII 148–51, answered by G. Darwin, IV 102; Walras's use of term, IV 47

Exchequer Bills, VI 116, 118

Exeter, British Association meeting (1869), III 237n3

Exeter, 2nd Marquess of (Cecil Brownlow, 1795–1867), Lord Chamberlain, I 72

'Experimental Legislation and the Drink Traffic', *see* Jevons, William Stanley, Works

exports (British): coal, VII 14, 24–25, 27, 28, 37; cotton goods to India, III 251n3; machinery to Australia, II 281; soap, II 40

reduced by rise in wages, IV 51

exports and imports

effect of foreign exchange on, VI 129, of taxation, VII 15

methods of payment, VI 108–11; in mercantalist and in 19th century views, 112–13

role of coal in, VII 24–5

statistics of, II 427

see also balance of trade

Eyre, Edward John, Governor of Jamaica, 1849–66, III 135

Eyre & Spottiswoode, publishing house, V 183n1

see also Spottiswoode, William

Eyton, R. W., *Antiquities of Shropshire* (1854–60), V 127

factories
coal for, VII 30
factory hands and farm hands, VI 35
married women in, V 161–7, 172–3
WSJ's first-hand knowledge of, V 164;
visits to manufactories, I 89, 92–3,
II 41–3, 435
see also manufactories
factory legislation: WSJ's interest in, 50;
Factory Acts, V 138n3, 172, examination question on, 152; proposed
crèches for infants of working mothers, 164
Fairchild, Charles Stebbins (1842–1924),
American financier, V 83–4
Fairfax, John, proprietor of *Sydney Morning
Herald*, II 250–1
Falbe-Hansen, Vigand Andreas (1841–
1932), Danish statistician, IV 43–4,
66, 244; WSJ meets in Denmark,
IV 206, 207, 244
letter from, IV 43–5
Falck, Georg von, economist, included in
list of Mathematico-economic writers, V 42
Falkland Islands: Brunel's *Great Britain*
sails *via*, II 60, rescued from, II
42n4
family budget of the poor (1872), III 256;
wages spent exclusively on bread,
VI 60–1
famines
as check to population, VI 58, 59
in India, IV 293n1, examination question on, VII 132
in Manchester (1842), VI 16
Faraday, Michael (1791–1867)
on decennial periodicity of sun-spots, I
24, 82
Friday evening lecture at the Royal
Institute, WSJ attends, I 81–2, 84,
87, II 243
'Oversight by Faraday' (WSJ, *Nature*,
10 February 1870), VII 126
Farey, Barnard William (1827–88), member of Institution of Civil Engineers: letter to WSJ on economical steam engines, III 187–90
farming
acres in crop for New South Wales and
other countries, VII 4
farmers' stocks of corn, VI 53–4

fertility differences, VI 90
gold coin for harvest wages, III 195–6
mutual aid from arable farming and
stock breeding, VI 15; stock-
farming, IV 241
subsidiary trades, VI 34
farms: a farmer's wife in Nepean Valley, I
148; fencing in Hawkesbury valley
farms, 138–9; Herbert Jevons's
troubles in Minnesota, II 413; Indian corn in Hunter River Valley, I
127
see also corn; Fishlocke; New South
Wales; vegetation
Farr, Dr William (1808–87), medical statistician, President of the Royal
Statistical Society, III 106n6
on the arithmometer, VII 89
Report on Statistical Science in England
(1863), III 49, *Serious Fall* noticed
in, VII 125
statistics of 1851 census, used by WSJ, I
17, VI 33n5
testimonial for WSJ, III 106, 114; his
neighbour in Hampstead, V 90–1
Farrer, Mr, bank agent in New Zealand,
III 74
Farrer, [Sir] Thomas Henry (1819–99),
Secretary of the Board of Trade:
letter on state control of industry, V
93; *The State in its Relation to Trade*
(English Citizens Series), V 137–8
Faucher, Julius (1820–78), IV 85
Faucher, Léon (1803–54), *Remarks on the
Production of the precious metals . . .*
(1852), V 58
Fawcett, Henry (1833–84), Professor of
Political Economy at Cambridge, I
37, 192n2, V 22; in the Ricardo-
Mill tradition, IV 122, ranked with
Adam Smith in Cambridge, V 78
WSJ and: quotes *Serious Fall . . .* in his
British Association paper, I 192n2,
III 36, 37, 42, 43, is converted by
WSJ's argument, 44–5; testi-
monials for WSJ, III, 106, 109
advocate of profit-sharing schemes, III
138, 143; at the Political Economy
Club, IV 202; a 'crotchety' exam-
iner, 240; supports proposed Fel-
lowship of Royal Society for Inglis
Palgrave, V 163; sponsors Civil

Service pension for Cliffe Leslie, 169n1

returned as Liberal M.P. for Hackney (1880), III 37n2, V 101n3; becomes Postmaster General, 93n2, 156, 161, speech in defence of postal notes, 101

Manual of Political Economy (1863), I 192n2; reviewed with *Serious Fall* in *Spectator* (16 May 1863), III 13n3; reviewed in *Westminster Review* (September 1863), 48n1; ed. 3, III 139n2; 'an abstract of Mill', 240, 241, 'Mill and water', VI 3–4; forced on students, III 246; definition of capital, VI 37, on fixed capital, 43; recommended to WSJ's students, VII 60

Free Trade and Protection (1882), VII 106–7

letter from, III 44

Fawcett, Millicent Garrett (Mrs Henry Fawcett): *Political Economy for Beginners* (1870), III 139n2, V 15, VII 146; used by WSJ in his classroom, III 241; reviewed by WSJ in *Glasgow Herald*, VII 126

Fawcett, Preston & Co., Liverpool engineering firm, II 201n3

Faye, Hervé-Auguste-Etienne-Albans, French astronomer, 'Sur la Météorologie Cosmique' (1878), V 13

F.C., writer of letter to *The Times* on the gold question, III 36

Fellows, Sir Charles (1799–1860), archaeologist, I 82

Fenians: their bold act in Manchester (1867), III 159; uprising in Ireland 90n2; outrages in London (1881), V 134–5

Fergusson, Dr Andrew (1787–1870), retired Inspector-General of Hospitals in the English Army, fellow passenger of WSJ on board the *Medway*, II 380, 385–6: lodges with WSJ in Peru, 388, 394; continues to Panama, 397

Ferniow, Mrs, II 8

Ferrara, Francesco (1810–1900), Professor of Political Economy at Turin, IV 69n5; on Walras's list for copies of *Theory of Political Economy*, IV 68, 84

Ferraris, Maggiorino (1856–1929), Italian journalist and politician: in WSJ's political economy class at University College, IV 302n1; on the origin of clearing houses, 302, V 153n2

letter from, IV 302–3

Field, Henry William (1803–88), resident assayer to Royal Mint, 'Queen's Assay Master', II 133n3; letters to WSJ on the standard of the coin, before and after 1851, III 221–3, 224; is sent copy of 'On the Condition of the Metallic Currency', 224

Field, Miss, schoolmistress, II 69

Field Naturalist and Scientific Student, The, V 195n4; 'Reflected Rainbows' (WSJ 1883), V 196,200

Field, Roscoe, and Co., firm of solicitors founded by Robert Roscoe, I 66n5

financial crises: (1696), IV 215; (1797), VI 118; (1825), VI 119n1; (between 1844 and 1857), VI 128; (1878), IV 293n1, 304n6; (1882), V 171n3

see also cycles

Financial Opinion (1877–1888), IV 216, 220n2; 'The New Post-Office Bank Note' (by 'M.'), IV 216n1

Fisher, Mrs, III 73

fisheries: Billingsgate fishermen, VI 32; Yarmouth fishing crews, IV 78

Fishlocke, New South Wales farmer, WSJ visits his farm, I 171, 172, 173–5

Fitzgerald, Maurice, V 123

Fitzmaurice, ancestors of Richard Cantillon, V 124, 125

Fitzroy, Robert(1805–65), chief of Board of Trade Meterological department, II 386

Fitzroy River, Australia, II 344; New Diggings at, 346, 350–2

fixed capital, VI 42–7, 105; Adam Smith's use of term, 40, 42, 45; Fawcett's instances of, 43; Mill's distinction between circulating and, 42–3; Ricardo's definition, 42; examination questions on, VII 135–6

Flanders, VI 69, 102

Flavelles, Sydney instrument sellers, II 344–5

flax, VI 33, VII 24
Fletcher, Francis (b. 1799), II 122n7
Fletcher, Hamilton, Liverpool shipowner, II 144
Fletcher, Henrietta, II 122
Fletcher, Maria, *see* Roscoe, Mrs Henry
Fletcher, Thomas (1767–1850), Liverpool merchant and banker, II 122n7
Flintshire coal mines, VII 14–15
Florence
 Marshall stays in, V 170n3
 merchant loans to Edward III, IV 215
 Thomas Jevons's visit to, II 199, 200
Floyd, John Buchanan (1806–63), Confederate General, U.S. secretary of war, II 431
fluctuations in commerce
 WSJ's study of: starts with Statistical Diagrams, I 35, 37, III 37–8, continues with sun-spots, I 48, VII 91, 92; Paper on, read at British Association meeting (1862), I 37, 188n1, III 304, VII 124; discussed in *Serious Fall*, III 64; lecture notes on, VI 115–26
 businessmen's profits from, II 445
 distinguished from crises (Adamson), IV 301
 and overpopulation, III 255
 not susceptible to mathematical measurement (Cliffe Leslie), VII 160
 see also cycles
Flux, A. W., revises *The Coal Question* for third edition, IV 235n2
fluxion theory of exchanges, *see* exchange, theory of
flying fishes, I 104, II 84–5, 97
Folk Lore Society, V 131
Fonblanque, Albany de Grenier (1829–1924), jun., *How we are governed* . . . (1858), IV 213
Fonblanque, Albany William (1793–1872), Head of Statistical Department, Board of Trade, III 181
Fontpertuis, Adalbert Frout de (b. 1825), French economist: translates WSJ's inaugural lecture (1877), IV 192, 276; sends his volumes on India and China to WSJ, 276–7, noticed by WSJ in *Journal of the Royal Statistical*

Society, 287–8; letters from, IV 276–7, 287–8
food
 and coal VII 24
 in economic theory: effect of cheap bread on consumption in general, III 55; and population, Malthus's theory qualified, VI 57–60; prices and wages, VI 63, price curves, III 54; primary and secondary demand for, VI 14–16; producers, in Mill's theory, VI 51, 53; stocks, as early capital, VI 37
 prices: in London, II 414, in Boston, IV 6; rise in, 1871–2, III 256
 at the table: Australian damper, I 143, 146, 172, 175; colonial, II 405; homegrown and imported, VII 24; pineapple flavour from tar, VII 20; Spanish, II 397–8; raspberry vinegar and buns, II 81; table d'hôte, II 177–8, V 148–9; too much eating at Aunt Jane's, I 64
 see also potatoes; rice
Forbes, James David (1809–68), Scottish physicist: earth-thermometer observations, IV 296–7
Forbes, Mr, of Sydney notoriety, I 224
Ford's Australian Almanac, II 174n2
 see also Waugh (and Cox) Australian Almanac
foreign exchanges
 'arbitration' of exchanges, VI 114–15
 and balances of trade and payments, VI 110, 111, 112
 and bank rate, IV 251–2, VI 129
 examination questions on, VII 131
 and international currency, VII 73–4
 nominal and real causes of variations in, VI 110
 operation under gold standard and inconvertible currencies, VI 108–15
 par of, III 207n2, VI 109n2, 110, 111, VII 69, 70, 110
 Piccadilly Circus rates for franc and sterling, V 149
 proper subject for mathematical treatment, VII 160
 short exchange, VI 111
 and tax on imports, VII 145
foreign loans: effect on exchanges, VI 112–13; 'foreign drain' on England,

1753-4, IV 241; 'swindling' loans of 1866-73, IV 236-7

foreign trade
associations of foreign traders, VI 69
examination questions on, VII 137
gains from total and final utility of, VII 143
gold coin for, VII 74
as means of increasing production, VI 22; inverse relation to home demand, III 142-3; England's dependence on, VII 74-5
see also commerce; exports; *and under* Jevons, Thomas

Forssell, Hans (1843-1901), Swedish Minister of Finance: letter to WSJ asking for his portrait, IV 233-4

Forster, William Edward (1819-66), Chief Secretary for Ireland (1880), V 179; resigns (1882), 179n6, 189; his coercion policy, 197

Fortescue, Hugh, 3rd Earl (1818-1905), IV 117

Fortnightly Review
articles by WSJ: 'Cruelty to Animals ..' (1876), IV 174n1; 'The Future of Political Economy', Introductory Lecture at University College (1876), IV 182n1, 190, 192; 'The Post Office Telegraphs and their Financial Results' (1875), IV 150, 172. Review of *Theory of Political Economy* (Cairnes, 'New Theories in Political Economy', January 1872), III 245, IV 58, VII 146-52, V 30
other articles: 'Economic Definition of Wealth' (Thornton, 1875), IV 114; 'The First and the Last Catastrophe' (W. K. Clifford, 1875), IV 207n4; Sidgwick on Benthamism, V 75; review of Cairnes, *Theory of Exchange Value* (G. Darwin, 1875), IV 81n1, 87, 99, 100, 102, 180
editor, John Morley, IV 273n9; 'Comtists who reign in', IV 250

fossils, II 133-4, 157, 331; fossilised wood, I 170

Foster, [Sir] Michael (1836-1907), physiologist, fellow student of WSJ at University College, London, IV 128

Foster-Barham, Alfred Garrett, husband of Eliza Jevons, cousin of WSJ, II 103, III 30

Foster-Barham, Mrs Alfred, *see* Jevons, Eliza

Foucault, Jean Bernard Léon (1819-68), French physicist: experiments with Pendulum, II 102-3, 104-5

Fourier, Jean-Baptiste Joseph, Baron (1768-1830): theorem of roots of equations, I 82; theory of motion of heat, IV 207

'Fourier's Law', V 35

Foville, Alfred de (1842-1913), French statistician: correspondence with WSJ on commercial crises, V 13-14, 16-17; obituary of Juglar, 17n1

Fowke, Captain, of the Royal Engineers: designs for Great Exhibition buildings (1862), II 430n12

Fox Bourne, H. R., *The Romance of Trade*, VII 103

Fox, Head and Co., Newport Rolling Mills: profit-sharing schemes, III 151-2, 165, IV 51, VI 77

Fox, William Johnston (1786-1864), Unitarian preacher, radical M.P. for Oldham: articles for *The Times*, II 445

Foxwell, Herbert Somerton (1849-1936)
collection of books on economics, IV 52n1, V 76, 84, 149, 159-60, 176n1
as examiner, V 185n1, fellow examiner with WSJ for Cambridge Moral Sciences Tripos (1874), IV 52-3, 69-70, (1875), 115-16, 133, 145, 146-7, 148, 239; examines with WSJ for Ricardo Scholarship (1881), IV 124n1, V 147, 149, 151-3; appointed Examiner in Political Economy for M.A., London University, IV 239-40
Fellow of Royal Statistical Society (1878), IV 232
lectureship at University College, London (1875), IV 109, 134n1, 135n1, 142, 143, 144-5, 146, 147, 239, his syllabuses, 232; extension lectures at Cambridge, IV 142, 145, inter-Collegiate lectures, V 22, 78; succeeds WSJ as Professor of Political Economy at University College, London

Foxwell, Herbert Somerton (*contd*)
    (1881), IV 52n1, V 117–18, 133,
    136–7, 147, 185
projected edition of Adam Smith, V 81–
    2, 106, 118, 160
sponsors pension for Cliffe Leslie, V
    169n1
and WSJ: dines with WSJ at Political
    Economy Club, stays with him at
    Hampstead, IV 223–4, V 179, 185;
    on WSJ's work, I 50; likes 'parts' of
    *Money and the Mechanism of Ex-
    change*, IV 133; on the irritation
    caused in Cambridge by ed. 2 of
    Theory of Political Economy, V 77–8,
    79; edits *Investigations* . . . (1884), I
    39, 51n1, 181n4, V 181n2, VII vii
obituary (J. M. Keynes, 1936), V
    106n2, 185n1
letters to, IV 52–3, 69–70, 101–2, 115–
    16, 133, 142, 143, 146–7, 147, 156–
    7, 173–4, 223, 223–4, 232, 237,
    239–40, 278, V 75–6, 76–8, 79–81,
    81–3, 84, 105–6, 117–18, 119, 120,
    129–30, 136–7, 147, 149–50, 151,
    159–60, 175–6, 179, 185–6, 187;
    letters from, V 185–6
also mentioned, V 83, 163n2
France
coal resources, III 71, 123, VII 27, 33,
    34, 50; wood as substitute for, VII
    18
currency system, III 186, VII 66–8;
    international money established,
    III 212
double standard, III 196–7, V 139,
    VI 100–2, VII 66, 67–8, or alter-
    native double standard, 66; mutual
    substitution of silver and gold, III
    17, gold substituted for silver, 21,
    186; proportion of silver to gold, V
    140; relative value, VI 102
gold coins, I 122, V 59, VII 66; franc
    and napoleon as international cur-
    rency, III 183–4, 207, 232, VII 69;
    report of American assayers on, III
    219
paper money, VI 98
silver currency, III 5, debasement,
    186; silver shipped to, in exchange
    for gold in 1825, VI 120n12
economists, VII 99; receptive to mathematical approach, IV 95, 103; use
    of term 'utility', VI 10, VII 79;
    WSJ's collection of French econ-
    omic works, V 149–50
and England: alliance with England in
    Crimean War, II 175n8; Cobden-
    Chevalier commercial treaty
    (1860), II 408, III 208n1, VII 14;
    movement of French capital to
    London (1877), IV 220; loan to
    Bank of England in 1839, VI 122;
    trade with Britain, V 50n4; rules
    the world with England, II 417;
    'hearty enemies', 418; all educated
    Englishmen read French, IV 290
hotels: in Callao, II 378, 387, 394; in
    Panama, 379, 397; Table d'hôte in
    Dieppe, II 177–8. *See also* Paris
Navy: iron ships for, II 428; Fleet or-
    dered to Alexandria (1882), V
    200n5
people: don't emigrate, VI 31; French
    singers at the Crystal Palace, II
    418; genius for originating, V 148;
    soldiers, II 63; working habits, II
    62
population: Laspeyres' statistics on aver-
    age length of life, V 52; deferred
    marriages, VI 58; child mortality,
    59; and acres in crop, VII 4
railways: electric railway, V 148n2;
    Paris and Orleans Railway Com-
    pany, VI 77
trade and commerce: crisis of 1701, IV
    295; iron manufacture, III 128,
    VII 49–50, Thomas Jevons's pro-
    jected iron business in, II 138, 143,
    145; John Law's Mississippi
    scheme, VI 116; national income,
    III 242; stock market, V 171n3;
    wine production, VI 32, period-
    icity of vintages, V 167
wages, Laspeyres' study of, III 126
war with Germany (1870), III 232n3;
    indemnity paid to Prussia, VI 98n7
wild strawberries, II 167
WSJ and: reads French, I 69, 78, prac-
    tises on Henny, II 57–8; continues
    his studies in Sydney, 225, 251, 255;
    takes French for his B.A., 415;
    speaking troubles, II 61, 62, 387,
    IV 192

visits to: studies assaying in Paris (1854), *see under* Paris; (1874) with Harriet, IV 33n2; (1878), IV 244; (1881), with Harriet in Paris, *see* Paris

also mentioned, II 415n3, 428, 431, 446, III 50, 53n1, VII 100

France, Emperor and Empress of, *see* Napoleon III, marriage to Eugenia de Montijo

Francis, William, joint-editor of *London, Edinburgh and Dublin Philosophical Magazine* . . ., II 306

Frankland, Edward (1825–99), first Professor of Chemistry at Owens College, II 50, 74n16, 316; succeeded by H. E. Roscoe, II 304, 315

Fraser's Magazine: articles by J. E. Cairnes (September 1859, January 1860), III 17, 18; 'The Principles of Currency' (Bonamy Price, May 1863), III 32

Fredericksburg, Battle of, II 454n7

Free Banking School, IV 112

Freeman, family of, WSJ's photographic friends, III 33

Free Masons, VI 69, 74

free thought, VII 42; freedom of enquiry upheld by Herschel and WSJ, III 60; free thought and the *Examiner*, IV 92

free trade
    American view of, III 239; overturned in Australia, VII 43; Dutch policy of, V 72; Manchester blames for trade depression, V 25
    argument for, V 73, VII 27; steady prices produced by, III 56; promotion of, vital to England, VII 75; not responsible for fluctuations in commerce, VII 91
    books on, VII 106–7
    Cobden's success with Emperor of France on, II 408; his Association for, V 41
    general election fought on (1852), I 86
    Gladstone's measures, I 18, III 88, 136, VII 14, in 1849, VI 139
    trade union view of, III 136; threatened by wage demands, VII 50
    between workers and employers, III 138, VI 79
    also mentioned, II 287, V 20

free will, I 157; and cause and effect, II 361–2

freight, international, V 27; effect on balance of trade, VI 113

Fremantle, Hon. Sir Charles William (1834–1914), Deputy Master of the Mint: estimate of gold circulation, V 92; suggestion for withdrawing light coin, 181; correspondence with Louis Mallet on WSJ and bimetallism, 187n4; also mentioned, II 133n1
    letter to, V 180–3; letter from, V 92

Freme, John Rowden, member of Renshaw Street Unitarian Chapel, II 169

Freme, Mr, nephew of John Rowden Freme, II 169

Frémy, Edmond (1814–94), French chemist, II 193

French flasks, III 51

French Revolution: proposed currency by weight, VI 99; double standard adopted, 100–1, VII 67–8; irregularity of crises due to, VI 118

Friedrich Wilhelm IV, King of Prussia, 1840–61, II 73n14

Friend of India, III 58

friendly societies, I 16, VI 69, 71, 79

Frout de Fontpertuis, Adalbert, *see* Fontpertuis, Adalbert Frout de

'Full Weight', writer of letter to *The Times*, V 87, 88

Fuller, Edward Harrison (1824–88), member of Manchester Statistical Society, letter to WSJ, IV 306

Fuller, Frank, 'mate' of Bolton and O'Connell at the gold diggings, II 364

funding system, IV 214n1; examination question on, VII 137

Funds, English, Diagram showing the Price of (second of 'Two Diagrams'), II 450

Fuseli, Henry, I 5

G—— author of letter on currency (*Economist*, 1875), IV 159n5

G——, Mme, WSJ's landlady in Paris (1854), II 70

Gabriel's Gully, New Zealand goldfield, III 74

Galignani family, founders of the *Messenger*, IV 9

Galton, Sir Francis (1822–1911), anthropologist
  letter to WSJ on law of reversion, IV 200–2
  supports Palgrave's candidature for Fellowship of Royal Society, V 90
  Walras's works sent to, IV 205, 214
  'Typical Laws of Heredity' (*Nature*, 5, 12, 19 April 1877), IV 200

Galvanism, II 72, 125: Roscoe Jevons's galvanic battery, II 193; galvanometer, II 193

Gardner, Percy, fellow examiner with WSJ in Cambridge Moral Sciences Tripos (1874), IV 69n1

Gardner, William, *An Enquiry into Deposits of Gold*, II 449

Garfield, James Abram (1831–81), President of the United States: attempted assassination of, V 143

Garibaldi, and the Sicilian insurrection, II 411–12

Garnett, Richard (1835–1906), editor of British Museum Catalogue: data on Indian grain prices, V 45–6; correspondence with WSJ on works of Cantillon, V 120–1, 130–1

Garnier, Joseph-Clement (1813–82), Professor of Political Economy in France, III 241n1, 261; editor of *Journal des Economistes*, IV 48, 85, 270, 271, V 21; his papers always in disorder, IV 288; copy of *Primer of Political Economy* sent to, IV 288
  Élements de l'économie politique (1845), V 39; *Traité d'Economie Politique*, III 241, IV 3, VII 107

gas supplies: London gas works, I 90; monopoly *versus* competition for, VI 133; New York Gas Co., V 71

gases, WSJ studies at University College, I 69; diffusion of gases, 70, 78

Gaskell, Mrs (Elizabeth Cleghorn Stevenson), III 94n3
  Life of Charlotte Brontë, quoted by WSJ on solitariness, I 30, 178, II 310n4, on visiting, I 178, II 337

Gaskell, Holbrook (1813–1909), partner of James Nasmyth, II 151n3

Gaskell, William (1805–84), Unitarian Minister, lecturer in English Literature at Owens College, husband of Mrs Gaskell, III 94

gaslight: from benzole, II 91; coal gas, 91, VII 20, 31; gas engine, VII 30, 31; gas fittings in Sydney, II 108, 113, 120, 175; in St George's Hall, Liverpool, II 103; from water, V 71

Gassendi, Pierre (1592–1655), mathematician and philosopher, IV 15

Genovesi, Antonio (1712–69), Professor of Political Economy, Naples, V 40

Gentleman's Magazine, IV 241

geography, I 66; H. E. Roscoe's lectures to working men on physical geography, II 332; and law of international traffic, V 28

Geological Committee, Royal Commission on Coal, III 154n2

Geological Magazine, III 63

Geological Society of London, II 298n11; *Quarterly Journal*, III 63n4

Geological Survey of England, III 63n1, 64

geology
  WSJ and: his chief reading (1854), I 98, 109, 114, goes to Lecture on, II 30; finds geology and scripture puzzling, I 156; observations on Australia, I 25, 125–6, II 273–4, 346; takes alluvial earth samples, I 144; sends rock specimens to Roscoe, II 356; articles on geology, I 25
  Thomas Jevons's interest in, I 118, II 188; associations with his iron business, 38; Tommy Jevons's geological discovery, V 154
  geologists, I 79n5, II 298, III 63, 154; Lyell's revolutionary ideas, I 66n4; Murchison's *Siluria*, II 131, his predictions on goldfields, 352
  see also minerals

geometry
  geometric mean *versus* arithmetical mean for index numbers, III 66
  geometrical increase of coal consumption, VII 13, 31–2, of coal production, 36, 37, of population, VI 55–7
  in mathematical treatment of political economy, IV 268–9, 281n1, VI 55n8

studied by WSJ, I 55, 90, VII 120
George, Henry: *Progress and Poverty* and *The Irish Land-Question*, V 151, 197
Gerhardt, Charles Frederic (1816–56), French chemist, I 87, II 228
Traité de Chimie organique, II 228n2
Germany
   banking and currency: Bank Act, IV 160; cheques, 178–9; gold coinage, V 58, change from silver to gold, VI 101, 102, 103; monetary crises, IV 163
   advances in chemistry, I 83nn2, 3, II 63, 71–3, 125; H. E. Roscoe studies in Germany, II 50, 71–3, under Bunsen at Heidelberg, 62, 63, 73, 124–5
   economists, III 82, IV 103, 190, 289, VII 99; no book on history of prices, III 61; mathematical theories not in vogue, IV 266, 277–8, gaining ground, V 144–5; historical school, IV 266; admiration for WSJ, 277; Roscher's *History of Political Economy in Germany*, 280; political economy not taught in schools, V 15–16, 29–30; German translations of economic works, V 144–5, VII 101
   Germans: read, but cannot speak foreign language, III 66; mortality among Germans in U.S.A., IV 55; Germans in Manchester, 110
   trade and industry: cheap labour, III 239; coal resources, 71; piano manufacture, V 190n5; post office, IV 185; trade with Britain, V 50n4, Thomas Jevons's plans for business connections in, II 138; wine production, VI 32, periodic vintages, IV 204n4, V 167
   University system of teaching adopted by Owens College, III 112
   war with France (1870), III 232n3; aggressive policy (1878), IV 225
   WSJ and: studies German, I 62, 78, II 5, 225, 251, 255, 306, III 185, VII 115, without much success, III 282, IV 185,.233, 278, 279, 281n1; reads Kant in German, II 438, finds Laspeyres hard reading, III 62, 66; visits to Germany, III 185, IV 244
   also mentioned, II 431, V 27

Germer Baillière et Cie, publishers, IV 288, V 22
   Bibliothèque scientifique internationale, IV 289, 290
Gibbons, James Sloan (1810–92), *The Banks of New York . . .* (1859), IV 43n3
Gibbs, Bright & Co., shipping firm, II 231
Gibbs, Henry Hucks, Baron Aldenham: *Correspondence . . on the Silver Question in India* (1877), IV 229, 231–2; joint author of *The Bimetallic Currency* (1886), V 191n1
Gibson, G. A., Professor of Mathematics at Glasgow University, I 65n6
Gibson, John, R. A., sculptor, his painted Venus, II 201
Giessen, Liebig's chemistry laboratory at, II 71–2, 305n3
Giffen, [Sir] Robert (1837–1910), statistician, assistant editor of *The Economist*, V 82, 175
   'On the Fall of Prices of Commodities in Recent Years' (1879), V 139; *Essays in Finance*, VII 105
Gilbert, J. W., *The Principles and Practice of Banking*, IV 12, 275, VII 106
Gilbert, Marie Dolores Eliza Rosanna, *see* Montez, Lola
Gillespie, Mrs Elizabeth Honeyman, loses suit against James Russel, coalmaster, II 50n15
Gillespie *v.* Russel, lawsuit over gas-coal, II 50n15
Giornale degli Economisti, IV 181; Nicolini on Ceva, V 21–2, 42
Giraldus Cambrensis (c.1146-c.1223), V 127–8
Gladstone, Herbert, defeated for Hampstead (1880), V 98n4
Gladstone, William Ewart (1809–98)
   attack on Disraeli's budget (1852), I 79n2, 86
   becomes Chancellor of the Exchequer (1853), I 79n2, 87; Budgets: (1853), II 40n1, 408n12, (1864), VII 14, (1866), I 44, quotes WSJ in speech, 45, 206, III 103
   policy as Chancellor: economy of public expenditure, I 44; Free Trade measures, I 18, III 88, 136, VI 139, VII 13, 14; plan for paying

Gladstone, William Ewart (*contd*)
    off National Debt, I 44–5, III 102,
    VII 11, 12–18, Terminal Annuities
    Bill (1866), I 206n3; Post Office
    Savings Bill (1861), II 430; speech
    on country-bank issues (1866), IV
    12, 14, 17; taxation, VI 136, 138–9;
    views on currency, IV 77
  Prime Minister (1868–74), V 179n7, VI
    137n7, 179n7; purchase of Post
    Office Telegraphs, IV 150n4;
    Trade Union Act (1871), VI 72–3
  returns to office, as Prime Minister
    (1880), V 97n1; his Cabinet, 97n3,
    135n4, 140n4, 150, 179n6; makes
    peace with the Boers, V 135
  Irish policy of conciliation, V 135n4,
    189n2; Land Act (1881), V 150–1,
    189; efforts to redress Ireland's
    wrongs, 150
  sends army to crush Egyptian
    nationalist revolt, V 200n5
  controversy with Herbert Spencer on
    natural selection, IV 38–9; address
    at Liverpool (1874), 36
  and WSJ: *Serious Fall* sent to, III 15,
    speaks of it with 'respect and
    praise', 114; impressed by *The Coal
    Question*, I 43, 44, III 95, 96, 123,
    quotes it in Budget speech (1866), I
    45, 206, III 103, VII 11; letter to
    Macmillan in praise of it, I 203, III
    84, asks for scientific assessment of
    its conclusions, 85; writes to WSJ,
    87–8, 89, letter used as testimonial,
    87n1, 107, 117; WSJ's draft replies,
    90–3
  Principles of Science sent to, IV 36, his
    'pleasant and interesting' reply,
    37–9, 41, conversation on, 222
  WSJ's visit to (1866), I 206n3, III
    120; conversation on vaccination at
    Political Economy Club, I 206n3,
    IV 222
  'Mr Gladstone's New Financial
    Policy' (WSJ in *Macmillan's Maga-
    zine*, June 1866), III 101n2, VII
    11–18
  letters to, IV 36, 41–2; letters from,
    IV 37–9
  writings: *Juventus Mundi* . . . (1869), VI
    95; *The Financial Statements of 1853*.

    1860–63, . . .(1863), VII 106
Glaisher, James Whitbread (1848–1928),
    mathematician, II 250; letter from,
    IV 221
Glasgow
  Anderson's Institution, II 315n3; WSJ
    refuses offer of lectureship at, 442
  bank failures, IV 293n1, 304n6; failure
    of muslin firm, VI 125
  British Association meet at (1855), II
    191–3, 229
  a Chinaman from, II 368
  the *Chrysolite* built in, II 372, 385
  Exchequer Bills sent to, VI 118
  oil distilled from coal, II 119
Glasgow Daily Herald
  review of *Theory of Political Economy* (16
    December 1871), IV 5
  Rylett's proposed letters to, V 111–12
  WSJ's notice of Mrs Fawcett's *Political
    Economy for Beginners*, VII 126
Glasgow University, II 66n12, 248n16;
    School of Theology, I 183n3
  WSJ's notebooks in the Library, I 65n6
glass manufacturing, II 41, VII 30; tax on
    glass, II 40; visit to flint-glass works,
    II 435
Gleeson, Mary, of Sydney, I 172, 173
Globe Insurance Company, I 180–1
Glyn, George Carr (1797–1873), Gover-
    nor of the Bank of England, evi-
    dence before Committee on the
    Bank Charter (1832), IV 265
Gmelin, Leopold (1788–1853), Professor
    of Chemistry at Heidelberg Uni-
    versity, I 83n3; succeeded by Bun
    sen, II 66n11
  Handbuch der Chimie, I 35, 83; translated
    into English by Henry Watts, II
    65n10
God, *see* religion
Godwin-Austin, Robert Alfred Cloyne
    (1808–84), geologist: paper on
    underground ridges, III 63
gold
  alloys, II 62, 232, III 194, 218, 222, VII
    68–9
  as a commodity, III 199, 202, IV 126,
    VI 141; an article of export, II 247;
    consumption and production, V
    58–9; increased supplies, VII 65,
    66, 68; sold abroad by weight, III

220; as a store of value, VI 95–6; trade in, I 21, 162, 'business of buying gold', III 4, WSJ purchases two ounces for assaying, II 55; utility, VI 84, used by gold beaters and gilders, VII 70
discoveries: from America, VI 78, California, III 2n6; Australia, II 42, 60, 146, VI 124, Melbourne, II 260, 279, New South Wales, 127–8, 279, 451, Victoria, 121; discoveries of 1851, II 53n7, 346, V 58, VI 91, of 1858, II 340, 346, 351–2; WSJ's 51 specimens, II 127; from New Zealand III 28; from Siberia, III 208; from Vancouver Island, II 439; in Wales and England, II 88–9, 92–5, 135, Britannia Mine, II 94n4, Poltimore mine, I 119, II 94, 128
effects of discoveries on distribution of wealth, III 17, on internal economy of Australia, II 205n5, on metallic currency of Europe, VII 66, on prices, I 181n2, III 21, 22–5, 53, 55, 68n1, IV 6–7, V 58, on price of silver, VI 101, on silver exports to Asia, III 208
see also assaying; coinage; currency
gold fields, I 123n3; co-operatives in, VI 75–6; geology, II 298n11, 350–2; price of gold on, II 127n3
diggers, I 229–30, 230–1, II 83, 219, 348, 350, 365; their intelligence and respectability, I 222, an 'utterly unintellectual race', 226; 'drunken set of devils', 227–8; civility, II 270–1; at dinner, facing p. I 15; on horseback, II 147; dress, 370; cruelty to aborigines, IV 174, 176–7; society in gold districts, II 48, III 74; Charles Bolton as gold digger, II 77n2, 340, 342, 346
diggings: expedition to Sofala (1856), I 227, 229–34, II 217, 218–21, 235, 256n2; 'dry diggings', I 228–9; Braidwood (1858), I 24, 33, II 358, 364–5; in Victoria (1859), I 24, 25, II 340, 346, 364–5, 366, 367, 370–2, 374; photography at, I 31, II 364–5; gold-digging town, 371, escorts from, I 252, II 247; in New

Zealand, III 28, 74
goldfield laws, II 122n2; insurrection of diggers, II 112, 122
gold hoards in India, IV 187
gold refining, III 50; chemically pure gold, 222
gold rush, II 405; in 1851, I 24, II 133n1, VI 91n6; in 1858, II 346, 351–2
gold shares, II 93–4; Thomas Jevons's losses in, I 118
gold and silver
circulation (1872), IV 10–11
constituted by nature for money, VI 96–7
cost governed by same laws as other commodities, V 140, 141–2
examination questions on, VII 131, 134, 138
exchange of, between France and England in 1825, VI 120n12
foreign exchanges of gold and silver producing countries, VI 111
replacement of silver by gold as currency, VII 74–5; substitution, III 17, 21
supplies: increased, in Europe (1849–65), III 209, depreciation caused by, III 18, VII 68; effect of increased supply of either on aggregate supply of both, III 17–18; relative proportion of, in countries with coins of both metals, V 139–40
trade in, VII 74
value: variations in, VI 97–8; relative values, V 188n4; relative variation, III 254; ratio of gold price to silver price, VI 101–2
see also gold; silver
gold and silver standard, *see* bimetallism
gold standard
in England, VI 100, 103, VII 67, 68
in France, adopted in effect, III 21, 186, 199; Wolowski on, 196–8, 198–200
in Germany, VI 101
not suitable for India, IV 187, V 141–2, 193
International Monetary Convention adopt, VII 68
supported by WSJ, III 198, VI 103
versus bimetallism, V 192–3
see also bimetallism; double standard

gold, value of
  fall in, proved in *Serious Fall* (1863), I 39,
    181n2, III 4, 5, 49n2, 54; news-
    paper controversy on, 36–8, 42–5,
    Cairnes's contribution, 36–7, 42–4,
    Fawcett's contribution, 36, 37, 42,
    43, 45
  not regulated by labour, VI 91–2
  standard value of gold, III 127, VI 99;
    below standard in Sydney, III 148;
    depreciation concealed in a bi-
    metallic currency, III 17–18, 208–
    9; depreciation in Denmark, IV 45,
    in ancient Rome, VI 102; WSJ's
    plan for 'a simple curve' of gold
    values, III 42; wage levels and
    changes in, VI 64
Gold, Colonel Charles Emilius (d. 1871),
  in command of colonial troops in
  Maori Wars, II 420
Goldsmid, Sir Julian (1838–96), M.P.,
  moves for Select Committee on
  Telegraph Department, IV 172
Goldsmiths Company, III 222
Gomme, [Sir] George Laurence (1853–
  1916), editor of *Antiquary*, founder
  of the Folklore Society, V 131
goniometer: WSJ's 'Reflective Goniometer', I 79
Gore, George (1826–1908), F.R.S., science master at King Edward's
  School, Birmingham: letter to, ac-
  knowledging copy of *The Scientific
  Basis of National Progress* . . .
  (1882), V 186
Goschen, Rt Hon. George Joachim, M.P.
  (1831–1907), 1st Viscount, V
  85n1
  Bankers Act Amendment Bill (1874), IV
    107n1
  estimate of circulation of sovereigns, III
    201
  figures on French real estate, III
    242
  Local Taxation report, III 242–3
  supports Palgrave's candidature for Fel-
    lowship of Royal Society, V 85, 90,
    91
  The Theory of Foreign Exchanges (1861),
    VI 111, 113–14, VII 105
Gossen, Hermann Heinrich (1810–58):
  Entwicklung der Gesetze des mens-

chlichen Verkehrs . . . (1854), early
  mathematical treatment of political economy, IV 267–9, 289, V 22,
  52, 55, 56, 80, 97; much like WSJ's
  theory, IV 272, 279–80, 281n1,
  282; examination question on, V
  152; account of, included in ed. 3 of
  Theory of Political Economy, V 60,
  61–2, 95; Walras proposes publication in *Bibliothèque scientifique internationale*, IV 289, and a French
  translation, V 21, 96; Walras's article on, 144, 145
Gothenburg, visited by WSJ, IV 206
Goulburn, Australia, II 367
government
  administration, an art, not a science,
    VII 55–6
  books on, for English Citizen Series, V
    138
  in economic and social affairs, I 49, VII
    159; justifiable interference, VI
    132–3, examination questions on,
    VII 136, 138; intervention in 1792
    to save firms, VI 118
  and population, VI 55
  promotion by, VII 62
  railway policy in New South Wales, VII
    9–11
  service in, II 343–4
  statistics of revenues, II 426
  see also Post Office
Government School of Applied Chemistry,
  II 250
Gowing, Richard, secretary of Cobden
  Club, VII 105
Graham, Sir James, IV 275; *Free Trade in
  Corn the real interest of the Landlord* . . . (1828), attributed to, IV
  275n8
Graham, John (d. 1869), Superintendent
  of the Coining Department, Royal
  Mint, III 165; death of, 224
Graham, Thomas (1805–69)
  as Professor of Chemistry at University
    College, London, I 13, 69, II 8, 13,
    35, 125; Herbert Jevons studies
    with, I 10: WSJ studies with, 65, 69,
    93, 94, his interest in molecular
    philosophy aroused by, 13–14, 101;
    demonstrates the 'Drummond
    light', 18; succeeded by Williamson

(1855), II 191

discovers laws of diffusion of gases, I 70, experiments on, II 315–16; attends British Association meeting at Liverpool, II 79, 94, 102; gives evidence in 'Torbane hill Case' on gas-coal, 350

Elements of Chemistry, I 65n1, 67, 83, 87, 114; vol. 2, edited by, with Henry Watts, II 316

appointed non-resident assayer at the Royal Mint by Herschel (1851), II 133n3, III 222–3; becomes Master of the Mint (1855), I 97n4, II 133, 161, 193, 228, III 224; Report on Sydney coins, II 231, 232; reports on *pyx* pieces, 261; assay methods, 345, III 218, 224; on dies for dating coins, 164–5; on light and heavy coins, 186–7, VII 70; strikes an aluminium medal, II 356; Report on Mintage (1868), III 210n2, 212, 215, VII 67

evidence before Decimal Coinage Commission (1857), III 187

sympiesometer based on his discoveries, III 147

H. E. Roscoe and, II 75, 122, 193

WSJ and: WSJ works in his private laboratory, I 19, 97–8, II 49, 51n1; recommends WSJ for Sydney assayership, I 96, II 46, 52, 54–5, III 103, gives him letters to friends in Paris, II 61, 65, to Sydney professors, II 131; his way with introductions, 79; provides apparatus for assaying, 74; is sent article on 'Clouds', 261, finds it 'conclusive', 304; suggests place as meteorological observer for WSJ, 392, 402, offers him a lectureship at the Andersonian Institute, 442

letters from, III 164–5, 186–7

personal: his practical and business-like character, II 49, 161; 'a little gim crack of a fellow', 102; his death, III 224n3

grain: imports, IV 211; prices of wheat in India, V 46–7, 51; also mentioned, VII 24. *See also* corn; vegetation

grammar: WSJ studies at College, I 54; Universal Grammar, III 94

Grantham, John, *Iron Shipbuilding: with Practical Illustrations* (1858), I 4

Granville, George Granville Leveson Gower, 2nd Earl (1815–91), Leader of Liberal Party in House of Lords: loses office as Foreign Secretary in Russell Ministry (1853), I 85; returns as Chancellor of Duchy of Lancaster in Aberdeen Ministry, 87

Chancellor of University of London, III 13; portrait, IV 123–4; at Political Economy Club, 222

also mentioned, V 187n4

graphical presentation: of the sky, II 245; of statistics, II 427, IV 8; distinguished from mathematical economics, IV 282–3

see also diagrams; statistics; symbolical statements

Gravez, Henri: French translation of *Primer of Political Economy*, IV 288n2, V 37

gravitation: and WSJ's atomic theory, II 159–60; measuring gravity, III 246–7, 253

Gray, John Edward (1800–75), keeper of the Zoological department of the British Museum: disbelief in du Chaillu's gorillas, II 436

Gray, Peter, articles on the arithmometer, VII 88

Great Britain

Admiralty: contract for Australian mail, II 133n1; Select Committee on (1861), 428n9; fleet and fortifications, 417–18, 428–9, steam war vessels, 234; Fleet ordered to Dardanelles (1878), IV 224n4, 225

Alkali Act (1863), II 305n3

coal, area of, III 189, VII 21, 22, 27, 34; statistics, V 143

emigration, IV 7, 8, VI 31; to Australia, II 267–8

foreign affairs, II 431

Anglo-American rivalry in South America, II 399n2; Oregon boundary dispute, II 408n14

Boer revolt, V 135n1

Cobden-Chevalier Commercial Treaty with France (1860), II 408, III 208n1

Great Britain (contd)
  Crimean War, see Crimean War
  Egyptian Expedition, V 200
  Palmerston's foreign policy, II 417–
    18
  scare over Constantinople, IV 224n4,
    225; Great Britain the only check to
    French and Russian aggression, II
    412
  foreign investment, in America, VI 124,
    125n5
  Foreign Office, V 140
  Government and constitution
    control over colony of New South
      Wales, II 205n5; do nothing to stop
      war against aborigines in Queens-
      land, IV 177
    general election of 1880, V 97–8,
      101n3, 111n2; Liberal victory,
      97n1, 115
    House of Commons, WSJ quoted in,
      III 210n1
    Inland Revenue, V 88
    Lords reject money Bill, II 412
    Russell's Whig-Liberal Ministry, III
      87n1; Reform Bill (1865), 130–1
    Treasury, Lords of, V 44
    see also under Disraeli; Gladstone, Wil-
      liam Ewart
  and India, V 140n3, 194n3. See also under
    India
  International Monetary Convention
    (1867): representatives at, III 213,
    VII 71; their Report, VII 67–70;
    Conference (1881), V 187n4, Brit-
    ish Government take no steps to
    reconvene, 194n3
  population: Celtic and other elements,
    III 243–4, rural, VII 5; census
    reports (1881), V 143; and im-
    prudent marriages, VI 58
  statistics, proposed arrangement in
    'Statistical Atlas', II 425–7
  workmen, British, IV 51
  see also England; Ireland; Scotland;
    Wales
Great Britain, Great Eastern, see Brunel,
  Isambard Kingdom
Great Exhibition of 1851, I 17, 51, 85n2, II
  179n1; the 'Palace of Glass', II 12,
  WSJ's Sunday evening walks to,
  23; exhibits from abroad, 12; or-

gans, 23–4; awards for exhibitors,
  50n1, 184n4; colonial agriculture,
  53n7; peat products, 119; Chubb's
  locks, 309n1. See also Crystal Palace
Great Exhibition of Paris, see Paris In-
  ternational Exhibitions
Great Exhibition, South Kensington,
  1862; WSJ visits, I 183–4, II 442;
  Fowke's designs for buildings, 430;
  type-composing machines on dis-
  play, VII 47
Great Oriental Bank, New Rush Creek, II
  371
Great Western Highway, New South
  Wales, I 145, 146nn1, 3, II 219
Great Western Railway, Canada, II 428
Greece, joins Latin Monetary Convention,
  VII 67
Greek language, see classical studies
Greeks, ancient, VII 135
Greeley, Horace (1811–72), founder of
  New York Tribune, II 421n6
Green, Alexander Henry, co-author of
  Coal: its History and Uses (1878), IV
  234n1
Green, Mr: Tommy Jevons attends his
  private school in Liverpool, II 34,
  44, 143, 167
Greenwich Hospital, prices index, IV 169–
  70
Greenwich Observatory, visit to (1874),
  IV 52
Greenwood, Frederick Francis (1830–
  1909), founder of Pall Mall Gazette,
  V 111n2
Greenwood, Joseph Gouge (1821–94),
  Principal of Owens College, Man-
  chester, I 41, 205n5, II 305, III 73,
  124, 233, 234
a favourite schoolmaster of WSJ's at
  University College School, III 5,
  39; arranges tutorship for WSJ at
  Owens College (1863), I 40, 47, III
  9, 10, 14, 29; asks him to take day
  classes for absent Professor, 75–6,
  104; and appointment of WSJ as
  Professor of Logic and Mental and
  Moral Philosophy (1866), I 207,
  III 89–90, 99, 120; testimonial for
  WSJ (1865), III 65–6; arranges
  leave of absence for him, IV 21;
  proposal to avoid WSJ's resig-

nation, 48–9, accepts his resignation in 1876, 163–4
is sent copy of *Coal Question*, III 89
letters from, III 75–6, 89–90, IV 21, 48–9, 112–13, 163–4

Gregory, expedition into interior of Australia, article on (WSJ, *Empire*, September 1857), VII 123

Gregory, William (1803–58), Professor of Chemistry at Edinburgh, II 50

Grenfell, H. R., Governor of Bank of England
opens debate on stagnation at Political Economy Club, IV 199n4, 202; proposes question on bimetallism, V 191, his extract on, 139
propositions on practical aspects of Silver Question, V 192–3
letters to, V 191, 193; letter from, V 192–3

Grey, Charles, 2nd Earl, IV 129n2

Grey, Henry George (1802–94), 3rd Earl, V 193

Grey, Maria Georgina (1816–1906), founder of Girls' Public Day School Trust, and Maria Grey Training College, IV 129; 'The National Standard of Education', paper read before British Association meeting, Bristol (1875), IV 129n2

Grey, William Thomas (1807–64), husband of Maria Grey, IV 129n2

Griffies, Elizabeth, *see* Moss, Mrs Thomas

Griffin, dealer in chemical apparatus, II 50

Griffith, R., bank manager in Ireland: letter to WSJ on gold coinage in Irish banks, III 190–1

Grimm, Friedrich Melchior, Freiherr von (1723–1807), V 120

Grose River, New South Wales, I 146, 147, II 253, 263, 264

Grosvenor, Hugh Lupus (1825–90), later 1st Duke of Westminster, honorary Colonel of the 13th Middlesex Rifle Corps, II 437

Grosvenor, Lady Constance (Lady Constance Gertrude Sutherland-Leveson-Gower, 1834–80), presents prizes to WSJ's Volunteer Company, II 437

Grote, George, *History of Greece*, III 11

Grove, [Sir] George (1820–90), editor of *Macmillan's Magazine*, member of Index Society, IV 298, V 176

Grundy, Francis Henry, civil engineer in Sydney, II 117–18, 129, 131, 140; WSJ shares his house, 166

Grundy, Rev. John (1782–1843), Unitarian Minister in Manchester, later in Liverpool, II 118

Grylls, Mr, solicitor, passenger on board the *Oliver Lang*, I 106, II 99, 112

Grylls, Mrs, II 112

Gua de Malves, J. P., *Essai sur les causes du declin du commerce* . . (1757), V 159

Guest, John, & Co.: Thomas Jevons acts as Liverpool agent for, I 12, II 11n3, 145

guilds: Saxon and medieval, VI 68–9; trade guilds, 69–70; guild masters, 69; now 'swept away', VII 48; once known as Universities, VII 48, 49

Guillaumin, Melle Félicité (1829?–85), takes charge of publishing house (1864), IV 261, 263

Guillaumin, Urbain (d. 1864), French publisher, IV 261n6; with Coquelin, *Dictionnaire de l'Économie Politique* (1854), V 13, VII 103

Guinness, Mr, of Dublin, traveller in Switzerland, II 187

guns, II 180
Enfield rifle, II 407, 436
'gunpowder and lightning', article by WSJ in *Empire*, VII 123
James Nasmyth's shell-firing guns, II 151–2
revolver and bullet moulds for Herbert Jevons, III 51
Whitworth rifle, II 431

Guthrie, Frederick (1833–86), later Professor of Chemistry at the Royal College, Mauritius: studies in Germany, II 72; demonstrator at Owens College, 315n3; applies for Professorship, 305; an old friend of WSJ, IV 128

Guy, William Augustus (1810–85), Professor of Forensic Medicine at King's College, London, V 90

gyroscope, II 102n1

Haarlem, the great organ of St Bavo, II 23n3

Hackett, James Thomas (1805–76), astrologer and mathematician, IV 275

Hagen, Karl Heinrich (1785–1856), early mathematical economist, IV 15, 278

Haldimand, William (1784–1862), London merchant: evidence before Committee on Resumption of Cash Payments (1819), IV 264

Halifax, England, telephone transmissions from, V 35–6

Halifax, Lord (Charles Wood, 1800–85), M.P. for Halifax, Chairman, Royal Commission on International Coinage, III 181n2; Chancellor of the Exchequer, I 85, II 157n2, V 192, VI 116

Halifax, Nova Scotia, WSJ stops at, II 390

Halifax currency pound and Halifax sterling currency, IV 161, 166

Hallé, Sir Charles (1819–95), pianist and conductor: concert in St James's Hall (November 1862), II 458; Berlioz concerts (1881), V 123, 131

Hallett, Thomas George (d.1919), college friend of WSJ, IV 128

Hamburg
tables of prices, III 21n6, 82; fluctuations in 1763, VI 117
WSJ's visit to, 1877, IV 206

Hamilton, Lord George, M. P. for Hampstead, V 98n4

Hamilton, Robert, Inquiry on the national debt (1813), IV 215

Hamilton, Rowland (d. 1897), Liverpool banker: sends WSJ copy of Money and Value . . . (1878), V 9; 'Money and Barter' (Journal of the Institute of Bankers, 1881), V 153; recollections of Liverpool business, 153–4
letters from, V 9, 19–20, 153–4

Hamilton, Sir William, III 113, 118; WSJ proposes writing on Mill and, I 205; his scholasticism, II 433; definition of pleasure, VI 119

Hamilton-Temple-Blackwood, Frederick (1826–1902), 1st Marquess of Dufferin and Ava, V 179

Hampstead Heath
botanical walks on, I 85, 95; wild flowers and the law, V 199
Field Day on, II 460–1

general election scenes, V 97–8
merry-go-round, IV 207
search for house to rent (1862), II 440–1; home with Harriet (1876), I 79n3, IV 182, 183, 184, 192, 212; organ installed, 189; runs on the Heath with the children, V 119, 123; meetings with Edgeworth, V 202

Handel, George Frederic, II 76, 314, 321
'Dead March' from Saul, at Duke of Wellington's funeral, I 75; Israel in Egypt, II 257, 313, 369; Judas Maccabeus, II 290n4; Messiah, I 79, II 224, 313, 328–9, 'Comfort ye' at the Temple, I 75

handicrafts, VII 22; straw plait, 22, 24; hand forging, 47

Hankey, Thomson (1805–93), M.P., formerly Governor of Bank of England: opposed to reduction of gold content of sovereign, III 211; letter to WSJ on gold coinage, V 58–9

Hannyngton, General, on the arithmometer, VII 88, 89

Hanssen, Georg (1809–94), German economist, IV 85

happiness: the only positive good, I 154n3; identified with progress, II 180, with exertion, II 67, III 3; friendship not necessary for, II 302, 336; WSJ 'exceedingly happy' with himself, 333
in WSJ's theory of utility, III 253, IV 152

Hardiman, Mr, see Haldimand, William

Hargreaves, John, miniature portrait of Mary Anne Roscoe, I 5–6

Harley, Robert (1828–1910), Vice-Master of Mill Hill School: letter to, V 116–17

Harman, Jeremiah, director of Bank of England, IV 265n5

Harness, Captain, Deputy Master of the Mint, III 222

Harper's Ferry, II 454n7

Harris, James, Hermes: or, a Philosophical Inquiry concerning Language and Universal Grammar (1751), III 94

Harris, Mr, II 135n11

Harris, Sir William Snow (1791–1867), Electricity (1848), I 87

Harrison, Frederic (1831–1923), Professor of Jurisprudence: at the Political Economy Club, IV 202, 224

Hartington, Spencer Compton Cavendish, Marquess of (1833–1908), Secretary of State for India: on currency plan for India, V 140, 194

Hartley, New South Wales: road to, I 146, 152, 238, II 254; township of Great Hartley, I 221, 222, 236; Little Hartley, 221, 236; Hartley Mail, 235; projected railway to, II 262, 265

Harvard University, VII 96; *Elementary Logic* used as textbook, III 239

harvests
    associated with commercial fluctuations, VI 121, 124; with sunspots, IV 291; with trade crises, 210, 211, 215, V 89; in India, V 48
    as circulating capital, VI 43
    in England (1855), II 167
    gold for harvesters' wages, III 195–6
    influence on demand for secondary goods, VI 15, on price fluctuations, 16, 89, VII 161
    Irish, V 150, VI 123
    labour for, VI 91
    and speculators, VI 84

Hastings: family holidays at Galley Hill, Bulverhythe, V 72, 142–3, 199–200; WSJ's death by drowning at, I 48

Hastings, George Woodyatt (1825–1917), M. P., co-founder of Infant Life Protection Society, V 167n8, 169, 173

Hauser, Miska (1822–87), Hungarian violinist in Sydney, II 250

Havana: WSJ's brief stay at, II 378, 381, 398, loses his Australian Journals in, I 25, II 374n1; a fellow passenger dies of yellow fever at, 401
    Directorio de la Habana (1859), presented by WSJ to British Museum Library, II 449

Hawarden Castle, Gladstone's home, VII 14

Hawkesbury River and Valley, New South Wales, I 134n3, 146n2, II 263; expeditions to, I 137, 143, II 252, 264, 280

Haydn, Joseph, II 313, 314, 321; *Creation*, II 224

Hayes, Catherine (1825–61), Irish soprano in Sydney, II 181

Hayward, classmate of WSJ at University College, I 54

Haywards Heath, home of William Jevons jun., uncle of WSJ, III 10, 11, 12, 69

Hearn, William Edward (1826–88), Australian economist, IV 91n3, VII 146; theory of wages, III 255; definition of political economy, VI 12, of labour, 18; territorial division of labour, 32; on the Government of England, VII 55
    Plutology, VI 32n2, VII 107; noticed by WSJ in *Spectator* (5 March 1864), VII 125

Heathcote, Mrs, of Sydney, II 174

Heeren, Arnold Hermann Ludwig (1760–1842), *Manual of the history of the political system of Europe . . .* (1846), VII 117

Heidelberg: holiday planned in, III 185; wine trade, VI 32

Heidelberg, University of
    Bunsen's laboratory, II 63, 125
    H. E. Roscoe studies under Bunsen at, II 63, 65–6, 118, 190, 193, 194, 324
    other students at, II 74n16, 392n18, 416n6

Heir, Robert James (d. 1868?), English actor in Sydney, later manager of Theatre Royal in Melbourne, II 257

Heir, Mrs Robert (Fanny Cathcart, 1833–80), Liverpool-born Australian actress, II 257–8

Helferich, Johann Alfonso Renatus von (1817–92), economist, V 42

Helm, Elijah (1837–1904), authority on cotton trade, President of Manchester Statistical Society, V 25, 26n2, 83–4
    letters from, III 206, V 83–4

Helps, Sir Arthur, *Friends in Council* (1847), II 223

Hemming, George Wirgman (1821–1905), mathematician, VII 152n1

Hendricks, Frederick (1827–1909), actuary: estimate of depreciation of

Hendricks, Frederick (*contd*)
  gold sovereigns, III 181; supports Lowe's gold coinage proposals, 211, 213, 215; supports metric system in evidence before Monetary Commission in Paris (1870), III 232, 233; on cost of converting bullion into coin, VII 70; pamphlet on decimal coinage, III 212, 213, 232n2, VII 66
Henslow, John Stevens (1798–1861), Professor of Botany at Cambridge: examines WSJ in botany at University College, London, I 56
  Principles of Descriptive and Physiological Botany (1836), I 54, 99
Herapath, John, editor of *The Railway Magazine and Annals of Science*, IV 274, 275n3; interest in cosmic cycles, 276
heredity: Galton's law of reversion (regression), IV 200–1; application to political economy, 202
Herefordshire, VII 23, 24
Herford, Edward (1815–96), Manchester City Coroner, V 167
Herford, Miss, IV 212
Herford, William Henry (1820–1908), educationist: letter to, on examinations, IV 212–13; also mentioned, V 167n9
Hermann, Mr, Henny's piano teacher, II 143, 169, 321
Hermes, see Harris, James
Herodotus, VI 101, VII 25
Herschel, Sir John Frederick William (1792–1871), astronomer
  as Master of the Mint: letter to Sydney Mint, II 49; rejects seignorage plan for gold coin, III 211, 216–17; on law of free coinage, 213; brings coinage up to standard fitness (1851), 222–3, abandons Trial Plates, 222, 224; succeeded by Graham (1856), 133n2, 161
  WSJ and: noted by WSJ at Faraday lecture, I 82; approves of *Coal Question*, 43–4, 200, III 95, letter on, 77–8; his letters used as testimonial, III 85, 107, 117, sent to Gladstone, 85, 87; preface to ed. 2 of *Coal Question* sent to, III 122–3; sees papers on

Clouds, II 432, finds them 'pleasing and elegant', 433–4; WSJ agrees with him on physical subjects, II 277, quotes his *Essays*, 308, 330, studies his works, III 80
  personal: thinks idea of substitute for coal chimerical, III 77, 90, 92, 124; notion for power from tides, 77–8, 122, 123–4; objects to metric system and spelling reform, 238; on principle of forced vibrations, VII 92–3; refuses to sign Theological Declaration of Scientific Men, III 60, or to join Society of Scientific Men, 237–8; his health, 122, 124
  Essays from the Edinburgh and Quarterly Review (1857), II 308, 330; *A Preliminary Discourse on the Study of Natural Philosophy*, VI 24; 'Meteorology' (*Encyclopaedia Britannica*, 1861), II 432n3, 434; 'Sound' (*Encyclopaedia Metropolitana*, 1845), VII 92
  letters to, II 432, III 60, 80, 83, 85, 122–3, 236–7; letters from, II 433–4, III 77–8, 83–4, 85–6, 123–4, 216–17, 237–8
Herschel, Mrs, III 122
Herschel, Sir William (1738–1822), astronomer, father of Sir John, II 432n1; conjectures on sun-spots, IV 189
Herschel's Weather Table, VII 95
Hertz, James (d. 1881), originator of Cheque Bank, IV 178, 179, 184n2, 186
Heswall, Cheshire, home of Mrs Timothy Jevons, II 4, 26n3
Heywood Bros, Manchester, III 257
Hickson, Mary Agnes (1826–99), Irish local historian: correspondence with WSJ on origins of Cantillon family, V 123–4, 125–6, 127–8, 131
  Selections from Old Kerry Records, . . . (1872), V 126
Higginson, Dr Alfred, family doctor of the Jevons family, I 60, II 143; gives talk on natural history to Liverpool Literary and Philosophical Society, III 89
Higginson, Mrs Alfred, *see* Martineau, Ellen

Higginson, Helen, *see* Martineau, Mrs James

Higgs, H., editor of WSJ's *Principles of Economics* (1905), I 51n1; edition of Richard Cantillon's *Essai . . .*, VI 18n2, 121n1

Hildebrand, Bruno (1812–78), Professor of Political Economy at Jena, IV 253

Hildebrandt, Albert, German civil engineer living in Manchester, IV 103

reviews in *Deutsche Allgemeine Polytechnische Zeitung*: WSJ's paper on mathematical theory of economics (1875), IV 103, 188; *Elements d'économie politique pure . . .* (Walras, 1876), 103, 188

Hill, Dr, schoolmaster in Oxford, III 49

Hill, Hamilton A., of Boston, IV 217n1

Hill, Sir Rowland, proposal for tax on coal, IV 55

Hincks, Sir Francis (1807–85), Canadian Finance Minister, IV 158, 166

early connections with Jevons family, IV 157

on banking and note issues in Canada and England, IV 158–62

letter from, IV 157–62

'The Bank of England and the Act of 1844' (*Canadian Monthly and National Review*, 1873), IV 157–9; unpublished letter to *Economist*, IV 160, 161

Hincks, John, brother of Sir Francis, IV 157

Hincks, Rev. William, brother of Sir Francis, IV 157

Hindus

Hindu ryots and the Lancashire cotton trade, IV 45

'Primers' for, IV 18–19

'Hiram, Le M.', *see* Limousin, Charles-Mathieu

Hirst, Thomas Archer (1830–92), Professor of Mathematical Physics at University College, London, I 206

historical school of economics, IV 266, VII 99, 100, 158, 162; examination questions on, V 152, VII 134

history: WSJ's interest in, I 50, 110, 159; studies for Matriculation, 54, does badly, 55, II 35; prefers to chemistry, I 61; studies for B.A., 62, Greek history, 69–70, II 45; takes second place to scientific subjects, I 78, 98; finds History classes dull, 90; can never remember a thing, II 291

History of Philosophy, WSJ gets gold medal for, IV 103

Hobbs, Alfred Charles (1812–91), American lock expert, II 309n1; Hobbs's lock, 309

Hodgson, Charles J., assayer: offers WSJ partnership in Melbourne, II 357; WSJ lodges with, 369

Hodgson, Mary Ann, *see* Roscoe, Mrs Richard

Hodgson, William Ballantyne (1815–80), headmaster of Mechanics Institute School, Liverpool, I 8n1, 13; WSJ's memories of, V 106–7; introduces social economy lessons, VII 53

appointed Professor of Political Economy and Mercantile Law at Edinburgh University (1871), III 235n1; WSJ's testimonial for, 235–6; likely to be interested in Walras's writings, IV 66; hopes WSJ will succeed him, 150; WSJ stays with, 167, 173, V 107

death at Brussels, V 106–7; his writings good, but too few, 108; translations, VII 46, 51, 59

letters to, III, 235–6; letter from, IV 167

Hoepli, Ulrico, Milan publisher: Italian translation of 'Primers', IV 248, V 37n3, 42, 53, 59; copyright fees, V 59, 60, 94

Hofmann, August Wilhelm von (1818–92), Professor of Chemistry at Royal School of Mines, I 64n2, II 50, 228

with Cahours, 'Note on a new Class of Alcohols', II 228n6

Hogarth, George, quoted by WSJ, I 30, 178

Hokatika, New Zealand, Herbert Jevons settles at, III 157, 158

Holborn, pickpockets, I 71–2

Holland

division of labour, VI 32

Dutch: excellence as linguists and economists, IV 74, 82; in Indian Archipelago, V 50

Holland (*contd*)
  gold coinage, V 59; ratio of gold to silver, VI 102
  periodic commercial crises, IV 224–5, 230
  taxation, IV 283–4, V 55–6, 72
  trade with Britain, V 72
  tulipomania, VI 117
  WSJ visits, I 211; his name familiar to Dutch authors, IV 280
Holme, James, building contractor in Liverpool, II 36n3
Holme, Samuel (*c.* 1800–72), building contractor, Mayor of Liverpool (1852), II 36
Holt, Bland (1853–1942), actor and producer, I 106n3
Holt, Clarence (*alias* Joseph), actor and manager, passenger on board the *Oliver Lang*, I 106, II 82, 83, 99, 112, 181
Holt, George, benefactor of Liverpool Mechanics Institute School, I 8n1
Holt, Mrs Mary (Mrs Clarence Holt), I 106n3, II 112, 181
Holyoake, George Jacob (1817–1906), Chartist, Cooperative social reformer: letter from WSJ promising contributions to the *Reasoner*, III 165
Homer, VI 95–6, 101; *Iliad*, II 329
Hong Kong, II 60; silver dollars, VII 68
Hooker, General Joseph (1814–79), in command of the Army of the Potomac: defeats Stonewall Jackson at Chancellorsville, III 16
Hooker, Sir Joseph Dalton (1817–1911), naturalist, President of the Royal Society, V 85, 91, 194
Hope, Beresford (1820–87), proprietor of *Saturday Review*, II 259n5
Hopkins, Albert B., of Aston, Birmingham: letter to WSJ on symbolic expression for utility, III 247–8
Hoppus, Rev. John (1789–1875), independent minister, Professor of Logic, University of London: testimonial for WSJ, III 106, 109–10
Hornblower, Rev. Francis, uncle of WSJ: WSJ stays with, I 64, 115, II 3n1, 4, 27; Lucy stays with, II 30n2; with Aunt Hornblower stays with the Jevons family, 36; illness and death (1852), I 88, 94; his love of Mozart, II 296
Hornblower, Mrs Francis (Jane Elizabeth Roscoe, 1797–1853), 'Aunt Jane', I 5, 242, II 155; WSJ writes to, I 59, stays with, 63–4, 115, II 3n1, 4, 27; Roscoe and Lucy stay with, II 16, 30n2; visits Jevons family, 27–8, 36, stays with them after her husband's death, I 88; illness, 92, 94–5, II 22, 26, 43; her good works, 22, letters, 27; death, I 95n1, II 405
Horner, L., 'Geological History of the Alluvial Land of Egypt', paper read before the Royal Society, II 330
Horse Guards, I 73, 74–5
horses
  as circulating capital, VI 47
  exports of, examination question on, VII 137
  horse-drawn vehicles, *see* coaches; omnibuses
  horse power, III 189–90, VI 25, VII 30, 35
  machine-made horse-shoes, VII 47
  trade in, between England and Wales, III 192
Horsfall, Thomas Berry (1805–78), M.P. for Liverpool, 1853–68, I 86n2
Horsfall, Thomas Coglan (1841–1916), town-planning pioneer: letter to WSJ on popular amusements in Manchester, IV 286–7; letter to *Manchester Guardian* on homes for workpeople, V 165, 166
houses
  as capital, VI 41, 54
  coal for heating and lighting, VII 30, 31
  'homes' and houses, V 165–6
  house market, IV 153–4
  improvements in slum dwellings, I 16–17, 68
  primary and secondary utility of, IV 138–41, 151–4
  rent, III 256
  tax on, I 86, VII 7
  Thomas Jevons's iron house, II 128, 129, 136
  weavers' windows, I 68

see also buildings
housewives, V 165
Houten, Samuel van (1837–1930), Dutch economist: Treatise on Value (*Verhandeling over de Waarde*), based on utility (1859), IV 73, 74, 75, 82, 88–9, 91
Howard, George William Frederick (1802–64), 7th Earl of Carlisle, distributes prizes at University College, London, I 54
Howard, Luke (1772–1864), manufacturing chemist: observations on clouds, II 161
Howell, George, *The Conflicts of Capital and Labour* (1878), VII 107
Howitt, Herbert Charlton, surveyor: drowned in New Zealand, III 158
Hubbard, John Gellibrand (1805–89), 1st Baron Addington, M. P., writer on currency and tax questions, IV 298; challenges WSJ on gold coinage controversy, III 211, 212, 213–5, quibbles over rule of three, 214, 221
Hudson River, WSJ's journey up, II 390, 401
Huggins, Sir William (1824–1910), President of the Royal Astronomical Society: WSJ dines with, at the Scientific Club, IV 293–4
Hull
gold coin received at Money Order Counter, III 179–80
a lecturer snubbed, III 229
WSJ sails from, IV 70
Hull Criterion, review of *Principles of Science*, VII 127
Hull, Edward, *The Coal Fields of Great Britain* (1861), III 63, 99n2, VII 14, 31, 36
Hull Forge Co., III 225n1
human machine, the, I 133–4; laws of human wants, VII 162
Humboldt, Alexander, *Travels*, II 332n2
Hume, David, on population, VI 54
Hume, Joseph: WSJ examines for Joseph Hume Scholarship at University College, London, V 105, 109
Hungary
coal, III 71
Kossuth declares independence, II

415n3; trouble in, 431
Hunt, Holman, IV 117
Hunt, Robert (1807–87), Keeper of the Mining Records Office: statistics of coal production, IV 127, 236, VII 25, 29, 32, 36
Hunt, Robert (1830–92), colleague of WSJ at Sydney Mint: goes with WSJ on trip to Wollongong, II 262; his sisters drowned on the *Dunbar* off Sydney harbour, 299, 301; goes camping on photography expedition with WSJ, 352–5, his skiff, *The Terror*, 353, 355; his easy cure for brittleness, III 50
Hunt, Messrs W. & Co., London, II 439
Hunter, William Alexander (1844–98), Professor of Jurisprudence at University College, London, V 23
Hunter, Sir William Wilson (1840–1900), Director-General, Statistical Department of India, V 45, 50; interest in sun-spot researches, V 57; 'Sun-Spots and Famines' (with J. N. Lockyer, *Nineteenth Century*, 1877), V 35
Hunter River: excursion to (1856), I 123–30, II 256n2; floods in 1857, II 298
Hunter River New Steam Navigation Co., I 123, 129
Huntley, Robert H. (Rob), surgeon, of Balmain, Sydney, II 47–8, 96, 129n; WSJ calls on, 131, 136
Husson, Mr, neighbour of Thomas Jevons at Llangollen, II 169
Husson, Mrs (formerly Mrs Beal, *née* Tate), at one time Henrietta's music teacher, II 169
Hutcheson, Francis (1694–1746), philosopher, teacher of Adam Smith, V 127
Hutchison, John, *The Practice of Banking*, VII 106
Hutt, William Wyatt, member of Index Society, IV 298
Hutton, Edward Malin (b. 1848), son of John Hutton by his first wife: goes to India, II 58; returns to school in Oxford (1866), III 149–50
Hutton, James (1726–97), Scottish geologist: 'Theory of Rain', II 245

Hutton John (1824–94), civil engineer, brother-in-law of WSJ
marriage to Lucy Jevons, I 11, 36, II 442n6; granite quarry at Penmaenmawr, I 11; financial difficulties, 45–6, 189n1, 199n1, II 458; things better, III 14, 30, 149; short of capital, 57, almost ruined with quartz mining, 205, with his copper mine, 210; proposes partnership with Herbert Jevons, II 441
his first wife (Eliza Malin), II 123n12; children of first marriage, I 189n1, III 58, 149; children of second marriage, I 11,241; home at Beaumaris, I 11, III 14, 57, 149; lets house, II 30; WSJ stays with, 26, 149, 185; suffers from tic, III 149; with Lucy, takes charge of WSJ's children at Hampstead, V 132, 148
also mentioned, II 14n3, 117, III 73
Hutton, Mrs John (Eliza Malin), II 123, III 58n3
Hutton, Mrs John (Lucy Jevons), see Jevons, Lucy
Hutton, Rev. Joseph, Unitarian preacher, father-in-law of Lucy Jevons, I 11, 36, II 14n3
Hutton, Mary Josephine (1867–1910), daughter of John and Lucy Hutton, I 11, 241, III 158, V 178
Hutton, Richard Holt (1826–97), brother of John Hutton, I 11
at London University: gold medallist, II 410; founder-member of University College Debating Society, I 39, 187n2; later Principal of University Hall, II 167n8; examines for Ricardo prize, II 416, for M.A. degree in Political Economy, III 111, 113
editor of National Review, II 416, of Inquirer, 416n6; sub-editor of Economist, I 36, II 416; co-editor and proprietor of Spectator, I 36, 37, 38, 182, II 416n6, 432n17; reviews Two Diagrams in Economist and Spectator, 448n3, 450, 459; reviews Serious Fall in Spectator, I 191n1, III 13, 15, 19n2
marriage to Mary Roscoe, II 26, 243; goes with her to Barbados, recovers

from yellow fever, 80; acts as trustee for Lucy Jevons (Mrs John Hutton), III 205
testimonial for WSJ, III 106, 111; letter from WSJ, II 450–1; obituary of WSJ, I 1
'Political Economy and the Gold Discoveries' (Spectator, 16 May 1863), III 13n3
also mentioned, I 35n2, 73n1, II 14n3, 30, 64n3, 123n12, 230, III 58n3
Hutton, Mrs Richard Holt, see Roscoe, Mary Ann
Hutton, Susan Katherine (Kate, 1850–1915), daughter of John Hutton by his first wife: WSJ proposes marriage to (1865), I 46; attends WSJ's lecture at the Royal Institution (1858), III 180
Hutton, Thomas Grindal (1862–75), son of John and Lucy Hutton, I 11, 241, II 462, III 57, 59, 150; dies of diphtheria, II 462n6
Huxley, Thomas Henry (1825–95): address to British Association (September 1870), III 236; and 'Science Primers' series, IV 192n3; also mentioned, VII 151
Hyde, Cheshire, lectures to Mechanics Institute, VII 54–65
hydraulic (accumulation) machines, VI 25–6, VII 30, 31; hydraulic Ram, III 124
hygrometer, WSJ's invention, II 250

ice, manufacture of, VII 30
Iceland: Daulby-Roscoe Icelandic Collection, I 59n5
Illawarra District, New South Wales: trip to (April 1857), I 159–78, II 256n2, 280; map of Illawarra, I 159n1, 160; vegetation, 163, 164–5, 170, 171–2, 174, 176, II 366; rocks, I 164, 170, 175, coal, 177; view of, 165–6; bread made from Chilean flour, III 20
Illustrated London News, II 197
articles on chess, II 445
'Probable Exhaustion of our coal Mines' noticed in (1868), III 180
imports, see exports and imports
income: distinguished from capital, VI 49–

51; distribution of, VI 60–8; national income, calculation of, III 242

index numbers, III 82n4; geometrical mean for, VI 55n8; Westergaard's problem concerning, IV 247–8. *See also* prices; statistics

Index Society (1878), IV 297–8
  index for *Investigations in Currency and Finance*, V 175; *Journal of the London (Royal) Statistical Society* 'carefully indexed', IV 224

India
  bridge construction, III 228
  currency, IV 163; advocates of bimetallism for, IV 186–7, V 140n3,142n2, of silver standard, V 141–2; gold standard not suitable for, IV 187, V 143n2, 193; problem of superfluity of silver, V 27, 59, 142n2, VI 103; cost of silver coinage, V 140; cowries as currency, V 141
  exchanges, IV 162, V 141; depreciation, V 142n2

India Office, V 48, 49n1, 140; Library, V 54

Indian Civil Service: examinations, V 68, WSJ examines for, 65

Indian Council, V 50, 140n3

Indian Mutiny, II 408, III 208, VI 125n5

Indifference, Law of, and WSJ's Law of the Substitution of Similars, I 210n1, III 168n2, cannot be two prices for same article in same market, IV 61

Industrial Conspiracy, Law of, V 138n3

industrial system of society, VI 35
  industrial organization, VII 100; partnerships, VI 76–7
  laws of industrial relationships, VII 38
  wealth promoted by industrial freedom, VII 44

industry
  classes and orders of, VI 21, 33–5
  coal for, VII 29–31; sited on coalfields, 21–2; industrial growth and coal exhaustion, III 65, IV 235, 236–7
  limited by capital (Mill), VI 38, 48, 62
  see also manufactures; trade

Infant Life Protection Act (1872), V 167

Infant Life Protection Society (1870), V 167n8

infant mortality: treated in WSJ's article 'Married Women in Factories', V· 154, 161, 167, 200, VI 59; among illegitimate births, V 173n2; attempts to get Government inquiry into, 168, 170–1; proposed discussion on, at National Association for Promotion of Social Science (1882), 173–4
crèches as remedy for, V 162, 164, 166, or exclusion of married women from factories, 163–7

inflation, IV 111, V 84

Ingram, John Kells (1823–1907), Fellow and Librarian of Trinity College, Dublin
  'The Present position and prospects of Political Economy', Presidential address to Section F, British Association, Dublin (1878), IV 272, 273n6, n8, 276, V 124n1, 125; supports historical, opposes mathematical, approach to economics, V 67–8, 78, 124n1
  letters to, V 126; letters from, V 124–5, 128

Inkerman, Battle of (November 1854), II 122n3

Inman, Dr, physician at Asylum hospital: attends Roscoe Jevons, III 204

innate characteristics, VI 30–1, of peoples and races, 31–2

inns and hotels encountered by WSJ
  in Australia: Ballarat Hotel, II 371; Bathurst Inn, I 234–5; Blue Mountain Inn, 237; Commercial Inn, Great Hartley, 236, Penrith, 238; Durants Inn, 235; Figtree Public House, 169; Gas Hotel, 233–4; 'The Golden Pippin', 228; Macquarie Arms, Windsor, 137, 140–1, II 252, 254; Mount Victoria Inn, I 220; 19 Mile Hollow inn, I 219; 'New Inn', 224; Russell's Marine Hotel, Wollongong, 162–3, 168, 177; Sofala Inn, 230; Springwood Inn, II 254; Wascoes old Pilgrim Inn, Lapstone Hill, I 152–3, II 254–5; Wyagden Inn, I 227, 234; unnamed, I 127, 128, 143–5, 225, 228–9, II 220, III 28
  in America, II 399; 'St Nicolas House',

inns and hotels (*contd*)
New York, 400
in Callao, II 394
in England: Barley Mow, near Staines,
II 9; Jack Straw's Castle, Hampstead Heath, stormed by the Volunteers, II 460; the Maypole,
Chigwell, I 55
in Havana, II 398
in Paris, Grand Hotel, V 148–9
in Wales, II 415
Inquirer, Unitarian newspaper, II 416n6,
VII 125; notice of *Two Diagrams*, II
443–4; Rylett's contribution to, V
114–15
insanity
Dr Conolly's lecture on Lunatics,
heard by WSJ, I 85
Henrietta's mental illness, I 11
lunatic asylum in Crown Street, I 8, 116,
II 25
Roscoe Jevons's insanity, I 7, 8–9, WSJ's
reflections on, 195
Institut de France, IV 37
instrument-makers, II 297n8; Flavelles, of
Sydney, II 344; Oertling, II 50, 62
instruments: Professor Neumeyer's II 372;
WSJ's, inspected by Lima customs
officials, II 387, 'idle' in London,
404
see also actinometer; barometers; goniometer; sympiesometer; thermometers
insurance: as an element in profit, VI
67, VII 142; utility and, IV 258
insurance companies, VI 119, 121
assurance societies, VI 71
and bubbles, IV 240
cooperative, on the mutual principle,
VI 75; working-class investment in,
VII 54; fire companies, VI 115;
WSJ advised to insure against fire,
II 118
Globe Insurance office, I 180–1
life insurance, WSJ given medical go-
ahead for, IV 106
intemperance
as check to population, VI 58
*Fourth and Fifth Reports of the Select Com-
mittee of the House of Lords on Intemperance* (1878), V 74, 165–6
Permissive Prohibitory Liquor Bill, VI
41
WSJ's article on (March 1857, unpublished), VII 117; 'Experimental Legislation and the Drink Traffic' (*Contemporary Review*, 1880), V
74, 166
interest: to be treated mathematically
(1860), VII 120; in *Theory of Political Economy*, II 411, determined by
last portion added, 422; Westergaard on, IV 255, Christie on, V
32, 33; expressed as 'a ratio of two
numbers', VII 142; theory questioned by G. Darwin, IV 24–9, 35,
63, by Adamson, 226–7, 230–1
on money at call, IV 133
as portion of the produce, VI 60, VII 62;
distinguished from profit, VI 67,
VII 64
and usury laws, IV 11, 17, VI 121
also mentioned, VI 104
see also rate of interest
International Coinage Commision, *see*
Royal Commission on International Coinage
International currency: gold coin for, III
183–4; controversy on (1869), 211–
21; Wolowski on, 198; U.S. assimi-
late gold coinage to international
standard, 232
article on, 'On the Condition of the Gold
Coinage of the United Kingdom,
with reference to the question of
International Currency' (WSJ,
1868), II 156n5, III 159n2, 195,
206–7, VII 65
see also International Monetary Convention; Royal commission on International Coinage
International Exhibitions, *see* Great Exhibition (1851, 1862); Paris International Exhibitions (1855, 1867,
1878, 1881)
International Institute of Sociology, V 3n1
international law, VII 55; and the
'Confederate Rams', III 53
International Monetary Association,
meeting at Mansion House, London (March 1882), V 175, 187n2
International Monetary Conventions,
Paris
(1865), III 212, VII 67

(1867), III 181n2; question of Great
Britain joining, 183–4, of assimilating coinage to recommended standard, 211, 212; recommendations
on seignorage, 211; British representatives in Paris, 213, Report,
215n2

 article on, 'On the International
Monetary Convention and the Introduction of an International Currency into this Kingdom' (WSJ,
1868), III 186, 191, 211, VII 65–75

 (1881), V 92n1, 139n5, 140, 187n4,
194n3

 (1889), V 92n1

International Monetary Standard
Association, IV 186n2

International Scientific Series: WSJ's contributions to, IV 34, 43, 98, 104:
publishers (P. S. King & Son), IV
148

 see also Jevons, William Stanley, works:
Money and the Mechanism of Exchange

International Statistical Congress (Berlin,
September 1863): *Serious Fall*
quoted by English delegate, III 49,
VII 125; adopts franc as international coinage, VII 66–7

international trade, VI 108–9; examination questions on, VII 134

and international telegrams, Madsen's
'Law of International Traffic', IV
243–8, V 27–9

international values: Marshall's pure
theory of, V 66; Mill on, VII
156

intuition, III 13

inventions, VI 21, 28–9; hindered by
workmen's attitudes, VII 46–7;
stimulated by division of labour,
VII 61

 see also calculating machines; logical
abacus; steam power

investment, VI 46–7

 contrary investment, VI 106

 and credit, VI 105–6

 examination questions on, VII 133

 in Government stocks, IV 110

 WSJ's investments: Booth & Co., I 210;
Brazil steamships, III 150; coal, V
139, 155, 179, 190–1; Government
debentures, II 232, 235; iron busi-

ness, II 232, V 155, 179; John
Brown & Co., V 155, 190; John
Hutton's quarry, I 210n2; railway
shares, III 50

'Invincibles', Irish terrorists, V 189n1

Iowa, II 419, 420, 427

Ireland

 Arrears Bill (1882), V 189n2

 banks, VI 125n5; bank notes, III 203,
IV 13, 18, 107n1, 161; gold coins in,
III 190–1, 201

 coal production, VII 27, 33; imports
from England, 22

 Coercion Bill (Act), V 132n5, 150, 151;
coercion a mistake, 179, 189, an
irritant, not a deterrent, 197

 earth tremors, I 71

 emigration to England, I 16, III 243, to
Australia, IV 7

 Fenian uprising (1867), III 190–1

 flax exports, VII 24

 Forster resigns as Chief Secretary for
Ireland, V 189

 Gladstone's Land Reform measures
(1881), V 135, 150–1, 179, 189;
opposed by Land League, 150

 Irish Church: blocks currency reform,
III 210; disestablishment, V
151

 Irish passengers on board the *Oliver
Lang*, I 105, II 98

 Irish Question, Rylett on, V 111–15,
196–7

 landlordism and evictions, V 54, 112,
150n3, 197; Eviction Bill rejected,
150

 origins of Richard Cantillon, V 123–8

 outrages in London (1881), V 134,
135n4; agrarian vendettas in Ireland, 150n3

 overpopulation, III 255; mortality, VI
59, of Irish in U.S.A., IV 55

 Phoenix Park murders, V 189

 potato famine, II 53n7

 Roman Catholics, V 127

 soap smuggled from, II 40n1

 WSJ's visit to, V 54; his 'Irish nausea',
115

 also mentioned, I 101, II 123, IV 154,
V 23, VII 100

 see also Dublin; Parnell, Charles Stewart

Ireland, Chief Secretary of, *see* Cavendish.

Ireland, Chief Secretary of (contd)
    Lord Frederick; Forster, William
        Edward
Ireland, Viceroy of, see Cowper, Lord
Irish Industry, Museum of, II 119n16
Irish Land League, V 150–1, 157
Irish Peat Company, Kilberry, II 118–19
Iron Founders and Engineers, in Liverpool, II 41
iron manufacture, II 38
    iron ore, VII 24–5; pig iron, IV 30, V
        85; pyrites, II 43
    iron and steel production in America,
        IV 30
    smelting, VII 19, 30, furnaces, I 93–4,
        VI 25
    works: coal consumption, III 124, VII
        19, 26; dependence on steam-
        powered engines, 20; from charcoal
        to coal, 22; Windsor Ironworks, II
        92n3, 94
iron masters, I 12, II 118, 138n4; blamed
    for secret system of trade, III 143;
    quarterly meetings, I 120, II 163–
    4; skills and rewards, II 38, 39;
    suggested as career for WSJ, I 88–9,
    117, II 38–9
'Ironmasters and Ironworkers', letter to
    The Times (WSJ, 17 December
    1866), III 141–3, 148
iron merchants: Herbert Jevons's career as,
    II 38; Thomas Jevons's view of, 38;
    Jevons family firm, 139, VII 49
iron products: bridges, III 141, 228; chur-
    ches, I 59; cottage, Thomas
    Jevons's plan for, II 128–30, 136,
    139; exhibits at Paris Exhibition,
    II 183
iron ships: Thomas Jevons's model boats, I
    3–4, 119, II 137–8; ironwork on the
    Oliver Lang, I 103, II 97; for the
    Navy, II 428–9; problem of fouled
    hulls, II 60; iron-shipbuilding
    yards, I 85, 93, II 41, 61, temporary
    suspension of building, III 142;
    Startled Fawn, II 144, 146. See also
    ships
iron trade
    competition from foreign trade, III 128,
        142–3, VII 49–50
    fluctuations in: depression (1854–5), II
        117, 138, 145; (1866), III 128, 142,

228; revival (1869), III 225n2, 230;
    collapse (1876), IV 210; depression
    (1880), V 107, 108; prospering
    (1881), V 155, 179; relapse (1882),
    V 190
Jevons family iron business, I 3, 12, II
    38, 137, 145, 259, III 128, VII 49–
    50; bankruptcy in 1848, I 12, II
    38n2; Thomas Jevons becomes
    manager for Dowlais Iron Com-
    pany, I 12, II 38, 117; family firm
    reconstituted, I 12, Thomas Jevons
    rejoins, II 117; plan to extend to
    Continent, I 119, II 138–9, 143,
    145–6, trip to France and Italy in
    aid of, II 175, 183; agency in
    America, I 119, II 138, 143, 145,
    150, 210; Herbert Jevons's career
    in, II 38, 448; WSJ invests in, 232;
    dwindling overseas business, III
    128. See also under Jevons, Henry;
    Jevons, Thomas Edwin
Isle of Wight, excursion to, II 432
Isnard, Achylle Nicolas (1749–1803):
    Traité des richesses (published
    anonymously, 1781), IV 260
Italia economica, IV 98, 103
Italy
    Bunsen's expedition to volcanic districts,
        II 229
    clearing houses, IV 302
    currency: adopts French double stan-
        dard system, VII 66; gold coinage,
        V 58, 59; international currency,
        III 212; paper money, III 199, VI
        98, 110
    economists, V 42, VII 99; receptive to
        new ideas, IV 47–8, 58, 68, 80, 84,
        95; demand for old English
        economical works, V 42, 74;
        working-class education in political
        economy, V 37–41
    translation of 'Primers', IV 248, V
        37n3, 42, 53, 59, 60, of Theory of
        Political Economy, IV 80, 94, 98, 103,
        154, V 40, of Walras, IV 261, 262,
        270
    Marshall recuperates in, V 170
    in Middle Ages, IV 215
    North and South, IV 154
    Puviani on, V 40–1
    savings banks, IV 154

Statistical Office, IV 48, 68, 298-9

Thomas Jevons's plan to extend family iron business to, II 138, 143, 145, 183; his business trip to, 139, 145-6, 173, 183, 309, towns in Italy visited, 175, 199; scares of cholera in Venice, 190; dies of cholera in Pisa, I 121, 122; English iron prices too high for Italian business, III 227

vintages, V 167

wars of liberation against Austria, II 417, V 37, VI 110n4; emancipation from Church and despotism, V 37-9

WSJ visits (1874), IV 22, 33n2, V 198

also mentioned, I 55n1, II 428, 431

see also Florence; Pisa; Rome; Venice

Jack, William (1834-1924), member of Macmillans publishing firm: consulted on Index Society, IV 298

letters to, IV 193, 238, 248-9, 251

Jackson, General 'Stonewall', II 454n7; killed at Chancellorsville (1863), III 16n6

Jamaica
copper tokens, IV 166
Director of Public Works, V 71
economic prosperity, V 70-1
Governor (Sir Anthony Musgrave), IV 126n1, V 270
rum, V 70

Janbecumberre gold diggings, II 365

Janssen, Pierre Jules César (1824-1907), French astronomer, V 86

Japan
represented at Paris Exhibition, IV 277
silk from, III 208

Jenkin, Henry Charles Fleeming (1833-85), Professor of Engineering at University College, London, later in Edinburgh: correspondence with WSJ on theory of Exchange, III 166-78, VI x; on list of persons interested in new economics for Walras, IV 66

The Graphic Representation of the Laws of Supply and Demand . . . (L.S.E. Reprints, 1931), III 166n4, IV 5n3, VII 146; 'On the Principles which regulate the Incidence of Taxes' (*Edinburgh Royal Society, Proceedings,* 1871-2), IV 5-6; 'Trade Unions. How far legitimate?' (*North British Review,* March 1868), III 166

letters from, III 167-72, 172-7, 178

Jennings, Richard, *Natural Elements of Political Economy* (1855), IV 91n3, VII 146

Jevon, family name of Jevons before William Jevon added 's', I 3n3, II 438

Jevon, Rachel, II 438

Jevons, Anne (Mrs George Worthington, 1796-1826), eldest daughter of William Jevons, aunt of WSJ, I 240, II 28, 47n2

Jevons, Annie (1825-1905), second daughter of William Jevons, jun,. cousin of WSJ, I 241, II 176-7, 446, III 73, 148, 180

Jevons, Arthur (1830-1905), third son of Timothy Jevons, cousin of WSJ, engineer and artist, I 241, II 10n1, 438, III 96; goes to Norway with WSJ, V 65

Jevons, Mrs Arthur (Catherine Castle Dawson, 1826-1906), I 241, II 10n1, III 96

Jevons, Eliza (b. 1832), daughter of Timothy Jevons, cousin of WSJ, I 241; marries Alfred Foster-Barham, II 103-4, III 30n4; a son, II 176

Jevons, Fanny (b. 1856), daughter of George Jevons, I 241, II 391n16

Jevons, Ferdinand (d. 1967), son of Thomas Edwin Jevons, nephew of WSJ, I 10, 241, IV 164, 291, V 65

Jevons, Frederick (1834-1916), fourth son of Timothy Jevons, cousin of WSJ, I 241: as a Unitarian defies command to pray, II 132; goes with Thomas Jevons's party to Paris, II 175, 179, 183, 202; with Rathbone Brothers, Liverpool shipping firm, II 391; travels in America, 391, 428, leaves as WSJ arrives, 382; stays with WSJ in London, II 454, goes on the loose with him, 455; marries Sarah Taylor, sister of Harriet Taylor, I 47, II 132n20, III 75; visit to WSJ and Harriet in Manchester, III 185; Harriet stays with, IV 150

Jevons, Mrs Frederick (Sarah Acland Taylor), I 47, 211n1, 241, II 132n20, III 185, IV 150n1, 216n1

Jevons, George (1818–1905), eldest son of William Jevons, jun., cousin of WSJ, I 241; in the family iron business, I 10, helps reconstitute firm after bankruptcy, 12, 56n9, II 38; marries Elizabeth Thornely, I 56n9, II 391n16; WSJ visits, II 391; at Brighton, II 444, III 69; is given copy of 'Two Diagrams', II 444; also mentioned, III 28, 69, 73

Jevons, Mrs George (Elizabeth Thornely, 1820–83), I 56n9, 241, II 391n16, 432n18, III 32; at Brighton, II 444, III 69

Jevons, George Walter (b. 1854), eldest son of George and Elizabeth Jevons, I 241, II 391n16, 444

Jevons, Harriet Winefrid (1877–1961), elder daughter of WSJ, I 241; birth, IV 211, 213; childhood, I 48, IV 291, 303, V 36, 66, 98, 123, 132, 136, at the seaside, 142, 185, 188, 190; a cold in the eye, V 200; also mentioned, V 149n1

letters to, I 49n2, 149n1; and the Jevons Papers, VI ix

Jevons, Henrietta (1839–1909), younger sister of WSJ, I 241

birth, I 6; childhood, 115, 116, 119, 120; catches crabs with WSJ, 56, goes to parties with him, 197; at Mary Roscoe's wedding, II 26; at boarding school, 67, 69, 109, leaves school, 276, 296; teaches charity children, II 277, 361, in a Unitarian school, 406, 458, III 57; 'learns' at Ladies College, II 406 'deep in a Novel', II 157, advice on reading, 291, 303; her essay, 328; bad handwriting, 363; her bedroom-study, 304; a Mudie box of books, IV 401–2; attends Liverpool meeting of British Association, II 434

musical talents and interests, I 11, 31–2, 67, 181, 217, 241, 277, 289, 295–6; plays double bass, II 29; piano lessons, 143, 169, 320, 321; advises WSJ to study thorough bass, 255;

singing, 257, 290, 363; concert going, 328

visits to friends and relations, I 38, II 413, III 30; WSJ disturbed by constant visiting, I 30, II 275, 276, 358, 441; her 'gay unsettled life', 337, 338, 358; has nothing else to do, III 30

in the Lakes, II 26; at Llangollen, 154; stays at Streatley with Lucy, 389, 391, 392, 393, 401; at Englefield, 389, 412, 414; sees London illuminated, III 6–8; at Beaumaris, 14, 32–4, 36, 149; visiting in Manchester, 46, 57, in Liverpool, II 414, III 75, 157–8

her 'heart-felt realities', I 154; self-forgetfulness, 189; happy, open disposition, II 338; views on religion, II 226, 241, 258, 296, has a leaning towards the Catholics, 277; misgivings, 323–4; in need of advice, 293

affinities with WSJ, I 11, 29, 223, 225, 241, 255, 303, 310, 311, 333, 358; a friend for him, II 275, 302–3, 307, 325; advice to her, on leading a useful life, 358–61; a pincushion for him, II 226–7, 289, a Chinese book for her, 368

WSJ's concern for her financial needs, I 45; her income, II 56, 414, III 40; shares WSJ's home after his return from Australia, I 11, in London, 33, 179n1, 189, II 389, 402, 406, 412; new arrangements (1862), 441, 442; plans for Manchester, III 29, 57; with WSJ in Birch Grove, 157

health: 'at times not quite well', II 406; suffers from having no occupation, III 30; would benefit from trip to New Zealand, 38–9, or from a present of clothes, 40–1; a bad leg, 97; well and cheerful, 158; at Roscoe's funeral, 205; a mental breakdown, I 11; hopes for recovery, III 227; 'not much changed for the worse', V 110; death, I 11

letters from WSJ, II 29–31, 57–9, 67–70, 76, 109–11, 158–9, 179–83, 212–14, 223–7, 240–3, 255–8, 274–80, 289–92, 294–9, 302–4, 306–8, 311–14, 317–22, 325–9, 333–9, 358–63,

377–81, 434–6, 440–2
letters to WSJ quoted, I 29–30, 26–7,
31–2, 154, VII 3, referred to, I 2,
11, 29, II 180, 223, 234, 237, 240,
255, 276, 280, 302, 319, 336, 358,
376, 382; a letter written on a
tombstone, II 294
letter from Thomas Jevons, II 177–9
also mentioned, I 182n2, II 4, 125, 145,
190, 216, 230, 238, 262, 342, 423,
425, 438, 444, 446, 459, III 70, 78,
80, 122, 148, 151, 159
Jevons, Henry (1827–1914), eldest son of
Timothy Jevons, cousin of WSJ, I
241
in the family iron business, I 10, 12, 38,
234; goes to America on business,
137, 138, 142, 145, 150; on the state
of the iron trade (1869), III 225n2,
226–7
marriage to Susanna Thornely, I 56n9,
his children, II 176; a rubber of
whist with Thomas Jevons, II 24;
manages family finance after
Thomas's death, 215, 38°, 391,
414, III 50, his letter strikes with
'the chill of money', II 348; takes
over family house in Chatham
Street, 216; plans for Tommy
Jevons, 391, 414; looks after
Herbert's affairs, 392, 404, III 30,
39, 40, Henrietta stays with, III 75;
care for Roscoe Jevons, 89, 204,
205; electro-plate silver tea urn
presented to him by the family,
205, 210
defeated in Liverpool municipal elections, III 227
letters from, III 226–7, 229–30
also mentioned, II 116, 341, 440
Jevons, Mrs Henry (Susanna Thornely,
1830–1915), I 56n9, 241, II
432n18, III 75; her children, II
176n11
Jevons, Herbert (1831–74), elder brother
of WSJ, I 241
birth, I 6; education: at Mechanics
Institution High School, Liverpool,
7; at University College, London,
Medical Faculty, 10, 13, 115n7, II
13, 26, intends to matriculate, 16;
abandons medicine, 78n4

in lodgings with WSJ in London, I 10,
13, 115, 116, II 1, 4–6, 7–8, IV 33;
moves to Aunt Richard in Richmond, II 8–9, 10–11, 14, 15–16,
arranges new lodgings for WSJ, 11,
13–14, 21; expeditions in and
around London, II 4, 9; visit to
Bonn, II 9; a picnic on Day of
Prayer and Fasting, 132
goes to Natal and India for his health
(1851–2), I 10, 116, 117, II 27n1,
174; sails for home, II 34, 35–6; in
London, I 76–7, 78, moves to Liverpool, 92
joins family iron business, I 10, 16, II 38,
56, 78, 143, 150, 154, 216, 234, 259;
his knowledge of business, II 405;
goes to Pisa on his father's death, II
213–14, 215
emigrates to Wayzata, Minnesota
(1858), I 10, 32, 189; WSJ visits, I
33, II 364, 377, stays in his log hut,
384, 400; his land, 384, 400, 404;
life in Minnesota, 392, 405, 409,
418–20; his fiddle and books, 404,
424; sugar making, 393, 423, 424;
becomes a school trustee, 409; his
'man', 409, 423, 424; farming
losses, 413; problems of being bred
a gentleman, 423
prefers America to British colonies, II
420, and American newspapers to
British, 421; on Americans and
British, 423; returns to England
(1861), I 10, 38, II 436, 440;
'strongly Anti-American', 438, 441,
his 'unfortunate expedition to
America', III 4; lodges with WSJ, I
179n1; plan to quarry in North
Wales comes to nothing, II 441,
442
emigrates to Australia (1862), I 10,
182n2, 189, II 446–7, 462, III 3,
15; Bank agent in Sydney, II 448,
III 4, 15–16, 28; fishing in Sydney
Harbour, III 31; plans to emigrate
to New Zealand, II 342, 441, 442
becomes Bank agent in Nelson, New
Zealand, III 33, 34; in Bank of New
South Wales, Dunedin, 40, 50–1,
57–8, 74, 158, 210; temporarily in
charge of bank at Tuapeka, 74;

Jevons, Herbert (*contd*)

gold buying, I 9, III 4, 28; assays, I 9, III 39, 58, 150, directions from WSJ, 48n2, 50–1; boxes from England, 39–40, 48, 50, 56, 158, 185; reads *The Coal Question*, III 74

goes to gold diggings at Hokatika, III 158, 185; speculates in quartz mining, 205, and in gold mines, 210; appointed Manager of branch bank at Grahamstown, I 9–10, IV 22

health, I 10, 116, 117, II 27n1, 174; illness in London, II 15, 21, has to drink Port wine, 16; injured by peculiar family disposition, II 337; thinks of trying water cure, 423; dies of cancer in Waiwera, New Zealand, I 10, IV 33–4, 42, 249–50

character, I 9; influenced by Arthur Clough, 65n4; matter-of-fact outlook, II 226; his theory of work, 447, III 3; social interests and hobbies, IV 33; fickleness of mind, 34

finances, II 16, 232–3, 298, 392, 405, III 30, 151, 204

letters to, II 202–3, 204–7, 215–18, 218–21, 230–3, 233–5, 238–40, 259–62, 270–4, 381–3, 388–93, 403 (2), 404–8, 409–12, 412–18, 421–2, 425–32, 442–3, 446–7, 451–4, 457–9, III 3–4, 5–6, 14–16, 28–31, 33, 33–5, 42–3, 48, 50–2, 52, 56–8, 58–9, 62, 68–9, 76, 88–9, 102–3, 148–51, 157–9, 182–3, 185, 195–6, 204–6, 209–10, 249, IV 21–2

letters from: to WSJ, II 44–5, 418–21, 423–4, III 38–41, 74–5; to Thomas Jevons, II 4–6, 8–9, 12–16, 16–18, 19–20, 21–2, from Thomas Jevons, II 185–90

also mentioned, I 119, II 8, 52, 75, 83, 88, 125, 131, 144, 157, 193, 240, 255, 256, 293, 341, 343, 444, III 32, 148

Jevons, Herbert Stanley ('Boy' 1875–1955), eldest child of WSJ, I 241

birth, IV 134n2, 146; named after Herbert Jevons, I 10; childhood, IV 150, 164, 194, 211, 213, 285, 291, V 99, 119, 123, 154; at the seaside, IV 271, V 142, 185, 188, 190, 200;

snowballing, IV 303; first lessons, V 36; his kite, 66; musical promise, 66, 108; enjoys election scenes, 97–8; making boxes, 132; a letter to Aunt Lucy, 136; on the Malvern Hills, 146, 147

lecturer in geology at Sydney University, changes to economics, I 114n2; presented with WSJ's posthumous medal for photography, I 31n1; family papers released after his death, I 7

Jevons, James Edward (1828–60), second son of Timothy Jevons, cousin of WSJ, I 241; farms in Natal, I 76n1, II 78n7, 174; returns to England, 78–9, 89; emigrates to Ceylon, dies there, II 89n7, 424

Jevons, Jane Emily (b. and d. 1827), eldest child of Thomas and Mary Anne Jevons, sister of WSJ, I 6, 241

Jevons, John Daniel Thornely (1861–7), younger son of George Jevons, I 241, II 391n16

Jevons, Lucy Anne (1830–1910), elder sister of WSJ, later Mrs John Hutton, I 241

birth, I 6; a 'mother' to the family after Mrs Jevons's death, 6–7, 11, 12, II 211, 238; her father's right hand, I 119, II 143, 209; unhappy remembrances of Roscoe's illness, I 9, III 205, 210; her household management, II 27–8, 36, 95–6, 276, 414, III 33–4

goes with Thomas Jevons to the Continent, I 11, II 139, 175, 177, 179, 183, 190, 202, 204; with him in Pisa when he dies, I 122, II 213, 215; writes to WSJ of his death, 209, 211

her sociable nature, IV 33; a picnic, II 4; parties, 10, 12; bridesmaid to Mary Roscoe, 26, to Elizabeth Jevons, 104, to Emily Malin, 142, 145; her many invitations, 216–17; visits to friends, 27, 227, 406, 412, 413; 'frequent *gaddings*', 276

visit to the Lakes, II 26, 27; abroad, 51, 56, homesick to return, 52; at Nantwich, I 66, II 27, 30; at Llangollen, I 120, II 154, 155, 157, 163, 165, 168; at Streatley with Henny,

II 389, 391, 392–3, 401; at Englefield, 412, 414; at Newton,
Lancs, III 26n2; escapes injury in a
railway accident, II 175–6
sketching, I 59, 63, II 83, 168, 254, 327;
her pictures hung in WSJ's Sydney
cottage, 294–5, 309; re-arranges
drawing-room pictures at home, II
172; painting, II 216, III 97; shares
Mudie box of books with Henny, II
401–2
advice and support for WSJ, I 11, 29, 39,
78, 186, II 238, 241, 381, 389;
recognises the 'dawning of a great
mind', I 13, sees the merit of *Serious
Fall*, 191; congratulates him on *The
Coal Question*, III 97; her understanding of him, I 47, II 310; a
friend for him, 303, 307; Henrietta
advised by WSJ to rely on her
cautions, II 223 and advice, 293
provides bun loaves and raspberry
vinegar for WSJ's voyage to Australia, II 81; shares in box for him,
289, her jam and plum pudding,
295; her old shawl used on camping
trips, 218, 220, 354; WSJ brings a
Chinese fan for her, 368
WSJ's concern for her, after their
father's death, I 32, 189n1, 199n1;
makes a home for her in London, I
33, 179n1, II 389, 402, 412; their
walks together, I 59, 60
breaks off engagement to Russell Martineau, I 11, II 392; marries John
Hutton (1862), I 11, 36, 38, 182n2,
II 442; her first child (Thomas
Grindal), I 11, 189n1 II 458, 462;
second child (Mary Josephine), I
11, III 158; her noisy children too
much for Henny, III 30; takes
charge of WSJ's children at Hampstead, V 132, 148; a birthday letter
from 'Boy', 136
her home at Beaumaris, I 11, III 158;
WSJ stays at, I 43, II 149, III 14,
33–4, 49, 57, 58, 59, 185, writes *The
Coal Question* there, III 97; the
house let, III 30; in Clynnog, I 11,
201n3, III 127, too dreary in winter, II 149; moves to Ludlow, I 11,
IV 33

financial difficulties, I 45, 189n1, 199n1,
II 458, III 210; her own income, II
56, 414, III 40; helps support old
family servant, II 441; trust settlement for her, III 205
health, II 143, III 57, 143; a cold, I 92,
II 29; thinks 'a little medicine and
medical advice' needed, II 425; not
well enough to attend Roscoe's
funeral, III 205
religious views, II 225, 327, has the
attitude of Faith, 337
diary, I 13; 'Recollections of my
brother', II 20n1, 21n7; material
for *Letters* and *Journal* provided by,
I 11
letters from WSJ, II 35, 105–6, 108–9,
146–7, 208–11, 237–8, 252–5, 288–
9, 299–302, 306–8, 309–10, 331–3,
339–42, 348–9, 352–5, 356–8, 364–
5, 366–70, 370–3, 373–6, 383, 384,
388, 422–3; to Mrs Lucy Hutton,
III 9–10, 18–19, 48–9, 62–3, 97,
101, 120–1, 126–7, IV 51–2, 80, 88,
93, 106, 146, 183–4, V 136, 146;
letters to WSJ referred to, I 9, 66, II
6, 25, 32, 204, 209, 211, 237, 255,
288, 336; letter to Harriet Taylor,
quoted, I 47
also mentioned, II 11, 14, 18, 22, 31, 48,
73, 74, 75, 121, 140, 214, 230, 240,
256, 261, 262, 299, 418, 436, 438,
III 73, 78, 80, 127, 151
see also under Hutton, John, Mary Josephine and Thomas Grindal
Jevons, Lucy Cecilia (b. 1880), younger
daughter of WSJ, I 241, V 122, 146,
154
Jevons, Mary Ann, wife of William Edgar
Jevons: *The Syrens: and other Poems*
(1880), V 190n1. *See also* Jevons,
Mrs William Edgar
Jevons, Mary Catherine (1827–1908), eldest daughter of Timothy Jevons,
cousin of WSJ, I 56, 241, II 440,
446, III 69, 97; goes to London
entertainments with WSJ, I 207;
stays with Thomas Jevons family,
II 141–2; goes with Thomas and
Lucy Jevons to Continent, 175,
177, 183, 213, acts as interpreter in
French, 184; death of her mother,

Jevons, Mary Catherine (*contd*)
II 391; sight-seeing in London, 412,
III 96; attends Roscoe's funeral,
III 205

Jevons, Reginald ('Rex', 1872–1907), eldest son of Thomas Edwin Jevons,
nephew of WSJ, I 241, V 110, 154

Jevons, Roscoe (1829–69), eldest son of
Thomas Jevons, brother of WSJ, I
241
birth, I 6, registered at Dr Williams's
Library, II 33n2; educated at
Mechanics Institute High School,
Liverpool, I 7; his early promise as
chemist and mathematician, 7, experiments in the coachouse, 7–8,
114n1, 194–5; poetical talents, 7,
194, 195; grief at his mother's
death, I 7, 8; his initials cut on a
tree, 193–4
enters family iron business, I 8, dislike of
life at the foundry, 195; onset of
insanity, I 7, 8, 12, WSJ's reflections on, 100n1, 194–5, 212, II
337; his father's visits to, in Liverpool asylum, I 8, 116, 120, II 16, in
Birmingham, II 163; visits from
WSJ, I 8, 9, II 391, III 30, 58, 89;
arrangements for annuity, II 55–6,
215; exclusion from family life,
II 27, 29
Henry Jevons's care of, III 89, 204, 205,
210; illness and death, I 9, 212, II
38n2, III 204, 210; funeral, I 11,
III 204–5; 'a sad chapter' in the
family history closed, I 9, III 206;
'best and noblest of brothers', I 212
diary, I 8, 194, 195

Jevons, Thomas (1791–1855), father of
WSJ, I 240
an iron merchant in Liverpool, I 2,
partner in family firm, 3; apprenticeship, 3n1; firm bankrupted, 12,
excluded from reconstituted firm,
12; becomes Liverpool agent for Sir
John Guest, of Dowlais Iron Co.,
12, 66, II 11, 117, 'a sort of servi-
tude', 38; returns to family iron
business (1854), I 12, II 117, 119,
120; also bankrupted as ironmaster
in South Wales, I 12; plans for
extending business to Continent, I

119, II 138, 143, 145–6, and to
Sydney, 139; attends quarterly
meetings of ironmasters, I 120, II
163–4
his household: Grandfather William
Jevons lives with, I 3, 8, II 4, 7n3, 9,
10, 27, 28, dies there, I 3, 116–17,
II 28–9; plays a rubber of whist
with him, I 116; marriage to Mary
Anne Roscoe, I 6, II 298, IV 157,
their children, I 6, her death, 6–7;
move from Park Hill Road to
Chatham Street after bankruptcy,
I 12, become the 'poor relations' of
the Jevons family, 12
family holidays: at Dolgelly, I 118, II
86–9, 92; at Llangollen, I 120, II
153–5, 163, 165, 167, 168–9
pleasures of home, I 121, as WSJ
remembers it, I 78, II 211, 212;
interior decoration, II 164, 172; a
new kitchen stove, 164–6; servants,
II 96, 176; guests, II 127–8, 132,
135, 141–2, IV 157; Professor
Graham invited to dinner or breakfast, II 79, 94, 102
Roscoe's desire to do his duty by his
father, I 195; visits to Roscoe in the
asylum, I 8, II 16, 163, provision
for him, 56; meets Herbert from
Natal at the Docks, I 76; hopes for
Tommy, II 214, 221
and WSJ: early expeditions together, I
56; surprises him reading the Gospels, 99–100; advice to him as a
schoolboy, 115; predicts a distinguished career, II 25, 43, 55;
encounters him in the British
Museum, II 30; accepts decision to
stay on at College (1852), I 61, 63,
to go into a Liverpool office (1853),
78; advice and proposals for career,
88–9, II 36–41, 43; visit to soap-
works together, I 92–3, II 41–2;
congratulates him on College suc-
cesses, 42–3, 58; lectures him on
book-keeping, II 78
consulted on Sydney assayership, I 96,
97; suggests conditions for accepting, 117, II 349; advice on getting
private work, I 118, II 91; views on
the post, II 46–8, 51–2, 255; disgust

at financial arrangements, I 120, 121, II 147–50, 173, 201; gives WSJ introductions in Sydney, II 47, 131, 136; suggests doing business in copper, 139–40, and writing articles for local papers, 172, 198; parting from WSJ, II 213, parting gift, 213, his photograph, 214, 227; other 'little things' left to WSJ, 233

WSJ on his father, I 3, 18, 59; his affection and goodness, I 115, 183, 195, humanity, I 155, II 327; knew WSJ but little, I 100; on the death of his father, II 208–11, 212, 213–4, 238; personal relations between father and son, II 21n7, 27, 54

continental journey on pleasure and business: plans for, I 119, II 138–9, 145–6, 173, 177; an opportunity for Lucy to see Italy, 139; members of the party, 175; first 'Table d'hote' in France, 177–8; Rouen Cathedral, 178; in Paris, I 121, II 179, 199, lodges in same house as WSJ, 179, 202; visits Exhibition, I 121, II 175, 183–4, and the Mint, I 121, gets WSJ's Assayers' Diploma and stamp, I 121, II 70n4, 184, 204; High Mass at La Madeleine, 179; crosses the Alps, I 121, II 199; in Switzerland, I 122, II 185–90, 199; in Venice, 190, 199–200; in Rome, I 121, 122, II 199, 200, visit to Gibson's studio, 201; the Ave Maria day, 201–2; collects gold coins for WSJ, I 122; his deep pleasure in the tour, 121–2, II 209–10; dies of cholera in Pisa, I 115n2, 121, 122–3, II 209–10, 227; buried in Protestant cemetery, I 22

finances: expenses for Herbert and WSJ in London (1850–3), II 7–8, 10–11, 14, 16, 17–18, 21, 33, 42; for WSJ's equipment and fares to Paris and Sydney (1853), I 117, II 55–6, 70–1, 78, 116–17, 144, 146; offers WSJ loan to build house, I 118, 120, II 130, 136, 139; loans repaid by WSJ, I 122, II 170, 201, 202

expenses of Grandfather William's funeral, II 29; expenses of Continental tour, II 139, 175, 183;

loses money in gold mines, I 118, 119, II 94, 164, 172; invests in silver lead mine, Pontgibaud Mines, France, 94, 164; buys patent for machine made horse-shoes, VII 47

dies at ease on money matters, II 210–11; disposition of money after death, II 55–6, 215, 232, 259, in his Will, I 117–18

inventive powers, I 3; his iron ships, 3–4, 119, II 137–8; design for model house, I 4, II 117; ideas for a corrugated iron cottage, II 128–30, 136; interest in decimal coinage and accounting system, I 4, 120, 122; the first man to use decimal system of accounts in England, II 143; suggests Bill making system compulsory, 155–6, his views submitted with William Brown's draft Bill, 157–8; on the Decimal Coinage of Italy, II 200; attends British Association meeting at Liverpool, II 102–3, describes experiment of M. Foucault, 102–3, 104–5; on a new invention for printing in colour, II 171–2

Unitarian faith, I 2; registers his children at Dr Williams's Library, II 33; at chapel, II 118, 134, 144, 151; attends Committee to approve Bust of William Roscoe, 128, 144; expects WSJ to attend chapel in Sydney, 131, 152; his religious opinions, 225, 327; 'we don't pray by command', II 132

general: on the earthquake at Birkenhead, I 71, 117, II 36; on health, II 101–2; executor for John Rowden Freme, 169; his collection of documents relating to Thames Tunnel, donated to British Museum, II 449, 450n2

writings: contributes paragraph, 'New Light' to *Mining Journal* (26 August 1854), II 91; *The Prosperity of Landlords not dependent on the Corn Laws* (1840), I 4, III 73; *Remarks on Criminal Law, with a Plan for an Improved System*, . . . (anon., 1834), I 4, 92n3

letters from: to WSJ, II 3–4, 6–8, 10–12,

Jevons, Thomas (*contd*)
23–5, 25–7, 27–8, 28–9, 31–2, 33–4, 35–7, 37–9, 39–41, 41–2, 42–4, 46–9, 51–4, 55–6, 59–61, 86–90, 90–6, 101–5, 115–19, 125–32, 132–6, 137–40, 141–4, 144–6, 147–53, 153–7, 163–9, 170–4, 174–7, 183–5, 199–202; his letters arranged, with comments, by WSJ, I 115–23, II 214

letters to Lucy Jevons, II 35, to Henrietta, II 177–9, to Herbert, II 185–90

letters to: from WSJ, I 101–9, II 20–1, 32–3, 70–1, 80–5, 96–100, 107, 108, 170, 195–9, 207–8; from Herbert, II 4–6, 12–16, 16–18, 19–20, 21–2; from William Brown, II 157–8

portrait photograph, II plate facing p. 12

also mentioned, II 31, 58, 75, 79, III 95

Jevons, Mrs Thomas (Mary Anne Roscoe, 1795–1845), daughter of William Roscoe, mother of WSJ, I 240, 242

youth at Allerton Hall, I 59n5, 193n5, 194; friendship with Emily Taylor, I 6, II 11n2; marriage to Thomas Jevons, I 6, II 298; children, I 6; insight into Roscoe's condition, 9, III 205

political economy included in her studies, I 6, reads *Easy Lessons on Money Matters* to WSJ, 157n4; encourages and teaches him in botany, I 6, 99, 113, II 256; teaches him his prayers, I 154, her 'saintly spirit' remains with him, 195; her present to him, II 209

portrait by John Hargreaves, I 2–3; Unitarian faith, 2; musical tastes, 4; published poems, 5; legacy from Aunt Moss, passed on to Lucy and Henrietta, II 56, legacy from Grandpa Roscoe, 405

death, I 6–7, 10, 75n2, II 211

Literary Diaries of Mary Anne Roscoe, I 6; quoted, I 201

also mentioned, I 53n1

Jevons, Thomas Edwin (Tom, 1841–1917), younger brother of WSJ, I 241

birth, I 6; childhood, I 115, 116, II 7, 29, 128; goes bathing with WSJ, I 56; at Mary Roscoe's wedding, II 26; acts a part in new chapel service, 32; skating, 118, 403, 424; picnic with Herbert on Fasting Day, 132; at Llangollen with the family, 154, his dish of wild strawberries, 167; at Mr Green's school in Liverpool, II 34, 44, 76, 143; fossils for, 157; present to WSJ, 195, from WSJ, 368

childhood illnesses: toothache, I 34; mumps, 60n3, 119, II 143, 145; cough, II 23; his more delicate constitution, 145

loss of his father, II 213, 214, left a 'delightful charge' to his brothers, I 117–18, II 56; WSJ promises a home for, 217, Lucy's care of, 238; goes to University College School, London, I 10, II 221–2, 230, 260, 293–4, lives with Aunt Richard, 223; goes on to University College (1857), I 10, 32

WSJ first sees him a grown man (1859), II 388; shares WSJ's lodgings in Porteus Road, London, I 33, II 389, 402, 413, 425, works with him for B.A., I 33, 34, II 341, 391, 402; financial arrangements, II 389, 391, 414; classes entered for, 389, 403, 406; gets 2nd certificate in College examinations, 415, 417, beats the Kossuth boys, 415; stays on to take B.A., 410, 412, 416, 421, III 13

walking tour with WSJ in Wales (1860), II 410, 412, 415

enters Rathbone Bros & Co. (1860), I 10, 182n2, on a five-year contract, I 10, II 391, 413, 414; arrangements for lodging with Uncle Timothy in Liverpool, 414, 435; learns Italian, 458; joins Liverpool Volunteers, 460; at Beaumaris, 446, 460, III 33; starts Debating Society in Liverpool, III 15; completes apprenticeship (1864), 57

stays in lodgings with WSJ at Wallasey (summer, 1863), III 12–13, 14, 18, then at Leasowe Hotel, 28–9, and at Beaumaris, 30, 33; ex-.

pedition to Allerton, I 193–4; tours Switzerland with WSJ, 75, 81n1; arranges shipment of box to Herbert in New Zealand, 50, 56

emigrates to New York as agent of Rathbone Bros (1865), I 10, III 78–9, 148, 185, 251; becomes partner in firm of Busk & Jevons (1868), I 10, IV 293

marriage to Isabel Seton (1870), I 10, V 146n1; children, I 10, IV 164, 291, 303, V 110, 154; settles in Long Island, I 10; his country home in the Adirondacks, IV 291; kindness to Will Jevons in America, V 190

visits to England (1867), III 158, (1873), IV 22, (1876), 164, V 110; tours Denmark and Sweden with WSJ (1877), IV 206–7, Norway (1880), V 110n1; sees Henny, 110; memories of changing money at Piccadilly Circus, 149

sends newspapers to WSJ, IV 42, and information on American currency, 43, 54–5, 56; his estimate of *Principles of Science*, IV 55; suggests tax on coal for Britain, 55, 222; enjoys article on Amusements, 293; is sent map of Afghanistan, 303, and *State in Relation to Labour*, V 200; sends WSJ notes for his collection of paper money, V 118, and two clocks, 178

his quick brain, I 10–11, II 56, 417; notions on logic, III 35–6; article submitted to *Macmillan's Magazine*, 160; his geological discovery, V 154

letters to, II 221–3, 292–4, 422–3, 433, 436–8, 460–2, III 6–8, 12–14, 29–30, 35–6, 49–50, IV 33–4, 42–3, 54–6, 56, 164, 221, 271, 291, 293, 303, V 36, 65–6, 110, 118–19, 122–3, 131–2, 134–5, 142–3, 146–7, 148–9, 154, 178–9, 180, 189–90, 198–200; letter from, III 78–80; letters from, referred to, II 260, 306, III 38, 48, IV 54, 221, 271, 291, 293, 303, V 65, 122, 131, 134, 142, 146, 154

also mentioned, I 51, II 4, 190, 225, 262, 280, 299, 304, 441, 443, 454, III 32, 33, IV 155n4, V 99

Jevons, Mrs Thomas Edwin (Isabel Seton), I 10, V 146, 155, 179

Jevons, Timothy, great-grandfather of WSJ, I 116–17, 240

Jevons, Timothy (1798–1874), uncle of WSJ, I 240

partner in family iron business, I 3; bankrupted, 12; taken back as partner in reconstituted firm, 12, II 38, 117, 143; recommends Herbert to iron merchant in Melbourne, II 448, 452; concerned at growth of trades union strength in iron industry, III 127–8, VII 49–50

takes WSJ over iron ship-building yard, I 93; travels with WSJ to London and Paris (1854), II 58, 61; gives him a travelling desk for Australia, 79; sends him the *Spectator* and *Examiner* in London, II 413, discontinues *Spectator* because it abuses John Bright, 432; recommends trying 'Diagrams' on *Economist*, 448; invited to WSJ's introductory Address at Queen's College, Liverpool, III 75; gratified by success of *Coal Question*, 95, 96, 97

homes in Liverpool: St James Road, Budget party at (1853), I 79, redecorated, II 141–2; Grove Park, WSJ stays at on return from Australia, II 388, 391, visits in 1861, 435, 448, Tom stays at, 414; St Michael's Hamlet, WSJ's weekly night at while lecturing at Queen's College, III 75, 76, the true logic discovered there in his sleep, I 204

takes charge of family affairs, with his son Henry, after death of Thomas Jevons, II 215, 341, 392, 440; thinks WSJ foolish to leave Sydney, 341; plans for Tommy's career, 341, 414, provides board and lodging for him, 414

death of his wife, II 391; takes his daughter (Mary Catherine) sightseeing in London, II 412; offers WSJ a bed in London, III 96–7; stays with WSJ and Harriet in Manchester, 185; attends Roscoe Jevons's funeral, 205

Jevons, Timothy (*contd*)
  letters to WSJ, II 448, III 75, 96–7, 127–8
  also mentioned, I 56n8, II 10n1, 89, 200
Jevons, Mrs Timothy (Catherine Lomax, 1798–1859), aunt of WSJ, I 240; visit to the Lakes, II 26; redecorates her home in St James Road, 141–2; goes with Thomas Jevons's party as far as Paris, 175, 177, 183; death, 391; also mentioned, II 4n3, 89
Jevons, William (1760–1852), grandfather of WSJ, I 2–3, 240; founds iron business in Liverpool, 3; bankrupted, 12; changes family name of 'Jevon' to 'Jevons', 3n3; marriage to Ann Wood, II 89n6; spends his last years in Thomas Jevons's household, I 3, 8, 116, II 4, 9, 27; his organ, I 79n3, II 7n3; evening rubber of whist with Thomas, I 116; his friends entertain WSJ in London, II 24n5, 25, visits William jun. in Birkenhead, 26; rather poorly, 28; dies a happy death, 28–9, 30n2; funeral, 29
  letters to WSJ referred to, II 24n5, 28
Jevons, Mrs William (Ann Wood, 1767–1846), I 240, II 28, 89n6, 152
Jevons, William, jun. (1794–1873), younger brother of Thomas Jevons, uncle of WSJ, I 183n3, 240
  starts as Unitarian minister, I 3, 183n3; bankrupted with family firm, 12; marriage to Fanny Worthington, II 47n2; helps Herbert with London lodgings, II 6; his home in Kenyon Terrace, Birkenhead, 26, WSJ as schoolboy dines at, 84; the house cleaned and renovated, 444
  receives copy of paper on 'Cirrous Cloud', II 304; sees WSJ on return from Australia, 391; on Herbert's Welsh quarry plans, 441n3; congratulates WSJ on *Two Diagrams*, 443–4, suggests sending copy to Mill, 445, 446; letter on his gold medal, 444; advises WSJ to try journalism or private tuition, 445–6; entertained by WSJ in London (1862), I 183–4, II 456–7; reads *Serious Fall*, III 10, 27, points out an error, 10–11, 12; offers loan of books, 27–8, 31, and his unfinished essay on Judgement and Reasoning, 31, 45–6; sees WSJ's name figured in *The Times*, 45; reads *Coal Question*, 72–3, and Mill's speech quoting it, 95–6; is sent paper on Prices, 71, and on Gold Coinage, 180; congratulates WSJ on Professorship, 121–2; reads his letters to *The Times*, 148
  winters in Brighton, II 177, III 10, 46, in Lewes, II 444; at Scrase Bridge, III 69; other visits, 72; his affection and calm, clear mind, I 183–4
  writings: *The Claims of Christianity* (1870), I 184, II 456, III 11n1, 46; 'The Expulsion from the Temple' (*Theological Review*, 1866), III 95; *Systematic Morality. . . .* (1827), I 183n3; 'Dissertations', III 11–12, 70 (and *see* above, *Claims of Christianity*); unpublished MS on planetary and solar life, II 456, 457; other writings, I 183n3
  letters to WSJ, II 443–4, 444–6, 456–7, III 10–11, 11–12, 27–8, 31–2, 45–6, 69–70, 72–3, 95–6, 121–2, 148, 180; letters from WSJ referred to, II 456, III 31, 45, 180
  also mentioned, II 38n2, 176n13, 405n5
Jevons, Mrs William jun. (Fanny Worthington, 1790–1871), aunt of WSJ, I 240, II 47n2, 176, 446, III 69, 73; at Brighton, II 177; ill with influenza, 444; a bad cold, III 70; her daughter wholly occupied about, 180
Jevons, William Alfred (b. 1820), younger son of William Jevons jun., cousin of WSJ, lawyer, I 241, II 405, 444, III 31–2, 45–6; consulted on settlement for Lucy Hutton, III 205
Jevons, William Edgar (1836–88), youngest son of Timothy Jevons, cousin of WSJ, I 241
  goes over soap works with WSJ, I 92, and an iron ship-building yard, 93; walks to Allerton with WSJ and Tom, 193; goes to London and Paris with WSJ (1854), II 58, 61; studies shipbuilding in Marseilles,

61, 304n5; joins Lucy at Pisa on death of Thomas Jevons, 214; copy of paper on Cirrous Cloud for, 304

an engineer in Glasgow, II 391; joins Volunteers, 407; at Englefield with WSJ, 414; ill in Penang (1861), 437; gives up sugar scheme, comes home (1864), III 49, no success with business, 158

marries Mary Anne Taylor, sister of Harriet Jevons, I 47n4, III 231n3; at Roscoe Jevons's funeral, III 204–5; holiday in Norway with WSJ (1881), V 143, 190n4; returns from America (1882), 190

his poems, V 190n4

letter from WSJ, referred to, II 235

Jevons, Mrs William Edgar (Mary Anne Taylor, 1840–1910), sister of Harriet Jevons, I 47n4, 241, III 231

Jevons, William Stanley (1835–1882)

BIOGRAPHICAL OUTLINE

1 September 1835, birth at No 14 Alfred Street, Liverpool, I 2–3; 17th birthday, 59; 20th birthday, II 180; 21st birthday, II 259–60; a Lancashire man, VII 22

family background, I 1–12, 240–3

childhood in Liverpool, I 12–13, 56–60, 78, 99–100, 113, II 211; *see also under* botany; chemistry; shells

1843 first lessons in political economy and botany from his mother, I 6, 99, VII 52

1845 death of his mother (Mary Anne Roscoe), I 6–7

1846 goes to Mechanics Institute High School, Liverpool, I 13, 88, V 107

1847 transferred to Mr Beckwith's school, Liverpool, I 13, 58, 115

1850 goes to University College School, London, I 13, 114, II 7–9, 12–15, 221–2; lives with Herbert Jevons in Hampstead Road, I 115–16, II 5–6

1851 moves to Mrs Mackenzie's boarding house in Gower Street, I 100, II 16, 17, 18–22

October, enters University College, London, I 13, II 30

1852 Journal entries, I 53–77

Easter, wins silver medal for chemistry in college examinations, II 31–2

July, matriculates from College in first division, I 54–5, 66, II 35, wins botany prize, I 58, 66

1853 Journal entries, I 77–95

February, plans for a business career in Liverpool, I 88–9, II 37–41

May, wins gold medal for chemistry in College examinations, II 42–3

July, offered and accepts assayership in new Mint at Sydney, I 18, 96–7, II 46

leaves University without taking B.A., I 16, 78

August, studies assaying in London, I 19, 97–8, II 49

1854 Journal entries, I 95–109

February–March, studies assaying in Paris, I 19, 121, II 61–3, 67–71

June–September, voyage to Australia, I 19, 101–8, II 80–5, 96–100, 111–13

September 1854–December 1858, for work on assaying *see under* Sydney Mint, for life in Sydney, *see under* Sydney

1855 Journal entries, I 109–15

November, death of his father in Pisa, I 22, II 209–14

1856 Journal entries, I 115–34; diary extracts, VII 115–16, 123

March, tours gold diggings at Sofala, I 212–38, II 217–21

May, excursion to River Hunter, I 123–30

July, 'The Railway Discussion' (*Sydney Morning Herald*), II 235–7

October, starts weekly meterological reports for *Empire*, I 23, II 243, 303

gives up idea of career in chemistry, II 244

Christmas, excursion to Richmond and Parramatta, I 134–54, II 252–5

other letters published in Sydney papers, VII 123

reading, plans for writing, including reading *Wealth of Nations* and under-

Jevons, William Stanley (*contd*)
taking a work on 'Formal Economics', VII 116
1857 Journal entries, I 134–78; diary extracts, VII 116–19, 123
February, April, letters to *Empire* on railway policy, II 262–8, 282–7
April, trip to Wollongong, I 159–78
much occupied with political economy, II 280, 292
June, starts monthly meteorological reports for *Sydney Magazine of Science and Art*, II 297n7
June, December, letters to *Empire* on land policy, VII 3–11
July, 'On Cirrous Clouds' (*London Philosophical Magazine*), II 193n14, 244n7
paper on a new Sun-gauge read before Sydney Philosophical Society, II 297n8
November, paper on Sun-gauge published in *London Philosophical Magazine*, II 297n8
December, 'On Clouds . .', paper read before Sydney Philosophical Society, I 23, II 244n7
other published letters, II 268–9, 281–2, VII 123
1858 diary extracts, VII 120, 124
January–September, works on climate of Australia, II 332, 340
April, 'On the Forms of Clouds' (*London Philosophical Magazine*), II 345
September, bankruptcy of *Empire* ends meteorological reports, II 341, 346
September, November, photography expeditions to Middle Harbour, II 342, 352–5
October, 'Canoona Diggings in a Scientific Aspect' (*Sydney Morning Herald*), II 350–2
December, offered and refuses partnership in Melbourne, I 33, II 357
other published letters, II 329–31, VII 124
1859 diary extracts, VII 124
January, photography expedition to southern diggings in New South Wales, II 364–5
February, article on Australian climate published in *Waugh's Almanac*, II 341n3, VII 124
March, leaves Sydney, travels overland to Melbourne, II 366; tours Victoria goldfields, 366–73
March–September, journey to England *via* Peru, Panama, Havana and United States, I 33, II 373–88, 394–401; stays with Herbert Jevons in Minnesota, II 384, 400
September, returns to Liverpool, II 388, 390–1
October, returns to University College to take B.A., I 33–4, II 389; lives with Lucy, Henrietta and Tom Jevons at 8 Porteus Rd, Paddington, II 393, 402
1860 diary extracts, VII 120
February, plans a Work on Political Economy, VII 120
June, joins Volunteers, I 36, II 411
strikes out the *true theory of Economy*, II 410, 422
July, has a 'sad reverse' in College political economy examination, II 415–16
October, takes B.A. in first division, I 34, II 421
December, wins Ricardo Scholarship, I 34, II 422–3
1861 Journal entries, I 179–81; diary extracts, VII 124
studies for M.A. in Political Economy and Mental Science, I 34, 179, II 433, 437–8
September, acts as correspondent for *Manchester Examiner* at British Association meeting, II 434–6
'On the Deficiency of Rain in an Elevated Rain-Gauge' read at the meeting, I 35–6
other articles published, I 35, VII 124
1862 Journal entries, I 182–8; diary extracts, VII 124
March, refuses lectureship at the Andersonian Institute, II 442
June, takes M.A. with gold medal, I 34, 188, II 438, 444
Two Diagrams published, I 181n4, II 444, 450–1, 458–9
July, attempts to earn a living as literary agent, I 39, 182, 189–90, II 445, III 3, 6
October, 'Notice of a General Math-

ematical Theory of Economy', and 'On the study of Periodic Commercial Fluctuations' read at the British Association meeting, Cambridge, I 188, II 452, 456, VII 124

other publications, I 37–8, VII 124

1863 Journal entries, I 189–92; diary extracts, VII 125

April, accepts tutorship at Owens College, Manchester, I 39–40, III 9–10

Serious Fall in the Value of Gold published, I 39, 191, III 10, 13, 17, 33

May, moves from London to Wallasey, III 18, 29; prepares lectures on logic and political economy, 29, 34

September, *Serious Fall* quoted in *The Times* and at the British Association meeting, III 36, 42

September, October, letters to *The Times* on the Gold Question, III 37–8, 43–4

October, first term at Owens College, I 41–3, III 45, 48

December, *Pure Logic* published, I 40, III 48, 104

other publications, VII 125

1864 Journal entries, I 192–8; diary extracts, VII 125

May, feels overworked after first session at Owens College, III 58, 63

June–September, in London, working on the *Coal Question*, I 43, 197, III 58, 63, VII 125

July, elected Fellow of University College, III 58–9

November, elected Fellow of the [Royal] Statistical Society, III 62

publications, VII 125

1865 Journal entries, I 198–201; diary extracts, VII 125–6

April, *The Coal Question* published, I 43, III 68

May, 'The Variation of Prices and the Value of the Currency' read before the Statistical Society, III 54n3, 69

appointed to Professorship of Logic, Mental and Moral Philosophy at Queen's College, Liverpool, III 64–6, 69

October–December, acts as substitute

lecturer in Logic and Philosophy at Owens College, III 75–6; appointed lecturer in Political Economy, III 68

November, Herschel writes in praise of *The Coal Question*, I 280, III 77–8

other publications, VII 125

1866 Journal entries, I 202–9; diary extracts, VII 126

February, Gladstone's letter in praise of *The Coal Question*, I 44, 203, III 84

March, paper on the Abacus read before the Liverpool Literary and philosophical Society, III 89, VII 126

'discovery' of the 'true logic of the future', I 204

April, *Coal Question* quoted by Mill in Commons debate, I 44, 205, III 119; WSJ now 'a recognised statistical writer', III 97

paper on Autumnal pressure in the Money Market read to the [Royal] Statistical Society, III 104

May, appointment to Chair of Logic and Political Economy, and to Cobden Professorship at Owens College, I 207, III 120–1

June, 'Mr Gladstone's New Financial Policy' (*Macmillan's Magazine*), VII 11–18

October, Introductory lecture as Cobden Professor, III 128–38, VII 37–54

second edition of *Coal Question*, III 121, 125, 139, with Preface, 122–3

letters to *The Times*, III 98, 101–2, 139–40, 141–3; to *Manchester Examiner*, III 131–2; to *Manchester City News*, 137–8

1867 Journal entries, I 209–12; diary extracts, VII 126

January, 'Partnerships of Masters and Men' (*The Times*), III 151–4

February, starts work on 'a complete work on logic', I 209, 211

summer, visit to Continent, I 211, III 158

September, engaged on construction of logical machine, I 211–12, III 157

October, engagement to Harriet Taylor, I 47, 211

December, marriage

Jevons, William Stanley (*contd*)
  articles published, VII 126
1868 diary extracts, VII 126
  March, correspondence with Fleeming
    Jenkin on 'fluxion' theory of ex-
    changes, III 167–78
  lecture to Royal Institute on the Coal
    Question, III 183, VII 28–35
  April, evidence before Royal Commis-
    sion on International Coinage, III
    181, 183
  June, visit to Germany with Harriet, III
    185
  paper on International Currency,
    read to Manchester Statistical So-
    ciety, III 186, 191, VII 65–75
  October, two lectures on 'The Exhaus-
    tion of Coal' to Newcastle Literary
    and Philosophical Society, III
    195
  November, paper on the Gold Currency
    to the Statistical Society, III 195,
    200, 202, 206–7
  other publications, VII 126
1869 Journal entry, I 212; diary extracts,
    VII 126
  March, death of Roscoe Jevons, I 212,
    III 204–5
  two lectures on political economy for
    working men, VII 54–65
  May, 'Depreciation of Gold' (*Econ-
    omist*), III 208
  June, WSJ's figures on light gold coins
    quoted in Commons, III 210
  July, visit to the Continent with Harriet,
    III 209
  August–September, letters to *The Times*
    on the gold controversy, III 212–
    15, 217–21
  November, Inaugural Address as Presi-
    dent of Manchester Statistical Soci-
    ety, III 256n1
  December, meeting with Robert Lowe,
    Chancellor of the Exchequer, III
    231
  other publications, VII 126
1870 diary extracts, VII 126
  September, President, Economic Sec-
    tion of the British Association,
    meeting at Liverpool, III 236, VII
    126
  publications, VII 126

1871
  October, *Theory of Political Economy* pub-
    lished, I 48, III 244n2, VII 126
  November, review of *Theory* in *Saturday
    Review*, VII 152–7; other reviews,
    IV 5
1872
  January, review of *Theory of Political
    Economy* by Cairnes, III 245–7, VII
    146–52
  April, review of *Theory* . . . . . ., by
    Marshall, VII 141–6
  September, *Principles of Science* ready for
    printing, III 249
  October, takes six months off College
    work on account of health, III 252,
    V 157
1873
  June, asks for leave of absence from
    Owens College, or offers resig-
    nation, IV 20–1, 22; provides sub-
    stitute lecturer, 22–4
  tours Norway with Harriet, IV 21, 22
1874 diary extracts, VII 127
  January, death of Herbert Jevons, I 10,
    IV 33, 42, 249–50
  January–April, travel on the Continent
    with Harriet, IV 35; again offers to
    resign from Professorship at Owens
    College, 48–9; gives up evening
    classes, 56
  April, *Principles of Science* published, IV
    36, VII 127
  undertakes Primer on Logic, IV 34
  May, letter from Gladstone on *Principles
    of Science*, IV 37–9
  June, holiday in London, IV 51–2
  July–September, in Norway with Har-
    riet, IV 56, 61, 65
  November, 'The Progress of the Mathe-
    matical Theory of Political Econ-
    omy', read before the Manchester
    Statistical Society, IV 81, 82, 100,
    VII 75–85
  December, examines for Cambridge
    Tripos in Political Economy, IV
    52–3, 69–70, 93
  other publications, VII 127
1875 diary extracts, VII 127
  June, proposes subject for discussion at
    Political Economy Club, IV 116–17
  August, papers on Sun Spots and on the

Coal Question read to British Association at Bristol, IV 55n6, 129, 188

September, *Money and the Mechanism of Exchange* published, IV 126

November, examines for Ricardo Scholarship, IV 124

December, accepts Professorship of Political Economy at University College, London, I 49, IV 149, 154

examines for Cambridge Tripos, IV 115, 146–9

birth of first child, Herbert Stanley, IV 150

Italian translation of *Theory of Political Economy*, IV 80, 94

1876 diary extracts, VII 127

February, final resignation from Owens College Professorship, IV 163–4

Hon. LLD conferred by Edinburgh University, IV 167, 173

March, letter to *Manchester Guardian* on the Telegraph Department, IV 171–2

May, 'The Alleged Poisoning of Natives in Queensland' (*Spectator*), IV 174–7

July–August, holiday in Norway, IV 182, 184

October, Inaugural Lecture as Professor at University College, London, IV 182, 183

moves from Manchester to Hampstead, IV 183

other publications, VII 127

1877

April, 'Cram' (*Mind*), IV 212n2

May, Rubenstein and Wagner concerts in London, IV 199

June–August, holiday in Denmark and Sweden with Tom Jevons, IV 192, 206–7

August, birth of Harriet Winefrid, IV 211, 213

September, 'The Silver Question', paper read at the American Social Science Association, IV 217–18, VII 127

second edition of *Principles of Science*, IV 184n2, 189, 208

November, project for a students' edition of *Wealth of Nations*, IV 218

December, 'John Stuart Mill's Philosophy Tested' (*Contemporary Review*), IV 192n2, 221

conversation with Gladstone at Political Economy Club, IV 222

1878

March, *Political Economy Primer* published, IV 208, 242; arrangements for Italian translation, 248

plans for second edition of *Theory of Political Economy*, IV 238, with bibliography of books relating to the mathematical treatment of political economy, 242, 259

May–June, travel on the Continent, IV 244, 263

August, family holiday at Eastbourne, IV 271

paper on Sun Spots and periodic crises read at British Association meeting at Dublin, IV 272, 273, 274

September, attends Library Association meeting at Oxford, IV 284–6

October, 'Amusements of the People' (*Contemporary Review*), IV 286–7, 291, 292

November, 'Commercial Crises and Sun-Spots' (*Nature*), IV 293, 294, 295, 296

December, 'The Solar Influence on Commerce', VII 90–8

1879

January, 'A State Parcel Post' (*Contemporary Review*), IV 303, V 3, 35

January, April, 'Sun Spots and Commercial Crises' (*The Times*), V 10–12, 44–8

February, 'Sun Spots and the Plague' (*Nature*), V 35n2

March, elected to the Athenaeum (proposed by Herbert Spencer), V 26, 36

April, 'Commercial Crises and Sun Spots' (*Nature*), V 44n1

additions to pamphlet collection, V 43

June, second edition of *Theory of Political Economy*, with Preface and bibliography of mathematico-economic books, V 24n3, 34n3, 52, 64; reviewed, 67–8, by Cliffe Leslie, VII

Jevons, William Stanley (*contd*)
157–62
examines for Indian Civil Service, V
65
July, holiday in Norway, V 65
August, work on Logical Exercises, V 69
September, plans for reprinting society
(Adam Smith Society), V 73–4,
82–3
December, 'John Stuart Mill's philosophy Tested', V 75n1
1880
January, 'Experimental Legislation and
the Drink Traffic' (*Contemporary Review*), V 74, 90
July, 'Postal Notes, Money Orders, and
Bank Cheques' (*Contemporary Review*), V 99, 101
trip to Norway, V 105
September, family holiday at Littlehampton, V 106–7
October, decision to resign Professorship
at University College, V 110, 116,
117
Studies in Deductive Logic published, V
107, 116
starts on *Principles of Economics*, V 107,
116
December, research on Cantillon, V
118–21; 'Richard Cantillon' (*Contemporary Review*), V 118n2, 120
birth of Lucy Cecilia, V 122
Preface to Cossa's *Guide*, VII 98–101;
other work in progress, V 116
1881
January, 'The Rationale of Free Public
Libraries' (*Contemporary Review*), V
123
continues research on Cantillon, V
123–31
Berlioz concerts in London, V 123,
131–2, 134
March, holiday with Harriet in Kent
and Sussex, V 132
works on 'Use and Abuse of
Museums', V 132
continues *Principles of Economics*, V
134, 135, 136, 144, 155
May, 'Bimetallism' (*Contemporary Review*), V 136
'Life' of WSJ printed in *Biograph*, V
136

hands over key of Professorial office at
University College to Foxwell, V
136–7
works on *State in Relation to Labour*, V
138, 151, 154
July, family holiday at Hastings, V 142–
3
trip to Norway, V 143
September, family holiday at Malvern
Wells, V 146–7
October, visit to Paris with Harriet, V
148–9; bookhunting, 149–50
November, examines for the Ricardo
Scholarship, V 147, 149
December, buys a piano, V 155
poor health, V 157
1882
January, 'Married Women in Factories'
(*Contemporary Review*), V 154, 161,
172; letter to *Manchester Guardian* on
the subject, 163–7
plans for volume of collected essays, V
158, 175, 190, 201
visit to Cambridge, V 160
poor health, V 160, 178, 191, 201
attempts to get Royal Commission on
treatment of children, V 168–9
March, declines examinerships on
grounds of health, V 180, 185
becomes ordinary member of Political
Economy Club, V 142n1
April, notes on recoinage, V 180–3
family holiday at Hastings, V 185,
187, 188, 190
letter to *The Economist* on bimetallism,
V 187–8
June, Wagner concerts in London, V
194, 198–9
'Reflected Rainbows' (*The Field Naturalist and Scientific Student*), V 196,
200
July, *The State in Relation to Labour* published, V 198
'The Solar Cycle' (*Nature*), VII
108–11
holiday at Hastings, V 198, 199;
drowns while bathing, I 48, V 201–2

character: self-examination in Journal, I
53, 110–11, 112, 131, 187–8, 189, in
letters, II 240–1, 335; lack of soci-
ability, I 46, 196, II 15, 238–9, 302,

308, 318, III 89, views on parties, I 79, 197, II 223, 275, 337, 460, attempts to become 'passably social', I 196-7, social and convivial at home, I 50; loneliness of his 'second nature', I 29-30, 200, II 237-8, 306-7, need for a real friend, II 275, a person better than himself, 312; reserve, I 100-1, 131, II 8, 240, 349, early timidity, I 115, II 3, 14-15, 19, 237; his 'secret soul', I 30, II 337

fear of public speaking, I 42-3, 186-7, 192, 196, III 34; attempt to overcome the fear, II 457-8; attempts at humour, 182; his nervous framework not framed for the platform, V 137

lazy ways, I 79, 90, 95, 188, II 275, 296-7, not naturally lazy, II 343

'principle of action', I 22, 131, II 241-2, 312; on the proper uses of life, II 358-62

as collector: collection of economic pamphlets, V 43, 87, 146, 148, 149-50, 159-60, VII 117. *See also* botany; coinage; minerals; paper money; shells

finances: attitudes to money, II 170, 180, 226, 338, 357, the 'chill of money', 348-9; his family always the 'poor relations', I 12; poverty and marriage, I 199; tips, I 124

annual expenditure as student in London (1852-5), II 205

attractions of salary as assayer in Sydney, I 97, prospect of savings, 110, 112; earnings in Sydney, II 113, 116-17, 196, 215-16, 228-9, 311; as Government servant can take no payment for writings, II 239-40, 244; expenditure on books & journals, VII 115-19 *passim*; invests savings in himself, I 112, II 280, 310; throws up salary to continue education, II 255-6

financial relations with his father, I 117, 118, 122; repays loans, II 170, 201, 202; legacy from his father, II 232, 298

living expenses for renewed studies in London (September 1859), II 389,

413-14, search for money-making employment (1862), 452, 457

as tutor at Owens College, I 185, III 3, 9-10, 14, 48, 52, 57, pays his way from earnings for the first time, I 197; as lecturer, II 68

as professor at Queens College, III 68; as professor at Owens College, I 206, III 88, 101, IV 135, 143; lives under his income, III 151; salary increased, IV 123; as professor at University College, 'almost an honorary post', IV 142, 146, V 117; earnings as examiner, V 65

income from writings: 'Two Diagrams' and *Serious Fall* published at his own expense, I 181n4, 191n3; his books pay, IV 80, V 69, 117; royalties from American sales, V 69. *See also* investments

health and spirits: low spirits (1852), I 58, (1855), I 110-11, II 150; melancholy (1856), II 242; self-distrust (1858), 341; periodic depressions (1862), I 182, 184, 185, II 457, (1864), I 43, 200, III 58, 63, fear of sharing Roscoe's fate, I 195, 197, 200, 201, (1865), I 199-200; (1866), gloom and despair his lot, I 202n1, 205; (1867), despair turns to joy with his engagement to Harriet, I 210-11; (1872), nervous exhaustion from overwork, III 249, 250, (1873), nervous and muscular weakness, IV 22; (1875), overwork and neuralgia, IV 106; (1876), congestion of the cerebellum and nervous depression, IV 182; (1881), nervous pains, 157; (1882), neuralgic pains, V 160

poisoned by arsenic in chemistry class (1853), I 94; concealed poison in French sauces (1855), II 59, lead poisoning, II 249; his delicate, feeble frame, II 334; indigestion (1864), I 201, 209; rules for the preservation of health, I 209n1; port wine for his health, III 195; cannot undertake extra work (1882), V 169, 180, or attend debate, 191, but cannot miss *Mastersingers*, 194

hobbies, *see* photography, *and above*,

Jevons, William Stanley (*contd*)
  collections
  music: 'a condition of existence' for him,
    I 31–2, II 181, 319–20, 'part of my
    soul', 313; playing music, like read-
    ing poetry, 225, 227; a link with
    Henrietta, I 11, II 223, 241, 257,
    263, 289, 295–6, 319–21, 363
    as performer: put off by his music
      mistresses, II 67; plays the family
      organ, I 79, II 7, 24, takes lessons in
      London, I 79n3, II 458; learns his
      notes, II 29; in Sydney: buys a
      harmonium, II 109, 147, 158, 162,
      sketch of, in his parlour, 271; his
      'programmes', 181, 224–5, 250,
      277–8, 313–14, 338–9; bothered by
      notation, 227, and by flourishes,
      227–8; copies music, 320, VII 166;
      extemporises, II 257; his met-
      ronome, 295, music-holder and
      music-stand, 309; sells his har-
      monium, 363; buys an organ in
      Manchester, I 79n3; re-establishes
      it in Hampstead, IV 189; buys a
      grand piano, V 155, 190
    music library: for Australia, II 76; buys
      Oratorios, 257, operas, 289, 321,
      Beethoven, 320, IV 56
    musical performances heard: in Amer-
      ican hotels, II 383; barrel organs in
      France, II 58, in England, 320, at
      the seaside, V 108; concerts in
      Copenhagen, IV 206; glees in Bris-
      tol, IV 130; Liverpool Philhar-
      monic concerts, I 60; in London:
      Richter's concerts, V 134, 198,
      music in St James's Hall, II 458, IV
      189, V 123, Saturday afternoon
      concerts at the Crystal Palace, V
      110, Temple Church choir, I 75,
      Wagner at Drury Lane, V 194, 198,
      199, Weber at His Majesty's Thea-
      tre, IV 304, Westminster Abbey
      organ, III 18; chamber music at
      Manchester, IV 164; oratorio in
      Melbourne, II 369; military bands
      in Paris, II 58, 63, 68, 69, and
      dinner to music, V 149; Bach *Pass-
      ion* in Salisbury Cathedral, V 43; in
      Sydney: Anna Bishop's farewell
      concerts, II 224, Catholic chapel

  organ, 109, opera, 181, 190n4, Phil-
    harmonic Society concerts, 250–1
  observations on concert halls in Aus-
    tralian gold towns, II 371, on
    pianos in Lima homes, 396; views
    on singing, II 257
  subscribes to foundation funds of
    Royal College of Music, V 178
  writes a book on music (unfinished), I
    32, II 243, 277
  as teacher, I 49–50, III 108–9, 111, 118;
    views on teaching logic, philosophy
    and political economy, III 104–5,
    VII 56; keeps politics out of priv-
    ate, but not public, lectures, III
    132, VII 41; his teaching methods
    explained to Brewer, IV 22–4; class
    discussions, VII 60; advice to his
    students, VI 22, on taking notes,
    VII 60; essay subjects, VI 18, 120;
    dislike of lecturing, V 106, 116;
    advice to primary school teachers,
    VII 38–40; praise from students,
    III 70, 99
  Rylett's transcriptions of lectures
    given at Owens College, IV 241,
    VI 3–140
  as thinker: search for laws and uni-
    formities, I 24, II 341n3, for gen-
    eral principles, 361; 'strong dispo-
    sition to classify', II 308; power to
    discover new and symmetrical pat-
    terns', 308; powers of concen-
    tration, I 201; faculty of exact and
    precise thought, III 111, 120, voc-
    ation for speculative research, III
    115; originality, I 14, 30, II 308, III
    120. *See also* 'sameness'
  as writer: pleasures of composition, II
    276; 'a confirmed scribbler', 303, 'a
    rage for writing', 345; tries writing
    for a living, 452, no talent for light
    writing, I 183, 185, 189, II 461;
    burden of writing a large book, V
    110; views on quality of his writing,
    III 111, 115, VII 143
  obituaries of WSJ: Richard Hutton (*Pro-
    ceedings of the Royal Society*), I 1;
    James Sully (*Pall Mall Gazette*, 17
    August 1882), I 50; A. W. Ward
    (*Manchester Guardian*), I 49–50;
    Edgeworth on his loss, V 201–2

WORKS

The Coal Question: an Inquiry concerning the Progress of the Nation, and the Probable Exhaustion of the Coalmines (1865), VII 125

work on, in London (June–September 1864), I 43, III 52, 58, 59, 65, 67, and in 'Rotten Row', Beaumaris, 97; published by Macmillans (April 1865), I 43, III 68; format, 240; terms, 241; sales, III 127, 139; copies sent to J. G. Greenwood, III 89, Tennyson, 98–9, J. B. Smith, M.P., IV 29–30

recommended in Presidential Address to Section F of British Association (September 1865), III 99; Herschel's letter of praise, I 43–4, 200, III 77, 80, 85, 87, 95; Gladstone's letter on, I 44, 203, III 84, 85, 87–8, 95, quoted in his Budget speech, I 45, III 103, VII 11; referred to, by J. S. Mill in parliament, I 44, 205, III 93, 94–5, 99, 103, VII 13, extract from his speech used by Macmillan as advertisement, III 96, 119; *The Times* on, I 44–5, accuses WSJ of misleading Gladstone, III 101, VII 13

reviewed in *Pall Mall Gazette*, III 96n1, in *The Times*, 125, in *Engineering*, 125n1; noticed in *Daily Telegraph*, III 93, in *Athenaeum* and *London Quarterly Review*, VII 125; other letters on, III 71, 72–3, 74; regarded as a model in Holland, IV 74

Royal Commission on Coal due to, VII 18; letter from Chairman of Committee, III 154; *Report* based on misapprehension of WSJ's figures, VII 37

contents referred to, I 44, III 78, 88, 101–2, 127n1, 255, IV 127, 234–7, VII 32; predictions likely to come true (1881), V 139, 143

second edition (1866), I 121, 122, 139, IV 234–5, Preface, III 122–3; third edition, revised by A. W. Flux, I 44, III 127n1, IV 235n2

also mentioned, I 198n3, III 104, 114, IV 222

Elementary Lessons in Logic (1870), for Macmillans' School Class Books, with questions and exercises, III 139, IV 80, 118, 184; format and terms of publication, III 139; copy sent to Herbert Jevons, 210; used at Harvard, 239; well-known in Edinburgh University, IV 173; Italian translation, V 68

The Match Tax: A Problem in Finance . . . (1871), VI 138n8

Money and the Mechanism of Exchange (1875), International Scientific Series, IV 148n1

work on (May 1874), IV 43, 54, 56, 102; proofs, 106, Inglis Palgrave's criticisms and corrections, 111–12; a 'semi-popular' book, IV 66, 173n3; finished, IV 118; in print, 126; sales, I 48n3

Foxwell on, IV 133; Hincks on, 159, 160, 161; Walras on, 180, 289; W. Langton's corrections from Canada, 165–6

contents referred to, IV 98, 105, 106n1, 118, 155–6, 185, 209n1, V 153n2, 187, Preface, IV 299n5; quoted in lecture notes, VI 4, 28, 30, 98–9, 103, 104, 107, 108

foreign editions, IV 149; French, 150, 180, 183; American, 156n4, read in America and Canada, 164; German translation, *Geld und Geldverkehr* (1876), VII 127

second edition, IV 289; fourth edition, IV 54n1

also mentioned, VI viii, 97n5

Primer of Logic (1876), in Science Primers series, IV 192n3

plans for (1874), IV 34; sales, I 48n3, III 240n2, IV 183–4; copies sent to R. O. Williamson, IV 177, to Walras, 192; praised by Walras and Sécretan, 196, 205

Italian translation, IV 248; translation into Indian vernaculars proposed, V 18–19

Primer of Logic (*contd*)
  also mentioned, IV 189, VII 127
Primer of Political Economy (1878), in Science Primers series, III 241n2, IV 192n3.
  plans for an 'Elementary Treatise' (1871), III 240, 241; work on *Primer* (1877), IV 177n2, 189, 205, 219; format, V 135; sales, I 48n3, III 240n2, 251; copies for Rylett and Brewer, IV 242, Robert Lowe, 243, Vissering, 233, Fontpertuis, 288; Walras on, IV 259–60
  contents referred to, IV 228, VI 71n3
  Italian translation, IV 248, V 37n3, 42, 53, 60, 62, copyright, V 59; French translation (Henri Gravez, 1878), IV 288, V 37; used as text book in Oakland, U.S., V 69
  also mentioned, VI viii
The Principles of Science – a Treatise on Logic and Scientific Method (1874), I 48
  first ideas for (1867), I 209–10; title chosen (1868), VII 127; work on (1872), III 252, IV 34, 94, V 157; terms of publication (September 1872), III 249–50
  copies sent to Gladstone, IV 36, to d'Aulnis, 82, 88, 94, 96; two copies in Balliol College Library, 286; adopted as University text book, 281; first edition sold out, IV 191
  reviews: *British Quarterly Review* (James Collier, April 1874), VII 127; *Hull Criterion* (July 1874), VII 127; *New York Times* and *New York Tribune*, IV 42; *Saturday Review* (25 May 1874), IV 55; Gladstone on, IV 37–8, 41, 222; R. Strachan on , 305; other letters on, IV 55, V 29, 52
  contents referred to, I 52, IV 207–8, VII 92; Inglis Palgrave's solution to logical problem, IV 31; puts WSJ on 'same platform' as Mill and Whewell, IV 173
  second edition, IV 184, 191, 205; format, 218, 219; contents, III 216n2, IV 31n3, Preface, IV 208n5; on sale in Oxford, 286; alterations due to Kingdon, IV 207–8; third edition, IV 291, 305n2; Dover edition (1958), IV 207n3

Pure Logic, or the Logic of Quality apart from Quantity, with Remarks on Boole's System and the Relation of Logic and Mathematics (1863), based on the principle of 'sameness', I 40, 197n5
  publication (December 1863), III 48; sales, 240n2, only four copies sold by August 1864, I 198n4, III 59
  noticed in *Athenaeum* by De Morgan, and in *Spectator*, III 108, VII 125; Alex Bain on, III 107, Bowen, 239, Cairnes, 108, De Morgan, 49, 52, 108, Hoppus, 110, R. Hutton, 111, Martineau, 111, J. S. Mill, 120, Sandeman, 52, A. J. Scott, 112–13
  contents referred to, III 49n3
  also mentioned, III 109
A Serious Fall in the Value of Gold Ascertained and its Social Effects, with Two Diagrams (1863), VII 125
  work on, in London, I 11, III 4, suggested by study of Newmarch's statistics, I 181n2; published by Edward Stanford (16 April 1863), I 39, 191n1, III 104, VII 125, at author's expense, I 191n3, III 33; sales, 33, 59
  copies sent to Gladstone, III 15, to Cairnes, 18, to Rowland Hamilton, V 9
  initial disappointment at reception, I 191n1, III 15; only Lucy has a word to say for it, I 191; success follows, I 43, 192, 197, III 49, 50, 52, 108, 113; establishes WSJ as economist, I 39, 192n2, III 114; importance recognised by Cairnes, I 192n2, III 49–50
  reviews: *Economist*, III 42, Cairnes's letter on, III 17, 18, 23, 25; *Spectator* (R. Hutton), I 191n1, III 13, 15, 19n2; *Westminster Review*, III 48n1 50, 52; advertised in *Athenaeum*, III 12; noticed in *JRSS*, VII 125, in *Melbourne Argus*, III 38, in *National Review*, VII 125
  mentioned at International Statistical Congress, Berlin (September 1863), III 49, VII 125; quoted by Fawcett in address to British Association, I 192n2, III 36, 37, 42, 109, correspondence in *The Times*

arising out of Fawcett's speech, 36–8, 42, 43–5

Bagehot on, III 19, 114; Mill, 120; Newmarch, III 15; praised by Gladstone and two Bank of England Governors, 114; correspondence with Cairnes on, III 16–18, 19, 20–5, 49–50; other letters on, III 10–11, 26

appeal to WSJ as author for decision on a French prize essay, V 3, 4, 6

contents referred to, III 22n6, 26n3, 49n2, 54, 64, 82, 252, D. M. Balfour on, 54–5, T. Hankey on, V 58; disputed by Laspeyres, III 62, 66n1, VII 125; index numbers, VI 55n8; conclusions to be tested by further study of price changes, I 197n3, III 42, 53, 59, 61

also mentioned, I 187n3, III 110

The State in Relation to Labour (1882), I 49

engagement to write a book 'on trade unions' for English Citizens Series (March 1881), V 132, on 'Labour', 143, 144, 147, 151; arrangements with editor for 'State in Relation to Labour', 138, 154; MS nearly ready, 159, 160; difference of opinion with editor, 178; proofs finished, 180, 185, 190; copy sent to Walras, 195; to Tom Jevons, 200

contents referred to, V 138n3, VI 72n4, 77nn7, 8; Foxwell on, I 50, V 185–6, 187

Studies in Deductive Logic, a Manual for Students (1880), V 94, 106, 107, VII 127; designed for College use, V 69, 'examination from beginning to end', 109; copy sent to Rylett, 111; reviewed in *Athenaeum*, 118–19; sales, 118, 123, 135, in America, 123; Harley's suggestion on exceptions, 116

The Substitution of Similars, the True Principle of Reasoning, Derived from a modification of Aristotle's Dictum (1869), I 41, 210n1, III 239

The Theory of Political Economy (1871), 'the first modern book on economics' (J. M. Keynes), I 48

origins and Fleeming Jenkin's fluxion theory of exchange, III 166, 167n2, IV 6

MS sent to Macmillans, III 240; format, 240; terms of publication, 238, 241; arrangements for mathematical symbols, 241; publication (October 1871), III 240n1; sales, 240n2, IV 238

copies sent to Bodio, IV 80, 95, Cournot, IV 68, Robert Lowe, III 245, W. L. Sargant, III 244, Walras, IV 41, 46, 50, 63, for distribution on Continent, 67, 68

reviews: *Academy*, IV 5, 62, VII 141–6; *British Quarterly Review*, III 246n3; *Evening Standard*, IV 5; *Fortnightly Review*, J. E. Cairnes on 'New Theories in Political Economy', III 245, IV 58, 62, V 30, VII 146–52, George Darwin, 'The Theory of Exchange Value', IV 99; *Glasgow Herald*, IV 5; *Manchester Examiner*, IV 5; *Manchester Guardian*, IV 5; *Saturday Review*, IV 58, 62, VII 152–7

neglected in England, I 48, IV 57, 80; arouses interest on Continent, I 48, IV 58, 83; approved by d'Aulnis, 57–9, 61, 89, 90–1, by R. O. Williams, 130–1, 132

contents referred to: exchange theory, III 167n2, reply to Cairnes's criticism, 245–7, IV 60–1, Williams on, IV 131, 151–4, Adamson on, 228; equations of exchange, IV 87

general law of the variation of the final degree of utility, III 247–8

labour, as measure of value, III 253–4; definition, VI 18

in relation to lecture notes, VI viii–ix, 16, 37n3, 41, 45n9, 47nn10, 11, 63, 92n7, 93n9; passages set for reading, 48, 64, 94

maxima and minima, IV 255–8

Preface, III 240n3; on calculus of pleasure and pain, I 35

relation of price to demand and supply, V 30–1, 32–4

rate of interest, V 156, Adamson on, IV 226–7; George Darwin on theory of interest, IV 24–9, 230n1

ratio of exchange of gold and silver,

The Theory of Political Economy (contd)
IV 254
rent theory, IV 254n2, Walras on, IV
197–8
utilitarian approach to economic behaviour, I 28; theory of utility, IV
58
wages theory, III 255, IV 227
work *versus* leisure, IV 254n3
French translation (H. E. Barrault and
M. Alfassa, 1909), IV 261n6; Italian translation 'La Teorica dell'
Economia politica . . .' in *Biblioteca dell' Economista* (Boccardo,
1875), IV 80, 94, 98, 103,
154
for mathematical aspects of *Theory of
Political Economy, see under* mathematical theory of political economy; mathematics; Walras, Léon
second edition (1879)
plans for (March 1878), IV 238;
collection of material for bibliography on mathematical method,
242, 249, 277–8, 279, V 22, 24, 55,
inclusion of passages from Walras,
IV 270, 281–2, 290; work on revision, 250, 259–63, 265–6, 272, V
29; MS sent to printer, V 52–3; in
proof, 53, 55, 63; Adamson's
suggestions, 60–2.
publication: to be treated as a new
book, V 64–5; format and price, IV
238; copies for French periodicals,
V 64, for Walras, 95; extra copies of
Preface and Appendices for distribution, V 64, 65
reviews: *Academy* (Cliffe Leslie), V 67–
8, VII 157–62; *Manchester Examiner*
(Broadfield), V 67; *Westminster Review*, VII 127
contents referred to, IV 177n2, 198n6,
V 156, Preface, IV 3n2, 244, 255n4,
267n1, V 24n3, 42n7, 61n1, 76n4,
109n3, 125; alterations due to
Adamson, IV 230n1, 231n2, V
61n1, 62nn2, 3, to G. Darwin, IV
230n1, to Walras, IV 198n6
Broadfield on, V 67; Foxwell on, 77–
8, answered by WSJ, 79–80;
Walras's criticism, 95–7
Walras's unpublished translation, IV

261, 263, 270, V 95
also mentioned, IV 173n3, V
66
third edition, V 129n2; fourth edition
(1931), IV 227n3, 228n5, V 156n2,
VI 37n3, 89nn3, 4; Preface, I 27n3,
IV 267n1, V 34n3; Appendix II,
V 156n3, Appendix III, I 188n1;
'List of Mathematico-Economic
Books', V 27n2; alterations and additions due to Christie, V 34nn2,
4
Two Diagrams (June 1862), published by
Edward Stanford, I 35n2, 37, V
159n1, at the author's own expense,
I 181, II 443
'Diagram showing Bank of England
weekly accounts since 1844. . . .', I
181n4, II 451, 459n7, III 33, IV 12,
17, 112
'Diagram showing Price of English
Funds . . . since 1731', I 181n4, II
450, 459n7, III 33
copies for William Jevons, jun., II 444–
5, 446, for Miller in Sydney, 459,
for Brewer, IV 14, for Inglis Palgrave, 112n2, used by him, IV
12n10, 14, 19
reviews: *Economist* (R. Hutton), II 448,
450, 459, III 4; *The Times* and
Exchange Magazine, II 459, III 3–4;
Spectator, II 459, VII 124
sales, II 443, 455, 459, 461, III 3–4, 33,
59
work continues on 'Statistical Atlas', *see*
below, works unpublished
republished in *Investigations . . .* , I
181n4

ARTICLES, LECTURES, PAPERS

'Amusements of the People' (*Contemporary
Review*, 1878), IV 286–7, 292, 293;
reviewed in *Spectator*, IV 291; proposal to issue as a popular Mudie
book, V 65, 68
'Augustus De Morgan' (*Encyclopaedia Britannica*, ninth edition, 1877), I 15n3
'Bibliography of Works on the Mathematical Theory of Political Economy'
Journal of the Royal Statistical

Society, unsigned, June 1878), IV 277n1; criticised by d'Aulnis, 282–3; republished as 'Bibliographie' in *Journal des Economistes* (December 1878), IV 289, 290, V 21
see also under Theory of Political Economy, eds 2 and 4

'Bimetallism' (*Contemporary Review*, May 1881), V 136, 187

'Brief Account of a General Mathematical Theory of Political Economy' (1862), I 28, III 166, IV 61n1. *See also below*, 'Notice of a General Mathematical Theory of Political Economy'

'The Clerk of the Weather Office' (*Spectator*, 12 September 1862), I 38, II 452, VII 124

'On the Cirrous Form of Clouds' (*London Philosophical Magazine..*, July 1857), II 193n14, 244n7, 261, 304, 306, 324; copy sent to Henrietta Jevons, 314, to Sir John Herschel, 432, 433–4

'On Clouds; their various Forms, and producing causes, with experimental illustrations', paper read before the Philosophical Society of New South Wales (9 December 1857), I 23, 25; published in *Sydney Magazine of Science and Art* (January 1858), I 23, II 244n7, 345n7; published in abbreviated version, 'On the Forms of Cloud' (*London Philosophical Magazine*, April 1858), I 23n2, II 193n14, 244n7, 345; criticised by Rev. W. Scott, II 345, answered by WSJ, 329–31; copy sent to Sir John Herschel, 432, 433–4

'On Coal', lecture delivered in the Carpenters' Hall, Manchester (16 January 1867), VII 18–28

'Commercial Crises and Sun-Spots' (Nature, 14 November 1878), I 48, IV 240n1, 293, V 47, VII 94, 108; correspondence on, IV 294–7, 305 Part II (24 April 1879), V 44n1, 45n3, 57, VII 108

'On the Condition of the Gold Coinage of the United Kingdom, with reference to the Question of Inter-national Currency', published version (*Journal of the Royal Statistical Society*, 1868), of paper 'On the Condition of the Metallic Currency..', VII 65; reprinted in *Investigations*, II 156n5, III 159n2, IV 16n3, VII 65

'On the Condition of the Metallic Currency of the United Kingdom, with reference to the Question of International Coinage', paper read before the [Royal] Statistical Society of London (17 November 1868), II 156n5, III 159n2, 195, IV 11n4, V 88, 181n2, VI 110n3, VII 65, 71; noticed in *Economist*, III 200; correspondence on, 200–4, 206–7, 224; figures used by Chancellor of the Exchequer in debate on Money Laws and in Report on Mintage, III 210, 211; quoted in ensuing Gold Coinage controversy of 1869, 211, 212, 213–15, 221

'Cram' (*Mind*, April 1877), IV 212n2

'Cruelty to Animals – a Study in Sociology' (*Fortnightly Review*, 1876), IV 174n1

'On the Deficiency of Rain in an Elevated Rain-gauge as caused by the Wind', paper read before the Mathematics and Physics Section of the British Association, Manchester (September 1861), I 35–6, VII 124

'The Depreciation of Gold' (*Economist*, 8 May 1869), III 82n4, 208

Dictionary of Chemistry, edited by Henry Watts, articles by WSJ (1861), I 20n5, 35, II 345n4, III 50n1, VII 124; *see also below*, 'Gold Assay'

'Early Presentiments of the Electric Telegraph' (*Spectator*, 27 April 1867), VII 126

'The Exhaustion of Coal', two lectures to the Newcastle Literary and Philosophical Society, (15, 16 October 1868), III 188, 195

'Experimental Legislation and the Drink Traffic' (*Contemporary Review*, 1880), V 74n3, 90, 166n6

'On the Frequent Autumnal Pressure in the Money Market, and the Action

'On the Frequent . . . (contd)
of the Bank of England', paper read
before the [Royal] Statistical Society of London (17 April 1866), III
102, 104
'The Future of Political Economy. Introductory Lecture at University
College, London, 1876' (Fortnightly
Review, 1876), IV 182, 190; French
translation by Fontpertuis (Journal
des Economistes, 1877), IV 192, 276
'Gold Assay', in Dictionary of Chemistry
(1864), I 20n5, 35, II 345, III 50,
51; written from a 'Methodical'
point of view, II 247
'On Industrial Partnerships', public lecture sponsored by the National
Association for the Promotion of
Social Science (1870), II 322n9
'On the Influence of the Sun-Spot Period
upon the Price of Corn', paper
presented to the British Association
(1875), IV 129, 199, VI ixn4; withdrawn from publication, IV 188-9,
272n2
'On the International Monetary Conven-
tion, and the Introduction of an
International Currency into this
Kingdom', paper read before the
Manchester Statistical Society (13
May 1868), III 186, 191, 211, VII
65-75
'An Introductory Lecture on the Impor-
tance of Diffusing a Knowledge of
Political Economy', delivered at
the opening of the session of Even-
ing Classes at Owens College (12
October 1866), I 207n3, III 128,
VII 37-54; controversy aroused by,
III 129-38
'John Stuart Mill's Philosophy Tested',
four articles in Contemporary Review, I
48, IV 167, 191-2, 223, 250, V 24,
74
I (November 1877), IV 221; II (1878),
IV 221n2; IV 'Utilitarianism'
(1879), V 75n1
'Light and Sunlight' (National Review, July
1861), I 35
'List of Selected Books in Political Economy', compiled for the Library
Association (Monthly Notes of the
Library Association of the United King-
dom, 1882), VII 101-7
'On a Logical Abacus', paper read before
the Manchester Literary and Philosophical Society (3 April 1866), I
204n4, III 104
'On the Logical Abacus and Logical
Machine', paper read before the
Liverpool Literary and Philosophical Society (19 March 1866), I
204n4, III 89, 104, VII 126
'Married Women in Factories' (Contemporary Review, 1882), V 154, 161,
167, 172, 173, 174, 200
'Meteorological Observations in Australia'
(Sydney Magazine of Science and Art,
January-February, 1859), II
245n11, VII 124
'Meteorological Reports', published
weekly in Sydney Empire (3 September 1856-August 1858), I 23, II
198n6, 239-40, 244, 256, 303, VII
3, 123
'Meteorological Reports', published
monthly in Sydney Magazine of
Science and Art (June 1857-June
1858), I 23, II 198n6, 297n7, 298
'On the Movement of Microscopic Particles in Liquid' (Quarterly Journal
of Science, April 1878), I 15n1
'Mr Gladstone's New Financial Policy'
(Macmillan's Magazine, June 1866),
III 101n2, VII 11-18
'Notice of a General Mathematical Theory
of Political Economy', paper read
before the British Association,
Cambridge (1862), I 28, 37, 183n2,
188n1, II 452, 456, III 104, V 80,
VII 77; summary printed in Report
(1862), I 37, 188n1, IV 40, VII
124; printed in full in [Royal] Statistical Society Journal (1866), I
188n1, III 166, IV 40, 58, 61, 71;
establishes priority of WSJ's mathematical statement over Fleeming
Jenkin's, III 166, over Walras's, IV
40; circulation of copies, VII 76;
section 15 later considered erroneous, IV 61
'Notice of Kirchhoff's Researches on the
Spectrum' (Philosophical Magazine,
July 1862), I 38n1

'On the Periodicity of Commercial Crises and its Physical Explanation', paper read before the British Association, Dublin (1878), IV 271–2, 273, 274, V 47, 57, 168, VII 94; printed in *Journal of the Statistical and Social Inquiry Society of Ireland* (1878), IV 273n8, V 47

'The Post Office Telegraphs and their Financial Results' (*Fortnightly Review*, 1875), IV 150, 172; reviewed in *Pall Mall Gazette*, 150

'Postal Notes, Money Orders and Bank Cheques' (*Contemporary Review*, 1880), IV 216n2, V 99, 101

'Presidential Address to Economic Section of the British Association at Liverpool (September 1870), III 236, 243–4, VI 59n14, VII 126; reported in *Nature* (22 September 1870), III 236n3

'On the Probable Exhaustion of our Coal Mines', paper read at the Royal Institution (13 March 1868), III 180, 183, IV 30n1, VII 28–35

'On the Progress of the Coal Question', paper read before Section F of the British Association for the Advancement of Science, Bristol (26 August 1875), IV 128n4, VII 36–7

'The Progress of the Mathematical Theory of Political Economy . . .', paper read before the Manchester Statistical Society (November 1874), IV 70, 81, 82, 102, 180, 270, VII 75–85; copies sent to d'Aulnis, IV 82, 83, to Walras, 84, Musgrave, 126–7, R. O. Williams, 136; noticed in *Deutsche Allgemeine Polytechnische Zeitung*, IV 103

'The Rationale of Free Public Libraries' (*Contemporary Review*, 1881), V 123

'On Reading and Study', Introductory Address at Queen's College, Liverpool (2 October 1865), I 198n2, III 75, 76

'Reflected Rainbows' (*The Field Naturalist and Scientific Student*, 1883), V 196, 200

'Remarks on the Australian Gold Fields', paper read before the Manchester Literary and Philosophical Society

(15 November 1859), I 187n1

'Remarks on Mr Baxendell's Law of atmospheric ozone', paper read before the Manchester Literary and Philosophical Society (1868), VII 126

'Remarks on the Statistical Use of the Arithmometer', paper read before the [Royal] Statistical Society (19 November 1878), VII 85–90

'Richard Cantillon and the Nationality of Political Economy' (*Contemporary Review*, 1881), V 118n2, 120, 121n1, 122, 123, 124, 125

'The Silver Question', paper read before the American Social Science Association at Saratoga (5 September 1877), IV 266–7; printed in *Bankers' Magazine*, (1877), IV 217–18, V 187, VII 127; quoted in *Economist* (April 1882), V 188n2; reprinted in *Investigations*, VI 102n14

'On the so-called Molecular Movements of Microscopic Particles', paper read to the Manchester Literary and Philosophical Society (1870), I 15n1

'The Social Cesspools of Sydney, No. I The Rocks' (*Sydney Morning Herald*, 7 October 1858), I 29, II 298n10, VII 124

'Some Data concerning the Climate of Australia and New Zealand' (*Waugh's Australian Almanac for the Year 1859*), I 23–4, II 240n4, 332, 340n3, 356, 363, IV 203

'Spectrum' (*London Quarterly Review*, April 1862), I 38n1

'A State Parcel Post' (*Contemporary Review*, 1879), IV 303, V 3, 155n2

'Statistics of Shakespearean Literature' (*Athenaeum*, 12 March 1864), VII 125

'On the Study of Periodic Commercial Fluctuations, with five diagrams', paper read before the British Association at Cambridge (1862), I 37, 183n2, 188n1, III 104, VII 124

'On a Sun-gauge or New Actinometer', paper read before the New South Wales Philosophical Society (8 July 1857), I 23, 25, II 297; published in

'On a Sun-gauge . . . (*contd*)
  Sydney Magazine (August 1857), II
    161n3, 297n8, VII 123
'Sun-Spots and the Plague' (*Nature*, 13
    February 1879), V 35
'Trades Societies: their Objects and
    Policy', lecture to Manchester
    Trades Unionists Political Associ-
    ation (31 March 1868), III 161n2,
    183, VI 71n3
'On the United Kingdom Alliance and its
    Prospects of Success', paper read
    before the Manchester Statistical
    Society (8 March 1876), VI 41n17
'The Variation of Prices and the Value of
    the Currency since 1782', paper
    intended for the British Association
    (1864), I 197, III 54; read before the
    [Royal] Statistical Society (May
    1865), I 197n3, III 54n3, 69, 104;
    printed (*JRSS*, June 1865), IV
    163, 170; Laspeyres asks for a copy,
    III 61, 81; copy sent to Broadfield,
    72; read by Walras, IV 45; quoted
    in lecture notes, VI 118n7

published letters
  Economist (15 April 1882), V 187–8
  Empire: 'The Railway Discussion' (19
    July 1856), II 235–7; 'The Western
    Line of Railway, and the General
    Policy of Government Railway
    Extension' (10 February 1857), I
    26, II 262–8, VII 116–17;
    'Meteorology and the Herald' (25
    February 1857), II 268–9;
    'Protective Humbug' (28 March
    1857), II 280n12, 281, VII 117;
    'Comparison of the Land and
    Railway Policy of New South
    Wales' (8 April 1857), I 26, 235n1,
    282–7, VII 117, 118; 'The Public
    Lands of New South Wales'
    (24 June 1857), I 26, II 297, VII 3–
    8; 'Railway Economy' (29 Decem-
    ber 1857), I 26, II 303, VII 3, 8–11,
    123; 'Cure for the Revenue' (1857),
    VII 123; 'On the Philosophical
    Society of New South Wales'
    (1857), VII 123
  Manchester City News, 'Trade Out-
    rages' (3 November 1866), III
    137–8
  Manchester Examiner and Times, reply to
    'British Workman' (22 October
    1866), III 131–2
  Manchester Guardiam, 'The Prospects of
    the Telegraph Department' (22
    March 1876), IV 171–2, VII 127
  Nature, 'On Timing a Star-transit' (18
    November 1869), II 216n2; 'A De-
    duction from Darwin's Theory' (30
    December 1869), VII 126; 'Mau-
    pertuis on the Survival of the Fit-
    test' (6 March 1873), IV 4, 15; *see
    also* VII 126
  Spectator, 'The Alleged Poisoning of
    Natives in Queensland' (27 May
    1876), IV 174–7, VII 127; *see also*
    VII 126
  Sydney Magazine of Science and Art (23
    June 1858), II 329–31
  Sydney Morning Herald, 'The Railway
    Discussion' (19 July 1856), II 235–
    7, VII 115, 123; 'Review of the
    Sydney Magazine of Science and
    Art' (October 1858), VII 124;
    'Canoona Diggings in a Scientific
    Aspect' (29 October 1858), II 350–
    2, VII 124
  The Times, (4 September 1863), III 37–
    8; (24 September 1863), III 43–4;
    (12 May 1866), III 101–2; 'Iron-
    masters and Ironworkers' (17
    December 1866), III 141–3, 148,
    150n2, 225n2; (22 December
    1866), III 144–7; on deep coal
    mining (20 November 1866), III
    139–40; 'Partnerships of Masters
    and Men' (19 January 1867), III
    151–4; on the Gold Coin controv-
    ersy of 1869 (24 August 1869), III
    212–15, (10 September), 217–21;
    'Sun-Spots and Commercial Crises'
    (17 January 1879), V 10–12, (19
    April 1879), V 44–8, 57n3; 'Light
    Gold Coin' (23 December 1879), V
    87–9

reviews and notices: on Fontpertuis'
  pamphlets (*JRSS*, 1878), IV 287–
  8; on W. Vissering's Chinese Currency (*JRSS*, 1877), IV 224; other
  notices, *see* VII 124–7

obituary of Cliffe Leslie (*Economist*, 4 February 1882), V 171

writings, unfinished and/or published posthumously
  The Principles of Economics: a new work 'on Political economy generally' contemplated (June 1876), IV 177, (March 1878), IV 238, (November 1879), V 80; ready to start on 'Principles of Political Economy' (September 1880), V 107, 110; in full progress, 116, 136, 137, 143, 155; draft finished (April 1881), 134; plans for printing a two-volume work, 135; interruptions, 160; a new start (March 1882), 180 Foxwell on the intended 'Treatise', I 50–1; fragments published, with preface by Higgs (1905), I 51n1; contents referred to, I 17, 28, V 118n2, 156n3, VI 33n5, 49n6 also mentioned, III 241n2
  'Sir Isaac Newton and Bimetallism', unfinished, published in *Investigations*, V 159n1, VII vii
  'The Solar Influence on Commerce', unfinished article intended for the *Princeton Review* (December 1878), IV 293, 304n4, V 8, VII vii, 90–8
  'The Use and Abuse of Museums', intended for *Contemporary Review*, published posthumously in *Methods of Social Reform* (1883), I 49, V 132
collected writings, published posthumously
  Investigations in Currency and Finance, edited by H. S. Foxwell (1884), I 39, 51n1, V 181n2, VII vii; plans for volume of collected essays (1881), V 132, under the title 'Investigations Concerning Currency & Finance', 155, 160, 178, 189, 191, 194, 198; arrangements for publication, 158, 175; diagrams, 158–9, 201; index, 175; copy sent to printer, 180; proofs, 190; specimen sheet of bibliography, 201; completed by Foxwell in 1884, VII vii references to articles included: 'Commercial Crises and Sun-Spots' (1878), IV 240n1, 295n1, V 44n1; 'Commercial Fluctuations' (1862), I 188n1; 'On the Condition of the Gold Coinage' (1868), II 156n5, III 159n2, 210n1, VI 110n3, VII 65; 'Gold and Silver' (letter to Wolowski, 12 December 1868), III 198; on index numbers, VI 55n8; 'On the Influence of the Sun-Spot Period upon the Price of Corn' (1875), IV 188n1, VI ixn4; *A Serious Fall in the Value of Gold . . .* (1863), I 191n1; *The Silver Question* (1877), IV 217n1, VI 102n14; 'Statistical Diagrams' (1862), I 181n4, VI 127n1; 'Variations of Prices and the Value of Currency since 1782' (1865), III 54n3, VI 118n7; Introduction by Foxwell, I 181n4, V 181n2
  Methods of Social Reform and other Papers edited, with Preface, by Harriet Jevons (1883), V 132n6, 174n2; references to articles included: 'Experimental Legislation and the Drink Traffic' (1880), V 166n6; 'Married Women in Factories' (1882), V 161, 174n2; Presidential Address to Section F of the British Association (1870), VI 59n14; 'The Rationale of Free Public Libraries' (1881), V 123n2; 'A State Parcel Post' (1879), V 155n2; 'Trades Societies: their Objects and Policy' (1868), VI 71n3; 'On the United Kingdom Alliance and its Prospects of Success' (1876), VI 41n17; 'The Use and Abuse of Museums' (1881), I 49, V 132n6
  Pure Logic and Other Minor Works (1890), edited by Robert Adamson and H. A. Jevons, I 52n5

works projected and abandoned
  1856: a book on music, I 32, II 243, 277; a work on 'Formal Economics', VII 116; 'Notes and Researches on Social Statistics, or the Science of Towns, especially as regards London and Sydney', I 17, 28, VII 116
  1857: 'Anthropology of Man' or 'Man in Society', I 27, VII 118, 119

works projected and abandoned (*contd*)

1858: 'Social Survey of Australian Cities', I 29, 159n1, II 297n10; MS published in part in *Sydney Morning Herald* (November–December 1929), I 29

1861: 'Statistical Atlas': first ideas, I 180; twenty-eight diagrams completed, 180; work on, II 425–7, plan of contents, 425n2; attempt to find a publisher, I 180–1; *Two Diagrams* published, *see above*; work on diagrams continues, I 461; plan for 'The Merchants' Atlas of Commercial Fluctuations', II 459, 461–2, III 4

1862: 'Volunteer History', I 186, II 461; study of relation between science and religion, I 51; 'Tenth Bridgewater Treatise', 52

1874: 'historical sketch of opinions bearing on utility and value', IV 82

1876: proposed investigation into volume of banking transactions, V 162, 165

1877: students edition of *Wealth of Nations*, IV 218–19, 248–9, 263n4, 298, V 106n2, 115, 116

1879: 'Handbook to the Literature of Political Economy', for the Index Society, IV 297n1

1880: analysis of Mill's philosophy, I 51, V 116; bibliography of logic, V 116, 117

bibliography of WSJ's writings, printed by Conrad in *Jahrbücher für Nationalökonomie und Statistik* (1878), IV 253n3

Jevons, Mrs William Stanley (Harriet Ann Taylor, 1838–1910), I 241

engagement to WSJ (October 1867), I 47, 211; marriage (19 December 1867), 47, their happiness together, III 195, her promise to join in and esteem WSJ's work, I 211; first home in Withington, Manchester, I 47, III 182–3; holiday in Wales and Germany, 185, 209, 210; at Ludlow with Lucy, 249; in Norway (1873), IV 21, 22, 24; in Italy and France (1874), 33n2; goes with WSJ to Cambridge, 93

her first child (Herbert Stanley), IV 146, 150; move to Hampstead, 182, 183; second child (Harriet Winefrid), 211, 213, 214; visits to sister in Birkenhead, 216n1, V 99; at Eastbourne and Matlock, IV 271; third child (Lucy Cecilia), V 122; Berlioz concerts with WSJ, 131, 134; tour with WSJ (1881), 132; leaves WSJ with the children, 136; feels maternal cares at the seaside, 142–3; visit to Paris with WSJ, 148–9; hears *Tristan and Isolde*, 199; at Hastings (1882), 190, 199

health, III 210, IV 205, 211, 213, V 154, 190

helps WSJ with copying and arithmetical work, III 182; catalogues his books, IV 285; edits *Letters and Journal*, I 1, 11, 43, 187n3, IV 244, 281n1, V 191n1, VII 54; joint editor of *Pure Logic and Other Minor Works* (1890), I 52n5, of *Theory of Political Economy*, ed. 3, V 129n2, of *Investigations*, V 159n1, of *Methods of Social Reform*, V 174n2

letters to, III 231, IV 116–18, 128, 129, 129–30, 148–9, 150, 173, 182, 206–7, 216, 285, 285–6, V 43, 99, daily notes to, IV 128; letter from F. Y. Edgeworth on the death of WSJ, V 201–2

letters from, referred to, IV 128, 130, 150, 207, V 43

also mentioned, I 46, IV 116, 147, 184, 189n4, 194, 303, IV 35, V 67, 84, 92, 110

Jevons, Winefrid, daughter of WSJ, *see* Jevons, Harriet Winefrid

Jevons family

WSJ's researches into origins, I 3, 179, II 10n1, 28n2, his 'genealogical book', II 462; change from Jevon to Jevons, I 3n3; Sedgeley Hall, ancient family seat, 3; family connections: genealogical tables, I 240–1; Dawsons, I 241, II 10n1; Huttons, I 36, 241, 243; Lace, I 242, II 176n10; Moss, II 44n4; Roscoe, I 75n2, 242–3, legacy from Roscoe estate, II 405; Thornely, I 56n9, 241, 243 seaside holidays at West Kirby, I 54n7, 56; attendance at Renshaw Street Unitarian Chapel, I 58n5; solidarity, after death of Thomas Jevons, I 12–13, family affection, II 451

cursed with a 'stupid simplicity of character', I 38, II 447; an 'unsettling earnestness of disposition', II 337; regarded as obstinate and stupid, 341; all rolling stones, 417; not half enough humbug, 452

a 'streak of tragedy', I 7; star of the family rising, III 34; cause to doubt the 'benevolent government of human affairs', IV 250

Jevons & Busk, *see* Busk & Jevons

Jevons & Son, family firm of Liverpool iron merchants, I 3; bankrupted (1848), 12; reconstituted as Jevons & Co., 12

for details of the firm *see under* George Jevons, Henry Jevons, Herbert Jevons, Roscoe Jevons, Thomas Jevons, Thomas Edwin Jevons, Timothy Jevons, William Jevons

Jevons & Wood, South Wales ironmasters: Thomas Jevons, partner in, bankrupted in 1848, I 12

Joachim, Joseph (1831–1907), violinist: WSJ at his concert in London (November 1862), II 458

Johnson, Andrew, President of United States of America in succession to Lincoln, II 453n6

Johnson, E. W., manager of National Provincial Bank of England, South Molton: letter to WSJ on circulation of gold, III 195–6

Johnson, Dr Samuel, VI 23
Dictionary, VI 11; *Rasselas*, II 154

Johnston, James Finlay Weir (1796–1855), Professor of Chemistry and Mineralogy, University of Durham, II 50

Johnstones Bay, Sydney, II 182

joint-stock banks, *see* banking system

joint-stock companies, III 134, 143, 153; bankruptcies, VI 126; as cooperative protective companies, VI 75

Jones, an imposter in Sydney, II 115

Jones, Jenny, the Maid of Llangollen, II 153

Jones, Rev. Richard, *An Essay on the Distribution of Wealth . . .* (1831), VII 105

Joplin, Thomas, monetary writer, IV 275

Joule, James Prescott (1818–89), physicist, President of Manchester Literary and Philosophical Society, II 66, 66n12; concern for men of science in relation to national affairs, III 236–7

Journal des Actuaires français, IV 270

Journal of the Institute of Actuaries, VII 88

Journal des Débats, IV 68, 85

Journal des Economistes
'Bibliographie' of mathematical economists (1878), IV 259, 262, 270, 282, 289, 290, V 21
Dupuit: 'Réponse à M. Dunoyer' (1861), IV 197, 205
Fontpertuis: translation of WSJ's Introductory Address (1877), IV 192, 276
Walras: correspondence with WSJ, IV 48, 50, 261, 263; 'Principe d'une théorie mathématique de l'échange' (1874), IV 39, 45, 48, 57n1; letter from (18 June 1874), IV 57; 'Un économiste inconnu, Hermann-Henri Gossen' (1885), V 144n2, 145n4
editor, Garnier, IV 48, 85, Limousin, V 4
also mentioned, V 7n5

Journal of the Institute of Bankers: 'The Proportional Use of Credit Documents and Metallic Money in English Banks' (Pownall, 1881), V 130n2; 'Money and Barter' (Rowland Hamilton, 1881), 153n1; 'Our Gold Coinage' (J. B. Martin, 1882), 181n2

Journal of the Royal Statistical Society (JRSS), *see* Royal Statistical Society Journal

Journal of the Statistical and Social Inquiry Society of Ireland: 'The Periodicity of Commercial Crises and its Physical Explanation' (WSJ, paper read before British Association, 1878), IV 273n8, V 47; Presidential address (J. K. Ingram), IV 272n3, 273n8

journeymen, VI 69, 70

Jowett, Benjamin (1817–93), Master of Balliol College, Oxford, IV 286

Juglar, Clément (1819–1905), French economist: theory of the business cycle, IV 300, 301; obituary, by De Foville, V 17n1

Des Crises Commerciales (1862), IV 300n2, V 13, 16, 47

Julius Caesar, VI 102

jurisprudence, VI 8, VII 55; penal jurisprudence, VI 8

juvenile delinquents: Mrs Hornblower's (Aunt Jane's) concern at floggings, II 22; Home Secretary's interest in, V 168, 169

Kane, Sir Robert, Director of Museum of Irish Industry, II 119n16

Kansas, II 419, 420

Kant, Immanuel (1724–1804), II 424, 438, V 61, VI 132

Critique of Pure Reason (1781), II 433, VI 132n2

Kay, James Taylor (1840–93), Librarian of Owens College, III 234n2

'County Government' (*Macmillan's Magazine*, 1882), V 176n3

Keegan, Mrs, and child, passengers on the Harteley Royal Mail, I 235

Keira coalmine, I 177

Kelly, of the Prestatyn Soda Works, II 41

Kelly, Thomas, a Fenian prisoner, III 159n6

Kelvin, Lord, *see* Thomson, Sir William

Kemp, John, and Co., Messrs: bankruptcy figures for U.S.A. (*Nature*, 15 December 1878), V 11–12

Kennedy, E. B., *Four Years in Queensland* (1870), IV 176

Kennedy, Mary (later Mrs R. T. Wright), pioneer woman student at Cambridge, IV 148

Kenrick, William (?1725–79), review of Cantillon's *Analysis of Trade* (1759), V 122n2

Kerry, Cantillon's connections with, V 123–4, 125, 126, 128

Kerry, Earl of, V 124

Kettle, Rupert, umpire in wages dispute, III 226

Kew Observatory, possible post for WSJ at, II 392n19, 402

Key, Thomas Hewitt (1799–1875), Headmaster of University College School: WSJ's first schoolboy interview with, II 5; remembers WSJ later, 222; rescues a man from the medicals, 407

Keynes, John Neville (1852–1949): his Tripos papers marked by WSJ, IV 149, V 105, takes first place, 177; applies for professorship vacated by WSJ, V 117, withdraws, 133; examines with WSJ for Joseph Hume scholarship at University College, London, V 105, 109, 177; appointed Assistant Secretary to Cambridge University Local Examinations Syndicate (1881–2), V 133; testimonial from WSJ for London University examinership, V 177

letters to, V 105, 109, 133, 177

Kilberry, Ireland, turf-distillation factory, II 119n16

Killarney, Lakes of, II 342, 348

Kimberly, Miss, *see* Wills, Mrs

King, Gregory (1648–1712), *Natural and Political Observations and Conclusions upon the State and Condition of England* (1696), VI 89

King, Mead, marriage to Kate Newton, II 142

King, P. S. & Son, publishers of International Scientific Series, IV 148, 149

King's College, London, I 65n3, II 402; Edgeworth applies for Chair of Logic and Metaphysics, V 98, 99n2. *See also* Rogers, J. E. Thorold.

Kingsley, Charles, II 403n1; *Alton Locke*, I 16, 90n3

Kingsley, Henry (1830–76), Australian experiences, II 403n1; *Geoffrey Hamlyn*, 403

Kingston, Canada, WSJ travels through, II 401

Kingston on Hull, cooperative retail society, VI 74

Kingston, Jamaica, gas supplies, V 71

Kinkel, Gottfried (1815–82), WSJ attends his lectures on modern painting and sculpture at University College, London, I 85

Kinsman, John, book-seller: catalogues of second-hand books, V 76

'Kitchener' range, Thomas Jevons buys the latest kitchen stove, II 164–6, 166–7

Knapp, Georg Friedrich (1842–1926), economist, Professor at Leipzig, IV 85, V 42

Knies, Karl Gustav Adolf (1821–98), economist, Professor at Heidelberg, IV 85

Knight, Charles, editor of *London* (1842), I 16, 67, 90n3

Knowles, James Sheridan (1784–1862), dramatist: *Virginius* performed in Sydney, II 278

'know thyself', VII 40, 49

Kolbe, Hermann (1818–84), Professor of Chemistry at Marburg University, II 72

'Critical Observations on Williamson's Theory of Water, Ethers and Acids' (1854), II 72n8

Korff, Mr, WSJ's first landlord in Sydney, II 107, 196, 197

Kortum, Dr Karl Joseph Hermann (1836–1904), nephew of Gossen, Professor of Mathematics at Bonn, V 96, 144n2, 145

Kossuth, Francis, son of Lajos Kossuth, beaten in Mental Philosophy at University College by Tom Jevons, II 415

Kossuth, Lajos (1802–94), Hungarian revolutionary, II 415n3

Kossuth, Louis, son of Lajos Kossuth, beaten in Mental Philosophy at University College by Tom Jevons, II 415

Kranichfeld, Dr H., correspondence with WSJ on Cheque Bank, IV 178–9, 184–6

Kroncke, Claus, contributions to mathematical economics, IV 5, 19

Kyeamba, Victoria (Australia), local wines, II 368

labour
'free trade' in, VII 50
holidays for workmen, VII 49
hours of work
duration and painfulness of labour, VI 19–21, 26–27, VII 158, mathematical formula for, VI 92
examination questions on, V 152, VII 133
longer hours worked abroad, V 172–3
proper subject for union discussion, III 137, VII 49, 71–2, 73
manner of employment, VI 22–4; monotony of repetitive work, 28
organised labour, relations with State, I 49; *The State in Relation to Labour, see under* Jevons, William Stanley, Works
Banfield on, VI 14
the 'Labour Question', III 127–8
rewards of, in new countries, II 282
versus capital, VI 72, VII 58
books on, VII 107
examination questions on, VII 133, 136
and taxation of rich and poor, III 239
see also division of labour; trade unions; wages; working-classes
labour, in economic theory
and capital: not capital, VI 40; capital invested in employment of, II 427, VI 46–7; examination question on, VII 135–6
definitions, VI 18; Adam Smith's, 19; in *Theory of Political Economy*, VII 143
demand for, Mill's view criticised, VI 48; supply and demand view, 61
examination questions on, VII 133, 135, 136, 138
as first element in production, VI 17–18, 19–22, 36, 60
Mill on, VI 21, 24
in *Theory of Political Economy*, III 246, VII 158–9
price of, IV 7; high, in New South Wales, II 283
dear labour the measure of efficiency, III 255
productivity of, VI 26–7; wages determined by, II 422, IV 227
productive and unproductive (Mill), VI 26, 52–3
in relation to interest theory, IV 226–7, 230–1
value and: as cause of value, view in 1860, VII 120; Rogers's error, VI 90–1

labour, in economic theory (contd)
   examination questions on, V 152, VII
      135
   Gossen's theory of, IV 268–9
   as measure of value, Adam Smith's
      view, III 253, IV 115n3, VI 90, 98,
      VII 77–8, 83
   in theory of utility, IV 258, VI 92–4,
      VII 83, 141–2, 159–60; the pur-
      chase price of utility, VI 12
   value of last portion of labour, VI 91–2
labour disputes, arbitration in, VI 78. See
   also strikes
labour saving, VII 143; calculating machines, VII 86–7, 88, 90
labourers: regarded as machines, VI 53;
   their political economy, VII 59
   see also working classes
Lace, Ambrose (1793–1870), solicitor and
   Bailiff of Liverpool, II 44, 176
Lace, Margaret (1787–1840), wife of Ed-
   ward Roscoe, I 242, II 44n5
Ladies College, Bedford Square, VI 16n6;
   Henrietta learns at, II 406
Laing, John (1832–72), of the Bank of
   England, letter from, III 161–2
Laing, John, Theory of Business for Busy
   Men, VII 105
Laird Brothers shipyard, Liverpool, III
   53n1
laissez-faire, IV 272n5, V 27; examination
   question on, VII 136
Lake Superior, II 419, 420
Lalor, John J., translation of Roscher's
   Principles of Political Economy, IV
   108n2, VII 102
Lamarck, Jean Baptiste (1744–1829),
   theories of origin of man, I 66
Lamarre, Clovis, classicist, IV 277, 288n1
La Marseillaise: in Paris, II 83; sung by
   Anna Bishop in Sydney, II 224;
   included in WSJ's 'cheerful pro-
   grammes' on his harmonium, 339
Lambe, Dr [George, 1766?–1862], attends
   Thomas Jevons in his last illness in
   Pisa, II 210
Lamoureux, Charles (1834–99), French
   violinist and conductor: concerts at
   St James's Hall, London, V 131–2
Lancashire
   ancient and modern, VII 22–3
   depressions, VII 91

   earthquake, I 71
   Gladstone's victory in, III 136
   manufacturers, and tropical meteoro-
      logical variations, V 10–11, 45
   WSJ a 'Lancashire man', VII 22
land
   Bastiat's opinions on, V 196–7; exam-
      ination question on, VII 138
   of different productive powers, VI 90; in
      fully settled countries, 91
   'free trade' in, III 138
   improvements in, as fixed capital, VI 40
   land policy in New South Wales, II 282–
      5, 286–7, VII 3–8
   land tenure system, historical approach
      to study of, VII 100
   peasant proprietorship, V 196–7
   as requisite of production, VI 36, VII
      158, 159
Land, Jan Pieter Nicolaas (1834–97), Professor of Philosophy at Leiden: approves Principles of Science, IV 83,
   94, 96; praises WSJ's new theory of
   economics, 83
Land Act (Ireland, 1881), V 150, 151, 179,
   189
Land League, see Irish Land League
landlordism, III 134; as system of land
   tenure, VII 100; in Ireland, V 112–
   15
landlords
   hereditary, and high rents, II 282
   landed proprietors and cheap labour,
      III 255
   landowners, in classification of trades,
      VI 33–4; in England, their im-
      mense wealth and social power, V
      197; and exhaustion of coal, VII
      12; people should be their own
      landlords (WSJ), V 196
Land Question, books on, VII 105
Lane, Henry (d. 1873), Irish Republican,
   once a French professor: on board
   the Oliver Lang, I 105, II 81, 98; dis-
   embarks at Melbourne, 112; later
   Under Secretary for Finance and
   Trade, New South Wales, II 81n4
Lane, Samuel, from Cork, father of Henry
   Lane, II 98n4
Lang, Dr John Dunmore (1799–1878),
   Presbyterian Minister and pol-
   itician in Sydney, II 248

Queensland, Australia, . . . with a disquis-
ition on the origin, manners and customs
of the Aborigines (1861), IV 174, 176
Lang, Joseph, German economist, IV 278
Langel, Auguste, Ingénieur des Mines:
copy of *Theory of Political Economy*
for, IV 68; reviews WSJ in *Le Temps*
(14 October 1874), IV 85
Langley, Edward, supporter of bimetal-
lism, IV 186; 'The Silver Ques-
tion', paper read at Manchester
Statistical Society (March 1879),
IV 186n2, V 26n1
Langton, Henry, joint Hon. Secretary of
Manchester and Salford District
Provident Society: annual appeal
for funds, III 256–7; presents WSJ
with copy of Manchester Bankers'
Memorial, IV 107
Langton, Robert, joint Hon. Secretary of
Manchester and Salford District
Provident Society: annual appeal
for funds, III 256–7
Langton, William (1803–81), Manchester
banker, a founder of Manchester
Statistical Society: sends correc-
tions for *Money . .*, IV 165–6; on
monetary policy and decennial
crises, 209–11, 214–15, 220, on
post-office orders, 216–17
letters from, IV 165, 209–11, 214–15,
216–17, 220
'On the Balance of Account between the
Mercantile Public and the Bank of
England' (Manchester Statistical
Society, 1857–8), IV 13, 232; 'The
New Post-Office Bank Note' (*Fi-*
nancial Opinion, 27 September
1877), IV 216
also mentioned, V 130n4
Lankester, Edwin (1814–74), Middlesex
Coroner, V 173; translation of
Schleiden's *Principles of Scientific*
Botany (1849), I 66n2
Lansdowne, Lord
included in Earl of Aberdeen's Ministry
(1853), I 87
his ancestors and Richard Cantillon, V
123
Laplace, Pierre Simon de (1749–1827), IV
147, V 52; his inductive method,
VII 93

Lapstone Hill, New South Wales: Pilgrim
Inn, I 152n1; romantic appearance, 153, 217n1, II 221;
coach ride down, I 238; proposed
railway plans for, II 264
Lardner, Dionysius, *Railway Economy*
(1850), I 27, VII 118
Laspeyres, Etienne (1834–1913), Professor
of Political Economy at Basel
essay on Hamburg and London prices
(1864), III 61, 62, with criticism of
Serious Fall, 62, 66n1, VII 125; continues work on prices, III 81–2, 126
visit from WSJ in Basel, III 81; moves to
Riga, 125, 126
essay on wages in France (*Der Einfluss der*
Wohnung auf der Sittlichkeit . . .,
1869), III 126
letters from, III 61, 66–7, 81–2, 125–6
also mentioned, IV 58, V 42
'last portion added'
degree of utility of last portion, VI 87
determines rate of exchange, VII 82,
141; determines rate of payment for
whole capital employed, II 422
in Gossen's theory, IV 268–9
N. G. Pierson's version of principle, IV
283
value determined by last portion of
labour spent, VI 92
see also marginal revolution
Latham, Alfred (1801–85), director of
Bank of England: assists WSJ in
inquiry into state of gold coinage,
III 161–4, 179
letters from, III 162–3, 163–4, 179
Latham, Messrs Arbuthnot, & Co., merchants and East India agents, III
161n2, 163n1
Latin, as an international language, V 30.
See also classical studies
Latin Monetary Convention (December
1865), III 211, VII 66, 67, 69
La Touche, Rev. James Digges, vicar of
Stokesay, V 75
Lauderdale, 8th Earl of (James Maitland,
1759–1839), *An Inquiry into the*
Nature and Origin of Public Wealth,
VI 13
Lausanne, Walras's home at, IV 271, 289–
90, V 56
Laveleye, Emile Louis Victor de (1822–

Laveleye, Emile Louis Victor de (*contd* 92), Belgian economist, III 197; in England, V 68; supports pension for Cliffe Leslie, V 169n1
Primitive Property (translated by G. R. L. Marriot, 1878), VII 105
Lavergne, Louis Gabriel Léonce de (1809–80), *Les Economistes français du XVIIe siècle* (1870), V 124
Law of International Traffic (Madsen), IV 243–4, 245, V 27–9; Westergaard on the 'law of distance', IV 246–7
Law, John (1671–1729), his Mississippi Bubble, VI 116, 117
Lawson's History of Banking, VII 106
Lawthwaite, Miss, encountered at Llangollen, II 155
Layard, Sir Austen Henry (1817–94), archeologist: excavations at Palace of Nimrud, II 18n1
Leach, Thomas (1818–75), vicar of Thornton, Yorks, letter of thanks for copy of *Serious Fall*, III 26
lead
    for assaying gold, II 175, III 51
    black lead: in Illawarra, I 174; in Borrowdale, VI 83
    lead mines: in Cumberland, New South Wales, I 175; in France, II 94; in Wales, II 93, 135n11
    lead pencils, II 134
    poisoning through lead water pipes, II 249–50
    prices, VI 120, VII 21; value of ore raised (1865), VII 24–5
    smelting, VII 30
leases: made in gold money, VI 95; proposals for, in New South Wales, VII 7–8
Least Squares, Method of, VII 87
Le Breton, Letitia, *see* Roscoe, Mrs F. J.
Leclaire, Paris, profit-sharing scheme, VI 77
Lee, General Robert E., II 454n7
Lee, William (d. 1610?), inventor of stocking frame, VI 29
Leeds, IV 145, V 29n2
Leeds Mercury, III 100
Lees, William Nassau, estimate of gold and silver circulating in Great Britain, III 201
legal tender, a problem of terminology, III

199, VI 100
    double legal tender, 100–1
Leghorn
    clearing houses, IV 302
    Thomas Jevons buried in Protestant Cemetery at, I 22
Le Gros, Raymond, ancestor of Richard Cantillon, V 123, 128
Leibnitz, Gottfried Wilhelm, freiherr von (1646–1716), II 433, 437
    La Monadologie, II 433
leisure *versus* work, V 254n3
Lemielle, M., machine ventilator for coalmines, III 146
Leonard, E. J., translation of *Histoire de l'Economie Politique en Europe* (1880), VII 102–3
le Pelletier, Jean (163?–1761), on the commercial crisis in France of 1701, IV 295
Les Baux, bauxite ore from, II 63n6
Leslie, Thomas Edward Cliffe (1825–82), Professor of Political Economy and Jurisprudence at Queen's College, Belfast
    at Political Economy Club, IV 116; article on Section F of British Association (*Academy*, 1878), 273; objects to use of mathematical techniques in economic reasoning, V 67n1, 68, VII 157–61; agrees with WSJ on Ricardo's deductive method, 162; exposes fallacy of Mill's wage-fund theory, VII 77
    his poor health, V 68, 169, 170, 184; friends petition for Civil Service pension, 169; death, 169n1, 171n1; obituary by WSJ (*Economist*, 4 February 1882), 171
    review of ed. 2 of *Theory of Political Economy* (*Academy*, 26 July 1879), V 67, VII 157–62
    introduction to Laveleye's *Primitive Property*, VII 105; 'On the Philosophical Method of Political Economy' (*Hermathena*, 1876), IV 272n1, VII 100n; *Essays in Political and Moral Philosophy*, (1879), IV 272n1, VII 104
    letters from, IV 272–3, V 67–8
Le Temps, IV 68, 85

Le Trosne, Guillaume François (1728–80), IV 91n3

De l'ordre Social . . . , V 150

Levantine Valley, II 188–9

Levant trade, IV 210, V 49

Le Verrier, Urbain-Jean-Joseph, French astronomer, V 13

Leveson Gower, Granville George, *see* Granville, Earl of

Levi, Leone, supports seignorage in gold coin controversy, III 211

History of British Commerce, IV 13, 14n14, 18–19

Levicks and Piper, Sydney firm, II 117n12

Levol, Alexandre, assayer to Paris Mint, II 71, 184

Levy, Joseph Hiam, *Wealthy and Wise* . . . (1879), V 76

Lewes, visit to, V 132

Leyden University, interest in WSJ's new theory of value, IV 71

Libbey, Jonas Marsh (1857–1922), editor of *Princeton Review*: sends WSJ a barrel of American apples, IV 303, 304

letter to, IV 304–5

Liberals

Gladstonian, I 18, 44, V 111n2, VII 154; purchase of Post Office telegraphs (1870), IV 150n4; victory in 1880, V 97n1, 101n3, 115n6, Morley's unsuccessful campaign in Westminster, 79; WSJ's sympathies with, 97–8

Liberal Christianity, V 114n5

Mill's form of Liberalism, III 132

libraries and museums

as a function of government, VI 133, a proper use for wealth, VII 28

public libraries, article on, V 123, and *see under* Jevons, W. S., Works

see also British Museum; Dr Williams's Library; Irish Industry, Museum of; *and under* Liverpool; Manchester; *and* Oxford

Library Association: Conference at Oxford, IV 284–6, Soirée in the Museum, 284, 285–6; WSJ a member, VII 101, his list of books on political economy compiled for, 101–7

'Library of Useful Knowledge', I 65; *Natu-*

ral Philosophy, 65n3, 113; 'Chemistry', 65n3, 113; 'Electricity', 87

licensing reform, V 166; intemperance and working wives, V 165

'Experimental legislation and the Drink Trade', *see* Jevons, W. S., Works

Liddell, Henry Thomas (1797–1878), M.P. for Liverpool, 1853–5, I 86n2

Liebig, Justus, Freiherr von (1803–73), Professor of Chemistry at Giessen, later at Munich: chemistry laboratory at Giessen, I 83n2, II 71n2, visited by Harry Roscoe, 71, at Munich, I 83n2, II 73; attends British Association meeting (1855), II 193

Chemische Briefe (1844), read by WSJ, I 83, 87; 'Lord Bacon as natural philosopher' (*Macmillan's Magazine*, 1863), III 78, 80–1

also mentioned, II 50n8, 72nn3, 4, 305n3, 372n1

Liebig, Justus, son of, II 73

Lima: WSJ's voyage to, II 373–5, 381; impressions of buildings and people, 376, 378–9, 381, 387, 388, 394–6, goes up a church steeple, 380

limitation of supply: a quality of wealth, VI 9, 10; of food, and Malthus's theory of population, 57; role in regulation of price, 83

Limited Liability Act (1855), later incorporated in Companies Acts, II 232n8, VI 125; WSJ's suspicions of limited liability companies, II 232, VI 67

Limousin, Charles-Mathieu (d. 1909), editor of *Journal des Economistes*: letter to WSJ seeking advice on a prize essay, V 3–7

Lincoln, Abraham: heads Republican administration (November 1860), II 404n2, 424, 'Honest old Abe', 418; WSJ's antipathy to, 453; dissatisfaction with his administration (1862), 454n7; appoints commission on the revenue (1865), III 200n2; also mentioned, II 421n6

Lincolnshire, VII 23, 24

Lindley, John (1799–1865), Professor of Botany at University College, Lon-

Lindley, John (*contd*)
    don, I 54n8; lectures on botany,
    79n4; advocate of natural system of
    classification, 63n5
    Elements of Botany (1841), read by WSJ, I
    54; *The Vegetable Kingdom* (1846), I
    79n4; chosen by WSJ as prize book,
    66
'linear arithmetic', William Playfair's
    graphical system, IV 8, 9
Linnaean system of classification, I 59, 63
literature, WSJ and: plans for studying, I
    78; early indifference to poetry, 98;
    begins to feel a liking for, 110
Litolff, Henry Charles (1818–91), French
    pianist: arrangements of Beethoven
    for piano, IV 56
Littlehampton, holiday at, with the
    children, V 107
Little Hartley, *see under* Hartley
Livermore, Abiel A., *The Four Gospels*
    (1850), III 45
Liverpool
  banks: Bank of England, Liverpool
    branch, II 55; Barned's Banking
    Co., Ltd, failure in 1866, VI 126;
    Liverpool Borough Bank, failure in
    1857, VI 125; Moss's Bank in Dale
    Street, II 44n4, 342; banking busi-
    ness around 1850, V 153–4
  Borough Gaol, I 79n4
  British Association meeting (1854) in St
    George's Hall, I 118, II 75, 79, 94,
    103, 434, lectures and demon-
    strations, 104–5; (1870), WSJ's
    Presidential Address, III 236, VI
    59n14, metric system advocated,
    III 238
  climate, II 77; earthquake, I 71, 117, II
    36; great storm of 1852, I 80
  cotton trade, III 64–5
  docks: WSJ sails from, I 19, lands in
    (1859), II 390–1, 401, his sun-
    gauge stranded in, 343; Herbert
    Jevons sails from, I 76,
    II 442
    gold dust nuggets brought to, II 42;
    emigrant ships sail from, 53–4, 141;
    mail ships from Australia, 203; 'for-
    est of masts', 370; coal for, VII 23
  general elections: (1852), bribery, I 86,
    election of candidates declared

    void, 86n2; (1874), Gladstone's ad-
    dress, IV 36
hospitals and medical services: dispens-
    ary, I 79n4; Liverpool Hospital,
    Ashton Street, Roscoe Jevons dies
    at, I 9; lunatic asylum in Crown
    Street, I 116n2; Medical Insti-
    tution, I 79
industries and manufactories, II 40,
    listed, 41; Soap Works, I 92–3;
    merchants, II 234; trade its alpha
    and omega, 383; early trade guilds,
    VI 69
Iron Church of St Michael's, Toxteth
    Park, I 59
Jevons family homes: 14 Alfred Street,
    birthplace of WSJ, I 2, plate facing
    p. 14; Park Hill Road, Toxteth
    Park, home of William Jevons, II
    7n3, of Thomas Jevons, I 12, 88n7,
    chemistry in the coach-house, 194,
    the back breakfast room, 195, its
    'diminished dignity', II 290, the
    road 'dreary and forsaken', 388;
    125 Chatham Street, I 12, 88n6,
    WSJ at home, 56, 99, 116n2, Uncle
    Hornblower's funeral, 88; family
    organ, II 7n3; chemistry in the
    cellar, 34; earthquake felt in, 36;
    Professor Graham calls, 102; the
    house 'burnished up', 172; mem-
    ories of, in Australia, 290, depicted,
    plate facing I 14; The Dingle, home
    of William Roscoe, I 59n3, walk to
    the shore below, 59, reminder of, in
    New South Wales, II 106, 110;
    Falkner Street, home of Uncle
    Hornblower, I 88; Grove Park,
    home of Uncle Timothy, II 388,
    389, 391, 446; Newington Street,
    Uncle Hornblower's shop in, I 88
libraries and museums: Derby Museum,
    II 155n4; Female Apprentices' Li-
    brary, II 22n1; Free Public Li-
    brary, II 155n4, III 73; Mechanics'
    and Apprentices' Library, II 22n1;
    Picton Reference Library, II 95n5
Literary and Philosophical Society, I
    59n8; WSJ's paper on the logical
    abacus (19 March 1866), I 204n4,
    III 89, 104, VII 104, 126
Mechanics Institute High School: atten-

ded by Roscoe, WSJ and Herbert Jevons, I 7, 13, 88, II 34n6, V 107, chemistry at, I 114n1; Queen's College housed in school building, III 68, 291n1

Mechanics Institution (Liverpool Institute), II 29n1, 235n1; Queen's College a department of, later amalgamated with, I 198n2; Ladies College founded by Directors, II 291n9

municipal elections (1869), Henry Jevons defeated, III 227

Philharmonic Hall: contrasted with St George's Hall, II 203; concerts, I 60, II 141, 181, 224

poverty, I 16

railway plans for, VII 23

Royal Institution: Debating Society founded by Tom Jevons, III 15

St George's Hall: opened during British Association meeting, II 95; concerts and oratorios, 95; gas-lit chandeliers, 103; nothing in Paris to beat it, II 63; like interior of La Madeleine, 179; spoken of in Parramatta coach, I 136

Henry Willis's organ, II 23n3, opened with recital by William Thomas Best, 142; Samuel Wesley's performance on, 152. *See also above,* British Association meeting

schools: Mr Beckwith's private school, attended by WSJ, I 13, 58, 77n2, 115; girls' school (1844), II 291n1; Mr Green's private school, attended by Tom Jevons, II 34, 44, 143, 167; Ladies College, founded in 1856, II 291. *See also above,* Mechanics Institute School

shipowners, II 111n3, 203

Social Science Association meeting (1858), VII 53

Unitarian chapels: Paradise Street, I 3n1, II 118n15

Renshaw Street, attended by Jevons family, I 58n5, II 134, 151; opened in 1811, II 118n15; WSJ writes his journal in, I 58; Mr Thom's altered service, II 32; memorial tablet to Thomas Jevons, I 22n1, monument

to Grandfather William Roscoe, II 128, 144; collection of books, II 52n6; trustees, 169n10; attended by Miss Cushman, actress, 134; demolished, replaced by Ullet Road Church, 128n8, III 204; Unitarian school attached to, II 28n2

Toxteth Park Chapel, burial place of Roscoe and other members of Jevons family, I 9, III 204

Walker Art Gallery, II 95n5; William Roscoe's collection of Italian and Flemish paintings, I 4; miniature portrait of Mary Anne Roscoe, I 5–6; Gibson's 'Tinted Venus', II 201n3

WSJ and: birth in, I 2; at school, 13, 88, II 115; plans to go into business in, I 78, 89; sails to Australia from, I 19, returns to, 33, II 390–1, 401; feelings on, 251; sale of 'Diagrams' in, II 461, 462, III 4; gives paper to Literary and Philosophical Society, III 89; *see also* Queen's College

Liverpool Academy, II 128n7

Liverpool and Birmingham Railway, II 44n4

Liverpool Botanic Garden: instituted (1802), I 60n2; specimens from, illustrated in William Roscoe's *Monandrian Plants,* 63n3; WSJ attends show at, 60

Liverpool Chamber of Commerce, II 38n2

Liverpool College of Chemistry, II 134n6

Liverpool Conservative Tradesman's Association, II 36n3

Liverpool Fire Office (later Liverpool, London and Globe Insurance Co.), II 60n4

Liverpool Institute, II 30n1; connection with Queen's College, I 198n2. *See also* Queen's College, Liverpool

Liverpool Iron and General Trades Association, II 38n2

Liverpool and London Fire and Life Insurance Company, Sydney branch, II 129n, 131, 140

Liverpool, Lord (Charles Jenkinson), 1st Earl, *A Treatise on the Coins of the Realm* (1805), V 182, VII 67, 71, 106

Liverpool and Manchester Railway Committee, II 44n4

Liverpool Mercury, II 36n3, 95, 446

Liverpool, New South Wales, II 267

Liverpool White Star Line, II 116n6

Livingstone, Dr, his explorations in Central Africa, VII 118

Livy, on ratio of gold to silver, VI 101

Llangollen: Jevons family holiday at (1851), II 47, (1855), I 120, II 153–5, 163, 165, 167, 168–9; WSJ and Tom spend three days walking round, II 415

Lloyd, Henry Humphrey Evans (1720–83), major-general in Austrian army, V 42; *An Essay on the Theory of Money* (anon., 1771), included in WSJ's bibliography of mathematico-economic books, V 42n7; Verri's abstract of *Essay*, 60

Lloyd, Sampson S., M.P., IV 251

loans, *see* credit

Loans to Foreign States, Select Committee of the House of Commons on (1875), VI 113n8. *See also* foreign loans

Locke, John: his unmarried state, I 192; on labour as cause of wealth, VI 19; definition of credit, VI 104

lock-outs, III 130, 132

Lockyer, Sir Joseph Norman (1836–1920), astronomer, editor of *Nature*, III 236; research on atomic theory of matter, IV 294; interest in sun-spot cycles, V 57; member, Solar Physics Committee, 103

letter from III 236

'Researches in Spectrum Analysis in connection with the Spectrum of the Sun', paper read before Royal Society (12 December 1878), IV 294n5; 'Sun-Spots and Famines' (*Nineteenth Century*, 1877), V 35

locomotives, VII 23, 30

see also railways

Lodge, [Sir] Oliver Joseph (1851–1940), physicist: applies for Chair of Applied Mathematics at Manchester, V 141

letter from, V 141

lodging-houses (common), I 16–17, 68

log huts: in Australia, I 139, 147, 253;

Herbert's, in Wayzata, II 384, 400

Logan, W. H., *The Scottish Banker* (1850), VII 106

logic

WSJ and: studies for B.A., I 34, II 415, reads Mill's *Logic*, I 30, 185, VII 119, a 'new exercise for his thoughts', I 185; gets gold medal in M.A. examinations, I 34, III 103

influence of De Morgan, I 16, first paper on logic sent to him, III 34; *Pure Logic* published (1863), I 40, III 48, 104, Herbert Spencer on, III 117; work on logic continues, III 29, 58; the 'chaos' of current logical thinking, I 41

appointed Professor of Logic at Queen's College, Liverpool (1865), I 198n2, III 104; substitute lecturer in logic at Owens College, Manchester (September 1865), III 75–6; discovers 'the true logic of the future' (1866), I 204, the principle of 'sameness', I 15, 35, 40, 208–9; will graft the new discovery on his published work, 208; starts on 'a complete work on logic' (1867), 209–10, 211; *The Substitution of Similars* (1869), I 210n1; *Principles of Science* (1874), I 48, 210n1; *Logic for Schools* (1877), IV 192; *Exercises in Logic* (1880), V 69

as teacher of logic: evening classes at Owens College, III 10, 14, 27, 28, 34, 45, IV 23, 156; his method, III 105, IV 22–4; Broadfield on his teaching, III 118, on his examination questions, 93–4; on the tyranny of established authorities, 246; 'oppressed' with the abundant exercises of his logic class, IV 80; recommends Mill's *Logic* to public primary school teachers (1866), VII 44

articles attacking Mill's logic, I 48, III 240, IV 116, 167, 192, 223, V 74, 75n1, 80, 89; 'John Stuart Mill's Philosophy Tested' (*Contemporary Review*, 1877, 1878), IV 192n2, 221; WSJ determined to 'upset Mill's logic altogether', IV 250; a maze of contradictions, IV 101–2, 167, V 24

status as logician, I 51, III 116, Cairnes on, IV 113; inherent mathematical and logical ability, I 195; relation to Boole's system, III 13, 34–5, 69, 116; on qualitative and quantitative reasoning, III 13, 117, 'no quantity in logic', 13; Natural system of botany 'the best of logical exercises', I 99; Law of Unity, III 35; Law of non-contradiction, V 24; logical method and definitions, VI 5; wide and continued use of his textbooks, I 48

inductive logic applied to solar theory of crises, VII 93–4

examinerships in, for M.A. degree at University of London, IV 239

logical abacus, I 198n3, 206, 211–12, III 76, 80, 104, 116; construction, III 69, 157, like a small piano, 185; demonstrated at University College, I 206; papers on, I 204n4, III 89, 104, VII 126

Lomax, Catherine, *see* Jevons, Mrs Timothy

Lomax, Harriet, *see* Wood, Mrs Henry

Lomax, John, of Heswall, Cheshire, II 26n3

London

  arrival of Princess Alexandra, I 190; illuminations for her marriage to Prince of Wales, III 6–8

  bankers, IV 187, 210; banking, VI 32; clearing banks, III 159n1. *See also* Bank of England

  Cattle Show (1877), IV 222

  City: explorations in, I 67, 83, 90, 181, II 10, III 6–8; city people, V 98

  clearing houses, IV 55, V 153n2, 154; Returns, V 25

  coal from Newcastle, VII 22

  docks: walks to St Katherine's Docks, I 76, 84, to West India Docks, 90; assaying acids sail from, II 77; mail boats to Australia, 132

  dynamiting outrages, V 135n1

  Egyptian Hall, 'The Ascent of Mont Blanc' shown in, I 76

  gas supplies, VI 133; gas works, I 90

geological excursions (WSJ), I 62, 84, 114

gold coin in circulation, III 193–4; sovereigns and half-sovereigns in London vaults, III 179

Government School of Mines, II 299

Guilds, or Corporations, VI 70

Hyde Park, I 74; Queens Own Rifles on duty in, I 190; Field Day in, II 407, 411, skirmishing exercises, 411, 461

improvements in East End, I 68, 90; new swimming baths, 68–' dirty water tanks', II 409; model lodging houses, I 68; new roads and Government offices, II 430

Kensington Gardens, VII 120; Kensington Workhouse, V 162

Lying-in-State and funeral of Duke of Wellington, I 72–5, 83, 84, II 35

Mansion House, II 10; attempt to blow up, V 132; International Monetary Convention meet at, V 187n2

manufactures: lucifer matches, I 84, 89; potteries and glue in Lambeth, I 90; shipbuilding, VI 64, iron ships, VII 21; silk in Spitalfields, I 67n4; watchmaking and jewellery in Clerkenwell, I 71, VI 32; territorial division of employment, VI 32

Merchants, Bankers and Tradesmen, petition on usury laws (1829), IV 279

Metropolitan Railways, II 9, 430; Midland Hotel, St Pancras, IV 212; Euston Hotel, III 231; Waterloo, II 9

money market, IV 220; foreign bills drawn on, VI 109, 115

Museums, II 63; South Kensington Museum, I 184, II 430n12. *See also* British Museum

music: concerts in St James's Hall, Beethoven, II 458, *Damnation of Faust*, V 123, 131, 134; oratorio, II 224, in Exeter Hall, 320, Messiah, 328–9; organ and singing at Temple Church, I 75; Wagner recitals and opera, IV 199, V 134, 194, at Drury Lane, 198–9

National Gallery, I 85, II 9, III 8

London (contd)
Portland Street Unitarian Chapel, II 20, 25n8
prices (1845–1865), III 61, 67n1, 82; price of coal and iron, VI 21; price of silver, V 141
Regents Park, skating, I 84, 89, V 91–2
Royal Exchange, I 84, II 10; *Two Diagrams* exposed for sale in, II 455
St Paul's Cathedral, I 84, II 58, 63, III 6; hung with black for funeral of Duke of Wellington, I 75; ship's lanterns on the Dome for Prince of Wales's marriage, III 7
the Season (May), II 409–10, 412, III 14, 104; dead season (September), V 205, 211
Serpentine, skating on, I 84, 89, II 403
Somerset House: WSJ collects Matriculation certificates and prize order from, I 66; illuminated for Prince of Wales's marriage, III 7
Stamp Office, II 117
stock exchange, V 171n1; stockbrokers, VI 32
Temple Bar, II 10; to be pulled down, IV 222; 'six omnibuses abreast', V 65; Temple, III 7, VI 32
weather: London skies, and winter gloom, II 403; murky streets, 413; dreariness, 460
WSJ and: interest in London as a town, I 17; plan to study, 28, reads Mayhew on, 28, 80–1, VII 116; observations on social conditions in, I 67, 68, 91; study of trade statistics, I 17, VII 116
explorations in, I 17, 62, 77, 95; 'dark arches' between Strand and river, I 67, 83; Spitalfields, 67–8, 83; Westminster, 68; Clerkenwell, 71–2; Bermondsey too frightening, 77, 84; Waterloo Bridge to Jacob's Island, 90; Whitechapel to Isle of Dogs, 90–1; reaches Bermondsey and Thames Tunnel, I 91, II 10; Paternoster Row to Charing Cross, I 180–1
homes in: Harrington Street, Hampstead Road (1850), lodging shared with Herbert, I 115, II 6, 7–8, 19;
Gower Street: (1851), Mrs Mackenzie's lodging house for school boarders, I 13, 63, II 13–14, 16–18, his uncongenial companions, I 100, II 17, 19, 20, 141n3; (June 1874), WSJ and Harriet take rooms in Gower Street, IV 51–2; 32 Norfolk Street (1854) with Uncle Timothy en route to Paris, II 58; 13 Albert Street, Camden Town (1854), solitary lodgings, I 98; 8 Porteus Road (1859–63), lodgings shared with Lucy, Henrietta and Tom, I 33, 179, II 393–4, 402, 405–6, 458, III 3, 5; housekeeping expenses, II 413–14; preparations for leaving, III 12–13, 14; move to Wallasey, I 40, III 18; Torrington Square, home of Aunt Henry Roscoe, II 4–5, 122, 191, 356
desire to return to, from Manchester (1874), IV 107, 110, 112, 123; househunting, 164, 169; removal to Hampstead, 182; the new address, 183. *See* Hampstead Heath
visits to, from Liverpool or Manchester, II 76, III 57; works on *Coal Question* at British Museum, I 43, 197, III 58, 63; sees Gladstone in London (1866), III 120; reads paper on Gold Currency to London (Royal) Statistical Society, 195
views on London: 'intolerable solitude' felt in 1867, I 211; returning to from Australia is to 'enter again the Battle of Life', II 242–3; a 'quiet sooty room' in, happiness itself, II 380; noise of London, III 29; 'an inhospitable place', 30; advantages of Manchester, III 9, of London, IV 107, 134; worry of life, V 157
also mentioned, I 76, II 72, 134, 177, 222, 251, 276
see also Crystal Palace; Great Exhibition; Royal Academy Exhibitions; Royal Mint; University College; University College School; Westminster
London Apothecaries' Society, I 85n1
London Armoury Co., Enfield rifle, II 436
London Astrological Society, IV 275

London Committee for the Abolition of the Slave Trade, I 59n5

London and County Banking Company, gold and silver coin received, 1867–8, III 193–4

London Directory, I 17, VI 33n5, VII 116

London Domestic Mission Society, Spitalfields, I 17, 68n3, II 25n8, 65n7; Harry Roscoe's lecture on chemistry at, I 84, 89–90; attempt to provide popular amusements, IV 292

London Figaro, V 87

London Gazette, III 81, IV 79

London Library, V 122, 129

London . . . Philosophical Magazine, III 155; editors, II 306n9
    articles by WSJ: 'On the Cirrous Form of Cloud' (1857), II 193n14, 244n7, 304; on the Sun-gauge (1857), II 297n8; 'On the Forms of Clouds' (1858), II 193n14, 244n7, 345, 433; 'Notice of Kirchhoff's Researches on the Spectrum' (July 1862), I 38n1; articles by WSJ in *Chemical Dictionary* noticed in (October 1863), VII 124
    H. E. Roscoe: 'On the Measurement of the Chemical Action of Light' (1856), II 229n13, 243
    also mentioned, II 250

London Quarterly Review
    'Spectrum' (WSJ, April 1862), I 38n1; review of *Coal Question* (April 1874), VII 125

London Statistical Society, *see* Royal Statistical Society

London and Westminster Bank, IV 159, 160

Long, Edwin Longsden (1829–91), A. R. A.: 'The Babylonian Marriage Market' exhibited in 1875, IV 117

Long, Mr, Stock Auctioneer, fellow passenger on the Sydney Mailcoach, I 236

Longe, Francis Davey, economist, VII 146

Longfellow, Henry Wadsworth, *The Song of Hiawatha*, WSJ cannot make out, II 233

Longman, William, interested in 'Diagrams', but not in publishing, I 180

Longmans & Co., publishers: 'Two Diagrams' tried on, I 180; 'Christianity without Miracles' (William Jevons, jun.,) submitted to, I 184; Index Society works published by, IV 297n1

Lonsdale, Henry, *The Worthies of Cumberland* (1867–74), IV 275, 276

Loomis, Professor, astronomer: on periodic variations of the sun, VII 92

Lord Chamberlain, *see* Exeter, 2nd Marquess of

Lord Chancellor's woolsack, VII 22

Lorrain, Jacques ('Go-Ahead'): prize essay on new taxation system (French), V 4n4

Louisa Creek, gold discoveries, II 351

Louisiana, John Law's scheme for, VI 116

Lovejoy, Owen (1811–64), American abolitionist, II 409

Lowe, Robert (1811–92), Chancellor of the Exchequer, 1868–73
    WSJ and: quotes WSJ's figures on light gold coinage, III 210, 211; interview (December 1869), 231; WSJ his unofficial adviser, 231n2, prepares report on pressure of taxation, 231n2; is sent copy of *Theory of Political Economy*, 245; reads *Primer* on political economy, 243
    tax reform (1869), VI 137; seignorage scheme, III 211, 212, 213, 214, 221, abandons proposal, 212; budget (1871), VI 137n7; supports metric system, III 232; at Political Economy Club, IV 222, 243n1; returned for University of London (1880), V 97; dropped from Gladstone's Cabinet, and created Viscount Sherbrooke, 97n3
    a trade unionist's view of, III 135–6
    letters from, III 245, IV 243
    also mentioned, III 181n1

Loyd, Samuel Jones, *see* Overstone, Lord

Lubbock, Sir John (1834–1913), banker: supplies figures on sovereigns in his banks, III 159, 160; arranges visit to London clearing house, IV 55; proposed as officer for Adam Smith Society, V 73, 82; supports Palgrave for F.R.S., 90
    letters from, III 159, 160
    also mentioned, V 97

Lübeck, visit to, IV 206
lucifer matches: visit to factory, I 84, 89; Harry Roscoe's lecture on, 89–90; match tax, VI 137n7
Luddites, VII 46
Ludlow, Lucy Hutton's home at, I 11, III 205; WSJ and Harriet visit, III 249
Ludwig I, King of Bavaria, II 182n10
Lugano, I 121, II 199
lunar influence on tides and men, VII 95–6
lunar rainbow, I 102, II 82
Lunn, Rev. Francis: 'Heat' (*Encyclopaedia Metropolitana*, 1845), I 65n2
Lunn, Mr, Miller's landlord in Sydney, II 197
Luther, Martin, II 72, 392n18
Lutwyche, Alfred James Peter, barrister: lawsuit against Proprietor of *Sydney Morning Herald*, II 250–1
luxury
    examination question on, V 152
    misuse of wealth on, VII 28
    taxation of, VII 15, of luxuries of rich and poor, III 239
    unproductive consumption and (Cazenove), IV 122
    and workmen's wages, VI 60, 72
Lyell, Sir Charles (1797–1875), pioneer geologist, I 66, III 63; attends Faraday's lecture at Royal Institute, I 82
Lyons, Lord (Richard Bickerton, 1817–87), 1st Viscount, British Ambassador at Paris, III 209
Lyons, Mr, and the 'great nuggett' of gold, II 127–8
Lytton, Bulwer, *My Novel*, I 27, 130–1

'M'., article in *Financial Opinion*, IV 216n1
MacAndrew, Robert, schoolfriend of WSJ, I 72, II 78
Macaulay, Thomas Babington, *History of England*, II 291
McClennan, General George Brinton (1826–85), in command of Northern Army of the Potomac, II 453; relieved of all commands by Lincoln, 454n6
MacColl, Hugh (1836–1909), logician and mathematician, V 116; WSJ visits in Boulogne, 148

McCormick's reaper at the Great Exhibition, II 12n6
McCulloch, Hugh, Secretary of U.S. Treasury, III 79n4; his report, 79; fellow guest of WSJ at Scientific Club, IV 117; his portrait on greenbacks, 117
McCulloch, John Ramsay, economist: unreliability of his figures, III 21, 25; on capital, IV 119, VI 41, definition, VI 37; errors in theory of rent, IV 197, 198n6; definition of political economy, VI 6; population statistics, VII 5; uses quantitative method without mathematics, VII 78; examination question on, 134–5
Commercial Dictionary, III 81, VII 104, article on 'Prices', IV 169–70; *Select Collection of Scarce .. Tracts on Money*, V 42, 44; sixpenny work on wages and labour, VII 51; *Literature of Political Economy*, VII 103; *Principles of Political Economy*, VII 103; *Descriptive and Statistical Account of the British Empire*, VII 115, 117
    edition of *Wealth of Nations*, IV 197n5, 219, V 81
MacCunn, John (1846–1929), first Professor of Political Economy at University College, Liverpool, V 145n1
MacCutcheon, WSJ's colleague at the Sydney Mint, I 174; goes with WSJ on photography expedition, II 352–5
Macdonald, William, housepainter, trade union pioneer: letter to *Manchester City News* protesting against WSJ's inaugural lecture as Cobden Professor, III 132–6; WSJ's reply, 137–8; further letters, 137n1, 150
The True Story of Trades Unions . . . a reply to .. Professor Jevons (1867), III 132n1
Macdonald & Co., Glasgow muslin producers, VI 125n5
Macdonnell, John, *A Survey of Political Economy*, reviewed in *British Quarterly Review* (1872), III 246; his treatment of Mill, IV 119–20, 122
The Land Question (1873), VII 105
Machiavelli, Niccolò (1469–1527), V 37

machinery
  beauty of machines, VII 86, 87, 88
  classification of types, VI 25–6
  coal for, VII 20, 30
  examination question on, VII 131
  as fixed capital, VI 40, 42, 43, 47
  at Paris Exhibition, II 183
  trade union opposition to, VI 74, VII
    46–8; machine-breaking, VI 71,
    VII 45
  the world as a machine, I 154n3, society
    as, VI 27, VII 41, 153
  also mentioned, VI 35, 51
  see also calculating machine; loc-
    omotives; steamboats; steam-
    engines; steam power
Machyntlleth slate quarry, II 132
MacIntyre, Captain, of the *Chrysolite*, II
    374, 385, 386–7, 394
Mackay, Charles, *Popular Illusions*, VI 116n3
Mackay, Donald (d.1880), Boston ship-
    builder, II 144
Mackeldy, Ferdinand, *Systema Iuris Romani
    Hodie Usitati* (1847), V 102
Mackenzie, Mrs, landlady in Gower
    Street, London, WSJ lodges with as
    a schoolboy, I 100, 115n7, II 13–
    14, 16–18, 19, 21–2; her other
    lodgers, II 17, 19
Mackenzie, William Forbes, M.P. for Li-
    verpool, 1852–3; election declared
    void, I 86
McKewan, William (1820–1909), General
    Manager, London and County
    Banking Company
  letter on gold coinage in circulation, III
    193–4
Maclagan, [Sir] Andrew Douglas (1812–
    1900), President of the Royal Col-
    lege of Surgeons, Edinburgh:
    speech at Edinburgh University
    Honorary Degree ceremony
    (1876), IV 173
Maclehose, Robert, printer of *Primer of
    Political Economy*, V 135
McLellan, Mrs, landlady in Hampstead
    Road, II 6; her terms, 7–8; Herbert
    gives notice, 14
Macleod, Henry Dunning (1821–1902):
    places WSJ in 'third' school of
    Economists, IV 115; on commer-
    cial crises, V 47; complains of Pre-

face to ed. 2 of *Theory of Political
    Economy*, V 76–7
  'On the Definition and Nature of the
    Science of Political Economy',
    paper read before British Associ-
    ation (1862), I 188n1, II 456; *The
    Principles of Economical Philosophy*
    (1872), IV 73, 115n1; *Dictionary of
    Political Economy* (1863), IV 214, V
    47, VII 146, article 'Bank', IV
    214n1; *Theory and Practice of Banking*
    (1855), VII 106
  letters from, IV 115
  also mentioned, IV 91
MacMartin, Barbara Mary (d. 1857),
    marriage to Charles Bolton, II
    77n2; *see also* Bolton, Mrs Charles
Macmillan, Alexander (1818–96), co-
    founder of Macmillans publishing
    house, III 84n1
  publishes *Coal Question*, III 93, VII 125;
    quotes Mill's speech in advertise-
    ment, III 95–6; sends letter from
    Gladstone on, to WSJ, I 198n2,
    202–3, III 84, 87n2; proposes
    second edition, 121
  commissions text book on logic (1866),
    III 139, 249–50; publishes *Primer of
    Political Economy*, III 240, 241; pub-
    lishes *Theory of Political Economy*, III
    240, IV 40, ed. 2 with Preface and
    appendix, V 52–3, 64–5; *Principles
    of Science*, ed. 2, IV 218n2; *Studies in
    Deductive Logic*, V 69, 94, 135; plans
    for *Investigations*, V 158–9, 201, with
    index, 175, published (1884), V
    159n1; *State in Relation to Labour*, V
    132, 143, 159; plans for *Principles of
    Economics*, V 135
  asked to publish works of Index Society,
    IV 297; WSJ proposes students'
    edition of *Wealth of Nations*, 218–19,
    V 81; translation of Cossa's *Guida*,
    V 59, 60, 106
  terms: half profits and no risk, III 139,
    241, 250, IV 238
  English Citizen Series, V 132n8, 137–8,
    178
  letters: from WSJ, III 124–5, 139, 160,
    240, 241, 249–50, IV 34, 218–19,
    297–8, V 52, 53, 64, 64–5, 68–9, 94,
    133–4, 135–6, 158–9, 175, 201; to

Macmillan, Alexander (*contd*)
WSJ, III 84; from Gladstone, I 203
also mentioned, V 65, 101n1, 102n2
Macmillan, Mrs Alexander (Caroline Brinley), V 101n1
Macmillan, Daniel, co-founder of Macmillans publishing house, III 84n1
Macmillan, Margaret, daughter of Alexander Macmillan: 'former lady student of the Cambridge Society for the Extension of University Teaching', VII 98, translates Cossa's *Guida*, V 53, 64, 69, 94, 101–2, VII 98, 101; on 'res fungibiles', V 102; marriage to Louis Dyer, V 101
letter to WSJ, V 101–2
Macmillan, Messrs, publishers, IV 94, 192, 110, 238, 242, 290; English Citizen Series, V 132, 137–8, 143, 178
Macmillan's Magazine, III 84n1; editors, David Masson, IV 173n4, George Grove, V 176
articles by WSJ: 'Mr Gladstone's New Financial Policy' (June 1866), III 101n2, VII 11–18; on Mill's logic, III 240; *Coal Question* announced in, VII 125
other articles and notices: 'Burnt Out' (1865), III 83; 'Of Boundaries in General' (W. K. Clifford, 1879), V 53n1; 'Co-operation in the Slate Quarries . . .' (Cairnes, 1865), III, 65, VI 39n12; 'County Government' (J. Taylor Kay, 1882), V 176; 'Lord Bacon as natural philosopher' (Justus von Liebig, 1865), III 78n4; Sidgwick's *Principles* advertised as *Theory of Political Economy*, V 133; III 65, VI 39n12; article by T. E. Jevons submitted to, III 160
Macquarie, Lachlan (1762–1824), Governor of New South Wales, I 137n1
Macquarie Arms, WSJ sleeps at, I 137n1, eats Christmas dinner at, 140–1
Macquarie plains, New South Wales, I 224–5, 226, 'flat, bare & hideous', 235; river, 235
Fort Macquarie, II 208
Madras
Herbert Jevons arrives from, I 76

Magnetic Observatory at Trivandrum, VII 92
periodic rainfall, V 51
also mentioned, II 205n4
Madsen, Christian Ludwig (1827–99), telegraph and telephone engineer: meets WSJ in Copenhagen, IV 206, 207, 244; reads *Principles of Science*, V 29
controversy with Westergaard on statistical analysis of telegraph trade, IV 243–8
'On the Law of International Telegraph Traffic', IV 243, V 27–9, abstract of paper, IV 245; 'law of distances', 246–8; paper included in 'List of Mathematico-Economic Books', V 27n2
letter from, V 27–9
magnetism
Faraday's Experiments on magnetic and diamagnetic force, I 81–2
magnetic perturbations and commercial crises, V 45, 103
magneto-electric machines, VII 31, 34
Tyndall's researches, II 250
also mentioned, VI 7
Magnus, Philip, fellow student of WSJ at University College, London, I 187n3
mail carts (coaches), *see* coaches
mail service
Admiralty contract with Black Ball and White Star Lines during Crimean War, II 133n1
to Australia and New Zealand, II 133n1; P. & O. steamship service, alternate months, 133n1; alternative overland route *via* Marseilles, 133n1
see also ships.
Maine, Sir Henry James Sumner (1822–88), jurist: supports proposed F.R.S. for Inglis Palgrave, V 163
Lectures in the Early History of Institutions (1875), VI 36
Maitland, New South Wales: excursion to, I 123–30, II 256n2; Northumberland Arms, I 127–8
Makins, Mr, II 392
Malden, Henry (1800–76), Professor of

Greek at University College, London, I 82, II 305n7; his extra Greek class, II 421, 422, 437

Malet, John Adam (d. 1879), Librarian at Trinity College, Dublin, IV 286

Malin, Eliza, *see* Hutton, Mrs John

Malin, Emily Sophia, *see* Roscoe, Mrs William Caldwell

Malin, the Misses, sisters of Emily Sophia, II 132, 135

Malin, William, of Derby, II 123n12

Mallet, Sir Louis (1823–9), permanent Under-Secretary of State for India, bimetallist: Indian delegate to International Monetary Conference (1881), V 140; correspondence with Fremantle on WSJ and bimetallism, V 187n4; on WSJ V188n4

Mallock, William Hurrell (1849–1923): 'Positivism on an Island' (*Contemporary Review*, 1878), IV 250

Malmesbury, Earl of, Secretary for Foreign Affairs in Derby Ministry, I 85

Malthus, Thomas Robert: Ricardian theory of rent anticipated by, IV 146; doctrine of underconsumption, IV 193n2; soundness as political economist, VI 3
Essay on Population: WSJ reads, I 27, VII 118, 119; lecture notes on, VI 54–60; his view too gloomy, 60; 5th edition, 57n9; *Principles of Political Economy*, suggested reading for students at University College, London, IV 143

Malvern Wells, holiday at, V 146–7

Man
WSJ's religion founded on, I 154n3, 155, 157, II 288, 312; his knowledge of society and, II 321–2, study of, to be his object, 335–6, 361–2; pessimistic view of (1858), II 334; proposed 'comprehensive work' on (1857), VII 119
Whately's view of Social instinct in man, I 158–9; Herschel on, II 308; evidence of early man, 330–1

management: as career for WSJ, II 39; earnings of, V 104n1

Manchester

abattoir, VI 36

bakers, struggle for improved conditions, III 132–3

banks: Bankers' Memorial on note issue, IV 107; County Bank, 110n1, 111; Heywood's Bank, 165n1; sale of cheques, 185; Salford Bank, IV 165nn1, 2; sovereign returns, III 160, VII 71–2; Union Bank, V 129n1

British Association meet at (1861), II 434–6, III 47; WSJ reports on, for *Manchester Examiner*, I 25, 35, II 434–5; his first paper presented to, 'On the Deficiency of Rain in an Elevated Rain-gauge', I 35–6, 187n1; telegraph exhibition, II 435

Carpenters' Hall, lecture on Coal given in (WSJ, 1867), VII 18

Chamber of Commerce, III 183; petition on Usury Laws (1831), IV 279; Conciliation Board established by, VI 78

children's playgrounds and other popular amusements, IV 286–7

Cobden, the immortal 'Manchester Manufacturer', III 131, V 41; his home in Quay Street, I 41

cooperative companies, VI 76; Cooperative Hall, III 183n1

cotton manufacture, VI 33; WSJ visits cotton mill, II 435

depression of 1842, VI 15–16; of 1879, V 25

Fenian activity, III 159

free trade, VII 27, 75; Free Trade Hall, IV 287

gas supplies, VI 133

Germans in, IV 110

general election of 1880, V 97; working-class support for Gladstone, III 136

'good society', III 9, 46

Ladies' Literary Society, IV 129n4

libraries: Chetham Library, III 9, 30; Free Public Library, III 30, V 195n1; Owens College library a benefit to Manchester, III 233, 234; Portico Library, IV 99

Literary and Philosophical Society: papers by WSJ: 'Remarks on the Australian Gold Fields (1859), I 187n1, 'On a Logical Abacus'

Manchester (contd)
  (1866), I 204n14, III 104, 'Re-
    marks on Mr Baxendell's Laws of
    atmospheric ozone', VII 126; Bal-
    four Stewart's paper on periodic
    rainfall, V 103; Presidents, II
    66n13, 305n3
machinery, VII 20
manufactories, visits to, II 435; WSJ's
    first-hand knowledge of, V 164;
    'Married Women in Factories'
    based on, V 161, 170–1; the
    metropolis of manufacturing dist-
    ricts, III 151
Mechanics Institution, II 322n2
Museum, IV 287; Churchill Collection
    of coins, IV 193n1
music: Hallé Concerts Society, III 70n1;
    orchestra, II 458n4, IV 189, V
    123n3, Richter becomes conductor
    (1897), V 134n2; Rubenstein's re-
    citals, IV 199
National Association for the Promotion
    of Social Science meet at (1866),
    III 127n1, 140
newspapers, IV 102, V 111; see also
    Manchester City News; Manchester
    Examiner; Manchester Guardian
Personal Rights Association, V 187n1
population, VII 21
public opinion, II 316n8; public spirit,
    III 151
Royal Institution, II 305n3
Shude Hill Market, VI 36
Technical School, IV 242n2
Telegraph Department, IV 172
trade: diversity, VII 22–3; early trade
    guilds, VI 69; trade disputes, III
    133n1
Trades Unionists' Political Association,
    lecture to (WSJ), III 161n2, 183;
    Trades Union Congress (1868), III
    132n1
Unitarians, Platt chapel, I 202; Cross
    Street chapel, II 118n15. See also
    Manchester New College
Volunteers, II 407, III 15
weather, II 347, III 9
Whitworth Art Gallery, I 47n3
Women's Suffrage Committee, IV
    129n4
WSJ and: his 'mission' in, III 135; views

on, III 6, 9, 10, 49, 151, IV 52; first
    lodgings at Birch Grove, III 48,
    daily walks, 158; 36 Parsonage
    road, with Harriet, I 47, III 182–3,
    185, his organ, I 79n3, IV 189;
    removal to London, IV 183, 184,
    regrets at leaving, 213. See also
    Owens College
Manchester Alliance, housepainters' un-
    ion, III 132n1
Manchester City News: letter of protest from
    W. Macdonald against Cobden
    lecture (October 1866), III 128,
    132–6, reply, 137–8, further letters,
    137n1, 150
Manchester College, York, I 183n3
Manchester Educational Aid Society, III
    63n3
Manchester Examiner and Times:
  WSJ and: is sent copies in Sydney, II
    413; reports British Association
    (1861), I 35, II 434–5; Coal Question
    announced in, VII 125; correspon-
    dence on Cobden lecture (October
    1866), I 208n3, III 128–32; review
    of Theory of Political Economy (15
    November 1871), IV 5, notice of
    ed. 2 (9 July 1879), V 67; report of
    paper to Statistical Society on 'Pro-
    gress of Mathematical Theory of
    Political Economy' (28 November
    1874), IV 82, 83, 84, 90
  other articles: Bastiat, 'What is seen and
    what is not seen' (1852), VII 46, 59;
    Mills's letter on Bimetallism, V
    138–9; Rylett's letters on Ireland,
    V 111
  editors, III 181n2, V 73n3
  also mentioned, III 70n1
Manchester Free School, VII 53
Manchester Geological Society, III 63n3
Manchester Grammar School, I 65n5;
    examined by Thorold Rogers, III
    67–8
Manchester Guardian
  WSJ and: marriage connections with
    Edward Taylor, founder of paper, I
    46n1, 47, IV 271n1; reviews of
    Cairnes, IV 60; review of Theory of
    Political Economy (22 November
    1871), IV 5; letter to (March
    1876), VII 127; 'The Prospects of

the Telegraph Department' (22 March 1876), IV 171–2, VII 127; 'Married Women in Factories' (10 January 1882), letters on, V 163–7, 168; obituary of WSJ (A. W. Ward), I 50

review of Cairnes (W. H. Brewer, 1874), IV 60; report of Helm's address, V 83

other contributors, V 165n3, 195n1

Manchester and Liverpool Railway, II 29n1

Manchester Martyrs, III 159n6

Manchester New College, Unitarian college for arts and theology, II 392n18, 421n4; transferred to London (1853), II 421–2

Manchester Omnibus Company, VI 133

Manchester & Salford Bank, V 25, 130n4

Manchester & Salford District Provident Society, III 256–7

Manchester & Salford Sanitary Association, V 168

Manchester Statistical Society
  WSJ and: President, III 244n2, 256n1, Inaugural Address (November 1869), III 256n1; 'On the International Monetary Convention' (13 May 1868), III 186, VII 65–75; 'The Progress of the Mathematical Theory of Political Economy' (11 November 1874), IV 70, 74, 76, 81, 94; reported in *Manchester Examiner*, 82, 83, 91n2, paper printed, 102, reprinted, VII 75–85
  other papers: E. Herford, V 167n9; E. Langley, IV 186n2, V 26n1; W. Langton, IV 232n1; John Mills, VI 132, VII 132; J. C. Ollerenshaw, III 251n3, V 45; G. H. Pownall, V 25nn1, 2; L. Robbins, 'The Place of Jevons in the History of Economic Thought', *Centenary Address* (27 February 1936), I 188n1; Thorold Rogers, III 47
  other Presidents, IV 110n1, 242n2, V 25nn1, 2, 83; John Mills (1871), III 140n1, 244; Secretaries, IV 193–4, V 129; members, IV 286n1
  also mentioned, IV 45

Manchester Theatre Company, performance of *Midsummer Night's Dream* in Edinburgh, III 126

Manchester University, *see* Owens College; Victoria University

Manchester Women's Suffrage Committee IV 129n4

'Manchesterismus' in Germany, IV 85n9

Mangoldt, Hans Emil von (1824–68), Professor of Political Economy at Freiburg: mathematical theory of exchange, V 104

Mann, Major-General James Robert (1823–1915), Director of Public Works, Jamaica, V 71

Manning, classmate of WSJ at University College, London, I 54

Manning, Captain, of the *Oliver Lang*: his sailing methods, I 103, II 82, 97, 113; quarrelsome habits, I 105, II 85, 112; disliked by all on board, I 106–7; marries an emigrating milliner, II 112; unable to get another ship, 203, obliged to take a mate's job, 231; also mentioned, II 80, 83

Mansel, Henry Longueville (1820–71), his version of *Artis Logicae Rudimenta*, II 433

Mansel, Spencer (1838–75), Vicar of Trumpington: examiner for Moral Sciences Tripos with WSJ (1875), IV 147; death, 156

Mantellier, Philippe (1811–84), French judge and antiquary: on comparative prices of silver and commodities, III 67

manufactories
  capital invested in, II 281
  in Liverpool, II 40–1; manufacturing chemists, I 61, 89, II 37, 39, 40, 41, 43, WSJ's proposed career as, I 89, 117, II 36, 37–8; soap, I 89, II 40, 41, visit to soap works, I 92–3, to soda works, II 41–3
  in London, I 71, 90–1; visit to Lucifer match manufactory, 89
  Manchester, visit to (1861), II 435

manufactures: and agriculture, III 255, VI 121; duties on, VI 136n6; increased orders (1879), V 84; start of manufacturing system, VI 70, improvements after 1843, 123; limit to demand for, IV 237

manufactures (*contd*)
  manufacturers, VI 12–13, 33, 105, VII 16
manures, VI 57; from coal, VII 31
Maori wars, II 420n3; skill of the Maories, III 41
Marburg, Kolbe's laboratory, II 72
Marcet, Mrs Jane I 6
marginal revolution: place of WSJ in, VI vii, x; marginal utility theory, I 26, 34. *See also* last portion added; *and under* ratios
markets
  Britain's lead in world markets dependent on coal, VII 27
  definition, in *Theory of Political Economy*, VII 143
  higgling of the market, VI 82
  market reports, VI 84
  market value, VI 83–4, VII 148
  specialised markets, VI 36
Marine National Bank *vs* National City Bank (New York, 1875), IV 155
Married Women in Factories, *see under* factories; article on, *see under* Jevons, W. S., Works
Marriot, G. R. L., VII 105
Marseillaise, *see La Marseillaise*
Marseilles
  Overland Mail from Sydney *via*, II 132, 133
  Willy Jevons studies ship-building at, II 61, 214
  also mentioned, II 65, 181n2
Marshall, Alfred (1842–1924)
  studies mathematics at Cambridge (1862), I 37; assistant to Fawcett in Economics, I 37; Cambridge lectures (1869), V 78, 80; considered as substitute lecturer for WSJ at University College (1875), IV 134; Principal and Professor of Political Economy at University College, Bristol (1877), IV 128n1, testimonial from WSJ, 204–5, resigns on grounds of health (1881), V 170; resumes Professorship after year in Italy, V 170n3; marriage to Mary Paley, IV 148n6; tours U.S.A. (1875), IV 134n1; testimonial for Foxwell, IV 145, 239
  first-hand study of poverty, I 17; state-

ment on final utility, III 248n2; graphical methods, IV 96, V 23–4, proposed book on curves, 66; notions of quantitative theory of political economy, IV 101, V 24n2, 66, use of geometric system, 24n3, mathematical treatment, 78
  and WSJ: his Tripos pupils examined by WSJ, IV 96, V 23; failure to meet in Cambridge (1874), IV 96; evening party in his rooms (1875), 148; 'substantive differences' between WSJ and, on Mill, IV 100, and on Macleod, V 77; question of priority in mathematical treatment of economics, V 78, 80; included in mathematico-economic bibliography, 63n3; reviews *Theory of Political Economy* (*Academy*, April 1872), IV 5, 62, VII 141–6; is sent copy of 'Progress of Mathematical Theory of Political Economy' (1874), VII 76; on WSJ as an economist, V 66, VII 141–6
  Principles of Economics, III 248n2; *Pure Theory of Foreign Trade* and *Pure Theory of (Domestic) Value*, IV 205, V 23–4, 63, 66; *The Economics of Industry* (with Mary Paley), V 66, 80, VII 102, reviewed in *Athenaeum* (8 November 1879), V 80, Foxwell's lectures on, V 78
  letters to, IV 95–6, 204–5, V 63; letters from, IV 100, V 66
Marshall, Mrs Alfred (Mary Paley, 1850–1944): WSJ meets in Cambridge, IV 148; lectures to women students, IV 148n6, V 63; marriage to Alfred Marshall (1877), IV 148n6; goes with him to Italy, V 170
Economics of Industry (with Alfred Marshall), V 66, 78, 80, VII 102; recommended by WSJ for Bankers' Institute Examinations, V 80
Marshall, John, Professor of History at Yorkshire College; co-author of *Coal: its History and Uses* (1878), IV 234n1; correspondence on the coal question, 234–7
Martha, Jevons family servant, II 16; given notice by Lucy, 36

Martiis, Salvatore Cognetti de (1844–1901), Professor of Political Economy at Mantua. IV 84

Martin, John Biddulph (1841–97), Hon. Secretary of Royal Statistical Society: paper on Gold Coinage read before Institute of Bankers (April 1882), V 181

Martindale, Captain, report on New South Wales railway system, VII 9–11

Martineau, Ellen (Mrs Alfred Higginson), I 60n3

Martineau, Harriet (1802–76), I 3n1, 60n3, 178, II 421n4; *Illustrations of Political Economy* (1834), II 292, VII 51

Martineau, James (1805–1900), Unitarian minister, brother of Harriet Martineau, I 11, 60n3, II 134n7, 292n12; his home in Liverpool, II 106n1; Professor of Philosophy and Political Economy at Manchester New College (London), II 421n4; WSJ attends his lectures on mental philosophy, 421, 424; testimonial for WSJ, III 106, 111; on definitions, VI 5
  Hymns (1840) and *Holy Songs* (1842), II 14n3

Martineau, Mrs James (Helen Higginson), I 60n3, II 13

Martineau, Russell (1831–98), son of James Martineau, II 392n18; Lucy Jevons breaks off engagement to, I 11, II 392

Martineau, Mrs Russell (Frances Bailey), II 392n18

Martineau family, I 3n1, II 392

Massachusetts, II 151

Masson, David (1822–1907), Professor of English Literature at University College, London, II 443; Professor of Rhetoric at Edinburgh, III 106; testimonial for WSJ, 106, 115; address on education in Scotland, IV 173

Master of the Horse, I 71

Master of the Mint, Sydney, II 114

Masterman Ready, II 332–3

Masters of the Royal Mint, *see* Royal Mint

Match Tax, proposal for, defeated. VI 137n7
  The Match Tax: a Problem in Finance WSJ, (1871), 138n8

matches, *see* Lucifer matches

mathematical theory of political economy
  early statements of WSJ: (1858), II 321, has taken to the 'Mathematics of Society', 335, (1860), II 410, VII 120, (1861), II 422; stimulated by Lardner's *Railway Economy*, I 27; first publicly stated in paper to British Association (Cambridge, 1862), II 452, III 104, 166, VII 77, 124
  mathematical approach making progress, V 22; in England, IV 103, V 144, in Cambridge, IV 101, 103; in Germany, IV 266, V 144–5; in Italy, IV 84, 95; in Switzerland, IV 85; distinguished from graphical method by d'Aulnis, IV 282–3, 284; algebraic formula as criterion of, IV 278; supported by George Darwin, IV 81, 99, 102
  mathematical economists pre-dating WSJ, IV 3, 5, 8–9, 46–7, 103–4, V 24, 67n1, 129; Gossen, IV 267–9, 272, 278, 279–80, 282; Macleod, II 456; Mangoldt, V 104; Simon Newcomb, IV 141n4; Von Thünen, IV 282, V 60; Walras's theory, IV 40–1, 180–1, VII 76–7, coincident with WSJ, IV 46–7; bibliography of, added to third edition of *Theory of Political Economy*, IV 242, 270, 282
  examination questions on, V 152, VII 134
  'Progress of the Mathematical Theory of Political Economy' (WSJ, November, 1874), VII 75–85
  see also economics; political economy; statistics; *and under* Jevons, William Stanley

mathematics
  WSJ and: studies under De Morgan at University College (1851–3), I 15, 16, 34, 62, 65, 67, 70, spends most of his time on, 67, 69; examinations (1852), I 54, II 33, (1853), I 55, 96; plans to continue study while in

mathematics (*contd*)
    business, I 78, 79; in Sydney feels
    lack of 'solid foundations' in math-
    ematics, I 109, II 291, a 'severe
    exercise of the mind', I 110; returns
    to De Morgan for B.A. (1859–61), I
    32, 33, 34, II 291, 403, 406, 415,
    421, III 103, 108, for M.A., II 410,
    422
  studies theory of equations, I 82, 87,
    II 406; algebraic geometry, I 90, II
    291; conic sections, I 91; differen-
    tial calculus, I 34, 94, II 403; keeps
    and uses Roscoe Jevons's books on,
    I 194–5; tutors in Mathematics at
    Owens College, III 29
  in *Theory of Political Economy* (1871),
    IV 65, 87, 101, 198, VI 17; printing
    arrangements for symbols, III 241,
    IV 238; criticised by Cairnes, IV
    81, 114, VII 83–4, 148, 151–2, by
    Cliffe Leslie, VII 159–61; Marshall
    on, VII 142, 144–6; Westergaard
    on, IV 255–8; *Saturday Review* on,
    VII 152–7; approved by d'Aulnis,
    IV 81–3, by Walras, IV 65
  as base for chemistry, II 66; Brodie's
    chemical calculus, III 155–6; ap-
    plied to international trade and
    telegrams, IV 243–4; in the logical
    systems of Boole and WSJ, III 13,
    110; for physics, V 167n2
Maupertuis, Pierre Louis Moreau de
    (1698–1759), mathematician and
    philosopher: 'Maupertuis on the
    Survival of the Fittest' (WSJ,
    Nature, March 1873), IV 4, 15; his
    principle of least-action, 15
Maury, Matthew Fontaine (1806–73),
    American naval officer and Pro-
    fessor of Physics: his wind charts,
    VI 23n10
Max-Müller, Friedrich (1823–1900),
    philologist, Professor of Compara-
    tive Philology at Oxford, IV 285;
    exchange of views with George
    Darwin in *Contemporary Review*
    (1876), IV 87
May, Sir Thomas Erskine: *The Consti-
    tutional History of England* (1861–3),
    IV 213
Mayhew, Henry, I 16; *Great World of*
    London, WSJ reads, 28, VII 116;
    London Labour and London Poor
    (1851), WSJ buys a dozen odd
    numbers, I 80–1
Maynard, Constance Louisa (1849–1935),
    first Girton student to take Moral
    Sciences Tripos at Cambridge,
    (1875), IV 149
Mayor, Joseph Bickersteth, Professor of
    Moral Philosophy at King's Col-
    lege, London, V 99n2
measurement: of properties in physics and
    in utility economics, III 246–7,
    253–4
measuring instruments: article on, in *Dic-
    tionary of Chemistry*, I 35; corn meter,
    VI 34
  see also barometer; goniometer; sym-
    piesometer; thermometers
meat, degrees of utility, VI 85, 86–8
mechanics, VII 45, 59; principle of forced
    vibrations, VII 92–3, 97; mechan-
    ical manufacturers, VI 121; use in
    iron manufacture, II 38
Mechanics' Institute, Hyde, Cheshire,
    WSJ lectures at, VII 54–65
  other Mechanics Institutes, *see under*
    Liverpool; Manchester
medicine:
  diseases as check to population, VI 58,
    59; cancer, IV 33n1; diphtheria, II
    462n6; dropsy, II 176; gall stones,
    II 425; influenza, II 444; mumps,
    II 143, 145; smallpox, VI 59; yel-
    low fever, I 80, II 390, 399. *See also*
    cholera; insanity
  physic: Lucy's need of, II 45; wine as, II
    176, III 195
  as a profession, VI 66; Arthur
    Ransome's 'Health Lectures', V
    168n1
  sick benefit, VI 73; sickness relief from
    Provident Society, III 256–7
Mees, Willem Cornelius (1813–85), Dutch
    banker and economist: approves
    Theory of Political Economy, IV 58,
    76, 83
  Leading Chapters of Political Economy
    (1866), IV 58n6, 73
  also mentioned, IV 74
Melbourne
  WSJ and: goes ashore at, I 19, II 100,

115–16; sea passage to Sydney from, II 105–6; overland journey from Sydney to, I 21, II 279n1, 366–72, 381; lodgings at Emerald Hill, II 368, 369, 370; refuses partnership in, I 33, II 357–8; sails from to Callao, II 372, 385, 394

appearance of town, I 109, II 100, 113, 369; going the same road as Americans, II 206

Botanical Gardens, II 370

Chinamen in, II 142

cricket match against Sydney, II 262

gold and cotton shipped from, II 60, 146; gold nuggets on display, 127; Sydney sovereigns refused, 206; send no gold to Sydney, 260, 279

Herbert Jevons lands in, II 447, 452

Lola Montez's adventures in, II 182–3

Melbourne cars, II 385; Mail, II 342

Mint opened (1869), I 21, II 279n11; assaying, 369

Observatory, II 372–3

Philharmonic Society, performance of *Israel in Egypt*, II 369; joint festival with Sydney Philharmonic Society, II 328

steamboat service to Sydney, II 267, 366

Theatre Royal, II 257n7

University, foundation of, II 75

Melbourne Argus, *Serious Fall* noticed in, III 38

Melbourne Directory (1859), donated by WSJ to British Museum Library, II 449, 450n2

Melloni, Macedonio (1798–1854), Italian physicist, his thermo-battery, II 193–4

Mellor, Joseph, Liverpool merchant, V 164n2

Mellor, Mr, headmaster of Manchester Free School, VII 53

Mellor, Ursula, *see* Bright, Mrs Jacob

Melvill, Thomas, discoveries in spectrum analysis, VII 124

Menai Bridge, II 38

Menander, VI 101

Mendelssohn, Felix, II 313, 314, 321, 328, 338; 'Mendelssohn night' at Liverpool, 328

Elijah, II 224, 257, 313, 314, 329; *Hymn of Praise*, 296; *Psalm 95*, 338; *St*

Paul 313, 314, 329; songs, 289; *Songs without Words*, 338

mental philosophy: included in WSJ's M.A. studies, II 406, 437; gold medal for, III 103; application for Professorship of, at Owens College, III 103; testimonial to WSJ as teacher of, 118–19; his syllabus, IV 22–3

mental sciences, III 103; pleasure of pursuing, II 319

mercantile theory, V 48, VI 112

merchants, V 19, VI 113, VII 16, 41; bills of exchange and Exchequer Bills for, VI 105, 114, 118; bank loans for, 129; desire for paper money, VII 45; not interested in international currency, 73, 75

economic statistics contained in mercantile houses, VII 145; their Political Economy, VII 59

merchandise as money, VI 96

corn merchants, VI 34; merchants' clerks, VI 77; wholesale merchants, VI 33

Merioneth, copper mines with gold traces, II 88n3, 135n11

Merriman, Mansfield, (1848–1925), *Elements of the Method of Least Squares* (1877), VII 87

Mersey

explosion of the *Lotty Sleigh*, III 49

shipbuilding, VII 21, Thomas Jevons's iron boat launched on, I 3

also mentioned, II 110

Messedaglia, Angelo (1820–1901), Professor of Political Economy and Statistics at Padua: copy of *Theory of Political Economy* for, IV 68, 84

metals

coal for, VII 19, 30

demand for, VI 126

distribution of metal trades, VII 22–3

prices, and commercial fluctuations, VI 119, 120, 122–3, 124, 131

see also individual metals

metaphysics, II 411, 422; WSJ as teacher of, III 99

meteorology

WSJ and: keeps 'meteorological journal' on board the *Oliver Lang*, I 114; sets up maximum and minimum ther-

meteorology (contd)
      mometers at Church Hill Cottage,
      114; twice daily observations, I 22,
      115, II 160–1, 172, 195, 196, 228,
      245, 269; becomes unpaid Mete-
      orological Observer for Empire, I
      23, II 244; weekly reports, I 23, II
      198, 239–40, 244, 269, 303, VII 3,
      123; monthly reports for Sydney
      Magazine of Science and Art, I 23, II
      198n6, 245n11, 297, 298, VII 124;
      involved in meteorology 'to an aw-
      ful extent', II 291–2; keeps mete-
      orological log on board the Chry-
      solite, II 374, 386, 394; likely post at
      Kew for, 392, 402; meteorology
      recommended to Herbert in Aus-
      tralia, II 404
   writings on: paper on a Sun-gauge
      (1857), I 23, II 161n3, 297, VII
      123; 'Meteorology and the Herald'
      (Empire, 25 February 1857), II
      268–9; 'Meteorological Obser-
      vations in Australia' (1859), II
      245n11', VII 124; 'Some Data con-
      cerning the Climate of Australia
      and New Zealand' (1859), I 23–4,
      II 240n4, 332, 340n3, 363, IV
      203n1; 'On the deficiency of Rain in
      an elevated Rain-gauge' (1861), I
      35–6, VII 124; articles on measur-
      ing instruments in Dictionary of
      Chemistry (1861), I 35; 'Clerk of the
      Weather Office' (Spectator, 1862), I
      38, II 452, VII 124
   H. E. Roscoe's meteorological instru-
      ment for research on light, I 169;
      Melloni's Thermo-battery, II 193–
      4; Piazzi Smyth on Pouillet's
      measurements of solar radiation,
      IV 296–7
   periodicity first observed in meteor-
      ology, I 24; solar and terrestrial
      radiation measurement, II 161,
      193, 297n8, glass sphere for measur-
      ing solar heat, 323–4; graphic
      register of wind and sky, with
      sketch (WSJ), II 245–6; investment
      in apparatus, II 244
   see also barometers; clouds; periodicity;
      rainfall; sun-spots; weather
metrical system, III 186, 232, VII 69;

      recommended for weights and
      measures by British Association
      (1870), III 238
   see also decimal coinage
Metropolitan Association for Improving
      the Dwellings of the Industrious
      Classes, I 68n4; their model lodging
      houses, 68
Mexican Company, VI 119
Mexico, annual gold product, IV 7
Meyerbeer, Giacomo (1791–1864), Les
      Huguenots, II 69, 224
Miall, Louis Compton, co-author of
      Coal: its History and Uses (1878), IV
      234nl
Michaelis, Otto (1826–90), German econ-
      omist and finance administrator,
      III 197
Middle Harbour, Sydney, expedition to,
      II 342, 352–5; Middle Head, 347,
      353; sketch, 347
middlemen, VI 34; examination question
      on, V 152
Middlesbrough: partnership scheme at
      Newport Rolling Mills, III 151;
      strike of ironworkers, III 142
Middleton, Sir Hugh (1560?–1631), con-
      struction of New River Canal, VI
      43
migration
   as alternative to unemployment, VI 64
   immigrants in Liverpool, I 16
   see also emigration
'mil', proposed unit for decimal coinage
      system, II 156, III 186n1
Milburn, William, Oriental Com-
      merce . . (1813), V 54
Militia Bill (1852), I 85, 86
Mill, James: definition of political econ-
      omy, VI 5, VII 55; doctrine that
      production creates demand, IV
      120, 122
   Elements of Political Economy, ed. 3 (1826),
      VII 55, 102
Mill, John Stuart (1806–73)
   as M.P. for Westminster: speech on Malt
      Duties (7 April 1866), VII 12, 17,
      urges reduction of National Debt,
      not of taxation, I 44, 45, III 94n1,
      draws attention to Coal Question, I
      44, 45, 205, III 93, 94–5, 95–6, 99,
      103, VII 13, his speech reproduced

in *The Times*, I 45; extract from speech, used as testimonial by WSJ, III 119

frightens Opposition on Coal Panic, III 103; advocates profit-sharing schemes, III 138, 143, 153, VI 75–6, 77; on sources of revenue from taxation, VII 8

political economy: three propositions on capital, VI 38–9, 62; on fixed and circulating capital, VI 42; never had any idea what capital was, IV 101; George Darwin's article on, IV 35; Musgrave's views on, IV 126, 127n6

'Demand for commodities not demand for labour', VI ix, 48, lecture notes on, 48–54

theory of international exchanges, VII 152, 156; regulation of price, VI 83; productive consumption, IV 122; rate of interest, IV 27; rent, I 26, V 109n3; value, V 61, VI 80, 82, VII 78, 141; wages fund, V 77, VI 61–2, VII 77; definition of wealth, VII 56

Principles of Political Economy: WSJ reads (1857), I 27, VII 116, 117, 118, 119; 'the great modern authority on political economy', VII 7; recommended reading for working men (1869), VII 59; forced on students in London University (1872), III 245–6; used by WSJ at Owens College, IV 23, VI ix, 3, in lecture notes, VI 3–4, 9, 12, 18, 21–2, 24, 26, 31, 38–9, 42, 43, 48–54, 61, 62, 64, 68, 77, 80, 82, 83, 84, 133, VII 77; progress in economics retarded by, VII 77; as much error as truth in, IV 146; in University College syllabus (1875), IV 143; set for Bankers' Institute Examinations (1879), V 80; necessary reading for the judicious student, VII 99; examination questions on, V 109, 152, VII 137

criticised by WSJ in 'Progress of the Mathematical Theory of Political Economy', VII 77, for his crude treatment of quantitative relations, 78; issue taken up in *Examiner*, IV

92, 94, 104–5; his crotchets, IV 134

Adamson on 'the mincemeat man', V 61, 62; Cazenove on, IV 119–22; d'Aulnis studies, IV 90, 91; Fawcett's *Manual* an abstract of Mill, I 192n2, III 240, 241, V 78, VII 60, 'Mill and water', VI 3–4; Marshall on, IV 100, 143, 144; Musgrave's article, 'Capital: Mr Mill's Fundamental Propositions' (1874), IV 126, 127n6, 167; Walras on, V 95; his reputation waning in Oxford, IV 286

inclusion in Bibliography of Mathematical Economists questioned by Conrad, IV 278, by Walras, 260; a graphical, not mathematical writer (d'Aulnis), IV 282

Logic: WSJ reads *Logic* (1857), I 30, VII 119; 'his great treatise' (1866), VII 44; proposed articles on, for *Macmillan's Magazine* (1871), III 240; letter to *Hull Criterion* on Mill's Logic (4 July 1874), VII 127; 'John Stuart Mill's Philosophy Tested' (*Contemporary Review*, 1877–9), I 48n2, IV 167, 191–2, 221, 223, 250, V 24, 74, 75n1, 80; notes for book on Mill's philosophy, I 51, V 89; his system unsound, IV 116, 156, a maze of contradictions, 101–2, 167, V 24; Walras on, IV 196

personal: residence in South of France, II 446; his sisters, 445; panegyric on his wife, IV 166; testimonial for WSJ, III 120; member of Political Economy Club, IV 134; his straightforward and zealous character, IV 167

Essay on Liberty, III 132, VII 42, French translation, IV 261; *Essays on some Unsettled Questions of Political Economy* (1844), VII 104; *Examination of Sir William Hamilton's Philosophy* (1865), I 205; People's Edition of his works, VII 51, 102

letter to, III 94–5

also mentioned, I 10, II 360, IV 73, VI 133n1

Miller, Arthur William Kaye (1849–1914), printing expert: consulted

Miller, Arthur William Kaye (*contd*)
on typography of Cantillon's *Essai*,
V 122

Miller, Francis Boyer, brother of William
Allen Miller, II 194; assayer with
WSJ at Sydney Mint, I 19, 31, 56,
II 49, 108–9, VII 115; meets WSJ
off the boat, I 109n1, II 115; arrangements over salary, II 116,
148, 149, 173, attends hearing on,
in Legislative Assembly, 260; shares
his cottage with WSJ, I 21, 22,
111n4, 120, II 162, 166; his dog,
182; at loggerheads with his landlord, 197; a new house in Double
Bay, 248, 261–2; sells apparatus
and takes pupils, 249; at the theatre, 279; too independent for Captain Ward, 344; refuses partnership
in Melbourne, 357; welcomes Herbert Jevons, 452, 459, gets him a
job, 448n2, III 4; is sent copy of
Diagrams, II 459, and of *Serious Fall*,
III 16; fishing with WSJ, III 31;
also mentioned, II 207, 217, 218,
295, III 38
letters to, II 385–8, 393–402

Miller, Mrs Francis Boyer, II 149; WSJ
shares her home in Sydney, I 21,
22, 31, 111n4, II 162; her dogs,
Flask, Billy and Bobby, II 182; a
bigot against Catholics, 277, 295; at
the theatre, 279; her brothers, 340,
404; pleased with Australia, 402;
welcomes Herbert Jevons, 452

Miller, William (1809–66), Chief Cashier,
Bank of England: investigations
into 'Quantity of gold coin in use',
III 161–2, 163, 179

Miller, William Allen (1817–70), brother
of F. B. Miller, II 194
Professor of Chemistry at King's College, London, I 19, II 49n3, 50;
takes chair in Chemical Section of
British Association meeting (1854),
II 102; at British Association meeting (1855), II 191; applies for London University Examinership, 229;
WSJ meets at King's College
(1859), 402
Non-Resident Assayer to the Royal
Mint, I 19, appointed by Herschel

in 1851, II 133n3, 218, 222–3, 224;
a 'blow-up' over gold assays, II 49;
WSJ's probationary course in his
assay office, 51–2; endorses
Graham's testimonial for WSJ, 55;
his assay methods, 345

Millington, William, & Co., iron manufacturers: business letter to Messrs
Jevons & Co., iron merchants, III
230

Mills, John (1821–96), banker: 'The Bank
Charter Act and the late Panic',
paper read to National Association
for the Promotion of Social Science
(1866), III 140–1, IV 12, 13; succeeds WSJ as President of Manchester Statistical Society (1871),
III 244, IV 203, invites WSJ to
silver debate, V 26; his retreat at
Bowdon, IV 189n4; 'On Credit
Cycles and the Origin of Commercial Panics' (1867), IV 228,
229, VI 132, VII 126; decides not
to join Royal Statistical Society, V
89; article on Postal Notes submitted to, for *Contemporary Review*,
V 101; letter on Bimetallism in
Manchester Examiner, V 138–9
letters to, III 140–1, IV 29, 188–9, 199,
202–3, 228, 229, 231–2, 240–1, 244,
273–4, 281, V 26–7, 89, 89–90, 101,
106–7, 107–8, 138–9

Mills, Mrs John, IV 189n4; note on WSJ's
change of view on bimetallism, V
138n1

Milman, Sir Henry Hart (1791–1868),
Dean of St Paul's, I 82

Milton, John: Letters and Papers of State
from his personal collections, V
128; *Paradise Lost*, II 329, VII 97;
sonnet on his blindness, I 204

Mind: first number (1876), articles by
Mark Pattison and John Venn, IV
156; 'Cram' (WSJ, 1877), 212;
Adamson's critical notice of
Schröder (1878), 231; editor,
G. C. Robertson, 239n3

mineralogy, WSJ's plans to study, I 62, 78,
II 53

minerals:
in Australia, II 282, 350–2; exhibited in
London, II 50

in British Museum, I 80, 83, 84, II 63

in Jardin des Plantes, II 63

rail freight on, VII 29

Welsh minerals, II 93, III 192

WSJ's collection, I 60, 61, 62, 67; specimens from Fishlocke's, New South Wales, I 175

Mineral Statistics, Committee E of Royal Commission on Coal, III 154

mining
in colonial economy, II 282
examination question on, VII 131
investment in, VI 44
in Mill's categories of labour, VI 21
Mining Acts, V 138n3
mining school, proposal for, III 150
steam engine for draining, VII 30
WSJ, proposed career as mining engineer, VII 38 9
see also under coal; gold; iron; silver

Mining Journal: Thomas Jevons's extracts from, II 89, 92n3, 94n4, 135, 140, 146; his contribution to, 91

Mining Records Office, IV 127n3, VII 25, 29

Minnesota: Herbert Jevons emigrates to, I 10, II 364; his log hut, 384, 400, plot of land, 404, 409, meatless diet, 405; visited by WSJ, 382, 383; Herbert leaves, I 189, II 455
railway, II 404; statistical report on the 'North Star State', 418–19; population growth, 430; not a cheering prospect ahead, 413, 431; Red Indians on the war path, 455
also mentioned, II 427

Minnetonka Lake, II 384, 400, 411

mint, *see* Paris Mint; Royal Mint; Sydney Mint; *and under* Melbourne; Philadelphia

Miolan, Marie Caroline Felix (Mme Carvalho), French operatic soprano, II 69

Mississippi
coalfields, VII 27
free navigation for Red Indians, II 455
goods traffic, II 419, 428
WSJ travels up, II 364, 400

Mississippi Bubble (1717), VI 116, 117

Mitchell, Sir Thomas (1792–1855), Surveyor-General of New South

Wales: map of Illawarra District, I 159n1, 160; exploring expeditions, 235

Journal of an Expedition into the interior of tropical Australia . . . (1848), I 235n3, II 332n2

Mivart, St George: 'Herbert Spencer' (*Quarterly Review*, 1873), IV 29

Moffat, Robert Scott, *The Economy of Consumption . .* (1878), Macmillans advised by WSJ not to publish, IV 193

molecular philosophy: WSJ's early interest in, I 14, 101, 114; discussed in lecture on 'Production', VI 24

Momerie, Alfred William, Professor of Logic and Metaphysics at King's College, London, V 99n2

money
and capital, VI 37–8; as circulating capital, 40, 42; gold money as fixed capital, 45
as a commodity, IV 126, VI 94, 99; purchase of, for foreign trade, 109–10
in depressions, VI 62; cheap and dear money, IV 211
and effective demand, VI 83
examination questions on, VII 133
as medium of exchange, VI 94
as measure of value, III 203, VI 94–5, a store of value, 95–6; changes in value, III 47
monetary unification, VII 67; *see also* International Monetary Convention
Musgrave's views on, accepted by WSJ, IV 126
notes on (Owens College lectures), VI 94–103, 133; in mercantile theory, 112
price of, in terms of goods, III 67; purchasing power (1680–1876), IV 168, 169–71

money: of account, II 200; circular notes, III 182; metallic, VI 99–103, mono-metallic, 99, 100, 103; representative, III 203, VI 96, 100; token, IV 126, 298–9; universal, gold and silver as, VI 96
see also coinage; currency; gold; paper money; silver

money market
  and banks, III 163, IV 77, 209, 211, VI
    126, VII 16; governed by bank
    rate, IV 252
  fluctuations in, IV 54; in 1866, III 142,
    149; in 1878, IV 273-4; sudden
    easing in 1882, V 178; disastrous
    effects of bubble companies, VI
    116; pressure on, from Budgets, 137
  London market, IV 220
money orders, III 179; proposed changes,
    IV 216-17
Mongredien, Augustus, *Free Trade and
    English Commerce, Pleas for Protection
    Examined*, VII 107
Monkwearmouth colliery, WSJ goes
    down, III 126-7
Monografia statistica della Città di Roma . . . ,
    IV 299, V 198
monopolies
  of the aristocracy, III 130, 136
  examination questions on, VII 132-3
  gas supplies, VI 133
  goods with monopoly value, VI 83
  of guilds, VI 70; trades societies and
    joint-stock companies, III 34
  Post Office, VII 57; telegraphs, V 93n2;
    controversy over telephones, V 93
  uniform upset-price of Government land
    in New South Wales, II 284, 287,
    VII 4
  in WSJ's theory of exchange, VII 156-7
Monro, C. J., IV 15
Montez, Lola (Marie Dolores Rosanna
    Gilbert, 1818-61), 'Spanish' dan-
    cer in Sydney, II 182-3
Monthly Notes of the Library Association:
    'List of Selected Books in Political
    Economy', compiled by WSJ
    (1882), VII 101-7
Monthly Repository, Unitarian periodical, II
    445n2
Monthly Review: review of Philip Cantillon's
    The Analysis of Trade (1759), V 122
Montijo, Eugenia de, Countess of Téba:
    marriage to Napoleon III, I 87;
    appears on the balcony in the Tuil-
    eries, II 69
Montreal, Great Victoria Tubular Bridge,
    WSJ walks into, II 384n1, 391, 401
Moormeister, Eduard (1845-94), Director
    of Realprogymnasium at Altkirch:

on the teaching of political econ-
    omy in German and English
    schools, V 15-16, 29-30; trans-
    lation of Cossa's *Guida*, VII 101
  letters from, V 14-16, 29-30
moral philosophy
  definitions, VI 8, VII 55
  WSJ and: discussions with Harry Ros-
    coe, I 66; reads for B.A., II 415,
    422, for M.A., 437-8; gold medal
    for, III 103, 113; takes evening
    classes in, at Owens College, III
    104; as teacher of, III 99, 104, 118-
    19, examination paper in, 94; ap-
    pointed Professor of Logic, Moral
    Philosophy and Political Economy
    at Owens College (1865), I 198n2,
    III 103, 109, 115, 118, 122
morals
  and nature, I 166
  and political economy, VII 159; moral
    effect of taxation, VI 134
  and religion, II 226; Christ a genius of
    morals, I 155; eternal nature of
    moral truths, II 225
  not antagonistic to science, I 203
  the 'selfish' theory of, I 132-4
  WSJ a 'dependent Moralist', I 66
moral sciences, VI 7
Moran, Andrew, Illawarra cobbler, his
    wife and children: hospitality to
    WSJ, I 172-3, 175, 178n1; sketch of
    their log cottage, 173
Moran, brother of Andrew, I 175; WSJ
    shares his bed, 173
Moreton, Lancashire, botanical expe-
    dition to, I 57
Moreton Bay, Australia, gold-bearing
    rocks, II 351
Morgan, Dr John Edward (1829-92), Pro-
    fessor of Medicine at Owens Col-
    lege, WSJ's medical adviser, IV 20,
    21, V 99; tells WSJ he can now
    insure his life, IV 106
Morley, Henry (1822-94), Professor of
    English Language and Literature
    at University College, London,
    editor of the *Examiner*, V 73
Morley, John (1838-1923), statesman and
    writer, editor of *Fortnightly Review*,
    IV 273; defeated as Liberal can-
    didate for Westminster (1880), V

79; as editor of *Pall Mall Gazette*, V
111n2

Morning Chronicle, II 251

Morpeth, New South Wales, I 123n3;
expedition to, 124, 125-6, 128

Morrison, Robert (1782-1834), Protestant
missionary in China: his Chinese
Library at University College,
London, IV 233

mortality rates, III 243n2, IV 55; life
expectancy, a problem in statistics,
V 52

see also infant mortality

Moses, F. & Son, outfitters, I 76

Moss, Dales and Rogers, Liverpool banking firm, II 44n4, 77, 342

Moss, John, of Otterspool (1782-1858),
connection by marriage with
Jevons and Roscoe families, II 44

Moss, Thomas (d. 1805), Liverpool merchant, great-uncle by marriage of
WSJ, I 44n4, 56n1

Moss, Mrs Thomas (Elizabeth Griffies,
1755-1838), great-aunt of WSJ:
bequest to WSJ's mother, II 56,
235, III 40, 75

Mouat, Frederick John (1816-97),
Inspector-General of Local Government: arranges visit to Kensington
Workhouse, V 162, 164; as Secretary of Royal Statistical Society,
asked to press for Royal Commission on infant mortality, 168, 170

letters to, V 168-9; letters from, 162,
170-3

'mountebank', IV 210

Mount Keira, surveying expedition to, I
163-6, 167, 175; Keira Coalmine,
177

Mount Kembla, barometer readings, I
166-7; beauty of its valley slopes,
169-71, 172

Mount Victoria, I 236, 237; proposed
railway through, II 263, 264

Mount Victoria Inn, I 220

Moxon, Thomas Bouchier (d. 1923), Manchester banker: sends WSJ his
pamphlet, *The Banks of the United
Kingdom* . . . (1875), IV 110-11

Mozart, Wolfgang Amadeus, I 155, II 296;
his struggles for existence, I 178;
place in hierarchy of music, II 76;

313, 321, 328; played on WSJ's
harmonium in Sydney, II 76, 257

Don Giovanni, II 224; *Figaro*, 224; *La
Clemenza di Tito*, 339; Masses, 224,
Requiem Mass, 256-7, 290, 295-6,
329

Mudie, Charles Edward (1818-90), founder of Mudie's Circulating Library,
II 401n5

Mudie's Circulating Library: country
boxes of books, II 401-2; Mudie's
popular books, V 65

Mueller, J., *Lehrbuch der Physik und Meteorol-
ogie* (1856-8), II 306

Muir, Sir William (1819-1905), member
of the Council of India in London,
V 50

Müller, Christian, organ-builder, II 23n3

Mundella, Anthony John (1825-97),
M.P.: proposes question on trade
depressions at Political Economy
Club (1877), IV 222; on limits to
world demand for manufactured
goods, IV 237, 243n1; also mentioned, VII 104

Mundy, Godfrey Charles: *Our Antipodes: or,
Residence and Rambles in the Australian
Colonies, with a glimpse of the Gold-
Fields* (1852), II 52-3

Munich, Liebig's laboratories, I 83n2, II
73

Murchison, Sir Roderick Impey (1792-
1871), geologist, I 82; predicts gold
discoveries in Australian cordil-
leras, II 352; Committee Chairman, Royal Commission on Coal,
sends WSJ copies of questions, III
154

Siluria . . . (1854), II 131, 132, 135, 140,
144, 146

Murchison Medal for geology, II
298n11

letter from, III 154

Murray River, Australia, I 235, II 367

'Murray's Choice Reprints': *Wealth of
Nations* (1874), V 81

Murrumbidgee, Australian internal river,
II 367

museums: in France and England, II 63

Museum of Irish Industry, II 119n16

'Use and Abuse of Museums', *see* Jevons,
W. S., Works

museums (contd)
  see also British Museum; and under
    Paris
Musgrave, Sir Anthony (1828–88), Governor of Southern Australia, 1873–7:
  his 'celebrated article' on Mill's
  fundamental propositions (Contemporary Review, 1874), IV 126, 127n6,
  VII 77; examination question on,
  VII 132
  as Governor of Jamaica (1877), on en-
    terprise in Jamaica, V 70–1
  Economic Fallacies: Free Trade v. Protection
    (1875), IV 126
  letters to, IV 125–6, 166; letters from, V
    70–1
music
  in economic theory, VI 10, 52; a necess-
    ary, 53
  foundation of Royal College of Music, V
    178
  music for the people, IV 291n1, 292
  Spencer's Treatise on, II 227
  and weather, V 35
  see also Jevons, William Stanley: music;
    organs; and under individual
    composers
Muspratt, James (1793–1886), founder of
  Liverpool College of Chemistry, II
  134n6
Muspratt, James Sheridan (1821–71), Liverpool chemist, II 134
Muspratt, Mrs James Sheridan (Susan
  Phillips Cushman, 1822–59), II
  134
Mutiny on the Bounty, II 332n2
My Novel (Bulwer Lytton), I 27, 130–1

nail-making, VI 28, VII 61; William
  Jevons (grandfather of WSJ) an
  agent for sale of nails, I 2
Nantwich: home of Rev. and Mrs Francis
  Hornblower, I 3n1; WSJ stays at, I
  63–4, 115, II 27, collects botanical
  specimens, I 64; visits from other
  members of family, I 16, II 23, 26,
  30n2; Uncle Hornblower the minister at Unitarian Church, I 88; also
  mentioned, I 93
Napier & Co., Glasgow engineering firm,
  Volunteer Corps, II 407
Napoleon Bonaparte, II 61, VI 118, 119

Napoleon III
  his aggressiveness evokes Volunteer
    movement in England, I 36, 186n1,
    naval reform, II 428, and fighting
    spirit, 417
  attempted assassination of, II 408n13
  exchange of visits with Queen Victoria
    (1855), II 175n8
  intrigues with Russia, II 412
  introduces Free Trade, II 408
  marriage to Eugenia de Montijo, I 87;
    appears with Empress on balcony
    at Tuileries, II 68–9
  raises loan for more soldiers, II 430–1
  also mentioned, II 177, 179n1
  see also Bonaparte, Louis Napoleon
Nasmyth, Gaskell & Company, II 151n3
Nasmyth, James (1808–90), inventor of
  steam hammer, friend of Thomas
  Jevons, VI 29; his Monster guns, II
  151–2
Nassau Lees, W., III 48n1
Nasse, Erwin, V 169n1; On the Agricultural
  Communities of the Middle Ages
  . . . (translated by Colonel H. A.
  Ouvry, 1871), VII 105
Natal: Herbert Jevons's visit to, I 10, 76n1,
  II 34; James Jevons farms in, I
  76n1, II 174, returns from, II 78–9
Natali, Agnesa and Francesca, operatic
  young English ladies on board the
  Medway, II 398
National Association for the Promotion
  (Advancement) of Social Science,
  founded 1857, II 322, 361, IV 134,
  V 168, VII 55; Cliffe Leslie's view
  of, IV 273; letter from the Secretary
  V 173–4
  meetings: (1858), VII 53; (1863), VII
    47; (1866), III 127n1, 140, John
    Mills's paper on the Bank Charter
    Act, 140; (1871), V 29n2; (1875),
    IV 181n4; (1882), WSJ's paper on
    Married Women in Factories in-
    tended for, V 161, 173–4
  WSJ's lecture 'On Industrial Partner-
    ships' (1870), under auspices of, II
    322n9
national character, as an economic factor,
  VII 100; nationality, V 40
National Debt
  Baxter's paper on, read before British

Association (Liverpool, 1870), III 242, IV 9

in England and Australia, II 266

examination questions on, V 152, VII 134, 137

included in plans for 'Statistical Atlas', II 426

as perpetual credit, VI 106

quarterly interest payments, VI 127

reduction urged in preference to tax reduction, by Gladstone, Mill and WSJ, I 44, 45, 203, 206n3, III 87–8, 89, 94n1, 102, VII 11; Gladstone's plan for paying off, VII 12–18

rendered transferable by issue of Stock Certificates, IV 106n1

National Debt Commissioners, IV 133

National Gallery, I 85, II 9, III 8

Nationaløkonomisk Tidsskrift, Danish journal: notices of WSJ in, IV 44n2; controversy between Madsen and Westergaard on telegraph trade and mathematics, IV 244

National Review: 'Light and Sunlight' (WSJ, July 1861), I 35; *Serious Fall* noticed in (1836), VII 125

editors, Richard Hutton, I 36, II 416n6, Walter Bagehot, II 416n6

natural agents, VI 31, 57; as requisite of production, VI 17, 18, 60

natural history: Francis Archer's collection, I 55n1, 79; specimens in WSJ's 'brown paper parcel', I 141, 152

natural laws, I 154, VI 24, VII 39, 158; governing capital and labour, rates of profits and wages, VII 46, 50–1, currency, III 202; laws of nature and workmen's combinations, III 137, VII 48–9

Natural Phenomena (S.P.C.K.), II 291

Natural Philosophy: WSJ's early interest in, I 61, 62, but not in mechanical parts, 67, 69; plans to continue study after leaving College, 78; 'doing' electricity, 83, 87; finds Hydrostatics dull, 90, only accoustics worth reading, 91; examinations, 55, 94, gets first prize (1852), III 110; tries reading in Library of Useful Knowledge

(1855), I 113; studies for B.A. (1860), II 415; also mentioned, VII 58

see also chemistry; physics

natural price: or exchange value, II 284; labour as, VI 90

natural religion, II 325

Natural Science, I 154, 156; Newton a genius of, 155

natural selection, Maupertuis's 'Memoir' on, IV 4

see also origin of species

natural system of classification, I 63, 99

natural value: or cost value, VI 83, 84; of inexhaustible new lands, VII 4, 6; Ricardo's unverified assumptions on, VII 162

nature: ordered, but unfeeling, II 288; nature, the machine, 326–7; ruling, by obeying Nature's power, VI 22–3, VII 40, 151

Nature

articles by WSJ: letter on timing of star transit (18 November 1869), III 216n2; 'A Deduction from Darwin's Theory' (30 December 1869), VII 126; letter on astronomical observations (27 January 1870), VII 126; 'Oversight by Faraday' (10 February 1870), VII 126; address to British Association (15 September 1870), III 236; 'Maupertuis on the Survival of the Fittest' (6 March 1873), IV 4, 15; 'Commercial Crises and Sun-Spots' (14 November 1878), IV 293, 294, 296, 305, V 47, VII 94; 'Commercial Crises and Sun-Spots' (24 April 1879), V 44n1, 57, VII 108; 'Sun-Spots and the Plague' (13 February 1879), V 35

other articles: Balfour Stewart, 'On the Long Period Inequality in Rainfall' (8 April 1880), V 103, 'Suspected Relations between the Sun and the Earth' (17 May 1877), IV 204n4; Brewer, on Maupertuis (27 March 1873), IV 15; notice of Electric Exhibition, Paris (May–November 1881), V 148n2; Galton, 'Typical Laws of Heredity' (April 1877), IV 200n3; Thomas Huxley and H. E.

Nature (contd)
    Roscoe, addresses to British Association (15 September 1870), III 236; Hyde Clarke, letter (21 November 1878), IV 295; Janssen, 'Notes' on Sun-Spots (18 December 1879), V 86; statistics of U.S.A. bankruptcies (5 December 1878), V 11-12; report of Schuster's paper, 'Some results of the last total solar eclipse' (January 1879), V 8; other notes and letters, IV 15n4, V 12, VII 126
    founding editor, J. N. Lockyer, III 236n1
Nauck, Ernst (1819-75), Professor at Riga Polytechnical School, III 126
Neate, Mr, motion on reducing the National Debt, VII 17
necessaries
    included in wealth, VII 159
    Ricardo's interpretation of, VI 60
    rise in price, III 256, and wage claims, VI 63
    taxes on, examination question, VII 133
negative value, V 22; Macleod's use of term, 77
Neild, Alfred, Treasurer of Owens College, IV 20; Chairman of the Council, IV 20n1, 21, 107
    letters to, IV 20, 107
Neild, Alderman William (1789-1864), Chairman of Owens College Trustees, IV 20n1
Nelson, New Zealand, Herbert Jevons's post in, III 28, 33; price of gold, 28
Nepean River, New South Wales
    expedition to, I 143-4, 147-50, 217, II 253; romantic appearance, I 144; deep alluvial soil, 144, 215, II 220; sketch of, I 149
    proposed railway by, II 262-3
    also mentioned, I 175n1, 225
Neptune, I 104
Netherlands
    new economic theories well received in, IV 58
    taxation proposals, V 55-6
    see also Holland, *and under* Vissering, Simon and Willem
Neumeyer, Georg Balthasar (1826-1909), German meteorologist at Mel-

bourne Observatory: WSJ's visit to, II 372-3
Nevin, Mr, manager of Steeles Soap Works, I 92, 93
New Brighton, Cheshire, II 155, 446, III 32
Newcastle
    British Association meeting (1863), III 36, IV 127
    coals from, VII 21-2; plans for special coal trains, 23
    WSJ: visit to (1866), III 126; gives two lectures to Literary and Philosophical Society on coal (1868), III 188, 195; *Coal Question* sells well in, III 127
Newcastle, Duke of, Colonial Secretary, III 41
Newcastle, New South Wales
    coal mines, I 123n3
    regatta, I 128
    WSJ and: trip to, I 124, 129, 130, II 235; 'Red Tape and the Newcastle Life-boat' (*Empire,* 20 November 1856), VII 123
Newcomb, Simon: 'The Method and Province of Political Economy' (*North American Review,* 1875), IV 141n4
Newfoundland, IV 114
New Harmony, VI 44n7
Newhaven, II 177
New Haven (U.S.A.), Mr Towner's store, II 390
Newman, Professor Francis William (1805-97), *Lectures on Political Economy,* VI 15-16
Newmarch, William, F.R.S. (1820-82), Secretary of the Globe Insurance Co., I 181n1; WSJ's first meeting with, I 180-1; not interested in WSJ's diagrams, 180-1; reads *Serious Fall,* III 15; testimonial for WSJ, as vice-president of Royal Statistical Society, III 106, 115-16
    President, Economics and Statistics Section, British Association (1861), I 36; his unreliable figures, III 21, 25; estimate of British currency, 201; at the Political Economy Club, IV 52n2, 117, 202; opposed to Bank Act, 159; Presidential address, National Association for the Pro-

motion of Social Science (1871), V
29; proposed as Treasurer for projected reprints society, V 73, as
President, 82; supports Royal Society Fellowship for Inglis Palgrave, V 85, 184; death (23 March
1882), 184
The New Supplies of Gold . . . (1853), I
180n1; *The Bank of England* (1872),
IV 158; other articles and papers, I
180n1, III 19, 23
see also Tooke and Newmarch, *History of
Prices*
New Rush Back Creek, 'mushroom town of
canvas', II 371
Back Creek Advertiser, II 371, 373
New South Wales
anniversary of founding, II 114, 208
assizes, I 234
coal production, I 123n3, 125, 127, 129,
159n1, II 134, 267, VII 27, 33
contributions to Paris Exhibition, I 121,
II 183–4
farming, I 127, 137–9, 148, 175, II 282;
dairy, I 159n1, 169; Indian corn,
127, 128, 214; orchards, 136, 139,
144, II 252; wine growing, VI 32
gold discoveries, I 24, II 53n7, 205n5,
346, production, II 127, 279, 451;
gold coins refused by Victoria
State, I 21, II 260, become legal
tender throughout colonies (1857),
II 127; gold duty Bill, II 260
government: Governor (Sir William
Thomas Denison), II 205–6; old
Legislative Council, II 270n2, its
last days, 205–6; grant of responsible government (New South
Wales Constitution Act, May
1855), I 2, 123n1, II 205n5, 247;
new Legislative Assembly (elected
Lower House), II 205, 206n5,
270n2, WSJ hears Mint assayers
praised by, 260, mishandle railway
issue, 265, 266; new Legislative
Council (nominated), I 25, II
206n5; interim arrangements, II
205n5; Opening of New Parliament (May, 1856), I 123, II 205,
247; Ministerial crises, II 247–8;
opposition a bunch of pure democrats, 247–8, 266; not ready for

self-government, II 122
imports, II 281; of flour, VII 4
land policy, letters and articles on, I 26,
II 282–7, 297, VII 3–8
Library of New South Wales, Sydney, II
131n17
log buildings and fences, I 138–9, 147–8,
173, II 253
population: emigration from Britain, I
24, II 267–8; Census returns, VII 4;
and acres in crop, 4; proportion of
town to rural, 5
prices, IV 114; of land, II 284, 286–7,
420, VII 4–6
railways: WSJ's papers on, I 25–6, 26–7,
II 206n6, 235–7, 262–8, 282–7,
VII 3, 8–11; WSJ always opposed
to extension, II 451
Sydney and Parramatta railway, II
206n6, 266–7, 270n2; WSJ travels
by, I 134–5, 213, II 176, 219, 252;
railway traffic, II 267, 283
roads, II 451; made with convict labour,
II 221; WSJ's travels on, I 123–30
passim, 134–54 *passim*, 159–78
passim, 212–38 *passim*, II 219, 221,
254
Select Committee on Roads and Railways (1854), II 206n6
steam mills, I 128
taxation: on occupation of land, II 284,
VII 4; tolls on railways, II 285–6;
ad valorem duties, VI 137; suggested
reforms, VII 6–8
towns, I 128, 142, 225–6, II 197, 297n10
WSJ and: tours, I 24–5, 112; excursion
to River Hunter and Maitland,
123–30; to Blue Mountains, 134–
54, II 252–5; trip to Wollongong,
Illawarra, I 159–78, II 280; journey to gold diggings at Sofala, I 24,
213–38, II 217, 218–21; photography expedition to Middle Harbour, II 342, 347–8, 352–5; Braidwood diggings, I 24, II 358, 364–5
takes part in life of colony, I 31; no
friend for him, II 275, no wife, 298;
will gain only 'colonial experience',
I 110, II 216
systematic study of, I 22–5; *see also
under* Australia; geology; meteorology

New South Wales (contd)
    articles on: 'The Railway Discussion'
        (1856), II 235–7; 'The Western
        Line of Railway' (1857), II 262–8;
        letter on railways and land regu-
        lations (1857), II 282–7; 'Com-
        parison of the Land and Railway
        Policy of New South Wales' (1857),
        I 26, II 282–7; 'The Public Lands
        of New South Wales' (1857), I 26,
        II 297, VII 3–8; on railway econ-
        omy (1857), VII 8–11
    see also Australia; Sydney
New South Wales, Bank of, see Bank of
    New South Wales
New South Wales Philosophical Society, I
    23, 25–6, II 357n1, VII 123; WSJ
    elected member, I 23, II 290; paper
    on Clouds read before (9 December
    1857), I 23, 25; 'On the Philosophi-
    cal Society of New South Wales'
    (WSJ, Empire, September 1857),
    VII 123
newspapers, II 43, 196, 197, VI 32, VII 17;
    sent to Herbert in America, II 409,
    413, 424, 431, III 62, 210; trade
    and market reports, VI 84, VII 26
    American papers, II 409, 421; New
        South Wales papers, II 195
    WSJ advised against newspaper writing
        as a career, II 438, advised to write
        for periodical press, 445; his news-
        paper collection, II 373, including
        paper from gold town, 371, 373
    see also individual papers and journals
Newton, Sir Isaac, I 111, II 360, IV 68; a
    genius of Natural Science, I 155; his
    unmarried state, 192–3; purchase
    of South Sea Stock, V 107
    reports on the currency (1717), V 44;
        'Sir Isaac Newton and Bimetallism'
        (WSJ, unfinished), V 159n1, VII
        vii
Newton, Joseph (d. 1888), Sydney Mint
    engineer, fellow passenger on
    board the Oliver Lang, I 106, II 88;
    WSJ makes friends with, II 85, 98–
    9, 106, 347
Newton, Mrs, friend of Uncle and Aunt
    Timothy Jevons, II 142
Newton, Kate, daughter of Mrs Newton,
    II 142

Newton Keats & Co., Lead works, Flint-
    shire, II 164
New York
    Bank panics (1873), IV 111; cheque
        system, 54; Clearing House, 43, 54;
        Money Market, 43; trade recovery
        (1879), V 65
    T. E. Jevons (Tom) emigrates to (1865),
        III 78–9, 158, 251; becomes part-
        ner in Busk & Jevons, I 10; marries
        in New York, V 146n1; settles in
        Long Island, I 10
    WSJ lands in (1859), I 33, II 378; spends
        a week in, 382, 399, at St Nicholas
        Hotel, 383, 390, 400; nine-storey
        buildings, and railways in the
        streets, 399–400; returns to
        England from, 384n1, 390, 401
    also mentioned, II 78, 420
New York Commercial and Financial Chronicle,
    IV 111
New York Evening Post, review of Principles of
    Science, IV 42
New York Gas Company, V 71
New York State, II 428; water cure estab-
    lishment, II 423
New York Times, review of Principles of
    Science, IV 42
New York Tribune, II 421; review of Prin-
    ciples of Science, IV 42
New Zealand
    coalfields, VII 26
    emigration to, II 54n7; not fit for English
        ladies, III 39; WSJ attracted by the
        'English-like Colony', II 417
    goldfields, III 15, 28, 57, 74, 'nobblers'
        and billiards, 74; gold product, IV
        7; price of Nelson gold, III 28;
        sovereigns, III 210
    Howitt's fatal journey through, III 158
    Herbert Jevons emigrates to, see under
        Jevons, Herbert
    quartz and copper, III 74, 205
    Union Bank, III 39, 50; branch banks of
        Bank of New South Wales, 40, 51,
        57–8, 74
    war in North Island (1863), II 41;
        Maori insurrection (1860–1), II
        420
    also mentioned, II 98
Niagara, II 391; Blondin's tight rope
    walk seen by WSJ, 401

Nicholls, Sir George (1781–1865), *History of the Poor Law* (1854), VII 107

Nicholson, James Holme (1825–1901), librarian at Owens College, III 234n2; Registrar, IV 21, 164n2

Nickolls, John (1710–45), antiquary: his collection of Milton letters, V 128

Nicolaieff, telegraphic messages sent to and from, II 435

Nicolini, F., article on Ceva, V 22n2, 42

Nieson, F. G. P., sen., *Contributions to Vital Statistics* (ed. 3, 1857), V 9n3

Nieson, Francis Gustavus Paulus (d. 1929), actuary, V 9

Nightingale, Florence, II 361

Nimrud, Palace in Nineveh, II 18n1

Nineteenth Century, V 35

Nineveh sculptures in the British Museum, II 18

Noble, John (1837–98): *The Queen's Taxes* (1870), V 55; *National Finance* (1875), VII 106

Nonconformists, I 39; *see also* Unitarians

Norgate, Frederick, Edinburgh bookseller, IV 297

Norman, George Ward (1793–1882), Director of the Bank of England: evidence before Committee on the Bank Charter (1832), IV 264, 265; founder member of Political Economy Club, IV 264n2, 265

Norman, John Henry, foreign-exchange dealer: letters to WSJ on relative proportions of silver and gold coins in the principal countries of the world, V 139–40, 141–2

North America: coalfields, VII 27, 34; production of coal, 33

North American Indians, II 455, VI 59

North American Review, IV 141

North British Review, 'Trade Unions . . .' (Fleeming Jenkin, March 1868), III 166

North Cheshire Herald, report of WSJ's lectures on political economy (6 February and 13 March 1869), VII 54

Northcote, Sir Stafford (1818–87), Leader of House of Commons, 1876–80: supports Royal Society Fellowship for Inglis Palgrave, V 90, 91
  Twenty Years of Financial Policy (1862), VII 106

Northern Daily Times, II 172

Northern Whig, Belfast paper, V 111

North Harbour, Sydney, II 347

Northumberland, VII 17

Norway
  fishing, IV 22, VI 37
  international trade, V 27
  money system, V 130; gold coinage, 59
  wages, examination question on, VII 138
  WSJ and: holidays in (1872), III 249; (1873), IV 21, 22, 24; (1874), IV 43–5, 56, 61, 65, 70; (1876), IV 182, 184, 194; projected (1877), IV 192, 205, changed to Sweden, 207; (1878), IV 271; (1879), V 54, 65; (1880), V 105, 110n1; (1881), V 143, 190n4; holiday life in, IV 291, V 104
  also mentioned, V 99, VI 53

Norwood, New South Wales, II 196–7

Nottingham: infant mortality, V 173–4; National Association for Promotion of Social Science meeting (September 1882), intended paper by WSJ on married women in factories, V 161, or on infant mortality, 173–4

Nourse, Benjamin F., IV 217n1

Nouvelles de la République des lettres (October 1701), IV 295

Nova Scotia, II 441; shipyards, II 111n3; tidal power in Fundy Bay, III 123

O'Brien, Lords Clare, ancestors of Richard Cantillon, V 123, 125

Observatories, IV 295–6. *See also under* Edinburgh; Melbourne; Solar Physics

O'Connell, Daniel, M.P., V 123

O'Connell, George, brother of Mrs F. B. Miller, II 404

O'Connell, Maurice, brother of Mrs F. B. Miller: walks with WSJ in and around Sydney, I 24, II 207, 274, 300, 340, 342; goes to Sofala gold diggings with WSJ, I 153, 230, 233–8, II 364–5, knocked up by the heat, I 226, 227, rests while WSJ inspects diggings, 230, searches unsuccessfully for paid employment, 233; becomes a gold-digger, II 340, 405; WSJ loses a friend, 340

Odessa, telegraphic messages sent to and from, II 435

Oersted, Hans Christian, isolates aluminium, II 62n6

Oertling, L., scientific instrument maker, II 50, 62

Ogden, Jonathan Robert (1806–82), 'Psalm-tune Ogden', II 14

Ogden, Mabel Martha, see Thornely, Mrs Thomas

Ogden, Thomas Bolton, fellow-lodger in Gower Street with WSJ, II 14, 25, 141n3; his bad reputation, 17, 19, a 'disagreeable' companion for WSJ, 20

Ohio River, II 383, 400

oil
    mineral oils from coal, II 119, VII 20, 31
    oil and colour manufacturers, II 41
    see also paraffin oil; petroleum

O'Kelly, James Joseph, Irish M.P., released from prison, V 189n2

Oldham, cooperatives, VI 76

Ollerenshaw, J. C., India trader, III 252; 'Our Export Trade in Cotton Goods to India' (1869–70), III 251, V 45

O'Malley, Patrick, IV 279

omnibuses: in New South Wales, I 126, 128, 135–7, II 195, 196, 252; in America, on iron rails, II 399; omnibus duty, VII 12. See also coaches

Ontario, Lake, II 384n1, 401

Ophir, gold diggings at Yorkey's Creek, II 217

Oregon and Canada boundary dispute, II 408n14

organs: barrel organs, II 320; organ grinders, V 108; Christian Müller's in Haarlem, II 23n3; in the Crystal Palace, II 23–4; in Melbourne, II 369, in Sydney Catholic chapel, II 109; organ builders in Liverpool, II 41; in Peru, II 379; in Temple Church, I 75, in Westminster Abbey, III 18

and the Jevons family: Thomas Jevons's connoisseurship, I 79n3, II 24; William's organ, I 79n3, 92, played by WSJ, 79, II 7; WSJ takes lessons on, I 79n3, II 458, buys a harmonium in Sydney as substitute for, II 162, buys an organ in Manchester, I 79n3, re-establishes it in Hampstead, IV 189
    see also music

origin of species, I 66; Darwin's theory anticipated by Maupertuis, IV 4, 15

Ormonde, 17th Earl of, II 153n1

Orsini, Felice (1819–58): attempts assassination of Napoleon III (1858), II 408; The Austrian Dungeons in Italy . . . (1856), II 259

Osler, Timothy (b. 1823), barrister, I 73, II 122; joins the Volunteers, II 407

Osler, Mrs Timothy (Henrietta Roscoe, 1821–69), cousin of WSJ, I 73, 74n2, 243, II 122

Otago, New Zealand, III 28, 33; gold diggings, 57–8, 74

Ottoman Empire, II 418n7; see also Turkey

Outlines of Social Economy, recommended by WSJ, VII 53n

Ouvry, Colonel H. A., VII 105

Ovens District goldfield, expedition to, II 366–9

Overend, Gurney & Co. Ltd., failure in 1866, III 102n1, IV 12n10, 210, VI 126

overproduction: d'Aulnis's theory of, IV 73; and law of reversion (Galton), IV 202; and sun-spots, V 11

Overstone, Lord: opposes decimal coinage, II 156n5, and seignorage proposal, III 211; 'Thoughts on the Separation of the Departments of the Bank of England', IV 32

overtrading, VI 117, 124

Owen, Robert: ideal community at New Harmony, VI 44n7; pamphlets, V 43; Robert Owen, and his Social Philosophy (W. L. Sargant), VII 105

Owens College, Manchester
    Foundation: tutorials and lectures teaching system, III 112, no theological doctrines to be inculcated, VII 41, Nonconformists admitted as teachers, I 39; plans for Engineering, Mining and Scientific Schools, III 150, new buildings opened (October 1873), IV 23, 'second foundation', 107; receives

Charter as University (1879), V
61n2, 67, becomes 'The Victoria
University of Manchester', 61
WSJ urged to apply for tutorship (1863),
I 39–40, 185, 186, 189, III 3, 5, 6, 9;
prepares for first session, III 15, 29;
terms of employment, I 42, 204n5,
III 9–10, 14; life as tutor, I 41, 192,
196, III 34, 65, 69, 70; evening
classes, I 43, III 10, 14, 34, 48, 76,
104, 206n1, IV 22–4, 49, 56, 113,
124, 156, questions and discussions
in class, VII 60; overworks as tutor,
III 57, 58, 63, 149
appointed lecturer in Political Economy (1865), I 45, III 68, does
duties of Professor, I 42, 205n5;
substitute lecturer in logic, I 45, III
48, 66, 75–6, 104, 112, 118
applies for new chair of logic and
mental and moral philosophy, and
Cobden Professorship of Political
Economy (1866), I 202n1, 205,
206, III 96, 101, 103–5; testimonials, III 85–7 88, 89–90, 99–
100, 106–20; appointed, I 46–7,
198n2, 27, III 120, 121–2; inaugural lecture as Cobden Professor (October 1866), I 207n3, VII
37–54, correspondence arising
from, III 128–38; college work as
Professor, III 149, 150, 195, IV
105, 147, 150, 156; lectures, in
Rylett's transcription, 241, VI 3–
140; overworks (1872), takes six
months off, III 252, V 157; offers
resignation, IV 20, temporary
withdrawal accepted, 21, 22; arrangements for substitute lecturer
(Brewer), 21, 49, classes and syllabus, 22–4; again offers resignation (1874), IV 48–9; continues
without evening work, 43, 56; sub-
mits resignation (March 1875),
107, 110, renegotiates stipend and
work, 112–13, 123; fails to get
weekly leave of absence to lecture
in London, 123, 124, 125, 132, 133–
4; accepts London professorship,
134–5, completes engagement with
Owens College, 144, resigns finally
(February 1876), I 49, IV 163–4;

Council resolution of appreciation,
164n2; professorship advertised,
157, 164, 167; Robert Adamson
appointed, 183
Chemistry Department, H. E. Roscoe
Professor of, I 39, 41, 185n7, II
50n9, 304–5, 315–17, 322, III 150;
his laboratory, II 305, 316n8, 317,
VII 71
Library: *Exposition universelle de 1867 à
Paris* presented by Chevalier, III
209; gift of Blue Books from University College, London, 233–5
Principals, *see* Greenwood, Joseph
Gouge; Scott, Rev. Alexander John
prize meeting, III 122, 124; Richard
Cobden prize, V 129n1
professors: R. Clifton, I 36, 41, III 5;
A. J. Scott, I 41, III 48; A. Schuster, V 167; others, I 41–2, III
206n1, 305n8, V 141n2, *and see
above*, H. E. Roscoe
Trustees, I 47, 204n5, 206, II 305, III
106, 150, 234, IV 20n1; letter to,
III 103–5
also mentioned, I 1, 65n4, II 74n16,
315n3, IV 95, VII 58
Owens College Magazine, 'Life' of WSJ, V
136
Oxford University
boat races, periodicity in, V 51
Bodleian Library, IV 285; price lists in,
286
colleges: All Souls, old ale and tea at, IV
286; Balliol, IV 285, 286; buildings
surpass Cambridge in beauty, IV
285
Library Association meeting at (1878),
IV 284–6; Museum Soirée,
284
teaching methods in philosophy and
law, V 22, 23; experimental physics, I 41; Brodie's research in
chemistry, I 81n2; Mill's reputation declining, IV 286
a trade unionist view of, III 134, 136
oxygen: lecture on, II 13; oxi-hydrogen
blowpipe, 18; and production of
gas, V 71
ozone, WSJ's observations on, II 245;
'Remarks on Mr Baxendell's Laws
of atmospheric ozone' (Manchester

ozone (*contd*)
  Literary and Philosophical Society, 1868), VII 126

Pacific Ocean, II 217, 354; wreck of the *Dunbar*, II 300; voyage across from Australia to America, II 373-6
Pacific Steam Navigation Company, II 379, 397
Paget, Sir James (1814-99), surgeon: 'Medical Students' (*JRSS*, 1869), VI 66
Pakington, Sir John Somerset (1790-1880), Colonial Office, I 85
Paley, Mary, *see* Marshall, Mrs Alfred
Palgrave, Francis Turner (1824-97), editor of *Golden Treasury of English Lyrics* (1861), IV 53n1, 54; suggested contribution to English Citizen Series, V 157
Original Hymns by Francis Turner Palgrave (1867), IV 53
Palgrave, Sir Robert Harry Inglis (1827-1919), banker, IV 10n1
  notes on *Money and Mechanism of Exchange*, IV 111-12; looks for substitute lecturer for WSJ, 135-6, 163; consulted on proposed reprinting society (Adam Smith Society), V 44, 73, 83; visited by WSJ at Yarmouth, V 157; defends WSJ on bimetallism, 188
  proposed translation of Roscher's Political Economy, IV 108, 109-10; not one of the 'Free Banking School', 112; working on prices, 162-3, 168-71; election as Fellow of Royal Society, V 85-6, 90-1, 163, 188, 193, 194, letter from WSJ in support of, 183-4; supports pension for Cliffe Leslie, 169, 170; proposes discussion on 'Bank Money', 192
  editor of *Bankers' Magazine*, IV 217-18, V 85, 129, 130n2; edits *Banking Almanac and Directory*, IV 105, V 90, 130; editor of *Economist*, V 72, 73, 129, 130n2, 157, 197
  articles: 'On the Local Taxation of Great Britain and Ireland' (Royal Statistical Society Prize Essay, 1871), III 242, V 184; 'Notes on Banking in Great Britain . . .'

(*JRSS*, 1873), IV 98n1, 112n2, V 184, correspondence with WSJ on, IV 10-14, 16-19, 79, 98n1; Analysis of the *Transactions of Bank of England 1844 to 1872* (1874), IV 30-2, V 184; 'The Effect of Superseding . . . Country Note Issues with the Notes of the Bank of England' (*Bankers' Magazine*, 1874), IV 76-7, 98n1, WSJ's comments, 105, 118; articles on Bank Reserves (1873, 1875, 1876), IV 168, 169; article in *Quarterly Review*, IV 13
  letters to, IV 10-13, 14, 53-4, 76-8, 98, 105, 107-8, 109-10, 111-12, 118, 135-6, 162-3, 165, 168-9, 169-71, 217-18, V 44, 72, 73-4, 85, 85-6, 90-1, 129-30, 157-8, 169-70, 171, 188-93, 193-4; letters from, IV 16-19, 30-2, 78-9, 168
Palgrave, Mrs Inglis, V 157
Pall Mall Budget, V 111
Pall Mall Gazette
  alarmist articles on market trends, V 171
  on Gladstone, VII 13
  Irish Question, V 111
  'Political Economy, New and Old' (J. K. Ingram, August 1878), IV 272
  WSJ and: *Coal Question* noticed in (4 January, 20, 21, 24 April 1866), III 96; 'Post Office Telegraphs . .' reviewed in (7 December 1875), IV 150; obituary (Sully, 17 August 1882), I 50
  editor, John Morley, V 111n2
  also mentioned, V 130, VII 126
Palmer Diggings, North Queensland, IV 177
'Palmer Rule', IV 264n2
Palmerston, Viscount (1784-1865): goes out with Russell Ministry (1852), I 85; resolution on Budget, 86; becomes Prime Minister (February 1855), II 163n6; orders enquiry into army and supplies services, 122n3; his aggressive foreign policy, 417-18, strong navy policy, 429; sleeping habits, III 149; definition of dirt, VI 17
Panama: WSJ stops off at, I 33, finds mail from England at post-office, II 364,

376–7, 382; spends two days in Panama town, 379, 381, 397; travels by Panama Railway, 379–80, 381, 397

also mentioned, II 439

Pangenesis theory of life (Galton), IV 200–1

panics

American: (1873), IV 111, V 11; (1875), IV 111; due in 1893, V 84

Autumn panics, III 102

banking panics, IV 110–11, 229, 232; (1825), VI 119–20; (1866), III 102, 140, VII 41, fall of Overend, Gurney & Co., IV 210, VI 125–6

'coal panic', III 102; colliers' agitation during panic of 1869, III 228

in Ireland (1867), III 190; in Manchester (1878), IV 287

over price of silver (1875–6), VI 102

'Sun-Spots and Commercial Panics' (*Times*, 14 January 1879, unsigned), V 10n2, 12n4, 91

see also crises; cycles; periodicity

Panizzi, Sir Anthony (1797–1879), Italian exile, Principal Librarian at the British Museum, 1856–66: letter to, offering collection of printed and MS documents, II 449

Papal States, VII 67

paper: repeal of tax on, II 412; WSJ's economy of, IV 221

paper money

general movement to replace by metallic currency, III 199; gold and silver money replaced by, VI 98

overissue and the Free Banking School, IV 112

postal notes and, V 101n3

in U.S.A., V 118; collapse of, in 1873, V 11, 147, VI 126; greenbacks, III 79–80, 199

variations in rate of exchange due to depreciation of, VI 110

WSJ's collection of, III 80, IV 194, V 118; books on, V 195

see also bank notes; bills of exchange; Exchequer Bills: money

paraffin oil, VII 20; candles, 20, 31

parcel post, VII 61; parcel companies, V 159, 195, 196; parcel traffic by rail, 155n2, 159

'A State Parcel Post' (WSJ, *Contemporary Review*, 1879), IV 303, V 3, 155n2; Willdey on, 155–6

Parieu, Felix Esquiron de (1815–93), and international currency, VII 66

Paris

WSJ and: assaying course at Paris Mint (1854), I 19, 118, 121, II 56n2, 61–2, 65, 68; his lodgings, II 57–8, 179, 202; impressions of Paris, 58–9, 63, Carnival, 67–8; sees Emperor and Empress, 68–9; at opera, 69; geological expeditions round Paris, I 114; visit in 1867, III 158, in 1881, with Harriet, V 148–9; dinner at the Grand Hotel, 148–9

boulevards, II 69; Seine bookshops, V 149

Bourse, VII 76

Cantillon's connections with, V 123, 125

Commission of Inquiry into the Monetary Question (1870), III 232. *See also* International Monetary Conferences

cookery, II 59; vin ordinaire, I 141

H. E. Roscoe visits, II 190–1

industry, inquiries into (1847, 1860), III 126

International Electric Congress, and Electrical Exhibition (1881), V 148

museums, II 62, 63; Louvre, visited by WSJ, II 58, 63, 68, by Thomas Jevons, 179

music: barrel organs, II 58; drums, 58, 63, 68; bands, 58, 68–9; *Les Huguenots* at Academie Imperial de Musique, 69; Grand Opera, V 131; concerts, 148; dinner with music, 149

Revolutions, I 105, II 98, 112

Societé d'économie politique, V 4; Statistical Society, 3n1

telegraphic communication with British Association (1861), II 435

Thomas Jevons stays in (1855), I 121, II 70n4, 173, 175, 178–9, 199; stays in same lodgings as WSJ, I 121, II 179; visits Exhibition, 183–5

Tuileries, II 58, 63, 68–9

visit of Queen Victoria (1855), II 175, 190–1

Paris International Exhibitions
  (1855), II 63n6, 179, 191, V 148; alu-
    minium exhibit, II 63n6, 175; gold
    specimens from Sydney, II 135,
    136, 149, 175, 184; 'Palais de
    l'Industrie', II 179; Thomas Jevons
    visits, 183–4, impressed by machin-
    ery exhibits, 183, and New South
    Wales timbers, 184; H.E. Roscoe
    visits, 191
  (1867), VII 67; WSJ visits, I 211, III
    158, V 148, sees Arithmometer,
    VII 86, 88; Chevalier's *rapport* of,
    III 209
  (1878), WSJ visits, IV 285, V 148;
    Fontpertuis' publications on
    foreign countries represented at, IV
    276–7, 287–8; Birdwood's *Handbook
    to British Indian Section*, V 49; Arith-
    mometer again on view, VII 86
  (1881) V 148
Paris Mint
  WSJ takes two months course at, I 19, II
    56n2, 61–2, 68; examinations, 62,
    70, 71; diploma, I 19, 121, II 70,
    184, 204, 234; Thomas Jevons's
    visit to, I 121, II 184, 204
  Assayer at Mint (Périgot), II 61, 62, 71;
    his staff, 62, English sovereigns
    checked by, III 223; Warden of the
    Mint (Cahours), II 64, 65; coining
    process, 65, III 219; Mint Charge,
    III 215, VII 70
Paris and Orleans Railway Company, VI
  77
Paris, Treaty of (March 1856), II 234
Parkes, [Sir] Henry (1815–96), poet and
    later Prime Minister of New South
    Wales, II 239n3
  as editor of the *Empire*: takes on WSJ
    as meteorological reporter, I 23,
    II 239–40, 260, gives him large
    type and reprints articles, 297,
    303, 346; *Empire* goes bankrupt,
    346
  heads democratic Opposition in Legis-
    lative Assembly, II 247–8; praises
    WSJ as assayer during debate on
    salaries, 260
  letter to, quoted, VII 3
Parkgate Iron Works, Rotherham, III
    166, 225, 229

Parliament
  (1852), opening of, I 70–1, 83; supplies
    voted for funeral of Duke of Wel-
    lington, 72; Queen's speech, 86;
    Disraeli's Budget defeated, 86; Mil-
    itia Bill, 86; changes of Ministry,
    85–7
  (1860), Queen's Speech, II 406, 408;
    House of Lords reject Bill for repeal
    of paper duty, 412; Gladstone's
    Budget, 408n12; Anglo-French
    treaty of Commerce, VII 14
  (1861), a dull session, II 428; paper duty
    repealed, 412n8; Bankruptcy Act,
    428
  (1864), Gladstone's Budget, VII 12
  (1866) *Coal Question* quoted by J. S.
    Mill in debate on Malt Duties, I
    205, 207n2, III 94n1, 96, 103, 119,
    VII 12, 13, 17, Opposition fright-
    ened by, 102; Gladstone's Budget
    statement on reduction of national
    debt, III 103, VI 11, 12; motion for
    Royal Commission on coal sup-
    plies, II 101, 102
  (1871) debate on Goschen's Local Tax-
    ation report, III 242–3
  WSJ's visit to Houses of Parliament, I 85
Parliamentary Papers: WSJ rummages
    through, in British Museum, II
    426; collection of, presented to
    Owens College, III 233–5
Parliamentary Reform, II 428; defeat of
    Reform Bill (1867), III 130–1;
    WSJ's views on Reform agitation,
    150
Parliament Fields, botanical specimens
    from, I 57
Parnell, leader of Irish Party: arrested
    (1881), V 151n4; released (1882),
    179n6, 189n2; advocates peasant
    proprietorship, 196n1
Parramatta, New South Wales
  expeditions to, by railway, I 135, 212,
    238, II 217, 219, 252; church and
    buildings, I 142, II 213, 219; on by
    omnibus to Windsor, I 135–6, II
    252
  Parramatta coach, I 154; Parramatta
    railway, product of railway mania,
    VII 10, proposed extension, II 219,
    262–3; Parramatta Road and

Street, Sydney, II 147

Parry, John, Liverpool schoolmaster and librarian, II 52

Partington & Allen, Manchester solicitors, IV 150n3

partnerships: between masters and men, VII 60, 64; industrial, examination question on, VII 135

 letter to *The Times*, 'Partnerships of Masters and Men' (1867) III 151-4

Pascal, Blaise, his calculating machine, VII 86, 88

Passy, Frédéric, V 7n5

patents, II 427, V 71n1

Pattison, Mark (1813-84): 'Philosophy at Oxford' (*Mind*, 1876), IV 156

Paul, assistant in Dr Graham's laboratory, II 49

Pauli, friend of H. E. Roscoe in Heidelberg, II 65, 73

pauperism, III 256n1, VI 131, VII 28, 35, 90, 91; examination question on paupers, VII 135. *See also* poverty; workhouses

Paxton, Sir Joseph (1801-65), gardener and architect: his 'Palace of Glass', II 11, 12n5

pea, from China, II 142

peaceful picketing, VI 73n5

Peacock, Mr, defaulting reporter on *Empire*, Sydney Newspaper, II 256, 269

Pearce, W., managing partner in a woollen mill: letter to WSJ on married women in factories, V 174-5

Pearson, Josiah Brown (1841-95), Fellow of St John's College, Cambridge: examines with WSJ for Moral Sciences Tripos, Cambridge (1874), IV 52, 53, 70

peasant proprietors: Jamaican blacks, V 70; for Ireland, V 114, 150n2, 196

 examination question on, VII 133

peat, II 118-19

Peel Brothers & Co., worsted manufacturers, Bradford, V 172

Peel, George F., director of Peel Brothers, V 172n1

Peel, New South Wales, an inn and an aborigine, I 227

Peel, Sir Robert (1788-1850), 2nd Baronet Bank Act (1844), IV 10, 13, 17, 32, 77, VI 123, 127, applied in Canada, IV 158; examination of witness, Committee on Bank of England Charter (1832), IV 264n3

 tariff revision (1842), VI 136n6, 138-9

 also mentioned, I 79n2, II 157n2

Peel, Sir Theophilus (d. 1911), director of Peel Brothers, V 172n1

Péligot, Eugène Melchior (1811-90), Professor of Applied Chemistry in Conservatoire des Arts et Métiers, and Assayer to Paris Mint, II 61, 62, 64, 71, 184; attends British Association meeting (1855), II 193

Pell, Morris Birkbeck, Professor of Mathematics and Natural Philosophy at Sydney University, I 25; paper on railway economics, 26, II 236, 285, VII 8

Penang, William Edgar Jevons in, II 437; returns from, III 49

Pengwerne, Jevons family holiday at, II 154-5; Pengwerne Hall, II 169

Peninsular and Oriental Steamship Co. (P & O), II 133n1

Penmaenmawr Quarry, John Hutton's troubles with, I 11, 45-6

Pennsylvania, II 428; coalfields, VII 27

Penny Cyclopaedia of the Society for the Diffusion of Useful Knowledge, I 63; 'Natural Philosophy', 213; 'Tontine', IV 215

Penrith, Cumberland, II 43

Penrith, New South Wales, I 137, 143nn2, 4, 215, 238; dinner at Perry's Inn, 153-4, tea at Commercial Inn, 238; Penrith road, I 145, 148, 213-14, II 219, 220, 221, 254; proposed railway extension to, II 263, 264

pepper, V 49, VII 12

Pepys, Samuel, II 5

periodicity

 principle of, VII 91-3; Boccardo on, V 32

 of crises, IV 224, 225, 230; discussed at Political Economy Club (1877), IV 199, 202-3; in writings of other economists, IV 301, VII 110

 of droughts, I 24, and epidemics, V 71

 of excessive fixed investments, III 65

periodicity (*contd*)
of human habits, VI 20
Indian corn prices, V 36, famines, 45–7
meteorological changes, IV 203–4, 299–300, VII 96; rainfall variations, IV 203, V 50–1, 103
panics, I 64
periods of excitement, based on low corn prices, VI 124
vintages, no trace of, V 167
articles on: 'On the Periodicity of Commercial Crises', IV 271–2, 273, 274, V 47, 57, 168, VII 94; 'On the Study of Periodic Commercial Fluctuations, with five diagrams', I 37, 183n2, 188n1, III 1–4, VII 124
see also cycles; sun-spots

Perkes, Samuel, London firm of mining machinery manufacturers, II 93n3; his Gold Reduction and Amalgamating Machine, 92, 92n3, 94n4

Permissive Prohibitory Liquor Bill (1864), VI 41

Personal Rights Association, V 187n1

Peru: WSJ visits (1859), I 33, II 375, 376; climate, II 387, 388, 394; coast line, 397; also mentioned, IV 296
see also Callao; Lima

Peto & Betts, London banking firm, failure (1866), VI 126

petroleum, VII 20, 31

Pettenkofer, Max von (1818–1901), biochemist, Professor of Hygiene at Munich, II 73

Petty, Sir William: his daughter, V 124, 125

Pfeiffer, Eduard (1835–1921), leader of German consumer co-operative movement, IV 85

Pfeiffer, Ida Laura (1797–1858), Austrian traveller, II 361

Pharmaceutical Chemist Act (1869), VII 57

Philadelphia
Academy of Natural Sciences, II 436n6
Botanic Garden, I 60n2
Mint: Assay Masters, III 223; cost of coinage, VII 70
pig-iron prices, V 86
trade its alpha and omega, II 383
WSJ stays in, II 381, 382–3, 399; hotel music, 383

Phillips, John Arthur (1822–87), geologist, I 79

Philosophical Magazine, see London . . . Philosophical Magazine

Philosophical Society of New South Wales, *see* New South Wales Philosophical Society

philosophy
WSJ's early interest in, I 33; takes M.A. in 'philosophical subjects', 34, 179, III 103; notes for book on Mill's philosophy, I 51; on idealism and materialism, II 411; Robbins on WSJ as philosopher, I 51–2
philosophical teaching in British Universities, V 22, 23, 94
see also mental, moral, and natural philosophy

photography
by artificial light, VII 31
Claudet's career in, II 62n5; H. E. Roscoe's photographs, II 73, researches on photochemical action of light, 243–4
WSJ and: photography in New South Wales, II 332, 342, 348, of gold diggings, 340, 346, 364–5, 371; photographing expedition, 352–5; works outdoors in a tent, 344, 364; sends photographs to Henry, 314, to H. E. Roscoe, 344
photographic apparatus and mahogany stereoscopic camera on three-legged stool, 309, inspected by Spanish customs officials at Callao, 387; camera borrowed by Francis Roscoe for Vancouver Island, 439;
plates taken by WSJ: I facing p. 15, II facing p. 13; WSJ 'Australia's first Pictorialist' (*Australian Photographic Review*, January 1955), I 31; gold medal awarded posthumously, I 31n1
photographs of WSJ, I frontispiece, II frontispiece, facing p. 44, p. 45; of Thomas Jevons, II facing p. 12; other photographs mentioned, II 294, 295, 309, III 33

physics
Fourier's theory of the motion of heat, IV 207–8

H. E. Roscoe adopts physico-chemical determination as his sphere, II 244
mathematics and, V 167n2
at Oxford, I 41, at Cambridge, IV 207n1
and solar variations, VII 92
Tait's thermodynamics, IV 208
WSJ studies at University College, III 103
Physiocrats, IV 115n3, V 95; examination question on, V 151n1
physiology, studied by WSJ for B.A., II 415
Pidgeon, N., *The Life Experience and Journal of N. Pidgeon, City Missionary* (Sydney, 1857), donated by WSJ to British Museum Library, II 450, 450n2
piece work, VI 71, 74
Piedmont, Kingdom of, Sicily declared part of (1860), II 412
Pierson, Nicolaas Gerard (1839–1909), Dutch banker, Professor of Political Economy and Statistics at Amsterdam University, IV 57, 58, 74, 83, admires WSJ's theory, 76, a constant reader of his books, 252, 266–7; note on *Theory of Political Economy* sent to, 89
inquiry into history of banking policy, IV 251–2, 263–5; claims to use mathematical treatment, 266–7, included in economic bibliography, 279; d'Aulnis thinks him only a graphical economist, 283
articles on wage fund theory and workers (1874), with diagrams, IV 89–90; *Gronbeginselen der Staathuishoudkunde* (1875), IV 266, 283; *Principles of Economics* (1896–1902, translated by A. A. Wotzel), IV 251n1, 266, 267n4
letters to, IV 263–5, 279–80; letters from, IV 251–2, 265–7, 280
Pilate, I 52n3
Pilkington and Wilson, White Star line, II 133n1
pins: Adam Smith's pin factory, VI 27, 28; Birmingham factories, VII 60
Piper, Frederick, of Levicks and Piper, Sydney, II 117
Piper, Mrs Frederick, II 117
Pisa: Thomas Jevons visits, II 199, 200,

dies of cholera at, I 22, 122, II 209; photograph of, II 295, 309
Pisey, Mr, of King's College, London, II 402
Pitt, William, the Younger: examination question on his sinking fund, VII 137
Pittsburgh, WSJ journeys through, II 382, 383, 400
Pitt Town, New South Wales, I 139–40
planetary theory of commercial crises (Balfour Stewart), V 8
planetary system and theory of heat, IV 208
plants, *see* vegetation
platinum, II 18, 62, 204; platinum salts, II 65
Plato, VI 4, 101; *Theaetetus* and *Gorgias*, required reading for M.A. at University College, London, II 437
Plautus, T. Maccius, his use of the word 'trapezita', IV 210
Playfair, John, IV 8; *Illustrations of the Huttonian Theory* (1802), II 245n10
Playfair, Sir Lyon (1818–98), Secretary for Science, Department of Science and Art: lecture on Pottery, I 85; attends British Association meeting at Glasgow (1855), II 191; Professor of Chemistry at Manchester Royal Institution, II 305n3
Playfair, William (1759–1823): *The Commercial and Political Atlas . . .* (1786), II 427; *An Inquiry into the permanent causes of decline and fall of powerful and wealthy nations . . .* (1805), IV 8–9, V 159
pleasure and pain
in the 'Selfish Theory of Morals', I 132–3; man's natural desire for pleasure, II 226; pain and pleasure equally prevailing in nature, II 288, VII 153
in Thomas Jevons's life and death, II 210–11, 212, 214, 215, 238; modes of pleasure, 318–19, of travel, 319, 344; pleasures of England, 402
in utility theory: problem of measurement, III 246–7, 253–4, IV 254, VII 149–50; units of, III 254, VII 153; labour as pain, III 253–4, IV 268–9, VI 18, 19–21, 92–3, as

pleasure and pain (*contd*)
means of warding off pain, 53;
Saturday Review on, VII 153–4, 159–
60
Gossen's theory of, IV 267–9; in Senior's
definition of wealth, VI 9, 10, VII
79
see also utility
Plener, Ernst Edler von, *English Factory
Legislation* (1873), VII 104
Plymouth, bank failure in 1825, VI 119
Plymouth Breakwater, VII 26
Poems for Youth, by a Family Circle (1820–1),
II 154n2
poets and poetry
WSJ and: entirely deprived of poetical
powers, I 195; reads Byron, II 225;
cannot make out Hiawatha, 233;
poetical elements in WSJ's economics (de Foville), V 17n1
poems by Mary Anne Roscoe, mother of
WSJ, I 5; Roscoe Jevons's desire to
be a poet, 7, 194; poems by other
members of Roscoe and Jevons
families, I 66n5, II 154, V 190n4
see also Clough, Arthur Hugh; Milton;
Shakespeare; Tennyson
Poggendorf, Johann Christian, *Annalen der
Physik und Chemie* (1855), II 191n4,
192, 192n11; (1838), II 306
Poland, II 431; bubble activity in 1720, VI
117
Pole, Charles, Deputy Governor of Bank of
England (1819), IV 265n5
police, VI 29, VII 61; as a profession, VI
67, VII 63
poliography, WSJ's idea of, anticipated by
Mayhew, VII 116
political economy
definitions, VI 4–6, VII 55–6, 157–8,
utility the subject of, VI 10; the
dismal science, VI 7–8
examination questions on, V 151–3, VII
131–8
and the franchise, III 130, VII 43
historical method, IV 266, VII 99, 158,
162; history of political economy in
English needed, V 82
laws of, VII 77; morals and, VI 8, VII
57, 159–60
principles and problems, III 152–3, 255,
VI 60, VII 45–6, 49, 160; foun-

dation in statistics, II 450; a deductive science, IV 114, VII 158–9
teaching of: elementary, IV 242; for
children, I 6, II 208n3, V 29–30,
VII 38–9, 51–4; Macleod's lectures
to sixth form boys at Christ's Hospital, IV 115; in Germany and
England, V 15–16, 29–30; in Italy,
V 37, 38
Cobden Lecture for primary school
teachers, I 207–8, VII 38–54, correspondence arising from, III 128–
38; for working men, V 37, VII 38,
42–4, 49, 51, 54, recommended
reading, 51–2
text-books, VI 3–4; Adam Smith,
WSJ's proposed students' edition,
IV 218–19, V 81; Cossa's *Guida,* V
94; Fawcett, III 139, 240, 246, VI
3–4, VII 60; Hodgson's translation
of Bastiat, VII 46, 51, 59;
McCulloch, VII 51; Marshall, V
78, 80; Miss Martineau, VII 51;
Mill, III 245–6, IV 23, 143, V 80,
VI 3–4, VII 59, 99; Thorold
Rogers, VII 60; Senior, VI 3; Dr
Watts, VI 51; Archbishop
Whately, I 6, VI 4, VII 52; WSJ's
Primer, IV 242, in America, V 69,
Italy, V 53, suggested for India, V 18
at Universities: WSJ at Owens College,
99, 104–5, IV 23–4, VII 60, classes,
III 9–10, 34, 48, 76, 104, Rylett's
lecture notes, IV 241, VI 3–140;
terms of Cobden Professorship, III
86, 105, additional courses proposed by WSJ, 105; WSJ at University College, London, IV 135,
142, 143, 144–5, 156, Ladies included in his classes, 216
Marshall's teaching at Cambridge,
IV 96, V 80, lectures on Mill, IV
100, V 78, 80; Foxwell's syllabuses,
IV 23, lectures on Marshall, V 78;
influence of Mill on University
teaching in England, III 93, 246,
IV 116, 143, 286, V 80–1, 109
in Italian universities, V 38
examinations: Cambridge Tripos, IV
52–3, 69–70, 115, 147, women admitted to, 143, 146; question
papers, VII 132–8; reading scripts

and settling lists, IV 148-9; London University: M.A. paper sat by WSJ (1860), VII 131-2, two examiners on his answers, III 111, 113; applications for examinerships, IV 239-40, V 177. *See also under* examinations

WSJ and: first lessons, I 6; reads Adam Smith, Mill, Malthus and Whewell (1856-7), VII 115-19; first published contributions to economic discussion (1856-7), II 235-7, 262-8, VII 3-11; political economy his chief concern, II 280, 292; his mission in (1858), 321-2; warned against by H. E. Roscoe, 323; studies for B.A. (1859), II 403; plans a work on (1860), I 184, II 120; takes M.A. in, II 406, gets gold medal, 445, III 103; wins Ricardo scholarship, II 406, 410, 422-3; finds the 'true theory of Economy' (19 February 1860), I 179n4, 184-5, II 410-11, 'a complicated mathematical problem', II 422, based on the last portion added, 422; resolves to 'let out' his theory (14 September 1862), II 452; 'Notice of a general mathematical theory of Economy' read before British Association meeting (October 1862), I 37, 188, VII 77; similarity to, but priority over, Walras's theory, IV 39-40, 48, 49-50, 71, 76-7; d'Aulnis undertakes to popularise the new theory, IV 57, 59, 62, 66, 67-8, 71, 72, 74

for WSJ's career in political economy, *see under* Owens College; Queen's College, Liverpool; University College, London. For his writings on political economy, *see under* Jevons, W. S., Works

see also economics; mathematical theory of political economy; statistics

Political Economy Club

WSJ an honorary member, IV 52, 55, 102, 134; elected an ordinary member (1882), V 142; intended speech on mathematical method (1876), IV 180, 181n4; dines at, IV 52, invites Foxwell to dinner at, 173-

4, 223, V 185

meetings: (5 June 1874), discussion on India, IV 52; (7 May 1875), on political economy as a science of wealth, IV 114; (4 June 1875), railway reform, proposed by WSJ, IV 102n3, 116-17; (2 February 1877), on relation of value to utility and labour, proposed by WSJ, IV 102n3; (1 June 1877), on periodic crises, IV 199, 202-3; (7 December 1877), on trade depressions, WSJ meets Gladstone, IV 222; (1 February 1878), on laws of industry, IV 224; (1 March 1878), on strikes, proposed by WSJ, IV 243n1; (3 March 1882), on bimetallism, V 191

other members, IV 117, 202, 264n2

Mill as, IV 134

publications, V 44

also mentioned, I 181n2, 206n3

political philosophy: definition, VI 8, VII 55; gold medal for, at University College, London, III 103

Poltimore gold and copper mine, Thomas Jevons's speculation in, I 118, II 94, 128, 142; goes bankrupt, 164, 172

Polynesia, II 181n2; gold product,

Polytechnische Zeitung, see Deutsche Allgemeine Polytechnische Zeitung

Ponsonby, Sarah (?1755-1831), Lady of Llangollen, II 153

Pontgibaud Silver Lead Mining & Smelting Co., Thomas Jevons's investments in, II 94; pays a dividend, 164

poor, the, VI 106, VII 6-7; and political economy, VII 45; labour their patrimony, 48; rich and poor, VII 38; incidence of taxation on, VI 135-6, 137, 138

poor laws, V 161, VII 45; workhouse relief, V 162n2; poor rate, VII 57; examination question on, VII 135

Pope Alexander, II 83

Pope Pius IX, II 408

popular amusements, IV 286-7

population
   and acres in crop, VII 4-5
   and coal, VII 21, 23-4, 37

population (contd)
  growth, VII 40–1, encouraged by cheap
    corn, VI 15
  Malthus on: WSJ reads, VII 119; lec-
    ture notes on, VI 54–60
  overpopulation through improvidence,
    III 255
  and railways, II 267–8
  statistics, II 426
  theory of, excluded from Theory of Politi-
    cal Economy, VII 158
  see also emigration
porpoises, I 104, II 84, 97
Port Curtis, Queensland, gold discoveries,
    II 340, 346, 350n1
Port Denison Times (1868), IV 176, 177
Port Hacking (or Hagen), I 161
Port Jackson, I 124, 136; its beauty, II
    105–6, 110, 217
Port Phillip, Melbourne, I 107–8, 109,
    124, 234, II 99–100; gold shipped
    from, II 260; voyage to Peru from,
    II 273, 385
Porter, George Richardson (1792–1852),
    The Progress of the Nations (1847), VI
    63, VII 104
Portugal
  British sovereigns legal tender in, III
    163, reflux of sovereigns from, 162
  gold standard, VII 68
  proportion of silver to gold, V 140
'postal notes', proposal for, IV 216n2;
    article on, 216n2, V 99, 101
Postmaster General: contests estimates of
    telegraph profits (1875–6), IV 171–
    2; proposal for 'Postal Notes', 216–
    17
  see also (from 1880), Fawcett, Henry
Post Office
  book post, IV 13; parcel post, V 155n2;
    in Jamaica, V 71; 'A State Parcel
    Post' (WSJ, 1879), IV 303, V 3,
    155n2
  and Government: an optional function,
    VI 133; a successful monopoly, VII
    57, multiplication of efficiency
    through, VII 61; revenue from, IV
    171–2, VI 133, VII 10
  international postal service, V 27–8
  postage: on overland mail via Marseilles,
    II 132–3; on papers, II 413, IV 50;
    penny postage, IV 171; policy on

  charges, II 265–6; postage stamps,
    IV 217
  postal orders, IV 216n2
  Post-Office clerks, VI 75n3
  Post-Office Money Orders, IV 185, 216–
    17; Post Office Money Order Act
    (1848), V 101n2
  also mentioned, V 53
  see also telegraph; telephone
Post Office Savings Bank, V 88
potatoes, II 332; failure of Irish crops
    (1846–7), VI 123; as item in cost of
    living, III 256; a substitute food,
    VI 17, 88; used in manufacture of
    cotton, III 206
Potter, Edmund, M.P., F.R.S., III 29n2
Potter, Lucy (1840–1910), marriage to
    H. E. Roscoe (1863), III 29n2. See
    also Roscoe, Mrs H. E.
Potter, Richard (1799–1886), Professor of
    Natural Philosophy and As-
    tronomy at University College,
    London: WSJ attends his classes, I
    65, 83, 87, 95, II 421; 'duller than
    ever', I 94; 'Potter's book', I
    67
pottery, see ceramics
Pouillet, Claude Servais Mathias (1790–
    1868): experiments on sun's heat,
    II 297n8, 306, VII 97; earth ther-
    mometer observations on solar
    radiation, IV 296–7
poverty: in Liverpool and London, I 16–
    17, signs of, on WSJ's London
    walks, 67–8; medical relief for, III
    256–7; as check to population, VI
    58
  see also pauperism: poor, the; workhouses
Powell, Baden (1796–1860), Professor of
    Geometry at Oxford, V 108n1
power
  from coal, VII 30, 35
  power-producing machines, or prime
    movers, VI 25; electricity as prime
    mover impossible, 24; power-
    averaging machines, 25
  sun-power, VII 34–5
  tidal power, III 77–8, 122, 123–4, VI
    24, 25
  see also horses; steam power; water power
Pownall, George Henry (1850–1916), ban-
    ker, former student of WSJ at

Owens College: paper on capital and labour read to Manchester Statistical Society, V 25, 26n; plans for inquiry into banking transactions, V 25, 129–30

'The Proportional Use of Credit Documents and Metallic Money in English Banks' (*Journal of the Institute of Bankers*, 1881), V 130n2

Hon. Sec. of Jevons Memorial Committee, V 25n1

letter from, V 25

Poynting, John Henry (1852–1914), physicist: tables on intemperance, V 165

practical men, II 335, IV 296, VII 14, 88; mathematical economists as, IV 284; and solar cycles, V 11, 12, VII 92, 95

WSJ's combination of practice and theory in economic investigations, III 115

prejudice, VII 45, 46, 54, 56, 58, 67

Prestatyn, visit to soda-works, I 93, II 41–2

Preston, Robert Berthon (1820–60), Liverpool engineer and art patron, II 201

Pretoria Convention (1881), V 135n4

Prevost-Paradol, Lucien Anatol, on conservation of coal resources, III 123

Price, Bonamy (1807–88), IV 126

'The Principles of Currency' (*Fraser's Magazine*, 1863), III 32; *The Principles of Currency* (1869), V 154; *Currency and Banking* (1876), noticed by WSJ in *Manchester Guardian*, VII 127

Price, Richard (1723–91): sinking fund, examination question on, VII 137

An Essay on the Population of England, VI 54

prices

Analysis of prices since 1782 (WSJ), I 197, III 21, 42, 45, 52, 53–4, 61, VI 118–19; temporarily halted (1864), III 59; paper on, read to Royal Statistical Society (May 1865), I 197n3, III 54n3, 61, 69, 81–2, IV 163, 170; a 'more extended enquiry' projected (1874), IV 54, 114, 171; calculations on average ratio of change (1730–1876), 168, 169–71; article: 'Variation of Prices

and the Value of the Currency since 1782', IV 170n2

'arbitrated' price, VI 114–15

in credit cycle, VI 128–9, 131

diagrams (WSJ), I 196, III 21, 42, V 58, in proposed 'Statistical Atlas', III 425–6; others, V 13

examination questions on, V 152, VII 131, 135, 137, 138

indexes: *Economist*, IV 170; Sauerbeck's, III 256n1; Soetbeer's, III 21, 82; WSJ's, III 82n4, 256n1, IV 247n3

lists and tables: Balfour's, in *American Almanac*, III 54, IV 6–7; Bodleian, IV 286; of grain in India, V 51; Greenwich Hospital series, IV 169–70; Milburn's, V 54; pig-iron in Philadelphia, V 86; WSJ's, IV 170

market price, IV 61, VI 82, 87, VII 148

as measure of pleasure and pain (or utility), III 246–7, 254; Walras's 'ratio of the rarities', VII 76–7

measurement of price: in *Serious Fall*, I 39, 191n1, 192n2, III 36–8, 43–4, 54, 82, V 58

monopoly price, VI 83; Walras on, IV 197

in New South Wales, II 162, 215, 264, III 20, IV 114; minimum upset price for Crown lands, II 283–5, 286–7, VII 3–6, 8

price movements: WSJ's study of secular change, I 35; and gold supplies, I 181n2, II 451, III 20–5, IV 6–7, 53, 55–6, 77, V 58–9, VI 128; moderating factors, III 208–9; curves, III 53–4, 55

regulating effect of demand and supply, III 21, V 30–1, VI 81, 83, 89

and wages, III 142–3, VI 63, 64, VII 49–50

war prices, II 194, III 53, 54, 55, IV 6–7

see also ratio of exchange; value

prices, history of: in Adam Smith, IV 170; Laspeyres, III 61, 81–2; Mantellier, III 67; in *Monografia statistica*, V 198; *see also* Rogers, J. E. Thorold; Tooke and Newmarch, *History of Prices*

Princess Royal, *see* Victoria, Princess

Princeton Review: 'Solar Influence on Commerce' intended for, IV 293, 304–5, V 8, VII 90; editor, J. M. Libbey, IV 304n1

Prinsep, C. R., III 27

Printers' Trade Society, VII 47n

printing press: Babcock's polychromatic press, II 171–2; compositors, VI 74, VII 47; multiplication of efficiency through, VI 30, VII 62; new type-composing machine, VII 47

private enterprise, V 93

probability
  examination questions on, V 153, VII 137
  theory of, I 15; in scientific method, 35, V 52; WSJ studies at University College, II 30–1; applied to gold finds, II 352; applied to study of commercial crises, VII 93
  Westergaard on, IV 258

Probyn, J. W., editor of Cobden Club publications, VII 105

Proctor, Richard Anthony (1837–88), Secretary of the Royal Astronomical Society: 'University Boat Races and Sun-Spot Cycles' (*JRSS*, 1879), V 51

produce: total produce divided into rent, wages and interest, VI 60, 67; equals profit and wages, VII 142; examination question on, VII 136, on producers, V 152; rate of profit determined by labourers' share (Mill), V 27

production
  of coal, *see* coal
  and demand, Cazenove on Mill, IV 120–1
  George Darwin's projected paper on, IV 99–100
  lecture notes on, VI 19–26; three requisites of, 17, 36, 60; labour as agent of, 17, 21–2, 26, VII 158; natural agents, VI 17; capital as requisite, 36–7
  and value, VII 83
  Walras on co-efficients of production, IV 198
  also mentioned, V 95
  see also cost of production

productive capital, VII 16; productive and unproductive spending, II 268, VII 16

productive services (*services producteurs*), IV 191, V 95

productiveness: of labour, IV 227, VI 92–3; and rate of interest, VII 142

profits
  determined by supply and demand, VII 64
  in distribution theory (early view), II 422
  distinguished from interest on capital, IV 227n3, VII 64–5
  examination questions on, VII 131, 135
  from new land in New South Wales, II 282, 285
  as portion of produce, VI 62, 67–8, VII 142, 152
  profit-sharing in industry, III 138, VI 75–7, VII 64; panacea for labour troubles, III 143; letter to *The Times* on (19 January 1867), III 151–4. *See also* Fox, Head & Co.

progress
  American, II 197, 429–30
  dependence on coal, VII 33, 35
  and labour troubles, VI 79, VII 43–4; hindered by working-class attitudes to innovation, VII 46–9
  Herbert Spencer's definition, V 28
  WSJ's belief in, I 51, 98, 155, II 180, VI 67

progressive economy, VII 31, 33; progressive taxation, VI 136

property
  as capital, VI 38, 41
  laws of, III 152; Puviani on, V 39–40; founded on property in one's own labour (Smith), VII 48
  also mentioned, IV 182

protection
  Alby's defence of, IV 126
  Cossa's errors, VII 100
  examination questions on, V 152, VII 137
  fallacies of, III 239, V 25, VI 134
  foreign tariffs a possible advantage to England, IV 306
  Gladstone's battle against, I 18; Derby Ministry and, I 85, 86
  and Imperialism, V 20

in New South Wales, VII 8, 43, 118, 123, II 451
'Protective Humbug' (WSJ, *Empire*, 30 March 1857), II 280n12, 281, VII 117
Protective League (New South Wales), II 280n12, 281
Providence, I 158, II 211, 226; and workmen's bonus, III 153
Provident Society, Manchester & Salford District, III 256-7
provisions, as circulating capital, VI 41
Prussia
coal: area of coal measures, VII 27, 34; production, VII 33
exhibits from, in Crystal Palace, II 12
incomes, III 242
population and acres in crop, VII 4
Prussians on parade in Berlin, II 73
Seven Years War, III 125n2
Prussia, Prince of, II 73
see also Friedrich Wilhelm IV, King of Prussia; Wilhelm Friedrich Ludwig, King of Prussia
public health
in England: sanitary reform, I 16; repeal of soap duty, II 40n1
in Munich, Chair and Institute of Hygiene, II 73n12
public opinion, II 316, VII 17, 55
Publisher's Circular, III 141
Puerto Rico, II 381, 398
Punch, I 17n3, II 73n15, IV 194n3; copies sent to WSJ in Sydney, II 259
'punts' or ferries, I 140, 143
purchasing power, IV 168-71
Purser, on board the *Oliver Lang*, I 106, II 83
Pusey, schoolboy lodger in Gower Street, II 17, 19, 20
Puviani, Amilcare (1854-1907), Italian economist: undertakes translation of *Primer of Political Economy*, V 37n3, 40, 53, 62-3
letters from, V 37-41, 62
Pyrheliometer, VII 97

Quack, Hendrik Pieter Godfried (1834-1917), Professor of Political Economy at Utrecht, IV 58, 214

quantity
economic quantities in *Theory of Political Economy*, V 22, 32n1, Christie on, 30-1, 34; statement that laws of political economy deal with quantities, VII 77-8, 145, challenged by Cliffe Leslie, 159-61; WSJ the chief author of quantitative reasoning in Economics (Marshall), V 66
in laws of supply and demand, VI 81; relation between quantity and price of corn, VI 89
no quantity in WSJ's theory of logic, III 13, 117
and utility, VI 90, 93, 95
quarries, *see under* Hutton, John
Quarterly Journal of the Chemical Society: 'Photochemical Researches' (R. W. Bunsen and H. E. Roscoe, 1856), II 191, 192n10, 229; editor (Watts), II 191n3
Quarterly Review
'Coal and Smoke' (1866), III 90, 92, VII 125
'Herbert Spencer' (St George Mivart, 1873), IV 29n1
'History of British Government' (Inglis Palgrave, 1873), IV 13
quartz
in Australia, I 176, II 351, 366, 371, at Sofala, I 220, 222, 224, 227; burnt quartz, II 351; cooperatives among quartz mines, VI 76
in New Zealand, III 74; Herbert Jevons's speculation in, 205
in Wales, John Hutton's troubles with, III 205
Professor Smith's paper on separation of gold from quartz, I 36
Quebec, loans made in grain, IV 162
Queen's College, Liverpool
opening ceremony (5 November 1857), I 54n2; housed in Liverpool Mechanics Institute, I 198n2, II 291n1, III 68, later amalgamated with Institute (1881), I 198n2
WSJ appointed part-time Professor of Logic, Moral Philosophy and Political Economy (1865), I 45, 198n2, III 64, 65-6, 68, 69, 104; introductory address, 'On Reading and Study', III 75, 76; weekly

Queen's College, Liverpool (*contd*)
 lectures, I 204n2, III 68n1; resigns
 (June 1866), I 198n2, III 122n1
Queensland
 gold rush, 1858, II 350n1; discoveries at
 Port Curtis, 340, 346, 350n1
 treatment of aborigines by settlers, IV
 174–7, VII 127
Queen's Own Rifles, Volunteer Corps
 WSJ joins (January 1860), I 36, 186n1,
 II 407, 418; on guard in Hyde Park
 for arrival of Princess Alexandra, I
 190; Field Days, II 411, 460–1;
 musketry instruction, 417, 431;
 WSJ's marksmanship, 436–7, 443;
 promoted sergeant (1862), 443,
 460–1; battalion drill, III 14, VII
 120; regret at leaving, III 15
Queens men in Vancouver Island, II
 440
 see also Volunteer Movement
Quekett, John Thomas (1815–61), Professor of Histology in the Royal
 College of Surgeons, II 50
Quetelet, Lambert Adolphe Jacques
 (1796–1874), Belgian astronomer
 and statistician, II 362; *A Treatise on
 Man* (English translation, 1842),
 VII 119

Radicals: criticism of Cobden Lecture, I
 207, VII 37–8; WSJ neither Radical nor conservative, I 208
Raglan, Lord, II 163n6
Railway Magazine and Annals of Science,
 edited by John Herapath, IV 274,
 275n3
railways
 American, II 390, 419; construction, VI
 125, collapse of boom, 126n9;
 plank-road system, VII 11; WSJ
 travels by, II 390, 400
 in England: leadership in, II 183;
 narrow-gauge construction, II
 206n6; construction mania (1844–
 6), IV 210, VI 122, 123, (1860s),
 125, demand for rails, 225n2;
 foreign navvies on, VII 50; goods
 traffic, carriage of coal, VII 23, 29;
 parcel service, V 155n2, 159, 160
 companies: meetings, VI 76; borrow-
 ing policy, VI 105; Great Eastern,

VII 23; Great Western, VII 23;
 London and North Eastern, shares
 in, III 50; London and North Western, VI 46, VII 23; Midland,
 proposed revival of second class
 coaches, V 87
 travel on by Jevons family, I 64, II
 391, III 10, Lucy's narrow escape,
 II 175–6; duty on, VI 138; col-
 lisions, VII 40
 in Jamaica, V 70–1; Panama, II 379–80,
 381; Peru, 378, 388, 394. *See also
 under* France; New South Wales
 international travel, V 27, 28
 see also locomotives
railways and economic theory
 capital investment in, I 27, III 142;
 proportion of capital invested to
 labour, VI 38; as fixed capital, VI
 43; railway shares as fixed or circulating capital, 45, 46; railway
 expenditure in credit cycle, VI 131
 cost of living and, IV 7
 debate on administration of railways at
 Political Economy Club (1875), IV
 102n3, 116n1
 examination questions on, VII 133, 138
 'The Railways and the State' (WSJ,
 1874), IV 116n1
 WSJ's concern with railways in New
 South Wales, I 25–7, II 8–11, 235–
 7, 262–8, 451
Railway Statistics, in Weale's Series, I 27
rainfall
 in England, I 75
 on board the *Oliver Lang*, II 82
 in Minnesota, II 419
 in New South Wales, I 138, 146, 147–8,
 150, 216, 218, 220, 226, II 300, with
 hail and snow, II 97, 355; autumn
 rains, 205; thunder showers, 203,
 254; on a photographing expedition, 354–5; in monthly reports,
 II 298
 periodical, IV 203, V 50–1, 103;
 statistics, V 52
rainbows, I 226, lunar, I 102; article on
 reflected rainbows, V 196
rain-gauge, article on (1861), VII 124
 see also meteorology; weather
Rammelsberg, Karl Friedrich (1813–99),
 chemist, II 73

Randle, William, railway contractor in New South Wales, II 206

Ransome, Arthur (b. 1834), Lecturer in Medical Jurisprudence at Owens College: takes up issue of child care, V 168

rarities (*raretés*), Walras's equivalent to 'degrees of utility', IV 40, 41, 46, 67

raspberry vinegar, II 81

rate of discount, IV 265; and commercial fluctuations, VI 121, 129; compared with price index for metals, 124; shown in Diagram of Bank of England Weekly Accounts, 127n1; in credit cycle, 131; banker's view of, VII 59

rate of interest
and foreign exchanges, VI 111, 112–13; Bank policy on, IV 251–2, 264
periodic fluctuations in, IV 31, 32, in relation to commercial fluctuations, VI 121; rise in (1866), VI 126, fall in (1876), VI 113
see also interest

Rathbone Brothers, Liverpool shipping and trading company, II 391n17, V 178; T. E. Jevons taken on for five years, I 10, II 414, III 57, becomes New York agent, 78, 158; American trade, III 78n2

Rathbone, William, III 78n2

ratio of exchange, IV 140n2, 151, VI 87, VII 82, 83, or exchange value, III 22, 167n2, 171–2, 177, VI 80, 95, VII 141, 143–4, 148, or quantities exchanged, VI 93, or price, VI 81; equation for, IV 40, 228; proportion between quantity of corn and, VI 89; varies inversely with final degree of utility, VII 149

ratios: calculated by machine, VII 86–7, 89; of marginal utilities, III 168n2 of rarities (Walras), VII 76–7
between supply and demand, VI 82
of utility, II 410

Rau, Karl Heinrich (1792–1870), Professor of Political Economy at Heidelberg, III 197, IV 8, 260, 278, 283; included in mathematico-economic list, V 55
Grundsätze der Volkswirtschaftslehre (1868), V 63, 66

raw materials, VI 33, 84; as circulating capital, V 41; taxes on, abolished by Gladstone, VI 139

Raynaud, A., Paris manufacturer of perfumes, founder of Société d'économie politique de Paris, V 4, 7n5

Read, Gabriel, gold discoveries in New Zealand, III 74n1

Reade, Mr, proposals for logic Primer (1874), IV 34

Real del Monte Company, VI 119

reason, I 158–9
reasoning machine, *see* logical abacus

Reasoner, co-operative newspaper, III 165n3; WSJ subscribes to, 166

Réaumur, René Antoine Ferchault de (1683–1757), his thermometer, II 435

Recess Studies, 'Graphic Representation of the Laws of Supply and Demand' (Fleeming Jenkin, 1870), III 166

Red Indians, II 384, 455

Reece, Rees, London chemist, II 119n16

Reed, Thomas German (1817–88), musician and entertainer, IV 223

Reed, Mrs Thomas German (Priscilla Reed, 1818–95), actress, IV 223

Reeves, Sims (1818–1900), English tenor: concert at St James's Hall, II 458

reform, *see* Parliamentary reform

Reform Club, I 73, III 34; its chef, II 360n4

Registrar-General's Office, VII 87, 89

Regnault, H. V., *Cours élémentaire de Chimie* (1849–50), chosen as prize by WSJ, I 66, 67, 69, 77, 83, 87, 92

Reilly, [Sir] Francis Savage (1825–83), Q.C., V 169

religion
WSJ and: records thoughts on, in Journal, I 53; a 'Dependent Moralist' himself, 66; Morgan's freethinking, 95; once thought of entering ministry, 99, undertook a history of Christ, 99–100; discards belief in revealed religion, 154–5, looks for God in Matter and Mind, 155, in the dignity and love of man, 157, II 288, 325–7; finds his creed in *Jane Eyre*, 310, 311–12; finds God in Unitarian chapel (1866), I 202;

religion (*contd*)
  believes in future life, II 213; on morals and religion, 225–6, 241–2, 296, on Christian mythology, 327; goes to church in Wallasey, III 18
  view of God, I 52; no place for, in world machine, 154n3; seen if anywhere in order of Nature, 155; a general Principle, not a person, II 258; embodiment of universal good, 226; God, the Carpenter, I 132; felt within, 202
  other views: Saintine's unacceptable conclusions, I 156–7; Whately's view, 158–9; Roscoe Jevons's religious faith, I 194; Thomas Jevons on religion and Rouen Cathedral, II 178, on High Mass at La Madeleine, 179; Henrietta's doubts, II 225–6, 241; Lucy's attitude of faith, 337; Spencer and Gladstone on God and evolution, IV 38–9
  Dissenters, II 33n2. *See also* Unitarians
  grace before tea, II 253
  Roman Catholics, II 296; in Ireland, V 127; Roman Catholicism 'very disgusting', II 277; idolatry of Spanish-American churches, 378–9, 395
  'Spirit's Knob', American Indian sacred stone, II 384
  temples in Chinese gold-fields, Queensland, II 367–8
  see also science and religion
Renouvier, Charles Bernard (1815–1903), editor of *La Critique philosophique* . . . , IV 85–6
rent
  arising from inequalities, V 61,62, from peculiar advantages, VI 68
  Gossen's theory of, IV 269
  landlordism and rents in Ireland, V 112–15, 189n2
  land rents in New South Wales, VII 7, 8
  as portion of produce, VI 60, 67, VII 158
  Ricardian theory of, IV 197, V 61; examination questions on, IV 146, 147, VII 138
  to be solved as mathematical function (1860), VII 120; in *Theory of Political Economy*, VII 152; George Darwin on, IV 26, 28; Walras on, 197–8; Westergaard on, 254n2
rentes, VII 76
Rentsch, Hermann, editor, *Handwörterbuch der Volkswirtschaftslehre* (1864–6), IV 301
reprinting society (Adam Smith Society), proposal for, V 44, 73–4, 82–3, 87
Republicans
  in Ireland, *see* Lane, Henry
  Republican view of education, IV 213
  Republicans and Democrats, *see* United States of America
res fungibiles, V 102
resumption of cash payments, Report of Select Committee on (1819), IV 264, 265
retail trade, examination question on, V 152; retailers, VI 33
  see also shopkeepers
Reusch, Johann Peter (d. 1758), *Systema Logicum*, IV 231
revenue: Ricardo's error on, IV 121; from taxation, examination questions on, VII 134, 135
  'Cure for the Revenue' (WSJ, 1857), VII 123
Revue des Deux Mondes, IV 68, 85, 126n4
Revue Philosophique, V 22
Revue Scientifique, IV 86, 288
Reynolds, Joshua, V 66
Rhoda, friend of Lucy, II 32
Ribot, Thomas, *Revue Philosophique*, V 22
Ricardo, David
  capital confounded with revenue, IV 121; on fixed and circulating capital, VI 42
  currency, IV 12n3
  diminishing returns, IV 266
  part of the orthodox creed, VII 77; his methods still rule in England, IV 95; necessary reading for students, VII 99
  price theory, VI 83; and cost of production, V 62, VII 152
  rent, 'so-called' theory, IV 146, 147, 197, V 61
  value: on the term, VII 85; exchangeable value, VII 83; labour theory of, IV 115n3, VII 83, 141; his ideas on value mathematical, VII 78

wages: natural rate of, VI 59–60, VII
144; as fraction of total produce, VI
61; wages fund, 61–2
Cliffe Leslie on, VII 160, 162; Walras
on, V 95
included in syllabus for lectures, University College, London, IV 143;
examination questions on, London
and Cambridge, IV 146, 147, V
152, VII 134, 138
also mentioned, IV 73, 91, 252, V 78, 80,
VI 48, VII 142
Ricardo Scholarship in Political Economy,
at University of London, II 406;
won by WSJ (December 1860), I
34, II 416n5, 422–3, III 103; WSJ
and Bagehot examiners for (1875),
IV 124, WSJ and Foxwell (1881),
V 147, 149, 151; question paper,
151–3
rice: prices, III 252, IV 6; effect of low
price on Lancashire cotton trade, V
45, VI 15; use of, in cotton manufacture, III 206; also mentioned,
VII 24
Richards, William Westley (1790–1865),
founder of Birmingham armaments
firm, II 431
Richmond, home of Dr Richard Roscoe,
uncle of WSJ, I 75, 76, 84, II 5;
Herbert Jevons lodges with, II 8–9,
11, 14, 15–16, 18, 19–20
Richmond, Melbourne, I 108n3, II 100
Richmond, New South Wales, I 137n1,
146n2, 147; excursion to, 134, 142–
3, 148, II 252, 253, 256n2; the
Richmond-punt, I 143, 147; railway extension to, II 262, 263
Richter, Hans (1843–1915), Wagner concerts in London, V 134
Rickards, Sir George Kettilby, VII 146
Rifle Movement: Volunteer plan of defence, II 406–7. *See also* Queens
Own Rifles
Rio de Janeiro, I 102, II 112; British
sovereigns legal tender in, III 163–
4
risk, IV 227; profit as reward of, VI 67, VII
64–5, 142; examination question
on, VII 137
River Alma, battle of (1854), II 103n4, 204
Rivers Wilson, Sir Charles (1831–1916),

civil servant, financier, II 133n3;
member, Royal Commission on International Coinage (1868), III
181; British representative at International Monetary Convention,
III 212–13, 215, VII 67
letters from, III 181, IV 106
Rivière, Ann, *see* Bishop, Anna
Rivista Europa, IV 65
roads
financial aspects, VII 118; as fixed capital, VI 43
as function of Government, VI 133;
examination question on, VII 138
plank-roads, VII 11
road locomotives, VII 30
see also under New South Wales
Robarts, classmate of WSJ at University
College, I 54, 58
Robberds, Charles William, Unitarian mi-
nister in Oldham, I 58
Robberds, Rev. John Gooch (1789–1854),
Unitarian minister, I 58n4
Roberts, Hugh W., Manager of North and
South Wales Bank: letter on glut
of gold coin in North Wales, III
191–3
Roberts, Richard (1789–1864), inventor,
VI 29
Robertson, George Croom (1842–92),
Professor of Logic and Mental
Philosophy at University College,
London, editor of *Mind*, IV 239
Laws of Thought (1864), noticed by WSJ
in *Spectator* (11 March 1864), VII
125
Robinson, of the Queens Own Rifles, in
Vancouver Island, II 440
Robinson Crusoe, II 332–3
Robson, John (1815–76), Secretary, Uni-
versity College, London, IV 143
letters to, III 234–5, IV 123–4, 124, 132,
133–4, 144, 149; letters from, IV
108–9
Rochdale Society of Equitable Pioneers,
VI 74
Rockhampton, New South Wales, gold
finds, II 350
Rogers, Edward, Liverpool merchant, II
44n4
Rogers, James Edwin Thorold (1823–90),
Tooke Professor of Economic Sci-

Rogers, James Edwin Thorold (*contd*)
  ence and Statistics at King's College, London (1859–90), III 47n1;
  Professor of Political Economy at
  Oxford (1862–7), III 32n3; examines Manchester Grammar School,
  III 68; WSJ dines with, in Oxford,
  IV 285; testimonial for WSJ, III
  106, 116; examination question on,
  VII 138
  paper on wages and prices read to
  Statistical Society, Manchester
  (1861), III 47; *A History of Agriculture and Prices in England, 1259–1793*
  (1866–87), III 47n3; vols 1–3, III
  47, 66–7, 82, 126, vol. 2, 67, publication of vols 1 and 2 (1861),
  126n4, of vols 1–4, VII 103; edition
  of *Wealth of Nations* (1869), V 81; *A
  Manual of Political Economy*, VII 60,
  error on labour as cause of value,
  VI 90–1
  letters to, V 163; letters from, III 47, 67–
    8
Rolleston, George (1829–81), Professor of
  Anatomy and Physiology at Oxford: WSJ dines with, IV 285; letter
  from, IV 284
rolling mills, VI 25, VII 20, 30
Romans (ancient), examination question
  on, VII 135
Rome
  decimal coinage, I 122, II 200–1
  'on the high way to', II 295
  Monograph of Rome and the Campagna, IV
    299, V 197–8
  Thomas Jevons's visit to the Eternal
    City, I 121, 122, II 199, 200–2, 209,
    212; WSJ visits, V 198
Rooke, John (1780–1856), Cumberland
  Worthy, writer on economic issues,
  IV 275, 276
Roscher, Wilhelm G. F. (1817–94), VII
  101; *Principles of Political Economy*:
  passage on WSJ's theory of value,
  IV 73; d'Aulnis's polemic against,
  75; Inglis Palgrave's projected
  translation, 108, 109; J. J. Lalor's
  translation, IV 108n2, VII 102;
  *Geschichte der Nationaloekonomie in
  Deutschland*, IV 266, Gossen not
  included, 272, 280, 282; on Rau

and von Thünen, 283
Roscoe family, WSJ's maternal relations, I
  56n9, 58n5, II 44n4; genealogy, I
  242–3; *Poems for Youth*, II 154n2
Roscoe, Alfred (Fred, 1841–62), youngest
  son of Robert Roscoe, cousin of
  WSJ, I 243; joins the Queens Own
  Rifles, I 36, II 407; passes first B.A.
  at University College, London,
  418; sudden death at Wadham
  College, Oxford, 440
Roscoe, Arthur (b. 1825), second son of
  William Stanley Roscoe, cousin of
  WSJ, I 243, II 123; a sawyer in
  Otago, II 405
Roscoe, Clara (Patty), daughter of Robert
  Roscoe, cousin of WSJ, I 243, II 32,
  145, 425
Roscoe, Edmund (1864–85), son of H. E.
  Roscoe, I 243, III 59
Roscoe, Edward (1785–1834), brother of
  Dr Richard Roscoe, uncle of WSJ,
  I 242, II 44n5
Roscoe, Eliza, cousin of WSJ, I 36, 243
Roscoe, Elizabeth Mary (b. 1856), daugh-
  ter of William Caldwell Roscoe,
  cousin of WSJ, I 243, II 230
Roscoe, Francis James (Frank, 1830–78),
  youngest son of William Stanley
  Roscoe, cousin of WSJ, I 193, 243;
  death of his mother, II 64; his
  Chambers in Austin Friars, 122–3,
  230, 441; joins Queens Own Rifles,
  I 36, II 407, 418, his marksmanship, 431, 436–7; marriage, III 59;
  returns to Vancouver Island, loses
  wedding presents in shipwreck, 62;
  M.P. in Canadian Parliament, IV
  157; death, V 178n1; also mentioned, II 123n10
  letter from, II 438–40
Roscoe, Mrs Francis James (Letitia le
  Breton), I 243, III 59n2; loses
  wedding presents, 62; a Christmas
  gift for, V 178
Roscoe, Harriet (b. 1835), sister of H. E.
  Roscoe, cousin of WSJ, I 243; sees
  lying-in-state of Duke of Wellington, I 72, and his funeral procession, 73; goes to Heidelberg with
  brother, II 63n7, travels through
  Germany, 71, 73; marriage to Ed-

ward Enfield, I 90n4, II 64, 75, 122, 140; visit to H. E. Roscoe in Heidelberg, 230; in London, 315; also mentioned, II 4, 5, 29, 31n8, 32, 80

Roscoe, Henrietta, *see* Osler, Mrs Timothy

Roscoe, Henry (1799–1836), barrister, father of H. E. Roscoe, uncle of WSJ, I 74n1, 242; his old Law Commonplace Book used by WSJ for his journal, I 2, 53; early lessons in chemistry, I 6; *Life of William Roscoe* (1833), I 59n3, 61

Roscoe, Mrs Henry, 'Aunt Henry' (Maria Fletcher, 1798–1885), mother of H. E. Roscoe, I 73–4, 242; schoolboy visits to, in Torrington Square, Camden Town, II 4, 5; looks for lodgings for WSJ, 11, 14, 16–18, 19; WSJ lives with while at University College, I 13, 97, II 29, 31n8, 32; gives WSJ her ticket for Faraday lecture, I 81; daughter's marriage, II 64; home at Oval Road, 122, 163, 251; sees WSJ's letters from Australia, 115, 118, 121, her feeling for WSJ, 140, 166; provides London home for Tom Jevons, 167

goes to Heidelberg with Harry Roscoe, II 63n7; tours Germany, 71; tact at a wedding, 123; at British Association meeting in Liverpool, 191, 193; on Thomas Graham, II 125

takes a house with WSJ in Manchester (1863), I 42, 197, III 29, 30, 46, 48

teaches water-colour painting, II 194n18; her water-colours on sale in Sydney, 194, II 195, 251, 346

also mentioned, II 80, 122n7, 135, 144n17, III 60

Roscoe, Henry (1830–99), eldest son of Robert Roscoe, cousin of WSJ, I 74, 243, II 230

Roscoe, Henry Enfield (Harry, 1833–1915), cousin of WSJ, I 243

career in chemistry, I 16, 61n2, in physical chemistry, II 229, 244; early experiments in fireworks with Roscoe Jevons, I 7–8; chemistry at Mechanics High School, Liverpool, 114; B.A. at University College, London, II 63n7; studies with

Bunsen at Heidelberg, 63, 66, 73, 118, 194; gets his doctorate (1854), 63n7, 65n8, 79; research on chemical action of light, 63n7, 74, 122, 124–5, 159, 190, 191–3, 228, 229, 243, 315, 356, on Platinum salts, 65, 75; gets grant for research, 192; leaves Heidelberg for Paris and London (1855), 190–1; returns to Heidelberg during vacations (1858–61), 63n7, 356

becomes assistant to Professor Williamson in London, I 57, 82, II 74n16, 191, 193, 228, 229; on Williamson as teacher of chemistry, I 14, 95; appointed Professor of Chemistry at Owens College, Manchester (1857), I 39, 41, II 50n9, 304–5, 315, 316–17, 322, 342–3, 347; his laboratory, 355, 356, VII 71; on management committee, and lecturer to workingmen's college, II 322; the moving spirit on extension plans, III 150; resigns Professorship (1886), on election as M.P. for Manchester South, II 305n2

lecture on matches at Spicer Street Mission (1853), I 89–90; gives a Friday evening lecture at Royal Institution (1856), II 229, 243; lecture on coal in series of 'Science Lectures for the People' (Manchester, 1871), VII 18, 21, introduces WSJ's lectures in series, 18

faith in science as basis of knowledge, II 316; leads movement for society of scientific men, II 236–7; questions Lockyer's work on atomic theory of matter, IV 294

as photographer, II 73, 79; photochemical research, *see above*; paper on quantitative photography, III 59n1

and WSJ: lifelong friendship, I 13, II 125, 317, 355; his social ease envied by WSJ, I 38, 182n4; skates with him, 89; discussions on moral philosophy together, 66; advises on examinations, II 32, on the Sydney assayership, I 96, 97; gives him introductions in Sydney, II 194;

Roscoe, Henry Enfield (*contd*)

WSJ's only scientific correspondent, II 163; is sent first Monthly Meteorological Report, 244, 297; arranges publication of articles on Clouds, II 193, 306, 315, 324; asks for mineral specimens from Australia, 324, 356; indignant at WSJ giving up chemistry, 406; reads WSJ's paper on Goldfields to Manchester Literary and Philosophical Society (1859), I 187n1; daily breakfast together at British Association meeting (1861), II 434

suggests tutorship at Owens College for WSJ (1862), I 39, 185, III 3, 5, discusses arrangements with him, 9, 10; and election of WSJ as F.R.S., III 249; lunch together at Scientific Club (1878), IV 293–4; on WSJ's remarkable mind, I 62n2

personal: sees lying-in-state of Duke of Wellington, I 72, and funeral procession, 74–5, II 191; stays with the Booths in Liverpool, I 77, II 191; tours Germany with his mother and sister, II 71–3, visits Liebig's laboratories at Munich, I 83n2, II 73, at Giessen, 71–2; joins the Volunteers, II 407; marriage to Lucy Potter (1863), I 42, III 29; his children, III 59

publications: with Bunsen, 'Photochemical Researches' (*Quarterly Journal of Chemical Society*, 1856), II 74, 191n4, 192n10, 229, 243; 'On the Measurement of the Chemical Action of Light' (*London . . Philosophical Magazine*, 1856), II 229n13, 243; translation of Bunsen's *Gasometry* (1857), II 74–5, 315; with Bunsen, 'Photochemical Researches' in *Philosophical Transactions* of Royal Society, Parts I–III (1857), II 192n11, 229, 315n2, Part IV (1859), 356; *Lessons in Elementary Chemistry* (1866), III 139; translated into Russian, 160; editor of 'Science Primers' series, IV 192n3 *The Life and Experiences of Sir Henry Enfield Roscoe . . written by himself* (1906), I 7–8, 14, 61n2, 62n2, 81n2,

114n1, II 31n8, 73n9, 305n7, 316n8, III 160n2

letters to, II 49–50, 61–3, 77–80, 159–63, 243–52, 342–8, III 59; letters from, II 64–6, 71–4, 74–5, 121–5, 190–4, 227–30, 304–6, 315–17, 322–5, 355–6

also mentioned, I 61n1, 243, II 4, 5, 29, 64n5, 133

Roscoe, Mrs Henry Enfield (Lucy Potter, 1840–1910), I 243, III 29n2, 59

Roscoe, Jane, *see* Hornblower, Mrs Francis

Roscoe, Jane, daughter of Thomas Roscoe, cousin of WSJ, I 243; marriage to Horace Roscoe St John, II 123; publications, 123n14

Roscoe, Laura (Poppy, b. 1828), daughter of Robert Roscoe, cousin of WSJ, I 243, II 6. *See also* Thornely, Mrs James

Roscoe, Margaret Henrietta (b. 1858), daughter of William Caldwell Roscoe, I 243, II 230n16

Roscoe, Mary Ann (1821–52), daughter of William Stanley Roscoe, cousin of WSJ, I 243; marriage to Richard Hutton, I 36, her wedding, II 26, 64n3; dies in Barbados of yellow fever, I 80, 81, II 416n6

Roscoe, Mary Anne (1795–1845), daughter of William Roscoe, mother of WSJ, I 242; published poems, I 5; 'Literary Diaries', I 6. *See also* Jevons, Mrs Thomas

Roscoe, Richard (1793–1864), medical doctor, uncle of WSJ, I 242; visits to, at Richmond, I 75, 76, 84, II 5, 6; consulted on schoolboy lodgings for WSJ, II 11, 17; Herbert Jevons lodges with, I 13, II 8–9; stays with Jevons family in Liverpool, I 92, II 43–4, 46, 47–8; gives WSJ Henslow's *Botany*, I 99, and a present from his mother, II 209; health, II 22; friend in Sydney, 47, 48, 96; reads WSJ's letters from Australia, 115, 118; asked to stump up by a nephew, 123; also mentioned, II 34, 44n5

Roscoe, Mrs Richard 'Aunt Richard' (Mary Ann Hodgson, *née* Bardswell, 1801–88), I 242; visits to, at

Richmond, I 76; arrangements for Herbert Jevons to lodge with, II 9, 11, 14, 15, 18, 21; friendship with WSJ's mother, II 9n2, with Mr Green, 34; stays with Jevons family in Liverpool, I 92, II 46, 48; reads WSJ's letters, 118; Tom Jevons lodges with (1856), 223; also mentioned, II 44n5

Roscoe, Richard (Dick, 1833–92), solicitor, cousin of WSJ, I 243, II 176, 438; joins Queens Own Rifles, 407, 418; marriage to Honora Worsley, II 65n7

Roscoe, Mrs Richard, *see* Worsley, Honora

Roscoe, Robert (1789–1850), uncle of WSJ, solicitor, I 66n5, 74n2, 242, II 6n6, 65n7, 176n10, 230n18; his family, II 418

Roscoe, Mrs Robert (Martha Walker, 1798–1884), aunt of WSJ, I 66n5, 242; stays with Jevons family in Liverpool, II 141

Roscoe, Robert (1831–46), fourth son of Robert Roscoe, cousin of WSJ, I 66n5, 243; his poem 'Chevy Chase', I 66n5

Roscoe, Thomas (1791–1871), fifth son of William Roscoe, I 242; speech at his daughter's wedding, IV 123

Roscoe, Thomas Stamford (b. 1826), third son of William Stanley Roscoe, cousin of WSJ, I 243; feeding cattle in Ireland, II 123; a sawyer in Otago, 405

Roscoe, William (1753–1831), of Liverpool, solicitor and banker, maternal grandfather of WSJ, I 2, 242; bank failure (1816), bankruptcy (1820), I 5, 12; cultural pioneer of Liverpool, 5, collection of paintings, 4, patronage of Fuseli, 5; cofounder of Liverpool Botanic Garden, 60n2; connection with Unitarian Chapel in Renshaw Street, 58n5, a trustee, II 169n10, memorial bust in, 128, 144; home at Allerton, I 5, 59n5, at Toxteth Park, 59n3; an influence on WSJ, I 16, II 25; collection of pamphlets, I 5, V 146; his forgotten Liverpool property, II 405

publications: 'The Butterfly's Ball and the Grasshopper's Feast', I 66n5; 'The Dingle', 59n3; *Life of Lorenzo de' Medici*, I 4; *Life and Pontificate of Leo X*, I 4; *Monandrian plants.* ., I 63; writings on criminal law, I 4, 5

Life of William Roscoe, by Henry Roscoe (1833), I 59n3, 61, Thomas Jevons's copy, II 213; *Life of William Roscoe*, by Chandler, I 59n5, 63n3

also mentioned, I 7, 37, 75n2, II 22n1, 44n5, 56n1, 64n3, 123n14

Roscoe, Mrs William (Jane Griffies, d. 1824), grandmother of WSJ, I 242, II 56n1

Roscoe, William Caldwell (1823–59), cousin of WSJ, I 36, 187n2, 193n6, 243, II 64n3, 405n4; at University College, London, I 73n1, cofounder of Debating Society, 39, 187n2; feeling hard up, II 123; marriage to Emily Sophia Malin, II 123, 132, 135, 142, 145; first child, 230; dies of typhoid fever, II 123n13

Roscoe, Mrs William Caldwell (Emily Sophia Malin, 1830–86), I 243; marriage, II 123n12, 132, 135, 142, 145; children, 230; family party at Christmas (1866), III 149

Roscoe, William Malin (b. 1857), son of William Caldwell Roscoe, I 243, II 230

Roscoe, William Stanley (1782–1843), uncle of WSJ, I 193n6, 242, II 64n3, 123nn10, 11, 12, 405n4; death, 123n13; *Poems*, II 154n2

Roscoe, Mrs William Stanley (Hannah Eliza Caldwell, d. 1854), I 242; death, II 64

Rose, Heinrich (1795–1864), Professor of Chemistry at Berlin, II 73

Rose, Henry J., I 65n2

Rose, Hugh V., I 65n2

Rose, Sir John, Bank director, IV 160

Ross, James, IV 15

Rossi, Pellegrino (1787–1848), scholar and statesman, V 40

Rossini, Gioacchino, II 314; *Stabat Mater*, II 224, 314

Roswag, C., estimate of gold and silver

Roswag, C., (contd)
  coined in England, III 201
Rota, Pietro (1846–75), *Principles of the Science of Banking*, IV 302, V 153n2
Rothschild, Meyer Armschel (1743–1812), founder of the House of Rothschild, VI 104n1
Rothschild, Nathan Meyer (1777–1836), founder of London branch of the House of Rothschild, VI 104
Rouen, II 178
Rousseau, Emile-Pierre André Joseph (b. 1815), chemical manufacturer, II 184
Rowland, J. H., III 46
Royal Academy Exhibitions: (1854), II 76; (1863), III 14; (1874), Elizabeth Thompson's painting, IV 52; (1881), V 136
Royal College of Music: WSJ subscribes to Founders' Fund, V 178
Royal Commission on Coal Supplies (1866), III 101, 123, 127; Questions prepared by Committees sent to WSJ, 154; outcome of *Coal Question*, VII 18; *Report*, VII 36–7
Royal Commission on International Coinage (February 1868), III 181, 196, 212, VII 69; WSJ gives evidence, III 181, 183, his letter on the coinage laid before the Commissioners, 181; *Report*, 187, 207, 213, 219. *See also* International Currency
Royal Engineers, I 18, II 249
Royal Humane Society, I 89
Royal Institution of Great Britain
  Faraday's Friday Evening Lectures (1853), I 81–2, II 243
  Galton on laws of Heredity (1877), IV 200n3
  Harry Roscoe's Friday Evening paper (1856), II 229, 243
  Tindall's lectures on electricity (1855), II 146n2
  Williamson's lecture on organic chemistry (1853), I 87
  WSJ's lecture 'On the Probable Exhaustion of our Coal Mines' (13 March 1868), III 180, 183, VII 28–35
Royal Lyceum Theatre, London, I 106n3
Royal Mail, New South Wales, I 234–8

Royal Mint
  Select Committee on (1837), *Report*, III 222; Royal Commission (1848), II 140n6; Mint Indenture superseded (1850), III 222, 223; reforms of 1851, III 218, appointment of non-resident assayers, II 133n3, III 222–3, ended in 1870, II 134n3; need for reform (1879), V 88–9, 92; the new Mint (1882), V 182
  Canadian coins minted at, IV 166; free coinage system, VII 70; gold coin supplied to Bank of England, III 164; and international coinage, III 184; relations with Sydney Mint, I 18, Master's Report on coin issued in Sydney, II 231
  mintage, III 211, 215, 217n3, 221, VII 72; and par of exchange, VI 110, VII 70; Lord Liverpool's objections to, VII 71; replacement of light coin, V 181–3; 'Remedy', III 217, 223
  WSJ works at assay office of Non-Resident Assayer, I 19, gold assays sent from Mint, II 49; correspondence with Queen's Assay Master at the Mint (H. W. Field), III 221–3
  also mentioned, II 135, 140, V 140
  see also assaying; seignorage
  Masters of the Mint, II 161n4; Mastership vacant, III 225; *see also* Graham, Thomas; Herschel, Sir John
  superintendent of machinery, II 50n11
Royal Mint, Hong Kong, VII 68
'Royal Prerogative of Mercy, The' (WSJ, *Empire*, September 1857), VII 123
Royal Society
  Catalogues, IV 3
  Copley Medal, awarded to Foucault, II 102n1
  economists as members, V 188; WSJ elected to (1872), III 249, intends exhibiting logical abacus at, 157, 185, feels cut off from, in Manchester, IV 134; G. Darwin, IV 221; election of Inglis Palgrave, V 85–6, 90–1, 183–4, 188; initiation ceremony, 194
  Thursday meetings, V 188; Lockyer's

paper on spectrum analysis (1878), V 35

Presidents, see Hooker, Sir Joseph Dalton; Spottiswoode, William

Philosophical Transactions, papers by Bunsen and H. E. Roscoe, II 192n11, 229n13, 315, 356

Proceedings: Obituary notice of WSJ, I 1n2; papers by Sir Benjamin Brodie, III 155n3; Horner's paper on Egyptian geology, II 330; Lockyer, IV 294n5; Piazzi Smyth, IV 297n5; Sir R. Strachey, IV 203n2

Royal Society, Sydney, II 329n1

Royal Society of Arts: paper on spelling reform (Alexander J. Ellis, 1870), III 238

Journal, 'The Quest and early European Settlement of India' (Sir G. C. M. Birdwood, 1879), V 48, 49

Royal Society of Edinburgh, IV 231, V 17

Royal Society of Literature, I 54n2

Royal Statistical Society (London Statistical Society)

WSJ and: elected Fellow (November 1864), I 197, III 62, feels cut off from, in Manchester, IV 134; seeks support from, on treatment of children, V 168, 169; outline of 'Statistical Atlas' owned by, I 182n, II 425n2; analysis of prices read before (May 1865), I 197n3, III 54n3, 69

Boccardo elected to, V 31–2, 42, 60; J. Mills declines membership, V 89; Cossa asks for membership, V 60

founders, VI 25n16; officers, III 243n1, V 162n1, 181n2

also mentioned, IV 262

Royal Statistical Society Journal (JRSS)

papers by WSJ: 'The Variation of Prices and the Value of the Currency since 1782' (May 1865), I 197n3, III 54n3, 61n3, 69, 72, 81, 104, IV 163, 170, VI 118n7; 'On the Frequent Autumnal Pressure in the Money Market' (April 1866), III 102, 104; 'Notice of a General Mathematical Theory of Political Economy' (1867), I 188n1, III 166,

IV 40, 50, 58, 61; 'On the Condition of the Metallic Currency . . .' (November 1868), III 159n2, 195, 200, 206, IV 11, VII 65; 'The Progress of the Mathematical Theory of Political Economy' (1874), IV 70n1, 102, VII 75; *Serious Fall* noticed in (1863), VII 125; notice of Vissering on Chinese Currency (1877), IV 224; 'Remarks on the Statistical Use of the Arithmometer' (November 1878), VII 85–90; notice of Fontpertuis' pamphlets (1878), IV 287–8; 'A Bibliography of Works on the Mathematical Theory of Political Economy' (n.s., June 1878), IV 277n1

other papers: review of Cossa's *Guida* (1880), V 136; G. Darwin on marriages between cousins (1875), IV 35; R. Everest on Indian wheat prices (1843), V 46; Rowland Hill, 'High Price of Coal . .' (1873), IV IV 55; Mundella, on threats to British commercial supremacy (February 1879), IV 237, 243n1; Newmarch, articles (1859–61), I 181n2; Sir James Paget, 'Medical Students' (1869), VI 66n11; Inglis Palgrave, Prize Essay on local taxation (1871), III 242, V 184, 'Notes on Banking in Great Britain' (1873), IV 10n2, 16–19, 79, 98n1, 112n2, V 184, 'Analysis of Evidence on Banks of Issue' (1876), V 184, 'Analysis of the Transactions of the Bank of England' (1873), IV 31, 168n1, V 184; Price Williams, 'The Coal Question' (1889), V 143n4; Proctor, 'University Boat Races and Sun-Spots . . .' (1879), V 51n5; Thorold Rogers, on wages and prices (1861), III 47; Shaw-Lefevre, Presidential address (1877), IV 241; Waley, on strikes (1867), III 153–4

Royal West Indies Mail Company, II 381

Rubinstein, Anton Grigorevich (1830–94), recitals in Manchester and London, IV 199, 203

Rücker, Sir Arthur William, co-author of

Rücker, Sir Arthur William (*contd*)
　　Coal: its History and Uses, IV 243n1
Ruggles, Samuel Bulkley, American representative at International Monetary Convention, VII 69
Rule Britannia, II 224
Rule of Three, III 214, 221
rum, III 252, V 70
Ruskin, John, letter to *The Times* on the gold question (1863), III 37
Russel, James, and Son, coalmasters: win their suit against Mrs Gillespie (The Torbanehill Case), II 50n15
Russell, H. C., 'Astronomical and Meteorological Workers in New South Wales, 1778–1860' (1889), I 24n1
Russell, Lord John, 1st Earl: his Ministry defeated (1852), I 85; Foreign Secretary in new Ministry, 87, II 417n7, III 53n1; Prime Minister (1866), III 87n1; gets coal returns from European countries, 91, 92, 93
Russell, William James (1830–1909), chemist, II 74, 305; 'On a New Method of Estimating Sulphur', II 75
Russia
　　assassination of Alexander II, V 143n3
　　coal, VII 26, 27, 33, 34
　　commercial crisis (1772–3), VI 117n6
　　currency, III 199; gold coinage, V 58, 59, American assay of coins, III 219; silver standard, V 142
　　and England: war with England (1854–56), II 75, 79, 114, VI 124, 129, retreat from Sebastopol, II 103n4, driven from Sea of Azov, 151; kept in check by England and France, II 417
　　exhibits at Great Exhibition (1851), II 12; none at Paris Exhibition, 183
　　foreign exchange and corn exports, VI 114
　　incomes, III 242
　　international traffic, V 27
　　Russian edition of H. E. Roscoe's *Lessons in Chemistry*, III 160
　　Russians and Americans, II 197; sale of Alaska to America, IV 153n6
　　steam engines, III 188
　　supposed threat to Indian Empire, V 50n4; threat to Turkey (1860), II 412; war with Turkey (1877–8), IV 210, 211, 224n4, 225, armistice (1878), 225n3
　　tariffs, IV 306
　　wages, examination question on, VII 138
　　see also St Petersburg
Rutter, Dr John, co-institutor of Liverpool Botanic Garden, I 60n2
Rydall, New South Wales, I 223, 235
Ryder, gold assayer at Dunedin, New Zealand, III 39
Rylett, Rev. Harold (1851–1936), Unitarian minister
　　in WSJ's political economy class at Owens College, IV 241n1, V 115, 197n4; his notes on WSJ's lectures, IV 241, VI viii, ix, x, reproduced, 3–140; his own note on Lecture vi, 35–6, on Lecture vii, 41n
　　in Ireland, IV 241n1, V 54; solution to Irish question, 111–15, 196–7; supports Irish Land League, 150; opposes Gladstone's Irish policy, 151
　　letters to *Manchester Examiner and Times*, V 111–12; letter to WSJ printed in *Economist* (December 1881), V 157, 197; publications in *Inquirer*, V 114–15
　　letters to, IV 241–2, V 54, 150–1, 196–7; letter from, V 111–16
Rylett, Mrs Harold (Louisa Boucher), V 116

Sadler, Thomas, Unitarian minister at Horsham, II 20n3
Sadler, Thomas, jun. (1822–91), Unitarian minister, II 20
Sage, Mr, iron merchant in Melbourne, II 448, 452; hospitality to Herbert Jevons, 448n2, III 30
sago, III 206, 252
Saintine, (Joseph Xavier Boniface, 1798–1865): *Picciola, or Captivity Captive*, WSJ's comments on, I 155–6
St John, Horace Stebbing Roscoe (1832–88), author and journalist, II 123
St John, Mrs Horace Stebbing Roscoe, *see* Roscoe, Jane
St John, James Augustus (1801–75), author and traveller, II 123n15

St Lawrence River, WSJ travels down, II 384n1, 401

St Leonard's, Hastings: Newsroom, V 143; holiday at (April 1882), V 188, 190

St Mary's town, New South Wales, I 215, II 220

St Michael's Hamlet, near Liverpool, home of Timothy Jevons, I 193; WSJ discovers the 'true logic of the future' while sleeping at, 204

St Paul, Minnesota, II 364, 382, 400, 404; rainfall, 419

St Paul's Cathedral, *see under* London

St Petersburg
electrical exhibition, V 148n2
steam-powered paper mill, III 188n4
telegraphic messages exchanged with British Association, II 435

St Thomas Island, West Indies: WSJ stays two days in, II 377-8, 381, 382, 397

Salford
evening lectures in political economy for primary schoolteachers, VII 38
Liberal victory (1880), V 115
plans for popular amusements, IV 286-7
see also Manchester and Salford

Salford, Mayor of, IV 287

Salisbury: music in the gas-lit Cathedral, V 43

Salisbury, Ann, nurse to Jevons children, II 183, 214

salt: boiling process, VII 30; as a necessary, examination question on, VII 133; salt trade, VII 19

Saltney, Henry Wood's Chain and Anchor works, II 89

'sameness' (likeness): WSJ's constant search for, I 15, 35, 179, 189; basis of his logic, 40, 186, 208-9; substitution of similars, 210n1

Sampson, Low and Co., publishers, IV 175

Sandeman, Archibald (d. 1893), Professor of Mathematics at Owens College, I 42, II 305n8; regards *Pure Logic* favourably, III 52; testimonial for WSJ, III 106, 116-17

Sanitary Association, V 166; Manchester and Salford Association, V 168

sanitary reform, I 16-17, need for, VII 41; sanitary science as branch of social science, VII 55. *See also* sewage

San Juan Islands, dispute over ownership, II 408

Sansom, Thomas, custom-house clerk and botanist, I 59-60

Santo Domingo, II 381, 398

Saratoga, II 390

Sardinia, II 61n3

Sargant, William Lucas (1809-89), small-arms manufacturer, author of economic works: is sent copy of *Theory of Political Economy*, III 244; influence on Marshall, V 77; *Robert Owen, and his Social Philosophy*, VII 105
letter from, III 244-5

Saskatchewan, II 419, 420

Saturday Review, II 259n5; sent to WSJ in Sydney, II 259, 330; WSJ advertises as literary agent in, I 182; mention of Rachel Jevon, II 138; review of *Theory of Political Economy* (anon, 11 November 1871), IV 58, VII 152-7; editor, II 259n5

Savage, Marmion, *The Bachelor of the Albany* (1848), WSJ reads, II 290, 295

Savin, Thomas, railway contractor, VI 126

savings: Mill's 2nd Proposition on, VI 39; destroyed by crises, VII 91, by rising cost of living, III 256; tradesman's view of, VII 45; working-class savings in credit cycle, VI 131

savings banks
Bodio's treatise on, IV 154
deposits, III 180; in Jamaica, V 70
funds held by National Debt Commissioners, IV 133
Gladstone's Post Office Savings Bank Bill (1861), II 430
included in 'Statistical Atlas', II 426
working-class investment in, VII 54

Saxon guilds, VI 68-9, origin of trade unions, 71

Saxony, coal production, VII 34

Say, Jean-Baptiste, III 197, VI 48, 89, VII 78; definition of utility, VI 10, 11, of labour, 18, of value, VII 83; production creates demand, IV 120, 122; *profits de la classe ouvrière*, IV 227
A Treatise on Political Economy (translated by C. R. Prinsep, 1823), III 27;

Say, Jean-Baptiste (*contd*)
    Cours Complet d'Economie Politique Pratique, V 38
scarcity value, VI 84, VII 78, 83, 161
Schäffle, Albert (1831–1904), German economist, IV 301
Schertzer, Dr Karl (1821–1903), Austrian explorer: fellow-traveller on board the *Medway*, II 380; chief scientific member of *Novara* expedition, 380n2, 397
Schiller, Friedrich von, II 251
Schleiden, Matthias Jacob, *Principles of Scientific Botany*, translated by E. Lankester, I 66
Schmidt, Herr, Prussian civil engineer, III 73
Schmitz, Leonhard, *History of Greece* (1850), I 83, 87
Schmoller, Gustav (1838–1917), Professor of Political Economy at Halle, III 197; at Strasburg, IV 85; his disciple, Knapp, 85n8
Schönbein, Christian Friedrich (1799–1868), Professor of Chemistry and Physics at Basel: research on ozone, II 245
schoolteachers: free lectures on Political Economy for, III 105, VII 38; low wages, VII 63
    see also education; Green, Mr; University College School
Schröder, Ernest von, *Logik kalkuls*, IV 231
Schumacher, Hermann, economist, included in bibliography of mathematical economists, V 42
Schuster, Sir Arthur (1851–1934), physicist: goes on eclipse expedition to India (1875), IV 108, 109; finds connection between sun-spots and vintage cycles, 204, V 9, 167–8; appointed to Chair of Applied Mathematics, Owens College (1881), V 141n2, his inaugural address, 'The Influence of Mathematics on the Progress of Physics', 167; ideas on interplanetary matter, 168
    'Some results of the last total solar eclipse', paper read to Cambridge Philosophical Society (18 November 1878), reported in *Nature* (January 1879), V 8
    letters to, V 8–9, 167–8
    also mentioned, IV 108n3
Schuster, Felix (1854–1936), younger brother of Arthur Schuster, IV 108; at Leipzig University, 109
Schuster, F. J., father of Arthur and Felix Schuster, IV 108n3, 109
Schwabe, Samuel Heinrich (1789–1875), German astronomer: sun-spot observations, V 91
Scialoja, Antonio (1817–77), Italian Minister of Finance, IV 302, 303, VI 110n4
science
    WSJ's overriding interest in, at school and college, I 78, 98, 99, II 361; will not be a scientific man, II 78, 244; prospects of, in Australia, 216, 242; encouraged to go on with by H. E. Roscoe, 306, 315, 323; determines to give up physical science (1858), 334
    two classes of, logical and mathematical, VII 159; pleasures of pursuing physical sciences, II 318–19, *Economy* a 'very contracted science', II 321
    popular lectures on science at Royal Institution, I 82n8; establishment of Department of Science and Art (1853), 85n2; advantages of a scientific education, II 244, 316n8; Anderson's Institution for scientific and technical education, 442n7; the March of Science, England lags behind, II 125; proposed association of scientific men for increasing Government support for science III 236–7, opposed by Herschel, 237–8; Royal Commission on relation of state to science (1869), *Report*, III 237n3; Gore's discussion on state support for research, V 186
    see also individual sciences
Science Lectures for the People (1871), VII 18
science and religion, II 288; WSJ's unfinished work on, I 51, 52; not antagonistic, 203; Theological Declaration of Scientific Men, III 60; Brunton's writings on, V 122n1

Scientific Club, WSJ a member, IV 116, 118, 293-4

scientific method: applied to social sciences, I 30, 35, to history, by Buckle, II 316, to the study of man, 335-6; 'Limits and Results' of (*Principles of Science*), IV 36

Scientific University College, plans for, III 150

Sclater Booth, George, M. P., III 211

Scotland

  banks: banknotes, III 203, IV 107n1, 161, circulation, IV 31, 32; crisis of 1857, VI 125n5; gold and silver coinage in, III 201; Royal Bank of Scotland, IV 210

  coalmines, VII 21, 22

  emigration (1852), IV 7, of coalminers, VII 17

  iron trade, VII 22

  population, Celts of the West, III 243

  Scotch crews and passengers on board the *Oliver Lang*, II 77, the *Chrysolite*, 394

  Scotch professors, IV 173

  universities, teaching system, III 12, V 22-3

  WSJ visits, for honorary degree at Edinburgh, III 73, 124-5, 126-7

  also mentioned, III 233, 234

  see also Edinburgh; Glasgow

Scotsman, II 50n15, V 111

Scott, Rev. Alexander John (1805-66): resigns Professorship at University College, London, to become first Principal of Owens College, Manchester (1850), I 65n4, II 305n6; Professor of Language and Literature, of Logic and Mental and Moral Philosophy at Owens College, I 41; WSJ takes his logic and philosophy classes, I 45, 205n5, III 48, 75-6, 112, 118; resigns as Principal, II 305; testimonial for WSJ, III 106, 112-13; succeeded on his death as Professor of Logic and Philosophy by WSJ, I 207n2

Scott, Captain, Superintendant of roads in New South Wales, I 237

Scott, Charles Prestwich (1846-1932), son of Russell Scott, editor of *Manchester Guardian*, IV 271n1

Scott, Lawrence (1844-1930), Unitarian minister, son of Russell Scott, IV 292

Scott, Miss, first wife of John Edward Taylor, I 47

Scott, Russel (1801-80), London businessman: WSJ stay with at Eastbourne, IV 271

Scott, Sir Walter, *Guy Mannering*, II 134n5

Scott, Rev. William (1825-1917), Government Astronomer in New South Wales, II 329n1; meteorological observations for the Government, II 269; reply to his criticisms of WSJ's paper on Clouds, 329-31, 345; his temperate reply, 345n7

Scrope, G. Poulett, *Political Economy for Plain People* (1873), VII 104

sea-sickness, I 129, II 80, 81, 82

Sebastopol, siege of (September 1854), II 103, 122n3, 162, 171; captured by the Allies (September 1855), 194, 204, 206

Secrétan, Charles (1815-95), Professor of Philosophy at Lausanne, IV 196, 198, 205; translation of Gossen, V 21n4

Sedgeley Hall, ancestral seat of Jevons family, I 3n3

Seebohm, Frederick (1833-1912), partner in banking firm of Sharples & Company, IV 11, 216n2

Seebohm, Julia, daughter of Frederick Seebohm, student in WSJ's class at University College, London, IV 216n2

Seeley, John Robert., *Ecce Homo*, I 203

seignorage: on gold coins, favoured by WSJ, III 184, 207, VII 70, 71, controversy on, III 211-21; on silver currency, V 183

Seine, II 178-9; book- hunting on banks of Seine, V 149

selfishness, I 130, II 45, 212, 238, 276-7, 240-1, 302; 'The Selfish Theory of Morals' (John Woolley), influence on WSJ, I 27-8, 132-4; Whately's principle of Individual Competition, 157-8; self-interest the basis of human action, VII 10, 57, 158

Senior, Nassau William (1790-1864): in the true line of economic science,

Senior, Nassau William (*contd*)
   IV 146; with Malthus, 'the soundest
   political economist', VI 3; definition of political economy, VI 6, of
   wealth, 8, 9; law of variety in human wants, 13; on rent, 68; wages in
   the mass, 64; crude notion of quantity, VII 78; true theory of utility, 79, 80; deductive method, 158
   An Outline of the Science of Political Economy
      (1836), recommended by WSJ to
      his students, VI 3, 5, 68; ed. 5
      (1863), 'indispensable as a
      student's textbook, VII 102
   also mentioned, IV 81
   services: a part of wealth, VI 9; in *Theory of*
      Political Economy, V 34
   services producteurs (Walras), IV 191, V 95
Seton, Blessed Mother, ancestor of Isabel
   Seton, I 10
Seton, Isabel, I 10; *see also* Jevons, Mrs
   Thomas Edwin
Seven Weeks War (1866), III 125
Severn, Mr, of the Sydney Mint, II 199
Severn Estuary, possible tidal power from,
   III 123
sewage farms, VI 58; sewage disposal, VII
   30
Seward, William Henry (1801–72), Amer-
   ican Secretary of State, II 453
Seyd, Ernest (1833–81), German banker
   in London: opposes reducing gold
   content of sovereign, III 211; im-
   pugns quality of coins, 217, 218,
   219, letters to *The Times* on, 217n4;
   confuses his figures on export of
   British gold coins, 219–20
   Bullion and Foreign Exchanges . . . (1868),
      III 194, 198, 200, 218
Shadwell, John Lancelot, Prizeman in
   Political Economy at University
   College, London (1870, 1871); his
   critical remarks on *Theory of Politi-*
   cal Economy answered, III 253–4;
   comments on his 'Theory of Wages'
   (*Westminister Review*, 1872), 254–5;
   on U.S. silver certificates, V 194
   Political Economy for the People (1880), VII
      107
   letters to, III 253–4, 254–6
   also mentioned, IV 91n3
Shaen and Roscoe, later Shaen, Roscoe

   and Bracewell, London firm of sol-
      icitors, II 176n10
Shaftesbury, Lord, social reformer, I 16–
   17
Shakespeare, William: a genius of humanity, I 155; WSJ finds 'con-
   genial', 179, 184, VII 118; Shakespeare 'encadré' in a Jevons equation, V 171n1; price of a folio edition, VI 83
   Midsummer Night's Dream, seen in Edin-
      burgh, III 126; plays seen in Syd-
      ney: *Much Ado about Nothing*, *Tam-*
      ing of the Shrew, *Winter's Tale*, II
      278, *Othello*, 258, 278, *Tempest*, 278,
      279; *Romeo and Juliet*, II 176; *Son-*
      nets, I 38, 183n, 191, II 453
   'Statistics of Shakespearean Literature'
      (*Athenaeum*, 12 March 1864), VII
      125
   also mentioned, II 329
shareholders, VI 61–2, 68; workmen as,
   75–6; in New South Wales railways, VII 10; ruined by bank failures, VII 91
sharks, I 104; harpooned and brought on
   board the *Oliver Lang*, II 85, 97–8,
   112; in Sydney harbour, 114; 'Big
   Ben', 239, 248, 273
Sharpey, William (1802–80), Professor of
   Anatomy and Physiology at Uni-
   versity College, London, I 82, II
   122; WSJ has tea with, II 35
Shaw, parlourmaid of Jevons family, II 96
Shaw, Stebbing, *The History and Antiquities*
   of Staffordshire (1798–1801), II 438
Shaw-Lefevre, Charles (1794–1888), later
   Viscount Eversley, Speaker of
   House of Commons, I 74
Shaw-Lefevre, George John (1831–1928):
   Inaugural Address as President of
   Royal Statistical Society (1878),
   IV 241; moves vote of thanks to
   WSJ, VII 90
Sheffield
   hardware, VII 19; steel trade, VI 32;
      manufacture of die stamps, II 117
   outrages of sawgrinders, III 129, 131, 135
   the Shambles, VI 36
   also mentioned, V 111
shells, WSJ's collection, I 59, 60; buying
   shells in Australia, II 195

Sherbrooke, Viscount, *see* Lowe, Robert

Shiel, Mr, teacher at University College School, VII 53

ship-building, VI 32; in Boston and Nova Scotia, II 111n3; iron ship-building at Marseilles, II 61, 214

ship insurance companies, VI 75

shipping
  division of labour on board ship, VI 35
  as fixed capital, VI 43; 'increase of balance' earned by, VI 13
  state interference with, V 138; Merchant Shipping Acts, V 138n3; international signals, 148n2

shipping lines, *see* Black Ball; Cunard; Pacific Steam Navigation Company; Peninsular and Oriental Steamship Co; White Star

Ships
  Beagle, II 386n2; *Biobio*, mail boat to Sydney, II 163, 165, 170; *Canopus*, to Sydney, II 232, 233; *Champion*, to Melbourne, II 446; *Chrysolite*, from Glasgow, WSJ sails from Melbourne to Callao on, II 372, 373–6, 385–6, 394, keeps Board of Trade Meteorological Log, 386–7, 394; *Collaroy*, paddle-wheel steamer on River Hunter, I 124, 125; *Constance*, brings gold dust and tallow from Melbourne to Liverpool, II 146; *Devonian*, from Madras, I 76, II 34, a foul bottom, 35; *Domino*, to Bergen, V 143; *Donald Mackay*, sailing ship, II 147; *Eliza*, mail ship to England, II 203; *Fletcher*, London to New Zealand, races alongside *Oliver Lang*, I 105n1, II 98; *Frances Skiddy*, Hudson river boat, II 390; *Great Britain*, Brunel's iron-hulled, screw-propelled ship, brings gold nuggets from Melbourne, II 42, 60, letters from WSJ, 115, 289, changes from North Atlantic to Australia run, II 42n4, 231n4; *Great Eastern*, VI 91; *James Baines*, fast sailing vessel, inspected by Queen Victoria and Prince Albert, II 146n3, record passage from Australia, 147; *Lightning*, brings letters from England, II 202; *Maid of Judah*, WSJ copies

Register of weather, II 203; *Marco Polo*, mail from home, II 215; *Medway*, steamship, from Callao to Panama, II 376, 379, 381, 397, from Panama to St Thomas, 377–8, 380, 381, 397; *Mermaid*, brings news of Thomas Jevons's death, II 208; *Nora Crenia*, paddle steamer, to Illawarra by, I 161–2; *Novara*, Austrian frigate, voyage round the world, II 380, 397; Ohio river steamship, with sketch, II 400; *Oliver Lang*, clipper, of Black Ball Line, II 111, WSJ sails to Sydney on, I 19, 101–7, 118, II 77, 80–5, 86, 96–100, 101, 111–13, 115, 116, 144, 347, *see also* Manning, Captain; *Omeo*, New Zealand mail boat, III 41; *Oneida*, mail boat, II 258, 261; *Red Jacket*, mail boat, II 171, 204; *Shalimar*, II 170; *South Carolina*, II 137; *Startled Fawn*, Black Ball clipper, II 132, ironbuilt, 144, 146; *Williams*, of Australian Steam Navigation Company, I 123n4, race with *Collaroy*, 124, 125, WSJ's return journey on, 128–30; other ships, II 381, 397, 399

see also steamboats

shipwrecks: *Dunbar*, wrecked off South Head, Sydney, II 299–301, 310, 315; *Lotty Sleigh*, explodes with cargo of gunpowder in the Mersey, III 49; *Shomberg*, total loss, II 235; sinking of the *London* and burning of the *Amazon*, VII 40; wedding presents lost in a foundering ship, III 62; shipwrecks and sun-spots, V 10n2

Shirreff, Emily, sister of Maria Grey, cofounder of Girls Public Day School Trust, IV 129n2

shopkeepers, VII 59; second-hand bookshops, I 81, in Paris, V 149; Mrs Stokes's toy-shop, II 28n2; Uncle Hornblower's shop in Newington, I 88

Siberia, gold from, III 208

Sicily
  Bunsen's projected expedition to volcanic districts, II 229

Sicily (*contd*)
  Garibaldi and the Sicilian Insurrection, II 411–12
Sickles, Daniel Edgar (1825–1914), American lawyer, II 382n1, 453n6; his residence in Washington, 382
Sidgwick, Henry (1838–1900), Professor of Moral Philosophy at Cambridge, IV 239, V 22, 63, 66, 77, 78; pioneer of higher education for women, IV 143; invites Mary Paley to lecture in economics at Newnham, 148n6; marriage to Eleanor Balfour, 157n4; on diagrams and symbols, V 23; sponsors pension for Cliffe Leslie, 169n1
  WSJ's respect for, IV 157; his ideas on WSJ's attack on Mill, V 24; letters to, V 23–4, 75
  The Methods of Ethics (1874), IV 96, V 22, 133; *Principles of Political Economy* (1881), WSJ protests against first choice of title, V 133–4; article on Benthamism, V 75
Sidgwick, Mrs Henry (Eleanor Mildred Balfour, 1845–1935): engagement and marriage, IV 157; Principal of Newnham College (1892–1910), IV 157n4
Siemens, Sir William (1823–83), inventor of regenerative furnace, VI 29
silk
  from China, VII 24, and Japan, III 208; silkworm disease in Europe, III 208
  manufacture, VII 24; weavers in Spitalfields, I 17, 68, VI 32; trade in, VI 33, 34
  tax on, VI 136, 137, abolished, 139; ancient tax on silk dresses, VI 134; the untaxed luxury of the rich, III 239
Sill, Edward Roland (1841–87), Professor of English at University of California, IV 130n1, 141
Sillar and Co., Messrs, gold melters, III 218
silver
  from America, VI 103; Carribou, Vancouver Island, II 439; France, II 164; India, IV 186; Nevada, V 59; Peru, II 378; South America, VII 24
  as a commodity: for assaying gold, II 175; in Lima churches, II 379, 395; for electro-plating, VI 45, tea urn for Henry Jevons, III 210
  demonetising silver, IV 187
  depreciation, III 5, 17; continued fall in value, VI 99, 103, panic, 102
  drain of, to the East, III 201, 208–9
  influence on value of gold, III 21; gold price of silver, 254
  silver assays, I 20
  U.S. silver certificates, V 194
  see also coinage; currency; gold and silver; India
silver standard, V 142, 193, 194, VII 67; in Belgium, VII 66; *see also* bimetallism
Simmonds, J. A., logic student of WSJ at Owens College, III 70
Simpkin & Marshall, London publishers, II 363
Simpson, dealer in chemical apparatus, II 50
Sinclair, Sir John (1754–1835): Exchequer Bill scheme, VI 118; *History of the Public Revenue of the British Empire* (1803), VII 106
Singapore, II 75, III 149; mail service to Australia *via*, II 133n1
sinking funds: as reserves for depreciation, VI 47; Pitt's and Price's, examination question on, VII 137; in partnerships between workers and employers, III 152
Sinnett, Frederick, *Account of the 'Rush' to Port Curtis* (1859), donated by WSJ to British Museum Library, II 449, 450n2
Sismondi, Jean Charles Léonard Simonde de (1773–1842), definition of political economy, VI 5, 6
skill and knowledge: in economic theory, VI 22–3, 91; as fixed capital, 40; as determinant of wages, 63–4, 66, 90; dexterity gained from division of labour, VII 61
slate: quarries, II 132, III 65, 192, VI 39–40; trade in Welsh slates, III 192; works, I 90
slavery
  in English law, VI 9
  slave agriculture, III 53, 56; labour, VI

19; *Slave Power* (Cairnes), III 53

slave colonies: Spanish, II 429; in U.S.A., II 390, 404n2, 428; abolitionists, II 134n7, 151, 409

Smedley, Edward, joint editor, *Encyclopaedia Metropolitana* (1845), I 65n2

smelting, VII 19, 30

Smith, Adam:, 'father of the science', VII 99; Malthus in the true line of, IV 146; his ranking in England, IV 95, V 78; Adam Smith Centennial at the Political Economy Club, Gladstone's speech, IV 222; projected Adam Smith Society, V 44, 81

Lectures on Justice, Police, Revenue and Arms, VI viii

Wealth of Nations, VI 6, VII 56, 102
    capital, IV 121, VI 38, 40–1; consumption of capital, VI 39, 40; fixed, and circulating, 40, 42, 44–5
    consumption, IV 75; limits to desires, VI 85
    higgling of the market, VI 82; price of corn, IV 170
    labour: definition, as origin of wealth, IV 115n3, VI 19; division of, VI 27–8, 31; free labour, VII 48; supply and demand for, VII 63; as measure of value, III 253, VI 90, 98, VII 77–8, 83
    population, VI 54
    utility, VII 78–9, 83; main difference with WSJ, III 254
    value: division of, VI 94; natural, VII 148; in use and in exchange, VI 79; labour as measure of, *see* above
    wages, VI 65, 66
    read by WSJ's mother, I 6, by WSJ (1856), 27, VII 115; recommended to Henrietta, II 280, 292, 321, to WSJ's students at Owens College, VI 3, 26, 31; examination questions on, V 152, VII 131, 133, 134, 135, 136
    editions: Murray's cheap reprint (1874), V 81; Playfair's notes to eleventh edition, IV 9; Thorold Rogers (1869), V 81, VII 102; E. Gibbon Wakefield (1840), VI 27n2, 34n8, VII 102

Foxwell's projected edition, *see under* Foxwell, Herbert Somerton; WSJ's proposed textbook edition for students, IV 218–19, 248–9, 263n4, 298, V 81, 106n2, 115
    also mentioned, II 360, V 41, 127n2, VI 6n15

Smith, Albert (1816–60), 'Ascent of Mont Blanc', I 76, 84

Smith, Mrs Egerton, II 14

Smith, Elder, and Co., publishers, V 111n2, VII 53n

Smith, George, member of Smith and Elder, newspaper proprietor, V 111n2

Smith, James, Treasurer of Manchester and Salford Provident Society, III 257

Smith, Dr John, Professor of Chemistry and Experimental Physics at Sydney University, I 25, II 136n12; WSJ's introduction to, II 75, 79, 152; barometer readings compared, I 163n1; starts Philosophical Society in Sydney, II 249, reads WSJ's papers to Society, I 187, II 297; his paper 'On the action of Sydney Water upon Lead', II 249–50; paper on separation of gold from quartz read at British Association meeting (Manchester, 1861), I 25, 36, II 435; note to Graham on post for WSJ, II 442
    letter to, III 4–5; WSJ's 'annual letters' to, 4

Smith, John Benjamin (1794–1879), M.P., Manchester cotton merchant, III 183n1; WSJ sees before giving evidence to International Coinage Commission, III 183–4; supports seignorage for gold coin, 211; letter to *The Times* (26 October 1869), on international coinage, 232, 233n7; copy of *Coal Question* for, IV 29–30; speech on the Budget (1873), 30

An Inquiry into the causes of money panics. (1866), III 140
    letters to, III 183–4, 232–3; letter from, IV 29–30

Smith, John Prince (1809–74), London-born economist in Prussia, III 197

Smith, Colonel John Thomas (1805–82),

Smith, Colonel John Thomas (*contd*)
F.R.S., former Master of the Calcutta Mint: supports Lowe's seignorage plan, III 211, 213, 215–16, the plan originally his, 221; co-author of 'Report on Mintage' (1868–9), III 210n2, 216
Remarks on a Gold Currency for India (1868), III 221; 'East Indian Currency and Exchange' (*Westminster Review*, 1881), currency plan for India, V 141
letter from, III 215–16
Smith, Miss, sister of a student at Owens College, I 197
Smith, Robert Angus (1817–84), chemist, runner-up with H. E. Roscoe for Professorship at Owens College, II 305
Smith, Thomas Southwood (1788–1861), sanitary reformer, I 16
Smith, William Robertson: 'Mr Mill's Theory of Geometrical Reasoning', IV 231; 'note' on Bain's 'Theory of Euclid', 231
smuggling, V 48
Smyth, Charles Piazzi (1819–1900), Astronomer-Royal for Scotland: continues Forbes's earth thermometer observations, IV 297; papers on earth temperatures, 297n5, V 8
letter from, IV 296–7
snakes, encounters with, in Australia, I 153, II 110, 239, 365, under the bed, 207–8
snobs: Australian, I 234; British Association members, II 436
soap: as circulating capital, VI 43; coal for boiling, VII 30; soap duty, II 40
Steele's Soap Works, I 85, 92–3; career in soap-boiling considered for WSJ, I 89, 117, II 41
social conditions of the people, I 16–17; WSJ's observations in London, 67–8, 71–2, 77, 90–1; wish to give course of lectures on, at Owens College, III 105; 'social condition of man' a rich field for research, II 336
see also infant mortality; houses; social reform
social economy, VII 44; instruction in, for

poor schoolboys, VII 38, 52–3
social reform, V 161; articles on, in *The Contemporary*, V 74, and *see under Contemporary Review*; Aunt Jane Hornblower's activities as social reformer, II 22
see also infant mortality; intemperance; poor law; sanitary reform
social sciences
or statistical science, VI 8, VII 55; compared with physical sciences, VII 44–6; 'economic sociology' distinguished from 'economics', VII 158
WSJ's early attraction to, I 16, 35, 179; application of scientific method to, I 30, II 361–2; strong urge to study, 322, 327–8
'Social Survey of Australian Cities', (projected and abandoned), I 29, 159n1, II 297n10
socialism
anti-socialist views of Individual Rights people, V 187
examination question on, V 152
Herford's socialist view of education, IV 213
and modern society, VII 90
socialist approach to economics (Foxwell), V 186; schemes for wages and promotion, VII 64
Société d'économie politique de Paris, prize contest for new system of taxation, V 4, 7n5
Société Vaudoise des sciences naturelles, Bulletin: 'Théorie mathématique du billet de banque' (Walras, 1880), V 96, 98; 'Théorie mathématique du prix des terres' (Walras, 1881), V 145
society: as a machine, VI 27, VII 41, 153; laws of, VII 49; economic sociology the general science of, VII 158; WSJ undertakes study of (1857), II 322, 361–2, VII 119
Society of Arts, II 11
Society for Promoting the Amendment of the Law, V 173–4
Society for the Promotion of Christian Knowledge, VII 52
Society of Telegraph Engineers, IV 243
soda works, visit to, I 93, 117, II 41–2

sodium amalgam, used for assaying, III 150

Soetbeer, Dr Adolf Georg (1814–92), of Hamburg: tables of commodity prices, III 21, 82

Sofala (Sŏfălă): excursion to (March 1856), I 24, 123n2, 128n2, 212–38, II 218–21; Sofala road, 222, 229; town, 142, 229; gold diggings (with sketches), 230–3

solar eclipses, II 435, VII 96; India (1875), IV 108, 109; Siam (1875), V 8n1, n3; article on total eclipse in New South Wales (1857), VII 123

solar origin of commercial fluctuations, *see* sun-spots

Solar Physics Committee (1879), V 103

Solar Physics Observatory, South Kensington, V 103n1

solar power, as substitute for coal, III 91, VII 34–5

solar radiation, IV 296–7, VII 96, 97; measurement by actinometer, II 124n16, by WSJ's own sun-gauge, 125n17, 161, 297, 344–5; Melloni's method, 193; Campbell's sunshine recorder, 323–4, 343; Pouillet's observations IV 296–7

'On a sun-gauge or new Actinometer', paper by WSJ read before Sydney Philosophical Society (8 July 1857), I 23, 25, II 297, VII 123

solar wind, V 168n4

Solomon, Sydney bullion broker, II 108, 115

South Africa
   Gladstone's policy, V 135
   Herbert Jevons goes to, for his health, I 10, II 27n1
   see also Natal; Transvaal Republic

South America
   cotton growing, VI 33
   gold production, IV 7
   salt imports from Cheshire, VII 19
   silver from, VII 24
   South Sea Bubble and, VI 116
   wars of liberation in Spanish colonies, VI 119
   see also Brazil; Callao; Lima; Peru

Southampton, II 71, 133, 136, 402

South Head, Sydney, I 161, 163n1, II 269;

the *Dunbar* shipwrecked off, II 300–1

South Sea Company (1711), VI 116, 117, 119
   'Bubble' of 1720, IV 225, 228, 229, 233, 237, 241, VI 116, 117; a 'premature' crisis, IV 232; 'in the series', 240

South Sea stock, V 107

South Staffordshire Railway, I 93–4

Soyer, Alexis Bénoit (1809–58), chef to the Reform Club, II 360; Soyer's field stove, 360n4

Spain
   coal production, VII 27, 33, 34
   gold coinage, V 58, 59; Spanish dollar, III 183–4, VII 74; ratio of gold to silver, VI 102; 'double standard', VI 101
   manufacture of sherry, VI 33
   translations of works on economics, VII 101
   also mentioned, V 125

Spanish colonies in South America: slave colonies, II 429; separation from Spain, VI 119; Spanish architecture in Callao, II 378, in Lima, 396; bullfight, 376, 396; Catholicism, 378; ladies and carriages, 395, 396, 398–9; Spanish town of Panama, 377, 379; style of living on a Spanish steamer, 381, 397–8

Speaker of House of Commons, *see* Shaw-Lefevre, Charles

Spectator
   editor, Richard Holt Hutton, I 36, II 416n6, 432n17, 450n1; offers to publish articles by WSJ, I 37–8, 182, 183; article on Gladstone's Budget, VII 12; article on Gold Discoveries, III 13n3
   Timothy Jevons's copies sent to WSJ in Australia, II 413, later cancelled, 432
   WSJ, articles: 'Clerk of the Weather Office' (13 September 1862), I 38, II 452, VII 124; reviews of Hearn (*Plutology*) and Robertson (*Laws of Thought*), March 1864, VII 125; 'Early Presentiments of the Electric Telegraph' (27 April 1867), VII 126; 'The Alleged Poisoning of

Spectator (contd)
    Natives in Queensland' (27 May 1876), IV 174–7, VII 127
    reviews of works by WSJ: notice of *Two Diagrams* (1862), II 459, VII 124; *Serious Fall* reviewed with Fawcett's *Manual* in 'Political Economy and the Gold Discoveries' (Hutton, 16 May 1863), I 191n1, III 13, 15; *Pure Logic* spoken highly of (1864), III 108, VII 125; 'Amusements of the People' reviewed (5 October 1878), IV 291

spectroscopic analysis, Lockyer's experiments, IV 294; spectrum analysis, III 236n2

speculation
    in America, V 147; in Brazil steam ships, WSJ speculates in, III 150; in bullion, VII 70; in corn trade, VI 123; in foreign loans, VI 121–2; in home enterprise, VI 113; in land, II 287, VII 5–6; in railway shares, VII 9, 11, not for WSJ, III 50; speculative boom in foreign countries, VI 119
    astrological speculators, VII 92; speculative companies, VI 77, 121; problems of speculators, VI 84
    and circulation of bank notes, IV 112; Corbet on, V 107; Marshall on modern economic speculation, VII 147; and periodic crises, V 11, 48, 171, VI 119, 123, 124, (1710–11), IV 237, (1792), VI 117–18; and prices, III 53, VII 160

Speeches, Letters, Articles etc. on the Gold Coinage Controversy of 1869 (1870), III 211–12, 232–3

spelling reform, III 238

Spencer, Charles Child, *A Rudimentary and Practical Treatise on Music* (1850), II 227

Spencer, Herbert (1820–1903)
    philosophy of creation, accepted by WSJ, I 52, IV 4, a 'new and true philosophy', IV 29, V 24; controversy with Gladstone over, IV 38–9, 42; definition of progress, V 28
    letter to WSJ on *Pure Logic* used as testimonial, III 107, 117; agrees with WSJ on two orders of reasoning, 117; arranges election of WSJ to Athenaeum Club, V 26, 36
    First Principles, III 117, 'persistence of force' puzzles WSJ, IV 29; *Principles of Evolution*, I 52; *Principles of Psychology*, III 117; *The Study of Sociology*, IV 38n2
    'Herbert Spencer' (St George Mivart, *Quarterly Review*, 1873), IV 29
    letter to, V 26; letter from, III 117

Spicer Street Domestic Mission: Harry Roscoe lectures on Lucifer Matches at, I 84, 89–90

spices, III 54, V 48, 49, VII 24; ginger, V 70; *see also* pepper

Spitalfields: silk industry, I 17, VI 32; weavers and weaving sheds, I 67–8; bird traps, 68

Spohr, Louis (1784–1859), II 314, 321; 'The Last Judgement', II 76, its gloomy strains, 314

Spottiswoode, William (1825–83), President of the Royal Society: letter to, V 183–4

Springfield, New South Wales, I 238

Springwood, New South Wales, on the road to, I 146, 147, 149, 150, 152

Stafford, Countess of, daughter of Richard Cantillon, V 130

Staffordshire
    ancestral home of Jevons family, I 2, 3n3
    chain makers, hostility to new machines, VII 47
    coal, VII 19
    iron trade, VII 22; ironmasters, III 226–7, 228; iron prices, VII 21; ironworkers, III 142, VII 17
    population, VII 23, 24

stagnation of trades (1877), discussion on, at Political Economy Club, IV 199n4, 202–3. *See also* depressions

Standard, VII 12; *see also Evening Standard*

standard of value, *see* value; for money, *see* bimetallism; gold standard; silver standard

Stanford, Edward, map publisher: publishes *Two Diagrams* (1862), I 35n2, II 459n1, IV 12n10, V 159n1, arrangements for publication, I 181, sends copies on sale, II 455, III 4, 33; publishes *Serious Fall* (1863), I 191n1, VII 125; other publications, IV 176

Stanhope's Syllogistic table, V 117

Stanley, Edward Henry (1826–93), 15th Earl of Derby: recommends *Coal Question* in British Association speech (1865), III 99

Stanley, Rev. George Heape (1818–91), Unitarian minister in Sydney, I 31, II 131; his chapel full of friends, 152; encounters WSJ at theatre, 258

Stanton, Edwin McMasters (1814–69), American Secretary for War, II 453

stars: periodic variability, VII 98; star-transit, III 216

Stas, Jean Serrais (1813–91), chemist, III 219

state, *see* government

Stather, Maria Moreton, *see* Clarke, Mrs W. B.

Statistical Abstract for the United Kingdom, VII 104; *Statistical Abstract of the Colonial Possessions of British India*, VII 104

Statistical Congresses, III 212

Statistical Society, *see* Royal Statistical Society

statistics
  and the arithmometer, VII 85–90
  in classification of trades, VI 33n5, VII 116, 119
  in comparison of races, III 244
  Dr Farr's system, VI 33n5
  geometrical approach to, VI 55
  Gregory King as statistician, VI 89n3
  of international traffic, V 27–8
  from mercantile books, VII 145
  and periodic panics, III 102
  political economy founded upon, II 450
  of population, VI 57
  of prices in India, III 251–2
  from tax returns, VI 134
  and theory of exchange, VII 83
  WSJ and: early progress on historical statistics, or time series, I 35, II 233, 323, VII 117; statistical atlas projected, I 35, 40, 180, 182, II 438, attempts to find a publisher, I 180–1, contents analysed, II 425–7; two diagrams published (1862), I 35n2, 37, 181n4, II 450–1, 444–5; WSJ accepted as a 'competent statis-

tician', I 198, III 97; statistics included in lectures on political economy (1867), I 211
  alternates statistics with logic, I 211, III 252, IV 54; applies statistics to coal study, I 197, to depreciation of gold, III 5; reads paper on Gold Currency to Statistical Society, 159n2, 195, 200, 202; his statistical library, IV 13
  other articles and papers: on statistics of Shakespearean literature, VII 125

Statutes of Labour, VI 69

steamboats, II 146n3, 183, V 27, 28, VI 23, VII 20, 30, 31; 'Auxiliary Screw' principle, II 230–1, screw steamers, II 114, 381, 399; from Lucerne to Fluellin, II 185–6; paddle-wheel, I 124; for overseas mail, II 132, 133; WSJ's speculation in Booth & Co., Brazil Steam Ships, III 150; Bessemer Saloon Steamship, VI 91

steam-engines, II 180, VI 25, VII 19–20, 97; studied in Natural Philosophy at College, I 91; God's Steam Engine at work (Thomas Jevons), II 87; portable, on wheels, for Welsh gold mines, II 88–9, 135n11; Donkin's Economical Horizontal Patent Steam Engine, III 188–90; steam-engine-indicator, 188n4, 189; governor, VI 26; bubble companies for, VI 115

steam power
  coal consumption, III 98, 188–90, VII 30–1; steam coal trade, VII 26
  coining presses, VI 28n5
  corn mills in New South Wales, I 128; paper mill in Russia, III 188n4
  ploughs, VI 44, VII 30, 31; Herbert Jevons's idea for, II 420–1
  as prime mover, I 133–4
  for pumps, VII 19, 30
  for weaving, VII 22

Steble, Lieut-Colonel Richard Fell, defeats Henry Jevons in Liverpool municipal elections, III 227n2

steel: assay stamps for, II 117; Bessemer Process, VI 29; Gorton steel works, VII 23; production in America (1872), IV 30

Steele, Mr, visit to his Soap Works, I 85, 92–3, to his Soda Works at Prestatyn, 85, 93, 117, II 41–2

Steelyard, VI 69

Steinthal, Rev. Samuel Alfred, Unitarian minister at Platt chapel, Rusholme, I 202

Stenhouse, Professor John, collects signatures for Theological Declaration of Scientific Men, III 60n2

Stephen, Sir James Fitzjames (1829–94), Professor of Common Law, Inns of Court: appointed Judge, resigns Professorship, V 23

Stephenson, George (1787–1848), railway pioneer, II 360; on coal as bottled sunshine, VII 97

sterling, VI 100; definition of £1 sterling, VI 98; Herschel on, III 216–17; ratio to franc, VII 67, 73

Steuart, Sir James (1712–80): An Inquiry into the Principles of Political Economy (1787), V 12, French translation, 19–20; essay on Money (1810), 20

Stewart, Balfour (1829–87), Professor of Natural Philosophy at Owens College, III 236, V 141n2; President of Physics Section, British Association (1875), IV 129; joint editor of 'Science Primers' series, 192n3; on sun-spots and periodic rainfall, 203–4; planetary theory of solar periods, V 8, 35, 57; member of Solar Physics Committee, 103n1; 'visible energy', VI 24
    'On the Long Period Inequality in Rainfall', paper read to Literary and Philosophical Society, Manchester (1880), V 103
    letters from, IV 203–4

Stewart, Mr, Demarara sugar planter, fellow passenger on board the Chrysolite, II 398; with WSJ in Havana, 398–9

Stillingfleet, Rev. H. J. W., tutor on Continental tour, II 187

Stirling, Patrick James, translation of Bastiat's Harmonies of Political Economy, VII 102

stock: 'stock of the country', VI 40–1; stocks as circulating capital, 42; devoted to immediate consum-

ption, 52; of corn, 53

Stock Exchange, VII 16

stock-jobbing bubble (1732), IV 229, 233, (1743), 241

Stokes, Miss, of Liverpool, II 28

Stokes, Mrs, toy-shop keeper in Liverpool, II 28n2

Stokes, Mr, ironmaster, II 28n2

Storch, Heinrich Friedrich von (1766–1835), definition of political economy, VI 6

Stowe, Mrs Harriet Beecher, Uncle Tom's Cabin, I 178

Strachan, Richard (1835–1924), of Meteorological Department, Board of Trade: letter correcting an error in Principles of Science, IV 305–6

Strachey, Sir John (1823–1907), co-author with his brother, The Finances and Public Works of India, IV 203n2

Strachey, Lieut-General Sir Richard (1817–1908), brother of Sir John Strachey: paper on rainfall and sun-spot periods, read before Royal Society, IV 203; career in India, 203n2; member, Solar Physics Committee, V 103n1

Strahan, Alexander (1833–1918), founder and editor of Contemporary Review, V 3; asks WSJ for articles, IV 250; series of articles on social reform, V 74
    letter to, V 74–5

Strasbourg, II 175, 185, 199

Strauss, Johann, the Elder, 'Waltzes' in WSJ's 'cheerful' programme, II 339

Streatley, Berkshire, WSJ stays in, II 388–9, 391, 392, 401

strikes, IV 211, VI 71, 74, 77, VII 51; against wage reductions in iron industry, III 128, VII 49–50; in coal pits, VI 126n8; to raise wages, III 161, 225, 226, 255; for shorter hours, VII 143
    a disastrous policy, III 142, IV 243, Pierson on, 266, 267; WSJ's 'partizan' view of, in Cobden lecture, VII 48–9, challenged by 'A Cobdenite', III 129–31, defended, 131–2; partnership between masters and

men as cure for, III 153–4, VII 60,
132
strike funds, VI 71; trade unions and,
VII 41
Waley's article on, III 153–4
Stubbs, William, *The Constitutional History
of England* (1866), IV 213
Sturm, Charles (1803–55), theory of roots
of equations, I 82
Styria, coalfields, III 71
subordination of wants, law of, VI 13–14
subsistence: and population, VI 55–60;
subsistence wages, 62
substitution of demand, VI 17, 88; substitution of similars, I 210n1
Sucher, Rosa (1849–1927), German operatic soprano, in Wagner concerts in
London, V 199
Suetonius, on ratio of gold to silver, VI 102
Suez Canal, purchase of shares, IV 150n4
Suffolk, VII 24
suffrage (franchise), working-class, III
128, 130, 135, 136, VII 42, 43
sugar
imports in New South Wales, II 281
prices, IV 6; price curves, III 54; and
demand, III 24–5, and supply, VI
16
production: in Jamaica, V 70, West
Indies, VII 24; maple sugar from
Herbert Jevons in Minnesota, II
393, 423, 424
refineries, in Liverpool, II 41, London,
VI 32; career in sugar refining
considered by WSJ, I 89
tax on, III 239, VI 139
Sullivan, Dr William, chemical officer of
Museum of Irish Industry, II 119n16
Sully, James (1824–1923), psychologist,
friend and neighbour of WSJ: applies for examinership in Logic, IV
239; as Professor of Chemistry at
University College, I 50
Summers, William (1853–93), M.P., student under Jevons at Owens College:
letter to *Examiner* defending WSJ
against anonymous article, IV 92–3,
94
letter to, IV 93–4; letter from, 91–3
Sumner, William Graham (1840–1910), *A
History of American Currency*, IV 43
sun gauge, *see* actinometer

sun-spots
and commercial fluctuations, I 48, IV
304–5, V 194; key to connection,
price of corn, IV 199, in India, V
36, 45, VII 108, 112; articles on:
'On the Influence of the Sun-Spot
Period upon the Price of Corn'
(1875), IV 129, 188–9, 199, 272n2;
'Sun-spots and Commercial Panics'
(1879), V 10, 12n4, 91; 'Sun-Spots
and Commercial Crises', letters to
The Times (17 January 1879), V
10–12, (19 April 1879), 44–8
decennial connection, IV 228, 230, 232,
V 10, 11, 45, 48, apparent irregularity of sun-spot curve, V 17, dating problem of 1878, IV 274;
Broun's estimate, IV 293n1, V 8,
11, VII 92, 94n109; Faraday's reference to decennial periodicity, I
24, 82; Piazzi Smyth's researches
on, IV 297n5, VII 109; Balfour
Stewart's view, IV 203–4, V 103;
Wolf's numbers, V 8, 11, VII 108–
9, 112; WSJ's estimate, V 8, VII 94
Edmond's theory, V 86, 100–1, 103;
Adamson's doubts, IV 299–301; de
Foville's scepticism, V 14, 16, 17n1;
Strachan's scepticism, IV 203n2,
305
proposed society to coordinate research,
V 56–7
sun-spots and rainfall, IV 203–4, V 103
see also cycles
superannuation funds, VI 71, 73
supply, VI 16–17, 90–4
supply associations, VI 75
supply curves, *see* utility
supply and demand
alterations in, effect on employment, VI
35
Christie on, V 30–1; Cournot's treatment, IV 5, V 24
Jenkin's treatment of, IV 5n3; correspondence on, III 166–78
market values governed by, VI 83–4, 90
old laws of, in WSJ's new law of utility,
II 410, 422, VI 88, VII 152, 157;
Cairnes on, VII 147; concerned
with quantities, VI 81; formula for,
in terms of ratio of exchange, III
246, VI 81–2, 88, VII 83, 84, 85

supply and demand (*contd*)
  wages should be governed by, VI 78,
    VII 63–4
  Walras on, IV 260, VII 76
surveying, I 163n1
survival of the fittest, Maupertuis on, IV 4,
  15; *see also* origin of species
suspension of cash payments (1797), VI
  118; (1847), VI 123; threatened
  (1866), VII 41
Swank, James Moore (1832–1914), statistician and historian: statistics of
  American iron trade, V 86
Swayne, Mrs, sick relative of Jevons family
  servant, II 176, 390–1
Sweden
  crisis of 1772–3, VI 117n6
  farmers, VI 53
  international trade, V 27
  square coins, IV 194, 195
  visit to (1877), IV 207, V 65
Sweetman, H. S., *Calendar of Documents
  relating to Ireland . . .* , V 125–6
Swiss Family Robinson, II 332–3
Switzerland
  deferred marriages, VI 58
  gold coinage, V 59; international
    money, III 212; 'double standard',
    VI 101, adopts French system, VII
    66
  marksmen beaten at rifle-shooting by
    London Volunteers, 431
  soldiers, II 186
  Thomas Jevons's travels in, I 122, II
    173, 175, 183, 185–9, 199; WSJ's
    Swiss tour (1865), III 75, 81,
    (1878), IV 244
  wages, examination question on, VII
    138
Sydney
  WSJ and: voyage to (June–October
    1854), I 19–20, 101–9, 114, II 80–
    5, 96–100, 111–13, his luggage, II
    76, 79, including apparatus, 77–8,
    120; arrival, I 109n1, II 15; self-
    distrust on coming out, II 341, a
    'sentence of transportation', 348, 'a
    gloomy anxious work', 452; his stay
    in (1854–9), I 19–32, II 107–365;
    his years there like a dream, 394, 'a
    pleasant souvenir', III 164
  first home, Charlotte Place, Church

Hill, two-roomed cottage, I 109,
  111, 114, 'cobwebs and rats', I 20,
  II 107; laboratory room, I 20, II
  107, 113, 171; library and furnish-
  ings, 113; 'Holy Land' on Church
  Hill, 109; lease ends, 196, 197;
  move to Annangrove Cottage,
  Petersham, *see* Annangrove Cottage; move to Double Bay, WSJ's
  third home, *see* Double Bay
introductions to Sydney citizens, II
  117, no mind to communicate with,
  160, 275, 310, 311, 318; attends
  public lecture at Mechanics School
  of Arts, I 27, 132, and classes,
  132n2; walks in and around Sydney, II 106, 110, 126, 196–7, 233;
  from Double Bay to the Mint, 272–
  3, 276; excursions into the Bush,
  114, 298, with his puppy, 206–7,
  208
study of Sydney town, I 24, 28–9, II
  297n10, VII 116; impressions of
  Sydney, I 142, II 110; 'Social Cesspools of Sydney' (*Sydney Morning
  Herald*, 7 October 1858), I 29, II
  298n10, VII 124
letters from Sydney, II 107–14, 120–
  1, 146–7, 158–63, 170, 179–83,
  195–9, 202–27, 230–304, 306–14,
  317–22, 325–55, 356–65
banks, II 117, 128, 129, 130; Oriental
  Bank, 203; bank holiday for taking
  of Sebastopol, 204; bank failures,
  279; Herbert's post in, 448n2, III 4,
  16, 28; *see also* Bank of New South
  Wales
Botanic Gardens, II 142; flower show, II
  130
concerts, II 250, 320, by moonlight, 203,
  Anna Bishop's farewell concert,
  224
cricket match against Melbourne, II
  262
gold prices, II 127, 248; prices and
  wages, II 264
iron from Jevons firm, II 139
lead poisoning from water, II 249–50
Mechanics School of Arts, I 25, 132n2,
  lectures, 27, 132
Mining Company, II 117n14
newspapers, II 95, 151, 298, 451; sent

home to England, 173, 195, 231, 298, 342; WSJ writes articles for, 198, his letters printed in, I 185. *See also Empire; Sydney Magazine; Sydney Morning Herald*

people, I 126, II 181, 208; alleged licentiousness, II 48, 53; convict highwaymen, II 170; in the rain, 182, on holiday, 262; population, VII 5

Prince of Wales Opera House, II 278, opera, 290; Prince of Wales Theatre, 278n9; theatre performances, II 170, 181, 257–8, 278; Royal Victoria Theatre, 278n9; incident at *The Tempest*, 279

Regatta, II 114, 208

Unitarian chapels, II 131, 136, 152; WSJ's rare attendance, 118, 258

University, I 25, 65n4, II 329n1, Herbert Stanley Jevons lectures in geology (1902), I 114n2; Library, II 131; professors, 136; *Magazine*, No. I (January 1855), offered to British Museum, 449

WSJ determines to leave, I 32, II 307, 310, 313, misgivings dismissed, II 332, 347, 348–9; packs up, 363; leaves by mail-coach (February 1859), II 366, 381, 385; thoughts on his achievements, I 185

see also Australia; New South Wales; Sydney Mint; weather

Sydney Almanac, II 173–4, 195

Sydney Harbour, II 114, 208, III 31; Dawes Battery, home of Captain Ward, II 114, 141, 145, 208; Miller's new house at Double Bay, shared by WSJ, 248, 270–3; bathing and sharks, 114, 273

Sydney Magazine of Science and Art
published by J. W. Waugh, II 363n8; Professor Pell's paper on railways, II 236n2, VII 8; reviewed by WSJ in *Sydney Morning Herald*, VII 124; set of, donated by WSJ to British Museum, II 449, 450n2

contributions from WSJ: monthly reports on meteorology, I 23, II 198n6, 245n11, 297nn7, 8, 298, VII 124; 'On Clouds', paper read to Sydney Philosophical Society (January 1858), I 23, II 244n7, 345n7; 'Letter concerning Mr Scott's criticisms' (23 June 1858), II 329–31, 330n2, 345n7, VII 124; 'On a Sun-Gauge or New Actinometer' (August 1857), II 161n3, 297n8, VII 123

Sydney Mail, *see* coaches

Sydney Mint

WSJ, career as Assayer to Royal Mint in Sydney, I 1, III 218; accepts offer of post, I 18, 96–7; letter of appointment, II 57; does assays for Mint in his private laboratory, II 78, 113, 126, his assay stamp, 204, 234, 295; becomes full-time regular officer of Mint, with fixed salary, 120, 148, 162, 170, salary maintained without cuts by Legislative Assembly, 260; hard work at first, 170, 105–6; little to do most of the time, I 21, 111, II 198, 203, 206, 238–9, 247, 248, 261, 272, 278–9, like a continual whole holiday, 225, assaying the least of his duties, 274; analyses earth samples at the Mint, I 144; constructs his sun-gauge there, I 23; has to teach Mint clerks to assay, II 249; asks for, and gets, a holiday, 217; determination to leave, 310, 313, 342–3; leaves (December 1858), I 33; article on Mint Assaying, II 247, 345

assaying process, III 50–1; specimens for Paris Exhibition, II 135, 149, from new diggings, 346; ingot assays, 206; *mudges* in assays, 162

building delays of Mint, I 111, II 56n2, 60, 88, 107, 113, 115n5, 171; completed, 196; starts functioning, 162

coinage, II 127, 170; coins refused by Victoria State, I 21, II 206, 247, 260–1; used throughout New South Wales, 247; legal tender throughout British Empire (after 1868), 127; sovereigns minted, 161, 162, 170, 198, 206, 238–9, 247, 260–1, Graham's satisfactory report on, 231–2, 238, 261; dies for, II 90, 238; cost of coinage, VII 70

decorations for Peace of Paris (1856), II 234

Sydney Mint (contd)
  gold prices at, II 127n3; has the Gold
    Escort, 247; Melbourne sends no
    gold to, 260
  holidays: Christmas, I 134; anniversary
    of Colony, II 114, 208
  laboratories, II 162, 201, 239, 248–9,
    311, 313; Mint machinery, I 106, II
    78, 88; coining presses, 98
  Mint officers, I 109n1, II 77n2, 79, 195;
    see also Bolton, Charles; Hunt,
    Robert; Miller, Francis Boyer;
    Master of the Mint, see Ward,
    Captain Edward Wohlstenholm
  New Zealand assays checked at, III 39
  Thomas Jevons's quarrels with Mint
    arrangements, II 48, 130, 140, 148–
    50, 168, 171, 201
  Mint closed (1926), I 21
Sydney Morning Herald
  copies sent to Thomas Jevons, II 127,
    130, 195; suggested 'paragraphs'
    for, 91, 142, 172; monthly sum-
    maries for abroad, 346
  law suit, Lutwyche v. Fairfax, II 250–1
  meteorological reports, article on, by
    WSJ, II 268–9
  railways, articles on, II 263, 265
  WSJ and: prints WSJ in small print on
    back page, II 346; leading article
    on Serious Fall (29 July 1863), III 38
  articles by WSJ: 'Social Cesspools of
    Sydney, No. 1, The Rocks' (7 Oc-
    tober 1858), I 29, II 298n10, VII
    24; 'Canoona Diggings in a Scien-
    tific Aspect' (29 October 1858), II
    350–2, VII 124; 'Review of the
    Sydney Magazine of Science and Art'
    (October 1858), VII 124; 'The
    Railway Discussion' (19 July
    1856), II 235–7, VII 115, 123;
    'Social Survey of Australian Cities'
    (November–December 1929), I 29,
    II 298n10; see also VII 116
Sydney Observatory: foundation (1856–
    8), I 22, II 269; WSJ urged to apply
    for vacant Observership, III 4–5
Sydney Philosophical Society
  Inaugural Meeting (May 1856), paper
    on 'Rail Roads' (Sir William De-
    nison, President), I 26, II 235
  WSJ elected a member, I 23, criticises

society as exclusive, II 249, ap-
  pends his name to monthly reports,
  290; papers by WSJ read to: 'On
  Clouds' (9 December 1857), I 23,
  II 244n7, 345n7; 'On a Sun-Gauge,
  or New Actinometer' (8 July 1857),
  I 23, 187n1, II 297n8; his papers
  read by Dr Smith, Secretary, I 25,
  187n1
other papers: Professor Pell (Railways
  and Political Economy), I 26, II
  236, VII 8; Rev. Scott (Meteorology), II 345n7; Dr Smith (Sydney water), II 249–50
becomes Royal Society of New South
  Wales, II 329n1
also mentioned, II 258
Sydney Post Office Directory (1857), donated by WSJ to British Museum
  Library, II 449, 450n2
Sydney Railway Company, II 206n6,
  270n2; railway traffic, 267, 283
see also under New South Wales
symbolical statements: in Theory of Political
  Economy, IV 177; symbol of mass, V
  34
see also diagrams
sympiesometer, instrument for measuring
  air, recommended for use in coalmines, III 147
Syria, civil war between Christians and
  Druses, II 417, 418n7

'Tabular Standard of Value', chapter in
  Money and Mechanism of Exchange,
  IV 159, V 9
Tagart, Rev. Edward (1804–58), Unitarian minister, II 25
tailor of Prince of Wales, in Saville Row,
  III 8
Tait, Peter Guthrie (1831–1901), researches on thermodynamics, IV
  207–8
tallow, imported from Australia, II 146;
  tallow dips, VII 20
tanners, II 41
tar, VII 20, 41; tar and turpentine distil-
  lers, I 91, II 41
Taranaki wars (1860–1), II 402n3
tariffs, V 172; Peel's Act of the Tariff
  (1842), VI 137n6, 139
Tarrengower quartz mines, II 371

Tasmania, II 205n4, 386

Tate, Miss, *see* Husson, Mrs

Tauler, Johann (*c.* 1300-61), *Life* and *Sermons*, II 295

taxation

in economic theory, VII 100; lecture notes on, VI 132-40; Adam Smith's four principles, VI 134, examination questions on, VII 131, 136; taxes as part of cost of production, VI 84; of the rich and the poor, III 239, VI 135-6; of imports, effect on rate of exchange, VII 145; cost of collecting, VI 137-8; books on, VII 105, 106

Peel's reforms of 1842, VI 136n6, 139; in Disraeli's Budget (1853), I 86; constitutional issue raised over repeal of paper duty, II 412; reduction of taxes *versus* reduction of national debt, Gladstone's decision, III 88, VII 11-18, Mill's view, I 45, III 94n1; 'Taxes and the National Debt in *Coal Question*', I 44; debate on local taxation (1871), III 242-3

direct and indirect, VI 139-40, VII 8, 115, examination question on, V 152; to be imposed on bulk or weight rather than *ad valorem*, VI 136-7; emigration to avoid, II 268; evasion, VI 138; on necessaries, examination question on, VII 133; progressive, VI 136; *versus* tolls for railway finance, II 236, 283-6; for revenue and for protection, VI 134, VII 6, 15

proposals for reform of French taxation system, V 4-7; proposal to introduce British Schedule C system into Holland, IV 283-4, V 55-6

taxes: on alcohol, VI 134, 136, 139, VII 8; on bachelors, VI 55; beer and tobacco, III 239, VII 8; on coal, proposal for, IV 55, 222; on glass, II 40; house tax, I 86, VII 7; income tax, IV 283, V 56, VI 137, examination question on, VII 131-2; on letter stamps, VI 136; omnibus duty, VII 12; on raw materials, VI 139; receipt stamp, VI 136, 137; on rent increase, VII 7; soap duty, II 40; on occupation of

waste land, VII 4; tea and malt, I 86, III 239, VI 136, 139

see also Corn Laws; customs duties; tariffs

Taylor, Emily (1795-1872), writer, friend of WSJ's mother, I 6, II 11, 18; Herbert Jevons calls on, II 13, 14

Taylor, Harriet, *see* Jevons, Mrs William Stanley

Taylor, Isaac, *Words and Places* (1865), III 243

Taylor, John Edward (1791-1844), father-in-law of WSJ: founder and proprietor of *Manchester Guardian*, I 47, IV 271n1

Taylor, Mrs John Edward (*née* Boyce), mother of Harriet Jevons, I 47

Taylor, John Edward, jun. (b. 1830), half-brother of Harriet Jevons, later proprietor of *Manchester Guardian*, I 47

Taylor, John & Son, of London, managers of Pontgibaud Mines, II 164

Taylor, Mary Anne, III 231; marries William Edgar Jevons (1872), I 47n4, 241. *See also* Jevons, Mrs William Edgar

Taylor, Mr, of Messrs W. Hunt & Co., II 439

Taylor, Philip (1786-1870), civil engineer, II 61

Taylor, Richard, London bookseller, I 66

Taylor, Russell (d. 1849), son of John Edward Taylor, I 47n2

Taylor, Sarah Acland, sister of Harriet Taylor, *see* Jevons, Mrs Frederick

Taylor, Sophia, half-sister of Harriet Taylor, *see* Allen, Mrs Peter

Taylor and Francis, London printers and publishers, II 306n9

Taylor & Walton, publishers, I 180

Taylor's theorem, IV 149

tea

in Australia: in camp, II 219; grace before tea, 253-4; imports, 281

from China, VII 24

demand for, III 24-5, and prices, IV 138; prices in relation to other commodities, III 54, IV 6

green tea at Uncle Timothy's, II 36; Uncle Hornblower's tea business in Newington, I 88

in Mincing Lane, London, VI 32

tea (contd)
Rathbones' American trade, III 79
taxation of, I 86, III 239, VI 136, 139;
no effect on export trade, VII
15
Tedder, Henry Richard (1850–1924), Librarian, V 83
telegraph
Dover-Calais cable, II 30n6; news of
Louis Napoleon's *coup d'état* received by, 30
international traffic, Madsen's 'Law' of,
IV 243–8, V 27–9
'is the world happier' for?, II 180
in Jamaica, V 70
London to Liverpool, II 48
purchase of Post Office Telegraphs by
Liberal Government (1870), IV
150n4; monopoly control, V 93n2
telegraphic *soirée* at British Association
meeting, II 434–5
transatlantic transmission of financial
contracts, IV 220; in U.S.A., II 420
WSJ, articles on: 'Early Presentiments of
the Electric Telegraph' (1867),
VII 126; 'The Post Office Telegraphs and their Financial Results'
(1875), IV 150, 172; 'Prospects of
the Telegraph Department'
(1876), IV 171–2, VII 127
telephone, V 108
controversy over private *versus* state control, V 93
'Crossley Transmitter', V 36n5; telephone transmissions from Halifax,
Yorks (1879), V 35–6
transmissions of opera in Paris (1881), V
148n2
United Telephone Company, V 93n2
telescopes: Henrietta Jevons's telescope, II
304; telescopic observations of solar
activity, VII 96–7
Templar, Benjamin, author of school text
books on political economy, V 29–
30; introduces social economy classes in Manchester Free School, VII
53
*Reading Lessons in Social Economy for the use
of Schools*, VII 53
Tennyson, Alfred (1809–92), 1st Baron,
Poet Laureate: is sent copy of *Coal
Question*, III 98–9; *Ode sung at the
Opening of the International Exhibition*,
VI 23n9; 'Ruling, by obeying
nature's powers', VI 22–4, VII
40
letter from, III 98–9
terrestrial radiation, II 161, 193
territorial division of labour, *see* division of
labour
Teutons, VI 31, VII 33
textiles: classes of trade in, VI 33–4; machinery, VII 46; manufacture of cloth
and yarns, IV 210
see also cotton; silk; wool
Thackeray, William Makepeace, *The
Newcomes*, VII 118, 119
Thames, I 144; Lucy's sketch, II 294–5,
309; lodgings at Streatley-on-
Thames, II 392
Thames Tunnel, I 91, II 61n3, VI 91;
Thomas Jevons's collection of printed and MS documents on, donated by WSJ to British Museum
Library, II 449, 450n2
Theological Review: 'The Expulsion of the
Traffickers from the Temple' (William Jevons, jun., 1866), III 95
thermodynamics, IV 207–8
thermometers: earth thermometers for
measurement of solar radiation, IV
297; Réaumur and Fahrenheit, II
435; WSJ's in Australia, I 114, II
113, 131, 271–2
The Times
1852 reports on earthquake in Liverpool (November), I 714n4
1854 troop movements to Crimea (February), II 63n10
1862 circulation of Bank of England
notes (August), II 451; notice of
Two Diagrams (City article, 8
October), II 459, III 4; notice of
WSJ's paper on a General Mathematical theory of Economy (October), II 456
1863 correspondence and editorials on
depreciation of gold (September–
October), III 36–8, 42–5; letters
from WSJ, (4 September), 37–8,
(24 September), 43–4
1864 correspondence on Theological
Declaration of Scientific Men (20
September), III 60n2

1865 report of Gladstone's speech on coal exhaustion at Mold (2 January), VII 15

1866 report and leader on Mill's speech on Coal question (18 April), I 44; leading article on coal exhaustion and national debt reduction (19 April), I 44–5; leaders on Gladstone's plan to reduce Debt (May 4, 5, 7), 45; accuses WSJ of misleading Gladstone, III 101, VII 12–13; letters on *The Coal Question*, III 98n2, 98, 101–2; review of *Coal Question* (26 June) III, 125; attack on trades unions (October), III 129, 131, 135, VII 41, condemned by Macdonald, III 135; rejects William Jevons's letter on Athanasian creed, III 148; letter from WSJ on deep coal mining (20 November), III 139–40; 'Ironmasters and Ironworkers' (WSJ, 17 December), III 141–3, 148, 150, 151, 225n2, reply from 'Employer', 148, 150n2, 151, 153; explosions in coal mines (WSJ, 22 December), III 144–7, 148

1867 'Partnerships of Masters and Men' (WSJ, 19 January), III 151–4; on the 'Manchester Martyrs' (19 September), III 159n6

1869 debate on Money Laws Bill (24 June), III 210n1; on gold coinage controversy (August–November), III 211, 233n7; letters from WSJ, III 212–15, 217–21; from Herschel, 216n1, 217n3; from Seyd, 217n4; J. B. Smith, 211, 232, 233n7

1875 obituary of Cairnes (9 July), IV 122n4

1878 notice of Ingram's Presidential Address to British Association (17 August), IV 272

1879 'Sun Spots and Commercial Panics' (unsigned, 14 January), V 10, 11, 12n4, 91; 'Sun Spots and Commercial Crises' (WSJ, 17 January), 10–12, 35, 44n1; 'Sun Spots and Commercial Crises' (WSJ, 19 April), 44–8, 50, 57n3; business reports, V 83; 'Light Gold Coin' (WSJ, 23 December), V 87–9

1880 report of Fawcett on postal notes (16 June), V 101n3

1881 Mansion House bomb incident, V 132n5

1882 elections of new Fellows of Royal Society, V 188, 193

WSJ's daily copy while on holiday, V 200

Weekly edition, V 111; correspondents, II 123n15, 445, III 141

also mentioned, IV 181, V 67n1, VII 160

Thom, Rev. John Hamilton (1808–88), Unitarian preacher, of Renshaw Street Chapel, Liverpool, I 58, II 134n7; his altered service, II 32

Thomas, Ernest G., editor of *Monthly Notes*, VII 101

Thompson, Elizabeth (Lady Butler, 1846–1933), painter: 'Calling the Roll after an Engagement in the Crimea', exhibited at the Royal Academy (1874), IV 52; 'Quatre Bras' exhibited (1875), 117–18

Thompson, Henry Yates, radical newspaper proprietor, V 111n2

Thompson, Thomas Perronet (1783–1869), II 23n4; his Enharmonic Organ, 23–4

Thomson, James (1768–1855), editor of *Encyclopaedia Britannica*, II 228n8

Thomson, Poulett, Lord Sydenham, Governor of Canada, IV 158

Thomson, Robert Dundas (1810–64), appointment as Examiner for Chemistry at University of London, II 228–9

Thomson, Sir William (1824–1907), later Lord Kelvin, Professor of Natural Philosophy at Glasgow, II 66, III 113; his definitions discussed in WSJ's logic classes, III 118; on Fourier's theory of motion of heat, IV 207–8

Thorne, E., *The Queen of the Colonies* (1876), quoted by WSJ on the treatment of aboriginals by white settlers in Queensland, IV 175

Thornely, Charles, artist, II 432

Thornely, Elizabeth, *see* Jevons, Mrs George

Thornely, James (1822–98), solicitor, I 243, II 32n4, 230n17, 432n18, V

Thornely, James (contd)
99n3; his new house at Knotty Ash,
II 141; consulted on settlement for
Lucy Hutton, III 205
Thornely, Mrs James (Laura, 'Poppy',
Roscoe, b. 1828), I 243, II 32n4,
432n18; visit from her mother, II
141; her children, 141, 176. See also
Roscoe, Laura
Thornely, John, II 230
Thornely, Susanna, see Jevons, Mrs Henry
Thornely, Thomas (b. 1855), second son of
James and Poppy Thornely, II
141n3, 176
Thornely, Mrs Thomas (Mabel Martha
Ogden, b. 1859), II 141n3
Thornely family, of Liverpool, I 56, II
141n3, 230n17, V 99
Thornton, Sir Edward (1817–1906),
Minister-Plenipotentiary to U.S.A.,
V 58, 59
Thornton, Henry: An Enquiry into the Nature
and Effects of Paper Credit (1802), IV
251–2, VII 107, 146; a second-
hand copy for 6d, V 84
Thornton, Samuel, director of Bank of
England in 1819, IV 265n5
Thornton, William Thomas (1813–80),
officer of the East India Company,
V 77n5; On Labour (1870), IV 90, V
77n5; 'Economic Definition of
Wealth' (Fortnightly Review, 1875),
IV 114; question on wealth at
Political Economy Club, 114n4;
attack on wages fund theory, V 77,
discussed in Theory of Political Economy, VII 143
Thorpe, Sir Thomas Edward, co-author of
Coal: its History and Uses (1878), IV
234n1
Thorwaldsen's Museum, Copenhagen, IV
206
Thünen, Johann Heinrich von (1783–
1850): Le Salaire naturel (translated
from the German by Wolkoff), IV
183, 190, 266, German commen-
taries on, V 42–3; Walras on, IV
190; 'Germany's Ricardo', 266
a graphical, not mathematical economist (d'Aulnis), IV 282, 283; included in bibliography of
mathematical-economists, IV 282,

mentioned in preface to ed. 2 of
Theory of Political Economy, V 60–1
Der isolierte staat in Beziehung auf Landwirt-
schaft und Nationalokonomie, vol. 1
(1826), IV 265, 266n1; vol. 2
(1850), 266n1, V 42n10
tidal power, VI 24, 25; Sir John Herschel's
notions on, III 77–8, 122, 123–4
timber trade, VI 33, 123
mine timbers as circulating capital, VI
47
timber as substitute for coal, VII 18–19;
tax on timber, VI 139
see also vegetation: trees
time
in capital theory, I 26, V 156, VI 42–3
and credit, VI 104, 114
and energy, VI 26
in investment, VI 46, 50–1
stability of value a matter of, VI 97
in Theory of Political Economy, V 32–4
time-saving, VII 61
time series, I 35
Walras on, V 97
tin, IV 276, VI 120
Tindall, Dr John, lectures on electricity at
Royal Institution (1855), II 146n2
tobacco
annual expenditure on, VII 54
primary and secondary utility, IV 137–8
tax on, III 239, VI 136, 139, VII 8
also mentioned, VI 81
Todhunter, Isaac: edits works by William
Whewell (1876), IV 104; Researches
in the Calculus of Variations (1871),
IV 256; introduces WSJ to
Cournot's Recherches . . . , V 24
Tomkinson, Samuel (1816–1900), Sydney,
later Adelaide, manager of Bank of
Australasia, II 47
Tomline, George (1812–89), M.P., IV
298–9; A Free Mint: addressed to all
Ratepayers and Working Men (1871),
IV 299n5; agitates for increased
silver token money, IV 299n5, V
89
tontine, IV 215
Tooke and Newmarch, History of Prices from
1792 to the Present Time (six volumes,
completed 1857), I 181n2, III 21,
23, 53–4, 61, 81, IV 12, 72, 300n1,
VII 107; views expressed on bank

issues, IV 77. *See also* Newmarch, William; Tooke, Thomas

Tooke Professorship at King's College, London, V 98n1

Tooke, Thomas: co-author of *History of Prices*, III 25, 125; errors on currency, III 21; tables of prices, used by WSJ, 53–4; speculations respecting the war years, 55–6; views on paper money, IV 112n3, and periodicity of crises, IV 275, 300, V 11

On the Bank Charter Act of 1844, IV 32; *Thoughts and Details of the High and Low Prices*, VII 107

tools, VI 21–2, 28; as circulating capital, VI 47; 'tool benefit', VI 73

Toongabbee village, New South Wales, I 214, 215, II 219

'Torbanehill Case' (*Gillespie v. Russel*), II 50n15

Tories, III 229, IV 150n4, V 150

Toronto, I 65n5; WSJ visits, II 384n1, 401

Torrens, Robert, *On the Production of Wealth*, VII 107

Townend, George, director of Peel Bros & Co., worsted manufacturers: letter to WSJ on married women in factories, V 172–3

Townend, Simon, worsted manufacturer, V 172n1

Towner, Mr, dies of yellow fever in Havana, with WSJ's Australian Journal in his possession, II 390, 401

towns

WSJ's study of, I 17, 28, II 327–8, of 'poliography', VII 116; study of Sydney, I 24, 28, II 297n10, VII 116; tours towns of Victoria, I 25

American towns, II 383; London gloom contrasted with Australian and American towns, II 403; town life 'dispiriting', II 413

see also under Australia; London; Sydney

Townsend, Meredith: joint editor and proprietor of *Spectator*, II 416n6; editor of *Friend of India*, III 58n3

trade

American, II 383; Anglo-Indian, V 49–50; trade statistics, Holland and England, V 72

classes of, VI 33–4; subsidiary, 34; pepper and spice trade, V 49

freedom of, VI 132, *see also* free trade; laws against restraint of, VI 70–1, modified by Trade Union Act (1871), 72–3

shift from traditional sites to coalfields, VII 21–2

trade guilds, VI 69–71, VII 48

see also commerce

trade depressions, III 64–5, IV 236, V 25, 45, VI 122, 126; debate on causes at Political Economy Club (1878), IV 222; fall in membership of Statistical Society due to, V 90; years of 'black' trade, VI 121

revivals, IV 211, V 90, 107; fictitious 'big' trade of 1866–73, IV 236–7; accompanied by demand for metallic currency, V 89; helped by discovery of Californian gold (1849), VI 123–4

see also cycles

tradesmen, VII 57, 59; tradesmen's books, VI 104

trade societies, III 133, 134, 135, VII 51; 'Trades Societies: their Objects and Policy', lecture to Trades Unionists' Political Association, Manchester (WSJ, 31 March 1868), III 161n2, 183n1, VI 71n3

trade unions

as benefit societies, VI 73, 79; distinguished from guilds, VI 71

discussions on, at British Association meeting, IV 129–30, at Political Economy Club, IV 222

examination questions on, VII 132, 136

Fleeming Jenkin's article on, VI 166

housepainters union, III 132n1

legislation on, VI 71; Trade Union Act (1871), 72–3; in *State in Relation to Labour*, V 138n3, VI 72n4

proposals for international society of unions, VI 74

restrictive practices, III 151n2, IV 213, VI 74, VII 59; in iron industry, III 128, 225, VII 49–50; attitude to machinery, VII 46; not responsible for cyclical depressions, VII 91

suspicions of profit-sharing, VI 77

Times charges against, III 129, 135,

trade unions (*contd*)
VII 41; trade unionist's defence,
III 133–5
WSJ and: lecture notes on, VI 68–73;
supposed attack on, in Cobden
inaugural lecture, III 129, 131,
135, 137, VII 41–3, 48; view of
their proper role, III 137–8, VII
49; thinks strike funds should be
invested in mills and factories, III
132, 138
Trades Union Congress: first Congress at
Manchester (June 1866), III
132n1
Trades Unionists' Political Association,
Manchester, lecture to, III 161n2,
183
traffic, *see under* international trade
Train, Enoch, & Co., Boston shipping
house, II 116n6
Train, George Francis (1829–1904), Sydney merchant, II 116
Transvaal Republic, V 135n4
Travers, Newenham, assistant master at
University College School, II 222
Treasury, I 44, V 182, 183
Trickett, Sergeant Joseph (d. 1878), of the
Sydney Mint: meets WSJ off the
boat in Sydney, I 20, 109n1, II 115;
superintends building of Mint,
115n5; repairs WSJ's office, 197;
becomes Colonial Architect, 196,
203
Trinity College, Dublin: Ingram's Fellow-
ship, V 68, 124n1; Library, 124
Tristan da Cunha, I 102, II 112
tropical countries, prices in, III 24, 54
Trübners, London publishers, I 184
Tunbridge Wells, visit to, V 132
Turgot, Anne Robert Jacques, Baron de
l'Aulne, on gold and silver as universal money, VI 96
Turkey
Crimean War (1854), IV 225; British
soldiers for, II 63; default on loan,
VI 113
gold coinage, V 59; Turkish notes for
WSJ's collection, IV 194
Russian designs on (1860), II 412; war
with Russia (1877), IV 210, 211,
occupation of Constantinople, 225,
armistice (1878), 224n2, 225n3

also mentioned, II 415n3
see also Levant trade; Ottoman Empire
Turner, Charles, M.P. for Liverpool,
1852–3, election declared void
(1853), I 86
Turner, Frederick H., student at University College, London, I 56, 58
Turner, J.M.W.: watercolours in Whitworth Art Gallery, Manchester, I
47n3; WSJ has no feeling for his
landscapes, 98, finds nothing 'surprising' in 'Garden of Hesperides',
99
Turon river, New South Wales, I 24, 229
Tuskar, II 80, 86
Twigg, John Hill (1841–1917), of Indian
Civil Service, V 45n3; letter to WSJ
on periodic rainfall in India, V
50–1
Tyndall, John (1820–93), Professor of Natural Philosophy at the Royal Institution: lecture on Slaty Clea-
vage, II 250
Tyne: chemical manufacturing, VII 19;
shipbuilding, III 228

unemployment: (1839–43), VI 122;
(1878), VII 90–1; attributed to
shortage of token coins, IV 299n5; a
necessary result of division of
labour, VI 35
Unitarians
WSJ and: a Unitarian by descent, IV
36, his Unitarian background and
relatives, I 2, 3, 29, 88, 183n3,
Grandfather William Roscoe's bust
in Renshaw Street Chapel, II 128,
144; limits to which he calls himself
Unitarian, I 52, II 242, 258, thinks
them nearest to the simple truth,
225–6; in chapel (1852), I 58,
(1866), I 202, goes little (1854–5), I
96, II 131; member of Sydney
chapel, I 31, II 118, 347
chapel music, I 75
'Christian mythology' accepted, II 327;
don't pray by command, II 132
Domestic Mission in Spitalfields, I 17,
68n3, IV 292
Monthly Repository, theological periodical, II 445n2
schools, II 28n2, 406, 458

Unitarian chapels and ministers, I 11, 58, 202n2, II 20, 134, 142, IV 292n1, n3; other Unitarians, II 65n7, V 167n9, 189n3. *See also under* Bristol; Liverpool; London; Manchester; Sydney

United Kingdom, *see* England; Great Britain; Scotland; Wales

United Kingdom Alliance, WSJ's paper on, to Manchester Statistical Society, VI 41n17

United States of America
   banking: law on national banks, IV 56n3; banknotes and greenbacks, IV 43, 56, 159; bankruptcies, V 11, VI 122; overissues of currency, III 79, IV 56; panics, IV 111; reserves, IV 159; suspension of specie payments (1857), VI 124, (1865), III 79, (1869), III 79n5, 202

   coal, VII 27, 33, 34; needed to replace wood for fuel, 18–19

   communities, VI 44

   copyright law, V 69

   crises in America, IV 300; speculation in 1792, VI 117; (1837), IV 210, VI 125; (1839), VI 122; (1857), VI 124, 125, 129; smash expected (1864), III 57; breakdown (1866), VI 126; (1872), VI 126; panic crisis (1873), IV 111, V 11, 147; decennial crisis (1876), V 11; (1877), VI 125; depression (1878), VII 91; (1879), V 83, panic expected, 84; outlook in 1881, V 147; twenty-year cycles, VI 125

   currency: 'currency question' (1865), III 79–80; greenbacks, III 199, 200n1, IV 117, and national bank issues, IV 43, 56, 159, issue of greenbacks limited by law, IV 56n2, withdrawal considered, III 79n5, IV 159, not cancelled, V 84; WSJ needs information on, for *Money and the Mechanism of Exchange*, IV 43, 54, 56; 'inferior quality and overabundance' of circulating medium, III 201; collapse of paper money in 1866, VI 126; Inflation Bill vetoed (1874), IV 43, 56n2; currency remains inflated, V 84; small notes, IV 161

   relation of gold to note issues, IV 159; gold coinage, V 58, 59; British sovereign legal tender, III 163; American gold coins legal tender in Canada, IV 161; cost of silver coinage, V 140; silver certificates, V 194, no free coinage, 194

   Lincoln's commission on the revenue, III 200n2; report on currencies of Great Britain, France and United States, 201; *Report of the Special Commissioner of the Revenue upon the industry, trade, commerce etc., of the United States for the year 1868*, 203n3

   expansionist policy: filibuster raid on Cuba, II 399; Oregon dispute, II 408n14; purchase of Alaska, IV 153–4

   foreign trade: Jevons family iron business with U.S., I 119, II 143, 145, 210, III 227; American market best to sell in, dearest to buy in, III 79; cotton trade, II 234n5, III 208, IV 429; British exports to, IV 215, advantage to Britain of American trade, V 50n4; credit arrangements, VI 108, 109; flour exports to Australia, VII 4; danger of competition from, VII 50; imports of colonial produce, IV 220

Jevons family in U.S.A., *see under* Jevons, Henry; Jevons, Herbert; Jevons, Thomas Edwin; Jevons family; *and below*, WSJ

Mint, III 184; Director, 203, letter on British sovereigns, 218; reports on foreign coins, 219

navy, II 234, 429; Confederate navy, III 53n1

population, II 267, 430; Irish immigrants, V 114; Irish and German deaths in U.S., IV 55

post office, IV 293

prices, III 24, 79, IV 6–7; of land, II 420; of pig-iron, V 86; fall in corn and cotton (1878), IV 293

progress, compared with England, II 429–30

railways, II 267, 404, 419; 'plank-roads', VII 11; WSJ's impressions of, II 399–400, travels by, 390, 400

relations with Great Britain: dispute

United States of America (*contd*)
over enlistment of American recruits during Crimean War, II 234;
English investment in American
property, VI 124–5; boundary disputes over San Juan Islands, II 408
Republicans and Democrats: Republican gains in elections of 1856, II
404n2; Lincoln's Republican administration (1860), 404, election
as President, 418; differences on
land policy, 420; start of democratic secession movement, 429, *see
also* U.S.A. Civil War; Democratic
newspapers, II 409
slavery: slave states, II 428; issue of
slavery, II 390, 404n2; Channing's
abolitionist views, II 134n7, 151;
Lovejoy's anti-slavery campaign,
II 409; Fugitive Slave Law, II
134n7, 151, IV 174n1, 177,
amended, II 151n2
statistics, III 204; government statistical
report on Minnesota, II 418–19; on
incomes, III 242; of American iron
trade, V 86; Census figures on
mortality, IV 55
tariffs, II 427–8, III 239, VII 43; export
duty on cotton, II 429; tariff on
brandy, IV 138; Britain forced to
pay gold for imports from U.S., IV
215, 306
taxation, VI 139
Treasury, calls in U.S. bonds held in
Europe (1877), IV 220
wages, III 251; examination question
on, VII 138
War of Independence, VI 117; threat of
war with Red Indians (1861), II
455. *See also* U.S.A. Civil War
WSJ and: plans to visit Herbert Jevons
in Minnesota, I 33, II 364; voyage
to America, I 25, 33, II 373–83,
385–8, 394–9; arrives in Baltimore
(July 1859), II 381, 399; stays in
Philadelphia, 381, 382, 399; visits
Washington, 382, 399; stays in New
York, 382, 383, 399–400; goes by
steamer to St Paul, 382, 383, 400;
on American hotels, 383, 399, 400,
on the lay-out of American towns,
383, 399; shares log hut in Wayzata, 384, fishes, 400; journey from
Wayzata to New York by Hudson
river steamer, 389–90, through
Chicago, 400; sees Blondin cross
Niagara, 401; by train from New
York to New Haven and Boston,
390, 401
refuses invitation to visit in 1878, IV
291; sale of WSJ's books in, I 48, V
123; receives present of American
apples, IV 303, 304
see also Americans
United States of America, Civil War
(1861–5)
friction between North and South, II
423–4, 427–8, 431; threat of secession, 424, 427, 429; relative
merits, WSJ's view, 427–9, 453–4,
break-up of Northern States pre-
dicted, 455, is 'strictly neutral', III
53; relative strength, Herbert
Jevons's view, II 438; Southern
Congress's offer to Western States
to keep out of war, 455; Northern
cause supported by *Spectator*,
432n17, and by Cairnes, III 53
course of war: Southern victories (Bull
Run, Harper's Ferry, Antietam,
Fredericksburg), II 453–4; block-
ade of Southern ports, III 11, 53n1;
failure to take Charleston, III 16;
death of Stonewall Jackson at
Chancellorsville, 16n16; war drags
on, 31; loss of men, IV 7
effect on trade: on Rathbone's American
trade, III 78n2; cotton famine, VI
125; effect on prices, III 5, IV 6–7,
on cotton prices, III 11, IV 6, on
periodic fluctuations, VI 125
also mentioned, II 134n7, 408n14
United States of America, Presidents, *see*
Buchanan, James; Garfield, James
Abram; Johnson, Andrew; Lincoln, Abraham
United States Census, IV 55
United Telephone Company, V 93n2
universities
or incorporated trades and guilds, VII
48, 49
influence of Mill's writings at, VII
77
Walras's inquiry into the teaching of

moral and political sciences, V 20–1, 22–3

see also Bristol; Cambridge; Dublin; Edinburgh; Glasgow; Heidelberg; Owens College, Manchester; Queen's College, Liverpool

University College, London

WSJ and: Journal entries relating to, (1852–54), I 1, 13, 14, 18, 53–8, 60–70, 77–83, 87, 89–91, 94–8, 100–1, (1859–63), I 1, 98–9

enters College (October 1851), I 13, 35; matriculates from College, 13, 54–5, 66, II 33, 35; examinations (1852), I 53–4; takes botany and chemistry for honours, 54n5, 55–6; passes in first division, 55n4, gets botany prize, 58, 66, 77, III 310; certificates in Latin, Greek, and mathematics, I 54

chemistry classes, I 62, 64, 67, 83, 87, 91, II 30; under Graham, I 13–14; under Williamson, I 69, 87n2, in Birkbeck Laboratory (1853), 89, 94 95, II 42; recommended for Assay post as best student in the laboratory, I 96–7, II 299; college examinations, I 54, 82, 90, 94, 117; gains silver medal (1852), I 16, 54n1, 61n5, 117, II 31, 34, III 110, gold medal (1853), I 16, 114, II 42–3, 44, III 110

history classes, I 54, with Professor Creasy, 69–70; does not go into examination, 83

Kinkel's course of lectures on modern painting and sculpture, I 85

mathematics, I 62, III 103; under De Morgan, I 15, 64–5, 67, 70, 82, 90, 91, 95; writes out fifth book of Euclid with De Morgan's proofs, 69; starts differential calculus, 94, probabilities, II 30, 31n7; placed 4th in examination, I 54, 96

natural science, under Professor Potter, I 65, 67, 69, 90, 91, 94, 95; experiments in electricity, 83, 87

leaves College without taking B.A., I 16, 18, 31, 78, 95n4

plan to return to College, I 112, II 349, 364, 377; returns to take B.A. (1859), I 32, 33, II 389, 394, 402,

410; catalogue of work for B.A., I 34, II 403, 415

Latin and Greek, II 403, 406, 421, 422; mathematics with De Morgan, I 15, 33, 34, II 403, 406, 421–2; mental philosophy, classes at Manchester New College, London, II 421–2, comes equal first in College examinations, I 34, II 415, III 109–10; natural science, Potter's lectures, II 421; political economy, I 179, his 'sad reverse' in college examinations, I 33–4, II 415–16, question paper taken, VII 131–2

takes B.A. (October 1860), I 179n2, in first division, I 34

works for Ricardo Scholarship in political economy, II 406, 410, 416; wins it, I 34, II 416n5, 422–3, III 103

stays on to take M.A., I 34, 179, II 410, 413; studies in Political Economy and Mental Philosophy branch, II 406, 410, 411, 422, catalogue of subjects required, 437–8; exercises in logic, I 185, II 433; takes M.A. (1862), I 182n2, 188, II 443, 444, III 13; awarded gold medal for Philosophy branch, I 34, II 438, 444, III 13, 103, 107, 113; Hutton on his Political Economy paper, III 111

misses Essay prize (1862), II 443; awarded special prize by Council of University College for essay on 'The Effect of Climate on Nations', III 115

other activities at College: joins College Debating Society, I 39, 187, speaks at debates, II 457; revives Literary and Scientific Society, I 38–9, 187, its first President, I 39, 187n3, III 15

elected Fellow of University College (1864), III 58–9, 103; returns to talk to old students on logical abacus, I 206

as Professor of Political Economy (1875–80); appointed in 1875 for session of October 1876, I 49, IV 108–9, 118, 146, 149, 150, 154, 163–4; negotiations for interim per-

University College, London (*contd*)
iod, IV 123–5, 132, 133–6, 142–3, 147, 163; formal application, IV 144–5

introductory lecture, IV 182, 183, 276; remuneration and lecture subjects, IV 135, 142, 143, 144–5; classes, 192, V 26–7, 105, 109, 119, ladies at, IV 216; examinations, IV 183, 291, V 65, 80, 108, 118; examines for Ricardo Scholarship with Bagehot, IV 124, with Foxwell, V 147, 149, question paper, V 151–2; for Joseph Hume Scholarship, V 105, 109; finds lectures even more hateful than examining, V 106, 116

resigns (1880), I 49, V 116–17, 118, 143–4; 'pangs of regret', V 110, 119; hands key of office to Foxwell, V 137

social life at College: snowballing, I 89; holiday for opening of New Houses of Parliament (1852), II 30; an incident at a meeting, II 407; his few friends, II 275, 302; Bellamy Clifton, I 41, III 5; C. R. Colville, I 54, II 114; F. B. Edmonds, I 54, II 111–14; C. Upton, III 205; Whittaker, II 114

Council, III 233n1; and appointment of WSJ as Professor, IV 124, 132, 142, 143, 144, 145, 146, 168–9; appointment of Foxwell as successor, V 136

Departments: Faculty of Science, first in England, II 3, 89n4; Geological Museum, II 228; Jurisprudence, V 22–3; Medical Jurisprudence, II 167n8; Natural Philosophy, I 61n4; Political Economy, day and evening classes, IV 156

foundation, I 3n1; Matriculation and B.A. regulations, II 389n4; M.A. syllabus, II 437

Library, I 59n5; Chinese Library, IV 233

prize givings, I 54, II 414, 443

professorships: printed regulations governing appointments, IV 132, 133; Nonconformists eligible for, I 39

Senate, III 233n1; and appointment of WSJ, IV 108–9

Trustees, gift of Blue Books to Owens College, III 233–5

see also under Jevons, Herbert; Jevons, Thomas Edwin

University College School

WSJ attends (1850–1), I 10, 115n7, II 4–5; arrangements for tutoring, II 17; chemistry at school, I 62n2, 114, II 20; German, II 5, 225; success in class, I 100, II 7, 12, 21, 24, 222; prizes, I 13, 61n5, II 116, 293, 417; friends, Robert McAndrew, II 78n5, Joseph Chamberlain, V 189–90; his 'nasty' schoolfellows, II 17, 19, 201; leaves for University College, I 13

boarding houses for schoolboys, Gower Street, I 13, 100, others, II 17; no means of lighting the school, II 20–1; members of staff, *see* J. G. Greenwood, T. H. Key, H. Malden, N. Travers; Mr Shiel's Social Economy lessons, VII 53

Tom Jevons at, II 34n6, 221–2; Richard Roscoe, II 176n10; other boys, II 270n2

University Hall, London, hall of residence for University College students, I 80, II 167n8; Manchester New College housed in, II 421–2

University of London

application for charter (1835), I 82n7

Board of the University at Somerset House, I 66

examinations in political economy, III 246; Examinerships, IV 239–40; WSJ as examiner for M.A., III 246, V 80, proposals for questions, IV 70; paper taken by WSJ as student, VII 131–2; other examiners, I 36–7

gold medals, II 410; awarded to WSJ in Philosophical Branch of M.A. degree (1862), III 103, 107

poll at general election (1880), V 97

Senate, attitude to examiners, IV 240, to testimonials, V 106

women admitted to degrees (1878), IV 224n3

unproductive expenditure, II 268, consumption, IV 122, labour, VI 52–3

Upton, Charles (1831–1920), Unitarian minister, College fellow of WSJ:

takes Roscoe Jevons's funeral service, III 205
Upton, Lancashire, I 57
uranium, II 61n4
use, duration in, VI 42, 44, 47
usefulness, defined, VII 161
usury laws: bills of exchange exempted from, IV 252n3; and rate of interest, IV 11, 17, VI 121; supposed Bank of England petition against, IV 252, 265, 279, 280; tracts on, IV 210
'Utilitarian', Bentham's first use of term, V 75; his utilitarian theory, VII 159; WSJ adopts utilitarian approach to economic behaviour, I 28
utility
  co-efficient of utility, in paper on General Mathematical Theory read to British Association (1862), I 37; Fleeming Jenkin on, III 171, 172; later termed 'degree of utility', IV 40, 46
  definitions, IV 89, VI 10–12, VII 79; distinguished from usefulness, VI 11, VII 84; as value in use, VI 80, 84; as wealth, VI 6; a relation, not intrinsic, VI 11, VII 79–81, 'an attraction between a wanting being and what is wanted', VII 80
  degrees of utility, VI 84–8, 92–3, VII 80–4, 148–9; distinguished from total utility, difference between Adam Smith and WSJ, III 254; general law of the final degree, varies inversely with ratio of exchange, VI 88, VII 82, 149, A. B. Hopkins on, III 247–8
  d'Aulnis on degrees of utility, IV 59, 72–3; Cairnes on, VII 153; Walras on, IV 64, identified with his 'rarity', IV 40–4, 46, VII 82; R. O. Williams on, IV 136, 140–1, 151–3
  of diamonds and coal, VII 21; of monetary medium, VI 96
  equilibrium of utility, IV 141, VII 81–2, 83
  examination questions on, VII 135
  labour in relation to utility, *see under* labour, in economic theory
  maximum utility, IV 262, 269, VI 12
  problem of measurement, IV 5n3, VI 95,

VII 150, 153–4; measurement by price, III 246, VII 150; a quantitative notion, VII 159
  prospective, VI 11, VII 141
  terminal, VII 150–1
  total, III 169, IV 151, V 34; distinguished from degree of utility, III 254; not proportioned to final degree of utility, VII 143
  utility curves, III 167n2, IV 5n3, VI 16–17, 85–7, VII 81; d'Aulnis' curves, IV 59, 62; Dupuit's confusion, V 95; Fleeming Jenkin's, III 167–77; Walras's, IV 64, 197, 270, VII 76
  utility of exchange (Fleeming Jenkin), III 167–77
  and value, *see under* value
utility, theory of
  evolution of 'marginal' utility theory, I 15, 26, 27, first statement of *ratio of utility* (1 June 1860), II 410
  in *Theory of Political Economy* (1871), IV 3, 60, 101, 127, V 78, VI ix; discussed in 'The Progress of the Mathematical Theory of Political Economy' (1874), VII 78–85; Cairnes's objections, IV 60–1, 62, 81, VII 83–4, 148–51, 161; Marshall on, VII 141, 143; Westergaard on, IV 256–8; attacked in *Examiner*, IV 92n, in *Saturday Review*, VII 153–7
  laws of the variation of utility, III 254, VI 16, VII 160; decreasing benefit from last portion, VI 90, VII 81, 120
  lecture notes on, VI 13–18, 26–7, 52, 80, 84–9, 95
  in *Money and the Mechanism of Exchange*, IV 104n11
  other theories: d'Aulnis, IV 72, 75; De Quincey, VII 78, 79–80; Dupuit, IV 192, 197; Garnier, VII 79; Gossen's theory of 'Werth', or utility, IV 267–9; Say, VI 10–11, VII 79, 83; Nassau Senior, VII 79, 80. *See also under* Walras, M.E.L.
Utrecht, University of, IV 229, 252, 282

vaccination, IV 222, VI 59n13
Valpy, Richard (d. 1889), Statistical Department, Board of Trade, letter

Valpy, Richard (contd)
from, III 181–2
value: a hopeless term to be avoided, VII
143; Christie on, V 34; definition,
VI 79; examination questions on, V
152, VII 135; Adam Smith on, see
under Smith, Adam
value, standard of: an economical ana-
logue to the mean sun, IV 19;
money as, VI 97–8
value, theory of
WSJ's theory of: first statements (February 1860), 'to be established
upon the basis of labour', VII 120
in Theory of Political Economy (1871),
VI viii–ix; criticisms of theory:
Cairnes, III 22, 246–7, IV 99, VII
83, 161; Cliffe Leslie, VII 161; Marshall, VII 141–2; Shadwell, III 253
aspects of theory: gold and silver as
store of value, VI 95–6
labour as cause of value, VI 90–4, VII
141–2, as measure, III 253, VII 83
limited in long run by cost of production, III 246, VI 90, VII 84
money as measure of value, VI 94–5,
VII 71
as a quantitative notion, VII 159;
attempt to make it a precise notion,
IV 71
a relative term, ratio between two
commodities, VI 80, 95, VII 143–
4, termed 'ratio of exchange', VI
80; 'values in exchange proportional to the rarities' (or degrees of
utility), VII 82–3
stability of value, VI 97–8
supply and demand, relation to value,
VI 80–4, VII 84–5, 161
and utility, VI 84–9, VII 81–3, 161;
value defined by, III 246, VI 95
other theories: Banfield, VI 14; Cairnes,
IV 87, VII 161; Dupuit, IV 249;
Mill, V 61, VI 80, 82, 83, VII 78,
144; Ricardo, VII 78, 83, 85, 161;
Thorold Rogers, VI 90–1; Say, VII
83; see also under Smith, Adam
see also utility
Vancouver Island, Britain's boundary dispute over, II 408n14
Van der Berg, C. P. J., V 76; De Theorie van
het arbeidsloon included in bibliog-

raphy of mathematico-economic
works, V 76n2
variety, Senior's law of, VI 13
variation of utility, see under utility
Varna, II 103n4
Vatican, V 37
Vauban, Sebastian Le Prestre de (1633–
1707), Projet d'une Dixme Royale
(1707), V 149
vegetation:
Australian
crops: Indian corn, I 125, 127, 128,
137, 138, 165, 174, 214, II 220; oats
and lucerne, I 138; potatoes, 127,
165
flowering shrubs and wild flowers, I
145, 167; geranium and sarsparilla,
II 253; goodeniads and orchids, I
151, II 353; ribus and violet, I 146
gardens and orchards, I 139, 140, 142,
144, II 106; fig tree, I 169; or-
angeries, I 136, 139; vines, II 368;
hinderberry, I 167
regional features: bush and scrub, I
166–7; ferns in a shady dell, II 353;
green sward and scorched plain,
224–5; a picturesque gully, 220–1;
'ruins of nature', I 150–1; sub-
tropical, 164, II 366; tableland like
an English park, 365, 66
trees: acacia, I 144, 145, 224, 225; box,
171; cabbage tree palms, 170, 171,
176, hats made of, 167, II 254;
casuarina, II 365; gum, I 125, 127,
135, 136, 139, 145, 150, 151, 164,
171, 174, 212, 216, 217, 221, 226,
237, II 158–9, 181, 219, 254, 273,
353, 365, 366, 368, WSJ's eyes
wearied with them, 384; tea trees, I
151; tree-barking, 151–2, II 254;
woods from New South Wales exhibited at Paris Exhibition, II 183–4
in Minnesota, II 384; ginseng, 419;
maples, sugar from, 423
Welsh yews, II 168–9
see also botany
velocity, V 32–3
Venice
Bank of Venice, IV 215n1
the Monte, or joint-stock fund, IV
215n1
in Thomas Jevons's itinerary, II 175,

199–200; cholera, 190

Venn, John (1834–83), Cambridge logician: WSJ stays with, IV 148

'Consistency and Real Inference' (*Mind*, 1876), IV 156

Venn, Mrs John, hospitality to WSJ, IV 148

Verdi, Giuseppe: his music puzzles WSJ, II 321; *Il Trovatore*, 321; *La Traviata*, 'downright trash', 321

Verona, Thomas Jevons visits, II 199, 200

Verri, Pietro (1728–97), *Meditazioni sull'Economia Politica* (1771), V 60

Versailles, II 61, 185

Victoria, New Zealand, gold yields, III 74

Victoria, Princess Royal (1840–1901), I 72

Victoria, Queen

opens Great Exhibition (1851), II 12n6

opens New Houses of Parliament (1852), I 70–1, II 30, 222

orders public funeral for Duke of Wellington, I 72, visits the lying-in-state, 72

exchange of visits with Emperor Napoleon III (1855), II 175n8; visit to Paris, 175, 190–1

Queen's Birthday (1856), I 123, 128

inspects the *James Baines* (1857), II 146n3

presented with gold nugget, II 128n5

speech to Parliament (1860): expresses approval of Rifle movement, II 406; alludes to San Juan affair, 408

relations with Gladstone (1866), I 44n2

buys painting by Elizabeth Thompson, IV 52n3

the Victorian world, I 51, 76n2

Victoria State, Australia

go-ahead Victorians, II 197

gold discoveries, I 24, alluvial gold, II 127n5; gold exports to England, I 21; diggings, II 404; rebellion of goldminers at Ballarat, II 122n2

lighthouse on Cape Otway, I 107–8

population growth, II 430

ruffianism in towns, II 48

Sydney coinage refused, I 21, II 247, 260

WSJ tours, I 25, 112, II 344, visits goldfields, 367–72, 381

Victoria University, Manchester, formerly Owens College, I 41, III 70n1, V 61, 177

see also Owens College

Victoria, Vancouver Island: Frank Roscoe becomes M.P. for, in Canadian Parliament, I 193n6; his business there, II 438–9; land prices, 440

Vienna, V 37; Electrical Exhibition, V 148n2

Villiers, Charles Pelham (1802–98), M.P., I 86; member of Political Economy Club, IV 202

vintage cycles, IV 204, 276, V 9; no periodicity traceable, V 167

Virgil: and WSJ's equations, V 17n1; *Aeneid*, III 77; *Georgics*, VI 22–3

Virgin Mary, in Lima Churches, II 379, 395

Vissering, Simon (1818–88), Professor of Political Economy at Leiden, IV 224n1; 'Het Groote Tafereel' (*De Gids*, 1856), 233; Finance Minister of the Netherlands, V 72; article on trade of Holland and England possibly his, 72, 73

Vissering, Willem (1851–1931), economist, WSJ's Dutch correspondent: *On Chinese Currency, Coin and Paper Money*, noticed in *Journal of the Royal Statistical Society* (December 1877), IV 224, WSJ's copy, V 195, 196; remarks on Chinese labour, IV 233; article on trade of Holland and England possibly his, V 72, 73

letters to, IV 224–5, 233

Vivian, Hussey, M.P., moves for Royal Commission on coal supplies, III 101n1

vivisection, V 122n1

Vogt, Gustav (1829–1901), Professor of Public Law at Zurich, IV 85

Voltaic electricity, I 87; Voltaic light, II 18

Volunteer Movement: 'home guard' formed in 1859 against Napoleon III's threat of invasion, I 36, 186n1, II 408, 429, 431; an 'upper class' activity, II 406–7, 417; the Queen's 'Gratification and Pride' in, 406; proposal for Corps at University College, 407; franchise proposed for all Volunteers, 411; brigade field day of Volunteer Corps, 411; Great Wimbledon meeting, 431; new regulations (December 1862),

Volunteer Movement (*contd*)
    amending and consolidating Act
    (1863), III 15; Parliamentary sup-
    port for, III 14; Volunteer band, 7
WSJ's proposed history of, I 36, 186, II
    461. For his activities as Volunteer,
    see Queen's Own Rifles
other Volunteer Corps, II 407, 411, 460;
    in U.S.A., II 455

Wade, John, *History of the middle and Work-
    ing Classes* (1833), III 27, VII 103–
    4
wages
  as circulating capital, VI 47, 61
  of coalminers, VI 126n8
  and degrees of utility, VII 143
  differentials, VI 64–7, VII 53, 63–4,
    141–2; variation with skill and ef-
    ficiency, III 255; equal wages not
    desirable, III 153, 255; wage
    ranges in England, VI 62
  examination questions on, V 152, VII
    131, 132, 133–4, 135, 136, 138
  and hours of work, VI 71, VII 143
  intemperance and, V 165–6; proportion
    of wages spent on drink and to-
    bacco, VII 54
  interest and, VII 142
  in iron industry, II 225, 226–7
  of married women, V 172
  in the mass, VI 64
  to be treated mathematically, VII 120
  and population, Malthus's view, VI 59–
    60
  as a portion of the produce, VI 60, 61,
    67, VII 62; in profit-sharing
    schemes, III 143, 152–3, VI 77,
    VII 62–3; Marshall on, VII 141–2
  and prices, IV 51, VI 63–4, VII 144;
    during depressions, III 142–3; ef-
    fect of rise in price of corn, VI 63;
    proposed sliding-scale for wages,
    VI 78
  and profits: in Mill's theory, IV 27;
    together equal produce, V 78; in
    Walras's theory, V 56; rates of,
    governed inexorably by natural
    laws, VII 46
  real and money wages, VI 60–1,
    63
  regulation of, VI 61, 72–3, VII 62–4;

cannot be regulated at the will of
    anyone, III 137; increases paid for
    by consumers, VI 72; can be raised
    only by new capital investment, III
    138; governed by efficiency of
    labour, III 255, IV 227; wages-
    fund theory, V 77, VI 61–3, Mill's
    version, VI 48n2, VII 77
  and rent, VII 61, 78, 80
  Ricardo on, VI 59–60, 61–2
  and strikes, III 137, 255, VII 50–1; in
    coal industry, VI 126; against wage
    reductions in iron trade, III 128,
    VII 49–50; in shipbuilding, VI 64
  union activity to raise wages, VI 71–4,
    77, VII 49
  von Thünen's investigations, V 60
Wagner, Adolf Heinrich Gotthilf (1835–
    1917), Austrian economist, IV 301
Wagner, Richard (1813–83), I 50, V
    131n2; recitals in London (1877),
    IV 199; Richter's Wagner concerts
    (1881, 1882), V 134, 198, an anti-
    dote to bimetallism, 194
  Flying Dutchman, V 198; *Lohengrin*, V
    198; *Mastersingers*, V 194, 198–9;
    Tannhauser, V 198, 199; *Tristan und
    Isolde*, V 198n2, 199
Waikato, New Zealand, invaded by Gen-
    eral Cameron, III 41n4
Wakefield, Edward Gibbon: 'Note' on
    division of labour in his edition of
    Wealth of Nations, VI 27, 34; theory
    of systematic colonisation, VII 3
Wales
  copper smelters, IV 276; copper mines,
    II 88n3, 93, III 210. *See also* Pol-
    timore mine
  emigration to Liverpool, I 16
  gold mines, II 92–4
  rail trade, III 226
  Saxons and Britons, II 89
  slate quarries, VI 30–40; Cairnes on
    'Cooperation in Welsh Slate Quar-
    ries', III 65, VI 39n12
  staple products, III 192
  Volunteers, II 417
  Welsh mountains, I 108, II 86–7, V 146
  WSJ holidays in, III 185
  see also Dolgelly
Wales, North
  earthquake, I 71

glut of gold coin, III 191, from tourists, 192, from specie payments for staple exports, 191–2

Welsh dealers, III 191, 192–3; cash payments preferred to cheques, IV 11

WSJ goes on walking tour with Tom, II 412, 415

Wales, Prince of, *see* Edward, Prince of Wales

Wales, Princess of, *see* Alexandra, Princess of Denmark

Wales, South
coalfields, VII 21; strike against wage reductions, VI 126; emigration of miners, VII 17; Welsh coals, III 189

iron trade, VII 22; Thomas Jevons as ironmaster, I 12; wage reductions of ironworkers, III 142; emigration of workers, VII 17

railway plans for, VII 23

Waley, Jacob (1818–73), Professor of Political Economy in University of London: testimonial for WSJ, III 106, 113; examines WSJ in political economy at University College, 113, examination paper set by, VII 131–2

'On Strikes and Combinations' (*Journal of the Royal Statistical Society*, 1867), III 153–4

Walford, Cornelius (1827–85), Director of the Accident Insurance Company, IV 240, 274, V 82; on the arithmometer, VII 89

Insurance Cyclopaedia, IV 240n1

Walker, Francis Amasa (1840–97), American economist: *Money* (1878), IV 298–9, VII 105; *The Wages Question* (1878), VII 102; *Money in its Relation to Trade and Industry* (1879), VII 105

Walker, George (1824–88), President of the Third National Bank of Springfield, Massachusetts: letters from, with estimates of metallic circulation in Great Britain, III 200–1, 202–3

Walker, Oliver Ormerod, M.P., candidate for Salford (1880), V 115

Wallace, Robert (1697–1771), on population, VI 54–5

Wallasey, Manchester: WSJ lodges in (1863), III 14, 18, 29

Walliker, William Samuel (1821–92), Postmaster of Birmingham: letter with information on gold coin in use, III 179–80

Walpole, Spencer Horatio (1806–98), at the Home Office in Derby Ministry (1852), I 85

Walras, Antoine-Auguste, father of Léon Walras, early mathematical economist, IV 46–7, 260

Walras, Madame Louise-Aline, mother of Léon Walras, IV 198, 214; note to, 212

Walras, Marie Esprit Léon (1834–1910), Professor of Political Economy at Lausanne

sends WSJ his article 'Principe d'une théorie mathématique de l'échange' (*Journal des Economistes*, 1874), IV 36–7, 39, 45, 54, 189; is informed of WSJ's mathematical theory by d'Aulnis, 45; asks for copy of *Theory of Political Economy*, 46, 50, 63; both theories discussed in 'Progress of the Mathematical Theory of Political Economy' (November 1874), IV 70n1, 102, VII 75–85, copy sent to Walras, IV 84; referred to, in introductory lecture as Professor at University College, IV 183, 190; his theory almost identical with WSJ's, IV 39–41, 46–7, 49–50, 57n1, 63, 64, 80, 190, complementary to WSJ's, 71; co-efficient or degrees of utility paralleled by *rareté*, IV 40–1, 46, VII 76–7, 82; equation of exchange corresponds to equation of maximum satisfaction, IV 46, 50; priority claimed by and acceded to WSJ, 50, 64, 71, 104; both anticipated by Gossen (1854), IV 278; correspondence on priority published in *Journal des Economistes*, IV 48, 50, 261, 263

theoretical points referred to: coefficients of production, IV 198; demand curves and utility curves, IV

Walras, Marie Esprit Léon (*contd*)
197, 270, VII 76; general equilibrium theory, IV 36n1, 65, 260n3;
the term 'entrepreneur', IV 262,
263; theory of capitalisation, IV
191
copies of WSJ's books sent to: *Theory of
Political Economy*, IV 46, 50, 63;
Money and the Mechanism of Exchange
(French edition), IV 180, 183;
Primer of Logic, 192, 196; *Primer of
Political Economy*, IV 259–60; *State
in Relation to Labour*, V 195
translates, but does not publish, ed. 2
of *Theory of Political Economy*, IV
261–2, 263, 270, V 95
correspondence with WSJ on bibliography of mathematical books on
political economy for Preface to
ed. 2 of *Theory of Political Economy*,
IV 259, 260–1, 262–3, 270–1, 281–
2, 289, 290; criticises Preface as
published, V 95–7; republishes bibliography, with amendments and
an introduction, in *Journal des Economistes* (1878), IV 259n2, 290, V 21
personal: friendship with d'Aulnis, IV
59, 91, 271; elected Rector of Lausanne University, IV 180; cerebral-
spinal affection, IV 180, 182, 190,
V 195; proposed visit to WSJ in
Hampstead, IV 192, 198–9, 205–6,
211–12, 214; invites WSJ to Lausanne, 271; gives WSJ's first letter to
an autograph collector, V 96; death
of his wife, V 94
writings
Eléments d'économie politique pure (1874,
1877), first volume of projected
Traité d'Economie politique et sociale,
IV 37, 261, V 96; proofs of 'Théorie
de la Richesse Sociale' sent to WSJ,
IV 46, 49
First (1874) instalment, IV 37, 47,
65, 67–8, 81, 261; copy sent to WSJ,
63, 65, 67, 71; section on Money,
65–6, 67; preface, 65; price, 69; not
written for public appeal, 71; discussed in 'Progress of the
Mathematical Theory of Political
Economy', VII 75–7, 82–3; reviewed in *La Critique philosophique*,

IV 85n12, in *Le Temps*, 85n11, in
Revue Scientifique, 86, in *Deutsche
Allgemeine Polytechnische Zeitung*,
103, 188; noticed by George
Darwin in *Fortnightly Review*, 102,
180–1, in *Money and Mechanism of
Exchange*, 104, 183; plans for new
edition, 261, 290
Second (1877) instalment, IV 195–
6, 198, 214; d'Aulnis's doubts on, V
56
Eléments d'économie politique appliquée, V
96
Eléments d'économie sociale, V 96
Quatre Mémoires on mathematical
theory of social wealth, IV 181
1. *see above*, 'Principe d'une théorie
mathématique de l'échange'
2. 'Equations de la Production', IV
180, 181, 189
3. 'Equations de l'échange', IV
181n6, 189
4. 'Equations de la capitalisation',
IV 181n6, sent to WSJ, 189–90
collected *Mémoires* sent to WSJ, IV
190, 191, 205, 281; extracts included in bibliography of mathematical books on political economy, 263, 270, 281–2, 289, 290, V
95; Italian translation, IV 261, 262,
270; German translation, V 144–5
articles: 'De la culture et de
l'enseignement des sciences morales et politiques' (*Bibliothèque Universelle et Revue Suisse*, 1879), V 21,
22–3; 'Théorie mathématique du
billet de banque' (1880), V 96, sent
to WSJ, 98; 'Théorie mathématique du prix des terres . .' (*Bulletin
de la Société Vaudoise des Sciences Naturelles*, 1881), V 145; 'Un nuovo
ramo della matematica . .' (*Giornale degli Economisti*, 1876), IV 181;
'Un économiste inconnu, Hermann-Henri Gossen' (*Journal des
Economistes*, 1885), V 144n2, 145n4
letters to, IV 39–41, 49–50, 65–7, 102–5,
182–3, 188, 191–2, 205–6, 211–12,
259, 262–3, 281–2, 290, V 21–3, 98,
143–4; letters from, IV 36–7, 45–8,
63–5, 67–9, 84–6, 180–2, 188, 189–
91, 195–9, 214, 259–62, 270–1,

289–90, V 20–1, 94–7, 144–5, 195
Walsh, Richard Hussey, on bills of credit, VI 107
war: as check to population, VI 58, 59; decennial cycles disturbed by, IV 210, 211; war prices, II 194, III 53, 54, 55, IV 6–7; (1861), in America, IV 7; (1864), III 54; a necessary function of government, VI 132
'impending' European war (1866), III 102
see also Afghanistan; Crimean War; Taranaki wars; United States Civil War; *and under* France; Germany; Russia; Turkey; United States of America
Ward, [Sir] Adolphus William (1837–1921): elected Professor of English Language and Literature at Owens College (May 1866), I 207n2, his Introductory address on 'National Self-Knowledge', VII 39; joint letter to WSJ on his resignation from Owens College, IV 163–4; on WSJ as a teacher, I 49–50; appealed to, on a point of terminology, V 61–2
Ward, Captain (later Major-General Sir) Edward Wohlstenholm (1823–90), of the Royal Engineers, Deputy Master of the Royal Mint at Sydney, I 18, 19, 97, II 51–2, 196, 197, 231–2, 260, 340; relations with WSJ at the Mint, II 78, 116, 161, 248–9; urges him to get private business, 90–1; offers full time employment on Mint staff with fixed salary, I 20, II 162, 170, WSJ's letter of acceptance, 120–1; allots room for laboratory, 201; grants a holiday, 217; Thomas Jevons's disgust with, I 120, II 148–50, 173, 175; devotion to service, 249, 343–4
parties at the Dawes Battery for Anniversary of Foundation of the colony (1855), II 114, 141, 145, (1856), 208; incident at the theatre, II 279
letter to, II 120–1; letter from, II 57
Ward, Mrs Edward Wohlstenholm, *see* Campbell, Annie Sophia
Ward, Hon. John Petty, father of Captain Ward, II 51n2
Ward, William (1817–85), 1st Earl of

Dudley: wages and prices policy in his iron business, III 226–7, 228, 230
warehouses, VI 21; warehousemen, VI 33; warehousing system, examination question on, VII 132
Warington, Robert (1807–61), Chemist to London Apothecaries' Society, lecture on Clays, I 85
Warrington, chemical manufactory, II 435
Wascoes old Pilgrim Inn, I 152–3
Washington, D.C., II 455; WSJ's visit to, II 382, 399; threatened by Confederate Army (1862), II 453, 454n7
water
    quantities needed for conversion into steam, III 188–90
    raised by steam pumps, VII 19, 30, 31
    utility of, VII 149; Adam Smith on, 78–9; value without labour, VI 91
water carriage, II 283, 419
water cure, II 423
water power, VI 24, 25, 31; used in Dolgelly gold mine, II 92; water wheels, VII 22, 97. *See also* tidal power
Waterhouse, Alfred, architect: his additions to Balliol College, Oxford, IV 285
Waterhouse, Theodore (1838–91), 'first student' at University College in 1860: ties with WSJ for prize in Mental Philosophy, II 415
Watt, James (1736–1819), inventor of the steam engine, II 360, VI 28
Wattle Flat, I 234
Watts, Henry (1815–84), assistant Professor of Chemistry at University College, London, II 65–6, 122, 316; editor of Chemical Society *Journal*, II 191
    Dictionary of Chemistry (1864), III 51; 'Gold Assay' (WSJ), I 20n5, 35, II 345n4, III 50, 51; other articles by WSJ, I 20n5, 35, II 345n4, VII 124
Watts, Dr John (1818–87): secretary of the Cobden Memorial Committee, III 131, 138; secretary to Owens College Extension Committee, IV 242;

Watts, Dr John (*contd*)
  cheap tracts for working classes, VII 51
Waugh (and Cox), Australian Almanac: (1855–6), II 174, 363n8; (1859), article by WSJ, 'Some Data concerning the Climate of Australia and New Zealand', I 23–4, II 240n4, 341n3, IV 203n1, VII 124
Waugh and Cox's Directory of Sydney and its Suburbs, VII 116
Waugh, James William (1820–67), Sydney bookseller and publisher, editor of *Waugh's Australian Almanac*, II 363n8, and of *Sydney Magazine of Science and Art*, I 23n1, II 297n7
Waverley Hills, New South Wales, II 217
Wayzata, Minnesota: Herbert Jevons tries farming in (1858), I 10, 32, II 364, 377, 404–5, 418; his log hut, II 392, 409; crops, 409, 413, maple sugar, 423, 424; becomes a school trustee, 409; WSJ visits, I 33, II 384, bathes and fishes in Lake Minnetonka, 400, 409
Weale, John (1791–1862), London bookseller, *Rudimentary Series*, I 27, II 227
wealth, VI 9–13
  accumulation of, VI 7, 8, 52, VII 57; general increase in, VII 68; promoted by industrial freedom, VII 57
  from coal, VII 27–8, 35
  definitions: McCulloch, VI 6; Mill, VI 9, VII 56; Senior, VI 6, 8, 9, 79; Adam Smith, VII 56, 159; WSJ 'matter in the right place', VI 17; capital defined as, VI 37, 52, 54
  examination questions on, V 152, VII 131, 136
  National Wealth, I 125
  production and consumption of, VI 5, 12, 17, 19
  the subject of political economy, VI 4, 7, 79, VII 56
  or utility, VI 6
  see also under distribution
weather: in the total machinery of nature, II 326; and music, V 35; Maury's wind charts, VI 23; observation of,

  a function of government, VI 133; and prices, III 55
  in Australia: at Christmas, I 137, II 253; close air, II 261, 272, 273; cyclone, 298; fog, I 220; a moonlight night, II 210; rain, I 220, II 182, 205; thunderstorms, I 147, 148–9, 218–19, II 203, 253–4, 355; winds, Brickfields or Southerly Busters, II 113, 245–6, 355, hot-gale, 245, sea breezes, 196, 245, 272
  in England: fog, II 6; smoke, II 402, 403; summers, II 92, 95, 167, III 72; winters, II 22, 118
  Herschel's weather table, VII 95
  Indian whirlwinds VII 124
  Irish 'Scutchers', V 115
  at sea: on the voyage to Australia, II 82–3, 84, 99, 100, 112–13; aurora australis, I 108, II 100, lunar rainbow, II 82; from Melbourne to Peru, II 374–5, 386–7
  see also clouds; meteorology; rainfall; *and under* cycles
Weatherstones, New Zealand, III 74
Weber, Carl Maria von (1786–1826), II 314, 321; *Der Freischutz*, II 224; 'Last Waltz', II 339; *Oberon*, performed in London (1878), IV 304
Wedgwood, Josiah (1730–95), IV 55n3
Wedgwood, Julia (1833–1913), writer: reads *Principles of Science*, IV 55
Weisz, Bela, of the University of Budapest: Essay on the mathematical method in political economy, IV 278
Wellington, Arthur Wellesley, Duke of (1769–1852); death, I 72; lying in state, 72–3, 83; funeral procession, 73–5, 84, 117, II 191, cost of his 'funeral obsequies', II 35
Wells, David Ames (1828–98), Special Commissioner of the Revenue, U.S.A., III 200–1, 202; annual reports, 251; translation of *Histoire de l'Economie Politique en Europe*, VII 102–3
Wells, Somerset, excursion to, IV 130
Welsh, John (1824–59), Superintendent at Kew Observatory, II 392n19, 402
'werth', or utility, IV 268
Wesley, Samuel Sebastian (1810–76), cathedral organist: the 'great Gun'

at public opening of St George's Hall, Liverpool, II 152

West, Alfred Slater (1846–1932), Examiner with Foxwell and WSJ in Moral Sciences Tripos, Cambridge (1875), IV 133, 143, 146, 147

West of England Bank: failure in 1878, IV 304n6; light gold coin held by, 87n2, 88

Westergaard, Harald Ludwig (1853–1936), Danish statistician: controversy with Madsen on statistical analysis of telegraph trade, IV 243–7; *Contributions to the History of Statistics*, 247n3; on problems of index-numbers, IV 247–8

meets WSJ in England, IV 243, 244, 247, 258; comments on *Theory of Political Economy*, 254–8

letters from, IV 245–8, 254–8

Westfield College, London, IV 149n9

Westgarth, W., letter to *Economist* on WSJ and bimetallism (28 March 1882), V 187

West Indies
American filibusters in Caribbean, II 399n2
climate, II 386, 416n6
sugar, VII 24
WSJ's voyage *via*, II 377–8, 397
woods exhibited at Paris Exhibition, II 184
see also Jamaica

West Kirby, WSJ botanises at, I 54, 56

Westminster
J. S. Mill, M.P. for, I 44, 45
Morley defeated for (1880), V 79
new Houses of Parliament, II 30, opened by Queen Victoria, I 70–1
Westminster Bridge, I 77, II 10
WSJ, exploratory walks through, I 68, 83; 'hung about' after *Coal Question* quoted in Parliament, I 44, 45

Westminster Abbey, I 84, 184; organ, III 18

Westminster Brigade of Volunteers, II 407

Westminster Hall, drills in, II 407

Westminster Review, II 23n4
review of *Serious Fall* (September 1863), III 48n1, 50, 52, VII 125; of Fawcett's *Manual* (September 1863), III 48n1; of *Theory of Political*

Economy, ed. 2 (January 1880), VII 127

'East India Currency and Exchange' (Col. J. T. Smith, 1881), V 141n1; 'Theory of Wages' (J. L. Shadwell, 1872), III 254

Westphalia, coal production, VII 34

whales, II 375; whale fishery, IV 305; whale trade, IV 155n1

Whately, Richard, Archbishop: *Easy Lessons on Money Matters for the Use of Young People*, WSJ's first text book on political economy, I 6, 157n4, VII 52; *Introductory Lectures on Political Economy*, I 27, VII 56–7, 107, 117n14, 118, 'Remarks' on (1857), I 157–9, referred to in Lecture notes, VI 4, 7, 94n10; *Elements of Logic* . ., I 185; also mentioned, V 41

wheat, VII 24
cycles, IV 276, and prices at Delhi, V 46–7
substitutes for, IV 138, VI 17
wheatflour used in cotton manufacture, III 206

Wheatley, Harry Benjamin (1838–1917), Clerk to the Royal Society, hon. secretary of the Index Society: *What is an Index?*, IV 298

Whewell, William, II 251, IV 19; WSJ put 'on the same platform' as, IV 173; examination question on, VII 138

History of the Inductive Sciences (1837), I 155, II 79, quoted, I 111; *History of Scientific Ideas* (1858), IV 69; 'Mathematical Exposition of Some Doctrines of Political Economy' (1829), IV 19n2, 69, 103–4; 'Mathematical Exposition of . . . Ricardo's "Principles"' (1833), IV 69; *Philosophy of the Inductive Sciences* (1840), read by WSJ, VII 116, 117n14, 'nothing but fog', I 185; Todhunter's edition of miscellaneous works, IV 104

Whitaker, William (1836–1925), geologist, member of Geological Survey of England: article on county geology in *Geological Magazine* (1864), III 63n5; at British Association meeting (1875), IV 128

letter from, III 63–4

White, Dupont, translation of Mill's *On Liberty*, IV 261

White, Horace (1834–1916), American journalist, editor-in-chief of *Chicago Tribune*, IV 117

White, J. M., translation of Orsini's *Austrian Dungeons* .., II 259n2

Whiteboy Acts, V 150

Whitehead, George (b. 1842), manager of Parkgate Iron Works, III 166, 227; letters to WSJ on the iron trade, 225, 228–9

White Star shipping line, II 116n6, 133n1

Whittaker, classmate of WSJ at University College, II 114

Whittall, Joseph, Assistant Secretary of the Royal Statistical Society, V 170

Whitworth, breech-loading rifle, II 431

Whitworth, Joseph (1803–87), inventor of Whitworth rifle, II 431n16

Whitworth, William Allen, *Choice and Chance*, VII 126

wholesale druggists, possible career for WSJ, II 41
drug and colour merchant, opening for WSJ as, II 43

Wight, Rev. George: *Geology and Genesis* (1857), II 330–1

Wilber, Mr, First Mate on board the *Oliver Lang*, I 107, II 81; met again in the Mint, II 231

Wilberforce, New South Wales, I 137, 140

Wilde, Mr, machine for making electricity, VII 34

Wilhelm Friedrich Ludwig, King of Prussia (1861), Emperor of Germany (1871–88), II 73n14

Wilkinson, Thomas Read (1826–1903), managing director of Manchester and Salford Bank, V 130

Will, Heinrich (1812–90), German chemist, II 72

Willdey, Charles John (b. 1844), Post Office clerk: letters to WSJ on parcel post scheme, V 155–6, 160–1
his father, Post Office superintendent, V 160

Willetts, A. & S., New York business firm, IV 155n1

Willetts, Edward B., New York merchant, letter to WSJ on cheques in U.S.A., IV 155–6

Willetts, Samuel, founder of A. & S. Willetts, IV 155n1

Williams, Dr Daniel (1643?–1716), nonconformist divine, founder of Dr Williams Library, II 33n2

Williams, Edmund Sydney (1817–91), Edinburgh bookseller, IV 297

Williams, Captain George, gold finds in Wales, II 135n11

Williams, Ralph Olmstead (1838–1908), suggestions on primary and secondary utility, IV 131, 136–41; is sent 'The Progress of the Mathematical Theory of Political Economy', 136 letters to, IV 177, V 69; letters from, IV 130–2, 136–41, 151–4

Williams, Richard Price (1827–1916), civil engineer: difference with WSJ on Coal Question, V 143, VII 36–7

Williams, Walter, jun., *Times* correspondent in Brussels, III 141; letters to *The Times* on foreign competition, 141n2; objection to profit-sharing schemes, 151, 152

Williamson, Alexander William (1824–1904), Professor of Practical Chemistry at University College, London, I 13–14, 57n3, II 74n16, 125, 229; brilliance as teacher, I 14, 69; exponent of atomic theory, 14, 51, II 159; on allotropy of ozone, I 69; gives course of lectures at Royal Institution on Chemical Philosophy, I 82, 84, 85, 87; his laboratory, I 89, 94, II 65n7, his elderly pupil, II 35

WSJ on, as man and chemist, I 95; Harry Roscoe on, I 14, II 64–5, 75, 122, 228, becomes Williamson's assistant, 191, 193, 228, deserts him for Bunsen, 244; elected to Chair vacated by Graham, II 191; recommends WSJ for assayership, I 96–7, II 46; Kolbe on his 'Theory of Waters, Ethers and Acids', II 72 marriage, II 228

Williamson, Mrs A. W. (Emma Catherine Key), II 228n3

Williamson, Stephen (1827–1903), Liverpool merchant: letter to WSJ on bimetallism for India, IV 186–7

Williamson, W. C., Professor of National History at Owens College, II 305n8

Williamstown, Australia, I 108n3, II 100

Willis, Henry (1821–1901), organ-builder, exhibits at Great Exhibition, II 23n3

Willoughby Falls, New South Wales, expedition to, II 353

Wills, Mr, of Birmingham, II 155

Wills, Mrs (formerly Miss Kimberle and children, holiday neighbours of Thomas Jevons at Pengwerne, II 155

Wilson, A. J., editor of McCulloch's *Commercial Dictionary*, VII 104; *Banking Reform*, (1879), VII 106

Wilson, James, founder of *The Economist*, IV 275n4; *Capital, Currency and Banking* (1847), IV 32, VII 105; study of periodicity, IV 275

Wiltshire, VII 24

Wimbledon, meeting of Volunteers, II 431, 461

Winckelmann, Hermann (1849–1912), operatic tenor, in *Tristan und Isolde*, V 199

wind power, VI 25, VII 20, 35, 97

winds, *see* weather

Windsor, New South Wales, I 137n1; Christmas expedition to (1856–7), I 134–42, II 280, by rail and omnibus, I 134, 135–6; four in a two-bedded garret, 137, II 252; Christmas dinner at Macquarie Arms, I 140–1, II 252

projected railway to, II 263, 264

Windsor Iron Works, London, II 92n3, 94

Windsor Park, England, II 401

price of corn at Windsor (1637–1700), II 170

wine

in Dieppe, II 178; at Kyeamba, in the Australian desert, II 368; in Paris, V 148n3; in Windsor, New South Wales, I 141

as medicine, II 16, III 195

monopoly value of rare wines, VI 83

orders of industry in wine production, VI 33

tax on, VI 137, 139

vintage cycles, IV 204, 276, V 9, 167

wine-growing countries, VI 31, 32, VII 62

also mentioned, III 191

Wirth, Max (1822–1900), on recurrent crises, IV 300

Wiss, Georg Eduard (1822–87), Berlin editor, III 197

Withington, Manchester, WSJ's first home with Harriet (April 1868), III 182–3, 185, 195; move to London (1876), IV 182, 183

Witt, Henry M., Assistant Chemist to the Government School of Applied Science: paper on Thames water, II 250

Wittwer, W. C., Münich chemist; experiments on chemistry of light, II 192; his errors, 192, 244

Wöhler, Friedrich, Professor of Chemistry at Cassel: aluminium research, II 62n6, 66n11

Wolf, Johann Rudolf (1816–93), Swiss astronomer: calculations on sunspot cycles, V 8, 11, 17, 100; his numbers used by WSJ, VII 108, 109, diagram, 112; on the star Argus Navis, VII 98

Wolkoff, Mathieu, French translations and résumés of von Thünen, IV 183, 190

Wollaston, William Hyde (1766–1828): invention of reflecting goniometer, I 67; estimate of relative strength of sun and moon light, VII 96

Wollongong, New South Wales: expedition to (April 1857), I 29, 159–78, II 262; the town, I 163, Russels Hotel, 168; Wollongong butter, 168, 169; Wollongong Five Islands, 177

Wolowski, Louis François Raymond (1810–76), French economist: pamphlets on monetary question and gold and silver, VI 102, sent to WSJ, III 196, 200; supports alternative standard for international currency, 196–8, 199, VI 102, WSJ agrees in theory, disagrees in practice, III 198; a Bullionist, 199; estimate of French incomes, 242

letters from, III 196–8, 198–200

Wolseley, Sir Garnet, defeats Arabi Pasha in Egypt (1882), V 200n5

women

in education: accepted for examinations at Cambridge, IV 143, 146, Tripos results, 148–9; admitted to degrees at London University (1878), IV 224n3; attend WSJ's classes at University College, IV 216; flock to the Economic Science and Statistics Section of British Association, IV 273n5, speak at meetings, 129

in industry: prohibited by Printers Trade Society from working type-setting machines, VII 47n; married women in factories, V 161–2, 163–7, 168–9, 'the best Hands in the mill', 172–3, their good morals, 174

legal disabilities of married women, V 164–5

skaters, IV 303

votes for women, IV 129n4, V 164

WSJ on a woman's field of action, II 360–1, 362, III 97

Women's Suffrage Journal, IV 129n4

Wood, Ann, see Jevons, Mrs William

Wood, Sir Charles, see Halifax, Lord

Wood family, cousins of Thomas Jevons, I 240, II 89n6, III 30. See also Jevons & Wood

Wood, George, WSJ's great-uncle, II 89n6

Wood, Henry, son of George Wood, cousin of WSJ, II 142; his Chain and Anchor Works, II 89

Wood, Mrs Henry (Harriet Lomax), II 89n6

Wood, Miss, of Liverpool, II 14

Wood, Townshend, cousin of Thomas Jevons, I 12

Woods, Mr, driver of a luggage van: breakfasts with WSJ in a convict village, I 220

Woodhouse, Mr, of Bank of New South Wales, III 16

wool

from Australia, II 146, VI 111, 114, profits from, II 282; in England, VII 22, 24

prices, IV 6, 241

statistics, II 427

wool trade, VI 33

Woolley, Rev. John, Principal and Professor of Classics in University of Sydney, I 25, 132n3, II 136n12; lecture on the 'Selfish Theory of Morals', I 27, 132

Woolloomoolloo Bay, II 106, 273

Wootton, Alfred Charles (d. 1910), pharmacist, letter to WSJ, IV 294–5

workhouses, arrangements for infants of working mothers, V 162, 164

working-classes

earnings and spending, VII 54

franchise for, III 130, VII 42–3

and machinery, examination question on, VII 131

political economy for, III 135, V 37, 38, 40, VII 38; for working-class boys, I 208n3, VII 38–9, 51–3; lectures on political economy for working men, VII 54–65; trade unionist view of class interest and political economy, III 133–6

power of, through unions, III 128

profit-sharing for, III 153

prosperity in Europe, III 208

WSJ's alleged attack on, III 130, 131–2

see also labour; trade unions

Working Men's College Rifle Corps, II 411

Worsley family, Bristol Unitarians, II 65n7; Christmas day with (1862), II 460

Worsley, Honora (1837–79), daughter of Philip Worsley, later Mrs Richard Roscoe, I 243, II 65n7

Worsley, Philip, of the London Domestic Mission Society, II 65n7

Worsley, Philip, jun., friend of H. E. Roscoe, II 65

Worthington, Anne Frances (b. 1826), cousin of WSJ, I 241, II 28n2

Worthington, Fanny, see Jevons, Mrs William, jun.

Worthington, Frederick, surgeon, II 47

Worthington, George (1787–1859), solicitor, uncle of WSJ, I 240, II 28n2

Worthington, George (b. 1825), cousin of WSJ, I 241, II 28n2, 47n2

Wotzel, A. A., English translation of Pierson's Principles of Economics, IV 267n4

Wren, Sir Christopher, VI 69

Wright, Liverpool dealer in minerals, I 79

Wright, R. T., marries Mary Kennedy,

pioneer woman student at Cambridge, IV 148n5

Wright, William Aldis (1831–1914), Librarian, later Master, of Trinity College, Cambridge, IV 148

Wurtz, Henry (1828–1910), New York consulting chemist: method of producing water gas, V 71n1

Wyagden Hill, New South Wales, I 234; Wyagden Inn, 227–8

Wyon, James, resident engraver at Royal Mint, II 90

Yankees, II 429, 439, 441; Yankeeisms, 404, 439

Yarmouth
  banking accounts, IV 16
  fishing fleets, quarterly payments of wages, IV 78
  Inglis Palgrave's home, IV 13, 105

Yarmouth and Suffolk Bank, circulation of notes, IV 79, 99

Yates, Anna Maria (1787–1866), of The Dingle, Toxteth Park, II 110n3

Yates family, I 3n1, II 24n5

Yates, Rev. James (1789–1871), Unitarian and Antiquary, I 3n1; educationalist and classical scholar, II 24n5

Yates, Jane Ellen (1794–1877), of The Dingle, Toxteth Park, II 110n3

Yates, Rev. John, Unitarian minister (1755–1826), sleeping partner in firm of Jevons & Son, I 3; his home at The Dingle, Toxteth Park, II 110n3

Yates, John Ashton (1791–1863), M.P.,

Liverpool broker: WSJ's schoolboy visit to, II 24n5

Yates, Richard Vaughan (1785–1856), son of Rev. John Yates, partner of William Jevons, I 3n1

Yates, Samuel Ashton Thompson, *Memorials of the Family of the Rev. John Yates* (1890), II 110n3

Yeats, John: three volumes containing graphical charts, presented to WSJ, IV 8, 15

York
  Free Masons lodge, VI 69
  Manchester College, I 183n3, II 421n5
  WSJ visits, III 127

Yorkshire
  coal, VII 19, 22; coal trade, V 107
  depression of 1878, VII 91
  Lucy and John Hutton settle in, II 443
  population of West Riding, VII 23, 24
  woollen trade, VII 22
  working men, III 229

Yorkshire College, IV 234n1, V 61n2

Young, Sir George (1837–1930), 3rd Baronet, II 187n1

Young, William Mackworth (1840–1924), possibly 'Sir Wm Young Bart', encountered by Thomas Jevons in Switzerland, II 187

Zambelli, IV 260

Zanon, Giovanni Antonio (1845–1920), physicist, Professor of Naval Architecture in Venice, IV 48, 103, 260

zinc, II 204, VII 30

Zollverein, coal production, VII 27, 33